Also by Herbert Weinstock

ROSSINI: A BIOGRAPHY
(1968)

WHAT MUSIC IS
(1966; a second edition, revised, of *Music as an Art*, 1953)

DONIZETTI AND THE WORLD OF OPERA IN
ITALY, PARIS, AND VIENNA IN THE FIRST HALF
OF THE NINETEENTH CENTURY
(1963)

CHOPIN: THE MAN AND HIS MUSIC
(1949)

HANDEL
(1946; second edition, revised, 1959)

TCHAIKOVSKY
(1943)

Collaborations with Wallace Brockway:

MEN OF MUSIC: THEIR LIVES, TIMES, AND ACHIEVEMENTS
(1939; second edition, revised, 1950)

THE WORLD OF OPERA
(1962; a second edition, revised, of *The Opera*, 1941)

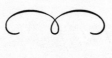

Vincenzo
BELLINI

Vincenzo
BELLINI

His Life and His Operas

Herbert Weinstock

Alfred A. Knopf · 1971 · New York

THIS IS A BORZOI BOOK
PUBLISHED BY ALFRED A. KNOPF, INC.

Copyright © 1971 by Herbert Weinstock
All rights reserved under International
and Pan-American Copyright Conventions.
Published in the United States by
Alfred A. Knopf, Inc., New York, and
simultaneously in Canada by Random House
of Canada Limited, Toronto. Distributed
by Random House, Inc., New York.
ISBN: 0-394-41656-2
Library of Congress Catalog Card Number: 70-111256
Manufactured in the United States of America

FIRST EDITION

"Incipite bucolicon, o dulces Musae, incipite carmen;
Tyrsis hic ille ab Aetna, et Tyrsidis haec vox est. . . .
Dulcior, o pastor, tuus cantus, quam que resonans
Illa a petra distillat superne acqua."

—Theocritus (First Idyl)

"What enchanted us in Bellini was the pure melody, the simple
nobility and beauty of song. Surely it can be no sin to assert
and believe this."

—Richard Wagner, in the Riga *Zuschauer*, December 19, 1837

"Chi non ama Vincenzo Bellini non ama la musica."

—Arrigo Boito, in *Omaggio a Bellini nel Primo*
Centenario dalla sua Nascita, 1901

"The sweet and elegiac character of his best music bewitched
everybody. It has bewitched many of his biographers, too. The
soft, fluffy portraits they draw are far removed from reality.
His letters reveal a much tougher personality, ambitious, intent
on his career and his fame ('la mia gloria'), suspicious of other
people's motives, without generosity of mind towards possible
rivals, egoistic and calculating even in his love-affairs."

—Frank Walker, in *Music and Letters*, London, January 1959

"Mio caro Florimo la nostra amicizia sarà d'invidia ai presenti,
ed alla nostra morte sarà lodata quando di noi si ricorderanno i
vecchi . . ."

—Bellini, in a letter of May 24, 1828, to Francesco Florimo

Acknowledgments

I HOPE THAT MY DEBTS OF GRATITUDE to many people and institutions are expressed fully in the back-matter notes. Here I wish, additionally, to thank old friends and former strangers whose willing and often essential assistance has provided special pleasure during the writing of this book. They have been so many that I am fearful of having omitted names that I would have wished to include. With that probability in mind, I express particular thanks to:

In England—Mr. A. John Watts of Croydon; Mr. Adam Harasowski, Mr. Henry Pleasants, and Mr. Andrew Porter of London; Mr. and Mrs. Richard Macnutt of Tunbridge Wells;

In France—Mr. Harold M. Barnes, signor Giorgio Camici, and M. Jean-Louis Tamvaco, all of Paris;

In Italy—Mr. Gene Galasso of Bologna; padre don Giosuè Chisari, maestro Roberto Pagano, the late professore Francesco Pastura, and dottoressa Maria Salmeri of Catania; dottore Dante Raiteri of Florence; signor Rodolfo Caramazza of Moltrasio; Mr. William Weaver of Monte San Savino; professore Francesco Bossarelli, signor Cesare Feoli, professore Terenzio Gargiulo, professoressa Anna Mondolfi, and marchese Lucio Parisi of Naples; dottore Guglielmo Barblan, signora Franca Cella Arruga, signora Luciana Pestalozza, dottore Victor de Sabata, signor Lorenzo Siliotto, Mme Wally Toscanini, and signorina Renata Vercesi of Milan; dottoressa Emma Alaimo, maestro Attilio Aronica, and signor Salvatore Minore of Palermo; signora Luisa Ambrosini, Dr. Friedrich Lippmann, professoressa Dina Masiello, the late maestro Giovanni Masiello, signor Fausto Rocco, signor Walter Talevi, and dottoressa Emilia Zanetti of Rome; and signora Margherita Antonelli and maestro Sandro della Libera of Venice;

In the United States—Miss Charlotte Greenspan and Professor Joseph Kerman of Berkeley; Professor Philip Gossett of Chicago; Dr. Richard J. Fauliso of Wethersfield; Mr. Jack Belsom of New Orleans; Mr. Wallace Brockway, Mr. Herbert Cahoon, Mr. Frank Campbell, Mr. Michael di Capua, Mr. Arthur Fierro, Mr. Donald M. Garvelmann, Miss Vera Giannini, Mr. Robert Gottlieb, Mr. Robert W. Gutman, Mr. Ben Meiselman, Mr. Fabrizio Melano, Mrs. Esther Mendelsohn, Mr. Richard Miller, Mr. Sam Morgenstern, Mr. Albert Parsons Sachs, Mrs. Susan Sommer, Mr. Floriano Vecchi, Mrs. Sophie Wilkins, and Mr. Stefan Zucker of New

York; and Mr. Richard D. Fletcher, Mr. Charles Jahant, and Mr. Edward N. Waters of Washington, D.C.

Among special debts of gratitude to archives, libraries, and other institutions, I have incurred particularly large indebtedness to: The Music Division of the Library of the Performing Arts of the New York Public Library; the Pierpont Morgan Library, New York; the New York Office of RAI (Radiotelevisione Italiana); the Bibliothèque Nationale and the Bibliothèque de l'Opéra, Paris; and—in Italy—the Biblioteca Ursino and the Museo Belliniano, Catania; the Biblioteca Nazionale, Florence; G. Ricordi e C. (and particularly the Archivio Ricordi), the Conservatorio Giuseppe Verdi, and the Museo Teatrale alla Scala (and especially the Biblioteca Livia Simoni), Milan; the Conservatorio di San Pietro a Maiella, Naples; the Biblioteca Comunale and the Conservatorio Vincenzo Bellini, Palermo; the Biblioteca Nazionale Vittorio Emanuele, the Biblioteca del Risorgimento, and the Conservatorio di Santa Cecilia, Rome; and the Fondazione Giorgio Cini, Venice.

I am very particularly grateful to my editor at Alfred A. Knopf, Mrs. Carol Janeway; without her patient sentence-by-sentence criticism and myriad suggestions this book would have been the poorer.

Without the pioneering labor expended upon the life of Bellini by the late Francesco Pastura, and upon his music by Dr. Friedrich Lippmann, I could not have written the present book.

—HERBERT WEINSTOCK

New York

Contents

PART ONE: THE LIFE

PART TWO: THE OPERAS AND NONOPERATIC COMPOSITIONS

Appendixes

Illustrations

ILLUSTRATIONS IN TEXT

An Introductory Note

HAVING PUBLISHED BIOGRAPHIES of Donizetti and Rossini, I naturally was
attracted by the idea—it came to seem almost a necessity—of writing a
Bellini. Before succumbing to that temptation, however, I hesitated for
some time, and for a special reason. Although I intensely admire Bellini the
composer of operas (I judge *Norma* to be the outstanding achievement of
pre-Verdi romantic Italian opera), I already knew that Bellini the man was
in many ways unattractive—and I therefore wondered not only if I could
face spending some years with him, but also if I could deal with him fairly.
My decision to make the attempt was taken after reading the Preface to
Roberto Ridolfi's *Life of Francesco Guicciardini* (New York, 1968; trans.
Cecil Grayson). Ridolfi earlier had published biographies of Machiavelli
and Savonarola, but had asserted that he would never undertake a life of
Guicciardini, and had given his reasons. But now he wrote: "But above
all the overt reasons why I was unwilling to undertake this work there
was another, which I did not express: that I have never managed to like
Guicciardini, though he is possibly the intellect I most admire. Thus I
was quite unable to make up my mind to write his Life, having always
thought, and having recently written, things like this: 'Love and affinities
help one to understand, and to look into oneself is always helpful. If a
constitution of the republic of letters were promulgated (awful thought),
it should compel biographers to portray only men in some way congenial to themselves: so many insincere or lukewarm books would be
avoided.' . . ."

Yet Ridolfi had written his *Guicciardini,* having decided to regard as
a challenge precisely that antipathetic cast of Guicciardini's character
which had delayed his decision. And because his book seemed to me to be
successful in portraying Guicciardini even-handedly, I decided—allowing
for the great differences—to accept the similar challenge. I still have not
managed to like Bellini in his relationships with other people, but I can hope
that I have evoked his character and his life as faithfully as if I had, and
that I have presented the winning and congenial aspects of his nature as
honestly as those I have found abrasive. For that reason, among other
reasons, I have let him speak, as often as possible, in his own words.

Something must be said about the translation of those words and the
words of others in this book—all translations being my own except where
otherwise specified. A translation always falsifies the original document to

some extent; despite all claims and appearances to the contrary, no two languages exist in complete parallel. Two possibilities face anyone trying to put into English a text from another language: he can stick very close to the original or he can attempt to recast it in the idiomatic English of his own era. With Bellini's letters, the problem is magnified greatly: he was an artless, incorrect, and often seemingly nonstop and all-but-incoherent writer of what must now strike most readers as spineless, gushing, over-romantic prose. Like nearly all of his Italian romantic contemporaries, that is, he now sounds very often like a "period piece."

I tried both methods of translation. And my final choice was to let Bellini speak for himself in as close an approximation as I could devise to the fulsome language of his time, to the heedless and frequently shape-less onrush of his own words. I ask my readers to note that those words were written long ago and in another country.

—H. W.

A Note on Notes

Despite a continuing conviction that a footnote should be just that—that is, should appear at the bottom of the page on which the indication of its existence occurs—here, as in my *Rossini*, I have decided against that sensible, comfortable system because of the very large number of notes and the amount of space they must occupy. Exceptionally, a few sub-stantive notes appear at the bottom of pages. But all the others, indicated by superior numbers ([1, 2,] etc.) in the text, have been put in the back matter of the book.

—H. W.

PART ONE

The Life

(I)

1801–1819:
Birth, Childhood, and
Adolescence in Catania

A FAMILY OF BELLINIS was established in the village of Torricella Peligna in the Abruzzi by the end of the seventeenth century.[1] By the early 1760's, records there show Rosario and Francesca Bellini —the composer's great-grandparents—as heads of a household of one girl and two boys. Their son Vincenzo Tobia (1744–1829) was musically inclined; when he was eleven years old, means were found to send him to Naples, metropolis and capital of the Kingdom of the Two Sicilies. There, on October 13, 1755, Vincenzo Tobia Bellini matriculated as a charity student at the Conservatorio di Sant'Onofrio a Capuana, where his known teachers were not musicians of imposing stature,[2] though he may have benefited from association with Nicolò Piccinni, then a *maestrino* (an advanced student charged with assisting his juniors), and with Antonio Porpora. By 1765, he himself had been made a *maestrino* and had composed an oratorio on a Metastasio text, *Isacco figura del Redentore*, the libretto of which was printed.

At some time during 1767–1768, Vincenzo Tobia Bellini, who had stayed in Naples for more than the ten years required at Sant'Onofrio a Capuana, left mainland Italy to settle in the east coast Sicilian town of Catania, which then had a population of about 30,000. There he took up a professional musical career. Not long after his arrival, Ignazio Paternò Castello, principe di Biscari, head of a wealthy Catanese family, chose him as household *maestro di cappella*, and assigned him a small pension that later Biscaris were to continue. Vincenzo Tobia's labors as private teacher of music, *maestro di cappella* to the local Benedictines, organist of the Sacro Collegio di Maria at nearby Misterbianco, and composer of occasional music for religious celebrations was to last more than sixty years. His compositions mostly have been lost or are now beyond identification, but printed librettos of some of his Masses and oratorios survive. His opera-oratorio entitled *Giosuè vittorioso sopra i cinque re di Cananea* was performed in Catania's piazza degli Almi Studi on the mid-August feast day of Agata, the town's patron saint, in 1772.

In 1769, when twenty-five, Vincenzo Tobia Bellini married Michela Burzì (Borzì, Wirzì, etc.) Napoli, a widow four years his senior. By her he had three sons and two daughters. Of these children of his first marriage,[3] the eldest was a son named Rosario (1775–1840) who took up his father's musical métier. A respected musical journeyman, Rosario Bellini grew up to assist his father, to compose occasional music, and to step briefly, sadly into history after the death in 1835, outside remote Paris, of his internationally renowned son. On January 17, 1801, Rosario Bellini married Agata Ferlito (1779–1842), a blue-eyed, blonde girl of twenty-two from a Catanese family of some substance.[4] When Vincenzo Bellini's adoring friend Francesco Florimo met Agata Bellini in Catania in 1832— she was then in her fifties—he described her as "intelligent and good-looking." She, her hard-working husband, and all of their other children were to outlive her famous firstborn. Toward his parents, as toward the other Bellinis and Ferlitos, the composer would display, after he left Sicily, a steady, affectionate attachment, intermittently intense. Among all his relatives, he eventually came to feel closest to his mother's younger brother, Vincenzo Ferlito.

Within little more than twelve years of their marriage, Rosario and Agata Bellini had four sons and three daughters. Their first child, born in Catania during the night of November 2–3, 1801,[5] was baptized in the Jesuit church of San Francesco Borgia. The names given him on that November 4 were Vincenzo, Salvatore, Carmelo, and Francesco—respectively that of his paternal grandfather; of the officiating canon of the Cathedral, Salvatore Scammacca, barone del Margo, who also had married the infant's parents; of his maternal grandfather; and of his mother's elder brother, Francesco Ferlito, who held him at the baptismal font.

The Catania into which Vincenzo Bellini was born had perhaps forty-five thousand inhabitants. As he first saw it, the town was relatively new. Situated on the Ionian Sea in volcanic, seismic territory, it had been damaged ruinously by a river of lava from Mount Etna in 1669,[6] and all but demolished in 1693 by an earthquake in which about sixteen thousand persons had died. As Ercole Fischetti wrote[7]: "Of our Greco-Roman and medieval town, of the later town surrounded by walls that old-time pictures show stretched out in starlike shape at the foot of the majestic bulk of Etna, nothing remained on the morning of January 11, 1693, but a pile of debris."[8] During Vincenzo Bellini's years in Catania (1801–1819), few of its buildings were more than a century old. Like Messina, sixty miles to the north, the town struggling back into existence was secondary to Palermo, which was the viceregal seat when not the refuge from tempestuous Naples of the king himself.

On the day of their marriage in January 1801, Rosario and Agata Bellini moved into rooms in the Palazzo dei Gravina Cruylas, close to what survived of the center of monumental Catania and hard by (in part, actually above) the ruins of the Roman-restored Greek theater and odeon. On one side, their rooms, now the Museo Belliniano, still face across a small courtyard toward the piazza San Francesco d'Assisi; they are reached from a back corner of the yard by stairs originally intended for use by servants. Beyond a tiny vestibule lies a room with an alcove that contained the large matrimonial bed upon which Bellini was born. On the other side of the apartment, two small balconies hang out over what was then the via della Corsa, the present via Vittorio Emanuele. As Francesco Pastura remarked[9]: "For a couple starting its married life, the apartment rented in the via della Corsa was somewhat large"; it strongly suggests that the Bellinis were not then feeling any immediate pressure from poverty.[10]

Until late in the nineteenth century, the musical life of Catania (in 1971 a bustling city of more than four hundred thousand people) was very restricted. The town enjoyed no public theater equipped to present opera until the Teatro Comunale was inaugurated in 1821 with a performance of Rossini's *Aureliano in Palmira*.[11] The few large-scale non-religious musical performances heard in Catania early in the century were given in the private theaters of the wealthier local nobility. No music school existed. Public music was limited almost entirely to church services, weddings, funerals, and popular celebrations. The teaching of music remained in the hands of the *maestri di cappella* serving the churches and a few families; lesser musical chores were performed by the musicians of the smaller churches. Catania did not produce a composer of more than local fame until Giovanni Pacini happened to be born there on February 10, 1796, because his parents were members of a visiting operatic troupe.[12] Vincenzo Bellini's birth followed Pacini's by almost six years.

Reliable records of Bellini's childhood are lacking, but anecdotes— semi-fictional and sometimes wholly apocryphal—are myriad. The Museo Belliniano in Catania preserves a brief, anonymous précis of his life, twelve hand-written pages probably set down for the instruction of a biographer.[13] It is the artless labor of a man or woman whom, following Pastura, I shall call L'Anonimo, and who had witnessed some or all of the events described. Pastura wrote[14] that its author was "certainly a relative or friend of the musician." From that manuscript, numerous picturesque details have come, such as, for example, that Agata Bellini did not breast-feed her firstborn and that a wetnurse who had been persuaded to abandon her lover in order to feed the baby left the Bellinis' employ after six months because the deserted man was threatening her. Thereafter, "the baby did not want to take milk from any wetnurse, and for a period of more than three months was fed on a simple diet of fish."[15]

Those portents of musical genius which have become stereotyped in biographies of composers run through the published lore of Bellini's childhood. L'Anonimo wrote[16]: "When he was scarcely a year old, his games all had to do with nothing but music paper; and whatever he saw Rosario, his father, doing, he tried to imitate by waving the paper in his hands in the pretense of wielding a baton; if he heard playing, he quickly ran toward it and thought of nothing else; if he heard some instrument outside, he left his play, his supper, and everything, and made a thousand noises indicating his wish to be taken to where the playing was going on; and then he remained satisfied."

L'Anonimo also reported that at about the time of the birth of Vincenzo's first brother, Carmelo[17] (May 9, 1803), "at the age of eighteen months he learned an aria by Maestro [Valentino] Fioravanti,[18] which he sang prettily to his father's accompaniment."[19] Tiny, attractive 'Nzudduzzu—the nickname was a diminutive of the dialectical 'Nzuddu or Zullo, for Vincenzullo—is said to have received his first lessons in literature from a priest named Antonio Neri,[20] but no such man appears in the local records. Also, the boy's father is reported to have instructed him in musical theory, but L'Anonimo adds that this training was "more in practice than in theory, as the child did not read very correctly."[21] The same writer asserts that "Vincenzo began to study the pianoforte at the age of three."[22]

One of L'Anonimo's anecdotes which often has been reprinted probably refers to 1804: "One evening, while the Forty Hours' Devotion was proceeding in the church of the Capuchins [later destroyed], beautiful music was performed by a large orchestra—as was always the case with the Capuchin Fathers, for dilettantes also took part without remuneration—Grandfather Bellini leading; and that evening the boy, who was always at his side, worked himself up into such a state of enthusiasm that he began to cry and shout. In short, he wanted to take the leader's part, to conduct. To please him, the grandfather was forced to cede the paper bearing the measures, and Vincenzo directed the orchestra so well that he amazed everyone, and especially the Capuchin Father Luigi Monte, who could not refrain from weeping!!"[23] If, as is implied clearly, Vincenzo Tobia Bellini was conducting music of his own, the child could well have been so familiar with it that his "conducting" of it would not have been impossible.

That Vincenzo Bellini as a child was beautiful in a delicate, feminine way is certain (indeed, he was so described as an adult—Heinrich Heine would write that he looked like "a sigh in dancing pumps"). That he was passionately drawn to music before the onset of his adolescence is also beyond argument. L'Anonimo asserted that he played the piano admirably when little more than five years old,[24] but Bellini never became so proficient a pianist as, for example, Rossini. Filippo Cicconetti, his second biographer, enlarged upon the boy's accomplishments[25]: "With what pleasure and assiduity he abandoned himself to study can be conjectured from this—that from the age of five, he played with considerable ability; at six, when other children had not even begun to exercise their reason, he wrote a musical composition in honor of the canon Innocenzo Fulci,[26] his Italian-language teacher, and—the meaning of the words having been explained to him—clothed in notes the 'Gallus cantavit' [The cock crowed] of the Evangel. . . ." A purported copy of that little piece is preserved in the Biblioteca Comunale Ursino at Catania. It is for a single voice and appears to have been written down in 1807; if it was indeed composed by Bellini at the age of six, much more than the meaning of the text must have been explained to him.

In one case, we can witness the garbling of an original source. Apparently on the basis of a passage in L'Anonimo, Cicconetti asserted[27] that "at seven [Bellini] wrote two *Tantum ergo*s, one of which was performed in San Michele Maggiore alla Trinità, some *romanze*, and Sicilian songs, two Masses with Vespers, three *Salve Regina*s, and other cantatas." L'Anonimo had specified that one *Tantum ergo* was "for tenor voice—clarinet obbligato played by a dilettante, Giuseppe Pizzarelli—performed in the church of San Michele belonging to the Minorite Fathers, which created a great effect; and the other at the Monastero della Trinità."[28] Still another chronicler, monsignore Giuseppe Coco Zanghy, spoke[29] of only one *Tantum ergo*, saying that Bellini conducted it on Christmas Eve at the Minorite Fathers' church and then repeated it "to applause" on December 30 at the "church of the Monastero della Ss. Trinità."

Of Rosario and Agata Bellini's seven children, only Vincenzo died young, but his apparent frailty as a child did not prevent his going to school. L'Anonimo stated: "From the age of seven on, he studied the Latin language with the canon, signor Don Francesco Strano, librarian of the University of Studies in Catania,"[30] and added: "He presented his grandfather with his third composition [not specified]," whereupon Vincenzo Tobia Bellini, "reduced to amazement, told him: 'If you study, I will give you three lessons a week.' "[31] Various writers, led by L'Anonimo, have asserted that the boy studied English, French, Greek, Italian, and philosophy. But, as Pastura pointed out,[32] the adult Bellini knew no English, spoke French badly, wrote Italian very incorrectly, never showed a sign of familiarity with Greek—and of philosophy had only that of "common sense, an atavistic inheritance from the millennary experience of the Sicilian people." Bellini never became a well-educated man; Pastura put the matter aptly[33]: "In literary matters, Bellini was not uncultivated: his culture—disorderly, perhaps, but his own—was acquired more by intuition than by study, assimilated more through his sensibility than through his intellect."

Other undocumented anecdotes clearly were intended to display the boy Bellini's thin skin and warm kindheartedness (the first characteristic remained with him always, the second much less so). One of his brothers seems to have told Cicconetti that when the boy once noticed a weeping woman being led to a police post by guards, he became so agitated that he rushed at the men, insisting that they let her go. The composer's sister Maria told Antonino Amore that Vincenzo once brought home two small children whom he had found in the street in the rain, fed them, gave them clothes, and then, having learned that they were orphans, wanted them to stay with him always.

Some of the confused, often incredible statements about Bellini's earliest years derive from monsignore Coco Zanghy, who, for instance, wrote: "At about the age of nine, he wrote a Mass that was performed for the Octave of Corpus Domini in the church of San Biagio. At ten, he played so well on the organ of San Nicolò l'Arena that he was applauded by priore Cordaro, the excellent Cassinese organist. Then he also composed a *Compieta* with *Salve*, and another *Tantum ergo*, and at thirteen, to round this off, he was the author of another Mass for a solemn religious service in the Monastero di San Benedetto."[34]

L'Anonimo's account of the organ-playing incident naturally does not mention Cordaro, who, in fact, had been dead for some time before Bellini was ten: "One day, together with his schoolmates, Bellini planned to go into the church of the Benedictines to play on the organ.[35] His friends said that he could not do it. He said: 'I'll bet you some candy that I'll do it.' In short, they went into the church and asked a church Brother to let him climb up onto the organ. He succeeded, but as he was small, he could not manage the pedals. The organ had five banks of keys, and he told his friends to play on the keyboards from the sides under his direction. Some of the church Fathers, pupils of Bellini's father, asked who was playing. The Brother replied that it was a stranger. [The Fathers] climbed up and discovered the little Bellini, which amazed them, and they undertook to instruct him in music."[36]

The adolescent Vincenzo was in demand for exhibition and coddling at parties in the palazzos of the local aristocracy, to which the musical activities of his grandfather and father would have given him access. Nor is his youthful composing likely to have been only of religious pieces: little profane compositions would have been in demand for social festivities—and would surely have earned him presents or small sums.

That Bellini's lifelong reputation as a constant, passionate lover began when he was only twelve resulted from one very detailed anecdote told by Agostino Gallo, whom Bellini met in Palermo in 1832 and whose reliability as a chronicler is very dubious.[37] Gallo's published story included the following[38]:

"The most precocious physical and intellectual development was hinted at in him, and seemed to foretell that his existence would be brief. In fact, at so tender an age, Bellini was [already] a little man, somewhat thin, but tall and well formed, with nothing of boyishness about him but the excessive charm of a pink-and-white complexion lined here and there with very fine veins, and of extremely blond hair that, like threads of curled gold, fell in waves to his cheeks and shoulders. . . .

". . . near his home lived a respectable gentleman [the family name was Politi], the fortunate father of several children, among them a girl named Marietta, whose instructor in the elements of music was our Vincenzo's father. She was one of those dear creatures who are all spirit and vivacity, and she was intelligent beyond her years. A brunette with a complexion heightened by beautiful touches of red; with very black eyes and hair, a mouth like living coral, a smooth, pathetic voice tempered with melody, and an extraordinary bent toward the art of harmony. . . .

"One day the father [Rosario Bellini] took his son to Marietta's home so that her parents could observe his progress in music, and perhaps to awaken in his pretty pupil a certain desire to emulate it.

"When these children became better acquainted, Vincenzo became her family's idol and often ate with them. Whenever the hours of his studies at school or at home ended, his impulse was to betake himself to dally with his *amica*. . . .

"One of their favorite pastimes was playing with the little puppets that in Catania are well modeled and formed in gesso. One day he said to his darling: it would be prettier to have our puppets act in a proper little theater: ask your father to have one made and your brother to write a little farce with a song and an intermezzo for your girl doll; I'll adapt musical motives for them, and that way we'll have fun and earn the right to be together more. She liked the suggestion and begged her father and her brother so persistently that she obtained the little theater, the farce, the song. The latter [*i.e.*, her brother] thus became aware of his sister's liking for the boy and, more as a joke than otherwise, alluded to her infatuation in his verses when portraying her as the doll.

"I cannot tell whether they were aware of that or not. Certainly, however, Vincenzo wrote down melodies of his own invention; her father, who had not been conscious of what was happening, was overcome with wonder and pleasure when he found out about it. At the same time, he often noticed the loving pair at the pianoforte, one of them accompanying the composition, the other singing it according to the admonitions and corrections of her beloved *maestrino*.

"One day, her father happened to surprise them in the act [*sic*]— and there you have the boy fleeing from her family shamefaced and refusing to play in response to suggestion or command. Nevertheless, as the song had been rehearsed so often in secret without the father's direction, Marietta sang it well at the performance in the little theater, and it won applause for her and the composer, and from then on it was taken as a sign that he would bring honor to his name, his art, and his fatherland."

Gallo published what he said was the song, asserting that he had taken it from an old manuscript belonging to the Bellini heirs in Catania. Charming if bland, the piano-accompanied "*La Farfalletta*" is for mezzo-soprano, a minatory detail in view of its supposedly having been composed for a very young girl. It is often listed as Bellini's first song, but its authenticity is questionable.[39]

To Bellini's fourteenth or fifteenth year belong nine *Versetti da cantarsi il Venerdì Santo*,[40] eight of them to texts by Metastasio, the ninth to a Biblical text in Latin. Tradition long held that Bellini composed them to order for a pious Catanese lady who wanted them sung in the church of the Padre Crociferi. The then organist of that church later removed to Messina, where he had Bellini's little compositions performed each Good Friday. They were well described by Pastura[41] as "a series of '*ariette*' of typical eighteenth-century flavor in both form and writing. All this demonstrates the influence of the teaching of the elderly Don Vincenzo Tobia, who remained precisely what he had learned to be at the Neapolitan conservatory in which he had studied half a century before."

The influence of Grandfather Bellini upon his talented grandson increased in 1816, when Rosario and Agata Bellini, taking six of their seven children with them, moved into a larger, yet less expensive apartment; Vincenzo then went to live with his grandfather, who continued to instruct him in music. L'Anonimo asserted that at about this time, too, Bellini "went to study at the University, [taking] the three-year course in medicine, and his father and mother said to him: 'Why waste this time?' [and] he said: 'To take up a profession.' "[42] Bellini never studied medicine: confusion almost certainly entered the mind of the anonymous writer because Carmelo Platania, who was said to have taught the child English, was a professor of medicine. That Bellini may have listened to some of Platania's lectures is suggested, however, by passages in his later letters in which he talks about curatives and even prescribes for his friends.

Bellini's *Sinfonia in re maggiore*,[43] for first and second violins, clarinets, horns, and doublebass, almost certainly was composed during his final years in Catania. Other compositions—like the *Sinfonia*, they were probably intended for performance by a small ensemble of amateur or semi-professional musicians at aristocratic soirées—included *"Ombre pacifiche,"* a setting of twenty-four lines of vapid verse for two tenors and soprano with small orchestra[44]; an *Allegro a guisa di cabaletta*, beginning *"E nello stringerti a questo core,"* for soprano and orchestra[45]; and a *Scena ed aria di Cerere*—a sort of *cantata da camera*—also for soprano and orchestra.[46] Pastura believed[47] that to Bellini's sixteenth and seventeenth years also belonged three four-voice Masses with orchestral accompaniment; two *Salve Regina*s, respectively for chorus and for solo voice; a group of *Tantum ergo*s for one or more voices; and other, unrecoverable and unidentifiable pieces. Several of those surviving bear the date 1818, contain the phrase *"Laus Deo,"* and have "Vincenzo Bellini Ferlito" or "Vincenzo Bellini 2°" on their covers.

L'Anonimo reported that, "the profession that conquered" Bellini having been music, he said: " 'Send me to Naples,' as in fact the family considered doing. . . . He had advanced so far in his studies that when he was seventeen, his grandfather, for his part, had no more to teach him, and said to him: 'You can leave.' "[48] But the cost of sending the boy to Naples was forbidding to the increasingly hard-pressed Bellinis. During 1818, Vincenzo had to busy himself with his studies and with composing sacred pieces for church and monastery.

Meanwhile, the Vallo (province) of Catania had welcomed a new *intendente* from Palermo: Stefano Notarbartolo, duca di San Martino (Sammartino) e Montalbo. Both he and his duchessa—Donna Eleonora Stattela, born a principessa del Cassero—were to act toward Bellini with intelligent and almost visionary benevolence. To her, seventeen years after her arrival in Catania, he would dedicate *Beatrice di Tenda*, telling her in a letter of June 14, 1835[49]: "I do not wish to stop to record in detail the very great influence that your protection had on the beginning of my studies in Naples; believe me when I say that my heart rejoices in the emotion of remembering it." For a time, Bellini supervised the musical education of the duchessa's brother, duca Enrico, an amateur flutist.

When the Bellinis and Ferlitos reached the decision that Vincenzo should indeed continue his studies in Naples, a document was prepared. Addressed to the duca di San Martino, it was written out by someone else, but signed by "Vincenzo Bellini Ferlito sup[plicante]." A request for public assistance,[50] it bears no date. But on May 3, 1819, San Martino forwarded it to the "*patrizio*" (presiding city father), the principe del Pardo, with this order: "Signore, let there be placed before the delibera- tion of the decurionate the enclosed petition from Don Vincenzo Bellini e Ferlito, whose request reveals laudable inclinations not unrelated to the Comune's name in the liberal arts."

The ten city fathers convened on May 5 under the chairmanship of Pardo, who read Bellini's petition aloud, stating that the *intendente* had passed it on to him and asking if the council wished to assign to Bellini a pension enabling him to go to Naples to study. The favorable response was unanimous.[51] The decurionate then granted Bellini for four years an annual pension of thirty-six onze (equivalent to 459 Sicilian lire of the period, about $275 in 1971 purchasing power). They stipulated his obliga- tion to send them each year a sample of his work and certificates from his instructors that he had been attending to his musical studies. They further specified that on receipt of each payment of his pension, he was to send them a signed guarantee that if he should not return to Catania, he would repay the entire amount.

That decision was received joyfully by Bellini, but with some sadness by his parents and his grandfather, who, given their faith in his talent, perhaps foresaw that they were about to lose him for more than the four stipulated years. Bellini gathered together the manuscripts of his best compositions.[52] He was armed with letters to several powerful individuals in Naples, including—from the duca di San Martino—introductions to General Naselli, minister of the interior, and to Giovanni Carafa, duca di Noja, *intendente* of the Real College di Musica di San Sebastiano and superintendent of the royal theaters and spectacles. Early in June 1819,[53] aged seventeen years and seven months, Bellini left Catania by diligence for Messina. There he remained for six days with his father's sister Anna and her husband, Filippo Guererra. Finally—it would seem on June 14— he sailed from Messina. After a rough four-day crossing of the Tyrrhe- nian Sea, he disembarked at Naples.on June 18. Very soon thereafter, he matriculated at San Sebastiano.

Bellini lived nearly all of the succeeding eight years in Naples. There he began to mold his operatic style and contracted an extraordi- nary friendship. During the rest of his life, he would return to Catania and see the members of his family only when making two brief visits to Sicily, the first very probably in 1825, when he was already the composer of an unusually successful student opera, the second in 1832, by when his Grandfather Bellini would be dead and he himself would have composed all of his operas but *Beatrice di Tenda* and *I Puritani*. Then he would visit Messina, Catania, and Palermo as a fêted hero.

(II)

1819-1825:
The Neapolitan Years, I

I N 1808, THE MUSIC SCHOOLS of Naples had been consolidated in the
Real Collegio di Musica di San Sebastiano, housed in a seventeenth-
century building adjoining the church and monastery of the Gesù
Novo, just southeast of the piazza Dante. The Collegio was ruled by a
triumvirate, with each of the three men handling specified duties. Since
1813, its artistic director had been Nicolò Zingarelli (1752–1837), a successful operatic composer who also, in 1816, had succeeded Paisiello as
maestro di cappella of the Naples cathedral. His associated directors were
the duca di Noja and a priest, Don Gennaro Lambiase.

The students lived in the Collegio and worked at their musical studies
six mornings of every week the year round: on "principal subjects" Monday, Wednesday, and Friday, on specialized instruction in voice and
instruments Tuesday and Thursday, and on combined vocal-instrumental
exercises Saturday. Their afternoons five days each week were in part
occupied with nonmusical studies called "literary," intended to round
out their education.

Following a custom in earlier Neapolitan music schools, attached to
the Collegio was a *teatrino* (small theater), of which the chief purpose
was to provide advanced students of composition with experience of
actual performance. Cantatas, oratorios, and brief operas of their creation
were presented in it. School discipline was very strict, but the *maestrini*,
unlike the younger students, were permitted to leave the Collegio at
stated times—to give lessons that could initiate future sources of income
for them; to attend operatic and other musical performances; and to ex-

ercise the individual freedoms that, as youths, they must learn to manage.
The prevailing artistic atmosphere of the Collegio was a slightly modified
conservatism. By the time of Bellini's matriculation there in 1819, that
meant anti-Rossinianism in defense of the immediate and more remote past
of the Neapolitan school of composition, and particularly of the styles
of Pergolesi, Jommelli, Cimarosa, and especially Paisiello, who had died in
1816 at the age of seventy-six.

At seventeen, Bellini was well beyond the customary age for admission to the Collegio. How, despite his age, he was admitted is not known.
What is known is that the ten compositions[1] that he submitted before
matriculating were found by Zingarelli and his aides to be proofs of his
talent, but also were judged so faulty in technical details that, though he
was billeted with the older students, he was assigned to beginners' classes.
Pastura took that to indicate that the pieces revealed concepts of harmony,
counterpoint, and form which Bellini had acquired from his grandfather—
who had learned them more than sixty years before, and "which did not
take into account the changes that, in the interval, musical technique and
expression had experienced through the influence of French and German
artistic movements."[2] Bellini appears to have accepted the decision calmly
as a temporary setback: on July 3, 1819, writing to his uncle Filippo
Guerrera, he said[3]: "My desires are satisfied to the full." And on October
13, he was able to write his uncle that two weeks earlier he had been
awarded one of the scholarships—one hundred of them—that royal de-
crees of 1806 had established at San Sebastiano.[4]

Very early in his conservatory life, Bellini became friendly with his
fellow-student Francesco Florimo (1800–1888), thus initiating an extraordinary relationship that lasted until his death in 1835, after which Florimo
spent much of his remaining fifty-three years in celebrating his lost friend.
The two youths were almost diametric opposites: Bellini mercurial, ruled
by swiftly fluctuating moods, extremely volatile and self-centered; Florimo
unimaginative, placid, steadfast, contentedly mediocre. The somewhat
ungainly boy from San Giorgio Morgeto in Calabria genuinely fell in
love with his very handsome, talented, and unpredictable friend; nothing
known about Bellini suggests that he was capable of responding in kind.
Except in practical matters, Bellini always depended much less upon
Florimo than Florimo depended upon him. Hundreds of ardent phrases
in their later correspondence inescapably suggest to modern readers a
homosexual attachment. No other suggestion of that possibility survives,
unless it be the fact that neither Bellini nor Florimo ever married. In
1826, the year before Bellini left Naples, Florimo was to become librarian-
archivist of San Sebastiano, a position that he would hold through the

Collegio's change of name and location and until his death in 1888, in those sixty-two years building the Naples Conservatory library into the rich depository that it has remained.

Among Bellini's and Florimo's fellow-students in 1819 were the future operatic composer and superintendent of royal military bands, Nicola Fornasini (1803–1861), the future operatic composer Francesco Stabile (1804–1856); the brothers Luigi (1805–1859) and Federico (1809–1877) Ricci, future operatic composers both individually and in collaboration[5]; and Francesco Saverio Mercadante (1795–1870), then already a graduate student and practicing operatic composer (the first of his many operas, *L'Apoteosi di Ercole*, was staged at the Teatro San Carlo, Naples, on August 19, 1819).

Life at San Sebastiano was regulated by the clock. The students were roused at 4:45 a.m. and were expected to wash and dress themselves quickly. At 5:30, they were at Mass in the school chapel. A quick breakfast—and then, from 6 to 9, three hours in which to prepare for the day's musical classes, held from 9 to 11:30. Noon found them at lunch in the refectory, after which they were permitted an hour for recreation or, during the summer, two hours for rest in bed. From 4 to 6 in the afternoon, they attended classes in nonmusical subjects, after which they were allowed a brief stroll, the younger boys under the surveillance of a *maestrino*. After attendance at ten o'clock chapel, they ate a simple supper and were sent to bed.

Bellini did not take vocal lessons, but did devote considerable time to the theoretical study of singing under one of the foremost practitioners of true bel canto, the sopranist and composer Girolamo Crescentini (1762–1846), whose many renowned pupils included Isabella Colbran, Rossini's first wife. Crescentini's *Esercizi per la vocalizzazione* (Paris, 1811) was a required text at San Sebastiano: Bellini came to know its contents very well. From it, as Andrea Della Corte wrote,[6] Bellini acquired "a technique in part traditionalist and in part modernist, which reflected the evolution from eighteenth-century methods to those of the nineteenth century, and a cantilena that departed from the Paisiellian, Cimarosian, and Mozartean and accepted some element of the especially theatrical taste for romantic impetuosity."

Bellini was more directly and permanently influenced by what he learned about composing for the voice than by anything else in his conservatory training: Crescentini's somewhat reactionary and anti-Rossianian attitudes helped him to avoid becoming another overt imitator of Rossini. Those attitudes were set forth forcefully in a letter that Crescentini wrote to Antonio Micheroux on December 29, 1836[7]: "You are right in saying that today music is nothing but the amassing of a myriad of excessively noisy notes, and the reason why the poor singer—who must fight with such a quantity of them and with the uproar of trumpets, trombones, and all those devilish wind instruments—must make a career of shouting and cannot rely upon smooth use of his voice even when he knows how to handle it. I hope for its return soon from the false road that it is now traveling, and also hope that, having reached the end of the style of cabalettas and crescendos that exist galore in every piece of music by our present-day composers in the wake of the Rossianian genius, we shall turn to a simpler, truer style that will give the human voice what is its own and belongs to it; that it will return to the feeling for singing, for declaiming, and not for sounding forth and shouting, which singers do today because they cannot help doing so when faced by the bad taste introduced into vocal composition."

Bellini has often been accused of orchestrating badly or ineptly. That charge mistakes the special nature of his operas and disregards his chief aim in composition, which was to assign the burden of expression to the text-words and their melodies, for which reason (*vide* Crescentini) he naturally avoided the richer, more designedly expressive orchestration that brought upon Rossini the accusation of being "too Teutonic." Bellini did not equal Rossini's originality in instrumentation; he lacked the acute feeling for appropriate orchestral (especially solo) colors that Donizetti had inherited from Giovanni Simone Mayr. But for Bellini's conscious purpose that originality and those colors were not required; except in very noticeable and exceptional instances, his orchestra was meant to fill out harmonies, supply rhythms, and support and help to project the meaning of the libretto. A tendency toward that kind of operatic texture was native to him, but it also was importantly intensified by what he absorbed at San Sebastiano, especially from the teachings of Crescentini and Zingarelli.

Among Bellini's early teachers at the Collegio were Giovanni Furno (in "*partimento*," or exercises in harmony and accompaniment); the octogenarian Giacomo Tritto (1733–1824), who had begun a mildly successful career as an operatic composer half a century earlier, and who taught counterpoint; and, as his (and Florimo's) *maestrino* and tutor for regular lessons with Tritto, Carlo Conti (1797–1868), whom Rossini once called "the best contrapuntalist of the day in Italy."[8] Bellini progressed rapidly in his studies: in the 1820 annual competitive examination, he won the right to enter the classes in harmony and counterpoint—and to free tuition. This latter prize left part of his Catania pension available toward the support of his family. Also, he could now wear the school uniform, a long blue smock with black silk epaulettes which must have become him very well. But he was not happy with Tritto's very old-fashioned and doctrinaire teaching; he later transferred to Zingarelli's class and found its much freer, less tradition-bound atmosphere more satisfying.

The student compositions that Bellini forwarded to the Catania de-curionate as the promised proofs of his work at San Sebastiano included a *Sinfonia* and a Mass.[9] The *Sinfonia*, labeled *Capriccio, ossia sinfonia per studio*, is for large orchestra; it is in C minor and of fuguelike texture. The autograph (now in the Museo Belliniano) is countersigned by Tritto, a fact that dates it before 1822, when Bellini left Tritto's classes. The Mass may have been the one in A major which Ricordi published,[10] possibly the one sung in the Catanese church of San Francesco d'Assisi, hard by Bellini's birthplace, on October 4, 1821, to celebrate the saint's day of the Emperor Francis II (Catania then being in Austrian hands).

The only recorded political involvement of Bellini's life occurred in 1820–1821. The mainland part of the Kingdom of the Two Sicilies was dotted with pockets of discontent with Bourbon absolutism, and the libertarian secret society known as the *carbonari* was growing rapidly. Demonstrations broke out in Naples, their purpose being to force Ferdinando I to grant his kingdom a constitution like the one that had been proclaimed for Spain eight years before by his nephew, Ferdinando VII. On July 9, 1820, at the head of troops allied with the *carbonari*, General Guglielmo Pepe finally entered Naples in triumph. The king then promulgated the desired constitution (July 23), thus very temporarily becoming a constitutional monarch. Huge crowds clogged the narrow streets of Naples to rejoice over that illusory victory.

Sixty years later, Florimo recounted the high points of his and Bellini's political lives during that exciting interval, writing them out for Michele Scherillo on the blank spaces of used envelopes[11]:

"In 1820, during that honeymoon of constitutional government, all the young men, as happens during revolutions, were electrified by the mere name of *liberty;* and, shouting 'Liberty!' they were possessed by the Devil! ! We, too, Bellini and I . . . students at the Collegio di San Sebastiano, took part in that revolutionary movement; and were among the first to glorify what we then believed to be a happy event, the first to be present at the entry of the country troops that moved into Naples from Monteforte. From a window on the lower floor of the Royal Palace, we saw them pass, and above us, on the grand balcony, was the King—that Ferdinando who was III and IV, and after 1815 became I—who, with the entire Royal Family, fanatically applauded those people, not uniformed but in their own clothes, who mixed with the regular troops to form a mass in comic disorder, pleasant to see, especially as it passed under the King's balcony.

"And at that time, partly because our friends urged us on, partly so as to swim with the current, we enrolled in the movement known as the *carbonari*. But the momentary enthusiasm came to an end with the entrance of the German [Austrian] troops in March 1821. The old order of things returned, and good-bye liberty, good-bye constitution: reaction showed itself everywhere and to everyone.

"But this is where the *scena buffa* begins.

"The Rector of the Collegio di Musica was don Gennaro Lambiase, an excellent priest, a benevolent and good-hearted man who loved Bellini and me in a fatherly way—but he was a realist and a Bourbonist to the marrow of his bones. One evening—I remember it as though it were yesterday—it was May 29, 1821—he summoned us to his rooms and gave us a solemn, paternal talking-to, concluding in a gruff way: 'You are *carbonari*—and don't deny it, as I have learned it from a reliable source— and therefore you are enemies of God and of our august King! I am going to give you advice for your own good; and I want you to listen to me, because if you don't, I don't know where you are going to end up. To- morrow is the saint's day of the King, our legitimate ruler; in the evening, you will go to the San Carlo to celebrate his *festa*, and will applaud loudly whenever the audience applauds, and will keep on shouting at the tops of your voices: "Long live our King Ferdinando, consecrated by God and by Right!" And make certain that you force the audience to notice you because of your shouting. In that way I'll have the cards in my hands (these are his exact words) to save you when facing the Minister of Police— who is a close friend of mine because at the time of the French military occupation we were imprisoned together in the State prisons as Bourbon- ists, with irons on our feet. We had reason to fear being condemned to death as enemies of the State because they accused us of plotting the re- turn of Ferdinando and of having been in secret correspondence with Queen Maria Carolina.* When I speak about you so as to be able to defend you, I'll be able to say that, being very young and inexperienced, you allowed yourself to be borne away by the current and became *car- bonari* without understanding what an evil thing you were doing, etc., etc.; and I am certain of winning not only pardon for you, but also per- mission to keep you on as students in this Collegio. But you must go to Confession at once and ask forgiveness of God for your transgressions and for having agreed to belong to a secret society that is an enemy of Him and of the legitimate Sovereign.'

"The more he talked, the more we felt a certain terror of prisons, galleys, the gibbet; but what chiefly made us tremble was the idea of being

---

* (Scherillo's note): It was King Ferdinando who, on his return to the throne, gave Lambiase the position of Rector of the Conservatory because of his proved affection for the Bourbon family.

expelled from the Collegio. And when evening came, we went to the theater and carried out the Rector's prescriptions to the letter.

"The next day, after Confession in the Collegio's church, we went to the feet of the confessor, a well-educated man who shone in the city by his vast knowledge, and especially because of his acquaintance with the Oriental languages. When he had heard that our sin was being members of the secret society, we foresaw his questions, which were aimed at discovering the names of all the people we knew in the *lodge* in which the *Good Cousins* (the name the *carbonari* used among themselves) foregathered. Almost as though we had agreed beforehand, we gave the same answer, which was that we had come to his feet to confess our own misdeeds, not those of others. Then the good priest, having probed that hard ground, changed his tone and gave us absolution. We immediately climbed back up the Collegio staircase and presented ourselves to the dear Rector Lambiase, who embraced us and invited us to supper. We were back in the good graces of God, of the King, and of the Rector!

"What a good-natured man! If he had not taken up our defense at that hour, we undoubtedly would at least have been expelled from the Collegio; and what would have become of poor Bellini, only nineteen years old and without the means to study music? The best that it would have been possible for him would have been a post as organist in some village."

During 1822, Bellini met for the first time Gaetano Donizetti and Maddalena Fumaroli, the first of whom was all unwittingly to become one of his chief bugbears, whereas the other was to cast a crazily disproportionate shadow of false sentiment over much of the future writing about him.

Donizetti (1797–1848), already the composer of nine operas (six of which had achieved performance), had reached Naples for the first time late in February or early in March 1822. Soon thereafter, in a demonstration of that astonishing speed in composing which later aroused Bellini's scorn, he prepared a cantata to signalize the birth of a daughter to Prince Leopoldo, King Ferdinando's brother, and was well along in composing *La Zingara*, an opera to a libretto by Andrea Leone Tottola. That earliest of Donizetti's Neapolitan operas was welcomed with enthusiasm on May 12, 1822, at the Teatro Nuovo, the first of its twenty-eight consecutive performances there that season.[12] Florimo later reported that its "success was splendid and complete" and that "it was given for a year, and always to increasing delight on the part of the public, which never tired of hearing it." He added:

"As is natural, it was attended eagerly by . . . those young men who meant to enter the same musical arena, not least among them the very distinguished composer Carlo Conti, who said to Bellini and me one day:

'Go to hear Donizetti's *La Zingara*, which I enjoy every evening, and increasingly; and among the other pieces, you will find a septet [it ends Act I] that only a pupil of Mayr could and would know how to create.' We hastened to go, and the septet mentioned, the opera's culminating number, was what caught the attention and admiration of Bellini, who soon obtained a copy of it and then, keeping it on the stand of his cembalo, studied it and played it every day. Shortly thereafter, he begged and urged Conti to introduce him to Donizetti, and I remember that the day when that introduction was made was a red-letter day for Bellini, who told me, when he returned from the meeting still in a state of enthusiasm: 'Besides the great talent that this Lombard has, he is also a big, handsome man, and his noble features, sweet and yet imposing, inspire affection and respect.' Those are his exact words, which I still remember."[13]

Bellini's admiration and affection for Donizetti did not survive: his later competitive, jealous, and vindictive remarks about Donizetti provide the least attractive passages in his surviving correspondence. Largely because of his feeling against Donizetti—and against the less admirable, less likable Pacini—Bellini was to say that it was impossible for two men practicing the same métier to remain true friends. That opinion would have astounded both Donizetti and Rossini, whom Bellini was later to woo so ardently.

Maddalena Fumaroli, the other new acquaintance of 1822 who was important in Bellini's life, was a young girl. The story of their simple, ill-starred infatuation has become so clouded by nonsense that its factual outlines can be discerned only with difficulty. Antonino Amore confidently published[14] a portrait of Maddalena which some later writers have reproduced. But Luisa Cambi unintentionally symbolized the fictional qualities of the Bellini-Fumaroli legend when she wrote[15]: "No portrait of her is known. That reproduced in the work of A. Amore (*Bellini: Vita*), and an enlargement of which is preserved in the Museo Belliniano at Catania, has served later for all other biographers. But it is thought to be an engraving based upon a copy *made from memory* of a *presumed* portrait."

Maddalena Fumaroli probably was born in Naples about 1802. She was the daughter of Francesco Saverio Fumaroli, a prominent jurist, and his wife Teodora, whose maiden name had been Geronimo Princerio. Having been a guest in the Fumarolis' home, Bellini was attracted to the girl and offered to give her singing lessons. They fell in love, a fact that for a time seems to have escaped detection by her parents. When the elder Fumarolis discovered the situation, they stopped the singing lessons, asked Bellini to their home less often, and finally forbade him to see Maddalena. As he was then about twenty-one, she about twenty, their acute distress can be imagined. According to Florimo,[16] who was aware of their infatuation at the time, the lovers found a means of exchanging letters.

In 1821, to artless verses possibly written by Giulio Genoino, the librettist of Donizetti's *farsa La Lettera anonima* (1822), who may have instructed Maddalena in literature, Bellini had composed the romanza *"Dolente immagine di Fille mia";* somewhat later, he set a *scena* (recitative, andante, cabaletta) beginning *"Quando incise su quel marmo/L'infede il nome mio."* Both became popular salon pieces when Girard (later Cottrau) published them in Naples not long after their composition.[17] Florimo's determination, later seconded by other commentators, to see these melancholy pieces as direct results of the Fumarolis' interference in their daughter's love affair is no more than romanticizing in view of the dates of their composition, which are too early.

The beclouding legend also would have it that when, in 1825, Bellini came to compose his first, student opera, *Adelson e Salvini* (not *Salvina*, as sometimes stated), he labored over it with the greater ardor because he was convinced that a success for it would soften the hearts of Maddalena's parents. When that success outran his most daring expectation, Bellini, acting against Florimo's advice, asked Giuseppe Marsigli, who instructed Maddalena in painting, to present his formal request for her hand to her father. Fumaroli rejected it, and not unreasonably. True, Bellini was by then the composer of an opera popular enough to be repeated every Sunday in the school's *teatrino*, but at twenty-four he had no firm hope of a stable future income or any other means of supporting himself, not to mention a wife. Urged forward by his intense ambition to win glory as an operatic composer, and perhaps by his desire to marry Maddalena, Bellini persuaded the duca di Noja to invoke a government regulation that conferred upon a notably worthy student of composition at the Collegio the right to have a cantata or one-act opera performed at either the Teatro del Fondo or the Teatro San Carlo.

Bellini elected to set an operatic libretto by Domenico Gilardoni entitled *Bianca e Fernando* (the opera became *Bianca e Gernando* when performed, for a reason that will become clear). Surely if that opera were to prove another public success . . . Like *Adelson e Salvini* in 1825, *Bianca e Gernando* won its audiences in 1826. The Fumarolis were approached again through Marsigli. "I recall," Florimo wrote,[18] "that Bellini awaited with me the outcome of this message, and you can picture with what anxiety; but Marsigli scarcely had appeared when he read the unhappy outcome on that friend's face—though he was trying to conceal it. I saw him blanch at his [Marsigli's] words, which confirmed those fears; I saw him quiver all over, but his strength of spirit quickly calmed him, and he assured me, clinging to my hand, that he would persist and win." In a book wildly unfair to Bellini as a person,[19] Giuseppe Tito De Angelis asserted that Fumaroli accompanied this rejection of Bellini's suit with a demand that the young man return all the letters that he had received from Maddalena—a demand that deeply wounded Bellini. The source of that curious bit of information is unknown.

But in April 1827, Bellini left Naples for Milan and bigger success at La Scala. At first, he kept in touch with Maddalena by letter. Then the frequency of the letters diminished: he was becoming more involved with, and more welcome in, the great world. Then someone—possibly Marsigli —took it upon himself to present Bellini's suit to Maddalena's parents a third time. It was accepted. Bellini was informed that Maddalena could and would marry him. Florimo wrote[20] that this unexpected news "found Bellini anything but enthusiastic. Still, he did not want to reply on the spur of the moment, and for some days he remained undecided about what to do. His will and his reason finally were stronger than the residue of his faded love, and by an energetic effort he made a firm resolution to reply negatively to the offer that had been made. Was this a virile determination to consecrate himself exclusively to his art? Was it because the old flame was guttering out in his heart? Probably both things, and especially the latter . . ."

Florimo asserted[21] that Bellini, "whether to justify himself or to bring some comfort to the poor deserted girl, wrote her a letter brimming with affectionate words, which she read while shedding the tenderest tears and kept jealously by her all the rest of her life because in it he promised her never to marry any other woman (a feeble consolation for someone in love and suffering) and assured her that the only rivals she need fear in the future would be his operas." The letter may have been sent, but it has not survived.

Four references to Maddalena Fumaroli occur in Bellini's correspondence for 1828. Writing from Milan on January 16, to Florimo, he said[22]: ". . . let us hope that everything will turn out well for *la Fumaroli;* as for me, I should never have been able to content myself with her because that is the way that the interests of my career and my finances would have it." Again to Florimo, on February 25[23]: "*La Fumaroli* has not, in fact, written to me about the way you spoke of Peppino [unidentified], and I am glad that she is beginning to persuade herself." Once again to Florimo, on May 12, from Milan[24]: "I have received two letters from *la Fumaroli*— very tardily because I was in Genoa when they reached here; I don't think that I shall answer or else I'll send the answering letter to you." On June 9, finally, he told Florimo[25]: "I enclose an answer to *la Fumaroli*'s three letters; she wants to marry me at any price, and I have neither the desire to take a wife nor the money to support one; and I have repeated all that a thousand times. She is still young, and she can change certain decisions that were made out of lack of experience. You can take the page to her— and let's hope that she will be persuaded." Nothing indicates that Bellini tried to see Maddalena when he visited Naples later. She died (of a "broken heart") in Naples on June 15, 1834. When Bellini, in Paris, learned of her death is not known, but his only mention of it in a surviving letter, to Florimo, occurred on June 7, 1835[26]: "The news of the death of poor Maddalenina distressed me terribly, and you see what chance *** moment that I stop *** of love *** . . ."

The story of Maddalena Fumaroli is very sad and very human—not least as revealing Bellini's absorption in his personal ambitions (he would have said "*la mia gloria*"). In his defense it can be said that circumstance had dragged out a naïve infatuation to the point at which, for him (but unhappily not for Maddalena), its original significance had been dispersed. For him to have married this apparently simple girl when his mind and emotions had moved so far away from her might seriously have damaged his peace of mind during the time left to him for composing. Very probably, too, he and she being what they were, marriage would have turned a more immediate face of unhappiness upon them both. That, rather than the inflated sentimental saga that Amore and other early biographers —but not Florimo—made of their sparse relationship, is the real meaning of Bellini's first adult love.

Early in 1822, Bellini had followed Florimo's lead in transferring from Giacomo Tritto's class to Zingarelli's. Unanimous testimony by those who studied under Zingarelli and knew him well pictures him as a gifted teacher with a special propensity for adapting his methods to the individuality and needs of any promising student. When one of his pupils displayed indications of talent for theatrical composition, he saw to it that the boy became familiar with dramatic verse and the ways and functioning of opera houses. Of Zingarelli's early handling of Bellini, Florimo wrote[27]:

"With that sense all his own, Zingarelli quickly understood the young Catanese's fine gift, and began with real interest and fatherly love to cultivate that elect talent, at first through the severity of hard study, then by guiding and directing it to consider in depth the works of the classic and renowned masters who illustrated the art so well." Having estimated Bellini's talent and lacks, Zingarelli told him to abandon work on counterpoint and fugued basses for the time being and to compose solfeggios,

---

*** This symbol will be used to indicate illegibility in an autograph—in this instance because the paper of the letter, in the library of the Naples Conservatory, has been partially destroyed.

lots of solfeggios, those wordless melodies which nevertheless could be developed into expressive musical fabric suitable for vocalization.

" 'If you make your compositions *sing*,' " Zingarelli told Bellini,[28] " 'then you can really be certain that your music will please. If, instead, you amass *harmonies, double counterpoints, fugues, canons, notes, counter-notes*, etc., the musical world will or will not applaud you after half a century but the public certainly will disapprove of you. It wants *melodies, melodies*, always *melodies*. If your heart learns to give them to you, study the ways to set them forth as simply as possible, and your success will be assured; you will be a composer; the other way, you will be nothing more than a good organist in some village.' " Advice more germane to Bellini's musical character would have been impossible to find. And, as if composing those solfeggios freed Bellini's mind and spirit, he composed about four hundred of them to lay before the astonished Zingarelli for criticism.

Because Zingarelli had quarters in the Collegio and was at home to favored students, Bellini came to be on very friendly terms with him, though the older man deliberately showed his most rigorous and demanding side in their teacher-pupil relationship. "Everyone remembers," Florimo wrote,[29] "that most of the time Bellini took two lessons each day, and he [Zingarelli] would say to him: 'You are so young! are you perhaps afraid that a lifetime will not be long enough to learn the art? Let's see this latest solfeggio (the second of the day), which I hope will be better than this morning's.' " Thus Zingarelli fortified Bellini's inborn tendency to assign the prime position among the materials of composition to melody, and most particularly to vocal melody.

Among the Bellini musical autographs preserved in the library of the Naples Conservatory, only two are dated 1823: a *Sinfonia* in E-flat major and a set of four *Tantum ergos*. The *Sinfonia* (*larghetto maestoso-allegro moderato*, for large orchestra) bears this inscription by Bellini: "*Sinfonia* in E flat—for large orchestra—written by Vincenzo Bellini—student at the Collegio di Musica—Naples, 1823." He remained sufficiently satisfied with the introductory section of this student exercise to adapt it for use twice later: in the *sinfonia* for *Adelson e Salvini* (1825) and in that for *Il Pirata* (1827). The *Tantum ergos* survive in a fair copy made by Bellini, on which he wrote: "Four Tantum Ergos—by Vincenzo Bellini—on October 10, 1823."

Because these 1823 compositions are the earliest in which suggestions of Bellini's future style appear importantly, the temptation arises to attribute to his close contact with Zingarelli that liberation into melodic expressiveness of a somewhat melancholy tinge. But to overpraise the *Sinfonia* and the *Tantum ergos* would be foolish: were they not by Bellini, they would be devoid of interest. Except for them and possibly the *Sinfonia* in E flat and the Oboe Concerto (in the same key),[30] 1823 seems to have been for Bellini a year of hard study devoid of exterior excitement. On November 26, the Catania decurionate, satisfied with his proofs of progress, extended his annual pension for three years.

Early in 1824, as a result of Bellini's showing in the annual competitive examinations, he was appointed *"primo maestrino"* (he had been a simple *maestrino*). This honor carried with it not only the duty of tutoring younger, less advanced students,[31] but also the right to have a room of his own in the Collegio and to go each Thursday and Sunday to an opera at either the San Carlo or the Teatro del Fondo. On one of these delighted-in visits to the San Carlo, Bellini heard Rossini's *Semiramide*[32] expertly performed by a cast including Joséphine Fodor-Mainvielle, Adelaide Comelli-Rubini, Giovanni Battista Rubini, and Luigi Lablache. He emerged from that extravagant entertainment stupefied and disheartened. Florimo wrote,[33] "Bellini was so affected after hearing it that, on his way back to the Collegio after the theater with me and other companions, he gave vent to sad words of discomfort to us as he dawdled near the Porta Alba, because it seemed impossible to him to write good music in the face of that classic music by Rossini." Many younger composers—among them Carlo Conti, Luigi Ricci, and Saverio Mercadante—would succumb to Rossini's strong influence and often be his more or less feeble imitators. Bellini himself would require time, experience, and resulting self-assurance to rid himself of that influence almost entirely: clear traces of Rossinian manners and gestures appear even in *Il Pirata*, the third of his operas (1827).

Bellini needed prolonged, intense inward concentration for the development of his own manner, his own music: after leaving Naples in 1827, he never again showed real interest in new music by others or in emergent composers. Artistically speaking, he was to live exclusively in the universe of the librettos he set and the music they evoked from him. Perhaps he was saved from overt Rossinianism by Zingarelli, who often fulminated against the ripples—which became waves and then began to look like a tidal disturbance—raised by Rossini's operas above the previously smooth surface of eighteenth-nineteenth-century Italian opera. Back in 1819, after a performance of young Carlo Conti's *Le Truppe in Franconia*, Rossini had congratulated not only the *maestrino*, but also his preceptor, Zingarelli. Florimo, who had been present, wrote[34]: ". . . Zingarelli, instead of expressing thanks for such warm words of praise directed at him by Rossini addressed him this way: 'My dear Maestro, you are ruining all these pupils of mine for me, for they want to imitate no one but you, only you.' Rossini, in turn, with that natural cynicism and joviality so native to him, answered: 'They could avoid ruining themselves, these dear young men of yours, venerated Maestro, by limiting themselves to imitating you, only you.' Zingarelli turned his back and said nothing more."

During early April 1824, Bellini and Florimo each felt sufficiently sure of himself and his purse to sign a contract for the purchase of a mahogany piano "with six pedals on the ground" for 160 ducati[35]—eighty ducati down, ten to be paid each month for eight months. Bellini would work on the composition of both *Adelson e Salvini* and *Bianca e Gernando* at this piano. In February 1828, when it had begun to seem that Bellini would not return to Naples from Milan, Florimo sold it for him.

Exactly when Bellini learned that he was to compose an opera for performance in the Collegio's *teatrino* by fellow students is not known,[36] but it was probably in the summer or early autumn of 1824. He either selected or was assigned a three-act *dramma* by Andrea Leone Tottola entitled *Adelson e Salvini*, which Valentino Fioravanti had composed eight years before.[37] The text was written in standard Italian except for the role of Salvini's servant, Bonifacio, which was in Neapolitan dialect.[38] Bellini worked at composing *Adelson e Salvini* through the end of 1824 in the belief that his opera would be presented on January 12, 1825, to celebrate the king's birthday. But Ferdinando I died during the night of January 4–5, 1825, and the first performance of *Adelson* could not occur until after the resultant ten-day period of mourning.[39]

Bellini's first opera, sung by students from Crescentini's class, was an undoubted success with its first special audiences; it became so popular that permission was granted for its repetition in the *teatrino* on Sunday afternoons throughout 1825. Of its première, Florimo wrote[40] that ". . . among the applauding audience was Gaetano Donizetti, who ran up onto the stage to embrace the young composer as soon as the spectacle was over, saying such flattering words that they moved Bellini to tears. Bellini (I was present), struck silent by pleasure, wanted to kiss his hand, but Donizetti, with heartfelt effusiveness, embraced him in a transport, and in solemn words predicted a happy future for him." Donizetti certainly was in Naples at the time, and the anecdote may be accurate; it is equally possible, however, that Florimo, writing many decades after the event, had confused the première of *Adelson e Salvini* with that of *Bianca e Gernando* fifteen months later. None of Donizetti's many surviving letters refers to *Adelson e Salvini*, and when writing to Mayr on May 30, 1826 in praise of *Bianca e Gernando*, he referred to it[41] as Bellini's "first production."

From Milan, on May 12, 1828, Bellini wrote to Florimo[42]: "Tell me whether you have revised [*accommodato*] *Adelson* for Barbaja," thus indicating that they had agreed earlier to refashion the opera in view of a possible staging of it under the aegis of the impresario Domenico Barbaja, very probably in Naples, and that Bellini either had entrusted Florimo with the revision or had left with him, or sent him, some revised or new materials.[43] The changes were not completed in 1828, for on March 14, 1829, Bellini wrote to Florimo[44]: "I have written you the changes that you should make in *Adelson*." How much of the reshaping was Bellini's, how much Florimo's, cannot be ascertained: no complete autograph of the revised version of the opera survives—if, indeed, one ever existed.[45] The existence of the two autograph revised act-finales now in the library of the Naples Conservatory suggests that Bellini wrote out only the most important revisions and new numbers and then sent them to Florimo, who incorporated them into the new two-act version according to a plan previously agreed upon.

Florimo wrote[46]: "However, he [Bellini] later held this, his first work, in no esteem, to the point of writing on its last page: 'End of the *dramma*, alias big *pasticcio*.' " The words appear where Florimo saw them, but whereas "End of the *dramma*" is in Bellini's handwriting, "alias big *pasticcio*" is not. Had he considered *Adelson e Salvini* worthless, it is unlikely that, when already the composer of both versions of *Bianca*, and of *Il Pirata*, he would have expended labor and time upon completing —or even helping to complete—a revision of it when he did not have in hand a contract guaranteeing that it would both reach performance and be cast so as to redound to his "glory" as a composer.

On October 10, 1835, seventeen days after Bellini's death, Giovanni Ricordi wrote to Florimo[47]; "Now I shall ask a favor of you. Wanting to make known to the musical world the first opera of our aforementioned friend, *Adelson e Salvini*, which he wrote for your conservatory there, I beg you to obtain a copy of it for me and forward it to me as quickly as possible . . ." Florimo complied with the publisher's request, probably forwarding a manuscript copy of the revised full score and a copy of the piano-vocal score, as well as his own piano-solo reduction, both of the latter containing only the important separate numbers. The Ricordi firm eventually issued the piano-vocal score and Florimo's piano-solo reduction, placing upon the title pages of both the misleading annotation: "Edition revised against the Autograph score existing in the Library of the Royal Conservatory of Music in Naples." No performance of the revised *Adelson e Salvini* is mentioned anywhere: Bellini's first opera seems (1971) not to have been staged since its performances in the San Sebastiano *teatrino* in 1825.

1825-1827: The Neapolitan Years, II; *Bianca e Gernando*; Milan; *Il Pirata*

NEWS OF BELLINI'S TALENT had begun to spread beyond the walls of San Sebastiano and outside Naples. In July 1825, while *Adelson e Salvini* continued to be heard each Sunday, he was invited to compose a *messa di gloria* for a church in Gragnano, a small community across the Bay of Naples, on the slopes above Castellammare di Stabia.[1] Which of several *messe di gloria* was prepared for this commission is not known: Pastura guessed that it was the one in G minor of which vocal and orchestral parts survive in the Naples Conservatory library.[2]

Bellini may have gone to Sicily in August to visit his family and friends in Catania for the first time since his departure for Messina and Naples more than six years before. Very little can be learned about this trip: the earliest printed reference to it was made by Cicconetti in 1859[3]; he placed it in 1825 and implied that Bellini was fleeing his bitterness and despair at the Fumarolis' refusal to let Maddalena marry him. For that reason, Cicconetti wrote, Bellini sought "the more tranquil affections of his family—which, on his return to Catania, he enjoyed during some August days . . ." But Cicconetti may have had no basis for mentioning the trip other than a statement by L'Anonimo that Bellini "thought of going to embrace his family after seven years of absence [*sic*],[4] as in fact, he betook himself to Catania on August 17, 1825, which was a great surprise to his family and his friends."[5]

That Bellini visited Sicily during the mid-1820's is proved by a passage in a letter that he wrote to "my dear uncle"—Filippo Guerrera of Messina—on September 27, 1828[6]: "Who knows but that in a few years I shall see my dear uncle, my affectionate aunt, and the lovable Cristina [the Guerreras' daughter] unexpectedly, as I did four years ago? I cherish that hope, and I shall realize it on the first favorable occasion that presents itself to me." Bellini thus placed this Sicilian trip in 1824, as did Giuseppe Arenaprimo when he wrote[7] that Bellini stopped off in Messina during that year and added: "It is remembered that . . . Vincenzo Bellini was advised urgently . . . not to try for the position of director of the Cappella Senatoria of our cathedral, as had been his intention . . . This episode survives in tradition: some have even added, on the testimony of several people of the time, that Bellini, a youth of not quite twenty-three, did present himself for the competition, and perhaps with results that were less than happy."

Whether or not those oral traditions reflect any factual foundation will never be known: that portion of the relevant Messina archives which a conflagration in 1848 had left intact was destroyed by the 1908 earthquake. Pastura confidently placed Bellini's brief Sicilian sojourn in 1825, after noting that Florimo had never mentioned it in print, probably because "for him it had the air of a visit made privately."[8] But a puzzling account of the trip was published in 1953 by Ottavio Tiby.[9] He too dated it 1825, but assumed that Bellini had left Naples intending not to return and had spent months in Catania, assumptions for which no documentation whatever can be found. "It is known that the crisis was one of short duration," Tiby wrote, "and the summons from Zingarelli, coming toward the end of the year, fortunately induced Bellini to change his mind. He left [Sicily], and the success of *Bianca e Fernando* at Naples, and then of *Il Pirata* at Milan set his life on the proper path."

What "summons from Zingarelli"? Why "toward the end of the year"? We know that during the summer or early autumn of 1825, Bellini began to compose the opera then scheduled for performance at the Teatro San Carlo in January 1826. The contract with the government held by the impresario of the San Carlo and Fondo theaters included the clause specifying that whenever the Collegio judged one of its students worthy, a cantata or a one-act opera must be ordered from him. The impresario was required to supply gratis the text to be composed and to pay its composer three hundred ducati; the composition was to be presented during a gala evening. The duca di Noja, in addition to being a member of the triumvirate governing San Sebastiano, was also superintendent of the royal theaters, and Bellini had been notified that this honor had come to him. Agreement was reached that he would compose, not a cantata—a prospect that bored him—or a one-act opera, but a full-length opera. Bellini certainly remained in Naples during the autumn and early winter of 1825.

The San Carlo management probably expected the student composer to set a libretto by Tottola, its official dramatic poet. But Bellini rejected that suggestion, perhaps because of his experience in setting Tottola's *Adelson e Salvini.* Instead, he suggested that the impresario commission a libretto from a young writer named Domenico Gilardoni. Although Gilardoni had never written an opera text, he thereupon was commissioned to prepare for Bellini's use one called *Bianca e Fernando.* He borrowed the framework of his story from a prose play that had been staged successfully at the Teatro dei Fiorentini: *Bianca e Fernando alla tomba di Carlo IV duca di Agrigento,* by Carlo Roti.[10] The play's Sicilian setting especially attracted Bellini, who is not known to have objected when the royal authorities demanded that the title of his opera be altered to *Bianca e Gernando* because no form of the name Ferdinando— that of the heir apparent to the throne—could be used on a royal stage in the Kingdom of the Two Sicilies.

Bellini was informed that the chief singers for whom he was to compose would be Adelaide Tosi, a Milanese soprano who had studied with Crescentini; the prodigiously gifted tenor Giovanni David; and that physically and artistically tremendous favorite, first of Naples and then of all Europe, the bass Luigi Lablache. The opera that he set about composing with roles suitable to their voices had to be ready for rehearsal by December. It was ready—and rehearsals had begun—when the new king, Francesco I, decided that the announced January grand gala must be canceled out of respect for his late father. The audience at the San Carlo on January 12, 1826, therefore heard a repetition of Rossini's *La Donna del lago,* instead of the new opera by Bellini. The evening to honor Prince Ferdinando was postponed to his name day, May 30, which meant a delay of five and a half months for the Bellini première.

Bellini next learned that two of the singers—Tosi and David, for whom he had composed the roles of Bianca and Gernando—could not remain in Naples until the end of May. So he had to set about revising many passages in his opera to adapt them to the very different voices of Henriette Méric-Lalande (a French soprano who had studied declamation with Talma, singing with Manuel del Popolo Vicente García) and Giovanni Battista Rubini, then entering the period of his eventually vast fame.

Final rehearsals of *Bianca e Gernando* probably began very early in May. Among those who attended one or more of them were—in addition to Florimo—the Neapolitan music publisher Guglielmo Cottrau; Pietro Romani, a successor to Tritto as professor of harmony at San Sebastiano—who sternly criticized technical lapses in the music; Donizetti, who was preparing his one-act *Elvida* for a July première at the San Carlo; and Giovanni Pacini, who in 1823 had followed Rossini as, in effect, artistic director of that theater.

Late in 1825, after the première of *Bianca e Gernando* had been post-poned, the annual competitive examinations at San Sebastiano were held in the presence of a high government official. Florimo wrote[11]: "The examination having commenced, the first student, Vincenzo Bellini, was called up. As soon as he presented himself, Zingarelli said: 'I believe that it would be superfluous, if not useless, to examine this young man, who within a few months will be tested by judges much more severe than we are—the public at the San Carlo, where he will give the opera that he is composing, *Bianca e Gernando*.' Everyone concurred in Zingarelli's opinion." Zingarelli probably intended not only to allow Bellini to return undisturbed to work on his opera, but also to prevent the other examiners from finding him deficient in compositional theory, full mastery of which, as Zingarelli had come to understand, was irrelevant to Bellini's immediate desires as a composer.

The first performance of *Bianca e Gernando* finally took place at the San Carlo on May 30, 1826. The hereditary prince, Ferdinando, in whose honor the grand gala was being offered, was present, as were other mem-bers of his family, including his mother, Queen Maria Isabella—but not his father, Franceso I, who was convalescing from an illness so lingering that it had threatened to cause a second postponement of this première.[12] The icy Spanish etiquette that surrounded the Bourbons required audi-ences not to applaud in the sovereign's presence unless he applauded first. Florimo specified[13] that on the first night of *Bianca e Gernando*, applause broke out after the section of the Bianca–Gernando duet beginning *"Deh! fa ch'io possa intendere"* after the king had given the signal, but as the king was not present, the applause must have been begun by either the queen or the hereditary prince. *Bianca e Gernando* was greeted with less inhibited enthusiasm at its next performance, and as more repetitions took place, its tall, handsome twenty-five-year-old composer became a lion in the Neapolitan salons. From Milan on August 4, 1828, Bellini himself would write to Florimo[14]: "I remember very well, and you can too, that *Bianca* made all the homes in Naples want me . . ." More signif-icant for his artistic future, that success won him his first important publica-tion[15] and a commission from Domenico Barbaja which promised him another payment of more than three hundred ducati.

Meanwhile, on June 13, the *Giornale del Regno delle Due Sicilie* had published the earliest extended critical review devoted to a Bellini opera. In it, the anonymous writer said: "Two young men, one a student of the art of music, the other of the poetic art, sig. Bellini of Catania and sig. Gilardoni of Naples, have given the first earnest of their emergent ability in the opera we are discussing. Youth's early attempts in the difficult arts always deserve praise; but they deserve special encouragement when, as in the present instance, they come crowned with happy success." Then, after entering well-founded demurrers to Gilardoni's libretto, he continued:

"Coming now to the music of sig. Bellini, his style appears stamped with the sometimes slightly immoderate vivacity of modern music, while it does not disdain a degree of control by the austere laws of the old music. In its harmoniousness it does not sacrifice feeling to meaning, and in our view that is a composer's chief virtue. Without rushing in to compare sig. Bellini to other maestros already well known, we shall say frankly that sig. Lablache's aria [probably *"Allor, che notte avanza"*], the trio of sig. *Lablache* himself, sig. *Rubini,* and sig[nora Almerinda] *Manzocchi* [*"Di Gernando . . . son le cifre"*], as well as the largo of the quintet in Act I [*"Ah che l'alma invade un gel"*] and the second-act duet between sig. *Rubini* and sig[nora] *Lalande* [*"No! no! mia suora . . . più non sei"*] are to be counted among the laudable pieces of new music enjoyed in recent times at the Real Teatro San Carlo."

On the basis of what Donizetti had heard at one or more rehearsals of *Bianca e Gernando,* he had written to Giovanni Simone Mayr, his former teacher, on May 30[16]: "This evening, our Bellini's *Bianca e Gernando* (not Fernando, because that is a sin) goes on stage at the San Carlo, his first production, beautiful, beautiful, beautiful, and particularly as this is the first time that he writes."

Many years later, Giovanni Pacini would write[17]: ". . . I busied myself with attending the rehearsals of *Bianca e Fernando,* the second child of our dear Bellini, which won a success that was, if not enthusiastic, certainly happy, so much so that I proposed to Barbaia—and I boast of this—that he accept as *maestro di obbligo** at the Teatro della [*sic*] Scala my celebrated fellow-townsman—who, in fact, in the autumn season composed for that illustrious stage *Il Pirata,* which, as everyone knows, had a really fanatical success even though my *L'Ultimo Giorno di Pompei,* given as the first opera of the season,[18] had been so popular as to force the management each evening to turn away a quantity of people wanting to get into the theater."

At about the time of *Bianca e Gernando,* Bellini conceived for Pacini a distaste so intense that it would lead him, with or without justification, to cite plottings by Pacini and his closest friends (notably a very odd woman, the contessa Giulia Samoyloff, for some time Pacini's mistress) as primary instigators of his own artistic discomforts and failures. That distaste was in part a response to Pacini's constant self-aggrandizement, the insensitive lengths to which he often went to assure

* Untranslatable, this term indicated the composer of an *opera d'obbligo,* a work commissioned especially to be the chief event of an operatic season.

production of his numerous operas, and his exaggerated claims to a leading role in the launching of Bellini's career.

On June 18, 1826, not quite three weeks after the première of *Bianca
e Gernando*, Bellini wrote to the civic authorities of Catania to inform
them of its success and to express his gratitude for their support: the
pension granted him for four years in 1819 and extended for an additional
three years in 1823 was now expiring.[19] His letter seems not to survive,
but a copy of the reply sent him in the name of the decurionate by
Giuseppe Alvaro Paternò, principe di Sperlinga Manganelli, is in the
Museo Belliniano: dated July 9, it expresses official satisfaction with
Bellini's activities and congratulates him on his recent success.

On July 19, Bellini wrote a long letter to his Messina cousin, Cristina
Guerrera,[20] telling her that he had sent her three pieces from *Bianca e
Gernando* rather than the cavatina that she had asked him for—one
that he had sung when visiting the Guerreras, but could no longer identify. He thought it unlikely that he would see her that year: a visit to
Sicily "seems to me a little difficult because of my being called outside
the Kingdom." Very probably, this last referred to a hope rather than a
certainty, the hope of being contracted by Barbaja, to compose an opera
either for La Scala, Milan, or for some other theater in northern Italy.

Bellini also asked his cousin to pray to God "that the other *opera
semiseria* that I shall be giving soon at the Real Teatro del Fondo will
prove successful," and "thus I shall send you the most beautiful of the
pieces that are received well." No indication exists that Bellini considered
composing a new opera for production in Naples in 1826: his otherwise
inexplicable reference to "the other *opera semiseria*" almost certainly
indicates a passing intention to produce a revised version of *Adelson e
Salvini* at the Fondo in the wake of the favorable reception of *Bianca
e Gernando*. The fact that the hoped-for commission from Barbaja
materialized quickly would have sufficed to make revision of *Adelson*
almost impossible for the time being.

How Bellini occupied himself between the première of *Bianca e
Gernando* (May 30, 1826) and the day of his departure from Naples for
Milan more than ten months later (April 5, 1827) is not known.[21] During
that period, the musical world of Naples was taking on the shape that
it would hold for decades—in many a detail, until now. In May 1826,
Florimo was appointed archivist-librarian of San Sebastiano. During the
rest of Bellini's life, Florimo remained his almost constant confidant and
became his representative in Naples, the sounding-board toward which he
directed a copious series of letters. After Bellini's death, Florimo became
the tireless, amateur, somewhat unreliable historian of Neapolitan music
from its beginnings. At the apex of that history he always placed Vin-

cenzo Bellini, whom he mourned, revered, and celebrated for more than fifty-three years.

More of the emerging new outline of the Neapolitan musical world came into view on September 19, 1826, when Francesco I signed a decree transferring the Real Collegio di Musica from San Sebastiano to the neighboring Convento di San Pietro a Maiella, where it and its famous library have remained. There, as at San Sebastiano, Bellini and Florimo each had a room from the time of the installation of the new Collegio in October or November 1826.[22] But Bellini's activities during the summer and autumn of 1826 and the winter of 1826-1827 remained undecipherable. The relevant questions were asked by Pastura[23]:

"It is certain that Bellini remained in Naples . . . but how did he spend those ten months? Did he compose music? If so, which? Should one place in that period those fragments of dialogue and *scene* which have survived, and notably the *scena* from that supposed *Ifigenia*?[24] Did he continue to carry out the duty of a *primo maestrino* at the Collegio? Did the shock of the success of *Bianca*, or the stronger one received from *presidente* Fumaroli's third refusal [to permit his daughter to marry Bellini] make him ill? Did he enter into negotiations to compose other operas for the San Carlo, the Nuovo, or the Fondo? Did he then begin to nourish hopes, or even have a promise, of being signed up for La Scala?" The questions are unanswerable; those ten months remain the most tantalizing gap in the biography of Bellini.

Barbaja's canny interest in the young man about to emerge from the Naples Conservatory was explained by Florimo[25]: "It was his system to offer contracts for the composition of operas for the Royal Theaters— the San Carlo and the Fondo—to all young pupils of the Collegio who showed any promise of success. He was in the habit of saying that with a small investment he found among those young men the one who would lead him to large profits. Whether he reasoned well or badly is demonstrated by [Nicola] Manfroce, Mercadante, Conti, Bellini, the two brothers [Federico and Luigi] Ricci, [Michele] Costa, [Lauro] Rossi, and others who, all at his invitation, composed their first or second score [for him]." The preliminary signal of *Adelson e Salvini*, and then the reception of *Bianca e Gernando*, naturally left Barbaja wanting Bellini to compose the *opera d'obbligo* for the next season at the most important of "his" theaters, La Scala.

Barbaja was not in sole command in Milan, but was only one member of a managerial group often referred to as Giuseppe Crivelli e Compagni, which ran two Milanese theaters—La Scala and the Teatro della Canobbiana—from 1826 on. Pastura believed that Bellini signed a contract with that group before he left Naples in April 1827, but it is more likely that he did not do so until later. Certainly, however, Barbaja promised him that such a contract would be drawn up, and that he would be paid 100 ducati each month from April 1827 to the following October, by when the new opera had to be ready. Barbaja would send Bellini off to Milan with a letter of introduction to Antonio Villa, the Crivelli partner who acted as artistic director at La Scala. The signing of the actual contract seems to have resulted from intervention by Villa, Saverio Mercadante—whom Bellini had known in Naples, and who was established temporarily in Milan—and Felice Romani, an official librettist of La Scala.

At an undetermined date during Bellini's last years in Naples, the painter and stage designer Giuseppe Cammarano[26] sketched a portrait of him. Obviously unfinished, the portrait must be considered reasonably faithful. The face is long, the forehead high, the nose prominent, the mouth rather feminine; but the arresting feature is the eyes, at once melancholy and very alive and admitting the possibility of youthful humor. Yes, one says, Bellini at twenty-three may well have looked like that.[27] The problem of what Bellini really looked like at any period of his life is insoluble: he lived before photography—and the few surviving portraits of him painted from life are extremely disparate. Throughout his life, however, he unquestionably was regarded by all who met him as unusually handsome (many people said "beautiful") and, for a Sicilian, unusually tall.

Preparing to leave Naples, evidently believing that he would return, Bellini gave into Florimo's keeping all the music in his room at San Pietro a Maiella, as well as his piano and some furniture.[28] Once those practical dispositions had been made, he set out on the seven-day journey to Milan by diligence on April 5, 1827, his name day. He traveled part of the road with Giovanni Battista Rubini and his wife, Adelaide Comelli-Rubini, a soprano who later was to cause him considerable anguish; but he reached Milan on Ash Wednesday, April 12,[29] without them, probably because they had gone on to their home near Bergamo.

Antonio Villa and Saverio Mercadante were surely the first people whom Bellini sought out in Milan.[30] Mercadante was at the point of supervising the dress rehearsal of his new opera, *Il Montanaro*, scheduled to open the spring session at La Scala on April 16. He was friendly and helpful to Bellini, directed him to lodgings in the contrada Santa Margherita, near La Scala, and introduced him very quickly to three people who were to be important to his future: Felice Romani, and Francesco and Marianna Pollini.

Romani (1788-1865), a Genoese of considerable literary and worldly sophistication (he had traveled widely through Italy, and in Spain,

Greece, and the German states), had begun his long fruitful career as an opera librettist in 1813 by writing for Mayr the texts of the two operas that have been considered Mayr's finest: *Medea in Corinto* and *La Rosa bianca e la rosa rossa*. By the time Bellini met him, Romani had also written librettos for—among many other composers—Michele Carafa, Carlo Coccia, Donizetti,[31] Mercadante, Meyerbeer, Francesco Morlacchi, Giuseppe Mosca, Pacini, Stefano Pavesi, Rossini,[32] and Niccola Vaccaj, and had become an official librettist to La Scala. He eventually wrote some 125 librettos. Unmarried, Romani lived in a courtyard apartment in the via degli Omenoni, not far from La Scala. He was a classicizer, a strong admirer of Metastasio and of the poet Vincenzo Monti, and a harsh judge of the new romanticizing then symbolized by Alessandro Manzoni's novel *I Promessi Sposi*. Romani was to become an intimate friend of Bellini, as well as his librettist elect. Before a quarrel severed their relationship in 1833, he would supply Bellini with the librettos of *Il Pirata, La Straniera, Zaira, I Capuleti e i Montecchi, La Sonnambula, Norma,* and *Beatrice di Tenda*.

In 1844, nine years after Bellini's death, the fifty-six-year-old Romani married Emilia Branca, one of the talented daughters of Paolo Branca of Milan, who, with his wife and daughters, presided over the most respected of the Milanese musical salons. In 1882, seventeen years after her adored husband's death, Emilia Branca Romani would publish a blindly partisan biography of him,[33] which ever since has been supplying misinformation and tendentious opinion about Romani himself, Rossini, Donizetti, Bellini, and the other composers with whom Romani collaborated. That her book is so prevailingly undependable is especially lamentable because Romani was by much the best of the Italian librettists—particularly in responsiveness to words and suppleness of versification—between Metastasio and Boito. An excellent summary of Romani's excellences was supplied by G. Mazzoni when he wrote[34]: "No one after Metastasio had brought to the stage so rich, fluid, and harmonious a vein of actions and forms exactly adapted to musical expression; he appeared opportunely just when Italian melody was singing its arias to the whole civilized world." He was ideally suited to be Bellini's librettist and collaborator.

Francesco Pollini of Ljubljana (1763-1847), an accomplished pianist, musical pedagogue, and minor composer,[35] had studied briefly with Mozart in Vienna, and then with Zingarelli in Milan. When the Milan Conservatory was opened in 1809, Pollini became its first professor of piano. By the time Bellini reached Milan, he had retired because of age and ill health. He had been the dedicatee of a manuscript Mozart Rondo for violin and piano; Bellini's *La Sonnambula* was to be dedicated "*al celebre Francesco Pollini.*"[36] Pollini's Milanese wife, Marianna, was a better-than-amateur musician; she sang and played the harp well. She was a longtime friend of Zingarelli, who often sent her from Naples young men recently graduated from the conservatory there and eager to enter musical life in Milan. Childless, she and her husband lived comfortably in the contrada Soncina-Merate. They soon became devoted to Bellini and provided him with a substitute for parental affection and care. Both of them shortly were addressing him, and referring to him, as "my dear son," and their undeviating friendship and sound advice were to prove of large value to Bellini as long as he remained in Milan, as well as in letters after he left Italy.

Emilia Branca wrote[37] that Romani immediately offered to fortify Bellini's position vis-à-vis La Scala by supplying him gratis with a libretto; she added that "the generous offer was not accepted," and the story may well have been accurate. She stated further that Romani had written: "I alone read in that poetic spirit, in that impassioned heart, in that mind eager to soar beyond the sphere in which he had been restricted by the school rules and the servility of imitation, and it was then that I wrote for Bellini *Il Pirata*, a subject that seemed to me likely— to put it this way—to touch the most responsive chord in his heart; nor was I mistaken. From that day forward, we understood one another, struggled together against the vicious habits of the musical theater, and with courage, perseverance, and love set to work, having agreed to extirpate them little by little." What Emilia Branca did not make clear was that those sentences were a condensed and inexact quotation from the obituary notice on Bellini which Romani had published in the *Gazzetta piemontese* in October 1835 (for a complete translation of that *Necrologia*, see p. 210).

The announcement of the autumn season at La Scala appeared on August 12, 1827. It stated that three *opere serie* would be heard, one of them "expressly composed by the Maestro Sig. Vincenzo Bellini." The opera was not named. That omission may or may not indicate that, four months after Bellini's arrival in Milan, he and Romani had not decided upon the subject of their first collaboration; but neither of the other promised *opere serie* was named either—nor was it rare to omit the titles of operas from such preliminary announcements.[38] Much more likely is that the Bellini-Romani collaboration had begun in May, and that by August the composition of *Il Pirata* was well advanced. Bellini certainly knew by May that he was to shape the chief roles in his opera for Henriette Méric-Lalande and Rubini (he was familiar with their special capabilities and lacks, having dealt with them in *Bianca e Gernando*), and for the twenty-eight-year-old Antonio Tamburini of Faenza, who was well on his way to occupying as leading a position among bass-baritones as Rubini occupied among tenors. Bellini very probably was also familiar with Tamburini's voice and artistry from having heard him in Naples in 1820 (Teatro Nuovo) and 1824 (Teatro San Carlo).

On September 18, 1827, the *Gazzetta privilegiata di Milano* announced: "The new opera of a young Neapolitan maestro is being readied. The school from which he has come bodes well . . ." Such an announcement commonly was made only after rehearsals had begun, and that was true of *Il Pirata*, the première of which had been set for Wednesday, October 24 (for unknown reasons, it later was postponed to Saturday, October 27). Bellini found it easy to lead Méric-Lalande and Tamburini into their roles as he had conceived them. But when he began trying to impose the character of Gualtiero upon Rubini, he was balked by the tenor's stubborn determination to rely for his usual success wholly upon projecting beautifully his sensuously beautiful voice.

Bellini, however, was well advanced in formulating what became one of his ruling beliefs: that, at least in a Bellini opera, the singers should sing characteristically rather than merely beautifully, should evoke the individualities of their roles and the shiftings of emotion as much by the way they sang as by the way they acted. Cicconetti, who seems to have learned from the singers themselves and from conte Giacomo Barbò di Castelmorano[39] what took place during the rehearsals of *Il Pirata*, wrote[40]: "Giulio [*sic*] Barbò related how, finding himself in Vincenzo's quarters one morning when Rubini was announced, he was asked by Bellini to retire to the adjacent room and remain there until some new pieces of music could be rehearsed with the tenor; then—the tenor having been brought into his [Bellini's] room—he asked: 'How are you this morning? Are you in the mood to do well today, and in my style?' 'Eh, dear signor Bellini,' the other answered, 'you need someone else to satisfy you; nevertheless, I'll do the best I can'—and they began to rehearse the duet between Gualtiero and Imogene.[41] But, behold, he [Bellini] encountered the same limitations and the same difficulties. Advice, prayers, repetitions were multiplied uselessly, whereupon Bellini could no longer contain himself: 'You are an animal,' he exclaimed. 'You don't put into it half the spirit you have; where you should be driving the whole audience out of its mind, you are cold and languishing. Show your passion; haven't you ever been in love?' The other answered not a word, but stood there confused. Then the Maestro adopted a somewhat gentler tone of voice. 'Dear Rubini,' he added, 'are you thinking about being Rubini or about being Gualtiero? Don't you know that your voice is a gold mine that hasn't been discovered yet? Listen to me, and some day you'll be grateful to me. You are one of the best singers. No one equals you in bravura. But that isn't enough.' 'I know what it is that you want, but I can't pretend to be in despair or to fly into a rage.' 'Admit it,' Bellini went on, 'my music doesn't please you because it doesn't provide you with the usual opportunities. But if it has entered my head to introduce a new sort of music which expresses the words very closely, and to make a unit of the words and the singing, tell me, must you be the one from whom I receive no help? You can do it. Enough. Forget yourself and throw yourself with all your soul into the character you are representing. Come along then, my friend.' And he began to sing. Although his voice had no special quality, nevertheless, with his face and his entire body animated, he produced singing so pathetic that it constricted the heart and brought so much fire to the breast that it would have torn apart the hardest of men. Moved, Rubini joined in with his stupendous voice. 'Bravo, Rubini, now you have understood me. I am satisfied. I expect you to do the same tomorrow. For the rest, remember to stand up when you practice and to accompany your singing with gestures.' And, having bidden him an affectionate farewell, he called back the friend who had overheard the colloquy in admiration, with laughter, and with fear."

Final rehearsals of *Il Pirata* were held at La Scala on October 25 and 26. On October 27, the *Gazzetta privilegiata* announced, under "Today's performances": "I[mperial] R[oyal] Teatro alla Scala. Performance of the new opera *Il Pirata*, music by Maestro Bellini, with the ballets *Eutichio* and *Alceste*."[42] When Bellini's opera was performed that night it had scenery by La Scala's great designer, Alessandro Sanquirico. *Il Pirata* was an immediate, and then an increasing, success. By Sunday, December 2, when the season ended, it had been sung to fifteen full houses.

Two days after the first performance of *Il Pirata*, Bellini wrote to his uncle Vincenzo Ferlito[43]: "My very dear Uncle—My parents and relations can rejoice together; your nephew has had the good fortune to produce such a success with his opera that he does not know how to put it into words . . . On Saturday, the 27th of the current month, it went on stage; from the dress rehearsal on, news was spread about that it contained good music; then the hour sounded which called me to the piano-forte; I appear, and the audience welcomes me with great applause; the *sinfonia* begins and pleases a lot, a lot; the introduction, consisting of a single chorus, which they said was somewhat bad, but as it occurs during a storm, the audience wasn't aware of it; but at the end, very little applause."

At his least coherent, Bellini went on: "Rubini's entrance [aria], such an inexpressible furor, and I arising at least ten times to thank the audience. The prima donna's cavatina also applauded; then a chorus of pirates, with echo, which gave so much pleasure because of the novelty of my having imagined the echo so well; and then, finally coming onto the stage, they go on singing for another thirty measures, diminishing constantly, the voices with another orchestra on stage, all of wind instruments; all that makes so much effect, and I have gathered so much applause, so much that I am seized by convulsive sobbing because of the internal commotion of so much satisfaction, and am scarcely able to control it after five minutes; then come the *scena* and duet of Rubini and Lalande, so that at the end the audience, all shouting like madmen, made an uproar that seemed infernal; then follows Tamburini's cavatina, which, though applauded, pleased but little—finally we attack the finale, and the largo has been much praised as a work of great art, and also for creating an effect because of domination by the principal song, and was much applauded—

"The curtain falls, and you can imagine the applause; and then calling me out onto the stage; I presented myself and received the general thanks of such a cultivated audience, which also called out all the singers after me.

"The second act starts with a female chorus, which I have harmonized well, but, as it was not well performed because the women were too few and sang off pitch, it is passed by coldly. We attack a duet between Tamburini, bass, and Lalande, and it pleases greatly. Then follows a trio for all the leading singers, and it creates a furor; then a chorus of warriors, which also pleases. Finally, Rubini's *scena* and Lalande's have aroused indescribable enthusiasm; and the Italian language itself has no words to describe the tumultuous spirit that takes hold of the audience as it calls me out, and I was constrained at least twice to go onto the stage, as were all the singers. Yesterday evening, the second performance, the applause increased and I was called out onto the stage three times, as on the first evening. Tomorrow will be the third, as this evening they are doing an act of *Mosè* to give Lalande some rest. These have been the visible demonstrations by the audience; later I shall send you the periodicals, which come out after the third evening, and we shall know what the criticism will be and the real good that they'll pick out.

"I am extremely content, as I had not expected so much of the joy of success; now these honors will spur me on to advance in my career honorably, and I'll accomplish that by study.

"You will give this news to all my friends, and if I have any enemies there, the newspapers will persuade them later.

"For the time being, it won't be convenient for me to return to

Naples until, through other proofs, I consolidate my reputation in these Italian towns first . . ."

When the reactions of the Milanese journalists appeared—especially those of the musico-theatrical periodical *I Teatri* and of the official *Gazzetta privilegiata*—they validated Bellini's own description. On November 5, the *Gazzetta* reported: "The Maestro and the singers, greatly applauded for each piece, are called out onto the stage each evening by the unanimous desire of the audience . . ." *I Teatri* of November 2, midway in a long review, began its praise with the *sinfonia*, distributed it lavishly to most of the separate numbers, caviled at one or two of them, and closed by saying: "Aside from the few defects that we have noted in this opera, we have no fear in calling it a work of perfect intelligence and taste; but we can well say to the worthy young man: *Macte animo . . . sic itur ad astra.*"[44]

After the Scala season closed on December 2 with the fifteenth singing of *Il Pirata*, the *Gazzetta privilegiata* added (December 5): "The season at the Gran Teatro drew to its close on Sunday with *Il Pirata*, by Maestro Bellini. Those parts of the spectacle which pleased most were repeated by popular demand. They are the cavatinas of Lalande and Rubini, with their duet and the latter's aria . . . Lalande, Rubini, and Tamburini, always greatly acclaimed during the course of the spectacle, came out again and again after the first and second acts to receive new and noisy testimony of unanimous approval . . ."

Giovanni Ricordi soon published a piano-vocal score containing the separate numbers of *Il Pirata*. Then, as its success at La Scala continued to grow, he issued a complete piano-vocal score. Bellini, having decided to remain in northern Italy rather than return to Naples, sat for his portrait at least twice: once to an unknown artist who used tempera to portray him in white pantaloons, cream-colored waistcoat, and light-blue coat[45]; the other time, at the instigation of principessa Cristina Belgiojoso, a leading Milanese *salonnière*, to her friend Ernestina Bisi. The latter is a pencil drawing. When Bellini sent a copy of it to Florimo on July 7, 1828, he asked that other copies of it be retouched[46]: ". . . of the head, have only the sideburns used as models and pay no attention to the rest, as it resembles me but little, especially in the hair, which is so sparse as to make me seem an old man; do you understand?"

In Naples, meanwhile, as 1827 ended, Francesco I allowed himself to be pushed by some of his advisers into curbing his Sicilian subjects' use—overtly and, in the adviser's view, sacrilegiously—of operalike music in Church services.[47] On December 8, the king signed a rescript ordering that no music be performed in Sicilian churches until it had been certified as appropriate by a commission of three established Maestros.[48] From churches all across the island, stacks of music began to reach Palermo with requests for the commission's approval. From Catania they included forty-six pieces by members of the Bellini family: six by Vincenzo, twenty by his father, eighteen by his brother Carmelo, two by his brother Mario. All but seven of these received approval. Of the rejected seven, one was by Vincenzo: on January 28, 1828, the commission issued this order:

"We, D. Natale Bertini, presiding member of the Commission for censoring church music, D. Giovanni Maggio, and D. Andrea Monteleone, associates on that same commission, having, in conformity with the Sovereign dispositions contained in the Royal Rescript of December 8, 1827, examined a Mass by the Maestro Vincenzo Bellini of Catania, have judged that its performance cannot be allowed because it is composed in theatrical style."[49] Bellini probably did not hear of these happenings until well after the commission's ruling had been made known. The commission itself endured only a little more than two years.

More immediate irritations came to Bellini late in 1827 and early in 1828. Barbaja was planning to stage *Il Pirata* at the Kärntnertortheater, Vienna, with the role of Imogene assigned to Adelaide Comelli-Rubini,[50] whose capabilities Bellini fiercely called unequal to it. On January 21, 1828, he wrote to Florimo[51]: "It is believed that they are going to do *Il Pirata* [in Vienna], and it is said further that Comelli wants to do the role of Imogene; imagine what a horror that would be; and so I have written to Rubini, and the least that I told him was that he must be careful lest the opera not please, as he knows that this is a role only for Lalande or a similar high soprano. . . ." Later in the letter, he referred to Comelli-Rubini as "that witch, his [Rubini's] asinine and ambitious wife . . ." His letter to Rubini seems not to survive, but Pastura, who copied it out before its disappearance, quoted it in full.[52] Without actually denouncing Rubini's wife to him, Bellini urged either Giuditta Pasta or Lalande for the role of Imogene, giving his reasons exhaustively. When he wrote to Florimo on January 21,[53] he was nervously awaiting word from Rubini. Whether or not it ever arrived, Bellini's urgent demands were ignored: *Il Pirata* was staged at the Kärntnertortheater on February 25, 1828, with a cast including Rubini, his wife, and Tamburini.

I Teatri, and a new triweekly periodical called *L'Eco*, printed the first reports of the Vienna *Pirata* to reach Milan. Both pictured it as a fiasco, *I Teatri* reporting that it had been withdrawn from the stage after a single performance.[54] Very quickly, however, the truth became known: both *Il Pirata* and its performers had been greeted happily in Vienna. That revised report was published, not only in the *Gazzetta privilegiata di Milano*, but also in both *I Teatri* and *L'Eco*.[55] The last said: "Reliable information and the testimony of someone who saw and heard assure us that Bellini's *Il Pirata* has created a furor. Rubini was called out three times, Tamburini had a great success, and Mad. Comelli was well received." On March 8, Bellini told Florimo[56]: "Yesterday I received a letter from Rubini in which he tells me that *Il Pirata* created a definite furor and that his wife performed a miracle of San Gennaro in performing the role of Imogene." Comelli-Rubini would never be a Pasta or a Méric-Lalande, but in Vienna she had exceeded herself (as she would do in Naples in the same role three months later). *Il Pirata* had won Vienna, which would hear Pasta as Imogene in 1830. Bellini's international fame had begun.

(IV)

1828-1829: *Bianca e Fernando*; Giuditta Turina; *La Straniera*

NO NEW OPERA BY Bellini was to be heard at La Scala between the première of *Il Pirata* on October 27, 1827, and that of *La Straniera* on February 14, 1829. As 1828 began, nonetheless, he could regard himself correctly as well advanced along a highway to success and fame (which he enjoyed to the full). On January 16 of that year, in a long letter to Florimo,[1] he reported: "The other day, Signor [Bartolomeo] Merelli, a theatrical correspondent,[2] came to see me at home and brought me the legal offer of a contract from the impresarios at Genoa for the coming Carnival: but because the roster [of singers] is not yet completed, I did not want to commit myself, and so replied that when they finish contracting the actors—and if they are to my liking—I shall accept their offer immediately; we left it that way, and in the meantime, taking advantage of the interval, I shall be able to work out a better contract in either Venice or Turin." In particular, Bellini was then negotiating a contract with La Scala to provide an opera for the coming Carnival season, when Rubini would be one of the singers.

Swayed in part by the fact that at Genoa his opera would inaugurate the new Teatro Carlo Felice, in part by failure of his negotiations with other theaters, Bellini finally accepted the offer transmitted by Merelli, probably signing the contract during the first week of February 1828.[0] By then, however, too little time remained for composing and rehearsing a new opera: the opening of the Genoa opera house was announced for April 7. Bellini therefore took advantage of the presence of Adelaide Tosi and Giovanni David on its first roster, suggesting that he would revise *Bianca e Gernando*, the title roles of which originally had been intended for them. When he assured the Genoa authorities that he would reshape the opera thoroughly and add to it both a *sinfonia* and three new vocal numbers, agreement was reached.[4] The opera could be billed as *Bianca e Fernando* this time: Genoa was in the dominions of the House of Savoy, in which there was no royal Ferdinando.

Bellini was determined that Romani should make the required revisions in Gilardoni's libretto and add to it. But Romani was in Venice putting the final touches to a libretto for Morlacchi,[5] and nothing could be arranged with him by post. So Bellini set to work to compose the promised *sinfonia*, designed to replace the brief instrumental introduction to *Bianca e Gernando*. Laboring steadily, he was ready by February 27 to send to Naples a detailed description of the revisions being made in *Bianca e Gernando*. He asked Florimo to tell Cottrau about them[6] and enclosed a letter to Gilardoni, whose request to be allowed to revise the libretto had been rejected by Bellini because he had become sure of Romani's great superiority. "With *Il Pirata*, up to the dress rehearsal, everyone was certain that it would be a fiasco, and yet it was the opposite; let us hope that about the same will happen with *Bianca* . . ." he told Florimo.[7]

Bellini was required by contract to reach Genoa by March 12, but on March 13 he was still in Milan awaiting Romani's return from Venice. Soon after that, however, they traveled together from Milan to Genoa. There Bellini had difficulties with Tosi, who arrived on March 22 and quickly expressed dissatisfaction with "her" cavatina, which she did not find a vehicle for displaying her good points at their best. Bellini had intended to revise only the cabaletta of this *scena*, but now, borrowing a melody composed originally for solo clarinet in Act II of *Bianca e Gernando*, he refashioned the largo as well. Writing from Milan, probably on March 13, he had told Florimo[8]: "I have done the largo and the cabaletta of the new cavatina for Tosi, and it is already orchestrated, awaiting Romani, who will do me some good words, which I'll put in place of some awful words that I myself had to write. This piece pleases me, and especially the largo, which I have taken from Ruggi's solo . . ."[9] Tosi did not share Bellini's good opinion of the new cavatina. Lamblike for the moment, he altered it again: the result was "*La mia scelta a voi sia grata*" as later published by Ricordi.

Rumors had reached Naples that Tosi was spreading her net to catch Bellini as a husband. When he wrote to Florimo from Genoa on April 5, he said[10]: "I don't know who is talking the nonsense about Tosi's casting eyes upon me; whereas neither she nor I have any thoughts of taking on a companion, and you can be certain that if I should marry, I'd never take anyone from the theater. It's true that we share the most perfect harmony and friendship; but perhaps that has come about because she needs me; as for me, I'd be ashamed to esteem anyone for ulterior motives, and it is as a person, not as a composer, that I am her friend. I should tell you that after she looked through her two new pieces at the pianoforte, she was unhappy with the first part of the cavatina, and I did a new one for her. She rehearsed the cavatina with the orchestra and then, after she had sung it like a dog and therefore had not found it effective, she wanted another, and at the same time she did not want [to sing] the *stretta* of the *scena*, which she said lacked any [opportunity for displaying] agility, and she called it music composed for children, saying that if I didn't change it, she would substitute one of her *pezzi di baule*[11] for it. I realized then that we were on the verge of quarreling . . . I replied that I would not change a note; not out of disrespect, but because I wanted my music performed with the tempos that I decided upon, and not at her caprice, and wanted it given exactly the shadings that I had imagined. She struggled for two days—[but] finally sang the pieces as I had handed them to her. My dear Florimo, they were so effective that she came to beg my pardon—and that cabaletta, which she told me I had composed for children, will bring down the house. Now we are the very best of friends, as though nothing took place. She is very happy and sings everything as I wanted it, and therefore the music makes the effect that I had imagined."

At that moment, Bellini's suspicious jealousy of Donizetti rose to the surface: "[Giovanni] David, however, told me that [Tosi's desire for] that change had come about through Donizetti, as I had suspected, as Tosi herself told me that when she had Donizetti look through her role, he said that the *stretta* of the aria was no good. I think that what he expressed was his own feeling, without malice and because he wishes her well. But then, his having suggested so many changes of tempo in the parts, and all of them opposite to mine, backs up my firm belief, which I've always held, that friendship within the same métier absolutely cannot exist; and the fact that he is going on stage after my opera does not lead me to believe that he is eager for my success. . . ."[12]

On April 5, the day of the dress rehearsal of *Bianca e Fernando*, Bellini described the preceding rehearsal to Florimo[13]: "The pieces on which I base my hopes are the three cavatinas and finale of the first act and the duet and two *scene* of the second; and Tosi's *scena* especially is indescribably effective; the first section consists of a largo, the second of the agitato that you know, and the third of a cabaletta of brilliant declamation that carries the listener away; in a word, we certainly won't have a fiasco. I don't think that the opera will produce much effect on the first evening because of the illumination [of the theater], the participation of so many outsiders, and the novelty of the theater; but as the second evening is Tuesday,[14] and it will make its effect better then, everyone can write about the outcome [on the basis] of the two evenings. Last evening, the duet made everyone there weep: David and Tosi sang it like two angels, and David in particular sang it much better than when I rehearsed him the first time here in Genoa. The second-act trio, which everyone likes very much, will be sacrificed because of the father, as the bass [Giuseppe Rossi] is very weak musically, for though he has a beautiful voice, he never can stay in time."

The new Teatro Carlo Felice was illuminated brightly on the evening of April 7, 1828. Carlo Felice, King of Sardinia and Piedmont, and his entire court occupied the royal loge and two other loges flanking it. The first music heard was an *Inno reale* that Donizetti had composed for the occasion.[15] The première of *Bianca e Fernando* followed, but was interrupted at the intermission by the dancing of *Gli Adoratori del fuoco,* a six-act ballet by Giovanni Galzerani in which the ballerina Elisa Vaque Moulin won an ovation.[16]

Bellini's chronicle of that première in a letter to Florimo on April 10 began[17]: "Here I am, and I'm no longer jittering. The opera produced the effect desired." Then, after noting that the inauguration of the theater itself naturally detracted from his opera, Bellini added that the pieces upon which he had rested particular expectations had proved effective, "so much so that the audience was left well satisfied, especially with the second act; and the King sent one of his chamberlains to thank the composer and the singers and [to say] that he was sorry not to have been able to applaud because he was present in state; in fact, yesterday evening he kept his word, saving his applause for the only time when court etiquette allowed it at a theater in Turin[18]—for the second-act duet, which they say is indescribably good; and he took in the rest of the music without ever raising his eyes to the singers, all of whom, without exception, pleased [the audience] very much, a lot." Two days later, again to Florimo, it was[19]: "*Matters are improving:* from evening to evening the furor over the opera is increasing. . . . The King has consistently applauded the duet every evening and has listened attentively to the rest."

But it was Bellini's nature to suspect inimical forces at work everywhere, cabals already in motion. On April 10, he had told Florimo[20]: "My enemies had begun to speak badly after the first evening, but after the King's applause [at the second performance], they decided to alter the thing by saying that Bellini's music must be heard several times if it is to be enjoyed, as happened in Milan with *Il Pirata;* but anyone with common sense knows that when pleasure cannot be expressed by applause, each person draws whatever conclusion pleases him. . . ." At least one critic praised Bellini for the very fact that his music improved with familiarity, writing[21]: "It is known among us too from experience that the delight aroused by Bellini's compositions never is greatest on the first, night; it was the same with Mozart." Despite Bellini's fears of "enemies," *Bianca e Fernando* was to be sung twenty-one times before the Carlo Felice's first season closed.

Of the composers who had been invited to Genoa to supervise the staging of their operas—Bellini, Donizetti, Morlacchi, and Rossini—only Rossini, then working on *Le Comte Ory* in Paris, did not appear. And when *Il Barbiere di Siviglia* became the second opera of the season, it was sung badly. Bellini told Florimo on April 16[22]: "*Il Barbiere* has gone on and has been an incredible fiasco; being badly partnered by a terrible donna and a very mediocre tenor,[23] it does not seem at all what it was in Milan. Tosi is still bothered by her throat, but it is hoped that she will sing tomorrow at least, and the King, not wanting to suffer from *Il Barbiere* any more, yesterday evening ordered that *Bianca* be given with the substitute [Elisabetta Coda], but she too was unwell, and the King replied that then it should be given without a donna, that it would be enough not to hear that horrible performance of *Il Barbiere*." The next opera heard was Rossini's *Otello*, with Brigida Lorenzani singing the tenor role of Rodrigo. On April 21, Bellini reported to Florimo[24]: "Last evening, the marchese Grimaldi, the musical director, crucified me by trying to persuade me to write a cavatina and a *scena* for Lorenzani—and I, being unable to fend him off directly, did so by demanding the rather high fee of one thousand francs, and up to now they have offered me five hundred; but I am sticking firmly to my guns and won't do a thing without a thousand francs. I don't know how the matter will turn out." He did not compose the cavatina and *scena* for Lorenzani.[25]

As for the "*Gran scena di aria finale—'Deh, non ferir, ah, sentimi'— in Bianca e Fernando*—Sung by Signora Adelaide Tosi . . ." it became entangled in a mesh of deceptions caused by the fact that Bellini had agreed to let Ricordi issue the separate numbers of the revised *Bianca*, thus reducing the commercial value of the partial piano-vocal score of *Bianca e Gernando* which Cottrau had published. Pastura well described the resulting tangle[26]: "Back in Milan, after having contracted with the publisher [Ricordi] for the printing of the separate pieces from the new opera,[27] Bellini remembered his first Neapolitan publisher—Guglielmo Cottrau—who in 1826 had printed *Bianca e Gernando* for him without requiring any recompense from him, a young man just emerging. And, seeing that in Italy no law existed to protect authors' rights, he decided to repay that friendly gesture with an act of faithlessness toward the

Milanese publisher. Entirely in his own hand, he copied out Tosi's *scena* and sent it to Cottrau as a means of bringing the old score of *Bianca* up to date by adding it to the pieces already known and having it printed before it could be printed in Milan."

Bellini had lingered on in Genoa: he did not leave for Milan until April 30. He was again without a commitment to compose a new opera. On April 10, he had written from Genoa to Florimo[28]: "I don't know yet what contract I'll have for the Carnival. I absolutely would not come to Naples, even if they covered me with gold [because of the Comelli-Rubini incident?]. I'd like to go to Venice, but the impresario hasn't been named there yet. . . ." Two days later, again to Florimo, he wrote[29]: "Yesterday, conte Ferreri, chief of the directorate of the Teatro [Regio] at Turin, wanted to persuade me to accept the Carnival contract for that theater for the fee of 3,500 francs, but I am determined on 4,500, without which I shan't compose; for that reason, matters remain undecided . . ." On Florimo's advice, Bellini later reduced his demand to 4,000 francs; but he never composed an opera for Turin, probably because his insistence that Romani write the libretto alienated the Turin impresario. He gave his own reason for not writing for Turin in a letter to Florimo on April 19[30]: " . . . but I won't compose even if they give me the whole Kingdom, as the company is extremely dubious, having [Violante] Camporesi, who, though good, is forty-five years old[31]; [Brigida] Lorenzani, and you know [about her]; and [Lorenzo] Bonfigli, who, I am told, has a good voice but is a sausage; and, to cap the climax, a rotten libretto; there you surely have all the ingredients of a big fiasco. . . ." He was determined to compose only Romani librettos, and them only for leading singers who could and would fulfill his perfectionist requirements.

On May 15, *Bianca e Fernando* returned to the Carlo Felice for additional performances. About five days later, Bellini wrote to Florimo from Milan[32]: "To please you more, I enclose a letter written to me from Genoa by the daughter of Lucien Bonaparte,[33] informing me of the return of my *Bianca* to the stage: she says everything in a word: *Bianca fait pallir Otello*—Bianca has turned Otello pale . . ." In Lady Christina's view, Bellini's opera had more vitality than Rossini's. Some days later, Bellini told Florimo[34]: "This morning I have answered *Lady Dudley Stuart*, and have sent her a *cavatinetta* of mine [identity unknown] as a way of reciprocating her favors." Bellini would see Lady Christina again in London in 1833.

Meanwhile, Luigi Lablache, arriving in Milan from Naples to sing at La Scala, disturbed Bellini by reporting that Barbaja was planning to give *Il Pirata* at the Teatro San Carlo with the cast that he had used in

Vienna. On May 12, in a fury, Bellini told Florimo to take every possible step to prevent Comelli-Rubini from singing the role of Imogene[35]: ". . . Lablache assures me that if Comelli should do it in Naples, they would kill her." Florimo thereupon made himself such a nuisance to Barbaja that the impresario finally barred him from the preliminary rehearsals with cembalo, which were held in Barbaja's home. But Comelli-Rubini sang Imogene at the San Carlo on May 30. With the royal family present, the first night was a mixed success, in part because Comelli-Rubini was suffering from jangled nerves. The second performance, however—with the king and queen present again—was a triumph. On June 14, *I Teatri* (Milan) reported[36] that Comelli-Rubini had improved immeasurably that second night. But even three days before the appearance of that report, Bellini had written to Florimo[37]: "I never would have believed that poor Comelli, after the misfortune of the first night, would have had courage enough to perform with her natural ability, which wrung applause from the Court and the audience." Again he— and this time Lablache with him—had been proved wrong about her.

On June 7, during that run of *Il Pirata* in Naples, Barbaja arrived in Milan intent upon repairing his relations with Bellini. On June 9, Bellini told Florimo[38]: "The day before yesterday, Barbaja reached here, and I avoided him until I received your letter telling me about the success of *Il Pirata;* but yesterday I finally went at a time when I knew that he would be out, and left a letter for him so as not to run into him and thus create a scene; because my present state of mind is extreme irascibility, and the insults that he wrote me after the Comelli fiasco were too cruel to me, and as a result, I'm not sure that if I laid eyes on him I might not lose my temper. . . ." Barbaja needed Bellini, however, and as a master impresario was also a suave diplomat.

Later in his letter of June 9 to Florimo, Bellini complained that Francesco Pollini did not want him to compose for the Milanese Carnival season because, for one reason, Henriette Méric-Lalande might not then be on the roster of singers at La Scala—and that neither Florimo nor he himself wanted him to write for Naples. ". . . and therefore I don't need Barbaja for this year, and I don't think that he needs me either, as they tell me that he has contracted Donizetti and Vaccaj, and Coccia for the autumn here, and, for the Carnival, they say, Pacini and Conti; for me, then, the only remaining hope is Venice; though there, too, they will have an unhappy company [of singers] and for prima donna, it is said, none other than [Caroline] Unger; so, see at what a crossroads I am. Idleness irritates me, the risk confounds me, to be a long time without composing displeases me, and so I am in consternation in a sea of doubts and don't know which way to turn. I am not even sorry that I refused

3,500 francs for the Turin contract, as that company is too feeble for any hope; and thus there is nothing for me to do but play the *cavaliere*, a thing that bores me greatly, and I wish that I had more money so that I could go to Paris to try fortune there, as it doesn't seem to have abandoned me up to now; enough, I can't do it, and therefore patience. We'll see what will happen. Write me what you think, to fill up the page if not for any other reason."[39]

Two days later, Bellini admitted to Florimo that he was happy to have been proved wrong about Comelli-Rubini; then, referring to Barbaja, he added[40]: ". . . but I want to tell you about my first encounter with him and the outcome, which I'm sure you must be anxiously waiting to hear." Then, reporting that Barbaja had discussed the difficulties with Antonio Villa and giving Villa's report of that conversation, Bellini described the meeting under the porticoes of La Scala the preceding day: ". . . and while we [Villa and Bellini] were chattering away, we saw Barbaja coming toward us, and he grasped my hand with a smile, saluting me in his usual manner and saying to me: 'Baron Busybody, did you receive my letter?' I answered coldly that I had not, and he, his face darkening, asked Villa if he had not sent the letter. Villa said that he had, and he [Barbaja], turning to me: 'And so?' In the same tone as at first, I told him that the opening of his letter had made me very certain that it was not addressed to me, and that therefore I had torn it up. Picture him all upset at my answer and wanting to hide his rage by means of a smiling mouth, telling me that he wanted to give me a copy of it so that I could reread it every morning. But I, always cold, cold, told him that such letters should be reserved for other people."

A long, confused report follows of what each of them said about each other, about *Il Pirata*, Comelli-Rubini, and Florimo, and of what Bellini later found in the copy of Barbaja's letter. Then Bellini writes: "I finish [by telling you] that he invited me to breakfast with him this morning and, when I was there, offered me several contracts; but I showed my inclination toward Milan in Carnival, though the company seems to me a little doubtful because it isn't known whether or not Lablache will remain, as that depends upon the King of Naples's allowing it; but, in any case, Tamburini will come here, and *** [41] this last, Lalande, and Vinter [Berardo Calvari Winter]. Pollini tells me that Rubini's not being here is good for me because it seems to him impossible that I could risk another *Pirata* for him [Rubini] without falling into resemblance to *Il Pirata* itself; but that, as I am obliged to compose for other singers, the change of genres may easily drive me on to novelty; so that, on all counts, I'll accept for here; whereas, the only other possibility being Naples, for which you tell me absolutely not to accept, in a few days maybe I'll sign the contract if we can get past the difficulties of the fee and other matters that could interfere with a good outcome. . . ."

On June 14, Bellini wrote Florimo[42]: "Yesterday I saw Barbaja again, and he told me again to choose between two theaters for Carnival, Milan and Naples, whichever I want to compose for: in Naples, Rubini, Tosi, and Lablache or Tamburini; and here, Lalande, Vinter, and Lablache or Tamburini; I lean more toward Naples, Rubini being there, whereas here I have no tenor[43]; but as you tell me not to come, I'll accept for this theater, and may God help me, as all my friends tell me that I'll never again compose another *Pirata*. . . ."

What follows in that letter to Florimo[44] is one of the most extraordinary outbursts of jealousy in Bellini's correspondence: ". . . therefore, even though on one hand it flatters my *amour propre*, on the other such a testimonal disheartens me; but if I stay here, I shall be very determined, to see that I do something to avoid a fiasco like the one that the Ecc.mo Sig.re Cav.re has brought forth in every way." Bellini is referring to the production at La Scala on June 11, 1828, of Pacini's setting of a Gaetano Rossi libretto, *I Cavalieri di Valenza*. "Florimo, this event has ruined him with the Milanese, who have demanded that Barbaja dismiss him for a year, in which case he could not compose in either Naples or Milan, and I think that Barbaja agreed to that, giving Pacini a compensation of two thousand francs out of the profit that he will make. Now, to give you some notion of the impression that the music *** on everyone's spirit, in a word I tell you that Pacini has not done anything worse than this in his life. The whole opera is in a continuous minor, and all stolen; the Sig.r Poet copies all the exact situations of *Il Pirata*, [as] I think that you'll see in the journals themselves; imagine, even down to the words. Now, the introduction begins with a hermit and then a chorus, after which comes the entrance of the tenor, the first tempo of which begins in the minor, and then four measures appear in the major; in short, the same procedure as in the cavatina of the *Pirata*, and in the second quatrain the words even say '*Nell'orror di mie* [sic] *sciagure*,'* etc., etc., the audience began to be ill-disposed upon hearing Vinter recall the great Rubini; thereafter, then, the donna's cavatina, preceded by a chorus and dance, which was whistled at, [the audience] not being able to bear danced interludes, which for the Milanese interrupt the pleasure of enjoying the action continuously; then, after the cavatina, which *la Lalande* sang very well, and for which she was applauded, came the duet between Vinter and Lalande, and that is in exactly the same situation as in *Il Pirata*, to the point at which, recognizing her first husband, instead of '*E des-*

* Near the beginning of *Il Pirata*, Gualtiero's cavatina contains the words '*Ma l'orror de' miei pensieri* . . .'

*so! !** she says 'Egli stesso,' and this last is orchestrated *talis qualis* mine; which further agitated the audience, and the duet, which is extremely bad, finished to little whistlings; then followed the entrance of Unger, who plays the second husband; although the opera is entitled *I Cavalieri di Valenza*, it seems to me to be the same as *Moglie di due mariti*[45]; then they attacked the finale, which is an unspeakable botch, in addition to which the largo is stolen from Meyerbeer's quintet in *Il Crociato* [*in Egitto*], 'O ciel clemente,' and with the same repeat; therefore, after the first act, which his partisans wanted to applaud, there were tremendous whistlings; after the ballet, the second act began with a quartet, which only his [partisans] applauded, and which was found to be a medley of many Maestros and ineffective; then a chorus of drinkers in the same tempo and layout as that in *Il Pirata*, which was interrupted by a chorus of women inside, like the one that follows in the trio of Rossini's [*Ricciardo e*] *Zoraide;* but little was applauded; then Unger's *scena,* and finally that of Lalande, who as usual sang it well enough, but it produced a really wretched effect, and the composition, all in minor, is a requiem; at the end, the spectacle closes with a naval battle,[46] after which there was applause and the singers and the Maestro came out. Neither the battle, with all the great spectacle that they had made, nor his friends' having called him out was able to make people come running the second evening; the theater was full [only] for *Adelaide e Comingio*[47] or *Il Matrimonio segreto;* in a word, it could be said that only the subscribers were there; picture the imprecations from Barbaja after so much expense; and [with] everyone having believed that even with only two good pieces it could have aroused the same furor as [*L'Ultimo Giorno di*] *Pompei* because of its spectacular staging; but not even two [pieces], not one, to be found, and the opera went up in flames; behold the end of the intriguers; neither Naples nor Milan is for him [Pacini] any longer[48]; if one doesn't compose good music, subterfuges achieve nothing; and for that reason I am keyed up to do as well as possible so as not to produce a fiasco; enough, may God help me."

It should be added that the Milanese periodicals, while commenting unfavorably upon obvious borrowings in Pacini's *I Cavalieri di Valenza*, did not accuse him of deliberate plagiarism—and that Bellini's statement that the opera had gone up "in flames" was wholly incorrect: in fact, *I Cavalieri di Valenza* was sung twenty-five times at La Scala that season, more often than any other opera.

On June 16, Bellini had more accurate news for Florimo[49]: "This morning, I signed a contract with Barbaja for an opera during the

---

* In Act I of *Il Pirata*, Imogene's last words before she begins to sing "*Tu sciagurato!*" are "*È desso, è desso!*"

Carnival in this Teatro della [*sic*] Scala. The singers will be Lalande, Lablache or Tamburrini [*sic*], and perhaps Vinter or someone else. After so much shouting on his part, the price agreed upon was one thousand ducati; to me that seems not a bad arrangement, and I think that you will find it good, as I had five hundred ducati for two operas in my last contract, and in the first, one hundred fifty; it seems that I have made a little upward jump, doesn't it?" The opera contracted for would turn out to be *La Straniera*. In Bellini's very long letter of June 14 to Florimo,[50] he had reported the confidential discussion with Bartolomeo Merelli concerning another contract, this one to compose the inaugural opera for the Teatro Ducale at Parma, negotiations that eventually would lead to the opera after *La Straniera*: *Zaira*.

Having to write a new opera for La Scala, Bellini faced once again the problem of selecting with Romani a subject that could be condensed into his sort of libretto. Writing to Florimo on July 7, 1828,[51] he mentioned having looked into several possibilities and said that he was about to read "*il Solitario* d'Alincourt [*sic*] "—that is, *Le Solitaire*, a novel by Victor-Charles Prevôt, vicomte d'Arlincourt, or, more likely, a dramatization of it in Italian by Giovan Carlo, barone di Cosenza.[52] But early in August he told Florimo[53]: "It appears that both Romani and I, as well as Pollini himself, lean toward D'Arlincourt's *La Straniera*,[54] an idea that you yourself gave me in one of your letters. Romani certainly will not follow the play, but will assemble all the best situations in the novel— that is to say (and don't breathe a word about this to anyone, lest some other poet get the idea), the arrival of Artur on the little island of Montolino . . . Artur's meeting with La Straniera at the fountain . . . the meeting of Valdebourgo with La Straniera, his sister, and the duel with Artur . . . the trial . . . the wedding . . . and the deaths of Artur and La Straniera. Perhaps it will all be divided into four very short acts so as to lend verisimilitude to the times and places"[55]

At this time, too, Bellini and Florimo had the first of several disagreements on the subject of being helpful to friends. Florimo's life was dominated by two passions—for friendship, particularly friendship with Bellini, and for the library at San Pietro a Maiella, and he often rose up against Bellini's self-centered, casual failure to be practically helpful to mutual acquaintances who yearned to get their operas staged. In 1828, Luigi Ricci left the Naples conservatory without a diploma, having broken a regulation prohibiting undergraduate students from having their compositions performed under commercial auspices outside the school.[56] Florimo asked Bellini to use his influence to help Ricci obtain a contract in Milan. On July 14, Bellini replied[57]: "My dear Florimo, it seems to me that affairs must be upsetting you at this moment, as you not only forget your Bellini, but also give vent to invectives that I don't think I deserve. I excuse them on the basis of your lack of experience of these places, and I say all this in connection with the Ricci matter; think about it a little and then tell me your idea: how can I promise my friends to obtain a contract for them? . . . Can you guess the amount for which that cheapskate [Carlo] Coccia composes?—for one-thousand-five-hundred svanziche, which are 300 ducati—[so] can you see poor Ricci leaving Naples without being known to the impresarios here and receiving 300 ducati, and—even supposing that they would give it to him—having to pay for his trip, lodgings, and even the cembalo? And how would they be able to give those 300 ducati to a beginner here when they give that price to a well-known Maestro of some merit?"[58] With justice, Bellini went on defending his failure to help Ricci. He cited the fact that young Luigi Rieschi,[59] "a poor fellow who has merit," could not get an opera performed in Milan without remuneration, even if he himself paid for the libretto. Bellini said that he had read Florimo's letter about Ricci to the Pollinis, who had thought Florimo wrong, but had excused his anger because he was not acquainted "with these towns."

Florimo was not mollified. In his view, one should do the impossible for one's friends. Writing to Bellini in Paris seven years later (August 15, 1835), he would say[60]: "Help Mercadante[61] as much as you can; always assist him; advise him on everything as you believe it. Show him friendship; it isn't necessary for you to introduce him to Ministers, Ambassadors, Peers of France; you will be able to introduce him to your society friends, of whom you have huge numbers, to families not at the very top. In short, in a thousand ways you can show your friendship and the trouble that you will go to for him. Don't upset me about this; please me by doing it, and don't act the egoist. Because you know that I abhor indifference when a demonstration of friendship is needed, and I plead with you not to treat him [Mercadante] as you treated [Carlo] Conti in Milan.[62] Don't fly into a rage; but be content with what I tell you. You don't always behave properly because you aren't always glad to remember the past. This is between us: but from today on, do things my way and you'll make fewer mistakes." Earlier, Bellini had promised to do what he could for Mercadante, but by the time he received that 1835 letter from Florimo, he was too ill to think of such matters or to defend himself as he had in 1828 with regard to Luigi Ricci.

Late in August 1828, Florimo sent Bellini news that he feared might be unsettling. In Naples, a composer named Andreatini[63] was planning with Bellini's old friend Domenico Gilardoni to make an opera from D'Arlincourt's *L'Étrangère*. But Bellini was not upset: on September 1, he told Florimo[64]: "Gilardoni and Andreatini—let them write whatever they wish: I'll go on stage ahead of them, and if they do a *Straniera* after I have composed one, it will look as if they are guilty of presumption, not I." On September 10, having told Florimo how he would handle one scene in the opera, he added[65]: "I don't know if Gilardoni has taken the introduction this way; but however he has taken it, and however beautiful the libretto he may make, and whatever music Andreatini may put to it, both Romani and I—and doing the worst possible—will always do better than they will. . . ." His final reference to the Andreatini opera (which may never have been composed or, if it was composed, may never have been staged) occurs in a letter to Florimo of September 24[66]: "I'm sorry for all that has occurred with regard to Gilardoni and Andreatini,[67] but I cannot help them. Romani found the subject the most susceptible [to libretto treatment] of all those I proposed to him, and that's reason enough not to argue with a Romani. All I needed was to have Gilardoni as a complete enemy; and the same for Andreatini. But it's not my fault."

Also to the period of gestation of *La Straniera* belongs the most often quoted of Bellini "documents": the so-called "Letter to Agostino Gallo." That incomplete, undated text reads[68]: "Because I have decided to compose few scores, not more than one each year, I use all the forces of ingenuity. Being convinced that a large part of their good success depends upon the choice of an interesting theme, upon the contrast of passions, upon harmonious and ardently expressive verses, not to mention effective *coups de théâtre*, I go to the trouble, first of all, to get a perfect text from an esteemed writer, and have therefore preferred Romani, a very gifted talent shaped for the musical drama. Once his work is finished, I study the characters of the protagonists attentively, the passions that rule them, and the emotions they express. Filled with the feelings of each of them, I imagine that I have become the one who is speaking, and I try to feel and express myself effectively in that guise. Being aware that music results from variety of sounds and that men's passions reveal themselves variously through modulated tones, I have extracted the emotional idiom of my art from incessant observation of them. Then, shut up in my room, I begin to declaim the part of the character in the drama with all the heat of passion, and meanwhile I observe the inflections of my voice, the haste or languor of pronunciation under those circumstances; in sum, the accent and tone of the expression that Nature gives man in the grip of the passions, and there I discover the musical motives and tempos adapted to demonstrating them and transmuting them into something else by means of harmony. Then I quickly rush them onto paper, try them at the clavicembalo, and when I myself feel the corresponding emotion, I judge that I have succeeded. Otherwise I go back to inspiring myself until I have achieved my purpose."

In part and at times, that may well have been one of Bellini's methods of creating vocal lines. But it is not his way of writing a letter. Neither the phraseology nor the intellectual tone and handling of the ideas resembles anything else of his that we have. Possibly Gallo was putting into epistolary form, in his own highflown language, assembled fragments of conversations that he had had with Bellini, whom he met in Palermo in 1832, and then retrospectively assigning it to 1828. But no autograph of either the Bellini "letter" or Gallo's own text ever has been seen, and what appears most likely is that, on the basis of personal acquaintance with Bellini and some of his operas, Gallo invented the "letter" whole. Its publication history is confused. It may have made its first appearance at Florence in 1843 in a Gallo pamphlet entitled *Sull'Estetica di Vincenzo Bellini, notizie comunicate da lui stesso al Gallo*. It may have been printed in a pamphlet published anonymously in Sicily at about that same time, no copy of which can be found: *La Musica ne' suoi principii nuovamente spiegate*. Pastura pointed out[69] that the Gallo "letter" is not mentioned in any of several writings about Bellini which Gallo himself published during the composer's lifetime.

Filippo Cicconetti quoted the "Letter to Gallo" in his *Vita di Vincenzo Bellini*, published in 1859, and it has been reprinted by almost every writer on Bellini since then. Emilia Branca flatly denied its authenticity, but—as Antonino Amore made clear[70]—for wrong, Romani-protecting reasons. When Luisa Cambi included the Gallo text in her volume of Bellini's letters because "of its notoriety and its diffusion through the Bellini biographies,"[71] she wrote: ". . . I confess that I, too, am very skeptical about the authenticity of this letter, not so much because of the question of the style, which is secondary [!], as because it is contrary to Bellini's habits to speak of his own way of working. No other example appears in his correspondence; nor are there other letters addressed to Agostino Gallo.[72] It must be added that the autograph was published first in Sicily,[73] where the legend had taken deep roots that Bellini was so little of a melodist, so little a lyricist, that he had dallied with the notion of setting Alfieri's *Oreste* to music just as it was,[74] all in continuous recitative. This letter seems to derive from the same source."

Pastura, evenhandedly setting forth the arguments for and against the credibility of the "Letter to Gallo," wrote[75]: "Let us not forget the episode narrated by Florimo, who really knew how much torment went into the creation of his schoolmate's operas. 'Asked one day by a group of people around him how he had worked to discover those angelic melodies in *La Sonnambula*, in *Norma*, etc., he smiled and answered modestly: "I don't know! and I can't even tell you; they came to me and I wrote them," '[76] and, sheltering himself behind that smiling modesty, he elegantly cut off every other question on that subject.

"I confess that if I had had no reason to change my mind, I too would have thought that way; but study of the autographs preserved in the Museo Belliniano suggested another possible solution of the problem to me. Depending partly upon the reserve that the composer always showed about making his own professional secrets clear, partly on the testimony of the autographs mentioned, I have reached the decision to consider authentic Bellini's statements, which must have been made during the course of one or more conversations among friends and which, collected by Agostino Gallo, were reshaped very much later and published by him— perhaps—in the form of a letter.

"These arguments and examination of the autographs induced Ilde-brando Pizzetti to believe, if not in the authenticity of the letter addressed to Gallo, in the truth of the system adopted by Bellini for the composition of his operas."

And there, for the time being—very probably forever—the unlikely "Letter to Gallo" must be left.

The first, and for some time the only, verses for the libretto of *La Straniera* which Romani delivered to Bellini were those of the choral barcarolle that opens the opera: "*Voga, voga, il vento tace.*" On September 9, Bellini wrote the date and the word "*Introduzione*" at the top of a page of music-paper; he completed the chorus that morning. The première of the opera had been scheduled for December 26, but on September 20, Bellini told Florimo[77]: "It appears that all the misfortunes of this opera of mine are bunched together, but I don't want to be distracted for that reason. Romani has been in bed with a fierce fever and inflammation of the bladder since Monday, and he has endured twenty-four leeches and four bleedings, and because of this interruption, I don't think that I'll be able to go on [stage] for the December 26th opening. I have prepared so many ideas already that if they suit the situations well, they should be very effective. It's true that Romani's illness is abating every day; but even if it continues that way, he'll not be able to apply himself for another ten days or so."

Continuing to share his thoughts with Florimo, Bellini remarked that he would be in despair if Romani should prove unable to complete the libretto; the alternative writer, Gaetano Rossi,[78] could write a good libretto, "but never, never will be able to versify like Romani, and es-pecially not for me, who am so bound to good words; just notice in *Il Pirata* how the verses, not the situations, inspire my talent, in particular in '*Come un angelo celeste*,'[79] and that's why I must have Romani."[80]

Bellini's reactions to the impossibility of moving ahead with *La Straniera* would have been more despairing if at the time he had not been plunged deeply into the most impassioned amorous involvement of his life. At a performance of *Bianca e Fernando* in Genoa—very probably the première—he had been introduced by the marchesa Giuseppina de' Lomellini Tulot to the twenty-five-year-old Giuditta Turina, who had come to Genoa without her husband to attend the inauguration of the Teatro Carlo Felice, and whom he had heard about from Marianna Pollini in Milan. Born Giuditta Cantù, the girl had been married when only sixteen to a wealthy silk-merchant, Ferdinando Turina, considerably her senior. She was to play a varyingly important role in Bellini's life for the next five years, as long as he remained in Italy. His special emotional attitude toward her had been manifested in May: sending a copy of the *scena* "*Deh, non ferir,*" from *Bianca e Fernando* to Cottrau in Naples, he had dedicated it "to Sig.ra Giuditta Turina."

By September 27, he was ready to tell Florimo all about Giuditta[81]: "Now listen with regard to my love affairs, which I believe have been distressing you; but you need have no doubts, for when I'm not with girls, they can't make me lose my head. When I came to Milan last year and made every acquaintance possible, I began to be received well, and I formed amorous connections; but of short duration because—as you know, being acquainted with my nature—I look for emotion with sensual pleasure; therefore, because in many of them it's clear that the latter quality dominates, that's enough to make me abandon them all, though remaining friendly. This life of leaving one girl and taking on another went on until I was in Genoa, where I met my present *amica*. . . ." This last was, of course, Giuditta Turina.

Continuing to explain everything to Florimo, almost as though explaining it to himself, Bellini added that Giuditta belonged to a "more than millionaire family,[82] her husband being the head of a firm that is among the richest in Milan, but as they have a silk factory in a village called Casalbuttano, forty-five miles from here, they spend most of the year there; the cognomen is Turina, and it is to her that I dedicated the rondo from *Bianca;* well, I met this young woman—she is scarcely twenty-eight [*sic*] years old[83]—beautiful, amiable, and strikingly sweet in manner. I was presented to her by the marchesa Lomellino [*sic*], and she received me with such generosity that she delighted me from that moment on; and because I spent a lot of time with the many Milanese who had come there [Genoa] for the opening, I found myself with her almost every day during the period in Genoa after I went on stage, but I began to be interested in her two days after I was introduced to her, when I went to call upon her the first time at her home, where she was with her brother [Gaetano

Cantù], the one person who accompanies her on her trips, as her husband always is occupied with his business affairs. Well, when she came in and saw me, she blushed scarlet, and I was surprised and enchanted by that unexpected phenomenon, and it was then that I had the thought of making love to her."[84]

Bellini had intimate details to share: "During the succeeding days, I continued to visit her until some great pains* forced her to keep to her bed, and I profited by her misfortune to demonstrate my amorous solicitude to her, keeping her company every day; and therefore there were hours when I was alone with her, and you know how conversations unintentionally turn when one has fixed thoughts in one's mind. In that way, we confessed to being enamored, but she expressed sharp doubts about my constancy because I have to move from town to town and she cannot always be in Milan. She constantly insists upon these points, and during her whole stay in Genoa the only pleasure we had was that of talking and of being together† for hours, embracing and immersed in amorous kisses, and constantly saying how much we loved one another. But she never ceased to have doubts about my love's being true, and on my side I also suspected that she was not like the other Milanese women whom I had approached."[85]

Then, deciding to withhold nothing from Florimo, Bellini continued: "Thus she left Genoa for Casalbuttano, promising to write me from there as soon as I returned to Milan, which I saw again eight days after she left Genoa. I wrote immediately upon my arrival, and had no answer; I wrote a second letter marked by coldness that could be wounding . . . and she replied in a letter complaining of my almost insulting tone. Then I answered her, but not with the amorous desire of the first letter, as I had begun to feel that my suspicions were justified. In fact, she answered me, though after some time, advising me that she would be in Milan the following Wednesday and hoped to see me at the opera house. Although I had resolved to think no more about her, and did not want to look like a man chasing women, I went to the theater when Wednesday came around, but saw no one in her loge. But I learned from some friends that she had been asking for me, and I told them that I would go to see her during the evening; but I kept to my determination, knowing that she would be leaving the next noon. I went to see her just before the end of the performance, did not sit down, wished her a happy trip, and found her enveloped in extreme irritation. But the next morning at eight, her servant turned up to tell me that his mistress wished to see me; and I

---

* Giuditta suffered from painful menstruation and appears to have had serious gynecological difficulties.
† Here Bellini crossed out the phrase "with our lips [together]."

went. And when she lamented my cold attitude, I answered that one does not play with love and that I thanked God, who still was in me, for not having lost my peace of mind. As an excuse for not having answered me immediately, she gave that of not arousing her husband's suspicions and lots of other things, so that I finally was convinced, but I remained wary the entire time. I left, and the next week she returned to Milan, where, so as to be with me, she seldom went to the theater. And after several evenings of amorous talk and embraces and kisses, I cut the blossom of love almost in passing, as her father was in the house, and there we were, with all the doors open. In the swoon of lovemaking, she said to me: 'Bellini, will you always love me? Will you love me still more?' "[86]

Thus began the clandestine sexual relationship with a married woman which was to occupy Bellini intermittently for four and a half years. The most important human connection of his life after his friendship with Florimo, it was to end badly, especially for Giuditta, and to cast an ambiguous, unpleasant light over Bellini both as a man and as a lover.

"I answered her," Bellini went on in the extremely long letter of September 27 to Florimo, "swearing that I would, that I should love her as long as she deserved it; in fact, though a very rich and beautiful woman full of the gifts that make people desire her company, she [said that] she had had no earlier diversion [*divertimento*], that she had not been asked, and that now she refuses everything, runs away from bustle, and enjoys herself only when she is with me, and that when, of necessity, she finds herself out among people, she is afflicted with melancholy. Thus, all indications are that she really loves me, and that's why I am telling you about it now, entrusting it to our secrecy. She doesn't want me to write to you because she is afraid that a letter may go astray,[87] but I cannot fail to talk about you to anybody, [so that] she esteems you highly, and is almost jealous of my affection for you. She wants to see a portrait of you, and constantly says to me: 'Bellini, let's go to Naples to see your friend'; and I tell her: 'Let's go'; and that's always my answer. She would like to read your letters, but I tell her that I can't let her [see] them all because affairs of yours do not allow that, and she thinks that you speak of some lover and that that's the reason I refuse it. In the end, we are in complete harmony, and I am like a happy lover and don't go wandering about from beauty to beauty. I have confided everything to *la Pollini*, a very worldly woman, and she sometimes advises me, as she has advised me on all the other matters I may tell you about in another letter. I didn't tell you about this earlier because I thought that it might alarm you needlessly, as the thing might vanish while being born. Now that it seems established, here is the honest report."[88]

The penultimate sentence of that letter of September 27, 1828, casts a revealing light on Bellini's character: "My dear Florimo, this love will rescue me from some marriage, and I believe that you will understand this because of my weakness for becoming infatuated to the point of folly." Direct human responsibility was not for him. Only after that odd confession did he end this letter, which stretches on to about seventeen hundred words: "Greet everyone, everyone, receive my embraces, the greetings of Sig. [Francesco] Pollini, and love me as I love you. *Addio.* Your Bellini."[89]

During the early days of his liaison with Giuditta, Bellini was thinking about *La Straniera* and trying to get on with it without verses from Romani. Because he was to design its leading roles for the singers whom Barbaja and his managerial colleagues in Milan would contract for the La Scala season, Bellini desperately wanted Rubini, to whom he continued to attribute an important part of the public's enthusiasm for *Il Pirata*. He enlisted Florimo and Guglielmo Cottrau to work on Barbaja in Naples with the aim of obtaining Rubini's release from his contract there. As early as September 4, writing to Florimo, he had quoted a letter from Cottrau: " 'Abandon all hope of having Rubini, as it is quite impossible that Barbaja would free him from Naples.' "[90] Suspecting that Cottrau was quoting Barbaja, Bellini accepted unhappily the prospect of having as his tenor Berardo Calvari, called Winter, whom a Scala audience had disliked in Pacini's *I Cavalieri di Valenza* and Donizetti's *L'Esule di Roma*[91] in July— and whom he himself referred to as "a dog." Winter would not do for the role of Arturo in *La Straniera*. Bellini had received good reports of the tenor Domenico Reina,[92] and therefore wrote to him at Lucca for details about his vocal range and technique. Near the beginning of his letter to Florimo of September 27, Bellini reported that Reina had replied courteously, saying that "his voice is virile, always on pitch, extends from the B flat below the staff to the A above the staff, all in chest tones, and up to high E in falsetto, that he has agility and sings evenly [*spianato*], and that his style will adapt well to my music, which he is disposed to study like a dog and to perform entirely in my manner as I shall teach him, for if Rubini had wanted to sing in *his* way and the Maestro to compose for him in *his* way, a *Pirata* would not have been a success, etc., etc., so many things of that kind that he made me picture him as a humble young man and one who will want to do himself honor; everyone tells me that his voice is beautiful, that he has all the acting and spirit that one could wish for, and that his only defect is shortness of stature, but there's no remedy for that."[93]

Bellini saw to it that Reina became the Arturo. The other leading roles in *La Straniera* were being shaped for singers whose characteristics he knew well. With them in mind, as soon as Romani had recuperated and had begun to deliver the libretto piecemeal, Bellini was hard at work on the new opera in his rooms in the contrada di Santa Margherita. Quoting Cicconetti, later writers have sometimes asserted that he composed all or part of *La Straniera* while visiting Giuditta Turina's family, the Cantùs, at Desio, some ten miles northeast of Milan.[94] But Pastura demonstrated the extreme unlikelihood of Bellini's having left Milan during that period except for the first week of October, when he certainly visited Burgo di Morgne (now Burago Molgora), probably with the Cantùs, having developed a friendly relationship with Giuditta's father, Giuseppe Cantù. He was not happy there, however, and by October 17 (perhaps a week earlier) was hard at work in Milan on *La Straniera*, which would occupy him at least until December 27.[95]

From Milan on October 27, Bellini wrote to Florimo[96]: "Two words, and I'll leave you, as I am behindhand in finishing the duet, of which he [Romani] gave me the *stretta* yesterday; this is the second time that he has redone it, and it doesn't please me at all, but so as not to weary him, I'm using the first, which is the following . . ." What follows thereafter is the text of Act I, Scene 3, of *La Straniera* almost exactly as finally set, but without the choral intervention (*"Oh! trieste festa . . ."*); and that of Act I, Scene 4, again in almost final form, but without the final interjection by the knights, Montolino, and Osburgo (*"Ritorna ai giocchi . . ."*).[97] After quoting Romani's lines, Bellini continued: "And then another quatrain for the chorus follows; now I find this final *stretta* cold, and Romani, having been persuaded to change it, has made it worse; all this between us. It is said that perhaps Maestro [Giuseppe] Persiani[98] has offered to compose the first opera for Carnival, in return for which he would scarcely get [even] a gift, and now people would have it that everything has been settled; it is all in my favor, as the more operas there are, the later I'll go on. My dear Florimo, I leave you because I want to do the *stretta* of this duet; the whole first section has come out very beautifully, which bodes well for the effect that it will produce in the theater; I hope to complete it all this morning . . ."[99]

On November 3, still from Milan, Bellini sent Florimo a copy of more of Romani's verses, this time for the Arturo-Alaide love duet in Act I, Scene 7 (beginning with *"Che ascolto? E fia verace dunque la fama? . . ."*).[100] In an undated fragment of another letter to Florimo, Bellini wrote[101]: "I thought that I'd be able to transcribe some poetry for you, but that blessed Romani has not given me anything for six days, and I hope that this evening or tomorrow I'll have the chorus of *huntsmen*, after which we'll see the trio, and then the second finale . . ." And on November 17, he told Florimo[102]: "Here is a chorus of huntsmen which I have done, which pleases me a lot, and Pollini is very well satisfied with it and says that it will make a great effect." The verses are those of Act I, Scene 8 ("*Campo ai veltri . . .*"). On January 7, 1829, as always to Florimo, he wrote[103]: "I am writing to you from the restaurant because the post is just about to leave . . . G.a [Giuditta Turina] is improving constantly; but still is not out of danger.[104] I am almost up to the 2nd act, the poetry of which I cannot transcribe for you because I am working very hard and scarcely have time to sleep; and then because Romani now has left for Venice, and therefore if he suggests something to me, there won't be anyone who can alter it. . . ."[105]

Cicconetti told an anecdote about the composition of *La Straniera* which lacks confirmation but sounds the genuine Bellinian tone. After saying that Bellini usually composed his music in direct response to text lines, Cicconetti added[106]: "From this custom he never departed except once, when he was about to complete this new work. One day he sat down at the pianoforte to compose the final aria [*"Or sei pago, o ciel tremendo"*], all that remained to be written. He read and studied the verses that Romani had prepared for him, but soon became aware that they did not warm his spirit, or move him to any real passion.* His need was for strong, robust conceptions and for the poet to take hold of the idea revolving confusedly in his [Bellini's] mind, and then he would have been stirred by his genius. He tried to see whether the musical idea would be born in him already worked out without the words that the poet would have summoned up, but nothing occurred to him. When Romani was with him, he told him what had happened and asked him to please him by altering the poetry. The poet promised it to him within half an hour, and brought it to him in even less time. When Bellini had read it, he did not say a word. 'You are not content with this either?' the poet asked. 'No.' 'Then I have enough spirit to write you a third one,' Romani replied. But neither it nor a fourth one satisfied the composer. So the other man, half astonished and half embittered, added, taking back the paper, 'Now I must confess to you that I don't understand your thoughts about this or what it is that you want.' Then Vincenzo, his face animated: 'What do I want? I want a thought that will be at one and the same time a prayer, an imprecation, a warning, a delirium,' and, running inspired to the pianoforte, he impetuously created his final aria while the other man, staring at him in awed stupor, set to writing. 'This is what I want,' the Maestro said. 'Do you understand now?' 'And here are the words' (the worthy poet replied, presenting him with them). 'Have I entered into your spirit?' Bellini embraced Romani, and that was how the renowned final aria of *La Straniera*, 'Or sei pago, o ciel tremendo,' was created."

When it became certain that *La Straniera* could not be made ready

---

* Here Cicconetti clearly reflects the "Letter to Gallo."

for rehearsal soon enough to be performed on December 26, 1828, the opening night of the La Scala season, it was postponed to February 1829, and Rossini's *L'Assedio di Corinto*[107] was given instead. Rehearsals of *La Straniera* began soon after New Year's day 1829, and the première took place as rescheduled, on Saturday, February 14, 1829, with the cast foreseen. Bellini's new opera was an immediate and resounding success.[108]

On February 16, after the second singing of *La Straniera*, the first page of the *Gazzetta privilegiata di Milano* said: "The new opera of Maestro Bellini had a clamorous success. The poet served the composer well, and the composer could not have served the singers better; all competed to render themselves pleasing to the public, and succeeded in such a way as to be applauded greatly during the course of the opera, and consequently at its close. . . ." On February 19, the same journal said: "Amid the irruption of the Rossinian torrent, it is no small thing that a young composer should signal the first steps in his career by attempting a genre that could be called new for the present period. Not only is he a restorer of Italian music, but also he—a modern Orpheus—has resuscitated the beautiful melody of Jommelli, of Marcello, of Pergolesi, with beautiful song, with splendid, elegant, pleasing instrumentation."[109]

The weekly *Corriere delle dame* devoted three pages to *La Straniera*. A publication intended for women, the *Corriere* dilated upon such details as that "all of elegant Milan" had attended the première, that the boxes had been priced at from two to nine zecchini,[110] and that among those present had been "the Archduke, the Prince Viceroy, and the Archduchess Vicereine," as well as a Signora Torchi who had shone in one loge because of "certain curls, thanks to the invention of the hairdresser Carlo Gerosa in the corsia San Giorgio 3223."[111]

A critical comment unusual in its underlying seriousness in that time of prevailingly superficial musical criticism was made in *I Teatri*[112]: "Seeing that for a stretch of fully sixteen or eighteen years, the public was accustomed to the extremely brilliant style of Rossini, it seemed impossible to discover another style that would entice it to enjoy melodies of an altogether different workmanship. But it seems impossible to doubt that a courageous young man, also Italian, is appointed to bring about a change in our habits, almost satiated with beauty as they have been, and incapable of finding new beauty."

On February 15, the day after that gratifying première, Bellini announced its success in a letter to Romani, who was still in Venice: "*La Straniera* outdid *Il Pirata* by not a little. Without exception, all the pieces were applauded. *La Lalande*, Tamburini, and Reina sang like angels. Tamburini is the pirate of *La Straniera.** *La Lalande* has never in her career had a role to make her appear as supremely excellent as the one in this opera does. The enthusiasm of the Milanese is beyond belief. I went out onto the stage seven times, the singers still more.

"My dear Romani, the thing went as we never had imagined it. We were in seventh heaven. The libretto provides poetry and effective *coups de théâtre* that one cannot imagine improved; and especially Tamburini's scene at the trial and Lalande's at the chapel are so divine that they were shouting in the theater and all the ladies were fluttering their handkerchiefs with joy. Burn this letter, as it won't do for us to detail our triumphs now. With it, receive my gratitude more than ever, as I owe half of my satisfaction to you, oh my good friend; don't change, and we shall be able to achieve an immensely luminous career [together]. *Addio.* Your Bellini."[113]

The next day (February 16), Bellini wrote to his uncle Vincenzo Ferlito[114]: "My *La Straniera* went on stage Saturday the 14th current, and I can't find words to describe its reception to you. It could not be called *furor, being praised to the skies, fanaticism, enthusiasm,* etc.; no: I assure you that none of those terms is adequate to express the pleasure that the music, all of it, aroused. Everyone was dazed because they had thought that I could not produce another *Pirata,* and to find this opera much superior astounded them all in such a way that they made me come out twice during the first act and five times during the second, a thing not seen since the Teatro della [*sic*] Scala has been in existence. All Milan is enthusiastic, and I am beside myself with pleasure. . . . Don't let anyone but my nearest relatives see this letter, and then tear it up; as it's not wise for me to praise myself; as soon as I have the journals, I'll forward them to you, and you have them inserted into the Palermo journal if that is possible. My dear Uncle, cheer my beloved parents, grandfather, and all my relatives with this very happy news, and tell them all that my glory has soared to the stars with this new opera and that I hope to raise it farther by my unceasing studies. . . ."

Bellini was not exaggerating: by February 16, Marianna Pollini was writing to Zingarelli in Naples to report surpassing news about his former pupil's new opera[115]: "No mere [good] reception, but furor, enthusiasm, was evoked by my Bellini's opera. You will have received a letter from my husband[116] giving you a description of the rehearsals I attended the dress rehearsal [and] the first singing, on the fourteenth. I don't know how to express myself better; I'll only say that Bellini's reception is un-

---

* Bellini meant that Tamburini's success as Valdeburgo paralleled Rubini's as Gualtiero in the earlier opera.

precedented, he was thanked twice during the first act; five times during the second he had to emerge onto the stage to lively, spontaneous acclamations and repeated shouts of delight; the poor young man almost fainted from pleasure and gratitude at receiving the salute . . . Lalande is an angel, every word is heard as declaimed, and nothing could be better; she enchants us in a very new way. Tamburini, another theatrical angel, bears himself well, very well, and sustains his role with a mastery generally unknown to singers. Reina the tenor carries himself with a most animated spirit, and my son [Bellini] is served in a way that one could not wish improved. . . . *La Straniera* is worth many *Pirata*s, and I wish that you had been with me at the theater that first evening so that we could have shared a pleasure, a joy, that makes one suffer greatly because it is too intense . . ."

On that same February 16, Tamburini wrote to Florimo[117]: "Oh what a furor! oh, what fanaticism! the opera of our mutual friend Bellini has raised! What can I tell you? The beauties of this opera are so many that I wouldn't know how to enumerate them." Then, after apologizing for having spoken slightingly of Bellini's music to Florimo in Naples, Tamburini added: "Long live Bellini, and may you enjoy his triumph with me, the like of which I cannot recall during eleven years in my profession. . . . Triumph, triumph, triumph! never before heard of in my time; to such effect that when the performance was over, I remained stunned for several hours by the audience's enthusiasm, which resembled a revolution. . . ."[118]

Considering the character of *La Straniera*, unique among Bellini's post-*Bianca* operas in both providing little obvious long-breathed "Bellinian" melody and depending largely upon action that is "melodramatic" in the English meaning of the term, those audience reactions now appear astonishing.[119] The press preponderantly shared the reactions of the audiences who crowded the repetitions of *La Straniera*, but a group of persistent detractors of Bellini viciously attacked both the opera and its composer. Forty-five years later, the fanciful Giuseppe Rovani wrote[120]: "The composers concentrated upon themselves, and became taciturn. Furthermore, it is well known that a certain somebody had said to the learned consistory: Gentlemen, we must do our utmost; the joke has taken on the dimensions of a whale. In fact, it is not to be borne. And then a deputy of the Sanhedrin, disguised in mask and domino, emerged in public with an indictment with which he seemed to announce that Bellini was otherwise not a genius, but a thief; and attacked him in the three departments of inspiration, technique, and esthetic. He observed that Valdeburgo's aria '*Meco tu vieni, o misera*' was nothing but a plagiarism of an ecclesiastical chant traditional in Rome and Bologna, '*Stave Maria languente/Ai piedi della croce*'; that the trio '*No, non ti son rivale*' was a reminiscence of a cantilena in Caraffa's [*sic*] *Gabriella di Vergy*, with—only the difference of a leap of a third; that Alaide's prayer in the second act, when the wedding takes place in the church, had originated in a trio for Zopiro, Seide, and Pamira in [Peter von] Winter's *Maometto* [*II*]; that the phrase '*Ogni speme è a te rapita*,' etc., in the first duet between Valdeburgo and Isabella [*sic*, for Isoletta] reproduced the gondolier's song in [Rossini's] *Otello*; that the stretta of the duet '*Un ultimo addio ricevi, infelice*' was only an echo of the popular Milanese song '*La sura Peppina*' and what follows; that, in a nutshell, Bellini's style was abstruse, discontinuous, distorted, and lacking in distinction, that it alternated among the *serio* and the *buffo* and the *semiserio* . . ."

Nearly a century and a half after its première, *La Straniera* seems most notable for its dramatic theatricality, and occasional relevant beauties. With it, Bellini had proved to the exacting audiences of La Scala that *Il Pirata* had by no measure exhausted his creative resources. Certainly he now stood, though in public esteem still below the thirty-seven-year-old Rossini, on a level with the thirty-four-year-old Donizetti as the foremost young Italian composer of opera. He was twenty-seven.

(V)

1829-1830: *Zaira*;
I Capuleti e i Montecchi

LITTLE MORE THAN FIVE MONTHS had elapsed between Bellini's notation of the first measures for *La Straniera* and its delirious first night. During that period, he had been invited to London to supervise a staging of *Il Pirata* and compose a new opera. The impresario of the King's Theatre, Pierre-François Laporte, had assembled a company of Italian singers for a season in 1830, and Jules-Prosper Méric, Méric-Lalande's husband, had suggested that he engage Bellini with it. On November 22, 1828, Bellini had outlined the resulting negotiations to Florimo in a letter that exhibits him as a businessman[1]: "You should know that Lalande's husband tried to make an arrangement for me with the impresario, who wanted me to adapt *Il Pirata* for [Domenico] Donzelli, Lablache, and *la Lalande*, and I would have to stage it as well as buy the score*; then to compose a new opera, the libretto for which I'd either have to write myself or pay for, and I'd have to go to London about the middle of the month of March [1830]. Well, my demand for all that was twenty thousand francs; he offered me fifteen, and I reduced my demand to eighteen, and he stuck to his proposition. Day before yesterday, then, I went to see *la* [Giuditta] *Pasta*,[2] who told me that I should not cede ownership of the score, or at least should keep half of it, she said, because even if the score should have a mediocre reception, the least that it will be sold for is 25,000 francs; and after that advice I was with Méric, and I proposed to him that I would be satisfied with 12,000 francs and keeping half of the ownership. But when that was transmitted to the impresario, he did not agree. My

* Rights in the use of the autograph full score remained with the *impresa* running La Scala.

dear Florimo, it seems to me that I cannot do it for less because I should have to pay for my trip there, and then perhaps for my return to Italy; I should have to pay for my lodging and food for almost three months, so that little would be left for me. And then, what can I do if Pacini has offered, as I am told, to stage all the operas and compose a new opera for them for only 10,000 francs? . . ." Bellini succeeded in convincing himself that a later year would bring better auspices for a visit to England, and in 1833 that belief was to be proved correct.

Before the première of *La Straniera,* Bellini had become involved in negotiations about composing another opera. A new ducal theater was being readied at Parma, and first offer of the contract to compose its inaugural opera naturally had been tendered to Rossini. But Rossini, then in Paris, where he was still under contract to supply the Opéra with a new work (*Le Comte Ory*), could not accept the extraordinary offer of 1000 louis d'or from Parma. As early as June 14, 1828, Bellini wrote to Florimo from Milan[3]: "Here I have run into the theatrical correspondent Sig.[r] Merelli,[4] who, in confidence, has the reputation of being an intriguer, and he told me that he has been commissioned by the Parma *impressario* [*sic*]* to deal with me for the opening of that new theater; and when he asked for my price, I replied with my wishes, and we'll see what will result from that. But I have little faith in this correspondent, and I imagine that he has made me this offer to get on my good side. I told [Francesco] Pollini about it, and he promised to find out personally whether or not the Parma impresario has such intentions toward me. My demand was for six thousand francs, and for that reason, if it is genuine, we'll get an answer. The price that I'll demand from Barbaja here will be the same *** if he will agree to give me 5,000 francs, which amounts to 1,135—I say 1,135—ducati, I'll compose; without them, I'll write no opera here or in Naples—with my style I must vomit blood."

By that last, lurid phrase, Bellini meant that whereas most of his contemporaries—Rossini, Donizetti, and Pacini included—were willing to rush out operas that could have been improved immeasurably by more thought, time, and effort, he was not. Because of the comparatively long period that he needed for composing an opera as he meant it to be composed, he had determined to demand remuneration proportionate to that expenditure of time, to ask for fees then considered exorbitant. Rossini composed (or, in some cases, substantially recomposed) thirty-nine operas in twenty years, Donizetti some seventy in twenty-eight years, Pacini about one hundred in forty-four years. In contrast, Bellini's creating operas

---

* Bellini consistently misspelled this word, unintentionally producing a comic effect: the Italian word *impressare* means to rush, to worry, or to torment, whereas *impresario* comes from *impresa* meaning enterprise, undertaking, or management.

at about the rate of one per year was looked upon as slow and finicking.

The new Teatro Ducale (now the Teatro Regio) at Parma had been begun in 1821 at the command of Marie-Louise, Napoleon's widow, who in 1817 had become Grand Duchess of Piacenza, Parma, and Guastalla. She had placed its management in the hands of a commission headed by her grand chamberlain, conte Stefano Sanvitale, and including Luigi Torrigiani, a lawyer and writer, as controller of theatrical spectacles.[5] Andrea Bandini, a Florentine, had been made its impresario. Merelli had told Bellini the truth: Bandini had indeed asked him to approach Bellini about composing an opera for the inauguration of the new theater. But after talking to Bellini in Milan, Merelli justified Bellini's suspicion of him by writing Bandini a letter in which he said[6]: "I spoke to our friend Bellini, who is now in such a presumptuous state that he has refused many occasions to compose because he wants 6,000 francs for a score, the amount that he also asks from you and which, to please me, he will reduce to 5,000 francs; but he will not accept one soldo less. . . . What got into your head to take up this beginner, who has only one opera (*Il Pirata*), which, furthermore, has no musical value, and which pleases because of Lalande, Rubini, and Tamburini? Did you know, furthermore, that his opera [*Bianca e Fernando*] was a fiasco in Genoa? Do you want to have the same experience? . . . There are Pacini, Generali, Coccia, Mercadante, all of whom, without exception, are and will be discreet."

But the members of the commission at Parma wanted Bellini, particularly after they had received a letter from Francesco Pollini in praise of him. Conte Sanvitale therefore bypassed Merelli, turning directly to Alessandro Rolla, director of the orchestra at La Scala, and asking him to tell Bellini that the commission intended the contract for the inaugural opera to go to him. On August 6, 1828, Bellini wrote to Florimo[7]: "This morning (keep this to yourself), our Rolla asked me confidentially if I was disposed to write for the opening of the theater at Parma, as Rossini cannot leave Paris, and he [said] that if the Archduchess, who is in Vienna, does not make some other arrangement, he will have the pleasure of signing me up. I replied that I am very eager for this occasion, which can do me much honor, but only if I can have the libretto by the beginning of January. Now Rolla will answer and God will think out the rest. That's why I tell you not to mention this to anyone, because of the intrigues that others could weave around me, and that way we'll get along. It will be a great stroke of luck for me if this works out." Seven weeks later (September 24), it was[8]: "As for Parma, I still don't know anything." But in a letter probably written on November 26, Bellini told Florimo[9]: "I give you the consoling news that at this moment the theatrical agent Sig.^r Merelli has brought me the contract to compose the opera for the

1

The room in which Bellini was born, now
part of the Museo Belliniano, showing the
"reconstructed" portrait of Bellini as
an adolescent, painted at the request of
Francesco Florimo by Federico Maldarelli,
the cembalo donated to the museum by the
composer's second cousin Pasquale Bellini; and
the stool returned to the Bellini family by
Rossini.

2
Portrait (oil) of Bellini painted before
April 1827 by Carlo Arienti, frequently
misattributed to Pelagio Palagi. It was
given by Bellini to Francesco Florimo, who
presented it to the Conservatorio di San
Pietro a Maiella, Naples.

3a
Presumed portrait (oil) of Bellini painted
before 1827 by Giuseppe Cammarano,
father of the librettist Salvatore
Cammarano.

3b
Portrait of Bellini (oil) painted in 1830 by Natale Schiavoni (often Schiavone), which Francesco Florimo called "the likest to Bellini" of all portrayals of him. When, in 1892, it was presented to Giuseppe Verdi, the composer wrote: "…it gives me pleasure to see the features of this sweet and sympathetic composer, who, in the Temple of Art, has a niche that is higher or less high, but his!"

4a
Portrait of Bellini (oil) painted by Giuseppe Patania during Bellini's April 1832 visit to Palermo.

4b
Bust (marble) of Bellini carved by
Giuseppe Pollet during Bellini's April
1832 visit to Palermo.

5a
Miniature portrait of Bellini painted by
Maria Malibran during Bellini's 1833
visit to London and presented to him by her.

5b
Bust of Bellini (plaster copy) carved in
Paris in 1835 by Jean-Pierre Dantan
jeune. Bellini sent this copy to his
friend Alessandro Lamperi, from whom it
descended to the late senatore Carlo
Rizzetti, who donated it to the Museo
Belliniano, Catania. Bellini sent three
other copies to Sicily: one each to his
uncle Vincenzo Ferlito, the duchessa
Eleonora di San Martino, and Filippo
Santocanale.

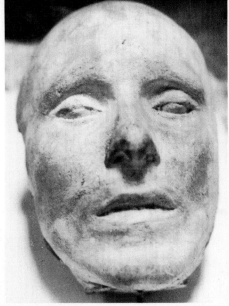

6
Death mask of Bellini taken at Puteaux
on September 24, 1835, by Jean-Pierre
Dantan *jeune*.

7
Francesco Florimo, lithograph by Ranetta
after an 1822 drawing by Tartini.

8
Francesco Florimo, portrait (oil) by
G. Simonetti, painted about 1843.

9a
Giuditta Turina, portrait (pastel)
by Luigi Bianchi, done about 1828.

9b
Giuditta Turina, anonymous drawing
(crayon) sometimes attributed to
Francesco Hayez, about 1838.

10
Felice Romani, lithograph by Bomben,
about 1830.

opening of the theater at Parma, which will take place on May 12, 1829. The price is 5,000 [actually 4824] francs, or say 1,135 ducati. It seems to me to be going well: in another letter I'll discuss it at greater length. . . ."

Florimo received added details in a letter dated December 1[10]: "Now let's get on to what you are most curious to learn. Well, in my last short letter, I gave you news about the Parma affair. Now you will learn about the company, which is Lalande, Lablache, [Teresa] Cecconi, and a certain [Carlo] Trezzini, a tenor described to me as good. The impresario would like to have me compose *Cesare in Egitto*, but as I have a condition in the contract that the book must satisfy me as a whole and in detail, I have refused, though it is a creation of the lawyer [Luigi] Torregiani [*sic*] of Parma, for the subject is as old as Noah[11]; and, as is also stated in the contract, the impresario is bound to send the poet to me in Milan early this month; upon his arrival, therefore, we'll agree on what subject I should compose. I'll be going on with my opera *La Straniera* not later than early February, and therefore I'll have almost three months for composing the one for Parma, and I think that that's enough, as the contract also requires them to deliver the book, all completed, by mid-January, and that way, having all the poetry, I'll be able to complete the opera easily without rushing."

When Merelli continued to insist upon *Cesare in Egitto*[12]—Torrigiani was, after all, the controller of theatrical spectacles—Bellini strongly recommended that he ask the writer to come to Milan to discuss the matter with him. Torrigiani reached Milan on December 6 and talked with both Bellini and Méric-Lalande. These explorations having proved altogether unsatisfactory to him, he returned to Parma and wrote to conte Sanvitale[13] criticizing Bellini acidly and making the bureaucratic suggestion that a commission be named to study his *Cesare in Egitto* and pronounce upon its merits. His notion was that such a commission was certain to find the libretto good—and that Bellini could then be forced to set it. At the suggestion of Count Adam Adalbert von Neipperg, the Grand Duchess's consort, Sanvitale replied to Torrigiani by sending the impresario Bandini to Milan to smooth Bellini's considerably ruffled feathers. Back in Parma, on January 8, 1829, Bandini wrote to Neipperg to say that Torrigiani's libretto could not be used[14]; further, finding Bellini and Romani disposed to collaborate on an opera on such a subject as "*Carlo di Borgogna oppure Giovanni da Procida*,"[15] he had signed a contract with the librettist for the reasonable fee of seven hundred francs, a contract that he enclosed.[16] Marie-Louise sent the wounded Torrigiani a consolatory draft for three hundred and sixty new lire to cover the expenses of his futile trip to Milan and added the gift of a gold box.

Once Bellini and Romani had arranged to collaborate on the opera for Parma, they appear to have done nothing more about it until after the première of *La Straniera* at La Scala on February 14; then Romani had to rush to Venice to work on the *Rosmunda* libretto for Carlo Coccia, the acting director of the Teatro La Fenice. He promised Bellini that he would provide him with a libretto about Charles the Bold, which he would send to Milan act by act. But the first packet of text which Bellini received from Romani proved to contain, not one act of that libretto, but part of one carved out of *Le Solitaire*, a novel by D'Arlincourt, from whose novel *L'Étrangère* Romani had derived the libretto of *La Straniera*. Bellini may have been agreeable to that substitution, though he had rejected the subject of *Le Solitaire* in favor of that of *L'Étrangère* in 1828, largely because Andrea Leone Tottola already had written a libretto from it for Stefano Pavesi. However he felt, Bellini wrote to Florimo on March 4[17]: "I'll have the first act for Parma in two days," but did not specify the subject. On March 14, he added[18]: "I'll already be in Parma when you receive this letter, as I'm leaving on Wednesday, the 17th of this month, hoping that I can take Romani with me, who arrives from Venice today, as the first act of *Il Solitario*, which he sent me, doesn't please me at all, and, as you have counseled me all along, I'm sticking to *Zaira*, and so already have worked out the plan of the pieces from Voltaire's tragedy,[19] and I find it most interesting; but everything depends upon whether or not Romani can be persuaded to treat it."

Romani having been persuaded to wrestle with Voltaire, Bellini and he left Milan together on the morning of March 17, 1829, and reached Parma that evening, putting up at the Trattoria della Tedesca, in the strada Santa Lucia.[20] Two days later, Bellini waited upon conte Sanvitale to inform him of the change from *Carlo di Borgogna* to *Zaira*, to demand that the orchestra for his opera include five cellos, and to announce that the first performance must be delayed because late arrivals by some of the singers would leave him only two weeks for rehearsal if the date originally announced were to be maintained. Thereafter, Romani fell comically foul of the Parma police. He had been wearing his customary moustache beyond the three days such facial decoration—then the very symbol of liberalism—was permitted to outsiders. When seen wearing it in a café and ordered to shave it off, he looked at his watch, stood up, refused, and announced his intention to leave Parma at once. Bellini was thrown into nervous agitation until conte Sanvitale persuaded Romani to wait a day, took the problem to Marie-Louise, and won her consent to Romani's moustache. Romani remained in Parma.

The composition of *Zaira* advanced adagissimo when it moved ahead at all. On April 17, conte Sanvitale wrote Bellini demanding explanation of the fact that the theater's coypist had not been receiving autograph score to work from; he added[21] that "so long a delay [librettist and composer had been in Parma exactly a month] . . . could entail unhappy results if it should continue any longer." Bellini's reply, which either was delivered in person or has been lost, did not appease Sanvitale, who returned to the attack in a second, more mandatory letter[22]: "I again invite you to be courteous enough to let me know when you will be in a position to give your opera to the copyists and [to tell me] the reasons for your delay in composing it. . . ."

One reason for Romani's slowness in producing text was his well-known propensity for tergiversation. Another was that Bellini's perfectionist demands had begun to irritate him, especially as he felt dangerously exposed to criticism for reducing to libretto proportions so long and hallowed a drama as Voltaire's *Zaïre*. Unquestionably, too, some of the delay reflected mental and spiritual lethargy on Bellini's part. Cicconetti wrote[23]: ". . . [the people of Parma] believed that they detected in Vincenzo clear evidence of a failure to fulfill with requisite zeal obligations that he had assumed toward the entire city. The fact that he was rarely to be found at home, that he meandered frequently through the streets of Parma, that he spent the evening hours in convivial conversations, caused a variety of talk about him. Those who were least stern and who set great store by Bellini said that the spirits of great men often fall into a sort of inertia as though forgetful of their powers—as a result of which, if they are disturbed, they react almost contemptuously by producing works that give clear evidence of fatigue and of lack of the divine fire requisite for artistic creation. On the other hand, others went about exclaiming: 'See how little the composer cares about his standing in this city and this theater, how little he believes necessary to win their favor.'" Pastura, often ready to defend Bellini against all comers, commented this way upon Cicconetti's remarks: "Today we cannot accuse Cicconetti of excessive imagination; some documents[24] that have remained unknown until now prove that a month after Bellini reached Parma, the opera had not made much progress."

Murmuring began to rise among the operagoers of Parma. Where was the promised Romani-Bellini opera? Why, seeing that librettist and composer had been on hand since March 17, had it been necessary to postpone to May 12[25] its première and (more important to them) therefore the inauguration of the new Teatro Ducale? Torrigiani, his friends, and the supporters of his pesudo-Metastasian style probably swelled the gossip, complaints, and increasing discontent that were to infect the audience by the night of the première of *Zaira*. In fact, the dress rehearsal did not take place on May 15.

Oddly, Bellini seems not to have deciphered the handwriting on the new walls of the Teatro Ducale: on the day of the première, writing to his uncle Vincenzo Ferlito, he began by reporting that he was very busy because his opera would go on stage that evening[26]: "Yesterday evening was the dress rehearsal, and I believe that *Zaira* too will be as fortunate as my other operas. Almost all the pieces were applauded; but those to impress a whole audience are a cavatina for Lalande, a trio and a duet in the first act; and in the second act a duet for Lablache and Lalande; Nerestano's rondo, which is sung by a certain [Teresa] Cecconi, who has a very beautiful contralto voice, and then Lalande's *scena*, Lablache's, and a quintet in the second-act finale. All this together flatters me into believing that this evening the audience will be able to rest content with a composition written—poetry and music—in a single month,[27] and up to now I am very satisfied, and especially with the trio, a piece that amazed everyone so much that I myself don't believe that I have ever composed so effectively in this manner . . ."

The irritability and fretful state of mind of many members of the audience at the Teatro Ducale on May 16, 1829, were intensified when, picking up copies of the libretto published for the occasion, they read Romani's "*Proemio dell'autore*," which, after apologizing for having dared "a confrontation with Voltaire,"[28] set forth all the difficulties of condensing the tragedy into a libretto and concluded: "I well know that the style should have been more careful, and that, here and there, certain repetitions of phrases and concepts should have been edited out; but the poetry was written in shreds while the music was being composed, in such a way that I was not permitted to go back over what already had been done; and poetry and music were finished in less than a month. I know furthermore that he who, with Molière's Alceste, makes time his excuse is always ready to shout that *le temps ne fait rien à l'affaire;* nevertheless, it should be observed that Molière's Alceste is a misanthrope. Whatever the public's judgment on this, my work, may be, I shall always be proud that it was made use of under such solemn circumstances; and the thought of the faith that was reposed upon my small talent will sweeten whatever bitterness I have had and may have to experience. Felice Romani."

That *Proemio* pleased no one but Romani. Some members of the audience at the Teatro Ducale might reasonably have felt that he was blandly saying that they were being offered a botched libretto that he had not wanted to write, but then had written in disjunct pieces in a damaging rush. Bellini saw that Romani's apologia cast a bad light on him and on *Zaira*, its score included. The authorities must have wondered, too, why Romani could not have persuaded Bellini to let him write a manageable subject and could not have taken time to produce it at the peak of his ability, especially as his own statement seemed to say that he had idled away the first of his two months in Parma. The audience that crowded the Teatro Ducale on the night of May 16, 1829, included friends and partisans of both Bellini and Romani; it also included friends and partisans of Torrigiani who still were angry because the librettos that he had proposed had been rejected. It was far from being a friendly, or even a receptively neutral, audience.[29] On that night, in the presence of Marie-Louise,[30] *Zaira* received the first of eight consecutive nightly performances, the last of which was to occur on May 24.

At the first performance of *Zaira*, Bellini sat at the cembalo, as was the decreasing custom. Exactly how the audience as a whole reacted to the opera and its performance remains unclear: apparently only the first-act trio and Nerestano's rondo were applauded. What is certain is that Bellini's second 1829 opera, the fifth of his career (sixth if both versions of *Bianca* be counted) was not a success. Cicconetti, who may either have heard descriptions of that night from people who had experienced it or have seen now-vanished letters, wrote[31]: "With Vincenzo therefore seated in the prescribed place, and the spectacle having begun, it soon became clear that this was destined to be neither the place of a triumph nor a judgment seat, but a sacrificial altar. For from the outset whenever applause was directed at the singers, behold some people making it clear that it was not intended to praise the Maestro. Whenever, during the course of the opera, his name was called out approvingly, even in some places rapturously, nonetheless it often died on the lips when voices were raised to cut off the joy and demand silence, seeking nothing better than to burst into signs of crude disapproval at each piece of lesser value, at each flaw in the performance. And if history did not demand truth and if it was not important to demonstrate the extreme strength of musical factions, the disdainful spirit would refuse to report that on that evening there were even some who broke into ranting abuse of the composer of *Zaira*."

The description of that evening by the official inspector of the theater reads this way: "The spectacle began at precisely eight-thirty and ended nearly two hours after midnight. The music in the opera seems not to have been received with pleasure, except for a first-act trio; but the singers were applauded extraordinarily. The ballet [*Oreste*, choreographed by Antonio Cortesi] won general approval."[32] During the night after the first performance, handbills, possibly the work of Torrigiani's supporters, appeared in the streets of Parma: "Anyone who finds the musical inspiration of signor Bellini is besought to take it to the boxoffice of signor Bandini, the impresario, and he will be treated courteously."[33] Bellini appears to have lost interest in *Zaira* as soon as he left Parma: even its name is all but completely absent from his later letters. It was never revived during his lifetime, and he transferred many of its best musical passages to later operas. From a remark published by Romani in 1835,[34] it is clear that some strain between Bellini and him developed at this time, certainly the result of recriminations and mutual accusations of responsibility for the failure of their latest collaborative creation. In fact, *Zaira* was the only enduring failure of Bellini's professional career.[35]

How long Bellini remained in Parma, whether he left there alone or with Romani, where he went first—none of these data can now be determined. Very strangely, almost none of the many letters he surely wrote to Florimo survives between one dated March 14, 1829,[36] and a letter from Paris dated February 14, 1834[37]—after which the surviving letters again become abundant. To be sure, we have some ninety letters that Bellini wrote to other people during those five years, but few of them begin to replace what must be lamented as the "lost letters to Florimo,"[38] especially as the lacuna occurs during the period in which Bellini composed all but one of his finest operas, visited London, and settled in Paris.

After studying this gap, Pastura wrote[39]: "It is therefore to be believed that many of the letters sent to Florimo were given to admirers who, passing through Naples and stopping by to render homage to the custodian of the Bellini memorabilia, did not fail to ask for—and obtain—some relics of the idolized Catanese musician; as, on the other hand, it is to be believed that at least two-thirds of the correspondence stretching from March 1829 to March 1834 formed part of that fire, lighted in honor of friendship, to which Florimo sacrificed historic truth in order to make Bellini the man resemble Bellini the artist in everything . . ."

But Pastura's well-documented belief that in later years Florimo gave away and destroyed Bellini letters does not explain why the years 1829–1834 should have been favored especially for that generosity and arson—or why, if Florimo gave away all but three of many Bellini letters of that period, more of them have not turned up in the possesssion of others. Nothing available in other sources suggests that during those years Bellini would have been reporting matters that even Florimo would have considered reprehensible, unless it was the evolution toward disaster and eventual collapse of his liaison with Giuditta Turina—which Bellini himself made so little effort to conceal that the story can be reconstructed from what he told other friends. Notably, too, Florimo failed to destroy later letters that Giuditta wrote him which cast a very poor light on Bellini. May not the Bellini letters of the 1829–1834 period have been kept in one or more packets that Florimo lost or failed to preserve from accidental destruction? It is as likely a supposition as any.

Late in the spring of 1829, Bellini went to Casalbuttano as the guest of Ferdinando and Giuditta Turina, who annually rented a very large villa there (her parents and her brother Gaetano often stayed there, too). While he was vacationing there, on June 8, in distant Catania his paternal grandfather, Vincenzo Tobia Bellini, his childhood protector and musical preceptor, died at the age of eighty-five. Bellini's reaction to that break with the past is known only as it appears in a notebook believed to have belonged to his sister Michela Marziani: "Immediately upon receiving news of the death of his grandfather, Vincenzo Bellini gave himself up to weeping bitterly over his loss. He wrote: 'I am beside myself with grief; my grandfather is dead. I am more beholden to him than to others, being indebted to him both for his having kept me for so many years in his home, where I learned the greater part of the dogmas of music, and for his always having showed me affection beyond that of a relative.' "[40]

Bellini probably left Casalbuttano and returned to Milan toward the end of June. He had to begin planning his immediate future. He held no contract for a next opera, but was inclined to tie himself to the Teatro La Fenice at Venice. In trying to negotiate a contract there, he again encountered the (to him) unpleasant existence on the operatic scene of his fellow Catanese, Giovanni Pacini.

On June 10, Pacini's opera *Il Talismano, ossia La Terza Crociata in Palestina*[41] had received its première at La Scala with a brilliant cast including Rubini, Giuseppe Frezzolini, and Tamburini. It had run successfully for sixteen nights (and would be returned to La Scala for eighteen more performances in October). Pacini therefore loomed up before Bellini—whose most recent opera had been a failure—as a very real present threat. On a crest of popularity, Pacini accepted two contracts for new operas for the 1830 Carnival season: from Turin and from the Fenice. But when the Fenice impresario learned that Pacini was also under contract to Turin, he told Bellini that if (as seemed very likely) Pacini should fail to deliver the promised opera for Venice on time, the contract would be transferred to him. Uncertainty, then. But, during that summer, Bellini had important matters in hand which could have kept him from worrying too much over not having a definite assignment for Carnival. La Scala was closed for cleaning and repairs from July 3 to the end of August, and *Il Pirata* was consequently being put on during a summer season at the Teatro della Canobbiana, with the leading singers who had helped it to success in 1827. That staging proved to be a psychologically healing event for Bellini. Starring Méric-Lalande, Rubini, and Tamburini, *Il Pirata* ran through twenty-four consecutive performances at the Canobbiana from July 16 to August 28, eight more than Pacini's *Il Talismano* had been given at La Scala two months earlier.

During those days, Rossini, fresh from the apparent triumph of *Guillaume Tell* at the Paris Opéra,[42] arrived in Milan with his wife, en route to Bologna. On August 28, Bellini wrote to Vincenzo Ferlito[43]: "I have not been able to make arrangements for Venice because Pacini has been unwilling to accept the penalty,* and therefore I am without work for this Carnival, and perhaps—who knows?—that may be better, as Romani has so many librettos to do that he would scarcely be able to apply himself to doing one well for me; at Venice not so many good voices as in Milan, and in Milan, after having succeeded with two operas that seem to me impossible to equal, it would be a great risk. The famous Rossini, after creating a furor in Paris with *Guglielmo Tell*, is here temporarily now, on his way to Bologna; having reason to call upon the lady who owns the house where I live, he learned from her that I was living in the same house, and thereupon begged her to take him to me.[44] In fact, I saw my door open and a servant enter, to announce a visit from Rossini, who had reached Milan the evening of [the] 26th, and as my landlady was the first to see him, nobody [else] knew that he was in Milan; you can picture my surprise, which was so intense that [I] was all atremble with pleasure; not having had the patience to put on a jacket, I went up to greet him in shirtsleeves, and therefore begged his pardon for the indecent manner in which I was presenting myself to him, justified only by the sudden pleasure of making the acquaintance of so great a Genius; he replied that it was of no importance, and added so many, many compliments about my compositions that he had come to know in Paris.

"And then, continuing, he told me: 'I have recognized in your operas that you begin where the others have stopped.' I answered that this eulogy from him would serve to make me immerse myself deeper in the career I have adopted and that I counted myself fortunate in having elicited a compliment from the musical man of the century. That evening, he came to hear *Il Pirata;* then he came back the next evening, which was the final performance of the season, and he has been telling all Milan that he found in the whole opera a finish and an organization worthy of a mature man rather than of a young one, and that it is full of feeling and, in his view, carried to such a degree of philosophic reasoning that the music lacks some peak of brilliance.

"That was his feeling, but I shall go on composing in the same way, on the basis of common sense, as I have tried it out that way in my wild enthusiasm. Yesterday, then, I was invited to dinner by the Cantù [Giuditta Turina's parents], where I found Rossini and his wife [Isabella Colbran]; he repeated his compliments to me, but said nothing about feeling

---

* Pacini, that is, was determined to compose the opera for La Fenice rather than pay a contractual penalty for failure to deliver it.

and brillance; but at our first meeting he had told me that from my music he understood that I must love a lot, a lot, because he had found great feeling in it, etc., etc.

"So in Milan they now talk about *Il Pirata*, Rossini, Rossini and *Il Pirata*, for each person says whatever pleases him, and the same thing with the singers. Meanwhile, I consider myself lucky for this incident because I get to know so great a man.

"My dear Uncle, I leave you, begging you to share this with the entire family and all the relatives. Receive an embrace, and believe me always Your most affectionate nephew Vincenzo.

"P.S. *Il Pirata* has had huge crowds for all 24 performances, and at the last performance it brought in a large sum of money because it is the custom then to repeat the pieces that have pleased most; they had to repeat the duet and the trio in the third act."

Thus the immediate operatic past—though no one then suspected that *Guillaume Tell* would prove to be Rossini's final opera—met something of the immediate operatic future. Later, in Paris, Bellini was consciously to nurse his acquaintance with Rossini into a friendship that became uniquely warm, protective, almost paternal on Rossini's side, but always remained wary and calculating on Bellini's. That ambivalent relationship would culminate in 1834–1835, during the composition of *I Puritani*.

The diminution in the number of Bellini letters available, caused mostly by lack of those to Florimo, becomes a total break in the correspondence from August 28 to November 3, 1829, a period during which occurrences related to him can be determined only from exterior sources. We know that La Scala reopened on September 1 with Vaccaj's opera *Saul*, which was followed four days later by Bellini's *Bianca e Fernando* with Méric-Lalande, Rubini, and Tamburini. Operagoers who had reacted with intense favor toward the revival of *Il Pirata* reasonably responded less eagerly to *Bianca*.[45] We know, too, that on September 28 a royal official wrote from Naples to Bellini[46]: "His Majesty [Francesco I] having instituted the Royal Order of Francesco Primo, he has deemed you worthy to be decorated with the silver medal of that Royal Order; and therefore has deigned to accord it to you. In the Royal Name, and to my pleasure, I call this to your attention and await forwarding the medal to you in the usual manner." Bellini would have felt special delight in receiving this honor from the ruler of Sicily.

In mid-October, Bellini made an unexplained short excursion to Turin, a fact unknown to his biographers until 1932, when Alessandro Luzio published an article[47] that includes seventeen letters written by Bellini between November 3, 1829, and April 29, 1835, to a Turinese friend, Alessandro Lamperi.[48] As Luzio suggested, Bellini may have met Lamperi at

Genoa in 1828, but is more likely to have met him during this brief visit to Turin in October 1829: in the earliest of the surviving letters to him, from Casalbuttano[49] on November 3, Bellini apologizes for writing to him directly rather than to "our mutual friend Grosson."[50]

While in Turin, Bellini foregathered mostly with musicians and others attached to the Accademia filarmonica. From a report in the *Gazzetta piemontese* of November 3,[51] we learn that because the concert season was not on, Bellini attended student exercises at the singing school to hear sections of Haydn's *Die Schöpfung* sung to the accompaniment of double string quartet and cembalo; also that the Accademia filarmonica made him an honorary academician. He outfitted himself with a new greatcoat from a tailor recommended by Lamperi. Bellini evidently was back in Milan by November 1, but the letter that he wrote to Lamperi on November 3 makes it clear that he had preferred to spend that day, his twenty-eighth birthday, with Giuditta Turina at Casalbuttano.

In Venice, meanwhile, Giuseppe Crivelli, an impresario of the Teatro La Fenice, had decided to commission Bellini to compose a new opera. Also, Alessandro Lanari, who often worked in association with Crivelli, suggested that *Il Pirata* be introduced to Venice during the 1830 Carnival season at the Fenice. Bellini signed a contract with Crivelli[52] and agreed to go to Venice to supervise the staging of *Il Pirata*, meaning that he would adapt the score to the capabilities of the cast, which was already determined. It may well have been at this time too that Lanari first suggested that, in the case of Pacini's likely non-appearance with the promised new opera, Bellini should also compose one for the Fenice for the coming season. Bellini clearly regarded his original contract with Crivelli and the eventual contract for *I Capuleti e i Montecchi* as two separate agreements.

Toward the end of October 1829, Giovanni Ricordi published in Milan *Sei Ariette per camera del maestro Vincenzo Bellini*.[53] The appearance of this collection of salon pieces further attested to Bellini's rapidly growing renown and popularity.

How long Bellini tarried in Casalbuttano in November is not known. He certainly returned to Milan, for on December 12 he set out from there, stopped at Casalbuttano again, and continued on to Venice on December 17. Two days later, he found that rehearsals of the season's inaugural opera, Giuseppe Persiani's *Costantino in Arles*, were in progress at the Fenice. He would have listened to them concentratedly: the chief singers were those who would sing in *Il Pirata*—Giuditta Grisi (with whom gossip quickly was picturing him in amorous intimacy), Lorenzo Bonfigli, and Giulio Pellegrini. Also, he soon met Giovanni Battista Perucchini, a leading Venetian amateur of music[54] who was to become his friend, as he was a friend of most composers who visited Venice, Rossini included.

The Teatro La Fenice opened on December 26, 1829, with *Costantino in Arles*. Rehearsals of *Il Pirata* began two days later. For eighteen days thereafter, Bellini was occupied with shaping the singers to his ways of performance and revising details of his score to accommodate their abilities and lacks.[55] By then, Lanari had good reason to doubt the prompt appearance of Pacini with the needed opera, and thereafter alerted Bellini. On January 5, 1830, Bellini signed a letter written out by someone else[56]:

"Signor Alessandro Lanari

"Should Maestro Pacini fail to fulfill his contract to come to write his operas [*sic*] at the Gran Teatro La Fenice, I, in response to your invitation to me, take on the responsibility of composing Romani's libretto *Giulietta Capellio* for you,[57] restricting myself to the honorarium of three hundred twenty-five valid napoleoni d'oro [about 8000 lire], I say napoleoni n. 325, with a special contract, but I am to have a month and a half of time between the day when I receive the libretto and going on stage.

"The present will have the force of a contract until the 14th of the current month, and believe me, in all friendship Your most affectionate friend Vincenzo Bellini."

Although no stigma then attached to reusing a subject or a title used earlier by one or more other composers, and though Bellini would have had no reason to feel any special regard for Nicola Vaccaj—whose successful setting of Romani's *Giulietta e Romeo* was then only four years old—he may well have experienced some twinges of discomfort over taking up a subject on which his teacher Nicola Zingarelli—now seventy-eight—had composed his most popular opera, another *Giulietta e Romeo* (La Scala, Milan, January 30, 1796).[58] Florimo, who strongly felt that Bellini ought to be experiencing such twinges, wrote[59]: "At that time, Bellini wrote a most thoughtful letter to Zingarelli, informing him of his difficult position, and at the same time begging his pardon for being eager to set to music a subject so happily dealt with by him, and with such well-merited success. Zingarelli, a man of spirit, answered him (and had the courtesy to read his reply to me before dispatching it), saying that he was not at all offended, and also urging him to study the subject well because it was very interesting in itself, offering, as it did, affecting situations very suitable for his pathetic music."[60]

On January 14, Bellini signed this codicil to the interim contract-letter regarding "*Giulietta Capellio*"[61]: "Venice, January 14, 1830. Because of delay by the couriers,* the present arrangement is extended to

* Extreme cold weather had left roads impassable and had frozen the lagoon between Venice and the mainland.

the 20th of this month." In a letter written the next day to Gaetano Cantù, he referred to Pacini as "that anti-gentleman" and said[62]: ". . . I have had to make a pact with the impresario until the 20th of this month: the day on which everything will be decided—and then, look, scarcely a month and ten days will remain for composing the opera and staging it, as it must go on by March 1 because the theater will close on the 20th of that same month. The libretto that Romani has done for Pacini—I don't know whether it is completed yet, as I have read [only] the first act and a portion of the second, and in intimate confidence between us, it is more tasteless than frigidity itself in person; enough, pray for me that God may either free me of this undertaking or help me make it succeed."

The first Venetian performance of *Il Pirata* was given on January 16. Four days later, Bellini wrote to Florimo[63]: "I now inform you that I am engaged to compose the opera for this Carnival, and this morning we shall confirm the contract with the management, which allows me a month and a half of time to compose and stage it. See what a strangling, as you well may think, telling me that I have done wrong; but demonstrations by the Governor and by almost all of Venice drove me to this dangerous enterprise. In the meantime, all Venice is pleased by this arrangement, and I hope not to do too badly. If I don't write to you often during the coming days or, indeed, [write] often but little, don't grumble, knowing in what a rushed period I find myself.

"The weather is constantly bad here: *Il Pirata* gives increasing pleasure. Romani, who is already here, having arrived yesterday, will rewrite *Giulietta e Romeo* for me, but will give it a new title and different situations [*sic*].[64] *Addio*, my dear Florimo. My health isn't bad; only I have a cold, and if this weather doesn't let up, I'll be unable to cure myself. Wish me well and receive my embraces. Your Bellini."

Juxtaposition of indifferent health with the malaise caused by having to rush the new opera to completion was more ominous than Bellini could know. The Venetian weather continued frigid; his cold would soon be raising his temperature to fever. The inescapable need to work up to ten hours each day under such conditions drained his never abundant physical resources until he came to feel that he was composing in a delirium, as perhaps, some of the time, he was. As early as January 26, he wrote to Giuditta Turina[65]: "Two pieces of the opera are completed and orchestrated: weariness from morning to evening, and it will be a miracle if I emerge without some illness." Illness was to follow. It may not be too strong to say that the composition of *I Capuleti e i Montecchi* during the harsh Venetian winter of 1830 was a directly contributing cause of Bellini's death. Also, it is more than possible that it was then that he contracted and began to suffer from the chronic amebiasis that would kill him in 1835. That *I Capuleti*, composed that way, should have followed the equally rushed *Zaira* was a double misfortune.

Romani lacked time to write a completely new libretto. In large part, he therefore simply recast his Vaccaj text,[66] not disdaining to insert groups of unchanged lines into the new libretto. Bellini, who must have realized that he could not compose a wholly new opera in six weeks, sent for the score of *Zaira*, perhaps believing that he could transfer whole sections of it *en bloc* to *I Capuleti*. Soon enough, he found himself struggling with the complex task of fitting existing music to a new text.[67] Kept constantly in his quarter by work and illness, he had to forego the public gaiety of the Venetian Carnival, when the piazzas—and especially San Marco—became stages peopled by brilliantly costumed revelers.

By those trials and those means, Bellini succeeded in completing and orchestrating Act I of *I Capuleti e i Montecchi* for rehearsal on March 3, when he wrote to Giuditta Turina[68]: "I'll be writing you few letters until I shall have gone on stage, as I must finish the opera—that is, still must do one scene of the second act. This morning, we rehearsed the first act with full orchestra, and it promises to be effective. The singers are caught up in it, and the music seconds them; Wednesday is the great day,[69] and who knows whether it will be famous as a fiasco or as a furor? I look forward to the latter, first because I feel that the music of the first act makes its effect, and second because all Venice is on my side.

"I am very happy that your health goes well, that you are permitted to take walks . . ."[70] I still cannot tell you that I am well, as from either cold or heat I am chilled or I am burning up; but I hope that after going on stage I shall improve. . . ."

The first performance of *I Capuleti e i Montecchi* occurred at the Fenice on March 11, 1830, with Giuditta Grisi as Romeo.[71] It was an unclouded immediate success. But the season was late: the new opera could be performed only eight times before it closed the Fenice season on Sunday, March 21.[72] The press chronicles turned up almost unanimously enthusiastic. *I Teatri*, for example, under the rubric "Lombardo-Veneto," reported: "Thus, after the first act, as after the second, there were called out onto the stage the composer of the music, Grisi, Romeo, Carradori [*sic*], Giulietta, Bonfigli, Tebaldo; Grisi twice after the cavatina, Carradori once after the aria '*Ah! non poss'io partire*'; the painter Gianni after the revelation of the tomb scene.[73] More and more letters agree in saying that, all things considered, this opera by Bellini has aroused as much enthusiasm in Venice as *La Straniera* aroused in Milan from the first evening on."[74] Florimo said that after the third performance Bellini was conducted to his quarters "by an immense throng of people with flaring torches, preceded by a military band that played the specially favored pieces from his operas."[75]

Bellini lingered on in conquered Venice about one week after the Fenice closed its doors for the season on March 21. Before his departure, he signed a contract with Crivelli to compose another new opera, to be staged at the Fenice during the 1830–1831 Carnival season. Then, on about March 30, he returned to Casalbuttano and Giuditta Turina. He did not get back to Milan until April 12. Awaiting him there were letters from Alessandro Lamperi saying that the management of Turin's Teatro Regio wanted him to compose the chief new attraction for its 1830–1831 Carnival season. Replying on April 14, Bellini wrote[76]: ". . . to my sorrow, I must tell you that I cannot enter into negotiations, being bound to Venice for that period."

Except for the serious drain on Bellini's physique, his four-month absence from Milan had been triumphantly rewarding. In the five years that had passed since the production of *Adelson e Salvini* in Naples in February 1825, he had composed five operas and revised one of them. Except for the parenthetic failure of *Zaira*, his artistic road had sloped constantly upward to the many-voiced accompaniment of swiftly mounting fame and adulation. Rossini remained operatically unproductive in his retreat at Castenaso, near Bologna. Some unwelcome threats persisted, of course—notably Donizetti and Pacini—but Bellini's personal star now gleamed, high and clearly visible, in the Italian operatic sky.

(VI)

1830-1831: *Ernani*, *La Sonnambula*, *Norma*

URING APRIL 1830, pleasing news reached Bellini from Catania. His uncle Vincenzo Ferlito wrote him that the decurionate's deliberations, begun in 1829, about coining a gold medal in his honor had concluded with approval of the project by the *intendente* of the Vallo di Catania.[1] Expressing his pleasure in this formal recognition from the authorities of his birthplace, Bellini later sent the Catania decurionate a specially bound, inscribed score of *I Capuleti e i Montecchi*,[2] accompanying it with an engraving made from a portrait of himself by Natale Schiavoni which Florimo called the most faithful likeness of his friend.[3]

Although Bellini remained relatively idle at Casalbuttano until about mid-April, his health improved little. Also, rumblings out of the Milanese world of opera soon required his presence in the city. The arrangement by which the "Società Crivelli e Compagni"[4] had been managing La Scala (and the Teatro La Fenice at Venice) was about to expire. A triumvirate consisting of the duca Pompeo Litta and two businessmen named Marietti and Soresi was trying to replace the Società Crivelli, and was eager to sign on singers—including Pasta and Rubini—and composers, notably Donizetti and Bellini. The three men were doing everything possible to acquire from Crivelli the contract that he held with Bellini for composition of an opera for the Fenice, and would finally succeed in buying it. In the surviving fragment of a letter that Bellini wrote to Vincenzo Ferlito, probably in April 1830, he said[5]:

". . . they have told me that they have bought my contract only so as to free me from Crivelli, and not to acquire me and my talents, and consequently that it was their intention to tear up the contract, which assigned me 7,000 francs for the opera that it bound me to compose for the Venetian theater, leaving me to decide about making a different demand, and that I am obligated to compose either for the Milanese theater or the Venetian, as now there is some question as to whether this Society will have the Milan theater or the one in Venice, adding that for Carnival I may compose no more than this single opera; well, that being my intention—an intention that I had made clear to them before they bought me from Crivelli—I have demanded a payment of 12,000 svansike [sic, for svansiche], equal to two thousand four hundred ducati, and a half interest in the score, which—if the opera should be a success—would bring me in a total of 3,000 ducati; they have granted me all these points; I have been extremely fortunate in this arrangement, as I shall earn almost twice as much as if I had composed for Crivelli[6]; Fortune still seems to want me as her favorite; I'll not abuse [the situation], as I always study . . ."

Despite these favorable negotiations, Bellini was far from happy. His worsening health was worrying him. In an undatable letter to Vincenzo Ferlito (it almost certainly was written very late in May or early in June), he said[7]: "I told you that I wanted to give you an account of the illness I suffered, and here it is: the chief cause was my having composed I Capuleti in Venice in twenty-six days, during which I applied myself for ten hours at a stretch during the morning [and afternoon] and four more in the evening. Sometimes my breath stank there as a result of very bad digestion; the nasty weather also added to my suffering; in April, I returned to Milan and had no appetite until May 21, when a tremendous inflammatory gastric bilious fever attacked me and made it necessary for them to give me a bloodletting and then an emetic: on the third day, [Francesco] Pollini, with the doctor's intervention,[8] wanted to take me to his home because my quarters consisted of narrow rooms with low ceilings, a thing that was dangerous because of the nature of my illness, which might degenerate into *** malignant: at the Pollini home, in a word, I was taken care of with such kindness and affection as I cannot describe. They are still out of pocket, as I have paid only for the doctor and the remedies; thus you can see what debts I acknowledge to this good family, which loves me more than a son."[9]

The only serious illness of Bellini's life, this one was to prove chronic, if intermittent (summer was an ominous season for him from 1830 on), and eventually mortal. Pastura said[10]: "Not an opera of Bellini's but is followed by a nervous collapse, if not also by an illness." The romantically perfectionist intensity that he invested in composing except when pressure of time forbade it always depleted his physical and nervous energies. Franca Cella acutely summed up the relationship between Bellini's nature as a composer and the relatively rapid ebbing of his physical resistance[11]: "He wrote ten operas, a very limited number if contrasted with the creative exuberance of the composers of the time, but sufficient to fill his life with labor, a life that was brief because, for him, creation required prolonged concentration and wearying application, as a result of which his physique was destroyed." Such destruction may well have been inevitable after the composition of *I Capuleti e i Montecchi* at Venice, during an iron winter under nerve-twisting conditions.

Just before (perhaps during) the crisis of Bellini's April–May struggle with intestinal inflammation, he negotiated two more contracts for future operas. One was with the Litta-Marietti-Soresi group, which had failed to replace the Crivelli-Lanari-Barbaja society at La Scala and in Venice, but was planning to defy La Scala by mounting a season of magnificent performances at a smaller Milanese theater, the Carcano.[12] Their daring would lead, on Bellini's part, to a plan to set a Romani libretto to be based upon Victor Hugo's *Hernani*, the discarding of that plan, and the eventual creation of *La Sonnambula*. The other contract, with the Crivelli group, provided that Bellini would compose an opera for the autumn season of 1831 at La Scala, another for the Carnival season of 1832 (these would turn out to be, respectively, *Norma* at La Scala and *Beatrice di Tenda* at the Fenice). His future looked secure on excellent terms for the next two years.

When Bellini's slowly improving health allowed him to travel, during the second half of June he went to spend the summer as a guest of either the Cantù or the Turinas or both at Moltrasio, on the west shore of Lake Como about five miles north of Como.[13] And in 1827, across the narrow lake at Blevio, Giuditta Pasta had bought the Villa Roda, which was to become her permanent residence and a place of pilgrimage for her admirers. Born Giuditta Negri at Saronno in Lombardy in 1797, married while in her teens to Giuseppe Pasta,[14] an ex-tenor who had become a lawyer, Pasta had made her operatic debut when only eighteen, at the Teatro degli Accademici Filodrammatici, Milan, in *Le Tre Eleonore*, an opera by her teacher, Giuseppe Scappa. Bellini very probably had heard her during the period from November 1826 to April 1827, when she had sung at the Teatro San Carlo in Naples—in Pacini's *Niobe*, Carafa's *Gabriella di Vergy*, and perhaps also in Pietro Raimondi's *Giuditta*. She was already an internationally renowned soprano when she sang in Naples for the first time on November 19, 1826, in *Niobe*, and it is likely, though not verifiable, that Bellini at that time met the future creator of his Amina (*La Sonnambula*), Norma, and Beatrice di Tenda. During the summer of 1830 at Lake Como, her propinquity was to be helpful to him. The exact date of his arrival at Moltrasio cannot be determined, but a letter to his brother Carmelo survives with the heading "*Como, 1 luglio 1830.*"[15]

That letter is peculiarly interesting for what it tells of Bellini's relations with his family and of his attitudes toward money. His family in Catania was not flourishing financially. Rosario and Agata Bellini still had four children at home,[16] and though Rosario had fallen heir to his father's meager musical perquisites, he required assistance both in his daily rounds and in keeping his family afloat, aid that he was receiving to some extent from his twenty-seven-year-old second son, Carmelo. Vincenzo Ferlito clearly had asked Bellini by letter if he too could make regular additions to Don Rosario's slender purse. Bellini's letter to Carmelo is a reaction to that plea. In part, he wrote:

"The description that our most affectionate uncle Don Vincenzo has given me by letter on your filial virtues impels me to write to you directly to make you understand my great gratitude for so much that you have done for our good family, to whom we owe our physical and moral being. Perhaps our Uncle has told you why, up to now, I have not done what you are doing, and the reasons are good ones, o my good brother, and I repeat them to you. But you must please me by not spreading throughout the city what passes between us, something I want you to recommend to the whole family; do you understand? Well, my plan is to amass enough capital to be able to assign a fixed amount of at least six tarì[17] a day to our family, so that they will never lack for it, and at the same time to have the means to maintain myself independently of my profession. But I cannot achieve this unless I put some savings together, which is why— as you have understood and still understand—I refrain from helping our family and may have to continue to do so if good fortune fails me even briefly. On the other hand, if I prosper, I'll need another four years to accomplish what I want. You should know that our uncle will transmit thirty onze[18] in August, and I guarantee that sum annually; if now, during this period, I should work out a contract for the coming year,[19] I'll forward another thirty onze in February, and in that way I hope to send on the same amounts during the same months each year. But that will always depend upon what income I'll have until such time as I can assure myself of a sufficient sum to put us in a position free of need. You continue to help the household as you do now, and I swear on my honor that your brother Vincenzo never, never will abandon you. And I assure you of this: there will be enough to guarantee you a life free from need in illness and old age—and this promise of mine will hold until I can have the means to fulfill it. Don't abandon our family, and go on being the good and worthy son you are. I hope that my arguments are convincing, and that it will prove better to suffer a little for another two or three years so as to be able to be sure of sufficient comfort after that. . . ."

That Bellini was also discussing with Vincenzo Ferlito both his family's needs and his plan to send sums to Catania regularly is proved by a sentence in the undated letter of April 30[20] already cited. A canceled passage in it reads: "If you decide that way for my family, don't say anything to them unless we have agreed upon it, as at the present time I can scarcely find a bit of money to keep myself until I can obtain the first payment for the Carnival; enough, be assured that I'll reply then about how we can put the whole plan into execution."[21] No documents tell us whether or when Bellini may have begun carrying out his plan to forward regular sums to Catania. After he settled in Paris in 1833, he sent money to Catania through the Rothschild Bank; that is all that we know. He has been depicted, with small justice, as avaricious and un-generous, but that appearance of selfish money-grubbing reflected deep-lying fears for his future and a determination to guarantee regular assistance to his parents and siblings in Catania.

In the summer of 1830, Bellini and Romani had to agree immediately upon a subject for the opera to be staged the following winter at the Teatro Carcano in Milan. Because Giuditta Pasta was to have its leading role,[22] Romani too went to Lake Como, where he could discuss possible subjects with both Bellini and Pasta. On July 24, 1830, Saverio Merca-dante wrote to Florimo from Milan[23]: ". . . Bellini (Signora Pollini has told me) is at Como, and I hope to see him tomorrow, as I must go there to see Romani with the object of learning if he has done for me the libretto that has been pending for a year. . . ."[24]

By July 15, Bellini, Romani, and Pasta had agreed that the subject for the opera was to be extracted from *Hernani*, the drama by Victor Hugo which had been played for the first time at the Théâtre-Français, Paris, on February 25 of that year and already had become a political and artistic storm center. That these three extremely competent operatic judges could have made themselves believe *Hernani* a reasonable source for an opera to be staged in Austrian-controlled Milan under the iron censorship then operative can be understood only in view of two sup-positions: that they saw in Hugo's drama the extractable outlines of a non-political libretto crowded with forceful confrontations and passionate action,[25] and that Pasta was willing, perhaps eager, to sing *en travesti* the title role, that of a handsome Spanish outlaw.

On July 15, Bellini wrote to Guglielmo Cottrau in Naples[26]: "*Hernani* pleases me mightily, and pleases just as much Pasta and Romani and all who have read it; at the beginning of September, I'll set to work." But once that subject had been selected, neither Romani nor Bellini appears to have given much thought to the required opera for several months. No word about either *Ernani* or the need to create an opera for the forthcoming Carnival season occurs in Bellini's surviving letters between July 15 and November. Nor could he begin composing the opera in September: Romani, who had agreed to work on the *Ernani* libretto while Bellini remained at Moltrasio, instead returned to Milan and began writing for Donizetti the text of *Anna Bolena*, the opera that was to open the Carcano's extraordinary season on December 26, 1830.

Nor did Bellini continue recuperating at Moltrasio. Disregarding advice that he prolong his rest, he went to Milan, where he signed the two-opera contract with Crivelli, and then to Bergamo to supervise the staging, at the Teatro Riccardi, of *La Straniera*. He reached that stronghold of Giovanni Simone Mayr and Donizetti on August 2. The next day, writing to Giuditta Turina to announce his safe arrival[27] (but failing to put the year after the heading "*Bergamo 3 agosto*"), he reported that the heat made him feel that he was in "a constantly boiling cauldron," but that he was in good health. He also wrote: "*Avrete inteso che la balena fece fiasco; felice io, e tutti quei che non andarono*" (You will have heard that the whale was a fiasco; happy I and all those who did not go). That innocent sentence, coupled with Bellini's omission of the year from the dating, gave rise to a train of comic misunderstandings and falsifications which lasted one hundred and thirteen years.

Florimo, putting together his collection of Bellini letters in 1882, assigned that one to 1830, but could make no sense of the reference to a whale. So he decided that what looked like "*balena*" (whale) actually was "*bolena*," and that therefore Bellini was referring—without a capital letter—to a performance of Donizetti's *Anna Bolena*. And then "*andarono*" (went) struck him as unsatisfactory as a verb for attendance at an operatic performance. So, capitalizing and italicizing "*Bolena*," he replaced "*andarono*" with "*sentirono*" (heard).[28] And, as though to complicate still more that piece of arbitrary "editing," when Antonino Amore reprinted the Bellini letter in 1894, he retained Florimo's "*Bolena*," but filled out the dating to read "*Bergamo, 3 agosto 1832*" and added this footnote[29]: "In the correspondence edited by Florimo, this letter carries the date of 3 August 1830, and that is evidently in error: 1st because *Anna Bolena* could not have been given at Bergamo on 3 August if it was given for the first time in Milan on 26 December 1830; 2nd because it is proved that *Norma* was given in Bergamo the 20th of August 1832*; as appears in the letters written [by Bellini] to the poet Romani and to conte Barbò."[30]

Amore, no less high-handed than Florimo, had decided that Bellini

---

* It was, but the evidence is irrelevant.

had written the letter during his 1832 visit to Bergamo rather than when he was there in 1830. But, as Luisa Cambi understood,[31] Amore should have noticed that ". . . there were ten other proofs to say that the letter was of 1830; and that one of them, a single one, a simple phrase, should have sufficed to annihilate his proofs. 'Before leaving Milan, I signed the contract with Crivelli for 20,000 valid svanziche for two operas, without other obligations.' " Crivelli died during the summer of 1831, so that Bellini's letter must have been written, not in 1832, but during his earlier visit to Bergamo, in 1830.[32]

Luisa Cambi also extracted from *L'Eco*, Milan, of August 2, 1830, an account that proved that Bellini had indeed referred to a whale and not to *Anna Bolena*.[33] At the Milanese Anfiteatro dell'Arena, the dancer-choreographer Louis Henry, a specialist in nautical effects, had staged an extravaganza of naumachy, the much-publicized chief attraction of which was a life-sized mechanical whale designed to swim about with all the appearance of nature, surrounded by "savages" in pirogues, swimmers, divers, and illuminated boats carrying acrobats and equilibrists. The whale had not disported itself as promised; the audience had expressed violent disapproval.[34] Not "*Bolena*," then, but "*balena*." But the comedy was not yet quite over. Pastura, not reading Luisa Cambi's article with careful attention, wrote[35] that Bellini's "*balena*" had referred to a live whale "exhibited in a large tank at Milan, and which died shortly afterwards," thus introducing perhaps the final error into this cautionary tale for editors.

At Bergamo in the heat of an especially torrid Lombard summer, Bellini worked hard with the miscellaneous forces gathering to perform *La Straniera*. He was the guest of his prima donna, Stefania Favelli—who was, he told Giuditta Turina in that August 3rd letter,[36] ". . . in your position, as she is having severe pains; I asked her why, and she replied that, like you, she suffered from her diplomatic credentials." The first Bergamo singing of *La Straniera*, delayed because of Favelli's indisposition, took place at the Teatro Riccardi on August 17.[37] Bellini did not tarry in Bergamo thereafter: on August 22, he wrote from Moltrasio to his Venetian friend Perucchini[38]: "With pleasure, I send you the news that at Bergamo, *La Straniera* was a very great success, though it went on stage with Favelli still very weak from her most recent indisposition."

A gap in our knowledge of Bellini's activities stretches from those hot August days to November.[39] He almost certainly first went from Bergamo back to Moltrasio and then, as colder weather came on, moved with the Turinas to Casalbuttano. What is certain is that in a letter of November 10 to Perucchini from Milan, he began[40]: "I have been in Milan since the day before yesterday. The situation in the country, where I have been up to now, kept me from writing to you . . ." Where "in the country"? And what "situation in the country"? We do not know.

Nor does Bellini's only other available letter from late 1830, which yields up other indicative information, answer those questions. On November 17, writing to Alessandro Lamperi, he said[41]: "Just two lines to tell you that I am still alive, because for some time now I should have answered your letter, but the country and the poet [Romani] have had me beside myself; the country because I had to send to Milan especially for anything I wanted, and the poet because, while thinking over the plan for the subject, he still has not been able to begin the libretto, and we are, as you see, at the 17th of November, and I haven't composed a note as yet. . . ." Nothing had been accomplished toward creating either the libretto or the score of *Ernani*.[42]

Bellini and Romani almost certainly outlined the *Ernani* libretto soon after Bellini's return to Milan on November 8. Romani delivered some verses of it to Bellini before December 1. On January 3, 1831, however, again to Perucchini, Bellini wrote[43]: "You know that I am no longer composing *Ernani* because the subject would have had to undergo some modifications at the hands of the police,[44] and that therefore Romani has abandoned it so as not to compromise himself, and is now writing *La Sonnambula, ossia I Due Fidanzati svizzeri*, and just yesterday I began the introduction; you will see that it falls to my lot to compose this opera too in a short space of time, as it must go on stage on February 20 at the latest."

In the 1880's, when music that Bellini actually composed for *Ernani* was not yet known to survive, the question of whether or not he adapted a little, much, or even all of it in his hasty composition of *La Sonnambula* became the subject of an intemperate, protracted public debate in which the chief arguers were the marchesa di Montezemolo (Romani's remarried widow, née Emilia Branca), Michele Scherillo, and Antonino Amore. Anyone curious to follow the tortuous episodes of that odd, somewhat loony polemic will find them recounted in detail by Pastura[45]; a résumé of the central episodes is given here in Appendix C, page 394. That Bellini did so adapt some of the music originally composed for *Ernani* is established. That he did so, and that he liberally transferred melodic and other musical ideas from one of his operas to another (see Part II, *passim*) disposes of the frequently made assertion that, *in toto*, the music of his operas always was a unique and immediate response to the text lines he was setting. The genuineness and stylistic importance of that response are not in question. But the fact remains that Bellini was as ready as most other composers of his era to reuse in a new situation musical passages created for a different, earlier one.

In December 1830, Bellini and Romani agreed not to proceed farther with *Ernani,* largely because threatened political censorship would destroy whatever of Victor Hugo's inflammable drama might remain in Romani's text.[46] For the Teatro Carcano, they would instead create an opera for which Romani was to derive the libretto from *La Somnambule, ou L'Arrivée d'un nouveau seigneur,* by Eugène Scribe and the choreographer Jean-Pierre Aumer. Filling only thirteen pages in Scribe's *Œuvres complètes,* that synopsis had been used by Louis-Joseph-Ferdinand Hérold for a three-act ballet-pantomime, *La Somnambule,* first staged at the Opéra, Paris, on September 19, 1827. Pastoral-sentimental in character, making a young girl's sleep-walking the cause of a love imbroglio that ends happily, Romani's text differed drastically in tone from the librettos that Bellini had set earlier. That *La Sonnambula* became one of Bellini's finest operas was owing in part to that very difference, but also, in large part, to the accumulation of operatic experience which both he and Romani brought to its creation. It was also possibly owing to the challenge to Bellini's intense sense of personal glory posed by the high quality and echoing success of *Anna Bolena,* much the finest opera that Donizetti had composed up to then.[47]

Returning to Milan on November 8, 1830, Bellini did not go back to his former living quarters. Instead, he became a guest of the contessa Giuseppina Appiani in her palazzo in the borgo Monforte, where he was to live through 1831. Born Giuseppina Strigelli in about 1797, the contessa Appiani was the daughter of a prominent politician, conte Antonio Strigelli. She had married a son (or perhaps nephew or even grandson) of Andrea Appiani, a well-known neoclassic fresco-painter and portraitist.[48] She was later to be very friendly to both Donizetti (who composed *Linda di Chamounix* and completed *Maria Padilla* while a guest in her palazzo) and Verdi. The inevitable result was gossip, apparently baseless, that she had been the mistress of one or more of these composers, though at the time of her relationships with Donizetti and Verdi she was a grandmother in her forties. Raffaello Barbiera, an unreliable witness, wrote[49] that she resembled Ninon de Lenclos in preserving her shapeliness into old age. A woman of strong intelligence and roving interests, Giuseppina Appiani had become a noted *salonnière* in a city and era of recognized salons. No one has asserted that in 1830–1831, still in her early thirties, she was also Bellini's mistress. That Giuditta Turina or, more likely, Giuditta's mother, Carolina Cantù—who was related to the Appianis—had asked her to invite the still-weak Bellini to live in her palazzo, as Pastura suggested,[50] is altogether likely. There he would have come into frequent contact with the titled, wealthy, and otherwise noted people with whom he enjoyed being associated.

Bellini was living in the borgo Monforte when he received from Romani the first verses of the proposed *Ernani* text; when he sent a few of them to Florimo in a letter; when the decision was made to create *La Sonnambula* rather than *Ernani*. The Appiani palazzo remained his home while he composed both *La Sonnambula* and *Norma*.[51] There, on January 2, 1831, he began the introduction to *La Sonnambula*. From there, on February 7, he wrote to Lamperi[52]: "I have completed the first act, and perhaps I'll start the second tomorrow if the poet gives me the words." On that same day, he sent a note to Giovanni Ricordi[53]: "In accord with your note, I have handed your brother the first act, lacking two cavatinas and a duet; in the meantime, within half an hour or an hour, I'll pass by your shop, where I beg you to have the contract ready for me, drawn up on tax-stamped paper; you already know the general terms: but you must add to them that the score cannot be sold to anyone without the approval of the three parties—that is, you, Soresi, and me. . . ." Because the only other known letter from Bellini dated in January or February 1831 mentions *La Sonnambula* merely to say that the time for its production is near,[54] no accurate schedule of its composition can be drawn up.

Nine weeks to the day elapsed between January 2, 1831, when Bellini began the introduction to *La Sonnambula*, and the première of the opera on March 6. But between February 8, the day when, he said, he might start on Act II, and the day of the première, only twenty-six days passed. Further, Bellini cannot have worked that long on Act II: rehearsals would have filled at least ten days. He must therefore have composed Act II in about two weeks.[55] The rehearsals proved stormy because of Bellini's unyielding insistence upon his sort of perfection. According to both Emilia Branca and Michele Scherillo,[56] at the dress rehearsal a choice still had to be made among several Romani texts for Amina's concluding cabaletta, "*Ah! non giunge uman pensiero.*"[57]

Emilia Branca drew the scene this way: "Then the orchestra was ready to begin, when the Maestro, very agitated, ran here and there on the stage, looking for his poet. Finding him at last, he laid siege to him, clung to him, and for the hundredth time begged him to satisfy him by redoing the final strophes, exclaiming: 'I want something that will exalt Pasta and raise her to seventh heaven!' Glowing with the flame that lighted his spirit, he was swimming *dans l'embarras des richesses*, and yet was asking for something new. Taken thus by surprise, Romani, who by then was bored, finally lost patience, picked out one of the inconvenient *strette*, and, mumbling some words in the direction of the young composer, shook his head, turned his back, and hastily left the theater. Bellini, who at times was so subject to painful sensitivity that he found the least contradiction insupportable, gave vent to actions worthy of a vexed boy. He remained angry for some moments, but then Giuditta Pasta invervened, and with commanding words calmed the fantasy a little. She observed that the strophes supplied by the poet were very expressive and sure of effect—above all, those written into the score."[58]

The première of *La Sonnambula* took place at the Teatro Carcano, Milan, on Sunday, March 6, 1831; it shared the customary double bill with Louis Henry's ballet *Tutto al contrario*. The cast of the opera included Pasta (Amina) and Rubini (Elvino). It was received with immediate, unrestrained enthusiasm. The next day, Bellini wrote to Lamperi[59]: "Here you have the happy news of the uproarious success of my opera last evening at the Carcano. I say nothing about the music; you will see that in the press. I only assure you that Rubini and Pasta are two angels who enraptured the whole audience to the verge of madness; and then De Angelis[60] will write you what it does not befit me to say."

In the Carcano audience that evening had been the "father of Russian opera," Mikhail Ivanovich Glinka, and he later wrote[61]: "Finally, at the end of the Carnival, there came what everyone had been waiting for: Bellini's *La Sonnambula*. Despite the fact that it was presented late and regardless of the envious ones and the ill-wishers, this opera did make a tremendous impression. In the few performances given before the theaters closed, Pasta and Rubini sang with the most evident enthusiasm to support their favorite conductor [*sic*]; in the second act the singers themselves wept and carried their audience along with them, so that in the happy days of Carnival tears were continually being wiped away in boxes and parquet alike. Embracing [Evgeni Petrovich] Shterich[62] in the Ambassador's box, I, too, shed tears of emotion and ecstasy."

On March 7, the critic of *L'Eco* said[63]: "If we had the time that we do not have to prepare an article describing this performance, we would not begin it when coming from the theater still deafened by the flood of plaudits, shouts, outcries, and acclamations. Indeed, we, who make a profession of not allowing ourselves to be seduced easily, could not help joining in the general enthusiasm. But the poetry of Romani, the music of Bellini, and the performances by Madama Pasta and Rubini demand to be described with greater care and with a calm that would enable us to make sense of the praise and evaluate it, and that is what we propose to undertake in our next issue. Examples of like applause have been few. The Maestro and the singers were called out twelve, fifteen, or twenty times— we really do not know—onto the stage. Bellini has sustained his reputation. Rubini sang like an angel, and it was reserved for Madama Pasta to transform the majesty of Semiramide and the profound sensibility of

Anna Bolena so admirably into the simple and ingenuous graces of a young country girl. After her duet with Rubini, it could truly be said 'That is the way to sing.' "

The writer kept his word: in the next issue (March 9) of his tri-weekly, he analyzed *La Sonnambula* and the performance more judici-ously, but with undiminished enthusiasm, pointing out that acceptance of Amina's somnambulism as credible might be difficult, but that once it had been accepted, the drama cohered and produced its effect.[64] In a third article (March 11), he described the individual musical numbers, praising them and the performers without stint. In closing, he wrote[65]: "Of Maestro Bellini I shall say nothing except that up to now each of his works has been a step upward toward greater glory for him." Other periodicals matched the praise in *L'Eco*. A critique quoted by Pastura said[66]: "This music—new in workmanship, and in fact new in style—has the chief merit of coherence and/or relevance to its subject, and, above all, the undeniable [merit] of pleasing extremely. Not another *Pirata*, not *La Straniera* again, not *I Capuleti e i Montecchi*, it contains no reminiscences of either [Bellini's] own operas or those by others; the vein was spontaneous, the result most fortunate." In an article of March 15, the same writer[67] acutely remarked upon the influence of Italian folk tunes in Bellini's new melodies and noted the appropriateness of his instrumentation to the character of the subject.

Only two of Bellini's letters are available between one of March 7, 1831 (the announcement to Lamperi of the successful first night of *La Sonnambula*), and another letter to Lamperi dated "*Como 23 Luglio.*"[68] One of them (June 7) is to Domenico Donzelli (see below); the other, of the same date, is to Giovanni Ricordi and deals with a situation disturb-ing to both Bellini and Ricordi[69]: "I return to you the duet '*Son geloso*,' etc., from my opera *La Sonnambula* as printed by [Federico] Girard,[70] which you gave me to examine, and I declare to you that it is nothing but a vicious counterfeit that preserves of my [music] only a part of the singing line, the rest being very different from what is performed, and that the accompaniment has not even a notion of what is in the score. I think, therefore, that this was composed on the basis of the singers' parts, which someone stole from the rehearsals, and that Girard had it orchestrated by someone else so as to get it onto the market first, a fact that grieves me a lot because music lovers and musicians will judge my composition from what they will see printed, and it makes me marvel that Girard should have preferred the profit of a few ducati to the friendship he has always showed me, because he must have realized the damage that is done to a composer's fame by grafting a completely foreign accompaniment onto his song; therefore, please have the kindness to transmit to your Naples correspondent the enclosed article, which he should get inserted into the *Giornale delle Due Sicilie* so that the public may be informed of this disaster, in which good faith was betrayed." No effective copyright law existed to be invoked; lacking that recourse as they encountered larger piracies later, Bellini and Ricordi would have to return to that irritating problem more than once.[71]

With *La Sonnambula* successfully staged,[72] Bellini and Romani faced the search for a subject for the other opera promised for 1831, the one that had been contracted by the Crivelli group at La Scala. The choice, made during the March 7–July 23 period, cannot be dated exactly, but probably was made in June or July. Bellini's letter of July 23 to Lamperi, already cited, contains these sentences[73]: "I have already chosen the subject for my new opera, and it is a tragedy entitled *Norma, ossia L'Infanticidio*, by [Alexandre] Soumet,[74] now being performed with clamorous success in Paris. . . . My opera at La Scala must without fail go on stage by December 26." Romani and he had almost four months. in which to create the new libretto and score and prepare the opera for rehearsal in time for a very particular event: the Scala debut of Giuditta Pasta.

Rubini was not to be the tenor of Bellini's next opera. As *primo tenore serio*, the impresarios had contracted Domenico Donzelli, another *bergamasco*,[75] five years Rubini's senior and all but his equal in ability and renown. From Paris, on May 3, 1831, Donzelli had written to Bellini to describe his voice and capabilities[76]: "The extension of my voice, then, is almost two octaves; that is, from the bass D up to the high C. Chest tones, then, up to the G; and it is in that range that I can declaim with equal strength and sustain all the force of the declamation. From the upper G to the high C, I can avail myself of a falsetto which, used with artistry and strength, is a resource for ornamentation. I have sufficient agility, but I find it very much easier when descending than when ascending . . ."

Bellini had answered from Milan on June 7[77]: "With your letter you have merely anticipated my wish to write you in order to learn all the precise details that you have given me about the nature and flexibility of your voice. Maestro Mercadante, my close friend, already has given me a clear notion of you, and also has spoken a great deal about the warm diligence with which you perform enthusiastically whatever music a composer entrusts to you; so, as I am already content, *having to compose my opera for a celebrated artist like you,* and at the same time for a man with your praiseworthy feelings, I shall therefore rack my brain to make you as pleased with me as I am with you. The only pillars supporting my composition are Donzelli and Pasta, so the

subject of the opera must be made to revolve about those two alone . . ."
That vagueness about the subject may well indicate (as does the absence
of any reference to *Norma* in the letter of that same day to Ricordi)
that the choice of subject had not been made by June 7.

Bellini spent the July and August of 1831 at the Villa Passalacqua,
Moltrasio. Another lacuna in the available correspondence stretches from
July 23 to August 3, except for two letters,[78] neither of which mentions
Norma. On August 31, back in Milan one day, Bellini had news of *Norma*
to send to GiudittaTurina, who had stayed in Moltrasio[79]: "Yesterday
Romani told me that he had done two pieces and that he will have me
read them this morning, and if they please me, perhaps I'll start composing
tomorrow." *Norma* may have been begun on September 1. On that day,
Bellini could write to Pasta, who was in Paris: "Now I must apply myself
to the opera, for which Romani gave me the scenario just yesterday. I
hope that you will find this subject to your liking. Romani believes it to
be very effective, and precisely because of the all-inclusive character for
you, which is that of Norma. He will manipulate the situations so that
they will not resemble other subjects at all, and he will retouch, even
change, the characters to produce more effect, if need be. By now you will
have read it, [and] if any suggestion occurs to your mind, write it to me;
in the meantime, try to bring figurines of the characters as they are done
in Paris. . . ."[80]

Frightening news reached Italy in July: cholera had broken out in
Austria. Several of Bellini's letters and many articles in periodicals speak
fearfully of the probable spread of the plague to Italy: this terror dragged
on through August and into September. In an undated letter to an unidentifiable correspondent which clearly belongs to this period, Bellini
wrote[81]: "My health is good, and I am already[82] applying myself to
the new opera that must be given at La Scala on the coming December
26. The subject is *Norma*, a tragedy by M. Soumet: I find it interesting,
and if Romani extracts some beautiful poetry from it, it will become a
good libretto; but I fear that my vein will abandon me this time because
my head is distracted by that doubly damned cholera which is menacing
all of Europe; enough, let us see how it will end." But in a letter to
Giuditta Turina dated at ten o'clock on the morning of September 7, he
said[83]: "I have almost finished the *sinfonia* of the opera and have sketched
an introduction chorus, and I am not displeased. . . ." Early in September,
Bellini spent a short time at Moltrasio with Giuditta,[84] perhaps allowing
Romani time to write verses for *Norma* in addition to the few he already
had delivered.

More than the threat of cholera was disturbing Bellini. Two of his
worries were discussed in a letter of September 19 to Florimo from

Como,[85] in which he enclosed a letter addressed to the principe di Ruffano, then superintendent of the Neapolitan royal theaters, who had invited him to compose another opera for the Teatro San Carlo, to be staged in 1832. To Florimo, Bellini said: "From the enclosed letter for Ruffano, you will learn of my agreement to come [to Naples] to compose the opera, and the conditions, which Barbaja will not accept . . . so that if Barbaja wants to pay me three thousand ducati, he will have me; otherwise he can have the others. In the postscript you will see my prayer regarding *I Capuleti: Misericordia! ! !* la [Marianna] *Lewis! ! !*[86] I think that Barbaja has gone crazy: a donna who is below mediocrity; does not know how to sing, is a sausage on the stage, so that at Venice they were content to pay her without having her sing, is to be received at the San Carlo, to be given the part of the protagonist in an opera! ! ! Don't compromise me, as I know her so well that when she wanted a letter of recommendation for someone in Naples, I didn't want to write it for her then, so as not to tell lies.—Report my feelings to principe Ruffano and tell him not to say that he learned this from me. . . ."[87]

Continuing to confide in Florimo, Bellini said:[88] "I am composing the opera [*Norma*] without any zeal because I am almost certain that the *Cholera* will arrive in time to close the theaters; but as soon as it threatens to come near, I'll leave Milan . . . Should I have to come to Naples to compose the opera, I'll be content with [Giuseppina] Ronzi [de Begnis] and Tamburini, but you will understand that a good tenor like Donzelli or Rubini would be extremely necessary; enough, let's hope that everything will turn out so that you and I can be together for some months. Signora Giuditta [Turina] feels fairly well and salutes you warmly."

The letter forwarded to Ruffano illuminates Bellini the man of affairs and foretells the reasons why he would never return to Naples to compose another opera there. It reads[89]: "My friend Florimo has hastened to forward to me Your Excellency's desire that I should come to compose an opera for the Teatro San Carlo next year, a desire I share. I therefore accept your kind invitation with pleasure, as I long for another occasion to dedicate myself to my native theater, which gave me my first chance in the difficult world of music. But the person who will be opposed to this devoted wish will be Barbaja, who will not want to grant me the price that all the other theaters give me, adducing frivolous reasons that never impress me because I want to maintain the level that I have reached.

"The Teatro della [*sic*] Scala is giving me 12,000 Austrian lire, equal to 2,400 ducati,[90] for the opera that I am composing, as well as half interest in the score and two hundred additional ducati if the same opera should be presented later in the Venetian theater controlled by the same Crivelli,

who is impresario of La Scala; now, from the half interest, should it
be a success, I could earn at least another 800 ducati, as happened with
my opera *La Sonnambula*; consequently, as it is not at all convenient to
ask Barbaja for that half because my situation does not allow me to stay
long in Naples, and I would therefore gain little from it, I would cede
it entirely to him; adding on all the costs of travel, lodging, and other
things that I should have to pay for—whereas here I have had a home
for many years—etc. I could not compose the opera for less than three
thousand valid Neapolitan ducati[91]; the libretto [must be] written by
Felice Romani; the company to be selected from the individuals announced in the *cartellone*[92]; entirely new scenery and costumes and an
uninterrupted month of rehearsals; when Barbaja agrees to these demands,
I shall be ready to apply myself during the hot weather.[93] My respected
Prince, I foresee that it will be very difficult to come to an agreement
on all this, and I am in the position of not being able to compromise
upon anything more, which would neither be in my interest nor befit the
dignity of my career. It seems to me that, everything taken into consideration, I am asking less from Barbaja than from the other impresarios
because of the [half interest in] the property; I want all the rest, which
seems incidental, for the good of the opera, and therefore of the public.
It would be a solemn commitment on my part, and therefore save this
letter in case the matter should be settled, so that questions cannot arise
later with Barbaja, who is always going about splitting hairs. For that
reason, I place myself entirely under Your Excellency's valued patronage,
which I have already experienced personally, so that justice would be
done me in case of unforeseen questions.

"I hope that everything will turn out so that I may come and again
see Your Excellency and thank you for the interest that you have always
taken in me. Accept my thanks, and believe me, full of gratitude, your
most humble servant Vincenzo Bellini. Milan, September 19, 1831.

"P.S. At this moment, I have received a letter advising me that signor
Barbaja wants to stage my *Capuleti e Montecchi* with a company that
as a group could only ruin the score, as he has taken the role of Romeo
from Ronzi-Debegnis [*sic*]; therefore I beg Your Excellency to prevent
such a stupidity, which would upset me greatly, and to do everything, at
all costs, to give the role of Romeo back to *la Debegnis*. And if the in-
trepid Barbaja should prove resistant to my just desires, that would make
it certain that he feels no interest in me personally, and therefore I should
retract my agreement to compose the opera, promising Your Excellency
instead to come to compose it under a new management in the year
1833,[94] as I do not want to have anything to do with an enemy of mine
who, with good individuals [singers] at his disposal, gives one of my

operas with bad ones to be found in the streets. Florimo will inform you of everything; I shall not write more because I might compromise others; but listen to Florimo, to whom I have written at length."

Partly at Moltrasio, partly in Milan, Bellini went on composing *Norma*.[95] He completed it as November gave way to December. On December 12, Mercadante, writing to Florimo from Turin, mentioned just having received a letter from Bellini[96]: ". . . and I think that you will be interested in my repeating to you a paragraph that made me laugh enormously—'Monday I'll begin the rehearsals of my opera *Norma*, and I believe that you will be doing the same.[97] I have made my Testament, and I thought of leaving you something if they should murder me; as the same thing could happen to you, I beg you not to forget me. . . .' "

During December, Bellini again became involved in problems of piracy. On December 5, *L'Eco* carried this "Musical Notice" signed by Bellini, though probably drafted by Giovanni Ricordi[98]: "In all justice I must advise all the Managements of the Theaters, the signori Impresarios and Dealers in music that a Theatrical Correspondent has permitted himself to have my Opera *La Sonnambula* orchestrated from the simple reduction of it for pianoforte solo, and to sell it as the one written by me in Milan for the Tearo Carcano the past Carnival. If these falsifications damaged only the financial interests of the artists, perhaps I should not try to protest; but they also damage their reputations in so far as they spread about imperfect, monstrous works that also damage those who acquire them in good faith, especially for use in the theater. That is why I turn to the Theatrical Managements, to the signori Impresarios and Dealers in Music, begging them to be willing to regard as spurious any score of *La Sonnambula* which may be offered them except the copies indicated by me or by signor Giovanni Ricordi, with whom the only original is to be found. In that way, they will act to guard my honor and their own interest and to teach such forgers that it is now time among us, too, to respect the properties of men of talent and not to compromise their reputation and dignity. Milan, 1 December 1831. Signed *Vincenzo Bellini*."

One or more letters also were addressed to the most important publishers and impresarios. In a copy of one of them, also signed by Bellini, much of the "Musical Notice" was repeated,[99] but proof was added that the counterfeit scores of *La Sonnambula* could not be complete: "Ricordi . . . has abstained up to now from publishing the piano reductions of the introductions, of the first finale, of the Quartet in Act II, and of the Choruses . . ." That the pirates were busy with other operas as well had been indicated as early as October 21, in one of the salvos that

Ricordi directed against his competitors Artaria and Lucca[100]: "Musical Notice. Giovanni Ricordi, publisher of music in Milan, again warns the Public, the Publishers of music, and the signori Theatrical Impresarios on every reasonable basis that he is the recognized proprietor of the following scores:

> *La Donna bianca*, of Maestro [Stefano] Pavesi[101];
> *I Capuletti* [*sic*] *e i Montecchi*, of Maestro Bellini;
> *La Sonnambula*, by the abovementioned;
> *Anna Bolena*, of Maestro Donizetti

as well as of every variety of reduction and of the so-called *arrangemens* [*sic*] that may be made of the same, as a result of contracts stipulated and of the notices inserted in the *Gazzetta privilegiata di Milano* on January 5, February 28, March 11, and May 30 of the current year." But Ricordi and his composers were waging a war that could not be won until decades later, when a unified Italy passed laws effectively protecting literary and musical copyrights.

Rehearsals of *Norma* began on Monday, December 5, exactly one week before Mercadante, wrote the cited letter to Florimo. As usual, difficulties arose during the rehearsals. Scherillo wrote[102] that Pasta refused to sing "*Casta diva*" because she found it "ill adapted to her [vocal] abilities.[103] The Maestro used all his wiles to persuade her; but he had little success. They made a pact: she would keep it for a week, going over it again each morning; and if at the end of seven days she still found performing it repugnant, Bellini promised that he would change it." Not only did Pasta sing the aria: she also confessed her earlier error by sending Bellini, some hours before the première, a parchment lamp-shade decorated with flowers surrounding warriors and maidens; a bouquet of cloth flowers; and a note[104]: "Allow me to offer you something that was some solace to me for the immense fear that persecuted me when I found myself little suited to performing your sublime harmonies; this lamp by night and these flowers by day witnessed my studies of *Norma* and the desire I cherish to be ever more worthy of your esteem. Giuditta P. your most affectionate friend."

On December 19, two weeks after the first rehearsal of *Norma*, La Scala published its *cartellone* for the season scheduled to open a week later. It listed this way the operas to be sung:

I) *Norma*, the new composition of Maestro Sig. Vincenzo Bellini, to a new libretto by Sig. Felice Romani; II) *Il Corsaro*, by Maestro Sig. Cav. Pacini (new for Milan)[105] and especially adapted and staged by the composer; III) *La Vendetta*, newly composed by Maestro Sig. Cesare Pugni,[106] to a new libretto by Sig. Calisto Bassi; IV) *Anna Bolena*, by Maestro Gaetano Donizetti;

V) To be written expressly by the abovementioned Maestro Gaetano Donizetti, on a new libretto by Sig. Felice Romani.[107]

The season will open with the *opera seria Norma*, in which roles will be taken by the signore Giuditta Pasta, Giulia Grisi,[108] and Marietta Sacchi and the signori Domenico Donzelli, Vincenzo Negrini, and Lorenzo Lombardi. With the grand ballet entitled *Merope* and the demi-character ballet *I Pazzi per progetto*. The second opera, *Il Corsaro*, with an entirely separate company, will be produced as quickly as possible.[109]

The season at La Scala opened as foreseen, on December 26, 1831, with the première of *Norma*. The cast was: Pasta (Norma), Giulia Grisi (Adalgisa),[110] Mari(ett)a Sacchi (Clotilde), Domenico Donzelli (Pollione), Lorenzo Lombardi (Flavio), and Vincenzo Negrini (Oroveso)[111]; the stage settings were by Alessandro Sanquirico. To the incredulous astonishment of everyone involved in its creation, production, and performance, *Norma* was received by its first audience with chill indifference. Writing that night to Florimo, very forthrightly Bellini said[112]:

"I am writing to you under the shock of sorrow; of a sorrow that I cannot put into words for you, but that only you can understand. I have come from La Scala; first performance of *Norma*. Would you believe it? . . . Fiasco! ! ! fiasco! ! ! solemn fiasco! ! ! To tell the truth, the audience was harsh, seemed to have come to pass sentence upon me; and in its haste wanted (I believe) my poor *Norma* to suffer the same fate as the Druidess. I no longer recognized those dear Milanese, who greeted *Il Pirata*, *La Straniera*, and *La Sonnambula* with happy faces and exulting hearts; and yet, I thought that in *Norma* I was presenting them with a worthy sister [of the other three operas]. But unhappily that was not so; I was wrong; my protagonists failed and my hopes were deluded. Despite all that, with my heart on my lips I tell you (if passion doesn't deceive me) that the Introduction, Norma's entrance and cavatina, the duet between the two donnas, with the trio that follows, the finale of the first act, then the other duet of the two donnas and the whole finale of the second act, which begins with the Hymn of War and proceeds, are pieces of music of a kind—and please me so much (modesty)—that I confess I should be happy to create their likes for the rest of my artistic life. Enough! ! ! I hope to appeal against the sentence it [the audience] pronounced against me, and if I succeed in changing its mind, I shall have won my case, and then I'll proclaim *Norma* the best of my operas. If I don't, however, I shall resign myself to my most unhappy fate, and in consoling myself will say: didn't the Romans, perhaps, whistle at the divine Pergolesi's *L'Olimpiade*?[113] . . . I leave with the courier, and hope to arrive ahead of this letter.[114] But either I or the letter will inform you of the sad news that *Norma* was whistled at. Do not grieve because of that, my good Florimo. I am young, and I sense in my spirit the strength to effect a vindication of this tremendous downfall.

"Read this letter to all our friends. I like telling the truth as much in good fortune as in adverse. Good-bye, and I shall see you soon.

"In the meantime, receive an embrace from your most affectionate Bellini. Milan, 26 December, 1831."[115]

The future success and enduring reputation of *Norma* throw a peculiar retroactive light upon that first Milanese audience's reaction (as, in an example of more violent first-night disapproval, future success and reputation do upon the case of Rossini's *Il Barbiere di Siviglia*). When attempting to explain it, Bellini himself, his friends and other contemporaries, as well as later commentators, have divided the causes between some innate in *Norma* and some external to it. Bellini cannot be thought an unjust judge of the internal causes when, in a letter of December 28 to Vincenzo Ferlito, he writes[116]: "On the first evening, an eruption was produced by the introduction, Pollione's entrance, that of Pasta. What did not please was the Pollione-Adalgisa duet, and that will never please because it doesn't please me either; the duet that begins the final trio pleased greatly, but the trio as performed did not; the singers were weary, having rehearsed the entire second act that morning, and therefore it was not enjoyed; thus the first act finished without anyone's being applauded and called out; in the second act, except for a chorus that pleased but little, the rest was so extraordinarily effective that the whole [adverse] faction was too cast down to recover at all, and I was obliged to show myself on the stage at least four times, both alone and with the singers. Yesterday evening [the second performance], because the singers projected the trio better, I was also called out in the first act [and] the second act was more effective than on the first evening, so much so that my triumph was even decisive enough to raise hopes that the opera to close the Carnival will be the persecuted *Norma*."[117]

Earlier in that letter, however, Bellini had written[118]: "Despite a formidable faction antagonistic to me because it is supported by a powerful personage and by a very rich woman, my *Norma* has dumbfounded [its audiences], more yesterday evening, the second performance, than at the first. The official Milanese journal yesterday reported a decided fiasco because on the first evening the adverse faction whistled while the unprejudiced applauded; and because the powerful personage is an owner and can order the journal to write whatever he pleases.

"The powerful personage does this because of enmity toward Pasta, and the rich woman because she is Pacini's mistress, and therefore my enemy; in the meantime, yesterday evening the opera was enjoyed even more, and the theater was crammed full, a true sign of an opera's success, and it was the opera alone that drew so many people to the theater, as the two ballets were horrible fiascos."[119] Later in the letter, after remarks about some of the opera's individual numbers and the way they had been sung, he added[120]: "Pasta is an angel, and that expression will suffice to tell you how she performs her role in both singing and acting. Donzelli does very well and sings well, but still doesn't know his role thoroughly; Giulietta Grisi in the role of Adalgisa is a little cold by nature, but still is good; the chorus is excellent. The public showers the journalist with imprecations; my friends jump for joy; I am very well satisfied, doubly content because I have discomfited so many of my vile and powerful enemies."[121]

The "powerful personage" whom Bellini suspected of having worked to dampen enthusiasm at the première of *Norma* cannot be identified certainly, but may well have been duca Carlo Visconti di Modrone, then superintendent of the Imperial and Royal Theaters of Milan, who shortly would succeed Crivelli as chief impresario of La Scala. And it is notable that Pasta—by then much the most famous soprano of the day—should have been singing at La Scala for the first time in 1831, though she had made her debut in Milan in 1815.[122] But no documents can be cited to prove either that Visconti nursed enmity toward her or helped to foment the first audience's manifest discontent with parts of *Norma*—if, indeed, it be sensible to suppose that a high official would try, in a theater under his control, to damage a costly new production of an opera by an increasingly prominent young composer. The "very rich woman" was the contessa Giulia Samoyloff,[123] who was openly Pacini's mistress, and whom Bellini called "that madwoman," though he dedicated the Ricordi edition of *Bianca e Fernando* to her.

In the letter that Bellini wrote to Perucchini on December 31,[124] he reported: ". . . my poor *Norma* was persecuted so cruelly that they wanted to drown it at birth with, as you will see, all the journals shouting fiasco, *fiaschissimo;* a formidable faction because supported by lots of money by that madwoman because a new opera by Pacini [*Il Corsaro*] will go on in a few days. Do I make myself clear?" No documentation of Bellini's suspicions can be cited. Here, as in other situations really or supposedly involving Pacini, Bellini may be seen as, at least in part, victimized by persecution fantasies, with Pacini as chief bugbear.[125]

Norma went on to be sung thirty-nine times at La Scala during that 1831–1832 season. It therefore was almost certain to become a popular opera elsewhere. How widespread its popularity became in less than fifteen years is demonstrated by an astonishing passage in Glinka's *Memoirs.*[126] Writing of a visit to Murcia in Spain in the autumn of 1845, Glinka said: "The children's theater consisted of a presentation of Bellini's *Norma*—which had indeed been written to be performed by children [*sic*]—for the diversion of their parents. We went to a rehearsal and thought the children sang pretty well. The eleven-year-old in the part of Norma sang with enthusiasm—though not really adequately, of course —and was an excellent little actress, besides."

After the first few performances of *Norma* at La Scala, Bellini could leave for Naples and Sicily satisfied with its reception. No matter how sure he was of the high quality of the opera, however, he could not, of course, foresee that it would become one of the standard operas of the rest of the nineteenth century and would still be awakening eager expectation whenever announced for performance in the twentieth. In his own mind, however, it already was—and would remain—the finest opera he had composed.

The *Gazzetta privilegiata di Milano* for January 7, 1832, listed among the travelers who had left Milan the preceding Thursday (January 5): "*Bellini, maestro di cappella, per Napoli.*" The thirty-year-old Vincenzo on his way "home" was a much more accomplished and worldly young man than the youth who had left Sicily for the first time more than twelve years before, a much more assured and honored composer than he had been when he had returned to Sicily for a very brief visit more than six years before. He was initiating a period of comparative idleness: in 1832, for the first time since 1827, no opera newly composed or freshly revised by him was to be staged anywhere.

(VII)

1832: Naples; Messina; Catania; Palermo; Bergamo

ELLINI PROBABLY TRAVELED ALONE from Milan to Naples. But Giuditta Turina and her brother, Gaetano Cantù, also went to Naples: she was at last to realize her repeatedly expressed wish to meet Florimo and to visit the scenes of her Vincenzo's Neapolitan life. It is possible that Bellini joined them at Rome.[1] The lovers would remain in Naples for about six weeks, after which Giuditta and her brother would stay on there while Bellini and Florimo paid a two-month visit to Sicily. Filippo Gerardi wrote of Bellini[2] that he left Milan in January 1832 "and, passing through Rome, spent some days there." No other mention of that Rome stopover has come to light, and Bellini cannot have lingered long anywhere en route to Naples, which he reached, in despite of the overnight stops and the fact that the horses had to be changed about every twenty miles, on January 11, only six days after leaving Milan.

In Naples, Bellini went to stay at San Pietro a Majella, in the room that had been his from October 1826 to April 1827. Florimo, describing his friend's reunion with the aged Zingarelli (who then learned that *Norma*, when published, would be dedicated to him) and his eager welcome by the conservatory students, quoted as Bellini's reply to adulation of his success: "My dear friends, what can I tell you? I have been lucky, and I thank God."[3] One week after Bellini reached Naples, a young man called Giovanni (his patronymic is not known) wrote to an "Uncle Ignazio" whom Pastura identified[4] as Ignazio Giuffrida-Moschetti, a Catanese friend of Bellini, a letter[5] that paints Bellini from life, if through adoring eyes:

"Naples, January 18, 1832

"To Your Excellency—a connoisseur and a lover of merit. I cannot remain silent to Your Excellency about two encounters I have enjoyed very much, and that will also, I know, delight my affectionate uncle. I speak of Bellini and Walter Scott.[6]

"This morning I went to call on the Swan of Sicily, or, to phrase it better, of Catania. He is living at the Collegio di Musica. That seemingly trivial fact reveals the man who, having won such loud praise throughout Europe, and who combines all the qualities that render him admirable, disdains everything pompous and showy, [and] goes to live in the very place that witnessed the birth of the glorious career that he has achieved so quickly; he is informal with his old companions, respectful toward his teachers; he prefers being loved by all to being an object of respect and veneration.

"I was prepared to speak diplomatically, not knowing Vincenzo's present attitude; in fact, I presented my respectful compliments, saying that I had thought it my duty as a Catanese to congratulate the signor Maestro.

"As I was proffering the compliment, Vincenzo was not sure who I was, but as soon as he recognized me, he flung himself into my arms, embraced me tightly, and kissed me several times, saying: 'My dear Giovanni, you in Naples?'—and, turning to Tatà Zappalà and Fortunato Giardina,[7] added: 'But you leave me beside myself with happiness.'

"I could not help feeling surprised and contented, my dear Uncle, at such familiarity and at a good heart not common among men whose merits have raised them so high.

"We spent two very happy hours. Among all the things that were said and discussed, I observed how much gratitude this divine genius continues to feel toward his homeland, which he will see again in March or, at the latest, April.

"He showed me the Catanese medal,[8] and though it was minted horribly, he holds on to it as the honor dearest and most precious to him, adding to me that he has showed it all over Italy as the triumphant wreath for those whose valiant deeds have earned them such honor. He ended by saying that Catania is the most beautiful town in the world and Sant'Agata the first Saint of Paradise. The Catanese who were there shouted in chorus: '*Viva Sant'Agata!*'

"I ended my visit with the commission that I had to carry out, it having been entrusted to me particularly by some Sicilian officials.[9]

"Bellini showed confusion, and with the humility that so distinguishes him, told me that he himself would go to the district, and that he would not permit them to be inconvenienced; but the commission was precise and, like all military matters, allowed of no interpretation, and so we had to set the day for that ceremony, which so distinguishes both donors and recipient.

"But this letter is finished, and Walter Scott has not reappeared in it. Truly, when one is speaking of Bellini, one can hardly bear to lay aside his pen. However, I will tell you that the famous novelist and historian reached Naples on January 1 [*sic*] and has showed himself only once, at the Teatro dei Fiorentini. Soon, my dear Uncle, you will learn all about that from your nephew, Giovanni."

No similar document pictures Florimo's reunion with Bellini or his introduction to Giuditta Turina. We know that while Bellini was in Naples, he attended at least one performance of *I Capuleti e i Montecchi* at the Teatro San Carlo, and that he was received in informal audience by the queen mother, Isabella di Spagna, the widow of Francesco I. *I Capuleti* had been performed at the San Carlo for the first time on November 29, 1831; it was sung there again (with Giuseppina Ronzi de Begnis as Romeo, Luigia Boccabadati as Giulietta) on January 10, 1832, almost certainly in the belief that Bellini would be in Naples by that day. According to Cicconetti,[10] no performance of it could be given on January 11, the day of Bellini's actual arrival, because of "I don't know what discord between Ronzi and Boccabadati." Rossini's *Elisabetta, regina d'Inghilterra* replaced *I Capuleti* that night, and though Bellini helped restore peace between the two donnas, he had to wait until February 5 to hear his opera sung at the San Carlo.

Of that performance of *I Capuleti*, the *Giornale delle Due Sicilie* reported on February 7: "This long-awaited performance attracted an extraordinary number of spectators. Further, it was honored by the presence of His Majesty the King Our Lord [Ferdinando II], together with His Royal Highness, the principe di Capua.[11] Interest was added by awareness that the famous composer of this music, Sig. Bellini, was in Naples, and by the supposition that he too would be an onlooker at his own opera. . . . Our august Monarch . . . at last deigned to applaud again; and that applause, intended for the score and the composer, served as the signal for general acclamations urging the Maestro to show himself upon the stage. In the meantime, he remained in modest seclusion in one of the fourth-tier loges.[12] But he agreed to accept the invitation to appear upon the stage; when he first showed himself, he was alone; then, called back by increasing applause, he returned leading out with him the two deserving actresses [Ronzi di Begnis and Boccabadati]. That was a real moment of triumph for Bellini. The composer of *Il Pirata, La Straniera*, and *I Capuleti e Montecchi* [*sic*] received from both the Sovereign and the Neapolitans the sweet reward for the myriad pleasures that performances of his immortal compositions had afforded us copiously for so long a time."

Although Bellini wrote Vincenzo Ferlito on February 3[13] that he was tarrying in Naples so as to be able to present himself to the royal family (and sent word that a draft for 180 ducati which had been forwarded to Catania should be added to his family's resources), and though he was received by the queen mother on February 8, he did not leave Naples until February 25.[14] Giuditta was unwell much of the time: on February 21, Bellini wrote Pasta that she had been in bed for three weeks because of "pains suffered"[15]—and no further public appearances by Bellini are chronicled. On February 9, he wrote Vincenzo Ferlito[16]: "Yesterday I was with the Queen [Mother], who also lavished kindnesses upon me, praising my music very highly." In the letter of February 21 which he sent to Pasta by the hand of a friend, he referred to Pasta's recent triumphs at the Teatro Carcano in Milan in "my persecuted *Norma*" and Rossini's *Otello*. On February 23, finally, he wrote to Perucchini, who had been trying to arrange for Bellini's return to Venice to compose another opera for the Teatro La Fenice[17]:

". . . I beg you to tell [Alessandro] Lanari that I cannot do it for less than the amount that [Giuseppe] Crivelli paid me for my last opera, which I composed for La Scala. I hear that he is negotiating with Pasta, and therefore I'd be happy with the company; but I still cannot decide about the thing until the first days of May, being in talks about the San Carlo with the minister of the interior; and if I still have not arranged the matter here, that is because I am not satisfied by the makeup of the company, for which reason the Minister has promised me to do everything possible to improve it, and that would be enough to make me compose, and as for time, I wanted all of April, also for determining the present state of [Giovanni] David's voice, as David is the tenor contracted for the theatrical year. For the rest, if Lanari is far from giving me the payment that I received for *Norma*, he is free to think about another maestro, as I shall be unable to compose either for him or for any other impresario for one lira less than I have received for my most recent scores. . . . Tomorrow I leave for Sicily. . . ."

A flirtation on Giuditta Turina's part so upset Bellini during those weeks of waiting in Naples that almost three years later (November 30, 1834) he recalled the incident to Florimo in a letter[18]: "I have had no news of Giuditta in almost two months: perhaps she was piqued by some phrase of mine in the letters that I wrote her, but what would you have? I don't want to return to the relationship with her, in which I suffered very much, and you had a proof of that in Naples; what anguish and what pangs didn't her coquetry give me, and involving whom? . . . an old man! Then imagine what pains she made me suffer when she acted that way with young men . . ." That incident had been only a passing irritation; the one to suffer sharply from the outcome of their relationship finally would be Giuditta.

No indication survives that Bellini had tried to see his onetime love, Maddalena Fumaroli, in Naples before he and Florimo boarded the steam-packet *Real Ferdinando* on February 25, bound for Sicily. They reached the Messina roadstead at about 6:30 the next evening, but had to remain aboard overnight because the port already was closed. On the Sicilian shore to greet them on the morning of February 27 were several members of Bellini's family, including his father. Then began an almost royal progress for the returning native son. Florimo was to write[19]: "I, who accompanied him on that trip, which could be called a triumph, was witness to the great and enthusiastic welcomes given him by Messina, Palermo, and especially Catania." Messina began them,[20] though Bellini, nervously eager to get on to Catania, remained there only two days. He was the guest of a Raimondi Calvi family, in whose villa he received many callers, particularly young artists, poets, and intellectuals, dedicated Bellinians because they were Romantics.[21] And on the evening of February 27, the impresario Antonio Giglio offered at the Teatro La Munizione a performance of *Il Pirata*.

The Messina journal *L'Osservatore peloritano*, which normally limited its columns to official notices and much-belated foreign news, extraordinarily ran an account of that evening. In part, it read: "*Il Pirata*, a masterwork of this distinguished Maestro, was the opera produced again on the boards of our Real Teatro della [*sic*] Munizione. The audience, certain that the composer would be present at the performance of his so-celebrated work, gathered in very large numbers, and in fact the theater was filled by an immense crowd, and—what is most confusing—we saw Bellini present among the others as a simple spectator. In the meantime, our actors[22] and instrumentalists, profiting by so fortunate an occasion, wanted to give incontrovertible proofs of their ability in the art, and therefore put forth all possible effort to win the unqualified favor of the audience and the desirable and genuine approval of so celebrated a Maes-tro. He, to tell the truth, showed the greatest signs of satisfaction with both groups, and especially with our gentle and excellent first actress, Sig.ª Angela Borroni, and with the tenor, Sig. Giovanni [Francesco] Boccaccini.

"For all that, Bellini remained modestly in the second-tier loge until the finale of the first act, in company with some of his relatives, who had come here expressly to meet him. Thereafter, having gone to that of the Sig. Intendente, to which he had courteously been invited, he had scarcely appeared when he was applauded—with loud shouts of pleasure, hand-clapping, and words of praise—by an audience which, until that moment had remained profoundly silent and extremely attentive because of his presence. . . ."

Three years later, Giuseppe La Farina was to read political overtones into *Il Pirata* and consequently into its reception by the *messinesi*[23]: "But what was *Il Pirata?* It was an opera depicting a part of Italy's past, demonstrating the tyranny of a duca di Caldora, the unhappy love of a miserable Sicilian. It was a moral lesson drawn from native chronicles. It was a canticle of sorrow over people oppressed by arrogant power. A display of divine vengeance. In sum, it was a drama by Romani and Bellini conforming to their feelings; an opera intended to serve the most sacred purpose of improving while delighting; and the delight was general; the improvement faint, but progressive." To prove that either Romani or Bellini had such unlikely ideas of political amelioration in mind when creating *Il Pirata* is, of course, impossible.

Two brothers, Giacomo and Antonio Galatti, gave a large reception in honor of Bellini on the evening of February 28. Arenaprimo said of it[24]: "Before the dancing began—this was repeated to me by my venerable friend Matteo Saija, by then blind and failing, who had been present —a full orchestra performed, as homage to the highly esteemed guest, the *grande sinfonia* to *Il Pirata*, and then that to *Norma*, which were received with indescribable demonstrations of reverence and enthusiasm by the others, among whom were to be noted whatever the town offered of the finest in feminine grace, beauty, and elegance, in aristocracy of talent, birth, and wealth."[25]

Bellini appears to have left Messina on February 29. The weather was very unfriendly, and the party did not reach Catania until Saturday, March 3, at about five in the afternoon.[26] At the northern entrance to his native city, Bellini was welcomed officially, and handed into the carriage of the principe di Sperlinga Manganelli while a band played pieces from several of his operas. Members of the decurionate, professors from the university, and other notables marched in the procession from there into the city. Followed by a large throng, it moved to the street outside the home of Bellini's uncle Vincenzo Ferlito in the present via Paternò: there was no room for him in his family's reduced apartment in the quartiere di San Berillo.

The thirty-three days that Bellini spent in Catania are thinly documented; he very likely passed much of the time with his parents, his brothers, and his sisters, and in visits with old friends and acquaintances.[27] The members of his immediate family remain shadowy figures at best during his lifetime, and only one of his letters—a note of thanks to someone he did not know—survives from his Catania sojourn. Two official functions were held in his honor, but no operatic performance signaled his presence.[28] Instead, he was honored at the Teatro Comunale (later Coppola), almost certainly on March 11, by a performance of a new tragedy by his fellow-townsman Gioacchino Fernandez. This was called *Atreo;* it was performed by a visiting *"compagnia lombarda."* Between its acts, a second-rate tenor named Luigi De Rosa, who had lingered on in Catania after the last preceding operatic season there,[29] sang the "introduction" to *Il Pirata,* and a number from *La Straniera.* Antonio Menza said of that evening[30]: "The theater was packed. Scarcely had Bellini been discovered in the loge of the principe di Manganelli when a thousand joyful cries of acclamation broke from the lips of all. Then many citizens went out onto the stage, whither, greatly feted, Bellini was taken.[31] The carriages awaiting the young musician and the most prominent personages were sent away, and all the people, applauding, accompanied him home with windblown torches."

On March 18, an evening of poetic recitations was put on in the grand salon of the Palazzo Municipale to honor the city's guest. It began with a fulsome, florid speech of welcome by Mario Musumeci in which praise of Bellini, political aspirations, windy philosophizing, and windier talk about beauty filled too many serpentine sentences. As Vincenzo Percolla told the story of that evening,[32] the single truly interesting remark made was Musumeci's announcement that the autograph score of *I Capuleti e i Montecchi* which Bellini had presented to the city was to be deposited in the library of the university. He also said that a medal was to be minted in Bellini's honor. Much to Bellini's irritation, this second Catanese medal never materialized.

Pastura commented aptly[33]: "But for the guest of honor it must have been a real torture to feel himself constrained to listen to them [the poets] and to smile or make modest gestures at each allusion to his own operas or to his own genius, with comparisons that disturbed both the pagan Olympus and the Christian Paradise, and at the close of each reading to rise to congratulate the author and thank him for having found in him merits that he did not in fact possess, etc., etc. The words of praise did not displease Bellini, but he was not a glutton, and such an evening must have struck him as resembling a tourney in which all the combatants won and only he was left smothered under the weight of the most massive avalanche of words he had ever had to listen to in his life."[34]

Bellini and Florimo left Catania for Palermo, perhaps with a sense of release, by diligence on April 5, in company with several members of Bellini's family.[35] Bellini had seen Catania for the last time. Florimo described their four-day trip through central Sicily; writing on April 16 to Angelica Paola-Giuffrida at Catania,[36] he said that he and Bellini were then "in Palermo, well and safe, but still exhausted, very much exhausted, from an exceedingly rough trip during which—sleeping badly, eating worse, and traveling in constant peril of our lives—we suffered more than all the Holy Martyrs, not excluding your excellent S. Agata, of ever-happy memory."

The weary travelers reached Palermo on April 9; on the morning of that day, evidently during a brief stop, Bellini had written a letter to Ignazio Giuffrida-Moschetti, dating it from "the gates of Palermo."[37] This letter contains the first reference by Bellini to Filippo Santocanale ("Russuliddu"), who was to become his close friend, very frequent correspondent, and adviser—and who, after Bellini's death, was to be named by the Bellini family as its deputy in Palermo to deal with business matters concerning the operas.[38] Ignazio Giuffrida-Moschetti seems to have been instrumental in introducing Bellini to Santocanale, in whose house Bellini lived while in Palermo.[39]

The official portion of Bellini's stay in Palermo lasted from April 10 to April 15. His first public appearance very probably was preceded by several duty calls: on the duca di San Martino, then Sicilian minister of the interior; on the viceroy, Prince Leopoldo, an uncle of Ferdinando II; and both on the duchessa di San Martino and on her mother, the principessa del Cassero. On April 11, a performance of *I Capuleti e i Montecchi* at the Teatro Carolino initiated his public appearances. The obvious success of that evening embarrassed the editor of the official Palermitan journal, *La Cerere*: a little more than two months earlier, he had reprinted —without citing the source—the biased, unfriendly article published by the *Gazzetta privilegiata di Milano* (January 3, 1832) after the fourth *Norma* at La Scala, and thus had seemed to ally himself with Bellini's detractors. Now he publicly ate humble pie: in his report of the evening of April 11 at the Carolino, which had been attended, in torrid heat, by government officials, much of the local aristocracy, and as many plebeians as could get in, he wrote[40]:

"But yesterday evening at the R. Teatro di Musica, Bellini completed his triumphal appearance, and was greeted with wild acclaim in the loge assigned to him; for that reason, his score *Giulietta e Romeo*, so often repeated and so often applauded, took on a new character and excited greater interest in his presence. The actors, anxious in one way and inspired in another, were stirred to great efforts; and the audience— all the while continually turning to stare at the source from which it had emanated—absorbed the full pleasure that Bellini's delicate music carries in its heart.

"The applause was loud and incessant, from the *sinfonia* to the end. At the close of each act, Bellini was called out onto the stage by ceaseless shouts; when he appeared, he often demonstrated his desire to share his glory with the leading ladies, but the laurel wreaths nevertheless were tossed at his feet."

Next, the Accademia filarmonica, on the evening of April 12, saluted Bellini with a concert in the palazzo of its president, the duca di Monteleone. Of that occasion, Francesco Guardione wrote[41]: "A painted transparency was to be seen in the spacious salon, at the back of which the bust of the illustrious musician appeared crowned by Fame, and, at its base, the Genius of Sicily was writing: To Vincenzo Bellini—the Accademia Filarmonica dedicates.

"In the salon, thronged by lovers of the art, with musicians and with numerous spectators, shouting and applause echoed when Bellini arrived, and the most distinguished ladies of the aristocracy and those most versed in art sought the honor of offering him enthusiastic welcomes. The features of his face, which had an angelic appearance, were suffused with a blush that rendered the famous young man more beautiful. . . ."[42]

On April 14, Bellini visited the Conservatorio del Buon Pastore, where, according to Guardione,[43] "From his various inquiries, many of those with him could gather how very insistent Bellini had been during that visit upon the study of the fundamentals of the art, because it seemed to him that true musical greatness drew support from those old pages exhaling classicism, which modern usage, to its detriment, has begun to find satisfaction in setting aside. . . . Generous with expressions of affection and encouragement to the young students, he saluted them with good wishes for the future . . ."[44]

The official period of Bellini's Palermo stay ended on Palm Sunday, April 15; he and Florimo originally had intended to leave the city by steam packet that day, and thus to spend Easter in Naples. But Florimo, in his letter of April 16 to Angelica Paola-Giuffrida,[45] wrote: "A sumptuous luncheon given him [Bellini] by eight *maestri di cappella* and the composers of this capital assembled some of the *palermitani,* who honored Bellini by their presence to the sound of a band playing pieces from *Il Pirata, La Straniera,* and *Giulietta* during the meal . . . We shall leave for Naples on either Holy Saturday [April 21] or Easter Monday [April 23]." Stormy weather had delayed the departure of the Naples packet.

During Bellini's stay in Palermo he sat for two portraits. One, in oil, by Giuseppe Patania, is now in the Gallo Collection of the Palermo Biblioteca Comunale.[46] The other is a marble bust by Giuseppe Pollet, now at the Palermo Conservatory. Also, according to Agostino Gallo,[47] Bellini paid one special nostalgic call: "Bellini did not forget his Marietta

[Politi, his childhood sweetheart, for whom, according to Gallo, he had composed "*La Farfalletta*" in 1813]; and, having come to Palermo in 1832 and learned that she was still living there, he wanted to see her again after so many years of absence, and accompanied her on the pianoforte in various pieces that she had chosen from his scores, correcting some mistakes in them; which she [later] wanted to show me, holding those musical pages as a precious and feverish [*affannoso*] souvenir of that angel of music, whose dear portrait is always before her eyes in her room."

Another undocumented anecdote of Bellini's visit to Palermo has him joining Filippo Santocanale and several other young men[48] in a practical joke on Cristoforo Licalsi, organist of the Convento di San Martino delle Scale, on April 17. They are pictured as entering the monastery chapel and introducing Bellini to Licalsi as an organ-designer just arrived from Catania. Invited to display the organ, the devoutly Bellinian Licalsi obliged with the final aria from *I Capuleti*, whereupon Bellini spoke slightingly of the music, thus arousing Licalsi's ire. The composer then seated himself at the console and played "*Casta diva*," and only when his friends clustered about him to express their enthusiasm did Licalsi realize who he was.

At about six o'clock on the afternoon of April 23, Easter Monday, Bellini and Florimo sailed from Palermo on the *Francesco Primo*. They reached Naples after "44 hours of a happy trip"—that is, at about 2 p. m. on April 25—as Bellini wrote to Santocanale on April 28.[49] In that letter, he also said: "I believe that I'll accept the Carnival contract for Venice, where Pasta will be singing; but as soon as the contract is arranged, I'll bring you up to date, you being my intimate friend." That opera would be *Beatrice di Tenda*. On that same day, Bellini also wrote to the future Beatrice's husband, Giuseppe Pasta[50]:

"My dear Peppino—

"Lanari has forwarded to me the contract to compose an opera for the Venice Carnival, and also a note from you in which you say that because Lanari is offering me what I named to you in a letter,[51] you are certain that I'll not have run into any obstacle; well, as I don't remember what I wrote you about the payment, do me the favor of sending me that letter of mine, or at least the passage regarding it, or address the letter to Ricordi or to Finzi [and] let me find it at Florence, through which I'll be passing about the 16th or 18th of next month. You may be certain that I'll accept the arrangement, and I have written Lanari to that effect, telling him that we'll arrange everything when I get to Florence.[52] . . . I think that I'll go to spend some months at the lake with Giuditta Turina, who charges me with many affectionate expressions for your Giuditta, Mamma Rachele, you, and Clelia[53]; being so close together, we'll be able to discuss and arrange everything, as I hope to start my work there. I am up to the minute on all the Milanese theatrical news. My Norma—having been portrayed by the Encyclopedic Angel [Pasta]—could not have failed to have a good reception[54]; enough, for when I begin to speak of that divine donna, my mind doesn't give me terms adequate to express what I feel in my heart. . . ."[55]

On or about April 30,[56] Bellini said farewell to Florimo and to Naples; he would not see either again. Probably traveling with Giuditta Turina and her brother in their carriage, he did not reach Florence until about May 20. The story that he stopped off in Rome for a visit is believable, though no documentary proof of such a stay survives.[57] One credible detail is that while in Rome, Bellini was received in audience at the Quirinal by Gregory XVI and presented with the gold crucifix that his family, after his death, gave to Santocanale.[58] Another reported detail is equally credible: that Bellini attended a performance of *La Straniera* at the Teatro Apollo on May 18, during that opera's first season in Rome.

An apparently insoluble mystery wrapped in a confusion of date is connected with Bellini's last visit to Rome. Alberto Cametti wrote[59] "Among the manuscripts of the Roman operatic poet Jacopo Ferretti preserved a libretto in one act, undated: '*Il fu ed il sarà*, to be performe with music by Maestro Vincenzo Bellini at the happy wedding of signor Camillo Giuliani P[astore] A[rcade] to signora Carolina Persiani.' The characters are described thus: *the phantom of the past, Colini,*[60] *primo basso assoluto; the hypothetical voice of the future, P[ietro?] Angelini, primo tenore assoluto; fecundity, Teresa Ferretti,*[61] *prima donna assoluta; Chorus of ancestors* and *chorus of descendants.*' The work is dedicated to Vincenzo De Libert P. A. (*Pastore Arcade*) and *tiberino* [Roman], his 'old friend and teacher,' to whom the author says: 'To you, who taught me to write librettos, I indite one written in a very few hours.' The marriage of Giuliani—he, too, later an operatic poet[62]—and *la Persiani* was celebrated on February 18, 1832. Precisely in that year, Bellini passed through Rome twice on that glorious trip to his birthplace which he undertook as soon as he saw the happy turn of the fortunes of his *Norma* in Milan. The first time, he passed through there on January 8 or 9, for he reached Naples on the 11th; Cicconetti and Florimo testify to his brief stay in Rome on the return trip, when he attended the second perform ance of *La Straniera*. Bellini left Palermo for Naples on April 22 [actually 23]; *La Straniera* was on the stage from April 30 to May 20[63]; from the contents of a letter he wrote to Giovanni Ricordi from Florence on May 24,[64] we can surmise that he had reached that city at least one day before that. We can set the outside dates of Bellini's Roman stopover approximately, limiting it to between May 1 and May 20. During that brief stay—and if that statement 'to be performed with music by Maestro Vincenzo Bellini' was not a jest by the Roman poet—did he [Bellini] really have time to set to music the short libretto that Ferretti had prepared for him? Or did the project remain entirely in the state of a pious wish? In fact, the date of Bellini's stop among us fits badly with that of Giuliani's wedding. Because we lack any datum or document regarding it, this question hangs unanswered for the time being."

Guido Pannain was more decisive[65]: "The opera in one act (scenic cantata) *Il fu ed il sarà*, to a libretto by J. Ferretti, privately performed in Rome on February 18, 1832 [but was it?], certainly was not an original work by Bellini. Probably we are dealing with a *pastiche* of pieces of music taken from Bellini's operas." And there, unless unlikely additional documents should be discovered, the problem of *Il fu ed il sarà* must be abandoned. No trace of a score of it has been found.

Bellini left Rome about May 20, probably with Giuditta Turina and Gaetano Cantù, and reached Florence on or before May 23: in his letter to Ricordi of May 24 from there,[66] he said: "Last night I heard a performance of *La Sonnambula*,[67] which really was unrecognizable. All the tempos at the gallop; la [Rosalbina] *Carradori*[-Allan] colder than ice itself; the chorus shouting like people possessed. The tenor [Gilbert-Louis] Dupré [Duprez] sang the second-act aria very well, as, in part, la *Carradori* did the first-act cavatina; the rest was horrible!

"I have arranged the contract with Lanari to compose the opera for Venice[68]; there I'll have the divine Pasta, and on the same terms as in the contract with La Scala for *Norma* except that, instead of asking for half the proprietary rights in renting out the score, I asked for all of them; but Lanari now has a contract with [Giacomo] Zamboni,[69] and could dispose only of half. I'll be in Milan very early in June, and we'll discuss everything. . . ."

Except for a letter from Milan to Filippo Santocanale dated July 1,[70] no Bellini letters are available between May 24 and August 1832. He very probably returned to Milan about June 1 and then spent that month at Moltrasio with Giuditta Turina, who continued to be unwell. In the letter of July 1 to Santocanale, he said[71]: "In August, I'll go to Bergamo to stage my *Norma*, which Pasta herself will sing, but I won't be away from Milan more than two weeks. There is no other news. . . ." He remained in Milan throughout July.

Although Bellini appears not to have mentioned the fact, there was news. On May 12, 1832, at the Teatro della Canobbiana in Milan, a new opera had begun a seasonal run of thirty-three performances. It was Donizetti's *L'Elisir d'amore*, with a cast headed by Sabine Heinefetter

(Adina), Giambattista Genero (Nemorino), Henry-Bernard Dabadie (Belcore), and Giuseppe Frezzolini (Dulcamara), which had instantly become a raging favorite with Milanese audiences. To have Bellini's comment upon it, even though comic opera was of little interest to him, would be fascinating; but no proof survives that he heard it, though it certainly was being sung while he was in Milan.

Bellini was to spend, not two weeks, but a month in Bergamo. He left either Milan or Moltrasio for there on August 11 or 12 with Giuseppe and Giuditta Pasta, but not with Giuditta Turina, who was too unwell to travel. The first opera played at the Teatro Riccardi during that August Fair season was Giacomo Meyerbeer's *Il Crociato in Egitto* (1824), which suffered from a mistaken belief by the *bergamaschi* that the Riccardi management was skimping on it, treating it as no more than a prelude to the excitedly awaited appearance of Pasta in *Norma*, about which Giambattista Pinetti wrote[72]: "The first performance took place on August 22. Bellini's opera was staged after imposing preparation unexampled earlier on our stages. The orchestra, chorus, and stage-band were augmented. Nothing was skimped. Giuditta Pasta aroused the spectators' enthusiasm by the smooth modulations with which she knew how to adorn her singing, by her noble presence, by her reasoned emotion. Domenico Reina, who we were afraid might be compared with the tenor [Domenico] Donzelli of 'La Scala,' was sublime, and so was [Elisa] Taccani in the role of Adalgisa. This fine cast produced a corresponding effect upon the audience, which, satisfied, repeatedly acclaimed the opera and its performers."[73]

On August 23, the day after the first *Norma*, Bellini wrote to conte Giacomo Barbò[74]: "*Norma* has stunned all of Bergamo, and I myself have found it something different. Everything is more alive and spirited since the singers have mastered their roles. Pasta made me shed many tears; Reina (though not endowed with Donzelli's voice) sang with such fire that if you would come here, I'd be delighted to have you hear the *stretta* of the cavatina, which everyone thinks I have changed: I can say the same of '*Sola, furtiva al tempio*,' which *la Taccani* sang as she was taught, and which drew widespread applause. The trio could not be performed better, and so it makes everyone shiver; I don't speak of the rest because I am hoping that you yourself will get to hear it all; meanwhile, the applause was great, spontaneous, and unanimous; so you'll understand that the singers [and] the composer [were] called out onto the stage, etc., etc., the usual things.[75]

"So come quickly before I leave Bergamo, which will be at the beginning of next week, to come to Milan. . . ."

But it was to Romani that (while repeating much of what he had told Barbò) Bellini really poured out his happiness. Writing on August 24, he told his librettist[76]: "Our *Norma* created a decided furor. If you heard it as it is performed here, you would almost think it changed; to me it seems a different opera; its effect strikes me as admirable. . . . And in fact I wept because of the strong emotions that my spirit experienced. I wanted you beside me to share them with me, my good counselor and collaborator, for only you understand me, and my glory and yours are not separate. . . . The trio could not be better performed: they act it well and forcefully; it makes everyone shiver, and they find it a beautiful finale even without the help of supers, Druids, Druidesses, and other choristers to make noise. You were right to be obstinate about keeping it like this. . . . P. S. Mayr[77] salutes you affectionately; he embraced and kissed me. And I am in Bergamo!" Whether feigned or real, Bellini's astonishment that Bergamo audiences would receive a non-Donizettian opera enthusiastically and that Mayr, Donizetti's first teacher and lifelong friend, should demonstrate affectionate regard for him too makes strange reading.

From Bergamo, Bellini went to Giuditta Turina at Casalbuttano: he dated a letter to Giovanni Ricordi from there on September 16.[78] Once again, he was involved in searching for an operatic subject: his next opera was to be staged at the Teatro La Fenice, Venice, almost fifteen months after the unsatisfying première of *Norma* at La Scala. By an arrangement with Lanari, apparently reached in September, the première of Bellini's new opera at La Fenice was to be preceded there by his staging *Norma* to open the Venice season.

1833: *Beatrice di Tenda;* The Break with Romani; London

Pasta would sing the leading role in the opera that Bellini was to compose for Venice. Its libretto therefore had to turn about a central female character adaptable to her artistry and worthy of it. The search for a novel or play—everyone assumed that it would have to be a French novel or play—containing materials transmutable into such a libretto proved long, and it irritated both Romani (upon whom most of the reading and assaying devolved) and Bellini. That neither of them had hit upon a suitable source by September 24, 1832, is proved by a letter that Bellini wrote from Milan to Filippo Santocanale that day. It is a strange, starchy, humorless letter that shows Bellini's professed conception of the duties of friendship to have been not very different from Florimo's. In part, it reads[1]:

"I have been told that at *la Manzocchi*'s[2] house—some days before she left Sicily—a rather vulgar satirical poem was sung, and that this cantata ended with a thousand toasts still lower than the poem itself, all directed against my and your friend Florimo. The chief organizers of that excessive *accademia* were, I was told, Ottavio, the *Baroncino*, Peranna, other admirers of Manzocchi's merits, and *Santocanale;* the last-mentioned may well have been present, but it isn't possible that he would have got involved in anything so childish! When I was told the story, this was my first reaction; true, your nature is merry, but your wisdom still predominates, and you could not have mocked a guest of yours and a dear friend of mine; but I must confess to you that I know you capable of preventing such an occurrence, and therefore responsible for those who drink from your glass and whom you load with the most refined and affectionate attentions. What saddens me most is the feeling that so many people should have treated Florimo, not as a friend of mine being disemboweled, but as a fraud, a 'character,' etc., etc. There was talk that Florimo had spoken badly to Marcellini of my music during his stay in Palermo, and other bits of that sort of gossip.

"I do look forward to the pleasure of a speedy explanation of such an event, which you, as a friend, will give me; I ask this because I esteem you very highly and should not for any reason want to see any alteration in the ties that bind us—not because of some childish pranks in which the Man-zocchian rapture was able to make Ottavio, the little *Baroncino*, and others lose their heads because they knew that Florimo does not share their enthusiasm for that donna; and he was proper, for he praised her for what deserved praise, as I myself did; but if he ever jested with Ottavio, he did so out of vivacity and never out of real conviction.

"I am certain that my Santocanale still esteems and loves Florimo as I esteem and love him—and believe Bellini [when he says] that equals of Florimo may exist but nobody exceeds him in affection for his real friends. The test of almost fifteen years of friendship is enough to make that certain. Tell all this to Ottavio and the others who are persuaded differently, and if all this never happened, or happened differently, write to Florimo and tell him their real feelings, for what I heard about it was reported to him, too, and that explains his silence toward you. I await your reply eagerly, as you can well imagine.

"My general health is good except for some boils that have been martyrizing my right elbow. My poet [Romani] still has not found the subject for the Venice opera. I'll stay in Milan another two months, but early in December I must return to Venice, where Pasta is to sing, and she will make her debut in *Norma*, which was very well received in Bergamo, as I think the journals will have told you."

On November 5, replying to Santocanale's answer to that letter, Bellini returned to the subject of Florimo, still defending him hotly. He finally said[3]: "Well, then, I believe that we are at peace: however, I await the happy news of clarifications between you and Florimo . . . I wish that you would trust Florimo's good heart more: he is something of a humorist, but he is good and sincere: believe Bellini; but if we don't exercise some forebearance in accepting our friends' defects, then I think that friendships and affections will be of very short duration, as we all have our weaknesses and blind spots."

In September, Romani seems to have been awaiting from Paris a shipment of recent publications from which he hoped to select a subject that would appeal to Bellini as possible libretto material, would provide Pasta with a role different from both Amina and Norma, and would not require secondary roles beyond the capabilities of the supporting singers contracted by Lanari. However, between September 24, when Bellini first wrote to Santocanale about the Manzocchi-Florimo imbroglio, and October 6, when he wrote to him about other matters, Romani, Bellini, and Pasta agreed upon a subject for the new opera. On the latter date, from Milan, Bellini told Santocanale[4]: "My health is not bad, for my arm is almost cured. I hope to compose the first note for Venice on Monday [October 8]. The subject is *Cristina regina di Svezia*, taken from Dumas; it seems interesting to me, and I have high hopes for it, being in the hands of a Romani, my expert and favorite poet." They had hit upon *Stockholm, Fontainebleau et Rome: Trilogie dramatique sur la vie de Christine*, a five-act trilogy in verse with prologue and epilogue by the elder Dumas which had been staged for the first time at the Théâtre de l'Odéon, Paris, on March 30, 1830, with Mlle George as Queen Christina.[5]

Precisely what happened to that Dumas project—which was almost certainly discarded before Bellini had composed any music for it—cannot now be discovered. On November 3, exactly four weeks after he told Santocanale that he hoped to begin working on it two days later, Bellini wrote to Pasta from Milan[6]: "You will be astonished, you will think me demented, but what is done is done, and I hope that it will lead to happy results. The subject has been changed, and we'll write *Beatrice di Tenda*. I had a hard time persuading Romani, but persuade him I did, and with good reasons. Knowing that the subject pleases you, as you told me the evening when you saw the ballet[7]; finding that the last scene of this story is very like the ending of *Maria Stuarda*, from which Romani can perfectly well copy the Schiller scene so attractive to you for the opportunity that it presents to an artist of your caliber, and realizing how interesting the whole subject is, all that satisfies one very well. Romani will handle it in such a way that no situation will recall *Anna Bolena;* he is a man of good will, and I want him to show it also in wanting to prepare at least the first act for me swiftly."

Bellini was wrong about the possibility of Romani's exercising good will toward him in this instance. Earlier in 1832, that willingly overworked man had written the libretto of Donizetti's *Ugo, conte di Parigi* (La Scala, March 13, 1832). In the autumn, he had accepted an invitation from the new manager of La Scala, duca Carlo Visconti di Modrone, to become La Scala's staff librettist (specifying only that he not be required to live in Milan), and had written, besides much else, the text for an opera by Mercadante: *Ismalia, ossia Morte ed amore* (La Scala, October 27, 1832). By the date of the shift from Queen Christina to Beatrice di Tenda, he had agreed to supply as rapidly as possible librettos to Carla Coccia

(*Caterina di Guisa*, La Scala, February 14, 1833), Luigi Majocchi (*Il Segreto*, Teatro Ducale, Parma, February 26, 1833), Mercadante (*Il Conte di Essex*, La Scala, March 10, 1833), and Donizetti (*Parisina*, Teatro della Pergola, Florence, March 17, 1833, long after its originally announced première). Yet Bellini seems to have hoped, perhaps even believed, that Romani would fend off the other clamoring composers and produce first the *Beatrice di Tenda* text for him.

November passed without Romani's delivering new verses to Bellini.[8] How Bellini occupied his time during those weeks is not known. On the evening of November 24, however, he acted as Pasta's accompanist when she sang at a reception given by the Austrian governor in Milan.[9] On that day, too, he wrote to Alessandro Lamperi that he would leave Milan on December 5. The list of visitors reaching Venice on December 8 published in the *Gazzetta privilegiata di Venezia* shows that he and the Pastas arrived there that day and put up at the Albergo Reale.[10]

During some part of the almost four months that Bellini spent in Venice, Giuditta Turina was there, too. This time she had difficulty in persuading her husband to agree to her trip: some time shortly before this, he had received an anonymous letter warning him that Bellini was his wife's lover. She appears to have believed that this was Turina's first inkling of her adultery, but it took considerable insistence on her part to change his decision that she must not go to Venice. Then, reaching Venice while Bellini was desperately occupied with the much-belated completion of *Beatrice di Tenda*, she became the center of gossip about her and still another man.[11] Her presence there was not a source of peace or comfort to Bellini, to her husband, or, at last, to herself.

For some time after Bellini reached Venice, he would have had little time for composing even if Romani had delivered verses to him: on Monday, December 10, he began rehearsals of *Norma* at the Fenice. By then, too, he was worried to the verge of despair: the performances of *Norma* were to be followed at the Fenice by stagings of Giuseppe Persiani's *Eufemio da Messina* and Rossini's *Otello*—after which, during the second half of February, *Beatrice di Tenda* was supposed to make its bow. On the day of that first rehearsal of *Norma*, Bellini wrote to Vincenzo Ferlito[12]: "I write you two lines merely to inform you that, after a happy trip, I have been in this original and beautiful city since Saturday after supper. My health is good, and today the rehearsals for *Norma* begin. I am desperate because of the poet, who does not give me verses; and in the meantime I have had to involve the Government in order to compel him." To Santocanale on that same day, he wrote[13]: "My health is good, and if my poet would give me materials to which to apply myself, I'd be in calm spirits too." On December 13, again to his Uncle Vincenzo, he wrote[14]: "The poet Romani has not given me any more verses: the Government has taken steps, and we'll see how it will end."

When the governor of Venice was informed that Romani was failing to keep his contractual promise to the Fenice, he sent the problem to the governor of Milan, who had his police summon Romani. The poet later asserted that he had protested this summary treatment, but he nevertheless went to Venice, arriving there about January 1, 1833. The Milan police functionary had ordered him to write out an explanation of his delay—or, to judge by the language of the resulting document, had himself written it out on the basis of what Romani told him, and then had ordered Romani to sign it: Pastura described it[15] as couched in "a special phraseology that had nothing to do with literature—the bitterest prose of his life."

After Romani reached Venice, tempers cooled for the moment. He said that he shut himself up in his quarters to concentrate wholly upon writing the libretto of *Beatrice di Tenda*. That action naturally delayed still longer his delivery to Donizetti of the text for *Parisina*. From Rome on December 18, Donizetti had written very bitterly to his father with reference to an anonymous writer who had attacked him[16]: "I don't know of anyone who doesn't make use of reminiscences [from earlier scores], and if he wants to be kind enough to reveal himself, I'll take him for a short amble through the scores of someone whom he doesn't name [Pacini? Rossini? Bellini?] and make him, with his own hand, pick out from whichever of them he chooses, not reminiscences, but whole pieces taken from I know where. . . . He says that I should compose to better librettos. Let him give them to me; let him find a theatrical poet who is less of a rascal than Romani about keeping his word, and I'll offer him one hundred scudi for whoever will write a good book. He has a lovely speech in that key. I don't live without expense in the homes of beautiful women[17] who can present me with the poet and who belittle others in order to satisfy their protégé, as is happening now, and which I have protested to Florence because of the libretto that I should have had in October, but still don't have today."

As the fuse on these potentially explosive arguments grew short, *Norma* opened the season at the Fenice on December 26, with Pasta as Norma, Anna Del Serre as Adalgisa, Alberico Curioni as Pollione, and Federico Crespi as Oroveso. Bellini found the singers mediocre, Pasta excepted, and therefore began to fear for *Beatrice di Tenda*, in which all of them were scheduled to appear. Pasta, conquering Venice as she had conquered so many other cities, carried *Norma* to some success, but Del Serre and Curioni were received indifferently by the audience and criticized adversely by Tommaso Locatelli, a knowledgeable writer on musical subjects who was editor of the *Gazzetta privilegiata di Venezia*.[18]

On January 12, 1833, Bellini wrote Santocanale a letter mostly about the reception of *Norma* at the Fenice, but opening on a *cri de cœur*[19]: "Two lines only, o my dear friend, to give you word about my health, which is at the breaking point from the great fatigue that I am experiencing because of having to compose the opera in a short time, and whose fault is that? that of my usual and original poet, the God of Sloth!" To Giovanni Ricordi, two weeks later (January 27), he reported[20]: "The *Otello* of yesterday evening would not have been allowed to finish with any donna other than the immense Pasta; let that tell you enough; but every time that this *divinissima* donna appears, she banishes the audience's discontent and exceeds every expectation: when Otello killed himself, the audience cried out 'May he never rise again! ! !'[21] *La Beatrice* moves forward. I hope to begin the finale of the first act if Romani will give it to me; but how my opera can get on this way, God only knows: what a terrible company! ! However, Romani has given me beautiful verses: I am putting my usual devotion into composing; if the music turns out not to be intrinsically bad, it could be decisive with another company; however, I hope for everything from Pasta: a sure anchor in any shipwreck. The first act contains, for her, a romanza, a cavatina, a big duet with the bass, and the finale, entirely dependent upon her; in the second act, the trial and her big final scene; it has these pieces, and if I don't do them badly, I hope in part to save myself. Let's await the outcome."

An undated letter from Bellini to Romani, headed "At home, Friday morning" (internal evidence strongly suggests that it was written on February 1), belongs to this hectic interval[22]: "Dear Romani, After having worked like a dog, believe me that it is too cruel for me to come all the way to your house only to find you not there; therefore, as it was our agreement that I'll always be there by four at the latest, I beg you that if more important matters than the libretto take you away from home, you will send word to me before three o'clock, when I am always in. I hope that today you will have me find everything that is missing from the first act, as I have promised to deliver it to the copying office tomorrow or the next day. Your Bellini. Greetings." Bellini is addressing Romani by the formal *voi* rather than the former intimate *tu*. That cool tone and the fact that the two men were living in different parts of Venice demonstrate their changed relationship.

In a euphoric moment on February 14, Bellini wrote to Vincenzo Ferlito[23]: "My health is good. Another three pieces of the new opera to do, and it will be finished. I'll not be sending you the money order before the middle of next month, the time when I'll be asking this management for additional money. For the time being, we won't think about investing more money until my return from London, which I easily can arrange to visit in mid-April so as to return to Italy at the end of August; but the matter is not decided; but if it comes to pass, I'll give you the details then. I hope to go on stage here on March 6[24] if I am able to finish the opera and prepare it [*concertarla*]. In the meantime, I embrace you and leave you because I must go out to ask the poet for poetry."

But three days later, writing to Santocanale, Bellini again was desperate[25]: "I am glad that your health is good, as well as that of all our friends; mine is the same; but my morale is terribly afflicted because my sluggard of a poet has reduced me to such straits that I despair of even completing the opera: having to go on stage in only two weeks, I have the whole second act to do! ! ! Oh, what a huge fiasco I foresee!" In fact, Bellini was able to get *Beatrice di Tenda* ready for rehearsal only by deleting sections of the libretto and several partially completed musical numbers, including a third-act duet with which he had intended to parallel the unconventional, successful finale of *Norma*.

Just before or just after the first rehearsal, the public's and Bellini's increasing dissatisfaction with the bass Federico Crespi necessitated his being replaced in the role of Filippo by Orazio Cartagenova. And that change required alteration of some of Filippo's vocal lines to fit them to Cartagenova's virtues and weaknesses, as well as extensive recomposition of three numbers. Those tasks increased the furious labor that Bellini was performing under intensifying pressure. Nor was he alone in that condition: Lanari, having to pacify his audience as delay followed delay, filled the first two weeks of March at the Fenice with performances of *Norma*, *Otello*, and—not originally announced, and therefore grumblingly received as stopgaps—Donizetti's *L'Elisir d'amore* and a single singing of Rossini's *Tancredi*.

Almost exactly a month after the date announced for *Beatrice di Tenda* and only eight days before the scheduled seasonal closing of the Fenice, the theater was able to present Bellini's new opera: on March 16, 1833, it shared a double bill with a new ballet listed as *L'Ultimo Giorno di Missolungi*. Pasta was the Beatrice; others in the cast were Anna Del Serre (Agnese), Alberico Curioni (Orombello), Orazio Cartagenova (Filippo), and Alessandro Giacchini (Anichino). The libretto published for the première included an *avvertimento* signed by Romani which told the history of the real Beatrice di Lascari, contessa di Tenda, and concluded thus: "The fragment of the present *melodramma* was based upon that history— which may be read in [Andrea] Bigli, in [Andrea] Redusio, in [Giuseppe] Ripamonti, and in several other writers of those times and ours. I say *fragment* because inevitable circumstances have altered the plot, the tints, the characters. It has need of the readers' full indulgence."

That apology did nothing to reduce the fever in which that first

Venetian audience, already in an unfriendly state of mind, received *Beatrice di Tenda*. Michele Scherillo wrote[26]: "The introduction began; but though it was beautifully shaped, the audience greeted it coldly. Pasta came on stage; no sign of warmth. She sang the beautiful cavatina '*Ma la sola, oimè, son io*' and the dramatic cabaletta '*Ah la pena in lor piombò*' amid indifference; at a given point, the audience even began to shout '*Norma! Norma!*' in the belief that it had detected a phrase from that opera. The phrase would return later on, and the composer was more than a little worried. But Pasta, like the great artist that she was, varied the repetition so ably that nobody noticed the subterfuge. At that moment, Pasta conceived a cordial hatred of that stupid audience, which, while giving vent to its preconceived displeasure with the composer, did not respect her as the most skillful artist-singer of the time. And when, in the midst of impertinent murmurings, she had to sing the duet with the duke (Cartagenova) ['*Duolo d'un cor piagato*'], instead of turning toward the actor, she faced the audience and scornfully, energetically accented the phrase: '*se amar non puoi, rispettami!*' [if you cannot love me, respect me!]. It is said that the audience understood and responded with noisy applause. But that did not make it change its attitude toward Bellini's opera."

The reactions of the audiences at the five later performances given of *Beatrice di Tenda*—the last of which closed the Fenice season on March 24—were friendlier. On the day after the closing, Bellini reported to Santocanale with his usual honesty about "failures"[27]: "I was waiting for some journal to appear so that, with some opinion expressed, I could inform you about the reception of my new opera, which, because of a series of unhappy circumstances, has been as unfortunate as that of *I Capuleti* was fortunate. The blame for the opera's having been delayed until the 16th of this month is laid upon me, whereas it was all the poet's fault; and the faction against Pasta, which is powerful and makes the most noise, was joined by the one directly adverse to me, and so at the first night made such a noise—shouting, whistling, laughing, etc., etc.—that a feeling that I was at a fair became so strong that all my Sicilian haughtiness took possession of me, and my undaunted appearance all but silenced some and enraged the others; for the audience called out for me after four or five very effective pieces, but I remained in my seat as though nailed there.

"At the other two performances,[28] there was applause for five or six pieces, and the crowd was so large that both times the management took in almost twice as much for tickets at as the première. I'll add only that *Zaira*, whistled at in Parma, was avenged by *I Capuleti; Norma*, which was disapproved of in part during the first performances in Milan, took its own revenge; *Beatrice*, which I judge not unworthy of her sisters, will, I hope, also find her revenge. In the meantime, at the first evening, some stupid people thought to show their spirit by shouting '*Norma!*' as if to say that I had copied that opera. The journal had the naïveté to say the same thing, and I had the comparisons printed so as to show everyone what reckless ignorance that was. Together with those comparisons, the *Gazzetta* carries an article demonstrating that the delay was to blame, and thus defends my integrity from the calumnies of the envious, who always strike out of the blue—the success or fiasco of an opera being a matter of no importance. Rossini has written sixty-four operas,[29] and I believe that scarcely twelve of them make the rounds of the theatrical world. Tomorrow I leave Venice and go to Milan, and from there, on about the tenth of April, I'll leave for London, where I go to conduct an opera of mine which is to be performed there. Receive my embraces and believe me Your affectionate V. Bellini."[30]

The journalistic storm over *Beatrice di Tenda* was about to evolve into the bitterest, most convoluted, and—at our distance from it—most amusing polemic in the annals of early nineteeenth-century Italian opera. It had begun three days before the première: on March 13, the *Gazzetta privilegiata di Venezia* had published a letter purportedly written to its editor by "A. B." of Fonzaso[31]; it was almost certainly fabricated by Tommaso Locatelli, the musically sophisticated man who edited the paper. The burden of that verbose complaint is: "But we are in Lent, the first and seconds weeks of which have now elapsed, and we are almost— more than almost—in the third week, and the new opera has not yet appeared." The writer knowingly asks why the opera was not presented during Carnival, when audiences could have enjoyed it more calmly and when, if it had pleased them, it could have been repeated often?

Locatelli's ill-will shows more certainly in the reply to "A. B." which was published in the *Gazzetta* the next day.[32] "Things, misfortunes, happen, and in that connection it will be remembered that *I Capuleti e i Montecchi* was given [only] five or six times three years ago, *Benjowski*[33] four or five years ago, *Ivanhoe*[34] three or four last year, so it would not surprise me if, continuing the same descending arithmetic progression, *Beatrice Tenda* [*sic*] were to be given this year only two or three times; nor would it surprise me in the least, either if it should be postponed until next year. . . . And it must be noted now that this *Beatrice* is not an opera to be had cheaply like any other, it must be made into a perfect work, satisfactory to every taste . . . especially as . . . this *Beatrice* must shortly cross the seas, and will find better quarters in London; here it will receive little more than a 'Bon voyage' or, we might say, a passport."

Locatelli had not finished. On March 18, the *Gazzetta* published another "letter to A. B.": dated "Saturday night, March 16"—that is, immediately after the première—it reported[35]: ". . . *Beatrice Tenda* [*sic*] had no luck. Poor girl! the audience did not turn a comforting, happy face upon her, and the Maestro, there between the violoncello and the violin, watched her rush to her destiny without anyone remembering him. Some of his admirers struggled to recall him to the people's memory, and his name was heard here and there; but then what? they were pious wishes, and were not welcomed; those admirers of his were reduced to silence." The writer again asserts that "*Norma! Norma!*" was shouted out because members of the audience thought that they recognized borrowings from that well-loved opera; he speaks well of the singers, of Pasta in particular; he singles out half a dozen numbers for praise—and in lauding two choruses, says that they would have succeeded well in an *opera buffa*. "And here, between you and me, I risk making a confidence that I would not utter in public for anything in the world: I think that in judging the new opera, the spectators also had in mind all the time that they had had to wait for it; and, truth to tell, they had the right to something better after a labor that was, or at least seems to have been, so unrewarding. The spectacle was staged with all splendor."

Critiques published during the succeeding week show clearly that *Beatrice di Tenda*, despite many passages of admitted excellence and the high quality of the performance, had not been received happily at its première.[36] Then, on March 26, a pro-*Beatrice* salvo was fired off in a letter to Locatelli signed "A friend of M. Bellini."[37] Publishing it, the editor introduced it thus: "The duty of impartiality and justice obliges us to insert the following letter, which we publish without further remark." The letter reads:

"In your purported Fonzaso correspondence, you have, if not directly, then certainly with full clarity for anyone who knows how to read, inculpated Maestro Bellini in the delay caused in performing his new opera, *Beatrice Tenda* [*sic*]. The accusation attacks his integrity rather than his *amour propre*, for if it were correct, it would demonstrate in him either unpardonable laziness or equally blameworthy temerity for having assumed an obligation that he was not in a position to carry out; but you had, rather, a duty to exculpate him by publishing the facts as they are, and which you are hereby given faithfully to understand.

"It is true that Maestro Bellini, by the terms of his contract, was to have the libretto from the poet *Romani* partly in October and partly in November; but it is also true that up to January 15, he had not received from him more than the *Duet* between *Del Serre* and *Curioni* and the *Cavatina* for *Pasta*[38]: for which reason the Impresario, Lanari, was forced to turn to the competent authorities. Romani, by his declaration signed before the Police of Milan, where he then was—and which, with letter No. 5396 of December 23 of last year, was communicated from the Ecc. I. R. Presidio of that Government to the Noble Sign. Dott. Avesani, Governing Director of the Teatro della [*sic*] Fenice—excused himself for the delay, advancing the change of subjects desired by the composer and his *obligation*—these are his own words—*to the Milan Theaters*. So that you may know what breed of change that was: the poet had presented to *Bellini* at the end of October, not an outline or a sketch, but merely the title of a *Cristina di Svezia* that did not please the Maestro; that rejection therefore did not require the other to discard a single verse.

"Once the poet had reached the scene, he submitted various pieces to the Maestro one by one, and the opera still could have gone on stage on February 20 if the poor reception of the preceding scores had not necessitated finding a new bass in Cartagenova, who could not arrive until late, and which [the change] forced the poet and the Maestro to alter at least three pieces of *Beatrice Tenda*.[a] The Maestro did not undertake changes greater than those customarily made by other composers, and which the poet makes in other scores.

"Further, so that the public can see what the imputation of reminiscences boils down to, through the kindness of the Maestro, I am sending you lithographs of the two pieces upon which the accusation chiefly fell."[39]

Infuriated, Romani fired the next shot: a letter published in the *Gazzetta privilegiata* of April 2[40]:

"Highly esteemed sig. Editor.

"I invoke the impartiality and justice with which you gave space in the *Gazzetta privilegiata* of the 24th of the current month to a letter from a friend of M.° Bellini—to the end that you should concede me a page in the same paper for a reply that can clear me of the charge made against me that I delayed the appearance of that most unhappy *Beatrice di Tenda*, which, for the honor of the Italian stage, should have been postponed another week. I will give the facts as they are: I alone, with visor up and without the help of friends.

"It is quite true, as the aforementioned friend said, that I should have delivered to Bellini a *melodramma* (which he calls a libretto) half in October, half in November; but it is also quite true (and the friend maintained silence about this) that Bellini had reserved the right to select the subject.

a [Locatelli's footnote]: Out of love for truth and for Maestro Bellini, we must add to our first article and to the history of this score that at the second performance, the Maestro was acclaimed by the audience at the places noted, and that the theater was also very crowded for the third performance.

Either Minerva was discourteous to him or he did not want to accept Minerva's advice; July passed, August passed, September ran out, and October and November finally came, and that blessed subject still had not been found, and the Maestro was not to be seen. He emerged when God willed it; but the time was past, and previous obligations, which I could not disregard, put me in the position of having to refuse Bellini my labor. Nevertheless, besought and re-besought by him, and inured to major sacrifices for him, I consented to write, and put my mind to a lyric tragedy entitled *Cristina di Svezia*. One fine morning, Bellini's Minerva relaxed her strictness and suggested to him the subject of Beatrice Tenda, and on another fine morning my fondness for Bellini and my respect for his Minerva[41] imposed another sacrifice upon me, that of accepting it. While I am occupying myself with Beatrice in Milan, Bellini leaves for Venice and, as a reward for my compliance, puts the blame for the delay upon my poor shoulders. I was far away, and those who are distant do not always succeed in making themselves understood. The impresario, who did not have the facts, had recourse to the authorities, and to the shame of impresario and maestro, what followed was my being summoned by the Milan police and my protest—not my excuse—to them, which Bellini's defender places in evidence in his way. Then I hastened to betake myself to Venice and to demand an explanation of that procedure. The Maestro blames the impresario, the impresario the Maestro; honeyed words from the one, a sigh from the other calm my anger, and I shut myself up in my house and write and rewrite and change and re-change, and they touch up my *melodramma* in a thousand ways until the evening of the première, when my *melodramma* finally . . . becomes a libretto.

"Now what does Bellini claim, *or who does so for him*? That time did not pass for me as it passed for the Maestro, that the lost months were lost only for him? That it was to this that my days, my person, and my mind had been reduced? That I should put aside all other work so as to occupy myself uniquely with his, as though the twelve thousand francs destined for him would enter my wallet? And if he must preserve his integrity and his *amour propre*, he should not for that reason attack others. And if he wrote hurriedly, I too wrote hurriedly, and was tormented every day by his caprices and tortured more than Orombello[42] by the pre-established harmonies of his abovementioned music. And if that music did not have the success that he had hoped for, what purpose is served by the lie imputing to me the blame for that loss of time, which was caused entirely by him? What purpose is served by raising such a hubbub over the failure of a score, a misfortune to which the great Rossini too was subjected, without thereupon having deafened the world by his outcries? But the reason for the fiasco was this—but the wrong was this—but the poet—but the time—Eh! as Molière says, time *ne fait rien à l'affaire*. The opera was composed in three months? Well, then: it is a *galimatias* made in three months. But Bellini can console himself: a tree does not topple from one blow. Of what does this misfortune deprive him? Compensation? The milords of the Thames await him. Reputation? He does not lack for celebrants or friends.

"And here I come to a full stop; thanking the good luck that kept me in Venice longer than I had foreseen—or than others had foreseen—thus giving me the opportunity to clarify the singular controversy that the public finds amusing, and to assure you, highly esteemed signor Editor, of my sincere devotion. Felice Romani."

Publication of that letter in the *Gazzetta privilegiata di Venezia* did not calm Romani. He sent an altered, more venomous version of it to *L'Eco*, Milan, where it was published on an undated supplementary page.[43] In it, when saying that Bellini "had reserved the right to select the subject," he inserted, after "right," the parenthesis ("forgive me the term"); he put the first allusion to Minerva in this form: "Either Minerva was discourteous to him, or some other Goddess [Venus?] took the place of Minerva." Then, having brought his version of the events up to November, Romani wrote: "In addition, Bellini had disappeared. A new Rinaldo, he was idling on Armida's island . . ." clearly a reference to Giuditta Turina. He asserted that he had written some verses for *Cristina di Svezia* and could publish them if he, too, wanted to make the [lithographic] stones weep. The sentence referring to his having been far away in Milan now became: "I was far away: and the distant are not present to contradict the liars." Now he had been "more tortured than Orombello" by the tyranny of Bellini's music. Now, after the rhetorical "The opera was composed in three months?" his comment was: "Well, then it is a stupidity [*bestialità*] made in three months." In this second version, the letter ends: "Of what does this misfortune deprive him? Money? He has received the twelve thousand francs. Glory? The milords of the Thames await him. Reputation? He does not lack for celebrants. Friends? He has them, and of what weight is demonstrated by the writer of the letter to which I am replying, a very generous champion; may God preserve him in good health as an eternal mirror of theatrical chivalry. Felice Romani. Milan, April 1, 1833."

The rebuttal that Romani must have foreseen did not come from Bellini—at least, not directly from him. It appeared in *Il Barbiere di Siviglia*, Milan, on April 11,[44] and was signed "Pietro Marinetti." The writer's style was bloated garrulousness, but he clearly had discussed details with

Bellini, a fact that suggests that "Pietro Marinetti" well may have been a *nom de guerre* used by a known friend of Bellini wishing not to be identified. His letter read:

"TWO WORDS

"FOR SIGNOR FELICE ROMANI

"Signor Compiler of *Il Barbiere.*

"I see at the top of your No. 13 that you give space in *Il Barbiere di Siviglia* to an occasional article of theatrical polemic. Here is one. Publish it [and] you will be doing a really good deed and will show how unworthy it is for a man of great talent to lose himself in loading with contumelies another, no lesser talent, and in subjecting him to the sarcastic smiles of the malign and of the enemies of any who rise above mediocrity.

"You certainly understand that I wish to speak of Signor Felice Romani, who, in the Appendix of No. 40 of *L'Eco,* inveighs against Maestro Bellini in such a way as really to evoke compassion in men of good will.

"Before stating my argument, however, I must protest that I do not mean now to defend Bellini from the accusations leveled against him (an undertaking reserved for him), but only to give vent to the displeasure given me and all sensitive people by the very sarcastic manner, full of personal rancor and hauteur, with which Signor Romani has undertaken to assail his antagonist.

"In his unfortunate and bilious letter, Romani begins by trying to hold Bellini up to scorn because he reserved the right to select the argument of the opera that he was to compose for Venice. Suppose that he did—and what would that prove except that Bellini is the sort of composer who studies all details so as to assure himself of the chief means by which he can emerge happily from his musical trials? Oh, that all would act like Bellini, who, before girding up his loins to compose an opera, thinks thoroughly about what source of poetic emotions and inspirations he should draw upon; then we would not see such frequent repetitions of those shabby musical delusions with which we all too often are favored! Nor will you, my signor Romani, with your indiscreet, jesting allusions to Bellini's Minerva, ever succeed in proving that if he was as late as you say in suggesting Beatrice Tenda to you, it was out of laziness of mind, or of anything else on his part. And was not your example, perhaps, before Bellini's eyes? And when you want to set aside his musical convenience, as you too often disregard your own poetic convenience, could he not quickly have chosen at random, as you do, a subject from among the numerous tragedies being published every day in France, and to which—permit me to say it—you repair with closed eyes, as is proved by your *Caterina di Guisa* and your *Conte d'Essex*,[45] misshapen play-subjects of which you preserved only the monstrous and strangely immoral aspect!

"You will tell us that when Bellini proposed Beatrice Tenda to you, you set aside the first sections of a *Cristina di Svezia* that you had begun and applied yourself to the new story chosen by the composer. And you want to make us believe the humbug that you did so to please your artist colleague. Oh, my poor fellow! And who will not believe that you yourself, persuaded that you had taken up a story poorly suited to your strengths, were very glad to be able to put it to sleep in your wastebasket and instead take up another one better adapted to kindling your inspiration? If the matter were otherwise, I would ask you why you did not go on to treat your *Cristina* rather than that unhappy *Parisina*[46] which you most recently presented to the Florentines, and which you yourself, with rare modesty, described in the preface as unworthy of your name.

"Because you show up with such feeble weapons for combat, you must be forgiven your joke about making the lithographic stones weep, with which you thought to punish Bellini for having taken the trouble to put into print a musical example showing the foolishness of the accusation made against him by the *Gazzetta privilegiata di Venezia*—that of having reproduced in *Beatrice* the accompaniment of the final scene of *Norma*. Oh, yes, truly! Bellini should not have become entangled with an ignoramus who finds signs of imitation in accompaniments, which from Viadana[47] to our own time have all been woven in more or less identical and conventional forms! But as for you, signor Romani, yours was the more corrupt injustice of wishing to mock that zeal which, if nothing else, served to confound and leave red-faced a man who gave proof of an envious and base spirit and of complete ineptness in speaking of musical matters.

"And you did wrong, o signor Romani, to wail that Bellini had tormented you with his caprices, and thus had forced you to rush, and therefore be unable to polish your work as you would have wished. Your malice would have been excellent had it sufficed to demonstrate that the blame for the blemishes and oddities to be found strewn throughout your *Beatrice* were all Bellini's; but unhappily your malice becomes gross to the point of proving that when you write bad librettos, the blame is not always that of the composer who forces you to work in haste and tyrannizes over you with his demands, [and] you have before you *Caterina di Guisa*, *Il Conte d'Essex*, and *Parisina*, *melodrammi* that you drew up for composers far from tryannical in matters of dramatic demands.

"You ask Bellini why he makes such a to-do over the failure of a score, but you fail to notice that by those words you are offering him the highest praise and yourself the least agreeable satire; everyone would be lauding you if you showed yourself full of a sense of honor and of delicate feeling, and therefore sorry for not having been able, just once, to please the public as much as your noble ambition would have wished, whereas you are found culpable for laughing gaily over not one, but four consecutive fiascos—I am not exaggerating, and I would be able to prove this to you in a short, amusing analysis of your four latest lyric tragedies, as you call them. And if those four latest lyric tragedies are rather bad than not, the fault does not lie in lack of talent on your part (for you, signor Romani, have plenty of talent, and nobody denies that), but precisely in your tactic of having many strings to your bow and thus earning a lot of money. Emulate Bellini, if not in anything else, at least in the talent that shows him how to earn a long but very honest profit from his genius.

"You exclaim with Molière that time *ne fait rien à l'affaire,* but you should realize, poor fellow, that you are in large part mistaken, and that to prove your error there always are at hand those four unfortunate dramas of yours, which, like Banquo's ghost at Macbeth's banquet, reprove your purblind haste loud and stridently. But it is easy to understand that by your quotation from Molière you hoped to wound Bellini's *amour propre* sharply by accusing him of having little ready talent. Ah, witticisms! Further, you concede to Bellini that he meditates over his scores as much as two years, so that he may give us music full of poetry, feeling, and dramatic force—as is usual with his music, not excluding various pieces in *Beatrice.** Oh, my signor Felice Romani! if Bellini sins in spending a lot of time producing little, but that little good, what will your sin be in spending little time producing much that is bad? But what am I saying? Like the pregnant mountain in the fable, you too, dear signor Felice, sometimes spend lots of time doing little, even doing nothing! Do you, my dear signor Felice, recall that big announcement, printed in Manini's types, which was pasted up many months ago at all of the city's hundred street-crossings, that big announcement in which the COMPLETE COLLECTION OF YOUR WORKS was promised, and which, with the resounding trumpets of reputation, summoned people to subscribe to them? Behold in that a very potent argument to persuade you that, on most occasions, time *fait beaucoup à l'affaire!* You promised wonderful things in that pompous blurb, but because blessed time, which you pretend to scorn, was lacking for you, you were unable to keep the magniloquent promises; and of your great collection, announced in special characters, what more did you publish, in the course of a year or a little less, than the subscription manifesto? Time, my dear signor Romani, does a great

* ["Marinetti's" footnote]: I can attest to this, having attended the first two performances, which took place in Venice.

deal *à l'affaire*, and if you still are not convinced, you could convince yourself by rereading the *avvertimenti* that you have placed at the beginning of most of your librettos, singing the usual song in them—that unforeseen necessity, that imperious and unhappy circumstances, that immoderate scarcity of time were the reasons why you could not offer to this or that audience works worthy of it and—which says it all—[offered works] unworthy of yourself, as you wrote in the little preface to *Parisina*.

"You say that the opera that Bellini composed in three months is a stupidity, and I retort that your remark is, yes, a stupidity, for anyone who proffers so shameless a judgment without proof, without in any way validating the assertion, gives evidence of having, not a friendly spirit or critical acumen, but blinding bile and base spite. And among many other proofs, you give evidence of blind bile and spite in your letter when, not knowing how otherwise to lash out against Bellini, you do not blush to allude to a certain subject which, as the cultured man that you are, you should have been unwilling to touch upon. I say no more about that because I have a great fear of awakening in you a remorse for your sin so bitter that it would only sour the glory that you imagine yourself to have acquired by your virulent letter; a letter that you, yourself, in a calmer state of mind, will come to abhor as a wretched exposure of your weakness. Pietro Marinetti."

This paragraph, by Giacinto Battaglia, followed the "Marinetti" letter in that issue of *Il Barbiere di Siviglia*[48]: "If, as editor of the journal, I may be permitted to add two words here, I shall say how saddening it is to see how two distinguished talents, from whom we might expect concord and friendliness concerted toward the best glorification of their names, to the advantage of their noble art, and to the honor of Italy, lose themselves instead in such puerile battles, scarcely worthy of feminine gossip. And, besides, how is the public well served, and to what delight does this chattering contribute, it being unlikely to accomplish anything but make the stupid laugh and divert the malicious and those who would expend a fortune if that would enable them to see these geniuses, whom they envy, collapse under the weight of private enmities and personalities? G. B.-a."

Soon after the appearance of the "Marinetti" letter, *L'Eco* fired off what proved to be the penultimate cannonade in the *Beatrice di Tenda* war.[49] The editor prefaced it with this note: "Having inserted in the Supplement to *L'Eco* No. 40 a letter from signor *Romani* in reply to certain accusations made against him in the name of Maestro *Bellini*, we cannot refuse to insert also what follows, which was provoked by an article that can be read in No. 15 of *Il Barbiere di Siviglia*."

Romani's final outburst reads:

"The champions of theatrical chivalry are born abruptly, like the warriors seeded by Cadmus. I scarcely finish off one of them when, behold, two others spring up; the first goes forth to battle under the name of Pietro Marinetti, a formidable name 'noted,' as Dulcamara[50] says, 'throughout the Universe and other places'; the second presents himself to me under the even more formidable name of G. B.-a; initials that signify something monstrous, as you will see. *Ser Marinetti* assails me *with two words* in three columns, G. B.-a. with a lash of his tail. The thing could scare one to death: except that, looking at the banner under which both of them rally, to the most joyous '*La le ra la*' of *Il Barbiere di Siviglia*, I permit myself to believe that a farce is being acted; and, borrowing the fife and drum with which bears are trained, I shout: ADVANCE, SER MARINETTI!

"And *Ser Marinetti* rushes in, as ferocious as a Captain Coviello,[51] and opens the sluices of his dialectic. Listen to him. He tries to discover if the delay of *Beatrice di Tenda* is owing to me or to *Bellini*. And *ser Marinetti* starts examining the question by protesting that he *does not wish to defend Bellini* because *that defense must be awaited only from him* [Bellini]; but *wishes to give vent to the regret* (gaze upon this pitiful fellow!) *felt by sensitive people at the way—full of sarcasm, personal rancor, and hauteur—I had undertaken to assail my* ANTAGONIST (for in his DICTIONARY[52] anyone DEFENDING HIMSELF is called ASSAILANT!). And he proceeds to demonstrate that *Bellini studies every detail in order to assure himself of the best way to emerge happily from his musical trials* (*Beatrice Tenda* bears witness); and *he speaks of poetic emotions and inspirations and of shabby musical delusions and of subjects chosen at* RANDOM *and of foreign dramatic works, from which tragedies* (and G. B.-a. stealthily inflates these words) *I preserve only the monstrous and immoral aspect.*

"But who delayed *Beatrice Tenda?* I ask. *Beatrice Tenda*, he answers us, *is full of poetry, feeling, and dramatic strength, for I attended the first two performances* (Venice knows it). And he labels as an ignoramus one who *asks* for novelty of motives in the accompaniments too, and speaks of VIADANA and of SOMEONE WHO BLUSHES—and calls *Caterina di Guisa*, *Il Conte d'Essex*, and *Parisina bad librettos* because Bellini did not set them to music—and baptizes them as *fiascos* because when Bellini *produces a fiasco*, all other composers, despite public applause, must also *produce a fiasco*—and he wants me not *to have many strings to my bow*, almost as if he fears for his own—and laments that I [do not] want to emulate Bellini in earning a *long* but *very honest profit from his talent*, as if profit should be only for composers.

"All right, all right . . . but the delay of *Beatrice Tenda!* I add.

"The delay, he goes on is . . . so that *Bellini can meditate for as long as two years over his scores*. And he flies into a rage because I promised *a complete collection of my works* (the adjective *complete* is a pious wish on his part); and he laments that I have not published it up to now, as if it were charged to his expense; and he is disdainful over my having announced it with *special*[53] type (special, Manini! ! !) and over my having *pasted up the manifesto at all the city's hundred street-crossings*, as if all of the city's hundred crossings belonged to him. And he calls me *poor fellow, impudent, blind*; and because I laugh at that, he finally calls me *bilious*!

"But, in short, I insist upon asking who delayed the performance of *Beatrice Tenda?*

"And he continues by feigning ignorance. And he accuses me of having LASHED OUT at Bellini [by mentioning] A CERTAIN SUBJECT, *a thing for which I should feel remorse! ! !* (*Misericordia!*), and calls my letter published in *L'Eco virulent* . . . and talks to me of *glory* . . . and of *weakness* and of so many other trifles that, bored by his logic, I interrupt him with a toot on the fife and . . . FORWARD, G. B.-a.!

"And G. B.-a. steps forward, wagging his tail, and with the air of Tartuffe: and to the question about the blessed delay of *Beatrice Tenda* answers . . . with a tear.

"*And it was really saddening*, he says, *to see* how two distinguished talents that concord and friendship should expect to see *concerted toward the best glorification of their names* and *to the honor of Italy, lose themselves instead in these puerile battles* . . . And, having said that, he forgets having been the wolf who made use of the cat's-paw to pull the chestnut from the fire . . . and I, nauseated more by the hypocrisy of G. B.-a. than by the fury of *ser Marinetti*, give a louder toot on the fife; and *ser Marinetti* and G. B.-a. retreat into their den, where I shall leave them, *o signori*, so as to say a small word to *Bellini*.

"FORWARD, Bellini!

"*Bellini* has disappeared once more . . . But I see a steamship crossing the English Channel with unusual speed, leaving a great column of smoke behind . . . The illustrious Pilgrim is on that ship . . . And I doff my hat to him and shout: Maestro Vincenzo! Again this time your Minerva has led you into error, both as to the nature of the quarrel and as to the strength of your defenders. May you be happier later on! May England help you to cancel out the errors that you have committed in Italy!

"And here the curtain falls, and I protest to certain Journalists that this is the final scene of the Farce; and that for all their slandering of me, and for all the digs that they are giving me, I shall continue my habit of laughing silently at our great men's hallucinations; and, disdaining the judgments of our present-day Aristarchuses, I shall say to them only: Do better, o wiseacres, and then . . . scream. Milan, April 12, 1833, Felice Romani."

To that high-spirited, irrelevant, and inconclusive outburst, Battaglia made only this brief rejoinder:

"THE EDITOR OF IL BARBIERE DI SIVIGLIA

"TO THE READER.

"To the letter of sig. P. Marinetti inserted in No. 15 of *Il Barbiere*, sig. Romani has replied in his favorite critical manner: stupidities and scurrilities manipulated without good manners or principle. I do not deign to answer him, but leave his foolish buffoonery of fife and drum to fall into the oblivion that so long ago swallowed his diatribes against *I Promessi Sposi*, etc., etc., G. B.-a."[54]

There the bloody engagements over *Beatrice di Tenda* ended—until echoes of them were heard in dying fall in letters that Bellini was to write to Romani from Paris in 1834.[55] The two men never met again.

Bellini almost certainly had left Venice on March 26. Where he spent the days from then until his departure from Italy is not known, but he passed some of them with Giuditta Turina in Milan. With her he left his household possessions, including his piano; the full-length portrait of himself against a cloudy sky painted by Carlo Arienti,[56] which he asked her to forward to Florimo as a gift; and some funds, on which she was to get him five per cent interest.[57] He apparently did not give up his rooms in the contrada dei Tre Monasteri: his intention was still to return to Milan in August.

Bellini set out for London on or about April 12, traveling with Giuseppe and Giuditta Pasta, and probably with other Italian members of the troupe that Pierre-François Laporte (recently lessee of Covent Garden and now impresario of the King's Theatre) had signed up for his season.[58] From an undated fragment of a letter to an unnamed correspondent,[59] it is known that Bellini stopped off in Paris en route to Calais and entered into negotiations with Dr. Louis Véron, director of the Opéra, about composing a French opera: "I have delayed my reply," he said, "for a month or two, or until I pass through Paris at the end of July."[60]

When Bellini reached London is not known, but he was there by April 27: on April 29, the *Morning Chronicle* listed as among those who, two days before, had attended a performance of Rossini's *La Cenerentola* at the King's Theatre: Bellini, Charles de Bériot,[61] Henri Herz, Johann Nepomuk Hummel, Maria Malibran, Mendelssohn, Paganini, Pasta, Rubini, and Nicola Vaccaj. Like the Pastas, Bellini settled into rooms at 3, Old Burlington Street. He was already something of a celebrity in London. *Il Pirata*, with Henriette Méric-Lalande in the role that she had created, had introduced him to His Majesty's Theatre on April 17, 1830, and had been followed by *La Sonnambula*, with Pasta as Amina, and *La Straniera*, with Giuditta Grisi as Alaide. At the time of Bellini's arrival, something that passed as *La Sonnambula* was being played at Drury Lane Theatre. This distortion, the vehicle of Malibran's debut in England (May 1, 1833), was an English translation by Samuel Beazley of Romani's libretto, to which Henry Rowley Bishop had "adapted" Bellini's score.[62]

The twenty-four-year-old Mendelssohn, having completed his A-minor ("Italian") Symphony in March, was in England for the third time, to conduct its première at a Philharmonic Society concert on May 13, during which he also played the solo in Mozart's Piano Concerto in D minor, K.466, using his own greatly admired cadenzas. On May 18, *The Spectator* reported that his audience had included Johann Baptist Cramer, Paganini, and Bellini.[63] Mendelssohn obtained for his English friend Sophy Horsley a measure of *Il Pirata* in Bellini's autograph, as well as signatures of Malibran and Pasta. But the contact between him and Bellini seems to have been entirely casual.

Among the other people whom Bellini met in London was Henry William Greville (1801–1872), a younger brother of Charles Cavendish Fulke Greville. This sprightly diplomat was being posted to the British Embassy in Paris, where he and Bellini would develop their friendship during the last two years of Bellini's life. In Greville's diary we read[64]:

"June 23, 1833: I have seen a great deal of Bellini, who is very attractive, very '*fin*,' and at the same time very unsophisticated and natural.

"Calais, Wednesday, June 26: My last three days [in London] were passed in hurrying after commissions and taking leave of friends. On Tuesday I dined with the Wharncliffes, and went for the last time to see *Norma*, and probably to see Pasta for the last time also. I went between the acts with Bellini to her dressing-room, when she invited me very cordially to visit her at her villa at Como. . . . Bellini and I then went and supped with the Duchess of Cannizzaro, after which Bellini and I strolled about the streets for a long while, talking over all sorts of musical subjects. I hope to see him again, for he is original and agreeable." They were exact contemporaries.

Of all anecdotes concerning Bellini, perhaps the most highly colored concerns his first meeting with Maria Malibran. Its only source is a purported letter from Bellini to Florimo, undated, published by Florimo,[65] who described it as having been written from London. No autograph survives, and considerable doubt has been expressed about the accuracy of Florimo's presentation. The anecdote follows Florimo's own description of Malibran's singing in *La Sonnambula* in Naples, and particularly of the end of the opera, after "*Ah, non credea mirarti.*" It reads:

"With regard to the *allegro* of this scene, I believe it suitable to report an anecdote taken from a letter of Bellini's which he wrote me from London: 'The day after my arrival in this great country of *gray sky*, which with much wit was called *of the leaden sky*, I read on theatrical posters (which are carried about by men walking through the streets) the announcement of *La Sonnambula* translated into the English language (with Malibran as the protagonist). More to hear and admire the Diva who, for herself, so occupies the musical world, and whom I did not know except by reputation, I did not fail to betake myself to the theater, having been invited there by one of the most highly placed ladies of the best English aristocracy, the Duchess of Hamilton, who, in parenthesis, sings divinely, having been a pupil of our Crescentini, who, as you know, gave me a letter of introduction to her. I lack words, dear Florimo, to tell you how my poor music was tortured, torn to shreads, and—wanting to express myself in the Neapolitan way—flayed [*scorticata*] by these . . .[66] of Englishmen, the more because it was sung in the language that with reason was called, I don't remember by whom, the language of the birds, and properly of parrots, and of which I still do not understand even a syllable. Only when Malibran was singing did I recognize *La Sonnambula*. But in the *allegro* of the final scene, and precisely at the words '*Ah! m'abbraccia*,'[67] she put such emphasis upon that phrase and expressed such truth by it that first it surprised me and then delighted me so much that, forgetting that I was in an English theater, and not remembering the social customs and the consideration that I owed to the lady on whose right I was seated in her second-tier loge, and disregarding the modesty that a composer should show even if he doesn't feel it, I was the first to shout, at the top of my voice: '*Viva, viva, brava, brava*,' and to clap my hands as much as I could. That southern, even volcanic, transport of mine, quite new in this cold, calculating, and stiff country, surprised and provoked the curiosity of the blond sons of Albion, who asked one another who the bold fellow might be who was permitting himself so much. But after some moments, when it was recognized (I wouldn't know any way of telling you how) that I was the composer of *La Sonnambula*, I was given such a welcome that out of discretion I must be silent about it even with you. Not satisfied with applauding me frantically—even I cannot remember how often—or I with thanking them from the loge where I was, they wanted me at all costs upon the stage, whither I was all but dragged by a crowd of young noblemen who said that they were enthusiasts of my music, and whom I didn't have the honor even of recognizing. Among them was the son of the already praised Duchess of Hamilton, the Marquess of Douglas, a youth who has all the poetry of Scotland in his soul and all the fire of the Neapolitans in his heart. The first person to advance to meet me was Malibran, and, throwing her arms around my neck, she said to me in the most exalted transport of joy, with those four notes of mine: '*Ah! m'abbraccia!*' and said nothing more. My emotion was at its climax; I thought that I was in Paradise; I could not utter a word, but stood there stunned, and I remember nothing more. . . . The tumultuous and repeated plaudits of an English audience, which becomes frantic once it has warmed up, called me to the front of the stage; we presented ourselves holding one another by the hand: you imagine the rest. . . . What I can tell you is that never in my life shall I be able to feel a greater emotion. From that moment, I became an intimate friend of Malibran; she shows me all the admiration that she has for my music, and I [show] her what I feel for her immense talent; and I have promised to write an opera for her on a subject to her liking. That thought electrifies me now, dear Florimo. Farewell . . .' "[68]

Reprinting that admittedly very circumstantial letter, Luisa Cambi included it, with other undated fragments of purported London letters from Bellini to Florimo, as "of dubious authenticity." Pastura cast doubt upon it less directly[69]: "No trace remains of this noisy episode in the letter written to [Bellini's] friend Lamperi on May 16—that is, not more than thirteen days after it had occurred. In that letter we read only[70]: 'My *Sonnambula* is being given at the Drury Lane in the English language, the protagonist being Mme Malibran, who performs it with great taste[71]; the opera has aroused constantly waxing fanaticism . . .' It seems very strange that Bellini does not mention to his Turinese friend that clamorous encounter, which had taken place so short a time before, and even stranger the fact that in the letter written more than a month later to Santocanale,[72] Malibran, her interpretation of *La Sonnambula*, and the episode of the meeting seem to have been forgotten completely. My observations are simply that; nor should I advance doubts about a fact depending wholly upon Florimo's memory and scruples."

That Florimo invented the letter, and with it the episode, seems unbelievable. That he "edited" it—which well may have meant bringing together, to form a new text, sections from several now unavailable letters—is likely, his lack of scholarly scruples when handling documents being, despite Pastura, beyond question. That Bellini met Malibran and admired her can be documented. What cannot be proved or disproved, but appears unlikely in the extreme, is the frequently repeated assertion that she and Bellini rushed into a brief, impassioned liaison. She had been living with Charles de Bériot for some time; he was with her in London; she was impatiently awaiting her divorce from Malibran so that she could marry him—and only three months before singing in *La Sonnambula* in London, she had had a son by him. The story of the Bellini–Malibran liaison is much less credible than the meeting reported with so much confirmatory detail by Florimo.

Before Bellini left London for Paris in August, Malibran gave him two miniatures that she herself had painted. One of them is an oval containing a likeness of him which Pastura described[73] as "noted above all for the curious stylization of his curly hair [which here resembles swirls of yarn], a good resemblance in the molding of the face and the feature of the self-willed jaw." The other, also oval, is a self-portrait set into a small gold brooch with a looped gold ribbon surrounding it. Bellini later often wore it at the knot of a silk cravat.[74] It shows Malibran with her right hand raised to touch her long, loosed hair.

Some of the London social life in which Bellini took pleasure is suggested further by side-glimpses of him in a letter of Giuditta Pasta's and in the memoirs of Lady Morgan. On May 6, Pasta wrote to her mother[75]: "Yesterday I was very much occupied with the rehearsal of *Tancredi;* the rehearsal of the concert of old music; then I sang at Hummel's concert, and in the evening at the grand concert of the Marchioness of Landsdowne [*sic*], which, Heaven be praised, went marvelously—and how should it not have? Malibran, Rubini, Tamburini, and *la* [*sic*] *Galli* were there. You already know that the aforementioned Marchioness always wants me to take part in her concert, for which reason I am even more pleased by her success. Bellini, who was there as an onlooker, nevertheless had the goodness to accompany me in 'Casta diva,' which pleased very much. San Quirico [*sic*, for Alessandro Sanquirico] (the famous scenographer) has arrived in the best of health, with Marietti (Milanese impresario).[76]

"I beg you to say many affectionate words for me to the dearest [Giuditta] Turina . . ."

Lady Morgan (née Sidney Owenson), an ardent Italophile and music-lover who had known Rossini in Naples, eagerly welcomed Bellini. In her diary for June 24, 1833, she wrote[77]: "To-day had a visit from Madame Pasta, more naïve than ever; she told us she was near getting into prison at Naples, for singing out of *Tancredi, Cara Patria;* and she said orders were given to omit the word 'liberta' in all her songs. . . . Bellini came in, and Pasta, Bellini, and José* went through one act of his *Norma.* Bellini was charmed with José's voice. . . ."

(July 1, 1833) "Pasta and Bellini jumped out of a hackney-coach at our door to-day, with a roll of music in their hands,—it was the score of the *Norma,* they came, Pasta said, from the second rehearsal. Bellini scolded his great pupil like a *petite pensionnaire.* . . ."

(July 6, 1833) " 'Do you,' I asked [Pasta], 'transport yourself into

---

* "José" was the nickname of Lady Morgan's niece, Josephine Clarke, later Mrs. Geale.

your part?' *'Oui, après les premières lignes. Je commence toujours en Giuditta (mon nom) mais je finis toujours en Medea ou Norma!'* [Yes, after the first lines. I always begin as Giuditta (my name), but I always finish as Medea or Norma]."

(August 4, 1833) "Yesterday Bellini and [Vincenzo] Gabussi[78] came, and sang and played like angels. Lucien Bonaparte came in as they were singing—

> 'O bella Italia che porte tre color
> Sei bianca e rosa e Verde co'un fiore!'
> [O beautiful Italy, which bears three colors,
> You are white and rose and green like a flower!]

Lucien exhibited a suppressed emotion that was very touching. . . ."

(August 15, 1833) "Yesterday was curious and interesting; people coming in to take leave of us. We had at the same moment, [Thomas] Moore, Madame Pasta, Bellini, Gabussi. . . ."

Fifty-three years later, on March 13, 1886, Mrs. Josephine Geale— "José"—wrote from Dublin to Florimo and Michele Scherillo, who were then preparing the *Album-Bellini*[79] that they issued later that year to signalize the unveiling of a monument to Bellini in Naples:

"In the Memoirs of my aunt, Lady Morgan, I read the following paragraphs:

" 'Bellini came in, and together with Pasta and José (the diminutive of my name) we read one act of his *Norma*. Bellini remained pleased with my niece's voice.[80]

" 'The news of dear Bellini's death reaches me! Bellini and don Idesfore de Trueba, those two superb emanations of genius extinct! Oh! to think that only the idiots remain here below to bore us eternally!'

"To my aunt's memories I add my own impressions of that unique genius.

"I shall never forget his noble and graceful person, those blond and curly locks of his, and his eyes . . . Oh! the eyes of the divine Bellini!— blue in color, of an absolutely incomparable placidity of expression.

"I could describe them with our phrase 'sleepy blue eyes.' And the entire appearance of the great artist gave me the impression of a fine English type.

"I shall never forget the singular expression of his body when, seated at our piano, he improvised notes that made palpitate in my young girl's heart the first and greatest musical impressions of my life!"

Laporte's season at the King's Theatre opened on one of the last days of April 1833,[81] with Pasta in one of her most famous roles, the Medea of Mayr's *Medea in Corinto*. On May 16, Bellini reported by letter to

Alessandro Lamperi.[82] In part, he wrote: "A cough that came upon me strongly during the steamer trip from Calais to London has subsided, but a little of it is still with me; however, the physician has not diagnosed it as influenza because no fever accompanied it. I thank you for the care you have taken of *la L. . . .*[83]

"Let's turn to the London news. It is useless to tell you about the city! be satisfied [to know] that it is the first in the world and can be compared only to ancient, wealthy Tyre. At the Drury Lane Theatre, my *Sonnambula* was presented in the English language, Mª Malibran taking the part of the protagonist and performing it with great taste; the opera aroused fanatical reactions and does so increasingly.

"Up to now, Pasta has sung *Anna Bolena* and *Medea;* she has been applauded incredibly in both operas. London has found her in stronger voice and younger. When we meet the next time, I'll tell you my feelings about Malibran and Pasta in confidence: for now, it's enough for you that the latter is incomparable, especially in the sublime-tragic.

"Today at 15, *Il Pirata* goes on stage, sung by Pasta, Rubini, and Tamburini, and it is for Rubini's benefit evening; *Norma* will go on at the beginning of June for Pasta's benefit evening.[84]

"I can report that I am amused here, and a lot, by the continuous balls, the theater, suppers, concerts, the country, etc. I know all London, and therefore they all invite me. So much that I am being suffocated by so many diversions. Because I don't know the language or the streets, I was unable to go this morning to see the signor conte Nomis di Pollone,[85] but tomorrow I'll call upon him to deliver in person the present letter, to be forwarded to you.

"So you see I naturally find myself in the midst of a world of beautiful women, and truly of celestial beauties; but I indulge in nothing but sentiment, and that is little for someone who must leave the country within two months, and therefore I put more value upon friendship than upon love, so as not to run the risk of acquiring a wife.

"*Addio*, my dear Lamperi. I'll write to you as often as possible, to give you the news of the day, as you'll do on your part. Receive warmest greetings from signora Pasta and her husband, and give thousands of mine to your kind wife, the Bilotti couple, the Grosson family,[86] the beautiful young lady who speaks to you of me, etc., etc. . . .

"When you see the Barabino family, all my respects to them, and tell *la Remondini* always to give you news of *la Lucchina*,[87] which you will pass on to me: in the meantime, all good and affectionate wishes on my part. *Addio*, my dear friend, receive an embrace from your Bellini."

After quoting sentences from that letter, Pastura wrote[88]: "In this description . . . one recognizes that particular euphoric tone which Bellini took on each time that he felt he had conquered a new ambiance in which he was admired and cosseted by people enthusiastic about his music and himself: the frivolous tone of that worldly Bellini whom Heinrich Heine would caricature in a year or so. His rapid renown in the great world of London probably was owing in largest part to the success of *La Sonnambula* and to the theatrical encounter—according to Florimo's report—with Malibran at Drury Lane, but in view of the ever-difficult high English society, it is much more likely that the means of his introduction into it, beyond his presentation by Pasta, had been the friendship of Lady Hamilton and of Lady Christina Dudley-Stuart,[89] whom he had known in Genoa in 1828 and had met again in London during that summer."

After the performances of Mayr's *Medea in Corinto*, Rossini's *Tancredi*, Donizetti's *Anna Bolena*, and *Il Pirata*—a Bellini opera already known to London—on June 21, the delayed *Norma* was played at the King's Theatre for the first time, with Pasta in the title role, Joséphine de Méric as Adalgisa, Donzelli as Pollione, and Vincenzo Galli as Oroveso. The next day, Giuseppe Pasta wrote to Rachele Negri, his mother-in-law[90]:

"*Norma* was performed last night as Giuditta's benefit. The best of London society crowded in. Neither *Medea* nor *Anna Bolena* can boast of greater success than this first performance of *Norma;* thanks to my insistence with Laporte and because of Bellini's having directed orchestra and choruses, this opera is mounted in a way unexampled at the Italian Theatre of London; the triumph therefore surpasses Giuditta's desire and Bellini's hope; the applause was extraordinary, and there were more than a few tears during the second act. Giuditta seemed possessed by the character, and displayed the strength of which her constitution is capable only when stirred by some extraordinary motivation. She accompanied Bellini onto the stage, and both of them were saluted with an expression of enthusiasm.

"The ladies were magnificently dressed and shone with diamonds, and on this occasion, the English public displayed such intelligence and so much taste that the third performance at the King's Theatre[91] seemed the twentieth of *Norma* at the great Teatro della [*sic*] Scala. Donzelli displayed all the power of his beautiful voice, and the cavatina ["*Casta diva*"] was considered the most enchanting piece in the first act. '*Costui, costui dicesti,*' '*trema per i figli tuoi,*' '*Il mio sdegno ruggirà intorno a te*' made an enormous impression; beginning then with the chorus '*guerra, guerra,*' and until the throwing of the black veil over Norma's head, each action, each word of Giuditta's was received with signs, now of surprise, now of affection, now of enthusiasm. Shortly I shall send you the journals, which certainly will say more than has been said up to now of Giuditta and Bellini."

The *Morning Post* was unreserved in praising *Norma* and the singers: the performance, it said, had been greeted "with enthusiastic applause that ended only when Madame Pasta, accompanied by the Sigg. Donzelli and Bellini, presented herself to receive reiterated indications of admiration from the packed spectators." *Galignani's Messenger*, however, sounded a discord: "A new opera finally has been given, Madame Pasta having selected Bellini's *Norma* for her Thursday benefit. We were not prepared to expect much from Bellini, and therefore the outcome did not disappoint us. The scene is set in Gaul, but the music in the opera is everything but Gallic. . . . Pasta sang and acted in her accustomed manner. We have often had occasion to speak of her very false intonation, but never, either from her or from any other well-known singer, have we heard this grave imperfection carried to greater excess. It would not be exaggerated to say that not a single phrase of the entire opera was sung on the correct pitch. In the first-act prayer [*"Casta diva"*], Pasta strayed so far from the pitch as to leave one almost fearing a change of key; and in the trio at the end of the prayer,[92] the strings had to follow her false intonation, whereas the flutes and the clarinets found themselves driven to silence. Fortunately, De Méric had to repeat the same passage, and her correct ear brought the orchestra back to the lost road. All the concerted pieces (the opera has no arias!) in which Pasta took part suffered from the same cause; and it required her power as an actress to save her from disaster. . . ."

The writer in *Gallignani's*, deaf though he seems to have been to the qualities of *Norma*, prejudiced against Pasta though he may sound, may well have had a sharper ear than his colleagues with regard to her intonation. For she more and more sang off pitch. As Eugenio Gara wrote[93]: "A certain wear and tear nonetheless began to show itself, the 'gray' evenings were more frequent. . . . At Paris too—autumn 1833—the most expert observers advanced serious reservations." Pasta was only thirty-five, but from a strictly vocal point of view, her greatest days were beginning to draw in. She sang in opera for about eight years more, but with varying results and with constantly increasing dependence upon her histrionic talent.

The Times, reporting after the second singing of *Norma*, generally praised the performers—and understood the opera itself as what it was: "Bellini rose, with his style, to a genre of composition more elevated than anything else he has done up to now, and succeeded in obtaining an effect full of nobility and beauty. His music moves along sublimely and with grandiosity, and could sustain comparison with various operas of Rossini in their passionate, well-coloured combinations. In any case, he excels Donizetti in the vigour and character of his music, and seduces the listener's mind with superior talents and feelings that Donizetti would not know how to master."

On June 28, *Norma* was repeated again as one part of Laporte's own benefit night. That astonishing program also presented Paganini, "who has obligingly offered his services" to play "some of his celebrated variations"; Act III of Rossini's *Otello*, with Malibran as Desdemona; the ballet *La Sylphide*, with Marie Taglioni in the role that she had created at the Opéra, Paris, on March 12, 1832; and a group of *pas de deux* featuring Fanny Elssler. The London correspondent of *L'Eco*, Milan (July 10, 1833), referring to Paganini as "the man-violin," reported that his success at this benefit had been "colossal."

On June 26, in a letter to Filippo Santocanale, Bellini wrote in part[94]: "*Norma* has gone on stage in the theater here, and, behold, I enclose the description of its success from *The Times* of June 23, 1833. A like success cannot be recalled in the English theater. Pasta is always prodigious. Donizelli sings very well, and the choruses not so badly. It is a magnificent city, and the first of the world; and such magnificence is to be beheld in the architecture, in the huge, very beautiful, luxuriously fitted-out carriages, in the houses, and in the evening parties, of which there are two, three, four each evening, and all to divert the most melancholy being on this earth. If it were not so far from Italy, I'd come back here often, both because the inhabitants [here] are very kind and because the women have an enchanting, ideal beauty—in a word, one leads a blessed life; still, it does not succeed in blessing me as much as I was blessed when I found myself in the bosom of my Sicily during those brief months! ! ! I still do not foresee returning here very soon; but I do not mean to let so much time pass again without seeing my native land. . . ."

"P.S. I think that I'll give *I Capuleti* in this theater at about the beginning of next month."

But not until Saturday, July 20, 1833 (replacing the announced *Beatrice di Tenda*)[95] was *I Capuleti e i Montecchi* sung in London for the first time, with Pasta (Romeo), De Méric (Giulietta), Donzelli (Tebaldo), and Galli (Capellio). *The Times* (obviously in the person of another critic) liked it only mildly and doubted that it would have the success won earlier by Zingarelli's *Giulietta e Romeo*; the writer added that Bellini's opera had been received indifferently on the Continent. Bellini, this anonymous writer observed, might be versed in the theory of his art, but manifestly lacked inventiveness; little in the opera was new; it contained imitations of operas both by others and by Bellini himself. Generously, however, this critic added that at least it was better than *Norma*.

The amount that Bellini earned in England is uncertain. On December 1, 1931, this notice appeared in the *Corriere musicale dei piccoli*, Florence (p. 17): "The archivist of Covent Garden, Richard Northcott, has acquired in Vienna the original contract that Bellini signed with Laporte, the impresario of the King's Theatre. In it, Bellini agreed to come to London on May 1, 1833, to direct all of his operas to be staged at the King's Theatre. Laporte promised to pay him 100 pounds sterling on his reaching London and guaranteed him a further compensation of 300." Luisa Cambi reported[96]: "When I wrote to the Management of Covent Garden for a copy of the document, I was told in reply that no such document existed at that theatre." Cicconetti asserted[97]—on what evidence he did not specify—that Bellini's contract stipulated that Laporte was to pay him 12,000 francs.[98] He did not, it is clear, match the financial accomplishment of Rossini, who during a seven-month stay in London in 1823–1824 had earned enough to lay solidly the basis of his future large fortune. Bellini is said, however, to have received two valuable gifts in England: from Queen Adelaide, a chased gold case containing a large gold ring set with diamonds, and from Lady Christina Dudley-Stuart a gold stiletto (paper-cutter?) inlaid with precious stones.

The date of Bellini's departure from London cannot be determined,[99] but he reached Paris for the second time in mid-August 1833. He was never to leave France again.

(IX)

1833-1835: The Break with Giuditta Turina; Paris; *I Puritani*

O N JUNE 21, 1833, the day of the first London *Norma*, Bellini added affectionate lines to a letter that Giuseppe Pasta had written to his mother-in-law[1]: "Dear *mamma* Rachele, Peppino always forgets to remember poor Bellini to you, but from today on, I'll do it myself in the letters that I write to Giuditta Turina, who always sends me most affectionate lines about the affection that you have showed her, especially during this last unhappy occasion . . ." That "occasion" had come about in May. It had been the discovery by Ferdinando Turina of compromising letters from Bellini to his wife and his consequent decision to eject her from their home and seek a legal separation.[2] When Bellini heard this disquieting news, gossip was busy implicating him in other "love affairs," and even in intentions to marry. He did not suggest that Giuditta join him in London or Paris. Rather, he saw her new situation as an opportunity to terminate his own thinned-out relationship with her. For him, enjoying a clandestine liaison with a well-situated married woman was very different from taking on sole responsibility for her. He did not mean to share his life with Giuditta, and she remained in far-away Milan. No evidence is available, however, to justify Luisa Cambi's assertion[3] that after Bellini's break with Romani over *Beatrice di Tenda*, "A cold hatred of Giuditta, the unintentional cause of it all, seized him. He bore her a grudge for having followed him to Venice, for having had, because of her, to break off all relations with a man who for him was not only a valuable collaborator, but also one of his dearest friends . . ." Giuditta certainly had not, in a pejorative sense, "followed" Bellini to Venice; she had not in any discoverable way caused any of his difficulties with Romani over

Beatrice di Tenda. And no sign of any emotion approaching "hatred" of her would be consonant with Bellini's nature.

The next reference to Giuditta in Bellini's surviving letters occurs in one that he wrote to Florimo from Paris on March 11, 1834[4]: "I constantly am being threatened from Milan with Giuditta's coming to Paris; but I still have received no reply to the letters that I wrote to the contessa Martini,[5] which I think will produce their effect; if they don't, I shall leave Paris, as I no longer want to be put in the position of renewing a relationship that made me suffer great troubles." A few other references to Giuditta appear in Bellini's later correspondence, and in 1834 they briefly exchanged letters.[6] It was again to Florimo, from Puteaux, that on August 4, 1834, Bellini wrote[7]: "I have no more news of Giuditta. I swear to you that I remember her with regret and see that I have not in fact forgotten her; but the mere notion of attaching myself to her still another time frightens me." She was a publicly accused adultress—and she was chronically unwell.

Giuditta's view of the matter naturally was different. Her attitude is preserved in a highly emotional letter that she wrote to Florimo from Milan on February 18, 1834[8]: "Only today did I receive a letter from you which reached here on January 26, but was delayed in getting to me by a mistake of the postoffice. You found the letter of my friend [*amica*—the contessa Martini] cold, but I do not understand why, as my friend wanted to show you, a friend of Bellini, the condition to which his behavior has reduced me. I, who know your heart, have no need to read the letter that you wrote Bellini in order to be persuaded of your friendship, of which I have had too many proofs to doubt it for a single moment.

"The expression 'to graze the still-aching wound when offering words of peace'—it is that everything I believe to be a reference to Bellini does me so much harm that I don't know how to put it into words; thus, your telling me to come to Naples made me think that you were trying to separate me from him, and I did not believe that it was because of my husband, whereas of all the troubles and losses suffered, I feel only the loss of Bellini's affection and am obsessed with him to my misfortune. When he was in Venice last year, there was a zealot there, the sort always to be found, who told Bellini that a certain man was paying court to me and that he stayed with me one night until two o'clock in the morning; I assured Bellini that it was not true, and I have a thousand witnesses who can attest to that; he treated me very badly almost as soon as I reached Venice, but everything worked out, and we were very happy together by the time he left for London. You must know that last year my husband received an anonymous letter speaking of our relations, and that he did not want me to go to Venice. Bellini wanted it, and so I insisted to my husband so much that I extracted his permission. That was a false step, and perhaps the beginning of the storm that broke in May, but what would I not have done for Bellini! He writes me from Paris that during the past eighteen months his love has cooled, so why, then, when I begged him never to write anything that might compromise me, did he instead write those letters which fell into my husband's hands, and then afterwards write blaming his great love, which could not be restricted to writing simple, neutral phrases? Why, instead of waiting until September [1833] to write me of his having cooled, didn't he write me the moment that he learned of my troubles with my husband? perhaps things would be very different; instead, he wrote that he hoped that if my husband abandoned me, I would not abandon him [Bellini], and I, what do I do? I tread underfoot interests, reputation, everything, and think only of Bellini, whom I always have valued above everything else, and when he begs my pardon for the troubles that he has caused me, what do I answer? that only the loss of his affection could make me unhappy, and he takes that away from me at the moment when it is my only support! and what are his motives? the jealousies at Venice and the other gossipings retailed in Paris, one of them in a letter, and I have authentic proofs of its falsity. I did not give Bellini any answer about those accusations, for I should have felt that I was degrading myself; all my friends, seeing to what a condition my health and my morale had been reduced, wrote him about my situation, but would you believe it, Florimo, he answered them all by defaming my reputation so as to excuse his behavior, and took not the slightest interest in my condition. Bellini should have known me well enough not to believe all the gossip of idle people; I'll say further that I am convinced that he doesn't believe it in his heart, but does so in appearance only because it suits him to do so and because the stories fit into his plans. He says his career *avant tout,* and that's the way he speaks to a woman who has sacrificed everything for him? to a woman who for five years has loved him with the ardor and purity with which the angels adore the Divinity? and who, in spite of his cruel and indelicate behavior, loves him still? Did I damage his careeer during those five years? it seems to me that everything moved forward under full sail. I did not require that he should neglect what Paris offered him; who more than I could have shared in his triumphs? He could have raised his reputation through music, but there was no reason for him to debase it by his behavior, whereas I assure you that the admiration of the Milanese for Bellini has been replaced by contempt, a thing that hurts me greatly, and I would like Bellini to be able to justify himself in the eyes of the public. To be the cause of my separation and then to abandon me, however, is a grievous and a cruel thing. If he believes that I, as a woman without ties, could perhaps have gone to Paris (a thing he would not have loved), that would be proof that he thought me very affectionate to be able to be- have that way, and he is to be censured all the more for treating me as he does. I took pleasure in my freedom as a way of dedicating myself ent' ·ly to him, and I would have behaved myself exactly as he would b   ·ed. He would have been able to compose part of the opera   another time, I should have been able to go to Switzerland to   , and without damage to himself or to me, and without trampling   so tender an affection, he would have been able to continue his   .er. But enough, Destiny willed it thus, but Bellini will not be able   ʝ avoid feeling remorse. In Paris, he will find women more beautiful than I am—but never, never will they love him with the strength of the love that I still feel. But forgive me, dear Florimo, for this long and tiresome letter; but I have not been able to do less than open my heart to the friend of the one who treats me so unjustly and so cruelly. I'll send you the lithographs.[9] Write to me from time to time, and believe me always the same Affectionate friend Giuditta."

Frank Walker wrote[10]: "This absorbing document leads us to the following conclusions:

(1) Giuditta's visit to Venice was occasioned by jealousy on Bellini's part, rather than on hers, as has been thought, and he cannot reasonably have "har- boured rancour against her for having followed him" if she did so at his own request.[11]

(2) The love-affair was concealed from Ferdinando, who, so far as Giuditta herself knew, first learned about it from the anonymous letter. She must have lied to him, denying that Bellini's role went beyond that of a *cavaliere servente*, if she finally obtained permission to go to Venice. Romani's indiscretions can, at the most, only have contributed towards awakening, or re-awakening, sus- picion in Ferdinando's mind, the real crisis following in May 1834 [*sic, for* 1833], when he discovered some love-letters from Bellini to his wife.

(3) Giuditta's obviously genuine distress disposes completely of any idea that Bellini's love was used merely as a 'pretext' to obtain a separation.

(4) Bellini suddenly broke off the relationship by letter in September 1834 [*sic, for* 1833], alleging infidelity on Giuditta's part, and maintaining that his own love had cooled eighteen months [*sic*] before—*i.e.*, at about the time of the visit to Naples [1832].

Bellini, on his part, would be mentioning Giuditta in a letter to Florimo only one month before his death in 1835.[12]

Bellini returned to Paris in mid-August 1833 with no determination to remain there: as late as June 26, he intended to stay only about three

weeks. One of his first efforts in Paris was to try to complete the negotiations with the Opéra which he had begun en route to London. "In fact,
after five months, I was in Paris again," he would write to Vincenzo
Ferlito from there on April 1, 1835,[13] "and, talking again with the aforementioned director [Louis-Désiré Véron], could not arrange anything
because of the divergence of our interests; then the management of the
Théâtre-Italien made me offers that I found it advantageous to accept,
first because the pay was richer than what I had received in Italy up
to then, though by only a little; then because of so magnificent a company; and finally so as to remain in Paris at others' expense."

With Rossini's approval, his friends Édouard Robert and Carlo
Severini—respectively director and administrator of the Théâtre-Italien
—had begun to pursue Bellini soon after his arrival from London. On
September 19, 1833, Severini wrote him in Robert's name to say that an
orchestra seat at the Salle Favart (Théâtre-Italien) had been reserved for
him for the duration of his stay in Paris[14]: "The Administration begs
you to be willing to accept [this] feeble testimony of its esteem for
your character and its admiration for your talent." Further, the Italien
that season would present both *Il Pirata* (October) and *I Capuleti e i Montecchi* (November). Because the roster of singers included Giulia Grisi,
Caroline Unger, and Rubini, the success of Bellini's operas was assured.

Pastura took the existence of the Robert-Severini letter as proof
that, by September 19, Bellini had decided to remain in Paris. But as
late as October 18, nothing had been arranged definitely: writing to
Alessandro Lamperi on that day, Bellini said[15]: "It seems to me that in
my last letter I said that I was almost resolved to spend the winter in
Paris, and perhaps I'll come to some arrangement with the theaters[16] with
which I am negotiating; for that reason, it is useless to talk further about
my coming [to Turin] to stage my *Norma;* meanwhile, I must not fail to
tell you that if [Giuseppe] Consul[17] thinks of paying me for my efforts
at the same rate that he will pay others, he must give up having me."

Bellini's alternately awestruck, worshipful, fearful, and sycophantic
attitudes toward Rossini—whose advice the men at the Italien constantly
sought—led him to beliefs for which no justification can be found, and
which ill match what we know of Rossini's nature. To Florimo, in a
letter dated at Paris on March 3–4, 1835, Bellini could write[18]: "It
was true, very true, that before I approached him, Rossini did not in
fact love me, and spoke badly of me, and ridiculed my music as much
as possible . . ." In the letter of April 1 to Vincenzo Ferlito cited above,
he said: "But in that period Rossini was my fiercest enemy, solely because of the profession, etc., etc."[19] That Rossini, who after four years

of operatic idleness, showed no intention of composing another opera, should have been jealous of Bellini (whose most recent opera had not been a success) is unlikely. The two certainly saw one another when Rossini returned to Paris after a summer stay at the country villa of his lavish patron, Aguado.[20] Bellini more than once climbed the narrow stairs to the tiny apartment above the Salle Favart in which Rossini was living. Too, he soon found it prudent to be noticeably polite to Rossini's recently acquired nurse-mistress, Olympe Pélissier.

Although Bellini's negotiations produced no contract to compose a new opera, he settled into three very small rooms in a group of buildings known as the Bains chinois. This was made up of houses of several shapes and sizes dominated by a tower painted in imitation of Chinese lacquer and including a public bath. It was in the boulevard des Italiens, not far from the Salle Favart. Bellini's rooms took up one floor of the tower itself. He would describe them to Florimo in a letter from Puteaux dated September 4, 1834[21]: "I have already written Giud.^tta [Giuditta Turina] not to sell everything, but to send [some of the furniture] to me to Paris to add to my furniture, with which I shall be able to furnish three rooms for five hundred francs, Parisian houses being tiny. I already have a pianoforte, which, with just two chairs, occupies a room in the Bains chinois; so you can imagine the tininess of the apartments. I'll have sheets, towels, silver, candlesticks, etc., etc. sent from Milan, and with a little I'll fix up a home." Those rooms on the boulevard des Italiens were to be his city home for the rest of his life.

As a notably handsome young bachelor, an internationally famous composer of opera, and an Italian away from Italy, Bellini soon was welcomed to the flourishing salon of that romantic exile, Cristina di Trivulzio, principessa Belgioioso, whom he had met in Milan. There, in the rue de Montparnasse, as Pastura pointed out,[22] he probably met such other habitués of her soirées as Victor Hugo, Alfred de Musset, George Sand, Alexandre Dumas *père*, Heinrich Heine, Jules Michelet, Louis-Adolphe Thiers, François-Pierre-Guillaume Guizot, Chopin, Liszt, Augustin Thierry, and—the principessa's special favorites—fellow-exiles from Italy, including Vincenzo Gioberti, Alessandro Poerio, Pellegrino Rossi, Nicolò Tommaseo, and—most important for Bellini—conte Carlo Pepoli of Bologna. As Bellini knew little French (he never learned to speak or write the language with even the approximate correctness of his Italian), he cannot have carried on more than superficial conversations with anyone who did not speak some Italian. But he never needed or sought stimuli among extra-musical ideas except from the situations, and especially the language, of librettos; what he required, as always, was a favorable contract, a good libretto, and assurance of a suitable roster of singers. His fame was growing constantly: very soon, he himself was a minor Parisian lion.

Of the other Italian musicians then in Paris, Bellini probably already knew—in addition to the reigning Rossini—both Michele Enrico Carafa and Ferdinando Paër. Of the Paris visitors from elsewhere, he became acquainted, if only superficially, with not only Chopin and Liszt, but also Friedrich Wilhelm Kalkbrenner and Ferdinand Hiller. Among the French musicians, he met the aged, ailing Boieldieu, Fromental Halévy, and Pierre-Joseph-Guillaume Zimmerman. The most imposing musical figure in Paris after Rossini was another Italian, the septuagenarian, much-feared director-dictator of the Conservatoire, Luigi Cherubini, who welcomed Bellini to his small apartment in the faubourg Poissonière and later (1835) invited him to write in his autograph album. In response, Bellini was to compose for the album a two-voice canon for soprano and contralto (or, alternatively, for tenor and bass), with piano accompaniment, to lines by Guid(d)icioni: "*Dalla guancia scolorita,/dalla torbida pupilla,/passa il duolo colla vita;/sol con essa ha fine amor . . .*" (From the faded glove, from the troubled eye, sorrow passes away with life; only then does love end . . .).[23]

On December 22, 1833, Bellini had written to Vincenzo Ferlito[24]: "I have just got out of bed, where I remained a whole week because of a high fever resulting from a cold. . . . I can't report anything new since the last letter I wrote you. *Il Pirata* and *I Capuleti* are still being performed and are still pleasing [audiences] . . . The other evening, Donizetti's *Gianni da* [*sic*] *Calais* went on stage and was a fiasco. . . ."[25] He had nothing to tell his friends about himself except that he had decided to tarry in Paris indefinitely. He had not composed anything operatic since March 1833, when he had written the last notes of *Beatrice di Tenda* in Venice. Finally, in January 1834, he signed a contract to provide the Théâtre-Italien with a new opera to be staged by the end of that year. That news calmed the nerves of Florimo, who had begun to denounce Bellini by letter for lazing away his time: Bellini's London friend Henry Greville had met Florimo in Naples and had complained to him of Bellini's protracted inactivity. On March 11, Bellini confessed to Florimo[26]: "I know about your meeting with Greville, who has written me to report the conversations about my laziness which he had with you; my dear friends, you are right, and I confess that I feel great remorse over all the lost time; but if you reflect for a moment that a young man in my position, in London and Paris for the first time, cannot help amusing himself immensely, you will excuse me. It is with great effort that now, after a year of real death, I can get used to reading music and writing a few notes. You can't imagine the opportunities for diversion to be met with in these places, things it is impossible to give up; therefore, while I try to apply myself seriously in the attempt to make up for the evil done, let's not discuss it any more."

At about the time when Bellini signed the contract with the Italien, the secretary of the society newly in charge of the Royal Theaters of Naples, a cavaliere Galeota, wrote to him, inviting him to compose an opera for the Teatro San Carlo for the Carnival season of 1834-1835. Answering Galeota on February 14[27] and sending an approximate copy of the letter to Florimo the same day,[28] Bellini wrote that he must decline the invitation because the contract with the Royal Italian Theater of Paris required him to compose an *opera seria* and stage it at the end of the year. He might, he said, be able to provide Naples with an opera by May 30, 1835. "Consequently, *signor cavaliere*, as soon as the Teatro [San Carlo] shall have fixed the 1835 company (for you know that I have never arranged a contract without knowing the people for whom I shall be composing) . . . you will be kind enough to advise me, and then we shall discuss the terms that the contract should include."

As soon as Florimo learned of the invitation to Bellini, he began to exert all possible pressure on him to accept it. He wrote about the extraordinary success of Malibran in *Norma* at the San Carlo in March and held out the powerful lure that she would be the chief protagonist of the new opera, the society having assured her presence during January 1835. However, Bellini remained cautious, writing to Florimo on March 11[29]: "Malibran's success in *Norma*, which you described to me, brought me great pleasure . . . I understand your opinion that because Malibran has been signed up for Carnival, I should agree to compose the opera for Naples for January rather than later; but what shall I do, my dear Florimo, to find librettos? I am about to lose my mind over the plot of the opera for Paris, as it has been impossible to find a subject suitable for my purpose and adaptable to the company; therefore it is not possible for me to risk accepting the two obligations, both the opera for Paris and the opera for Naples, places that are very important because this is the first time that I shall be composing an opera with a realization of the expectation that both places rightly feel. You are correct that to have Malibran is already a likelihood of success, but do you also know that, having to compose for May, I might perhaps have both Rubini and Tamburrini [*sic*], with [Giuseppina Ronzi de] Begnis? . . . Now tell me why the Management or the Society doesn't make a contract with Romani; not for just one libretto, but by the year, calculating a thousand francs per libretto, with the understanding that he come to live in Naples; thus he could write the libretto for me as the only poet attached to the theater, and if they want to negotiate

with him, they can commission me to arrange it; I'd like to return good
for evil to that wrongheaded and very talented man. . . ."

In that letter, too, Bellini said: "In the meantime, I want to see how
conte [Carlo] Pepoli will do this libretto for Paris; I hope that he will
succeed, and perhaps very well, as he makes good verses and does them
easily." In a letter of March 12 to conte Giacomo Barbò, Bellini was
more specific[30]: "I am looking for the subject, and hope to find it
quickly, or to choose among three or four that have been proposed to
me. Conte Pepoli will write the poetry for me. He is well known in
Italy, as you are aware, and therefore something is to be hoped for. . . ."
Conte Carlo Pepoli (1801–1860), whose family had been prominent in
Bologna for centuries, was in exile because he had served in a provisional
revolutionary government in 1831. As a clever versifier, he had been
praised by Leopardi, but he had written nothing for the theater. Bellini
and he had become friends after meeting in the salon of the principessa
Belgioioso. He would supply Bellini with the libretto of *I Puritani*, but
only after a considerable struggle, which at least once became so bitter
that communication between them temporarily was broken off.

When Bellini and Pepoli began to read and sift possible sources for
the much-desired libretto, Bellini plunged somewhat feverishly into
Carnival celebrations. On February 12, he had written to Lamperi[31]:
". . . forgive my brain, upset by so many Carnival distractions, which
are so numerous in this Paris that they reach boredom, so much so that
I am thanking the Almighty that we have entered Lent." And to
Santocanale on February 13, he confessed[32]: "My health has been more
than a little upset by the great distractions that Carnival offers in Paris,
where, I being a foreigner and not the least of men, these Parisians have
overwhelmed and still overwhelm me with kindnesses; and indeed the
soirées, balls, suppers, etc., etc., brought on me a sort of *crisis*, which finally
seems to have vanished, and now I can say that I am well. . . ."

By April 11 Bellini at last was able to write to Vincenzo Ferlito[33]:
"I have now chosen the story for my Paris opera: it is of the times
of Cronvello [Cromwell], after he had Charles I of England beheaded."
Then, after outlining the plot, he added: "Giulia Grisi will do the
girl, Rubini the husband, Tamburini a rival with sublime emotions, and
Lablache a relative of the girl. . . . I am enthusiastic about the subject; I find it right for inspiration, and Wednesday [April 15] at the
latest, I'll begin to compose the music, hoping that the poet (conte
Carlo Pepoli of Bologna) will give me the verses. . . . I am awaiting news
from Naples or a response to conclude the contract, but I think that
they will encounter difficulties because of the price I have asked, four
thousand ducati for an opera; it's a lot, that's true, but one must know

how to sell what God has conceded to him. That's why I'm awaiting the reply."

The subject upon which Bellini and Pepoli had agreed was a French drama described upon its title page when it was published in 1833 as "Roundheads and Cavaliers [*Têtes Rondes et Cavaliers*], historic drama in three acts, with interpolated singing, by Mm. [Jacques-Arsène] Ancelot and Xavier [*i.e.*, Joseph-Xavier Boniface, called Saintine], played for the first time at Paris at the Théâtre National du Vaudeville, September 25, 1833."[34] In turn, Ancelot and "Xavier" certainly had borrowed freely from Sir Walter Scott, though their play cannot have been based, as is often stated in books written in English, upon his novel *The Puritans of Scotland* for the reason that he wrote no novel so entitled.[35] As the scene of both play and libretto is Plymouth, and as none of the characters so much as mentions Scotland, the reasons for many references to the opera as *I Puritani di Scozia* are unclear. Pepoli, following a scenario drafted by Bellini, reduced the thirty-nine "scenes" of the drama's three acts to manageable proportions, the number of characters from nine to seven—and at the same time changed the protagonists' names to provide more singable syllables.

In May, perhaps in part to put distance between himself and the distractions and temptations of Paris, Bellini went to stay in Puteaux, a banlieue on the left bank of the Seine a very short distance northeast of the city. There he was the guest of a young English Jew named Samuel Levys[36] and a woman who either was or was not Levys's wife, and whose maiden name seems to have been Olivier. These odd, but almost certainly harmless, people were to play a strange role in the rest of Bellini's life. Mr. Levys, who is sometimes said to have been a retired colonel of considerable wealth dabbling in the bourse, was to invest some 30,000 francs for Bellini with temporarily disastrous results. Writing to Florimo on August 4, 1834, Bellini explained[37]: "Did you know that I am in danger of losing some 15,000 francs in Spanish investments? As I wrote you, I invested about 30,000 francs in those funds on the advice of practical people; now, because there are disturbances in Spain, a reduction by half is feared: all hope is not lost yet, however, as the funds rose today: if I escape this time, I don't want to put myself in such a position while nations are as desperate as an Italian poet. Don't think that this threatened misfortune bothers me very much; you know whether or not I love money. I am young, and I still have strength and arms for working and for making a future for myself." Eventually, the value of the funds having climbed back up slowly,[38] his loss was to be very small.

On May 26, 1834, Bellini dated a letter to Florimo from "*Puteaux, rampe de Neuilly, 19*[bis], *environs de Paris*" and said[39]: "As you see, my dear Florimo, I am in the country near Paris, a half hour by road. I am well lodged in the house of an English friend of mine. I compose without being disturbed by anything, and therefore hope to complete my opera more carefully. The introduction, as I wrote you in another letter, is all planned, with Tamburini's entrance. Pepoli is at work, and to keep him moving ahead costs me a lot of weariness; he lacks practice, which is a great thing [to have]."

Some time before April 15, when Bellini began to compose *I Puritani*, he learned that the management of the Théâtre-Italien had invited Donizetti too to provide an opera for the coming season. That news set his teeth on edge. On March 11, to Florimo, he wrote somewhat incoherently[40]: "I thank you for the journal that speaks of the last performance of *Norma* in Rome. Then it created such a furor? I am very pleased. *Viva la Norma!* Opera over which my enemies thought to chant victory. Oh! the poor imbeciles! You must know that they are advising Donizetti to betake himself to Paris and to accept at a price that I'll know *** a contract that Rossini could give him to compose an opera—he too—for the Théâtre-Italien, and he has done everything already, and I think that he'll be signed up, I don't know for what pay. Some people believe that it isn't the same in Paris as it is in Italy—that is, that if he composes for Paris and I do too, it seems that his genius will be found increased and mine will vanish; then I say that each of us fights with his own weapons, as in Italy, and that the journals never can make a reputation, but only can consolidate it; and therefore I hope that I and he will do what each of us has done in Italy, and that if one of his operas, like the revised *Parisina* at Florence, was applauded, he had some tremendous fiascos in other theaters."

More than a year later, after both the popular and the critical success of *I Puritani* greatly had exceeded that of Donizetti's *Marin Faliero*, Bellini still was able to write to Vincenzo Ferlito[41]: "Although it was not the custom to sign-up paid composers at the Théâtre-Italien, Rossini, who really has lots of influence in Paris, and especially with all the journals, conceived the idea of having Donizetti contracted, too, so that, set up in contest with me that way, he might suffocate me, exterminate me, supported by his [Rossini's] colossal influence, etc., etc." (Actually, when Rossini urged Robert and Severini to sign up both Bellini and Donizetti, he was simply advising them, for the good of their theater, to commission operas from the two most accomplished Italian operatic composers then active.) Bellini went on pouring out his suspicions to his uncle: "In fact, at the announcement that Donizetti had been contracted too, I had a fever for three days, understanding the plot that was being hatched against me; and in fact, an acquaintance of mine told me not to hope for a good reception in Paris, and that if there was to be a success, it would be that of Donizetti because he had been brought by Rossini. Then, once the first impression had passed, I took heart and began to think how to bring about the disappearance and overthrow of those diabolic intrigues, which could have compromised me before all Europe: and that's what would have occurred if I had become the victim. I meditated and resolved above everything else to study my new score more than usual, and then to pay court to Rossini and approach him in order to make him realize how much I valued his immense talent, etc., etc.; also to approach a friend [*amica*: Olympe Pélissier] of his and, by seeing both of them often, to put myself on such an intimate basis that they themselves would decide to protect me instead of persecuting me. I didn't have to make any effort to do all that, as I have always adored Rossini, and I succeeded, and happily; meanwhile, I was working with might and main shut up in the country, well lodged in the house of a close English friend of mine, Mr. Lewis [*sic*].

"Having won Rossini's friendship, I said to myself: now let Donizetti come! That was the third time that I found myself composing in the same theater with him: at the Carcano in Milan, I believe it was in '31, he wrote *Anna Bolena*[42]; I replied with *La Sonnambula;* the next year, at La Scala, he wrote *Ugo* [*conte di Parigi*],[43] I gave them *Norma;* finally, I found myself here with him and, having tamed Rossini's hatred, I no longer was frightened, and finished with more courage that work of mine [*I Puritani*] which won me so much honor: a prognostication that Rossini made three months before the staging." This almost incredible letter, running to about 2,500 words, rambles disjunctly on.

As April 1834 lengthened, Bellini worked hard on *I Puritani*. On April 30, for example, writing to an undetermined duchess—very probably Camilla Litta, née Lomellini—when sending for her autograph album an arietta [now unidentifiable] that he had composed to a poem that she herself had transcribed and forwarded to him, he said[44]: "I am indebted to you for the interest that you always take in my daughters. I have begun to generate a new one, and I hope that she will not be unworthy of her sisters." On that same day, Bellini wrote Pepoli a congratulatory note about some libretto lines that the poet just had sent him, saying[45]: "Today I hope to finish scoring the introduction. . . ." The next surviving dated letter from Bellini is one to Lamperi of June 14; the only reference in it to *I Puritani* reads[46]: "I have no news: only that I have composed four pieces for my new opera and am constantly racking my brain to find those little motives which seem scarce in Europe now."

In a third letter of April 30—this one to Florimo—Bellini explained why his composing was inching forward so slowly[47]: "I have been sick, and I don't remember if I have already written you to thank you for the good oranges and cheeses [*casciocavalli*] that you were friendly enough to send me; if I didn't, accept my thanks now.

"My health was attacked by a gastric fever, I think, but everything is going well now, and I have begun to take up my work on the opera for Paris again." That brief indisposition, which had been recurring almost every year at the onset of warm weather, was a signal—unheeded or misinterpreted—from the chronic amebiasis that would end Bellini's life fifteen months later. By mid-June, however, he would have the complete libretto of *I Puritani* in hand from Pepoli, as is indicated by a description in the Charavay catalogue of a letter that he wrote to conte Rinaldo Belgioioso.[48] Pepoli was not an overcommitted writer like Romani.

Bellini was again in correspondence with Giuditta Turina. In his letter of April 30, 1834, to Florimo, he said[49]: "I have written to signora Giuditta Turina, and for that reason I don't ask you to send her my regards." In another letter to Florimo, written from Puteaux on June 24, he explained[50]: "Giuditta, though she wrote you about her contempt for me, tells me in a letter of the 9th of this month that she cannot transform into friendship the love that she still feels for me: and goes on like this—'Accept it, and I guarantee that I won't annoy you and will submit to having cold friendship from you,' etc., etc. Her entire letter is most affectionate, and if it weren't for my duty to pursue my career, I'd be resolved to take up again the relationship that linked me to her; but with so many engagements, and in various countries, such a relationship would be *fatal* to me, as it would cut short my *time*, and even more my *peace of mind;* for that reason, I shall send an evasive letter in reply, without hurting her if I can avoid it." He was even more explicit to Florimo in a letter of October 4[51]: "*La Giuditta* still writes me from Milan, and I can report that she is well; I see that she constantly thinks about having me back; but I, my dear, now that I've got out of the fire have no wish to fall back into it: I feel, and feel profoundly, that I should not be happier with her: I should be more jealous than before, and a woman, my dear, born a coquette will never be able to change; so now I want her friendship, and with much pain see that I am constrained to renounce her love so as not to lose my peace of mind again and compromise my future." Six days later, Bellini told Florimo that Giuditta was carrying out negotiations for him at La Scala.

The first available document of Bellini's attempt to re-establish a working relationship with Romani consists of three half-pages in his script.[52] They contain several incomplete sections, not all of them related to Romani, and the first draft of a letter to him. They almost certainly resulted from Carlo Balocchino's having forwarded to Bellini a letter that Romani had written to Bordesi (or Bordese), a mutual acquaintance of librettist and composer, which included some indication of willingness to enter again into friendly relations with Bellini. The fragments are not dated. One of them reads: "Signor Balocchini [*sic*] having sent me your letter to Bordese, and having sent it on unsealed as you forwarded it to him, and by its contents ~~I see that signor Bordese is telling me that truth,~~[53] I was more certain about what signor Bordese tells me."

In 1894, Antonino Amore published[54] an incomplete Bellini letter dated June 11, 1834, footnoting it this way: "Unpublished—It lacks the address; but I believe that it was sent to sig. Bordese, who was the peacemaker." It reads[55]: "Tell my dear Romani that I still love him even though he is a cruel man, and that my heart knows how much, and better than I myself, that whosoever looks me in the face sees my spirit there, and that I can tell him, if he likes, that if he felt for me what I feel for him, I'd want nothing more. But who knows whether he thinks about me for a single instant, whereas I do nothing but talk about him to the entire universe. Who knows if that poor portrait of me has been brought out of that closet where I saw him hide it; I have no need of one of him, having his image carved upon my heart. There is another poet who is enamored of me, but conte Pepoli never can hope to replace Romani; that is impossible. Give him a kiss for me."

The longer sketch, an undated preliminary draft of a letter to Romani,[56] was published for the first time by Amore, who said that it dated from late July 1834. But on May 26 of that year, Bellini wrote to Florimo[57]: "When Bordese the father returns, I shall ask him if Romani answered him, and I shall try to make peace; I myself have great need of him if I want to compose for Italy again; after him, nobody else can satisfy me; therefore, without demeaning myself, I'll do whatever is possible to establish peace . . ." That suggests that Amore's date is at least two months tardy. Also, a letter to Romani which was clearly a rewriting of that sketch is dated May 29. As first published by Raffaello Barbiera,[58] that revision reads:

"My dear Romani,

"From what signor Bordesi tells me of the conversation that he had with you in Milan, and following upon your letter to the aforementioned Bordesi, which signor Balocchini [*sic*] sent me, and unsealed, I see that your affection for me has not been extinguished any more than mine for you; and because signor Bordesi is in London at this moment, I have been unable to resist the promptings of my heart, and without calculating whether or not it is decorous of me, I myself have wanted to answer you, on my own to pour out my bitterness to you yourself, who caused it.

"I did not harm you: I defended my innocence before the Venetian public—which I recognized too late to be small and gossipy—which accused me of a secret understanding with the impresario to give my opera [*Beatrice di Tenda*] at the close of the season. What proofs could I adduce, if not those that you were the principal cause? I did not need such proof, as the whole world knows that the large number of librettos ordered from you always prevents you from satisfying composers and impresarios, and that was the case with me; but you—what a ferocious article you hurled against your friend! And you say that you have always loved me, and you wrote just that to Bordesi: 'Nonetheless, I have not ceased to love him, for I recognize that the blame was not all his, that he was incited by thoughtless friends, that he was deceived by more than one person who had it in his heart to divide us!'

"And if you were convinced of that truth, should you have written and published a ruthless libel in all the journals, as you did? And did your conscience allow that? Wasn't I at your door all of June, July, and August up to the tenth? After the month of August, up to September 10, I was in Bergamo to stage *Norma;* didn't I go to Milan and stay there until December 7? To select the story, didn't you assure me that you were waiting for dramas from Paris? And then didn't you add needless and irrelevant insults? And you say that you have loved me very much?

"I believed you entirely, but my heart wept—Pasta and Papadopoli[59] and Cartagenova are witnesses—when I met you in the streets of Venice during that unhappy period, which I'll never in my life forget; yes, I ran into you, and with bitter pain said to myself: should I break off, then, with the man who won me so much glory? who was the friend of my most secret thoughts? But the final lines in your preface to *Beatrice* [*di Tenda*] and the state of my mind, which was irritated then by the multitude of misfortunes oppressing it, would not have persuaded me to reprint that unhappy article in the Venetian journal.

"But let us draw a veil over everything that happened; and if you love me, let us think of repairing, and with dignity, the evil that was done, and let us rekindle our scarcely cooled affection, which has not been extinguished despite our very great irritation, which brought joy to not a few. Let's go back to being better friends than we were, and let us be worthy of one another! You don't lack the talent to write an article for insertion by common consent into the journals: 'that, after the steps taken by some friends, Romani and Bellini [are] reuniting for new works; they believe, not wanting to repeat all the insulting expressions to be found in the articles on this question, etc.'

"What I am suggesting to you is the formula employed in France when the seconds meet to settle duels; the journals announce the quarrel ended in the way I suggest above; thus, neither of us will emerge degraded; or, to put it another way, each of us will be worthy of the other.

"We have no need to avoid a duel; but to embrace each other again and to be joined in fond friendship; therefore consult your heart as I have consulted mine, and decide as a wise man.

"I would gladly have come to Milan to arrange everything in person; but right now Milan presents me only with serious discords, and it is imperative for me to remain far away for my peace of mind; and then, I have given my word to [conte Carlo Pepoli][60] for the libretto that he is writing. This poor young fellow has a lot of talent; but the theater is very difficult, and I am even more difficult than the theater itself. I hope to carry the thing through, but I suffer a lot without your verses and your talent, and then, then, oh, don't talk about his lack of expertise, so as not to discourage him more than he is discouraged already.

"I have been invited to compose an opera for Naples for the coming spring; if you agree, I shall be in Milan in January, and then, if it is our destiny to become friends again, we shall write.

"Farewell, my dear Romani; if you do not reply, this will be the last one that I shall give you. Your Bellini. Send your letter to Mons. V. Bellini."

If Bellini kept to his decision not to write to Romani again unless Romani answered him, then Romani replied—for, as said above, Bellini wrote to him again on July 11. We do not know what, if any, other letters passed between the two men from July to October or what plans for future collaborations may have been suggested then. But on October 4, Bellini told Florimo in a letter[61]: "Romani answered me with an affectionate letter; telling me that he is content to resume a friendship that never died in his heart, and that his having been decorated by his King and engaged for Turin[62] has put him in the position of no longer needing the theater, and that he offers himself for the sole pleasure of writing librettos for me, if I think to begin with Naples (at Milan, they believe that *** already is signed up for three operas at Naples). Now I shall answer, thanking him from the heart and promising him that when I come to compose the first Italian opera, I shall go to seek him out in Turin and stay with him until after it is completed. I assure you that this reconciliation gives me enough courage to say that Italy is mine again if Paris should not work out."

On or about October 7, Bellini again wrote to Romani[63]:

"It is with much satisfaction that I see our old and good friendship reborn, and I thank you. To me it seemed impossible to exist without you.

I approve of the steps that you suggest to me, and I'll not compose more Italian operas with any poet but you; you therefore will have Bellini at your side. Tell me, then, if you are going to live in Turin, or whether you will travel between Turin and Milan. If you settle in Turin and I should have to compose for Naples or Milan, or again for Paris (seeing that I no longer have amorous relations with any woman), I'll come to Turin to compose the opera, or go wherever you will be. Now that you are a royal employee, I want to be able to hope that you will not want to accept so many obligations to compose librettos. Write for Turin or for wherever, write *for me alone: only for me*, for your Bellini.

"Demand double what you have received in payment up to now; that way, you will earn money, will devote more time to making a libretto what you wish it to be, and—your librettos being rarer—not only will you be paid better for them, but also will again produce masterpieces, and without flaws, for the theater. I have advised you this way a thousand times, and by now you would have earned the same amount with half the effort. Didn't I perhaps do it that way after I became known? Thus, you should have listened to me! Enough, let's not discuss it further.

"Let me know how many librettos you'll write during this Carnival, and for what date and for whom. I don't mean those which you will be obligated to do, but those which you believe you certainly will bring to light. Tell me, too, the subjects that you will treat; I have prepared three or four that would make a big noise if written by you; they are subjects of a new kind, too. I hope that singing actors (the good ones, understand) will not be lacking. Enough: we'll see! I had all but signed a contract with the impresario of the French Opéra; but that didn't turn out well because of the staging period that he wanted to impose upon me; the time was too short, etc., etc. Perhaps I'll compose an opera for Naples, perhaps it will be for Milan, perhaps also for Paris—see all the offers that have been made to me up to this moment: I'll restrict myself to accepting the ones that can serve the interests and glories of us both. Now that I am back with you, o my great Romani, my distinguished collaborator and protector, I feel at ease and content.

"I send you this letter by my friend signor Alessandro Lamperi, whom I have asked to accept any letters that you may want to write me, for he can get them to me in Paris. Now make use of this method wherever you are, in Milan or in Turin. Signor Lamperi is as excellent a young man as could be, full of talent and extremely goodhearted, and you can trust him, as he is an official attaché in your King's Ministry of War. Write to me quickly and, I repeat, forget our past dissensions as I am forgetting them; they should never have existed. I can never forget the benefits and the glory that I owe you. Now let's begin another life together, more beautiful and more filled with glory. I know that your king has made you a *cavaliere;* I say nothing to you about your new position and the decoration that you have received: you have well earned it, and it honors you as it honors the king himself, who gave it to you. Farewell, my dear friend, and believe in the affection of your always grateful Bellini.

"P. S. Write to me immediately and tell me where you are, whether in Milan or in Turin, so that we can see each other again soon. I don't know [when] the hour to embrace you [will come]."

No other letter from Bellini to Romani is known to survive.

A curious echo of that much-discussed broken friendship was heard in 1882, when Emilia Branca, Romani's widow, published the strange book that she called *Felice Romani and the Most Renowned Musical Composers of His Time.* Bellini had died on September 23, 1835. On October 21 of that year, Romani had published in the *Gazzetta ufficiale piemontese* a "Necrology of V. Bellini." Full of exalted praise of both Bellini and himself, Romani's obituary article had contained a reference to the disturbance of their relationship at the time of *Beatrice di Tenda*— and then this sentence: "This last was a period of which we both felt ashamed." Quoting the obituary in her book forty-seven years later, Emilia Branca deleted even that small amend on Romani's part.

Early in 1834, Bellini was busy trying to transmute Pepoli into Romani. In a letter dated only "Monday morning," but certainly written in the late spring of 1834, Bellini told Pepoli that he was expected for dinner the next evening, and then continued[64]: "Don't forget to bring with you the libretto *** so that we can finish discussing the first act, which, if you will arm yourself with a good dose of monastic patience, will be interesting, magnificent, and proper poetry for music in spite of you and all your absurd rules, which are good subjects for chatter, but never will convince a living soul initiated into the difficult art that *must bring tears through singing.* If my music turns out to be beautiful and the opera pleases, you can write a million letters against composers' abuse of poetry, etc., which will have proved nothing. Deeds, not tittle-tattle that deludes because of a certain polished eloquence; in the face of that fact, everything else becomes *very watery soup.* You can call my reasons all the names you like, but that won't prove a thing. Carve in your head in adamantine letters: '*The opera must draw tears, terrify people, make them die through singing.*' It's a defect to want all the pieces to be equally accomplished, but a necessity that they all be molded in such a way as to render the music intelligible by the clarity with which they are expressed, as concise as it is *striking.* Musical con-

trivances murder the effect of the situations, more so the poetic con-
trivances in a *dramma per musica;* to make their effect, poetry and music
demand naturalness, and nothing else; anyone who turns off that road
is lost, and in the end will bring to light a ponderous and stupid opera
that will please only the sphere of the pedants, never the heart . . . and
do you know why I told you that a good libretto is the one that does
not make good sense?[65] because I know what a ferocious and intractable
beast the man of letters is, and how absurd he is, with his general rules
of good sense. . . . Farewell, an embrace from your incorrigible Vincenzillo." Unhappily for *I Puritani,* Pepoli, too, was incorrigible: he could
not be transformed into Romani.

At an early stage of the discussions with Pepoli, Bellini wrote out a
rough scenario for the libretto (two pages from it are given in photographic reproduction in Tomasino D'Amico's *Come si ascolta l'opera*
and cited in Pastura's documentary biography, pp. 418–419). Crosswise of
the second page, Pepoli wrote: "Maestro Vincenzo Bellini had melody in
his soul and considered it queen. An excellent man for goodness, but
sometimes eccentric by nature. At times he called me *an angel, a brother,
a savior,* and at times, when he was altering the melodies of his music
for the third and fourth time, to an observation of mine about the difficulty and impossibility of changing the composition of the drama or
changing the verses, he would fly into a rage, calling me a man without
heart, without friendship or feeling; afterwards, we would go back to
being better friends than before. C. P." Their collaborative work was
nonetheless well advanced by June 26, when Bellini dashed off a note
to Pepoli[66]: "Having completed the whole duet, and lacking something
[*i.e.,* some text words], I wish that you would take the trouble to come
to Puteaux to arrange everything, and at the same time give me [verses
for] Rubini's entrance. I'll expect you on whatever day and at whatever
hour you wish."

The half-abandoned negotiations with Naples had surfaced again in
letters to Alessandro Lanari, who had written Bellini on April 10, 1834,
to say that he had become director of the Royal Theaters of Naples and
hoped that Bellini would compose three operas, including the already
projected one for the Teatro San Carlo.[67] On July 25, Bellini copied into
a letter to Florimo[68] the text of one he had written to Lanari, in which,
after alternately bitter and facetious bantering, he had said.

"Let's turn then to the conditions that the contract should contain,
supposing that you won't find other objections (to which I'll no longer
know what to reply). 1st. I will stage my opera at the beginning of
February 1835; composed for Malibran, [Gilbert-Louis] Duprez, [Carlo]
Porto, and, where the story allows it, for all the people contracted by the

Royal Theaters. (I cannot give the opera earlier because of the time that will be taken up by the trip, the composition of the opera, and perhaps my having to go on stage in Paris in December if the management wants it; but as I have completed the first act of the opera that I am writing, I hope to finish it in mid-September so as to turn immediately to the one for Naples, and in case the management here thinks of staging it in November, I'll come to Naples immediately, and it will be possible to go on before February; but never on gala evenings, which are worse than *cholera* for the musical effect.) 2nd. If the Society *finds the theaters*,[69] I'll give the second opera in January 1836; the third in that of 1837, but in case the Society's contract with the government should end with the Carnival of 1836, I'll give the second in July 1835 and the third in January 1836; thus the contract would be settled for three operas; otherwise I'll not be able to do it for that price. 3rd. I'll be in Naples one month before the staging of the first opera; for the others, about a month and a half, to attend the rehearsals.

"4th. I'll take responsibility for the librettos; the management will pay one thousand francs for each one, the price Romani asks and which the Théâtre-Italien is paying Pepoli; should it be for less, the Society will make a profit; because I will always keep it up to date as to the choice of the poet, as of the subject, which will always avoid a tragic outcome; thus, we will exchange very useful information. 5th. I will cede ownership of the three operas to the management. I shall not be required to be present on the first three evenings of the operas, at the piano forte, as was the custom (special proviso). 6th. In return, etc., etc., the Society will pay me 10,000 ducati divided into six equal install-ments; the first when I reach the scene, the 2nd after the rehearsals, the others divided in the same way, etc., etc. I await either the contract to be signed or *a no*, but I too am prepared, having answers to give: do you understand, my dear Lanari? Think it over well, and remember Mazzarino [Cardinal Mazarin], who tells us *to think in advance so as not to have regrets later on*."

In the accompanying letter to Florimo,[70] Bellini said: "I have finished the 1st act of the opera; I still must compose the finale, which is already all thought out. I have asked Pepoli to reduce the two remaining acts to one for me, as this way the opera seems endless: there are nine pieces of music in the first act: imagine, then, what fun."

At the end of July, also, the director and the administrator of the Opéra-Comique called at the Bains chinois, but found that Bellini was summering in Puteaux. On August 1, therefore, they wrote inviting him to compose a three-act opera to a libretto by a writer of his selection who would be paid by them.[71] Informing Florimo of that development on August 4, Bellini wrote[72]: "Yesterday I received a flattering letter from the directors of the Opéra-Comique, who invited me, with intense prayers, to compose an opera for them. I shall answer them that I cannot reply now because I have contracts under discussion with Italy; but if I don't come to an agreement with Naples, perhaps, perhaps I'll accept and compose a libretto by *Scribe*." Had Bellini lived, then, he might— like Cherubini, Rossini, Donizetti, and Verdi—have composed one or more operas to a French libretto.

As Bellini meandered on in that extremely long letter to Florimo, he was taken by nostalgia for the past and for Naples: "This evening of August 4, I recall an evening of the same date on which we had run after a certain carriage through the Toledo and you finally left me at the Teatro Nuovo, where they were giving *Elisa e Claudio*[73]; the next day, *presidente* Fumaroli came from the Rector, and then . . . etc., etc., isn't that so? I remember that we found ourselves near the piazzetta della Marina, opposite the palace of Leopoldo [principe di Siracusa], with divine moonlight: isn't that so? Oh, dear ideas and innocent age of illusions, how you have vanished! ! ! Still, I am not unhappy now. Not having any amorous passion keeps me tranquil, but it is a vegetation with regard to that gender. I know a beautiful woman who loves me to extremes: I cannot say the same for myself; but I find her beautiful and amiable and very docile, so much so that she does not disturb me in anything; sometimes I see her, make love, and then think about my opera."

Very late in August, Bellini received from Naples a counterproposition that he accept 7,500 ducati (2,500 ducati each) for the three operas; he thereupon terminated the negotiations. Nor was anything to come of his pourparlers with the Opéra-Comique, the management of which strangely had suggested that he agree to compose a one-act operetta. Finally, he could not persuade the Opéra to offer him the terms that it had accorded to Rossini, and so would not compose for it either.[74] On September 21, he wrote to Santocanale[75]: "And now I don't want to negotiate with anybody until I see what success my opera will have." That day, too, in a letter to Florimo, he said[76]: ". . . in Paris up to now I am judged the best after Rossini, and I hope, if I do not deceive myself, to reinforce that idea by my new opera, which seems to me to be turning out well. Further, I have orchestrated it with such indescribable care that I feel very great satisfaction on looking at every piece that I complete."

In that letter to Florimo, Bellini listed in detail the sections of *I Puritani* which he had finished and those he still had to compose, pull together, or orchestrate: ". . . yesterday I told all this to Rossini, as if to ask him for his advice, and he answered that I am doing well to complete everything first and compose the two abovementioned pieces [a duet and a trio] at the end. I expect to complete everything in October, though Rossini tells me that the date as set is a formality, and that now, because I am so far advanced, I should work without agitation . . ." On October 6, Henry Greville entered in his diary[77]: "Yesterday I went to Puteaux, where Bellini is living: he played to me a good deal of his forthcoming opera, which is full of beautiful melody, and which I hope is sure to succeed."

After the middle of October, outside events impinged upon Bellini's quiet at Puteaux. On the 23rd, *La Sonnambula*, as supervised by him, was presented at the Italien with Giulia Grisi and Rubini. The outcome was that opera's happiest success to date in Paris.[78] The day after that performance, Castil-Blaze[79] wrote Bellini to say that in an article in the preceding Sunday's *Revue de Paris*, he had discussed the furor being created in Madrid by Bellini's operas—and that he was authorized by the director of the Madrid Opera to negotiate with Bellini to come to that city and compose two new operas and direct his older ones.[80] Like every other possibility suggested to Bellini for post-*Puritani* accomplishment, this one came to nothing.

At about the time when Bellini extended for another year his lease on the rooms in the Bains chinois (to which he returned from Puteaux on November 1), his interrupted negotiations with Naples revived in still another form. Florimo had written him that changes in the directorate of the Teatro San Carlo had altered the situation there—and that he would shortly be receiving a proposition from one of the new men, a cavaliere Colle. On October 13, Bellini answered Florimo in a very long, rambling, but in part highly particularized letter[81] preceded by this sentence: "Read this letter of mine when you are alone, as it contains things not to be communicated to anyone, no matter whom."

Bellini's chief points were: that he was prepared to sign a contract with the San Carlo to stage *I Puritani* and to compose two new operas for a total fee of 9,000 ducati; that the Opéra-Comique had asked him to compose a one-act operetta by May 15, and then—when he had declared that to be impossible—within one year; that the Comique was demanding that he promise not to compose for Italy, for which reason he wanted to complete arrangements with Naples first and then face the Comique with the *fait accompli*, in the face of which it would have to drop the proviso; that he would go to Naples for *I Puritani*, but not for either of the new operas to be composed later; that he would adapt *I Puritani* for the Naples company, which was to include Malibran,[82] Duprez, Porto, and a baritone of Tamburini's power[83]; that he was sure that the Neapolitan censor would pass Pepoli's libretto "because it is very moral and does not touch upon politics"—which latter statement was not true; that the two new librettos were to be written by Romani, who was to be paid 1,000 ducati for each of them; and that he would deliver the first of the new operas in either August or November 1835, the second in January 1836 or in November of that year. In passing, he described the role of the heroine of *I Puritani* as "very interesting because it is of a genre like *La Nina pazza*[84] and . . . has heart-rending situations . . ."

One of Bellini's self-protectively half-serious plans to marry is echoed near the end of that letter[85]: "I have written to Pasta, [and] from her answer I shall see if it will be possible to revive my and her first ideas about her daughter; but all that must be treated with extreme delicacy; do you understand?" Clelia, the Pastas' only child, was then just sixteen years old—and nothing was to come of this unlikely plan. On November 30 Bellini told Florimo[86]: "I don't know if I wrote you that I received an answer from Pasta to that letter I sent her to Bologna: she had her husband answer me (because she never replies), and imagine, he addresses me as most esteemed friend; in a word, a very polite letter, but icy and very far from leaving me any hope that their matrimonial project has remained in their minds . . ."[87]

In that extraordinarily prolix letter to Florimo of November 30,[88] Bellini announced flatly: "Then my mind is made up about finding a wife." After disposing of one candidate, an English girl of whom there had been some vague talk—she was already twenty-five or twenty-six years old, he did not love her, her brother wanted to give her a dowry of only 150,000 francs ("and, my dear, 150 thousand francs of dowry without love are little"), and he did not feel at all inclined toward "that union . . . perhaps the desire will rise again; but I think that difficult"— he ticked off another problematic possibility:

"A lady, and an old lady, the baronessa Sellyere [Sellière or Sellières], wants to marry me to an eighteen-year-old girl who is, she tells me, very pretty and has a fortune: two or three hundred thousand francs of dowry; she is an only daughter, and at present not in Paris, but in Rome with her father and mother; for her father is the celebrated painter [H]Orace Vernet,[89] who will return to Paris at the end of the coming January. I confided this jest of the baronessa's to Greville, who has been here for some months, to find out if he had met the girl: he told me that he had made her acquaintance in Rome; that she really is very comely, the head especially is something that resembles Canova's *Madonna Laura*, that she is also well educated. She knows music, drawing, and languages to perfection—that, in a word, if the dowry were to be no less than two hundred thousand fracs, he advises me to contract this union: because I will be taking something valuable both in spirit and in talent, and still more so because she is unaffected, that she seems to be of a good disposition and of unequaled sweetness: in my view, these details from Greville, which he gave me only yesterday, turn what I had thought a jest into something I now deem possible, and I find myself in a state to obey the baronessa, who will be enchanted to arrange this matrimony because she wishes me well and (she told me) loves the girl too; for that reason, I am telling you about it because, my dear Florimo, I do not hide the smallest of my projects from you, never.

"Now my plan is as follows: by contracting a union with a young girl who by her dowry will place me in a certain state of independence, I can remain in Paris and compose for the Grand Opéra and also for the Opéra-Comique, investing in each opera as much time as I want; because I won't have need for quick earnings to keep myself going. Having a young girl, too, pretty and well educated, will mean that I won't take up relations with women who are not mine and therefore bring continuous rancor upon me. With my wife, further (should she too possess the craving to coquet[90]), I'll be the master; I shall receive whoever appeals to me and whom I like; I shall also take her on trips if the notion seizes me, etc., etc. But I don't think that I shall be driven to that pass; I know myself; if I marry a comely and spirited girl, one who has a good figure and is good at the same time, I think that I shall supply her with most affectionate company. Well, women, all of them without exception, don't deceive their husbands except when their husbands deceive them; therefore, I foresee happiness for myself now; it could turn out that it would last as long as the happiness I imagined with the English girl . . ."

That dim chimera, marriage to a very young, very pretty, very docile, and wealthy girl, was still materializing in Bellini's surroundings in February 1835, when he wrote to Florimo[91]: ". . . you know that I am looking toward contracting a marriage in order to render myself independent of all need; two hundred thousand francs as a dowry would be enough for me. I had found them with a young girl of eighteen, enamored of me, but not I of her, as I observed her character, which is diabolic, lively, and imperious; but I spoke to you once of a certain lady, the baronessa . . .[92] This old woman loves me madly. If it had depended upon her, she would have had me marry an adopted daughter of hers, to whom her ambitious husband will give a dowry of two or three millions; but the girl is thirteen years old and too elegantly educated, to the point of losing her head, so that her nature may turn out despotic, as is to be feared already. But I never thought of such castles in Spain or, as is said, in the air. The baronessa has a niece, a young girl of eighteen, sweet, well educated, who belongs to relatives in reduced circumstances, without a soldo because of her father's vices. This girl is the daughter of the baronessa's sister, and she adores her—and, also adoring me, would like to adore the two in one by having us marry. But the baronessa knows that I haven't a soldo and don't want to compromise my present happy state by a moneyless marriage. She . . . is trying to persuade her husband to endow her niece with 200,000 francs, that is, to give her 10,000 francs annually during his lifetime and the capital of 200,000 after that. Also, this poor old lady has money with which, she tells me, she will think of furnishing me an apartment; or perhaps I shall also have quarters in her own house and also a very faint hope that if her husband should pre-decease her, she will be left beneficiary of the fortune, which pays 400,000 francs annually, and the old lady constantly repeats that if things should turn out that way, she would make me a millionaire. Very good! Her husband might have consented already, but he fears that I, a theatrical man, would bring into his house all the singers in the world, or else would fall in love with all the prima donnas, whom he describes as the most seductive women of the Inferno. I say (because I speak of these matters only with the old lady, who always weeps) that I have never taken up with such women, who seem seductive to others, but never to me. There you have the state of all my plans, which perhaps will go up in smoke because of my chattering. The young girl, however, seems to me quiet, not a coquette, and perhaps would be the woman to suit my tranquil life as a composer. To have rich relatives isn't bad. In short, I find her agree-able, not very beautiful, and then if I should love her, and she me, love—and especially mine, which would be faithful, once I married—would do her so much good that it would improve her health, as now she is somewhat delicate. She is called Amelia, is sweet, and would make love very well. During the summer I shall be living near her in the country . . .[93] There you have all of my plans that you wanted to know about, which I write you jestingly, confiding them only to my pen; and as for the rest, if it happens, that will be better; if it doesn't, that won't matter much. . . ."

Bellini, whose fame was international and whose radiant good looks were a subject of very frequent remark, certainly could have married if he really had wanted to marry. But a wife meant responsibility, both moral and financial, and that he clearly avoided. What he really desired was a very attractive, very young sexual partner who otherwise would leave him free to devote himself absolutely to composition and to the private furthering of his glory, and who would bring him, if not wealth, at least complete freedom from financial worry. He was not really self-deluded: he told the truth unmistakably when he wrote Florimo, in that almost endless letter of November 30, 1834: ". . . I love the woman whom I have no project to marry and I become bored when such a project faces me; if such an impression should prove constant, you see very well that I'll never take a wife. Amen . . ."

On November 20, 1834, the contract from the Teatro San Carlo reached Bellini. He accepted it with a single change: he would not promise to be in Naples in January 1835 to stage *I Puritani*. Writing to Florimo the next day, he explained why[94]: ". . . I am not certain of being able to come in January for two main reasons, both because of the French opera[95] (though I haven't signed anything yet, I have promised upon my word of honor); but the most terrible would be the time of my going on stage here with *I Puritani*; and if they put me on late, what can I do? I cannot obligate myself without risking my opera, and then if just one of the actors I have should become sick, what would we be able to do?" He asked Florimo to arrange his being allowed to come to Naples later, for the two new operas. "Therefore," he continued, "tomorrow I begin to make all the necessary adjustments that the opera requires [they actually occupied him from December 20, 1834, to January 4, 1835]: transpose Tamburini's role for [Francesco] Pedrazzi. I will order [the text for] the cavatina for Malibran from Pepoli; in a word, I'll arrange things for myself so that I'll be able to deliver—on January 1 at the latest—all of the score *without glue and without threads* (so that it won't be subject to staining) to the person whom principe Ottajano[96] will designate to me in case that I cannot come. I'll also send him the designs for the settings and, if I can, those for the *costumes*. Anything that I must change during the rehearsals [in Paris] I'll send you by *letter*. I'll rule this fine paper, on which I'll write to you in small characters the phrase or the new piece that I shall have done, this in case that the steamer from Marseilles should prove unable to arrive in time. . . .

"At this moment, I come from the theater, and I hear that Gabussi's opera[97] finally will go on on Tuesday, the 25th instant; after it, they must prepare [*concertarsi*] *Semiramide* and *Anna Bolena*, each of which operas will take up at least two weeks; therefore my rehearsals will not begin before December 10 or 15, illness not intervening. Judge from that whether I am wrong in fearing that I shall [not] be able to come to Naples in time to stage the opera. . . ."

In a second postscript, Bellini added: "I hope to come to Naples, if not in January, then in June or July of next year, to rehearse and direct my new opera if the Society will put it on at that time. . . . *Gustave III*[98] is interesting and full of spectacle, it is historical, and I should think that the censors could accept it if one did not have Gustave killed (if that should be what they'd want), but the situations are beautiful, very beautiful, and new. Then there is *Un Duel sous Richelieu*,[99] which is dramatic and extremely effective; I should like to compose them both; put your mind to persuading everyone, including the minister of police, who in the end hasn't so many prejudices. . . . I'll send you the libretto when it is finished, which I find it difficult to believe will be in a few days; but let them keep calm. Into it enters *neither religion nor iniquitous love nor any politics.* If the title *Puritani* displeases them, let them give it that of *Elvira* or else *Le Teste rotonde ed i cavalieri;* this latter is too long; we selected the first because it is famous because of the Puritans of Valter-Scott [*sic*]. . . ."

Meanwhile, Bellini's carefully plotted siege of Rossini's defenses was being carried forward successfully. On September 4, writing to Florimo, he had said[100]: "I think Rossini will be pleased: he has arrived here[101]; he received me very well: I hear that he speaks well of me. He urged me to do myself honor. He was content with the stage I've reached with the opera, of which the first act is finished, and of the second I still have to do a trio and the stretta of the finale: of the third, a duet and the final scene: imagine—I still have three months; therefore I'll have time to polish and re-polish. I have delivered all the first-act choruses. Carafa found the introduction and the finale very well orchestrated; in short, I am proceeding steadily and well. Pepoli himself has made a very beautiful trio for the two basses and *la Grisi,* as interesting as the fourth act of *Nina,* and is making a duet between Rubini and *la Grisi,* whose largo and cabaletta I have, and which should turn out excellently as a situation and, I hope, also as music. I seem to find Rossini more affectionate: he told Pepoli that my open character pleases him and that, as my music shows, I must feel profoundly: Pepoli answered that my greatest gift is to speak well of all artists without exception (and since I left Italy, I have kept myself from making the slightest observations about operas by other maestros), and then many other things that Rossini agreed with. Then I told him to advise me (we were alone) as brother to brother, and begged him to wish me well: *But I do wish you well* (he answered). *Yes, you wish me well; but you must wish it for me more* (I added). He laughed and embraced me! We'll wait for circumstances to show whether he's telling the truth or not."

To Santocanale on September 21, Bellini reported[102]: "I saw Rossini yesterday, and he asked about you, etc., etc." On that same day, he told Florimo[103]: "Tamburini is enchanted by his cavatina and by a trio: I am the same about almost everything that I've done up to now. . . . Rossini is satisfied, and always tells me that they have done badly, very badly, to describe me as slow and lazy."

On October 4, Bellini's word to Florimo was[104]: "You should know that (in order to pay Rossini court and, further, because I believe him capable of giving me precious advice) I begged him to condescend to look over my opera and give me some opinion: he told me that he would do it: a mutual friend had told him not to deny himself the pleasure that he knew I had asked him for, as it would honor my modesty and his greatness: Rossini told him that he would do it tactfully; but that he consoled himself with the fact that he already had seen a piece (he was speaking of the prayer [*"La luna, il sole, le stelle"*]) which told him that I am constantly studying, he having found the voices well placed, and that he now feels able to say something to me about the instrumentation. This has pleased me, and if I have Rossini's protection, I'll be situated well; although up to now he has said only bad, very bad, things about me, namely that the one who has the most talent in Italy is Pacini and, as to the laying out of the pieces, Donizetti, and those stupid journalists pay attention and always have listened to Rossini as an oracle, and he has dealt badly with those who have cast their shadow on him and has praised his followers, [those] shameful plagiarists, to the skies. . . . I'll tell you about the conversations that I'll have with Rossini when I go to show him a piece, and as I believe that he will do my art good whether advising me or praising me, I do it with the greatest pleasure; because his advice will be to my advantage, his praise will encourage me."

Bellini, though nervously inventing Rossini's "hatred" of him, was correct in believing that before reading through parts of the score of *I Puritani*, Rossini had not always rated him very high. The remark about advising Bellini concerning orchestration in indicative: the composer who had advanced from the relatively thin (though almost always appropriate) instrumentation of his own early operas to the more nearly "symphonic" orchestra of *Le Siège de Corinthe* and *Guillaume Tell* tended to find Bellini's orchestration somewhat reactionary, a trifle underdeveloped. As Andrea Della Corte wrote[105]: "Therefore, the preoccupations with the Rossinian criticism, proceeding from actual cases in point, with objections that were reasoned and therefore grave and damaging, were not then unfounded in the spirit of the still-youthful Catanese." Forty-three years after Bellini's death and ten after Rossini's, the Roman painter Guglielmo De Sanctis published an account of his meetings with Rossini in Passy in May-June 1856.[106] One evening, he said, he had interrogated Rossini about his opinions of various Italian composers. Part of the old man's reply had been[107]: "Bellini is great above all in *Norma* and *I Puritani*. He had a very beautiful spirit, exquisitely delicate; but he lacked abundance of ideas when composing. It was true, however, that he had not had time to display himself in full, having died while still young and at the most beautiful moment of his artistic life." Clearly, Rossini did not harbor, and certainly never expressed publicly, at least before *I Puritani*, that unreserved admiration without which Bellini believed any man to be in a real sense not a true friend.

From Puteaux on October 24, Bellini wrote to Florimo[108]: "Within a week I'll go back to Paris, to the Bains chinois, and then I have asked Rossini to grant me some moments so that I can let him hear what I have done, and now that has been arranged. Now they are saying that Rossini has the Théâtre-Italien for five years more. If this man really abandons jealousy now, having a need for new operas every year, perhaps he'll make me propositions, and perhaps he will be able to pay me about twenty thousand francs for one opera each year. Then I'll stay on in Paris, for I'll be able to compose for the French theaters, too; and then, if I were to be paid well, with a magnificent company, I swear to you that the thing couldn't be more favorable, and that's why I call all these desires something like *castles in the air*, as perhaps Rossini's opinion of me will never change, and his amour propre won't ever let him believe that his own operas no longer can support this theater."[109]

Bellini's conquest of Rossini went according to his plan. On November 18, he was able to tell Florimo[110]: "Now let's speak of Paris and the news. The most beautiful is that Rossini (don't tell a soul) loves me very much, very, very much. The other day, then, he began to examine my introduction, and found it magnificent, so much so (and miracles do happen) that he has ordered an organ to be procured for me at the theater to accompany the quartet of the prayer in that piece, etc. He found it all orchestrated in such a way as he himself had not believed that I'd know how to do it. He found Tamburini's cavatina charming, the duet of Lablache and Grisi very beautiful: the chorus that precedes Rubini's entrance instrumented with great taste and very brilliant; that entrance beautiful and well carried out . . . So Rossini is enchanted: he speaks well of me to everyone, as others have repeated to me, and has expressed such opinions that I see that I haven't deceived myself this time. The other day, after he had looked at the introduction, he said to me that he clearly foresees that I'll remain in Paris, that if this opera is a success, the directors of all the theaters will make me rich offers; that it would be good for me to remain in Paris and think no more about Italy: I answered that if he would be affectionate toward me, advising me, helping me both with my comportment and with my composing, I would swear to him to follow his advice; in sum, that, certain of his benevolence, I'd remain in Paris, [but] without it, never: he answered that he always had felt affection for me; I answered that I did not doubt his having had that benevolence which honest people feel for the person closest at hand; but that I was speaking of that of a father for his son, of a brother for his brother: he promised that he would feel that way about me, and I that I'd not do anything without his advice."

In fact, Bellini very probably submitted the finished score to Rossini for final criticism. Florimo wrote[111]: "Completed as it was, he sent it to Rossini as director of the Théâtre-Italien, accompanying it with a most modest letter conceived this way: 'Here you have my poor completed work, which I present to you, my excellent Maestro: make of it what pleases you most: cut it, add to it, modify the whole thing if you think it necessary, and my music will always profit thereby.'" In a footnote, Florimo added: "This passage is literally transcribed from a letter of his which he wrote me from Paris under date of December 14, 1834." Although no trace of that letter can now be found, no reason exists for doubting that Bellini wrote the quoted sentence or something closely resembling it.

Writing on November 24 to Filippo Santocanale in Palermo, Bellini was feeling surer of Rossini[112]: "I don't want to fail on this occasion to implore you to attend to Rossini's affairs and to tell you and beg you to interest yourself greatly in them, as he wants once and for all to see them taken care of so that he will not merit the bad humor of his wife [Isabella Colbran], who is the owner [of properties in Sicily]. I now receive continuous politeness from Rossini, as he now protects me and wishes me well, and I can repay him at this moment only by giving you this plea, about which he doesn't know. But in the meantime, sure that you will grant this prayer from me, I can feel the satisfaction of being able to repay with interest the friendship that this immense man demonstrates for me; do you understand? If his protection becomes stronger, my glory will profit very much, as in Paris he is the musical oracle."

Reasonably assured about Rossini's all-important attitude toward him and toward *I Puritani,* Bellini began rehearsals of the opera during either the last days of 1834 or the earliest of 1835. On January 21, he sent Florimo a report of the preceding day's dress rehearsal[113]: "The music was found very beautiful *al non plus ultra*! ! ! I can tell you that I never felt more pleased in my life. All of high society, all the great artists, and everyone most distinguished in Paris were in the theater, enthusiastic; and one embraced me on this side and one embraced me on that, not excluding my very dear Rossini, who now really loves me as a son. I enclose two articles from journals that came out this morning. Tonight should have been the first performance, but Tamburini is un-well, and maybe it will go on on Tuesday [January 27], and that displeases me; but patience, it will finally go on at its own good time. I am at the peak of joy! and you?—I well believe that you will rejoice as much as your Bellini. Let our friends read the enclosed journals and then, quickly, on the same day, send them on to my poor family, which will be palpitating for this success. . . ."

Tamburini must have recovered sooner than foreseen: the première of *I Puritani* took place on Saturday, January 24, 1835, at the Italien, with Giulia Grisi (Elvira), one or the other of two sisters named Amigo (Enrichetta di Francia), Giovanni Battista Rubini (Lord Arturo Talbo), Sr. Magliano (Sir Bruno Roberton), Antonio Tamburini (Sir Riccardo Forth), Luigi Lablache (Sir Giorgio), and Sr. Profeti (Lord Gualtiero Valton). In an undated letter postmarked at Paris on January 26, Bellini overflowed to Florimo with heedless disregard of syntax[114]:

"I cannot find words to describe to you the state of my heart. My opera finally went on stage on Saturday, and the effect, even though it corresponded to that of the dress rehearsal, still *** me unexpected. The introduction, effect; the cavatina of Tamburrini [*sic*], graceful and applauded; the duet between Lablache and Elvira, a very great furor; Rubini's entrance, much effect; the duet, great pleasure; the *quartetto a polacca*, fanaticism; the trio applauded in the solo *a solo* of Rubini; the finale, a huge furor. Second act (we have divided the opera into three acts, putting Grisi's aria before the duet of the two basses and after the piece that closes the second act because no effect could survive that made by the duet); then the chorus pleased; Lablache's romanza the same; a huge furor, Grisi's *scena* and all the first section especially, where she is mad and passes from thought to thought; also, Grisi sang and acted like an angel: the entire theater was driven to tears because in particular the appearance of the 6/8—when she believes that she is going to her wedding and the ball—lacerates the spirit. I can't tell you anything more about the effect of the two basses. The French had all gone mad; there were such noise and such shouts that they themselves were astonished at being so carried away; but they say that the *stretta* of that piece acts directly on everyone's nerves, and really [it does], for the whole pit rose to its feet at the effect of that *stretta*, shouting, containing itself, but then shouting again. In a word, my dear Florimo, it was an unheard-of thing, and since Saturday, Paris has spoken of it in amazement. The audience[115] (not according to custom, as only at the end of the spectacle is it permitted to call out, not the author, but only the name . . . neither Spontini nor all the others who followed him have had the honor of presenting themselves on the stage; and Lablache had, so to speak, to drag me out onto the stage; and, almost staggering, I showed myself to the audience, which shouted as though insane: all the women waving handkerchiefs, all the men shaking their hats in the air . . . After that, the curtain fell (understand that they had to repeat the duet), and I swear to you

that a half hour of rest was not enough. When the curtain was raised for
the third act, we saw the audience still excited. Rubini's romanza, greatly
applauded, was found long because of the repetition and the long recitative; thereafter the duet made a very great effect (but since the last
rehearsal I already had removed its middle largo because it was long),
and it was particularly so in the recognition [scene], and then of very
great effect in the cabaletta; the finale, a great furor, and the audience
called Bellini and the singers with great shouts, so much that for the
second time we were forced to show ourselves. . . . I'll enclose whatever
journals I find this morning. I think that they'll all be favorable to me,
my success being on every tongue without any opposition; they all shout
that this is an opera to bring me great honor. Oh, my dear Florimo, how
effective the instrumentation is. . . . Oh, my dear Florimo, how satisfied
I am! What bounds we have exceeded, and with what success? I still
am trembling from the impression that this success has had on my morale
and my physique. The impression was such that at some moments I am
like a fool. The Court wants a performance of the choruses from *Norma*,
and I'll do everything possible to make them go well. . . . They wanted
pieces from *I Puritani* to be played at their concert on Wednesday, but
that can't be because I shall need orchestra rehearsals, and there is no
time. The Queen had someone write me that she will attend the second
performance tomorrow. I count upon having the dedication offered to her
(and don't tell anyone) . . . Lablache sang like a god, Grisi like a little
angel, Rubini and Tamburini the same. . . ."

Florimo—who very probably had the description in a letter from
Bellini—wrote[116]: "The morning after the first performance, the boulevard des Italiens, where he lived *aux Bains chinois* (now demolished) was
crowded with an immense number of carriages; and the most elegant
and distinguished ladies of the aristocracy and the most eminent persons
rushed to offer him coronets of flowers." Immediately popular, *I Puritani*
quickly became the rage of Paris. Its four leading singers were long
referred to as the "*Puritani* Quartet." Its seventeenth singing would end
the season at the Italien on March 31, nineteen days after the happily received première there of Donizetti's new opera, *Marin Faliero*,[117] which
was not to be as popular as *I Puritani*.

Bellini's written reactions to *Marin Faliero* were distorted by jealousy. Four days after its première, Donizetti had written to his Bergamo
friend Antonio Dolci[118]: ". . . I think of sending you also two words about
the second and third evenings, which were very brilliant; Rubini sang as
I've never heard him sing, and for that reason had to repeat the cavatina
and the aria on both the second and third evenings. Bellini's success with
I Puritani made me tremble more than a little, but we are opposites in

style, therefore we have both won good success without displeasing the public." Bellini had not waited four days: on the day after the Donizetti première, he had written to Vincenzo Ferlito[119]: "The new opera by Donizzetti [*sic*] that went on stage last night, *Marin Faliero*, had a semi-fiasco; perhaps the journals will not be unfavorable to him, but the audience was left discontented; and the proof will be the imminent [re-] appearance of *I Puritani*." Bellini's "proof" materialized; whereas his opera was to be performed seventeen times before the Italien's season ended, Donizetti's seems to have been sung only five.

But Bellini was not assuaged by his own greater popularity. Tormented by the belief that Rossini still was pushing Donizetti forward to the detriment of all other composers, himself included, he returned to the attack on April 1, writing Vincenzo Ferlito an unbalanced letter (it wanders on through more than 3,750 words) of dangerously paranoid tone, returning again and again to denunciations of Donizetti, of *Marin Faliero*, and of Donizetti's 1832 opera *Ugo, conte di Parigi*, which had followed the première of *Norma* at La Scala by a little more than two months. Hacking at Donizetti in language that seems to rise from a cankering fear of persecution, he told his uncle: "The good things that he [Rossini] has said about Donizetti strongly influenced the journals; and the partisan frenzy was manifest when *Marin Faliero* went on stage on March 12 . . . at the dress rehearsal (as at mine) the management had invited an endless number of guests, with a difference: for me (for mine), people asked for the tickets, but for Donizetti's, the management offered them to people who did not want them. Therefore at the dress rehearsal there was immense applause, so much so that both of us—I was in a loge with Rossini—laughed at that furor, whereas at all the [other] rehearsals, the opera had been condemned to a short, a very short life because it is the worst of those which Donizetti has composed up to now, which have reached the number 48. . . .[120] The effect of *Marin Faliero* was mediocre. At the second performance, it seemed worse, at the third, everyone judged it a real funeral. . . .[121] But what an opera this is which he has written! It is something incredible—he who showed talent in *Anna Bolena*! This one for Paris lacks all novelty, is extremely common and vulgarly orchestrated—without concerted numbers: in a word, worthy of a young student. . . . *I Puritani* now has placed me in the position that I deserve—that is, first after Rossini. I say it that way because Rossini had made everyone believe that Donizetti had more talent (because he did not fear him) than Bellini, but now Italy, Germany, and France accord me the position that I have acquired by so much assiduous study, and which I hope always to improve."

Later in 1835, three days after Bellini's death, *Lucia di Lammermoor* was to have its première in Naples—and still farther into Donizetti's future lay *Roberto Devereux, La Fille du régiment, Les Martyrs (Poliuto), La Favorite, Linda di Camounix, Don Pasquale, Maria di Rohan,* and several other operas. But Bellini would not have need much longer to worry over Rossini's attitude toward him and toward Donizetti or ever to face another "contest" with Donizetti: without having begun a successor to *I Puritani,* he was to die almost exactly eight months after its radiant première at the Théâtre-Italien. That final period of his short life was to be so amorphous and disorganized that Francesco Pastura aptly entitled a chapter about it "Projects like Phantoms."

(X)

1835:
"Projects like Phantoms"

ON JANUARY 31, 1835, King Louis-Philippe, at the request of Louis-Adolphe Thiers, his minister of the interior, signed the appointment of Bellini as a *chevalier* of the Légion d'honneur.[1] Bellini never mentioned when or where he received the decoration, but a circumstantial account, which there seems no reason to disbelieve,[2] had Rossini presenting the decree and the ribbon to him on the stage of the Théâtre-Italien on the evening of February 3. Soon after that, Bellini had word from Naples that Ferdinando II had awarded him the cross of the Order of Francesco I. Telling Santocanale about the French honor, Bellini added[3]: "I leave you now because I am going to Court to see the Queen, to whom I want to offer the dedication of *I Puritani*, which is still creating a furor. Tell me what Rossini has written you, and do me the favor of writing him that I have communicated to you how much I feel indebted to him in this situation for the advice that he has given me, etc., etc. In a word, let's try to have him as a friend, even despite himself."

To Florimo, on February 6, Bellini reported[4]: ". . . yesterday I presented myself to the Queen to thank her for her protection, etc., and I begged her to accept as a token of gratitude the *Dedication* of the Opera; she was pleased to accept the offer with great satisfaction, so *I Puritani* is now dedicated *To the Queen of the French*, a legend that I also want to have stamped on the separate pieces that *Cottrau* will reprint from the Parisian ones: do you understand? Also, on Wednesday, the 11th current, the Court will give a grand concert, which could be said to be in my honor, as nothing but my music will be sung: the first part will be made up of five or six pieces from *I Puritani*, and the second part of a like number of pieces from *Norma*, which the Court had me informed of its particular desire to hear because everyone speaks of it to them with enthusiasm[5]—I am invited to be present, and when there shall thank the King for the great favor showed me on this occasion."

Bellini was to be condemned bitterly in Naples for having dedicated *I Puritani* to a member of its increasingly hated Bourbon dynasty, Queen Marie-Amélie being a sister of the late Francesco I of the Two Sicilies. Even Florimo expressed that displeasure: answering him on February 27, Bellini said[6]: "Before being displeased by something, it is essential, my dear, to be acquainted with a nation's customs: there never has been an example here of a score, an opera that has made a big stir, being dedicated to private persons. Spontini dedicated his *La Vestale* to the Empress Josephine, Rossini his *Guglielmo* [*Guillaume Tell*] to Louis XVIII, and I could only dedicate mine to the woman to whom I have dedicated it, and do you know when and how I offered her that dedication? . . . That our enemies should picture this in a different light now, that's of little importance to me." Bellini was riding high: as he told Florimo on February 18,[7] the impresarios of the Théâtre-Italien wanted to stage *Norma* the following year if he would enlarge the tenor part for Rubini, the father's role for Lablache ("who now adores me"), and he believed that he could obtain a fee of 6,000 francs for merely composing two new numbers and slightly retouching the orchestration.

Bellini had been away from Italy for nearly two years, and after the feverish excitement following the première of *I Puritani*, he began to feel a pressing, constantly increasing need for a warmth of personal contact which he had shared with no one in Paris—a need, most of all, for Florimo. In the letter of February 6, 1835, to Florimo, he had said[8]: "All Paris is content, and when even people who don't know me hear *I Puritani*, they exclaim: *He has well earned the honors that they have given him*. Florimo, how I'd like to talk with you! ! ! to tell you how satisfied my heart is, and how yours will be too, and then about my dear parents, and then about all our true friends." Thereafter, he bombarded the strangely unresponsive Florimo with invitations, which gradually became demands, that he come to Paris. On March 13, Bellini ended a letter (in which he spoke of the "constant, boring success of *La Juive*"[9]) with this sentence: "Will I be embracing you soon or not?" On April 29, it was[10]: "They [mutual friends named Mericof] are leaving for London in three weeks: I have promised them that if you come, we'll go to visit them on the Rhine at Frankfurt, where they'll spend all of July."

But Florimo showed no sign of intending to visit Paris, though he admitted that he was bored by his life in Naples. Instantly, Bellini seized upon that remark, replying on June 16[11]: "You tell me that you are oppressed by a monotonous life; but what would be better for you than to come to distract yourself a little in Paris?" But Bellini slowly began to understand that something other than a lack of funds—which he several times offered to supply, though saying that he himself was not in good financial condition—was preventing Florimo not only from coming to Paris, but even from advancing the real cause of that refusal. On July 1, he burst out[12]: "But why don't you come here for a little? Why at least don't you give me the reasons clearly? Why leave me in this doubt, which upsets me? You would get to know Paris, the new career that I'm attempting to open up for myself, and finally you would embrace me after three years during which we haven't seen one another. The fact that you send me things by way of other people leads me to suspect that for you to come to Paris would be difficult for the time being. At least, I repeat, tell me the reason: that will calm me or give me the grounds for calling you stupid. Do you understand?"

Florimo was in some sort of difficulty, whether external or private, internal, and subjective remains unknown. Pastura, who knew much about Florimo which he never had reason to publish, wrote[13]: "But at that time Florimo must have been prey to one of those 'moral seizures' [*mali morali*] to which he frequently was subject. Precisely of what it consisted we do not know, as it is probable that he had not spoken of it to Bellini up to that time. To his friend's insistence, he must have felt driven to reply with no more than a hint that he felt oppressed by a monotonous life: to [adduce] something general, in short, which explained nothing and began to make Bellini apprehensive." Perhaps significantly, Bellini's letter of July 1, one of the letters that Florimo left to the Naples Conservatory, is physically mutilated at the end, where we can read[14]: "At this moment I have received your letter, from which I learn that you have been ill, and I had good reason to tell you above that I had not heard from you for many days—are you really well now? Further, I am sorry that you will not be able to come to Paris now: I asked you a thousand times to tell me your reasons. I believe that they are a misguided delicacy on your part because you'd have to make use of a few soldi of mine. Whatever the reason, as I have *pro* *** you have the thick head of a *calabrese*, I do not *** you *** I no longer ask for reasons, and I'll see you when I see you. Amen. . . . Addio, my dear Florimo: you drive me crazy, but your Bellini always loves you."

When Bellini first had begun to suspect that Florimo would not come to Paris, he had turned to others. On March 19, he had written to Santocanale[15]: "Do you count on arriving this month? Do me the favor of bestirring yourself for once, and come to Paris, as it's only a tiny trip. Start out on the journey and you'll see; but come soon." But the most elaborate of his projects for importing companionship from Italy appeared in a letter of March 18 to Vincenzo Ferlito[16]: "Get ready, then, to come to me in Paris; because if I have a success with the French opera, I'll come to Catania, and then you and Aunt Sara will return with me, so as to see all of Italy, France, and England." The Ferlitos could afford to travel, whereas Bellini's parents and siblings could not.

Bellini's intermittent negotiations with Naples had come to life once more in 1834 because court officials, other important people in Naples, and friends of his had been putting pressure on the management of the Teatro San Carlo. Finally, his demands had been met, except that he was to receive, not 10,000 ducati, but 9,000, for three operas and that the first of them was to be delivered early in January 1835. Then Bellini had made a new suggestion: as *I Puritani* would not have been heard in Italy, why should he not, as the first of the promised operas, supply the San Carlo with a new version adapted to its singers—which to him most notably meant Malibran? Some time in October 1834, he received a favorable response from Naples, but with the worrisome proviso that the revised Act I of *I Puritani* must reach there by January 12, 1835, the second not more than eight days later.[17] He had accepted the amended arrangement and had received the contract on November 20.

The next day, the première of *I Puritani* at the Théâtre-Italien had been postponed to January, and it had become clear to Bellini that he would be unable to fulfill the contractual clause requiring his presence in Naples for the staging of the opera there. He foresaw no decisive difficulty over that. On November 30, he wrote to Florimo[18]: "Certainly I'll write a new cavatina expressly for Malibran.[19] In a few days I'll start adapting the opera according to the plan that I have worked out, and I see that it will be excellent for [Francesco] Pedrazzi,[20] Duprez, Porto (to whom you will take the trouble of teaching his role), and the powerful Malibran, whom you will go to see for me and, after having shouted loudly at her because she didn't ask me to see her when she passed through Paris,[21] you will give her my thanks for the care that she has taken, and still takes, in performing my operas . . . Tell *** I'll adjust and adapt *I Puritani* to her voice, that she should not have any fears about the role . . ." He confided to Cesare Pugni the copying-out of those sections of the score which would remain unchanged in Naples.

Bellini intended to send the complete refashioned score[22] to Naples by sea from Marseilles. But he learned that no steamer would leave there until January 10 [1835], which at best meant that the first act could not reach Naples until January 15—three days after the contractual date by which it had to be delivered and only five before the date specified for the delivery of Act II. On December 21–22, he wrote to Florimo[23]: "I am working like a dog to have everything ready for the 28th current, and to send it off immediately. Here we shall go on stage about January 15." The combination of preparing the Paris staging and the Naples adaptation in so short a time proved too much for him. But he completed the revision of Act I and delivered it to a shipping agent for forwarding to Marseilles. On January 5, 1835, he delivered Act II, which was to be sent from Marseilles quickly. But he was told that cholera had broken out in southern France, as a result of which the steam packets that should have left Marseilles on December 30 and January 1 had been held in quarantine at Nice: Act I would be late in reaching Naples. To Florimo on January 5, he wrote[24]: "I begged him [the shipping agent] to write to Marseilles at once to have it sent by post; and according to the stories, it will reach Naples between [January] 20 and 24; I have had the rest of the second act posted here today, and they will have it between the 18th and 20th. It is true that you have told me that the Society will not accept the score after the required date; but I want to make them see that I have done everything corresponding to their wishes, that a misfortune of *force majeure* has prevented the first act from reaching Naples on January 8 and the second on the 17th . . ."

On February 9, sixteen days after the brilliant Paris première of *I Puritani*, Bellini received word from principe Ottajano of the Naples management that the opera would not be performed at the San Carlo because of the tardy arrival of the score. The letter also dissolved the rest of his contract with the Society. Malibran, who intensely wanted to sing the role of Elvira as Bellini had reshaped it for her, threw her considerable influence into an attempt to persuade the Società dei Reali Teatri di Napoli to alter its abrupt, unreasonable decision. On February 18, Bellini wrote calmly to Florimo[25]: "I am sorry about all the events that have prevented *I Puritani* from being given, and I appreciate how much that dear *donna di Malibran* has done to get it performed; and if one thing in all this misfortune displeases me, it is that the angelic Malibran has been unable to make those Neapolitans enjoy my *Puritani*; but what can one do? you well ask: no force suffices against destiny; therefore let's not talk about it any more, and come what must come." Florimo bore off the two volumes of the revised score and kept them in the library of San Pietro a Majella until his death. They are now in the Museo Belliniano at Catania. But that version of *I Puritani*[26] never has been performed as Bellini intended it.

During March 1835, Bellini appears to have remained almost completely inactive. On the 31st, he attended the seasonal closing of the Théâtre-Italien, the seventeenth singing of *I Puritani*. That last visit to the Italien was also the last time he heard a performance of one of his operas. On April 1, he wrote a curious, highly informative letter to Vincenzo Ferlito. Running to more than 3,000 words, it amounts to a recapitulation of his life from his departure from Italy in April 1833 to April 1835, with asides on related subjects.[27] He recounts his first brief stopover in Paris en route to London; his stay in England; his return to Paris; the impossibility then of composing in French for the Opéra; his decision to work with the Italien. He returns to Rossini's original "enmity" toward him and to the attempt to "suffocate, exterminate" him by contracting Donizetti. He speaks of working with all his strength while living in the country "well lodged in the house of my close English friend, Mr. Lewis." Again he returns to the inflammatory subject of Donizetti, details the three times when they had composed simultaneously for the same theater, and goes into the "failure" of *Marin Faliero* and the refulgent success of *I Puritani*.

"Yesterday, what is more," he goes on, "something fantastic and unheard-of happened. While Rubini was singing alone on the stage, a note was thrown to him and many voices called out at the same time: 'Read it, read it.' The orchestra stops, Rubini picks up the letter, reads it to himself, turns toward the audience, and says: '*Messieurs, avec grand plaisir.*' Then the whole theater breaks out into the greatest applause. I ran to ask what the letter said: it was from many subscribers asking Rubini to sing, between one act and the other, the aria from *Il Pirata* which he had sung on his evening a month before, and had sung like a god. Then Rubini sang that aria, and there is nothing to say about the effect and the applause. In a word, yesterday evening *I Puritani* gave such pleasure that it altogether persuaded the Donizetti party that *Marin Faliero,* dead since Sunday and from the 12th to the 31st of March, must be sent to the cemetery!"

Thereafter, Bellini continued for another two paragraphs about the struggle in his own mind between Donizetti's opera and his own, closing the first paragraph by saying "and he [Donizetti] left the 25th, I think for Naples, convinced of his fiasco."[28] The next paragraph begins: "There you have the story that has cost me so much pain, so many sleepless nights, and so much diplomatic care to influence minds in my direction and thus dissolve a diabolic conspiracy created to ruin me. But I did not want to speak of it for fear of dismaying you, and poor Florimo, who knows it all, was frightened to death for almost a year, suffered almost constantly from fever considering the danger I was in. . . ." Again he returned to the unquestioned and unquestionable success of *I Puritani*, reporting that the closing night of the season had been "a real celebration, an evening of a brilliance never seen at the Théâtre-Italien." Continuing obsessively, the succeeding short paragraph contains the sentence, already cited, about his having won the position due him: first after Rossini. Then he gives his uncle a glowing account of his comportment and social success:

"Would you like to know how I have comported myself? My system always was to frequent the best society of the place where I was. At Naples, then at Milan and London, I did not give up that system, and I have followed it in Paris, a city that is more susceptible and values the *comme il faut*. Therefore, as soon as I reached Paris, I was introduced by the English ambassadress, whom I had known in London, to the most distinguished people in Paris, to ministers of France, to all the ambassadors, and to all the first families that came to the ambassadress's house; consequently, in a single evening I understood what could be made most useful to me and bring me the most honor. At the same time, I made the acquaintance of the leading musicians and painters, etc., etc. and of many men of letters. Now I find myself welcome in all those houses, and no week passes that I don't dine with some minister; particularly the minister of the interior [Thiers] and the one of commerce and public works wish me madly well.

"See what very curious coincidences occur: on Shrove Tuesday, I dined at the home of monsieur le comte de Hahault,[29] where the [other] dinner guests were the ambassadors of Austria, Naples, Switzerland, and England, and many other important personages; that evening, at a ball [given by] the barone Selliegre,[30] the richest man in Paris; and finally at a great supper at the house of the *Ministre de l'Intérieur*. Invited to a soirée every evening, every day to dinner by distinguished men or ministers or talented artists. In short, my reputation is established: everyone loves me personally because they all say that I am good, distinguished, and behave like a gentleman." At this point, Bellini realized that he was beginning to sound a little silly, for he threw in parenthetically: "(What foolishness, my repeating such things to you; but you wanted it, and I hope that you won't show this letter to anyone.)" But his strong, unsure ego was not to be put down so easily: the next sentence reads: "In short, I have their *comme il faut, et voilà tout*."

That extraordinary flood was not yet ready to abate. "What I owe to myself truly is my actions, that is, that never, nowhere, am I seen with scoundrels or debauchees [*mascalzoni o debioscati*], never in a gambling house or one for bad women; no one ever heard of my being involved in quarrels about money, I have never compromised anybody; but instead I have done what my resources allow for the needy, particularly in Paris, where there are so many Italian immigrants. Therefore I can assure you that I respect and love everyone in such a way that you would have had never to know me in order to fail to respond to my respect and love. My frequenting high society has made the theater people think that 'I am a little proud and haughty,' but I let them say so; enough that I am humble in manner and do my duty; it never has been a question of pride to scorn bad companions and choose them from among people of honor. There you have my present position. My future plans are to be able to arrange a contract with the French Grand Opéra and remain in Paris, making it my home for the present, and to reap all the advantages that such a city promises me, not refusing [to compose] some scores that Italy will want from me."

Finally, after reporting the recovery of about 5,000 francs of what he had thought lost in Spanish funds, Bellini devoted a long paragraph to the chimera of marriage.[31] Which of the suggested candidates for his hand he refers to as "a rather pretty young girl, sweet, of good family" is not entirely clear—it was probably the adopted daughter of the Sellières whom he had discussed with Florimo—but the impression he wanted to make upon his uncle is unmistakable: "She is not rich, but she has an uncle and aunt who are: if they will give her 200,000 francs, I'll marry her; and I think that I'll be truly happy, as she is good like Aunt Sara, very religious, of good principles, and very well educated; further, she has rich and important relatives and comes from a family loaded with honor. We shall see: I am in no hurry. Only that sort of marriage could put me in the position of being independent of everyone and everything: to have 10,000 francs of income and a good wife is to have a refuge from all ills, for with 10,000 francs, one lives well anywhere in the world. But I repeat to you that I am in no hurry and am waiting reflectively. Up to now, God has protected me; I hope that he will always inspire me."

Having portrayed himself as he wished others to see him, Bellini ended that autobiographical revelation this way: "Milan and Venice are asking me for operas, and the Théâtre-Italien wants me to enrich *Norma* with other pieces. I hope shortly to give you news of my decision. Many affectionate greetings to papa and mama, and I am grateful to both of them for the immense interest that they have taken in this new success of mine; also to all my dear relatives and friends. To you an embrace from your most affectionate nephew Vincenzo."

Early in the spring of 1835, Bellini sat for a bronze portrait-bust by Jean-Pierre Dantan *fils*. At least seven copies of it were made in gesso, Bellini having had one of them sent to Alessandro Lamperi in Turin and six to Santocanale—one each for himself and the duchessa di San Martino in Palermo, two for Florimo in Naples, and two for Vincenzo Ferlito in Catania.[32] Benedetto Condorelli, the first director of the Museo Belliniano, considered Dantan's bust an especially reliable likeness. Bellini had delayed sending a copy of it to Florimo for some time, hoping and perhaps believing that Florimo would come to Paris and then could carry it back to Naples with him.

On about May 11, Bellini returned to his second-floor rooms in the Levys' house in Puteaux. There, on May 13, he took up again what he called his "daily studies," noting down melodies and other musical ideas that might be adapted for future use. Shortly thereafter, Florimo was overwhelmed by rumors spreading through Naples that Bellini had been killed in a duel with a jealous husband. Frantic, particularly because he had not received recent word directly from Bellini, he immediately wrote both to Bellini and to others, begging for reassuring news. Bellini began a letter to him on June 5, but did not finish it[33]: "A real fabrication has caused you so much sorrow over the supposed duel and my death. You know me well, and understand that only a point of honor or a fatal misfortune would call me out onto the field—" On June 7, however, he sent a letter beginning with the passionately desired news of his survival[34]: "A real bit of nonsense, my dear Florimo, my duel. I see a few women, but husbands are systematically opposed to duels. You know that I avoid people with bad natures; so I never expose myself; I don't like playing the Don Giovanni or the Don Quixote, and therefore I hope to die in my bed as the most peaceful of men; so when such news reaches you another time, quarantine it before believing it."

The letter is badly mutilated at this point, but clearly deals with the death of Maddalena Fumaroli (of which Florimo seems to have informed Bellini very belatedly). After saying that he could not weep a single tear, he adds: "Giuditta's behavior has closed my heart to any abandon; but at such sorrowful news, on reading the poems that you have set to music [*Due Speranze*], I wept bitterly and saw that my heart is still susceptible to pain; enough, let's not discuss that any more. Have a poem done for me by the author of the one in the *Due Speranze*[35] relevant to Maddalenina's virtue and tenderness, which I can set to music. In that way, I'll respond to whoever wants a song of mine dedicated to her memory; let it be an answer to the two hopes [*due speranze*]; for certainly it will be tender, and have it so that I can speak to her beautiful spirit! !"[36]

The first London performance of *I Puritani* occurred at the King's Theatre on May 21 under the direction of one of Bellini's former classmates at Naples, Michele (later Sir Michael) Costa. This time, it followed rather than preceded a production of Donizetti's *Marin Faliero*, which had been mildly successful. On May 25, Bellini gleefully wrote Florimo[37]:

"Here I am to announce to you the unheard-of furor on the London stage of our *Puritani*, which was given on Thursday, the 21st current. Behold, the opera, despite some uncertainty on the part of the chorus, *had such a triumph, such enthusiasm, such a furor, that many people shouted, and never was so much applause recorded in a London theater.* They encored *Arturo's entrance*, the *Polacca*, and the *duet between the two basses*, and all the pieces were applauded repeatedly.

"They write me that Costa performed miracles of work because the impresario wanted the chorus to learn the opera *in six days' time*, and those poor people did what they could, but it was impossible for it to go well. They also write me that Princess Victoria (heiress presumptive to the English throne) was seen to clap her hands at the great duet of the basses and to call out *bis* before anyone else. . . . It seems to me that I wrote you that *Marino [Faliero]* was a fiasco when given in London the past Thursday, a week before *I Puritani*, and that the abovementioned journals[38] spoke of it on the 15th current, and the articles speaking of *I Puritani* are dated the 22nd." Bellini's first informant about that success had been one Doca, a theatrical agent who was acting as co-director of the King's Theatre and who would write him again on July 26, this time in humorous vein[39]:

"In fact, I am, we are, sick of hearing in every corner of England, and I shall say, only partly in jest, even in the diligences, the music of *I Puritani*, and one day, finding myself in a horticultural garden [where] the seven or eight military bands played almost nothing but *I Puritani*, I left that place in despair, and the guard on the diligence played the duet of the two basses on a valve horn; I went to the city, and there I heard it being hummed in the streets; at public and private concerts; and even in dreams one hears *I Puritani* being sung."

In a P.S. to Florimo on May 25, Bellini had reported[40]: "They write me from London, too, because it happened that for a whole week *La Sonnambula* was given in three theaters, two English [theaters] and the Italian Theater. The Queen of England [Adelaide] has ordered a performance of *I Puritani* for Tuesday because she is going to the theater to hear it again." No doubt was possible about Bellini's popularity in London. But when Doca went on from his humorous report on *I Puritani* to discuss a staging of *Norma*, he did not spare Bellini's feelings[41]: "*Norma* was born and—let it be said between us—died, and let it remain buried in friendship's bosom. Our good friend Pasta had greater dignity, but though poor Giulietta [Grisi] did everything she could to do well, it was to no avail when she was surrounded by an Adalgisa who gives one the tertian fever and a barbarous tenor who is finished as far as the glory of the Italian theater goes—I mean poor Curioni—without rehearsals and in the face of a thousand obstacles; period." Bellini's comment upon the London failure of *Norma*, in a long letter of July 1 to Florimo, was this[42]:

"Also another piece of news, that *Norma* was given in London with Grisi as the protagonist and was a solemn fiasco. The journals say that she sang and acted less well than in any other opera, and they remember Pasta with great sorrow because she was not in this performance. Oh! my dear Florimo! you cannot imagine the pleasure afforded me by the fact that Grisi made this experiment in London rather than in Paris, because, my dear, you cannot believe the damage that a fiasco with *Norma* [here] would do me; everyone extols it as the best of my operas; everyone wants it and demands it loudly, and you can see, can't you, that if they were to give it and produce a fiasco, that would take away all the French fame that I have acquired with *I Puritani*. . . . Do you think that I would have refused 8,000 francs to adapt it [*Norma*] if hope were *** for a big success? I heard Grisi sing the Cavatina [*"Casta diva"*] badly, and that was enough for me to judge her incapable of the rest, as I had seen her in *Anna Bolena*, [in] which, if you take away the tender part, [she] was unbearable in the rest, and especially in the tragic. Give her *La Sonnambula*, *I Puritani*, *La Gazza* [*ladra*], and a thousand operas of simple and innocent style, [and] I can swear to you that she will be second to none; but as for noble characters, she does not understand them or feel them because she does not have that instinct or the training to bear herself with the nobility and lofty style that they require; thus, it would be my feeling that in *Norma* she would be nothing, and that the role of Adalgisa is the only one suited to her character. I hope that what happened in London will rid her of the desire to do it in Paris, too, and that it will be reserved for Malibran to make it please the French."[43]

In Bellini's letter of May 25 to Florimo, these sentences appeared near the close: "No result as yet with the Opéra. Rossini advises me to have Scribe do me two poems, one for the Grand Opéra, the other for the Opéra-Comique, and thus to begin applying myself and not waste more time; I'll remember to tell you what I decide regarding this advice after I have spoken with Scribe."[44] All decision-taking at the Opéra had been suspended by bureaucratic complications and the fact that its new director had not been appointed.

As summer came on, Bellini's psychological and physical character and nature unquestionably began to alter. His grip on reality appears, on the evidence of his surviving letters of this period, to have been relaxing. He seems only half to believe in the many, often fragmentary projects that turn slowly in his mind. Also, as Pastura wrote[45]: "During the whole summer period of 1835, Bellini appeared always to be in a dark mood; perhaps because he still had not been able to establish contact with

the management of the Grand Opéra because of the continual postponement of the nomination of its new director, perhaps because he was without work and not in a flourishing condition financially. Florimo accused
him outright of having become lazy, tried every means of urging him on
to regularly scheduled composing even in the absence of a contract—
which merely demonstrated some lack of understanding on Florimo's part
of his friend's whole nature." As anyone who has struggled with Bellini's
extremely difficult script will have realized, it is never easy to decipher;
now it became, as Pastura said,[46] "more minute, more nervous, often undecipherable; sometimes a double page is not enough to contain all that
he has to say to the friend, and he writes lengthwise—across the lines
already written—in red ink. Long letters, crowded with projects, ideas,
reveries that the hand seems to have trouble restraining." Both the handwriting and the statements, ideas, and plans it sets forth inescapably suggest a man deeply disturbed physically, psychologically, or both.

One of the aspiring candidates to the directorship of the Opéra had
been Charles Duponchel. In his eagerness, he appears to have made promises to Bellini about future contracts in the hope that in some manner
Bellini could influence the decision in his favor. And late in June, Duponchel was named director. But nothing materialized for Bellini, in part
because he continued to insist upon a very high fee, but also because he
now became determined to obtain also what earlier was called a *prime:*
a sort of premium that had been paid to invited composers at the time of
their engagement. Duponchel did not want to pay a *prime* to Bellini, not
because of the sum itself, but because he did not want to re-establish the
precedent. By September 2, Bellini would be telling Florimo[47] that he
might have to go over Duponchel's head to the responsible minister in
his determination to obtain the *prime* too. By that date, however, time
had run out for Bellini.

On July 1, in another of those very long, wandering letters to
Florimo, Bellini said[48]: "Oh! if Rossini were to leave Paris permanently,[49]
that, too, would be the good fortune of my Italian operas, as perhaps the
impresarios [Robert and Severini] would come to me to counsel them
about the direction of the Théâtre[-Italien], and also, even though Rossini does not compose, he damages all the maestros, as the journals use
him as a support in speaking badly of the others, repeating a thousand
times: *why does the great Maestro not wake up and flatten his competitors
with a single blow!*" During this period, Florimo often complained of receiving no letters from Bellini; on July 18, Bellini replied[50]: "It is needless
for me to reply to you that not a week passed without my writing, and
believe me, it will be because of the Cholera that the letters are either
lost or delayed. You will know that this disease is wreaking havoc in

Toulon; but thanks be to God, it is far from Paris, and no rumors of it are heard here."

On July 28, the Corsican conspirator Giuseppe Maria Fieschi attempted to assassinate King Louis-Philippe by firing at him—from an upper window in a building on the boulevard du Temple, through which a parade honoring the July Revolution was to march—an infernal machine consisting of twenty-four gun barrels rigged to shoot simultaneously. The king escaped, but eighteen other people were killed.[51] In the aftermath, all places of public entertainment, including the opera houses, were closed, and that fact further complicated Bellini's lengthening period of waiting. To those weeks belong, as closely as can be determined, only four short compositions: the two ariettas *"L'Abbandono"* and *"Il Sogno dell'infanzia,"* the canon for Cherubini's album, and the one dedicated to Zimmerman.[52] We do not know whether or for how long during that summer Bellini may have kept up his intermittent practice of writing-out wordless musical ideas for possible future use.

On August 16, signing himself "Your most affectionate brother Bellini," he wrote from Puteaux his last letter to Santocanale.[53] From there, too, on September 2, he wrote his last-known letter to Florimo[54]: he had approached the responsible minister with regard to his difficulties with Duponchel and the Opéra: "Now let's wait a few days to find out what the Minister will do, and then I hope at any cost to end my idle life and begin to work again by accepting what they will offer me." This letter contains the first reference to what would evolve rapidly into Bellini's mortal struggle with his chronic illness: "For three days I've been slightly disturbed by a diarrhea; I am better now, and think that it's over, but I still have a slight *** of the head."

On a table in Bellini's apartment after his death was found an incomplete letter dated September 3 and clearly intended for Giovanni Ricordi. It deals with Cesare Pugni, who underhandedly had made for his own purposes an extra copy of the score of *I Puritani* while copying the autograph so that Bellini could send the "Malibran version" to Naples[55]: "Yes, I have heard everything from Severini, the infamous action of sig. Pugni, after I did everything for him that I could, not to mention the five-franc pieces that I often had to give him because he, with his wife and children, was dying of hunger. I gave him two hundred francs for copies he made for me of only four pieces from *I Puritani* for Naples; then I paid him 250 francs for a complete copy, though the Society did not need it and we still have it, and he did it only when I begged him, etc., etc. I gave him clothes that were almost new so that he could dress himself during the past winter, as during this summer; I begged the Ladies for cast-offs for his wife, and sent him two packages of things, etc., etc. I recommended him to Rossini, who got him some pupils and would have given him the position of chorusmaster, which is well paid, if he had known how to play the piano, etc., etc. . . ."

The nexus of this problem was that Pugni had conveyed the pirated score to La Scala, which was intending to stage *I Puritani*. On December 30, 1835, the Roman periodical *Lo Spigolatore* would remark[56]: "It is known that the I. R. Teatro alla Scala will present as the first opera of the imminent Carnival season *I Puritani*, by Maestro Bellini, not from the copy now found in the possession of the dealer Ricordi, but from another mutilated, tainted, and bungled copy that, with grave injury inflicted by one of our *maestri di musica*, now resident in Paris, was sent months ago from that City in pretended good faith, as though it were the authentic copy of *I Puritani* written by Maestro Bellini, no thought having been given, in regard to such behavior, to the damage to his own honor, to the standing of the purchasers, to the interests of the Management, to the expectation of the public, to the glory of the author, which will rise up to throw this act of ingratitude in the face of the indelicate Maestro."[57] Actually, the first performance of *I Puritani* at La Scala—which occurred four days before the Roman article was published, though three months after Bellini's death—almost certainly used the authentic score.

Feeling himself recovered from the attack of his annual summer illness, Bellini seems to have made trips from Puteaux into Paris to attend social gatherings. Among the people whom he saw either then or earlier was Heinrich Heine, whose description of Bellini shows the German's wittily malicious power of observation at its usual keenness. In answer to the question: "Was he good-looking?" Heine replied[58]:

"He was not ugly. You see, we men cannot answer affirmatively such a question about one of our own sex. He was tall, slenderly built, moved gracefully—I would say coquettishly, always self-consciously; he had regular features, somewhat elongated, and a pale rosy complexion; light blond, almost golden hair combed into thin little curls; a high, very high, noble forehead; a straight nose; pale blue eyes; a well-formed mouth and a round chin. There was something vague, an absence of character in his features, something milky; and sometimes a sour-sweet expression of sorrow would appear on that milk-face. That expression of pain took the place of a spirit [*Geist*] that was missing from Bellini's face. But it was sorrow without depth; it quivered in his prosaic eyes and flickered without passion on the man's lips. It seemed as though the young Maestro wanted to embody that flat, dull pain in his whole demeanor. His hair was combed in such a romantic, melancholy way, he carried his little Spanish cane in such an idyllic manner, that he always reminded me of one of the young shepherds who simper about coyly in our pastoral plays, with little pastel jackets and breeches and beribboned crooks. And his gait was so virginal, so elegiac, so ethereal. The whole man looked like a sigh in dancing-pumps."

Bellini was both attracted and repelled by Heine, who himself recorded the ambivalent aspect of their relationship[59]:

"I prophesied jokingly that in his capacity as a genius he would die soon, upon reaching the dangerous age. Strange! Despite the jesting tone, that prophecy frightened him; he called me his *jettatore* [possessor of the evil eye] and always made the *jettatore* sign [upraised index and small fingers of the right hand]. He so wanted to live, and had an almost passionate aversion to death; he did not want to hear of dying. He feared it like a child afraid of going to sleep in the dark. He was a good, sweet child, sometimes a little naughty, but one had only to remind him of his early death and he became meek and supplicating, and would make the *jettatore* sign with two fingers. Poor Bellini!"

Among the other people whom Bellini had seen during that summer were Lady Charlotte Hunloke (Hundlocke), principessa Cristina Belgioioso, and Mme C. Jaubert, and it is from them that we learn many details of his last weeks. In her *Souvenirs*, Mme Jaubert wrote[60]:

"One of the victims upon whom Heinrich Heine's mischievousness fell most persistently was the *simpatico* composer Bellini, another one of the guests who were sometimes invited to the country by the principessa Belgioioso. . . . Unfortunately, Bellini had confessed candidly that he was superstitious; at that time, our German poet, who wore black spectacles to rest his weak eyesight, was thus furnished with one of the essential attributes of the *jettatore*. You would have had to see him taking advantage of the young Italian's confessed weakness, to see all the Mephistophelean grimaces with which he accompanied this little war; when they played billiards against one another in the morning in the country, the fearful Maestro never stopped making the horn gesture to drive away the evil spirit."

Mme Jaubert reported that during supper one evening, after the guests had played at experiments in the occult, Heine said to Bellini: " 'You are a genius, Bellini, but you will pay for your great gift with a premature death. All the great geniuses died very young, like Raphael and like Mozart.'

"Bellini interrupted him. 'Don't say that, for the love of God! don't talk like that.' But Heine went on: 'Let's hope, my friend, that the world has been mistaken about you, and that in fact you are not a genius. The good fairies, what is more, gave you a thousand other gifts: they granted you the face of a cherub, the candor of a boy, and the stomach of a stork. Let us hope that the evil fairy didn't intrude among those good ones and ruin everything by stirring in genius . . .'

"Nevertheless, the Maestro, who had not enjoyed that macabre wit at all, did not hide his grudge against Heine. In order to reconcile them, I thought of bringing them together again at my home with the principessa Belgioioso and some other friends.

"When dinner time came on the date set, Bellini did not appear. 'He really is afraid of the *jettatore*,' they said jokingly. But the door opened. It was he . . . No, it was not he; in two written lines, the composer of *I Puritani* expressed his displeasure at being too ill to join us.

" 'That worries me,' the principessa said. 'That he has given up coming must mean that my poor Bellini is very unwell. He was so pleased about this dinner.' "[61]

The principessa sent Luigi Montallegri,[62] a physician, to Puteaux to take care of Bellini. In 1888, the catalogue of the Raccolta Succi at Bologna published the text of five notes that Montallegri thereafter wrote to Carlo Severini of the Théâtre-Italien[63]:

"There has been no appreciable improvement in our Bellini. His condition is still alarming; nonetheless, tonight he has had six fewer evacuations of mucous and blood and has slept a little. The vesicants promise to work, and I await a beneficial crisis from them. With esteem, I am Montallegri. Rue Tivoli,[64] 15[the hour]–20 September."

The second note reads: "The vesicants have begun to bring on a crisis of perspiration. During the past night, our Bellini was less restless and agitated. The slightly less frequent evacuations have permitted him sufficient rest. Montallegri. 21 September."

As Pastura noted,[65] the "breath of optimism" in the second note became hope in the third:

"Bellini's beneficial crisis continues. The matter has diminished enormously and the consistency has changed. We hope to declare him out of danger tomorrow. Montallegri. 22 September, 1835."

That welcome news is said to have reached Rossini in the country outside Paris just as he was preparing to go to see Bellini. As he himself wrote later, he thereupon decided to stay where he was.

Montallegri's fourth note, however, turned very pessimistic: "The thirteenth day has come, and has been alarming. Bellini passed a very restless night because the crisis of perspiration did not occur as on the two preceding days. I remained with him all day and all night so as to see the 14th [day] in. I'll write you something more definite tomorrow. I am, with esteem, Montallegri. Puteaux, 23 September."

Shortly after Montallegri had sent off that fourth note, Bellini's extreme agitation became a terrifying convulsion, and Montallegri understood that death was near. Wanting to inform Severini as quickly as possible, he wrote a note in very incorrect French (the first four had been in Italian) to Bonnevin, a pharmacist in the rue Favart—where the Théâtre-Italien was—asking him to deliver it to one Bianchi, very probably a staff member of the theater: "Mr. Bonnevin, Get this note to Mr. Bianchi at once and tell Mr. Severini of the approaching end of the unhappy Bellini. A convulsion has left him unconscious, and he may not live until tomorrow. Montallegri. Puteaux, 23 September." In the margin, Montallegri scribbled in Italian: "Our [friend] is lost; a convulsion has put his life in danger."

The other primary references to Bellini's final days appear in the diary, in French, of barone Augusto Aymé d'Aquino, an attaché in the Paris embassy of the Kingdom of the Two Sicilies and a nephew of the composer Michele Carafa; he had been on friendly terms with both Bellini and Florimo[66]:

"(September 11)

"On the 11th, a rumor spreads that Bellini is ill at Puteaux (where I saw him during the past few days). I find him in bed. He has, he tells me, a slight dysentery and will not be long in returning to Paris. At this moment appears Mme Lewis, whom I know under the name of Mlle Olivier. She scolds the patient sharply, saying that he needs absolute rest. The reproach clearly being addressed to me, I take my leave. I describe my visit to my uncle Carafa and to all our friends.

"The 12th. I return to Puteaux. The gardener [Joseph Hubert] appears at the gate to the house, but gives an order. Nobody is being received.

"The 13th. I return there with Mercadante; the same order.

"The 14th. Carafa passes himself off as a Court physician. He gets in to see Bellini, whom he finds in bed.

"(September 22)

"The 22nd. Nobody having been able to see Bellini for days, the dissatisfaction of his friends breaks out at Lablache's this evening. There is even talk of having the King's prosecutor intervene . . .*

"The 23rd. Having to go to spend the day at my sister-in-law's in Rueil, I leave early on horseback. At the pont de Courbevoie, I stop in Puteaux. The gardener is still inflexible. During the day, an appalling storm breaks out, and at about ten minutes after five, completely drenched by the driving rain, I knock at the house of M.ʳ Lewis. No answer . . . I push the gate, and it gives way. After having tied up my horse, I enter the house, which seems completely abandoned. I find Bellini on the bed, seemingly asleep . . . but his hand is ice-cold. I cannot believe the hideous

* Points of omission in the diary entries appear in the published version.

truth . . . The gardener reappears and tells me that Signor Bellini breathed his last at 5 o'clock, and that because M.ʳ and Madame Lewis had gone to Paris, he had had to go out to call someone and obtain candles . . . Bewildered and frantic, I rush as fast as possible to Lablache's, rue des Trois Frères, whence the fatal news spreads through Paris. This evening, at General Manhès's, I meet Mercadante and Donna Sofia. All of us are afflicted.[67] Giulio Alary turns up unexpectedly.[68] He tells of a touching melody for which Garofolini has just written the words:

> 'Weep, unhappy Catania,
> And the world weeps with you . . . etc.' "[69]

Bellini died, then, at about five o'clock on September 23, 1835, six weeks before his thirty-fourth birthday.[70]

Immediately, rumors drifted across Paris: Bellini had been poisoned; he had been murdered by Mme Levys, who had been his mistress and had become lethally jealous of another woman to whom Bellini had been paying attention. This nonsense was believed the more easily because many who had known Bellini, or merely had seen him, found it impossible to believe that so apparently healthy a young man could have died of mysterious natural causes. Rossini, who returned to Paris to take charge of the funeral arrangements and make certain that Bellini's estate would be cared for properly, saw to it that an autopsy was performed (in response to an order from the king) by a Doctor Dalmas, a member of the Faculté de Médicine sufficiently distinguished to have been awarded the Légion d'honneur. Finding no traces of poison in Bellini's body, Dr. Dalmas wrote[71]: ". . . it is evident that Bellini succumbed to acute inflammation of the colon, compounded by an abscess in the liver. The inflammation of the intestine had produced violent symptoms of dysentery during life."

What Dr. Dalmas did not try to explain was the source of that inflammation, that abscess—the real "cause" of Bellini's death. After noting Bellini's record of hot-weather diarrhea and studying Dr. Dalmas's report of the autopsy, Dr. Victor de Sabata wrote (1969)[72]: "I have good reason to suspect that the terminal episode was what our Latin forefathers called *inspissatio sanguinis*, i.e., thickening of the blood (caused by severe loss of water and electrolytes due to diarrhea) to the point at which it could not circulate through the smaller blood vessels, particularly in the brain and lungs." Earlier in his commentary, Dr. de Sabata wrote: "From the description given by the worthy Dr. Dalmas some 135 years ago, it is quite obvious that Bellini died of a terminal flareup of chronic amebiasis. It is, indeed, a wonder to me that the cause of Bellini's death still can be regarded by some as 'mysterious.' The preceding history of attacks of diarrhea, recurring for several years during the hot season, is itself sufficient, if not to diagnose the trouble with absolute certainty, at least to make any practicing doctor strongly suspect amebiasis. And then the findings at the autopsy are so typical of chronic amebiasis with amebic abscess of the liver that Dr. Dalmas's description could be lifted as it stands and printed in a treatise on pathological anatomy."[73]

But why, at least during Bellini's final hours, perhaps longer, had the Levys couple left him unattended in their Puteaux villa? Why had the gardener been instructed not to permit anyone to see Bellini? Almost certainly because the Levyses—and very probably Dr. Montallegri as well—suspected that Bellini was suffering from cholera, which is extremely infectious, and which was epidemic in southern France at the time. That Dr. Montallegri believed that Bellini was suffering from cholera is likely because Bellini's external symptoms resembled more than a little those of a victim of that plague. We may even speculate that Montallegri had told the Levyses that Bellini had contracted cholera, and had instructed them neither to visit him nor to allow other people to do so.

Was Dr. Montallegri with Bellini when he died? We cannot know, though it seems unlikely that if he had been present, the gardener Joseph Hubert would have failed to mention to Aymé d'Aquino his departure only some ten minutes earlier. If he did leave the dying patient alone, why did he do so? Again, we cannot know. Montallegri may well have been the bungler that he has often been accused of being, but his failure to diagnose Bellini's condition properly and his consequent application of useless vesicants may indicate nothing more than the general vagueness of internal medicine in 1835. Nothing whatever suggests that he was a villain who would knowingly have dashed away to let Bellini die unattended. What remains, then, is a mystery for which no final solution can be proposed.

The *Journal de Paris* for September 25 reported[74]: "As soon as monsieur Dantan *fils* heard of Bellini's death, he betook himself to Puteaux to the house of monsieur Levys, where Bellini died, and there proceeded to the operation of taking a death-mask of the young Italian composer: the able sculptor succeeded perfectly in portraying his appearance. The young Maestro is recognizable at first glance, and his friends will be happy to have the portrait that monsieur Dantan will make from the original in happier times."[75]

Rossini, fortunately, took firm charge of all arrangements for Bellini's funeral and tomb and of the proper distribution of his belongings in Paris and Puteaux. After the autopsy, Bellini's body had been placed temporarily in the Levys' family tomb. Rossini now appointed a commission of distinguished musical people which quickly sent out a circular letter[76]:

"Gentlemen.

"A premature death takes Bellini from the arts and from his friends.

"We have thought that it falls to France, which received his last strains and final breaths, to act as his family and homeland.

"Consequently, it has been decided to open a subscription destined for the erection of a monument to his memory.

"Aware of your love for the Arts, we hope that you will wish to join in this act of generous hospitality.

> "*The Commission*
>
> "Rossini–Cherubini–Paër–Carafa–[Fromental] Halévy–[François-Antoine] Habeneck–[Auguste-Mathieu] Panseron–[Adolphe] Nourrit–[Jean-Baptiste-Marie] Chaullet [Chollet]–Rubini–[Eugène] Troupenas."[77]

Adding the names of the two responsible directors of the Théâtre-Italien, Robert and Severini, the Commission also sent a letter to *"Messieurs les Artistes de l'Orchestre de l'Opéra."*[78] It contained these sentences: "We approach you to ask for the participation of your talents in the execution of a Mass in music which will be celebrated on Friday, October 2, in the Chapel of the Hôtel des Invalides. We dare to hope that you certainly will want to respond to our appeal and prove that musicians from all countries form a single family."

Two letters from Rossini to Santocanale, written respectively four days after Bellini's death and one day after his funeral, relate with the conviction of immediacy what took place. The first is dated at Paris on September 27[79]:

"I have the sorrow to announce to you the loss of our mutual friend Bellini. This unhappy man died on Wednesday the 23rd of this month at three o'clock [*sic*] in the afternoon. A dysentery, increasing constantly to inflammation for eighteen days, left every resource of the [medical] faculty useless. I am inconsolable over the loss of a friend, and equally so in thinking of the pain that this [letter] of mine will bring you and the sorrow that his parents will experience. All Paris weeps for him, and if in misfortunes of this sort (which are irreparable) there is any certain compensation, it is that the emotions demonstrated by such cultivated and civilized people as the Parisians must greatly alleviate our sorrows. I loved him and helped him while he was alive, and I now tell you what I have done since his death so that you can give an account of it to his family, and without losing any time. I came back from the country, where I spent the summer, a few hours after our friend's death [and] found that the justice of the peace had put his seal on all the effects belonging to the deceased. I had Bellini's body embalmed, and I had them hold aside his heart, similarly embalmed; so that if the relatives or his native city should want the heart, everything would be preserved. There was a written record of the *autopsy*, which I enclose in this [letter] of mine so that you may know about his illness. I at once formed a Commission of the principal musicians of the three Royal Theaters of Paris, and of which I am President, with the intention of having a Mass performed at the Invalides with all the pomp necessary to honor our friend; the members are the following: Cherubini, Paer, Caraffa [*sic*], Alevy [*sic*], Panseron, Nourit [*sic*], Chaulet [*sic*], Rubini, Troupenas, etc., etc.

"I immediately drew up circulars to open a subscription for the purpose of raising a monument to Bellini, with the fruits of which (once we have paid the expenses of the embalming and of the funeral ceremonies, which will be worthy of the deceased), we can do him honor, and thus save money belonging to our friend's relatives. As of now I cannot tell you the amount of the fortune that Bellini left, as his papers cannot be examined, for, as I told you, they are under seal, but from what he often said to me I think that his substance amounts to about 40,000 francs— that is, 10,000 in the hands of Sig. Levy [*sic*], an Englishman (in whose house in the country he died, and where he had unequaled care), another 20,000 in coupons of Spanish funds; there ought to be ten or twelve thousand francs in Milan with the Turinas, to whom I have now written for information. But I repeat to you that all this is approximate because I have not been able to examine anything, which I shall do when the family sends me the power of attorney, the form for which I hope to send you tomorrow if no difficulties arise because of the French formalities. You will offer my services to his family, and if I am not to be designated in the power of attorney, please beg them to leave some latitude to the designees to concede to the people who were most affectionate to Bellini some small objects belonging to the deceased—be it clearly understood, of very small value, because, you see, I am doing what I can to carry things out with the required pomp without its being detrimental to the family. I believe that the ceremony will take place on Friday, October 2. When sending you the form for the power of attorney, I shall give you the program of what will be done. As of now, I [can] tell you that I have at my disposition all the singers of the Grand Opéra, of the Théâtre-Italien, and of the Opéra-Comique, and I can tell you frankly that everyone finds it a pleasure and a duty to take part in this solemn and sorrowful ceremony. I don't know if my present emotional state leaves clear what I am writing. Be lenient in judging me, and tell the relatives and friends that the only consolation remaining to me is that of dedicating my careful attention to honoring a friend, a compatriot, and a distinguished artist. I had arranged something excellent for Bellini at the

Grand Opéra; that was [to be] his consolation, and death has cut it all off. Believe me, your most affectionate friend G. Rossini. Paris, September 27, 1835. Later I shall ask•you to have the relations write some letters of thanks to the people who will have *** ."

Rossini's letter of October 3 to Santocanale reads[80]:

"Most esteemed friend;

"I have the sad satisfaction to tell you that the exequies of our defunct friend were carried out with general love, with extraordinary eagerness on the part of all the artists, and with pomp that could have served equally for a king: two hundred [*sic*] voices performed the funeral Mass; the leading artists of the capital vied to sing in the choruses; after the Mass, we set out for the cemetery (where poor Bellini's body will repose until a new dispensation); a military band of one hundred twenty musicians escorted the cortège; every ten minutes a blow on the *Tam Tam* resounded; and I assure you that the numbers of people [and] the sorrow seen depicted on all faces were beyond description; I cannot tell you how great the affection was which our poor friend had inspired. I am in bed, half dead, because I don't hide from you that I wanted to be present until the last word was pronounced over Bellini's tomb; and as the weather was as bad as possible, it having rained unceasingly all day, but that did not discourage anyone, not even me, though I had been unwell for several days, so that staying there in the mud and covered with water left me more indisposed; I'll take care of myself, and I'll be altogether recovered in a few days. I send you Paër's oration, which appeared in *Le Moniteur universel*, and I also send you the oration by Fornari, a young Sicilian doctor and friend of ours, who showed a big heart and much zeal in this situation; this second oration was printed in *Le Temps;* I send you only these two because it is useless to have you spend on postage what I suppose that you will receive later. An oration by Professor Orioli produced a great effect, a poem by [Émilien] Pacini[81] was a like success. Finally, a modest sonnet that I did not want to have recited because it was mediocre, but I yielded to the poet's wishes and put aside the [question of] merit. Thus everything went divinely, and though still full of tears, I can feel the joy of having showed my poor friend the affection that he reverently bore me. The subscription for the monument is growing, and I hope to be able to announce to you shortly that the expenses of the funeral (which are not small) have been covered.[82] I had planned to open subscriptions in the Italian capitals, but not knowing definitely where Bellini's body will rest, I do not dare to do it for fear of having little success; and as we have time, for that reason, give me your opinion about this matter and I'll put it into execution.

"I have received your last letter; I thank you a million times for the trouble that you have taken for me[83]; I hope one day to be able to prove my gratitude; whenever you want to send me any sums, you can use the House of Rothschild. Tell Bellini's parents[84] for me that I am at their disposition for the little that I am worth, and that I should be happy to prove of service to them.

"Forgive me if I address you as *Voi*[85]; but in such circumstances I assure you that I think only with my heart and forget all the polite usages; further, I know that my nature must deserve your friendship. You do so much for me! Your Rossini."

When the casket containing Bellini's body reached the Court of Honor of the Invalides on October 2, the Chapel was filled by a large proportion of the most noted musicians and other artists then in Paris; the royal princesses also were present. The pallbearers were Carafa, Cherubini, Paër, and Rossini. After the soft intoning of the Gregorian Requiem, the rest of the Mass was sung by a chorus of three hundred and fifty voices and a quartet of great opera singers: Nicholas Ivanoff, Lablache, Rubini, and Tamburini. To the text of the Lacrymosa, the four men sang an adaptation of "*Credeasi misera*," Arturo's solo from the finale of *I Puritani*. In continuous rain, the hearse and eleven carriages set out at one o'clock for Père-Lachaise: over the Seine, through the rue Royale and the boulevards dark with onlookers. At the graveside, many words were spoken, as Rossini indicated. After the casket had been lowered into the ditch, the feeble seventy-five-year-old Cherubini, supported by Auber and Halévy and visibly weeping, threw onto it the first wet lump of earth. Then the mourners and the curious onlookers drifted away and the new grave was left to absorb the continuing downpour.

Commemorations of many varieties were held in Paris, Catania, Naples, Milan, and other Italian cities. Donizetti, happily unaware of Bellini's jealous disdain, wrote to Giovanni Ricordi from Naples on October 20, 1835[86]: "I am very happy that I shall be able, in Milan, to give the final proof of my friendship to the shade of poor Bellini, with whom I found myself composing four times, and each time our relationship grew much closer. It was I who showed the Filarmonica why it should do something to attest to our common grief. The departure of one instigator left the matter suspended. Now I should conduct a Mass at the Conservatory, and I have already begun it, but as the performance will take place in December, I am prevented from conducting it, and that grieves me. Everything that I had planned was canceled out by Destiny, which has turned me toward Milan—and, very happy to do this, I am awaiting good verses from the most distinguished [Andrea] Maffei, who will now have two reasons for tears—that is, the death of a friend and the marriage of his verses to my music. I have a lot to do, but a proof of friendship for my Bellini precedes everything else."[87]

At Bellini's grave in Père-Lachaise (between the graves of Grétry and Boieldieu), a monument by Carlo Marochetti, an Italian sculptor living in Paris, was erected. Thereafter, despite several movements to have Bellini's remains transferred to Catania, nothing was done until 1876. Then the city of Catania, with support from the government of united Italy, arranged the reburial. The casket was removed from the tomb in Père-Lachaise on September 15, 1876, and placed in its permanent place of honor in the Duomo of Catania on September 26,[88] resting upon a monument in marble and bronze designed by Giambattista Tassara into which this line from Romani's libretto for *La Sonnambula* is incised: "*Ah! non credea mirarti si presto estinto, o fiore*" (Ah! I did not think to see you extinguished so soon, o flower).[89]

Of the uncountable posthumous tributes to Bellini which appeared throughout Europe, by much the most interesting, especially in view of its source, is the *Necrologia* by Felice Romani[90]:

"The 24th [*sic*] of September was the last day of an illustrious Italian, and closed, in Pateaux [*sic*], near Paris, a brief life of thirty-three years blossoming with hopes and irradiated with Glory. Vincenzo Bellini is no more! . . .* a tear falls on these words, but I cannot blot them out.

"Catania, where he was born; Naples, where he had his schooling; Milan, which produced the beautiful wreath with which his youth was adorned; Paris, which was generous to him with hospitality and glory—every place, in short, into which the light of the arts, the flame of talent, and the love of the beautiful penetrate—will lament this untimely extinguished torch and weep for the loss of the sublime young man as for a common loss. But no one, perhaps no one so much as I, will be able to measure the emptiness that he leaves, because no one so much as I penetrated into the most hidden recesses of that noble intellect and discerned the source from which emerged the spark that inspired him.

"I was his companion, collaborator, and friend; to him I was guide, counselor, support; to him I was more than a brother. When he reached Milan from Naples already marked by his first studies, but devoid of all experience and not yet freed from the conventions that shackled him in his first theatrical work, *Bianca e Fernando*, I alone read in that poetic spirit, in that impassioned heart, in that mind childishly eager to soar beyond the sphere in which he was held by the school rules and the servility of imitation: I perceived that a different *dramma* was wanted for him, a poetry very different from that which had been introduced by the

* Points of suspension in the original text.

bad taste of the times and the tyranny of the singers and the ignorance of the theatrical poets and that still greater innocence of the composers of music. It was then that I first tested the young Bellini, writing for him *Il Pirata,* which seemed to me a subject likely, so to speak, to touch the most responsive chords in his heart. Nor was I mistaken.

"We understood one another from that day forward, struggled, struggled together against the vicious routines of the musical theater, and set out in accord to extirpate them little by little with courage, perseverance, love. From that marriage of intentions and forces were born *La Straniera, I Capuleti e i Montecchi, Norma,* and *La Sonnambula;* when that marriage was less close for a moment, first came *Zaira,* then *Beatrice di Tenda,* less happy operas that made it clear that thenceforward in Italy music could not deviate from poetry. This last was an epoch of brief discord of which we were both ashamed.[91]

"Others more educated than I am in what concerns the combinations of the art, the most varied theories, the practices, the examples of progress in the matter of knowledge, will analyze Bellini's works, his style, his procedures, his resources; they will tell of the path that he opened after the great *pesarese* [Rossini] and will investigate [the question of] where the latter stopped, where the former took a step forward: I limit myself only to asserting that few composers in Italy, and perhaps no composers other than ours, knew as well as Bellini the necessity for a close union of music with poetry, dramatic truth, the language of emotions, the proof of expression.

"In Bellini, death snuffed out more than a composer of music; it cut short plans that perhaps will not be carried out so quickly in Italy. I knew them all, and their full scope. When the biographers, who will not be lacking, and the masters of the art and the assayers and the critics will have paid their tribute of both praise and study to the generous young man for whom I weep and always shall weep, it will be my part to rectify some opinions, to inspect some judgments, to recall the past, to cast a glance into the future: then I shall publish our projects, our conversations, and the hopes nourished jointly despite the distance that separated us.[92]

"Alas! Perhaps those hopes are altogether dead. I sweated for fifteen years to find a Bellini! A single day took him from me! And that spirit which responded to mine is mute. Anyone who wishes to find in these words a text with which to accuse me of vainglory or to misrepresent my intentions in any way—such a person never knew Bellini; he does not deserve to understand my sorrow."

PART TWO

The Operas and
Nonoperatic Compositions

Adelson e Salvini

I. DRAMMA SEMISERIO in three acts with some spoken dialogue. *Libretto:* An adapted version of Andrea Leone Tottola's libretto for Valentino Fioravanti's *Adelson e Salvini* (Teatro São Carlos, Lisbon, 1815; Teatro dei Fiorentini, Naples, Carnival, 1816).[1] *Composed:* 1824–1825. *Première:* Student performance in the *teatrino* of the Real Collegio di Musica di San Sebastiano, Naples, during Carnival 1825, almost certainly between February 10 and 15. *Original all-male student cast:*

NELLY, *an orphan*	Giacinto Marras
FANNY, *young dependent of Adelson*	unknown
MADAME RIVERS, *governess in Adelson's house*	Luigi Rotellini
SALVINI, *friend of Adelson*	Leonardo Perugini
LORD ADELSON	Antonio Manzi
STRULEY, *a proscript nobleman*	Talamo
BONIFACIO, *servant to Salvini*	Giuseppe Ruggiero
GERONIO, *Struley's confidant*	Ciotola (Ciotala?)

Apparently never performed elsewhere; never published. Incomplete autograph score (lacking a *sinfonia* and part of Act I, Scene 1[2]) in the Museo Belliniano, Catania; fifteen pages of full autograph score (numbered 276–290) in the Bibliothèque Nationale, Paris. Autograph sketches and separate pages, as well as early manuscript copies, in the Museo Belliniano,[3] the library of the Naples Conservatory, and the archives of the Accademia filarmonica, Bologna. In 1970, ten pages of autograph score corresponding to pages 15–19 of the Ricordi piano-vocal score of Version II (plate numbers 10895–10896) were in a private collection in Europe.

II. Drastically revised version in two acts, with the libretto altered (possibly with help from Felice Romani) and with *recitativo secco* replacing the original spoken dialogue. *Prepared:* 1827–1829? by Bellini and Francesco Florimo, with the roles distributed as follows: Nelly—soprano, Fanny—contralto, Madame Rivers—mezzo-soprano, Salvini—tenor, Lord Adelson—baritone, Struley—bass, Bonifacio—*basso comico*, Geronio—bass. Apparently never performed; however, a two-act libretto in the Naples Conservatory library, published by the Stabilimento Musicale Partenope (with "Londra Boosey, Roma Scipione de Rossi, Parigi Choudens"), reads *"Musica di Vincenzo Bellini,"* does not list a cast, and shows Bonifacio's lines in standard Italian; it appears to postdate 1825 considerably. No complete autograph exists. A manuscript copy in full score is in the Naples Conservatory library; some text-words, agogic and instrumental indications, and stage directions are in Bellini's script. Another manuscript copy is in the British Museum, London. Two manuscript copies of the piano-vocal score are in the Naples Conservatory library, as are Bellini autographs of the two revised act-finales: "Chorus in the Finale of the First Act," running to the end of the act, and "Finale of the Second Act," running from *"Ecco al fine quel caro oggetto"* to the end of the opera. The latter bears this notation signed by Francesco Pastura: "This lacks Nelly's invocation *'Salvini alle tue piante,'* later adapted in the finale of *'Bianca'* as revised for Genoa." (That section is probably lacking because it had not yet been composed when this act-finale originally was written.) *Published:* In piano-vocal score without recitatives by Schonenberger, Paris, with plate number S.2184, indicating publication between 1843 and 1875 (the *sinfonia* is that for *Il Pirata*); in piano-solo transcription and in piano-vocal score (1903) by Ricordi, Milan, both with plate number 10896 except for the *sinfonia*, which has 10895–10896.[4] For full, detailed data on autographs, manuscript copies, and publications of *Adelson e Salvini*, see Friedrich Lippmann: *"Vincenzo Bellini und die italienische opera seria seiner Zeit,"* in *Analecta Musicologica*, 6, Cologne/Vienna, 1969, pp. 367–374.

THE LIBRETTO. Setting—Lord Adelson's island castle in Ireland, seventeenth century. Adelson has as a guest his friend the Roman painter Salvini, who has conceived a violent passion for his host's fiancée, Nelly. Colonel Struley, Nelly's uncle and former tutor, shares his family's enmity toward the Adelsons, from whom he once abducted Nelly. He returns to Adelson's island secretly, again intending to deprive his antagonist of Nelly—who is eagerly awaiting Adelson's return. She becomes aware of Salvini's passion for her, and is horrified. The inflamed Italian, hearing in the distance the noisy welcome being given Adelson by his dependents and followers, rushes distractedly away.

Struley, learning of Salvini's feeling for Nelly, decides to turn the knowledge to his own advantage. He convinces Salvini that Adelson's family has forced him to marry a London girl of noble family—and that Salvini can win Nelly by telling her of Adelson's falsity and persuading her to run away with him in a boat that Struley has concealed nearby. When Adelson encounters Salvini and detects the signs of his friend's intense emotion, he interprets them as indicating a passion for the painter's pupil, Fanny. At once Adelson tells Salvini that he shall have the girl; Salvini, convinced that Adelson already is married to the London girl, thinks that he means Nelly.

Struley has ordered Geronio to set fire to the house in which, near Adelson's castle, Nelly lives; he plans to abduct her with Salvini's help during the ensuing confusion. As soon as Adelson's retainers rush off to fight the fire, Salvini shows Nelly a letter (forged by Struley) purporting to prove that Adelson is married, and urges her to elope with him. Nelly is beginning to believe him when she sees Struley and divines that he is behind these machinations. Realizing that his plans are misfiring, Struley then attempts to carry off Nelly by force. But Salvini, now aware that Struley has duped him, dashes into the flames to rescue Nelly. In the ensuing melée, Struley fires a pistol at Nelly, whereupon Salvini wounds him, at the same time killing Geronio. When Nelly swoons, Salvini believes that he has killed her too.

The people return. Salvini reappears in ranting despair. Still convinced that he has killed Nelly, he begs Adelson to take just revenge upon him. Adelson, however, knows that Nelly, who has not been harmed, is hiding in a pavillion. He is more eager than before to arrange the marriage of Salvini and Fanny, but Salvini remains convinced that Nelly's inert body will be found. When he finally sees Nelly alive, he begs and receives pardon from Adelson and decides to marry Fanny and take her back to Rome. Preparations are begun for the marriage of Adelson and Nelly.

The most interesting character in Tottola's libretto as Bellini first set it (he is not equally interesting in Bellini's music) is the Neapolitan servant Bonifacio, whose involvement in the central plot is tangential. He had almost certainly been written into Tottola's libretto to provide a partly spoken, partly sung role for Carlo Casaccia, called Casacciello, a second-generation member of a classic dynasty of dialect buffoons. Bonifacio, who pretends to be timorous and slow-witted, sings and speaks in Neapolitan dialect, and that trait lends him a small individuality.[5] But farce was not in Bellini's nature in 1825, or ever. His unoriginal, Rossinian treatment of Bonifacio fails to raise the first version of *Adelson e Salvini* above mediocrity. In the second version—in which the second and third acts were abbreviated and run together—Bonifacio was deprived of most of his Neapolitan flavor: he now sings in standard Italian set in the variety of *recitativo secco* native to *opera buffa*.

Some interest also attaches to the very "Italianate" painter, Salvini, though, again, more in the libretto than in Bellini's score. At a later date, Bellini might have made much of Salvini's raging and unconquerable emotions and near-tragic acts. Even amid the flat, uncharacterized pages given him here, passages stand out which would not mar the tone and texture of a mature Bellini opera. But the other characters in both versions of *Adelson e Salvini* are stiff replicas of protagonists from standard operas of the then-recent past. The surviving interest of the opera inheres in its position as Bellini's first, composed when he was twenty-three and twenty-four, and in the passages from it that he later adapted for other, better operas.

Version I of *Adelson e Salvini* is in effect a Neapolitan *opéra-comique:* a row of separate sung numbers interspersed with spoken dialogue. Act I contains six numbers and ends with the return of Adelson; Act II consists of four pieces, in the last of which Salvini accuses himself of having killed Nelly; Act III has only three pieces. Version II is somewhat more unified and continuous, and is a true *dramma semiserio*. It too contains thirteen numbers: eight in Act I, five in Act II (the former acts II and III).

THE OPERA. *Sinfonia:* The overture to *Adelson e Salvini* begins *andante maestoso*, in D major, 4/4 time. After ten measures of fanfare, the introduction presents a repetitive melody (p. 2*) that Bellini adapted from a student *Sinfonia* in E-flat major (shorn of its first ten measures, much of this *andante maestoso*, beneficially altered, would be transferred to the *sinfonia* for *Il Pirata* [p. 128 of piano-vocal score] and would be echoed again in the opening of that opera's final scene). A modulation to D minor (p. 3) leads into a long allegro made up of a Rossinian D-minor first theme in triplets (p. 3) and a second, F-major theme (p. 7) tinged with the disembodied melancholy of many later Bellinian pages. As Andrea Della Corte noted,[6] one part of this F-major theme houses a conscious or unconscious borrowing from Rossini's *L'Italiana in Algeri:*

---

* Parenthetical numbers refer to the Ricordi piano-vocal score of the revised, two-act version, it being unlikely that the original three-act version will ever be published or staged. For differences between Version I and Version II, see Lippmann, *Vincenzo Bellini, op. cit.*, pp. 372–373. See also, herein, pp. 45–48.

A rapid pianissimo theme in continuous eighth-notes follows: this would also reappear in the overture to *Il Pirata* (p. 6 of the Ricordi piano-vocal score). After overextended reiteration of themes, the *sinfonia* concludes with a crescendo *à la Rossini*, from pianissimo (p. 13) to a noisy fortissimo (p. 14).

Act I: "A pleasant park, dotted with delightful flowerbeds. To the right, a castle; to the left, a pavilion; at the back, a wood. Fanny, seated upon a grassy hillock, is occupied in painting." The "Introduction: Ensemble Piece" is made up of a brief aria for Fanny (*"Immagine gradita del ben che tanto adoro,"* p. 16)—an arietta in praise of painting, old-fashioned when composed, pre-Rossinian in facture and effect; of interjections by Madame Rivers and Geronio (p. 21) and by the male tenants and peasants (tenors and basses, p. 22); of a trio for Fanny, Madame Rivers, and Geronio, with choral support (p. 25); and of a longish passage in *recitativo secco* for the same three (p. 28), the purpose of which is to establish Adelson's love for Nelly, his imminent return to the island, and Fanny's infatuation with her painting-teacher, Salvini. Except for the smudged charm of Fanny's opening arietta, it is an unpromising introduction.

In the cavatina for Struley which follows (*recitativo stromentato*—*"Geronio ancor non viene!"* p. 33—leading into the aria per se—*"Io provo un palpito per tal dimora,"* p. 35), the disparity between words and music almost comically displays Bellini's lack of experience. Story-forwarding *recitativo secco* ensues for Struley and Geronio (*"Ah se trovassi alfin il colonnello!"* p. 40): Struley is beginning to activate his scheme. Bonifacio enters (p. 46), encountering a courier with a letter. Launching into a full-fledged *scena*, Bonifacio first answers the courier's question as to his name (the cavatina *"Bonifacio Beccheria qui presente,"* p. 46). After the courier's departure, Bonifacio reads the letter aloud (" 'Fuggi! fuggi!' Perchè?" p. 49): his brother-in-law is warning him from Naples to be on the watch for infuriated, pursuing creditors. The *scena* culminates in a long stretch of *recitativo secco* (*"In Napoli, il far debiti,"* p. 58) to round out the time-honored *buffo* self-introduction (cf. Leporello's *"Notte e giorno faticar"* in *Don Giovanni*, Figaro's *"Largo al factotum"* in *Il Barbiere di Siviglia*).

The ensuing scene for Salvini and Bonifacio (*"Speranza seddutrice,"* p. 63) is a series of alternating snippets of soliloquy. The monotony inherent in its providing, in effect, a third successive cavatina is lightened by the emotional heightening in the cabaletta-like "*Oh! quante amare lagrime*," sung by Salvini (p. 74).[7] Before the change of key leading to this near-cabaletta, however, the near-duet includes (p. 66) an orchestral cantilena above which Salvini sings "*Nelly, che pena, oh Dio*": that cantilena would reappear in *Il Pirata*, subtly adapted, in the choral prayer "*Nume che imperi*" (p. 24 of the piano-vocal score). Bonifacio's reasoned comment on what he has heard of Salvini's distracted sorrow is (p. 73): "*Se non sarà Nellỳ, sara Mariannỳ, Rosì, Peppì, Checchì, Fannỳ, o Carolì . . . e tutti gli altri diavoli con la cadenza in ì*" (If it won't be Nellỳ, it will be Mariannỳ, Rosì, Peppì, Checchì, Fannỳ, or Carolì . . . and all the other devils with the cadenza on ì).

The finest character-illustrating music in Act I of *Adelson e Salvini* is the opera's most obviously Bellinian passage: Nelly's F-minor romanza "*Dopo l'oscuro nembo*" (p. 88), from which Bellini later would borrow for Giulietta's G-minor romanza in *I Capuleti e i Montecchi* (Act I, Scene 4), "*Oh! quante volte*." There, condensed and shorn of inert ornamentation, it was bettered immeasurably.

Nelly's confrontation with Salvini follows. He reads her the supposed letter from Adelson saying that his uncle is forcing him to marry a rich girl of noble family ("*Amabile Nelly*," p. 94); he offers himself as a replacement for the "faithless" Adelson ("*Felice istante*," p. 98), also telling Nelly that he is in love with her ("*T'amo, Nelly*," p. 101). When she reacts in horror, they express disparate emotions ("*Ah! se non vuoi, mio ben*," p. 106). The scene is well conceived, but less relevant to the drama than the succeeding trio, "*Questa buona signorina che venir fa l'acquolina*" (p. 116), for Nelly, Salvini, and Bonifacio (it is preceded by recitative: Bonifacio's "*Signorina*" and Nelly's "*Oh Dio! vien gente*," both p. 110). Nelly's phrase (p. 116) "*Oh qual raggio di speranza*" was to recur to Bellini when he was composing *I Capuleti e i Montecchi*; altered, but in the same key and using the same principal notes, it there became Romeo's despairing cry "*Svena, ah svena un disperato*" (Ricordi piano-vocal score, plate no. 42043, p. 118). Did Donizetti retain this page of *Adelson* in his memory when, nearly seven years later, he composed Doctor Dulcamara's "*Io son ricco e tu sei bella*," in Act II of *L'Elisir d'amore?* The resemblance is close, particularly as both passages are in B-flat major.

The "*Coro e finale*" closing Act I are played in a "Courtyard of Adelson's Castle." Fanny, Madame Rivers, and the male chorus are preparing to welcome Adelson; they sing a pastoral chorus, "*Qui, qui l'attenderemo*" (p. 126), in which Geronio joins. Musical phrases from the ensuing Adelson–Nelly duet ("*Obbliarti! abbandonarti!*" p. 140) were to reappear in Ernesto's entrance aria, "*Sì, vincemmo*," in Act I, Scene 7, of *Il Pirata*.[8] In neither location do they add materially to either dramatic or musical effect.

Act II: "The scene is that of the preceding act except that one sees garlands of flowers attached to the trees, and that the inscription 'They are united forever' hangs from the pavilion. Above it, one reads the ciphers of Adelson and Nelly. These indicate the wedding celebration."

The act opens with a plot-developing scene (pp. 167–187) involving, first, Struley, Geronio, the tenants, and the peasants; then (p. 181) Madame Rivers, Bonifacio, and Fanny; finally (p. 185), Adelson, Nelly, and Bonifacio. The chorus hails Adelson's return ("*È già Adelson ritornato*," p. 169); Struley shows Geronio the inscriptions on the pavilion (p. 176); Geronio informs Struley of Salvini's state of mind and his actions ("*Udite: ero poc'anzi nel vicino boschetto*," p. 177); and Struley instructs Geronio to set fire to the pavilion, adding that he will seize Nelly, and perhaps Salvini as well ("*Or m'odi*," p. 179). This scene is notable for its foreshadowing of the closeness with which, in later operas, Bellini's musical ideas often would cling to his characters, their shifting emotions, and their mental states.

In the duet-dialogue for Bonifacio and Nelly which follows (p. 188), Bonifacio tells her that her beauty is to blame for having inflamed the susceptible Salvini ("*Poni l'esca a contatto del fuoco*," p. 188); in contrast to the preceding scene, this one suddenly, deadeningly lacks feature and profile, and therefore seems overlong. Adelson leads Salvini in by the hand ("*Ah, sciagurato!*" p. 204), having just prevented him from committing suicide. Their *recitativo secco* conversation serves principally to reveal Salvini's volatility and Adelson's Metastasian *nobiltà*. Their duet, "*Torna, o caro, a questo seno*" (in which Bellini appears to have been recalling the *Qui sedes* of his A-minor Mass), might have been more effective had it not been divided very squarely between an opening *allegro maestoso* (p. 208) and a following *allegro assai* ("*Amico, contento, contento pur sono!*" p. 218), both of which are repeated. The prelude to the confusion—Adelson offering Salvini Fanny's hand, Salvini believing that his friend means the hand of Nelly—is expertly managed (p. 217) despite the inherent incredibility of the situation.

Struley, Geronio, Salvini, and Bonifacio discuss matters in recitative, during which Struley hands Salvini the "letter from Adelson's uncle" (Lord Belmont) announcing that Adelson already is married to "Milady Arthur," and therefore cannot marry Nelly (pp. 230–242). Lord Belmont's purported letter ("*Signor Colonnello*," p. 232) is followed by Struley's insinuations that Adelson nonetheless intends to seduce Nelly ("*Io qui son giunto per strapparla all'iniquo seduttor*," p. 233). Genuine humor informs the recitative in which Bonifacio momentarily wonders if the armed and menacing Struley may not be one of the creditors pursuing him (*"E chi è questo, bufalo?"* p. 236). Irony is added to the Adelson-Salvini friendship when Adelson tells Bonifacio that his uncle has promised to present his talented painter-friend to the King (*"Sì, quest'-uomo benefico promise di presentarlo al Re,"* pp. 255–256).

Perhaps the feeblest number in *Adelson e Salvini* is Bonifacio's protracted aria *"Taci, attendi, e allor vedrai,"* p. 243, which is followed by an "Ensemble Piece" (pp. 255–295) for Adelson, Nelly, Madame Rivers, Fanny, Bonifacio, and finally Salvini. This includes the climactic moment when Adelson makes clear to Salvini that he has been offered, not Nelly, but Fanny (*"Porgi a lui, Fanny, la mano,"* pp. 259–260). It also includes an effective section (pp. 262–271, which begins with Adelson's *"Che pensar, che far degg'io?"* p. 262), which grows from a solo into a duet, a trio, a quartet, and then into an impressive quintet and sextet. The hubbub aroused by the fire breaks out *allegro agitato* (*"Al foco! al foco!"* p. 272). Salvini tells Nelly that Adelson is already married (*"E Adelson maritato,"* p. 282), evoking violent disbelief (*"M'inganni, scellerato,"* p. 282). Struley confronts Nelly and Salvini (*"Nè cede ancor costei!"* pp. 284–285); Nelly pleads with Salvini to recognize Adelson as his true friend, Struley as a monster driving him to excess (*"Ah! Salvini, alle tue piante,"* p. 286)[9]; Nelly's reaction opens Salvini's eyes to Struley's perfidy (*"Vendetta sol ti guida? or veggo il tuo disegno,"* pp. 289–290). Salvini vows to have revenge (pp. 294–295).

The Finale begins with the tenants and peasants returning joyfully from the extinguished fire (p. 296). Bonifacio recounts Salvini's wounding Struley in the neck with a pistol shot and stabbing Geronio to death; Nelly has fainted (pp. 299–300). Salvini happily turns the rescued Nelly over to Adelson in a delicious aria-like passage (new in Version II): *moderato assai*, it is *"Ecco, signor, la sposa"* (p. 301), a recognizably Bellinian melody that would lead a richer life in *La Straniera* as Valdeburgo's *"Meco tu vieni, o misera"* (p. 184 of the Ricordi piano-vocal score). Salvini says that he intends to marry Fanny and take her to Rome (pp. 302–303). The jubilant final ensemble begins (*"Segni con bianca pietra,"* p. 305) with Nelly, Fanny, Salvini, Adelson, and the chorus. Bonifacio soon joins in. By the last measure, all of the protagonists except Struley, Geronio, and Madame Rivers have exulted, *alla vivace*, that *"qui regni pace e amor"* (here peace and love reign).

Della Corte aptly wrote[10] that when Bellini adapted ideas and passages from *Adelson e Salvini* in *Bianca e Fernando*, *Il Pirata*, *I Capuleti e i Montecchi*, and *La Straniera* (he failed to mention *Norma*), he "correctly judged which of his pages" were "best achieved. . . . The frequenters of the Conservatory *teatrino*, the relatives, friends, and teachers of the composer, the singers, and the instrumentalists, were not showing themselves excessively indulgent when they applauded warmly." At twenty-three and twenty-four, Bellini, though not displaying such originality as Rossini had displayed at eighteen when composing *La Cambiale di matrimonio*, had taken a few wavering first steps into the art of composing his own sort of opera.

Beatrice di Tenda

TRAGEDIA LIRICA (*opera seria*) in two acts. *Libretto*: by Felice Romani.[1]
Composed: 1833. *Première*: Teatro La Fenice, Venice, March 16, 1833
(restaged there in 1838, 1843, 1844, 1871, and 1964), on a double bill with
the "*ballo serio*" *L'Ultimo Giorno di Missolungi* (sometimes called *La
Caduta di Missolunghi*), choreographed by Antonio Cortesi to music by
Luigi Viviani. *Original cast*:

BEATRICE DI TENDA, *wife of Filippo* *Maria Visconti*	Giuditta Pasta
AGNESE DEL MAINO, *loved by Filippo, but* *secretly in love with Orombello*	Anna Del Serre
OROMBELLO, *Lord of Ventimiglia*	Alberico Curioni
ANICHINO, *onetime minister of Beatrice's* *first husband, friend of Orombello*	Alessandro Giacchini
FILIPPO MARIA VISCONTI, *Duke of Milan*	Orazio Cartagenova
RIZZARDO DEL MAINO, *brother of Agnese,* *confidant of Filippo*	unknown

The original settings were by Francesco Bagnara. *Published*: Issued in full
score (the only Bellini opera so issued during his lifetime), *circa* 1833,
by the Stamperia di Pietro Pittarelli e Co., Rome, with a publisher's
dedication to the marchese Gaetano Longhi; in piano-vocal score three
times by Ricordi, Florence and Milan: (1) 1833, with plate numbers
6880-6950-6970; (2) with plate numbers 35566-35585; (3) with plate
number 45541; in piano-vocal score by Girard (later Cottrau), Naples,
with various plate numbers (the *Preludio*, 2650); in piano-vocal score by
L'Euterpe Ticinese, Chiasso, Switzerland, a pirating operation shared by
three publishers (Lucca, Artaria, Bertassi); in piano-vocal score by both

A—"*Cartellone*" for the première of *Beatrice di Tenda*.

Pacini and Launer, Paris. Dedicated by Bellini to the duchessa Eleonora Statella di San Martino.

Autograph score, of which ten pages are nonautograph, in the library of the Accademia di Santa Cecilia, Rome. Two manuscript copies also in that library; three in the Naples Conservatory library; two in the library of the Munich Conservatory; one in the archives of the Teatro La Fenice, Venice. Autograph and copyist's sketches in the Museo Belliniano, Catania, including autograph sketch of an aria for Beatrice ("*Nè fra voi si trova*") in the first-act finale, a musical idea from which appears in her terminal aria in the published versions; a sketch for a Beatrice—Agnese duet intended to precede the trio (beginning with Orombello's "*Angiol di pace*") in the second-act finale[2]; and a sketch for Beatrice's final aria.

PERFORMANCE DATA. *Beatrice di Tenda* was staged at the Teatro Carolino, Palermo, on March 1, 1834, with a cast including Marietta Albini,

Giovanni Basadonna, and Ignazio Marini. Writing from Paris (April 11, 1834), Bellini told Filippo Santocanale[3]: "So my *Beatrice* was well received? I am pleased, and I see in the Neapolitan papers that the *palermitani* applauded this unfortunate opera of mine, which, furthermore, I myself did not believe deserving of the fate that befell it in Venice, and I was convinced that outside reasons induced that audience to disapprove of it when it appeared. I admit that the subject is horrible; but by means of the music, coloring it now tremendously and now sadly, I tried to correct and banish the disgust that Filippo's character arouses." To Florimo two months later (June 14, 1834), he said[4]: "*Beatrice*, whistled at in Venice, has been found not unworthy of her sisters in Palermo; and the Duke of Devonshire (whom I know well) tells me that people in the theater wept at the moment of the second-act quintet."

Both within and outside Italy, *Beatrice di Tenda* was played well into the 1870's. It was heard at the Teatro del Fondo, Naples, on July 18, 1834, and at the San Carlo there on November 18 of that year, with Fanny Tacchinardi-Persiani (Beatrice), Anna Del Serre in the role that she had created in Venice (Agnese), Berardo Calvari Winter (Orombello), Domenico Cosselli (Filippo), Revalden (Anichino), and Antonio Sparalik (Rizzardo). It reached La Scala, Milan, on February 14, 1835, with Giuseppina Ronzi de Begnis (Beatrice), Antonio Poggi (Orombello), and Orazio Cartagenova (Filippo, the role that he had created at Venice), initiating a seasonal run of twelve performances.[5] During the Lenten season of 1835, *Beatrice* was staged at the Teatro La Munizione, Messina, and on May 30 of that year at the Theater in der Josefstadt, Vienna. At Rome, the opera was presented at the Teatro Apollo on January 28, 1837, when the cast was headed by Caroline Unger (Beatrice), Domenico Reina (Orombello), and Domenico Cosselli (Filippo).[6] On July 21, 1837, the Accademia filarmonica romana gave the first of several announced concert performances of Beatrice; but cholera was epidemic in Rome, and the later performances were canceled. With Unger as Beatrice, the opera was staged at Trieste in the autumn of 1837 as *Il Castello d'Ursino*. On November 14 of that year, it was heard at the Teatro Comunale, Bologna, the Filippo being Giorgio Ronconi, who repeated his admired characterization when the opera was presented there again, with Amalia Schütz-Oldosi as Beatrice, on November 3, 1837.

At Faenza in 1840, Giuseppina Strepponi sang Beatrice, with Ronconi as Filippo. At the Nuovo Teatro Comunale La Fenice, Sinigaglia, in 1841, the splendid cast of Erminia Frezzolini, Antonio Poggi, and Ronconi assured the opera's success. On April 26, 1845, the Teatro della Canobbiana, Milan, staged *Beatrice* with a second-flight cast and ran it through twenty-five singings; reviving it, again without star singers, on

May 27, 1847, the Canobbiana added eleven more performances, for a total of thirty-six in little more than two years. The opera was being sung at Sinigaglia as late as the Carnival of 1866. Many other stagings occurred throughout Italy.

Beatrice di Tenda was sung at Vienna on March 15, 1836, at the Theater in der Josefstadt, in a German translation by Georg Ott (*Das Castell von Ursino*). It was staged in London on May 22, 1836, and also during that year, in German, at Graz (June 11), Prague (August 19), and Berlin (Königsstädtischestheater, December 29). In 1837, *Beatrice* was presented at Lisbon (May 8) and at Barcelona and Madrid (December 12). Budapest heard it in German on April 28, 1838. During 1840, it was staged at Valletta, Malta (Carnival), Clausenburg (Hungarian translation by István Jakab, April 9), Athens (summer), and Zante (December 30).

Paris heard *Beatrice di Tenda* for the first time, at the Théâtre-Italien, in 1840.[7] In 1841, it was staged in Mexico City (September) and Havana (autumn). Its first performance in the United States occurred at the St. Charles Theatre, New Orleans, on March 5, 1842. Earlier that year, it had been sung in Italian at Berlin (Königsstädtischestheater, January 29); in December, it was heard at Copenhagen. During 1843, *Beatrice* was offered at Agram (March) and Lugano (October); during 1844, at Bone, Algeria (Carnival) and New York (March 18). It was staged in St. Petersburg on November 29, 1845 and in Stockholm during the summer of 1848. It was the first Bellini opera heard in Buenos Aires (April 8, 1849). Brussels had it on October 9, 1851; Bucharest in 1858; Corfu in 1862. *Beatrice di Tenda* has never been staged at the Opéra, Paris; Covent Garden, London; or the Metropolitan Opera, New York.

During the centennial commemoration of Bellini's death, the Teatro Massimo Bellini, Catania, presented *Beatrice di Tenda* in January 1935, when the cast was led by Giannina Arangi Lombardi; it was heard there again on April 7, 1966, when Vittorio Gui conducted and the cast included Raina Kabaivanska (Beatrice) and Giuseppe Taddei (Filippo). The Teatro Massimo, Palermo, presented it on January 12, 1959 (see p. 237), again with Gui; the cast included Consuelo Rubio (Beatrice), Juan Oncina (Orombello), and Taddei (Filippo). The revival at La Scala, Milan, followed. Joan Sutherland's New York debut took place when she sang Beatrice in a concert performance of the opera by the American Opera Society at Town Hall, New York, on February 21, 1961; with her were Marilyn Horne (Agnese, also a New York debut), Richard Cassilly (Orombello), and Enzo Sordello (Filippo); the performance was greeted so enthusiastically that it was repeated twice at

Carnegie Hall (March 3 and 11). Sutherland also was heard as Beatrice at the Teatro San Carlo, Naples, on May 4, 1962, when she was supported by Margreta Elkins (Agnese), Renato Cioni (Orombello), and Mario Zanasi (Filippo).

Bellini's "unfortunate opera" returned to the Teatro La Fenice, Venice, on January 10, 1964—one hundred and thirty-one years after its lackluster première there—with Leyla Gencer (Beatrice), Antigone Sgourda (Agnese), Juan Oncina (Orombello), and Zanasi (Filippo). It was sung at the Teatro Coliseo Albia, Bilbao, on September 13, 1968, when the title role was taken by Rita Talarico and the Agnese was Anna Maria Rota. At the Teatro Comunale Giuseppe Verdi, Trieste, *Beatrice* was presented on January 25, 1969; the production had been borrowed from Palermo, and the cast included Talarico (Beatrice), Ileana Meriggio-li (Agnese), Pietro Bottazzo (Orombello), and Giulio Fioravanti (Filippo).

THE LIBRETTO. Setting[8]—The action unfolds at the Castle of Binasco, near Milan, residence of Filippo Maria Visconti and his wife, Beatrice de' Lascari, contessa di Tenda and widow of Facino Cane. To the dissolute young duke, his marriage has guaranteed lordship over the dominions brought him in dowry by Beatrice. His ambition largely satisfied, he is finding his mature wife a heavy chain upon him, both because he has been attracted by Agnese del Maino, one of Beatrice's ladies-in-waiting, and because the great deference still paid to Beatrice by their vassals diminishes him in his own eyes.

Act I: Scene 1. "Internal courtyard of the Castle of Binasco. View of the façade of the illuminated palace." In a castle arcade during a fête, a group of courtiers encounters Filippo, who has come from the party. To friends who ask why, he replies that Beatrice has palled upon him, that he can no longer tolerate her presence because the deference shown her constantly reminds him that in reality she still rules.

At this moment, the seductive voice of Agnese is heard singing a *canzone* in the festive hall. Her voice arouses Filippo's sensuality, and he swears to break his link to the woman he does not love. But Agnese is secretly enamored of Orombello, the young Lord of Ventimiglia and relative of Beatrice, to whom he feels drawn by more than familial devotion. Agnese has sent Orombello a note inviting him to her quarters this night, and he has assumed that it is from Beatrice.

Scenes 2–4. "Agnese's quarters." Orombello, astonished to find Agnese where he had expected to meet Beatrice, unwittingly reveals his infatuation with Beatrice to the inflamed girl. Realizing that he now has put both Beatrice and himself in Agnese's power (and additionally having

learned from her that Filippo is in love with her), Orombello pleads with
Agnese to protect Beatrice's name. But she decides to take revenge by
revealing to Filippo what she supposes to be an adulterous liaison between
Beatrice and Orombello.

Scenes 5–8. "A grove in the ducal garden." In a quiet corner of the
garden, Beatrice tries to calm the pain caused her by her husband's
hostile, contemptuous attitude. In view of the accusation made by
Agnese, Filippo now believes that he holds proof of Beatrice's infidelity,
and he attempts to add equally baseless accusations that she is intriguing
to deprive him of all power. The duke has acquired possession of
petitions addressed to their lady by vassals asking her to end her husband's
debauched conduct. He shows the stolen portfolio to Beatrice, openly
accusing her of treachery. Proclaiming her innocence, she demands
justice.[9]

Scenes 9–12. "A remote part of the Castle of Binasco. At one side,
the statue of Facino Cane (Beatrice's first husband). Orombello, also
accused of adultery and treason, is being trailed by Filippo's men-at-arms.
He finds Beatrice in a solitary spot, where she is kneeling before a statue
of her first husband, seeking help from his spirit, feeling herself abandoned
by everyone. To her astonishment, Orombello protesting his devotion to
her, also announces his love, which she can only reject. The two are
discovered together by Filippo and the courtiers. Beatrice's desperate
protestations of innocence go unheeded; she and Orombello are swiftly
arrested and removed to imprisonment.

Act II: Scenes 1–7. "Gallery in the Castle of Binasco ready for the
sitting of a tribunal. Guards at the doors." The trial of Beatrice leaves
no doubt of the fate of the tormented woman. Orombello, at last unable
to bear the tortures to which he has been subjected, has made a false
confession of his own guilt, declaring Beatrice guilty with him. When the
judges are ready to pronounce sentence, Filippo enjoins them not to give
way to futile, unmerited feelings of pity, but to pronounce just sentence
of punishment upon the guilty pair. Beatrice's demeanor is noble and
heroic; undaunted, she denies every accusation and rebukes Filippo.
Brought in to face sentence, Orombello takes heart upon seeing Beatrice
and, before judges and courtiers, retracts his confession, solemnly proclaiming Beatrice innocent, himself ready to die to save her.

Beatrice's firmness and Orombello's retraction have aroused feelings
of the harshest remorse in Agnese, inducing her to beg Filippo for the
lives of Beatrice and Orombello and to accuse herself of having defamed
them. Even Filippo momentarily hesitates to sign the death sentence
as, in fleeting repentence, he recalls what Beatrice did to give him honors
and power. But the voices of vassals, who beg grace for their lady,

obliterate all feeling of generosity in the duke; he signs the sentence condemning Beatrice and Orombello to death.

Scenes 8–9. "Ground-level vestibule above the castle prisons. Beatrice's maidens and servants emerge from the cells. All are in mourning. Sentinels everywhere." In the dungeon in which she has been tortured, Beatrice has spent her final night in prayer. When she emerges, she seems transfigured by a light of superhuman goodness. Proudly announcing that under torture she has said nothing, she exhorts her ladies not to weep for her, but to inveigh against her slanderers, whose punishment will be a lifetime of remorse. These words evoke a suffocated cry from the top of the stairs; it is from Agnese. Unable to alter Filippo's decision, she is in despair; now she casts herself at Beatrice's feet, confesses her guilt in the purloining of Beatrice's portfolio, and begs for pardon.[10] The voice of Orombello, heard emerging from his cell, exhorts Beatrice to forgive as he has forgiven. She does so. The lugubrious death procession, announced by a funeral bell, enters with the executioner.

Beatrice and Orombello move toward their death, while from the kneeling courtiers the motive of forgiveness resounds, sung first by Orombello, then developed in trio (Beatrice, Agnese, Orombello).

THE OPERA. If the years in which Bellini's operas were composed be kept in mind, *Beatrice di Tenda* can only appear, despite several passages of pure Bellinian melody, as one of the least successful of his works musicodramatically. The chief reason for its theatrical failure, leaving aside the very unfavorable circumstances under which Bellini composed it, is certainly its libretto. Although the text provides many of Romani's usual verbal felicities and several examples of his masterly confrontations, it suffers mortally from the extreme dullness of Beatrice, who for the duration of the entire opera merely suffers, complains justly, and responds nobly to events beyond her control; from the fact that Filippo is only intermittently realized as a human being; from the fact that Orombello awakens no response but gratitude in Beatrice; and from the fact that the only multidimensional character, Agnese, plays a minor role in the evolution of events as presented upon the stage. It is not possible to consider Beatrice a "worthy sister" of Norma—or even of Imogene and Alaide—and her inertness, her undeviatingly sacrificial role, and her uninflected nobility combine to weaken the drama to the verge of boredom. Only at those moments when Bellini's melody takes over despite the libretto story (though clearly in immediate reaction to Romani's words) can this opera be believed in as a composition created by Bellini between 1831 (*La Sonnambula* and *Norma*) and 1835 (*I Puritani*).

Preludio: Beatrice di Tenda begins with a simple sectional prelude, neither of its chief divisions being repeated; much of its musical material recurs during the opera. Beginning in E-flat major, allegro, pianissimo, it presents a first, rushing semimelody (violins and solo clarinet) that swells quickly to a fortissimo and then gives way to a marchlike second theme largely in on-the-beat chords. *Più moderato, quasi la metà,* but again pianissimo the second section presents, *"con grande espressione,"* an essentially Bellinian cantilena that will reappear in the first-act finale, where Beatrice sings it to the words *"Deh! se mi amasti un giorno"* (p. 106*). This in turn leads back to a concluding fortissimo restatement of the marchlike theme.

Act I: Scene 1. "Internal courtyard of the Castle of Binasco. View of the façade of the illuminated palace." After a short orchestral andante in common time marked by an insinuating, repeated, pastoral melodic fragment (it would not be out of place in *La Sonnambula*), a group of courtiers (two-part chorus—tenors and basses) moves across the court-yard to encounter Filippo (p. 6). When they ask why he has left the splendid fête so early, he at once launches (p. 6), in the insinuating phrase already heard, into a vituperative explanation of his unbearable dissatis-faction: *"M'è importuna . . . io la detesto,"* which openly expresses his dislike of Beatrice (and incidentally establishes him as an unmitigated villain). In a curiously Verdian chorus, the courtiers sycophantically egg him on, siding with him against Beatrice. They are interrupted (B-flat major, *andante assai sostenuto,* p. 15) by a harp (lute) arpeggio from inside the palace; to a rocking accompaniment, pianissimo (p. 16), Agnese is heard singing: *"Ah! non pensar che pieno sia nel poter diletto,"* the melody of which must have been concealed in Verdi's memory when he composed Amelia's *"Come in quest'ora bruna"* in Act I of *Simon Boccanegra.* Because the words of Agnese's *canzone* say that without affection "a heart suffers even upon a throne," the courtiers comment that she reflects Filippo's mood. If only he were free! *Andante amoroso,* he replies to their rather bellicose commentary. *"Con grande espressione,"* then *"con abbandono,"* with a melodic line that in part closely resembles that of Agnese's *canzone,* and with an accompaniment that can only re-call that of *"Casta diva,"* Filippo soliloquizes about Agnese (p. 20): *"Oh! divina Agnese! . . . Come t'adoro . . ."* He will find a way to break the fetters binding him to his wife.

Scenes 2–4. "Agnese's quarters":

Scene 2 (p. 29)—"Agnese seated in agitation at a table upon which a lute lies." Scenes 2 and 3 are for Agnese alone as she thinks amorously of Orombello, preluding upon the lute as she awaits his ardently hoped-for response to her invitation.

* Page references here are to the Ricordi piano-vocal score, plate number 45541.

Scene 4 (p. 30)—"Orombello enters, hurried and wary; when he sees Agnese, he stands still, astonished and looking about him." He has come expecting a rendezvous with Beatrice. In recitative, at cross-purposes, Orombello and Agnese slowly discover that she believes him to be as enamored of her as she is of him. When (p. 32) she speaks of his rival for her love (meaning Filippo), Orombello innocently repeats the word *rivale*, not believing that Beatrice has another suitor. Agnese then reveals that his "rival" is Filippo and proclaims (*"Nulla è un regno,"* p. 33) that she values Orombello's love more than a kingdom. Puzzled by his lack of ardor, she asks if he has not received a letter. Astonished that she should know of it, he replies that he has—and unwittingly reveals that he believes it to be from Beatrice. Agnese instantly is convinced that guilty love exists between Orombello and the duchess. He beseeches her to have pity, to spare the reputation of the innocent Beatrice, but she is beside herself with frustration and rage. "Bursting forth in all her sorrow" (p. 39), *allegro giusto, alla breve*, she sings (*"E la mia . . . spietato!"*) that she will be capable of pity only if Orombello can kill her passion for him. Repeating the melody that she just has sung (p. 41), Orombello replies that she is neither insulted nor scorned. Unmoved, she repeats the melody a second time, her first words unchanged, and then furiously dismisses Orombello.[11]

Scenes 5–6. "A grove in the ducal garden. Beatrice runs in, her maidens following her." Allegro, E major, 4/4 time, the scene opens (p. 48) with a repetition of the marchlike theme heard in the *Preludio*. In recitative, Beatrice discusses (p. 56) with her ladies (soprano chorus) the grief that Filippo's actions has brought upon her; her distraught state is manifested well in ribbons of *fioriture* (pp. 59, 61). After a sorrowing passage in C major, Beatrice sings (E major, *largo sostenuto*, p. 57) the intensely emotional aria *"Ma la sola, ohimè! son io,"* and—as her agitation rises—its cabaletta (*allegro moderato*, p. 60), *"Ah! la pena in lor piombò,"* while her ladies try vainly to give her a vision of a happier future.

Scene 7 (p. 66). "As Beatrice is leaving with her maidens, Filippo and Rizzardo [Agnese's brother and Filippo's confidant] enter, observing her in silence from a distance." In recitative (A minor, 4/4 time, *allegro maestoso*), Rizzardo says that Beatrice is disdainfully fleeing Filippo, who replies that she will not escape his watchfulness; he then sends Rizzardo to spy upon her. (One of the flaws in Romani's libretto is its failure to make clear whether or not the duke really believes in his wife's unlikely guilt or simply is pretending more and more to believe in what he himself has invented.) Alone (p. 66), Filippo wonders why betrayal by Beatrice would wound him—has he not been seeking proof of it?

Scene 8 (p. 67). "Beatrice and Filippo" (the scene continues on from

11a
Giovanni Battista Rubini as Gualtiero in the original production of *Il Pirata* (Teatro alla Scala, Milan, October 27, 1827): *"Pietoso al padre! e meco eri si cruda intanto!"* (Act I, Scene 6).

11b
Giovanni Battista Rubini and Adelaide Comelli-Rubini as Gualtiero and Imogene in *Il Pirata*, lithograph after a drawing by G. Cenestrelli: *"Ah! è mio … è figlio mio … Pietà!"* (Act I, Scene 6).

Enrichetta Meric Lalande

Straniera

12a
Henriette Méric-Lalande as Alaide in the original production of *La Straniera* (Teatro alla Scala, Milan, February 14, 1829): "*Questo almeno ti renda propizio sacrifizio che il core ti fa*" (Act II, Scene 13).

12b
Antonio Tamburini as Valdeburgo in the original production of *La Straniera* (Teatro alla Scala, Milan, February 14, 1829): "*Bando a terror…miratemi: l'aura vital respiro*" (Act II, Scene 4).

12c
Adelaide Tosi as Alaide in *La Straniera*: "*Or sei pago, o ciel tremendo*" (Act II, Final Scene).

Antonio Tamburini

Straniera

ADELAIDE TOSI

13

Homage" to the performances
opera at the Teatro
arcano, Milan, in 1830-1831.
ottom, left to right:
aetano Donizetti, Giuseppe
rezzolini, Felice Romani,
ellini; *top, left to right:*
lippo Galli, Nicola
olinari, Giuditta Pasta,
ouis Henry, Giovanni
attista Rubini. Issued by
pimaco and Pasquale Artaria.

14a
iuditta Pasta as Norma:
*Pace v'intimo...e il
cro vischio io mieto"*
Act I, Scene 4).

14b
omenico Donzelli, Giulia
risi, and Giuditta Pasta
Pollione, Adalgisa,
d Norma in the original
roduction of *Norma* (Teatro
la Scala, Milan, December
5, 1831). The background is
y Alessandro Sanquirico
ee Plate 18a).

15a
Giulia Grisi as Norma.

15b
Giulia Grisi and Luigi Lablache as
Elvira and Sir Giorgio in the original
production of *I Puritani* (Théâtre-
Italien, Paris, January 24, 1835).

16
Designs by Alessandro Sanquirico for the
original production of *La Straniera* (Teatro
alla Scala, Milan, February 14, 1829):

a
Courtyard of the Castle of Montolino
(Act I, Scenes 1–5).

b
A Remote Place (Act I, Scenes 11–15).

17
Designs by Alessandro Sanquirico:

a
I Capuleti e i Montecchi, first Milan
production (Teatro alla Scala, December
26, 1830), Final (tomb) Scene.

b
La Sonnambula, original production
(Teatro Carcano, Milan, March 6, 1831),
Final Scene. Note absence of the now
traditional bridge or catwalk above
the millwheel.

a

ABITAZIONE DI NORMA
nell'Opera Norma

b

18
Designs by Alessandro
Sanquirico for the original
production of *Norma*
(Teatro alla Scala, Milan,
December 26, 1831):

a
Norma's Dwelling (Act II,
Scenes 1–3).

b
Temple of Irminsul (Act II,
Scenes 6–10) with Oroveso
(hand raised), Norma
(kneeling), and Pollione
(alone).

19
Theaters of some Bellini
premières:

a
The Teatro alla Scala,
Milan, in 1828.

b
The Teatro Carlo Felice,
Genoa, in 1828.

c
The Teatro Ducale (later
Regio), Parma, in 1832.

d
The Théâtre-Italien (Salle
Favart), Paris, in 1830.

a

b

c

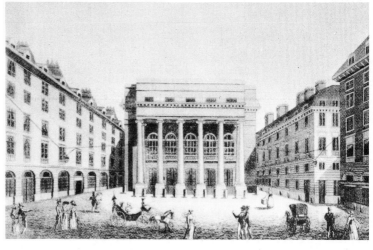

d

20

Bellini's letter of December 31, 1831, to Giovanni Battista Perucchini (first and last pages), announcing the "failure" of *Norma*. This letter was transcribed incorrectly in BE, pp. 296–7; it was described (and again transcribed incorrectly) in Alberto Basso, ed.: *Autografi di musicisti* (Turin, 1962), pp. 35–7, where the now missing final sentences are quoted.

Scene 7 without interruption, change of key, or a new time signature). In recitative, Filippo brutally accuses Beatrice, to her confusion and sorrow. At the beginning of their duet, the key shifts to G major (p. 69) as Beatrice begins (*allegro moderato, con espressione,* p. 70) "*Duolo d'un cor piagato,*" the accompaniment for which includes an oboe melody in thirds which was borrowed from a clarinet melody in thirds in Scene 2 of Act II of *Zaira*, where it precedes Orosmane's "*Donna che più di te ne meriti.*" Disregarding Beatrice's attempts to calm him by invoking sweet reason, Filippo answers (p. 71) by accusing her of inciting their vassals against him and of loving a younger man. He has, he finally says (pp. 73-74), proof of her guilt: it is in a portfolio that he has had filched from her quarters. As he enragedly repeats himself, she continues pleading with him.[12] When she asks for death rather than such treatment, he replies (p. 81): "*Attendila*" (Wait for it). This theatrically very effective finale, in reality an alternation of brief solos and passages *a due*, ends (pp. 82-90) with Filippo threatening revenge, Beatrice relying upon just judgment from the world. An especially telling touch is the modulation from G major to G minor (p. 77) just before Beatrice's "*Questi d'amanti popoli.*"

Scenes 9–12. "A remote part of the Castle of Binasco. At one side, the statue of Facino Cane":

Scenes 9–10 (p. 91)—"Chorus of men-at-arms" (tenors, basses). In B-flat major 4/4 time, *allegro moderato*, the soldiers discuss Orombello's fate, sure that he will betray himself under torture. For Bellini, this chorus is a nadir: it lacks both melodic distinction and dramatic relevance. In an *allegro moderato* passage (p. 97), however, a foretaste is given of the Verdi choruses in *Il Trovatore*.[13]

Scene 11 (beginning of the first finale)—The orchestra preludes conspiratorially (B-flat major, 4/4 time, *allegro moderato*, p. 104) before setting forth, "*con grande espressione,*" the cantilena of the second section of the *Preludio*. Beatrice kneels before the monument to her late husband, and to that same melody sings (p. 106) "*Deh! se mi amasti un giorno.*" As she is completing it, Orombello enters and hears her lamenting that everyone is abandoning her (pp. 107-108). Saying that he has not abandoned her, he asks her to flee with him—to which her distracted reply is that her faith in him has been mistaken for love by others. This leads him (p. 112) to confess his love, "*con tutta passione,*" in the aria "*Ah! d'immenso, estremo affetto*" (p. 113), whereupon she orders him to leave. Beside himself, Orombello asserts that he must have her forgiveness or die.

Scene 12 (continuing on from Scene 11 with only a change of time to 2/4—As Beatrice goes on insisting, *allegro moderato*, that Orombello leave her, Filippo enters (p. 113) with Agnese, Rizzardo, Anichino (a friend of Orombello and former minister of Facino Cane), courtiers, and men-at-arms (five-part chorus, s1, s2, t1, t2, bs). Pointing out Beatrice and Orombello in impassioned conversation, Agnese asks Filippo *"Vedi?"* (Do you see?). Filippo shouts *"Traditori!"* and in a featureless quintet with chorus (*"Oh, vil rampogna!"* p. 115), Beatrice, Agnese, Orombello, Anichino, and Filippo express diverse emotions repetitively and at length. Then (p. 122), with interjections from the others, Beatrice and Agnese, in thirds, largo, sing *"Ah! tal onta io meritai,"* Beatrice saying that she has deserved this shame, Agnese exulting in it. Beatrice's vocal line becomes more and more ornate (pp. 127-128) as the ensemble continues (to p. 137) without adding much relevance or excitement.

Filippo (adagio, p. 138) orders that Beatrice and Orombello be chained and held under guard. When Orombello tries to defend Beatrice, Filippo says that it is he himself he must defend. Thereafter—though orchestra, the five soloists, and the five-part chorus all sing on busily—nothing occurs but repetitions of what has occurred earlier (except that the courtiers now express some belief in Beatrice's innocence). The music whirls along ever faster (*più mosso*, p. 153; *incalzando il tempo*, p. 154; *più stretto* and *ancora più stretto*, p. 155; *più stretto ancora*, p. 156) through noisy pages for which the only, inexact explanation is lack of inspiration induced by absence of usable ideas in the libretto. When, welcomely, the act ends, "Beatrice and Orombello are surrounded by guards."

Act II: Scenes 1-7. "Gallery in the Castle of Binasco readied for the sitting of a tribunal. Guards at the doors":

Scene 1—After a brief, somber orchestral introduction (B-flat major, 3/4 time, andante), Beatrice's maids-of-honor (soprano chorus) and some gentlemen of the court (two-part chorus, t and bs) discuss the trial and bemoan the terrible tortures to which Orombello has been subjected, tortures that have extracted from him both a confession of his guilt and an admission that Beatrice has been his accomplice in it. Then they leave, agreeing that no one can save Beatrice.

Scene 2 (p. 169)—Filippo, Anichino, men-at-arms. After an orchestral introduction (D major, 4/4 time, *allegro assai maestoso*), Filippo and Anichino discuss Beatrice's fate, Filippo insisting that the law must decide it, Anichino warning him that the people of the surrounding countryside have heard what is happening and are incensed. Filippo orders the men-at-arms to close the gates of Binasco until dawn. He will not heed Anichino's pleas.

Scene 3 (*scena*, chorus, quintet)—The judges enter (p. 172) and seat themselves; they will be presided over by Rizzardo. Filippo occupies a high seat as lords and ladies, Agnese among them, crowd in. *Assai moderato,* the orchestra plays an abbreviated variant of the introduction to Scene 2. Anichino regrets that Orombello had not shared his earlier fear of what might happen. Agnese, though waiting for the hour of vengeance, is much disturbed. After Filippo charges the judges to do their duty, they order Beatrice brought in.

Scenes 4–5—Beatrice appears (p. 175), and after an angry, agonizing exchange between her and Filippo, the judges summon Orombello. A plaintive, fragmented melody (*maestoso lento,* p. 177) is introduced. In Scene 5, Agnese's agitation increases. "Orombello appears, staggering a few steps." Supported by guards, he advances slowly. Beatrice calls out *"Orombello!"* (p. 179) and then upbraids him for having betrayed her. Recounting his torture (p. 180), he firmly retracts his false confession. As Beatrice, Filippo, Agnese, Anichino, and the judges react to this reversal, a lento modulation (p. 183) leads to the finest pages of the opera. Almost symphonic in expansiveness and development, this quintet with three-part chorus is begun larghetto as Beatrice sings *"Al tuo fallo ammenda"* (p. 184) and the others join in.

Guido Pannain, judging *Beatrice di Tenda* very severely ("It is a wave of perfumes in which everything vaporizes; touched, the flowers are cardboard"),[14] well wrote: "There remains the opera's best page, which was so judged from the first moment, the second-act quintet preceded by the affecting scene between Beatrice and Orombello (*'Tu morrai con me'* [p. 179]), in the onrush of that typical song-dialogue which, in Bellini, is both interruption and continuity, uniform and various, linear and pregnant, and which here, in a special way, echoes *Norma.*"

Filippo has wavered again, and now is ready to have the sentencing of Beatrice and Orombello suspended. But when Anichino suggests releasing them, the judges forbid the action and order the prisoners interrogated again under torture. Now Filippo is deaf to Beatrice's anguished demand that he and the judges allow her to plead her innocence. She and Orombello are led away by the guards (p. 214). In an allegro passage (p. 202), Filippo—beginning *"Ite entrambi"*—sings a melodic phrase that well may have been in Verdi's mind when he composed the conte di Luna's *"Per me ora fatale,"* in Act II of *Il Trovatore.*

Scene 6 (p. 215)—In recitative, the remorseful Agnese tries to persuade Filippo to forgive Beatrice, saying that what she herself deserves is the veil of a penitent rather than a crown. Denying her prayer, Filippo sends her away weeping.

Scene 7 (p. 217)—The orchestra briefly introduces (F major, 4/4 time, *andante assai sostenuto*) Filippo's *scena ed aria.* Struck by Agnese's remorse, Filippo soliloquizes in fearful confusion and listens unwillingly to the distant voice of Beatrice as she is taken from the torture chamber back to her cell. His truncated semi-aria (p. 218), "*No . . . da terror percosso,*" unhappily lacks the melodic force required by its text. Anichino enters (p. 219) to tell Filippo that Beatrice has not confessed under torture, but that the judges nonetheless condemn her to die and now want him to sign the death warrant. When the courtiers ask him to relent (p. 220), he at first refuses. But then, in the fine, expressive aria, "*Qui m'accolse oppresso*" (p. 222), he wavers in remembering Beatrice's goodness to him. He is about to tear up the warrant when (modulation to A-flat major, p. 224) noise from outside proves to be an attack upon the castle by Facino Cane's faithful men, who are demanding that Beatrice be surrendered to them. Again enraged, Filippo signs the warrant (p. 227). In a cabalettalike passage (*allegro moderato,* p. 228), he asserts that she is condemned, not by him, but by her own wickedness and that of others; he also declares that as long as she and he both live, the realm cannot be truly united (this political theme, introduced sporadically and fragmentarily as it is, can only seem extraneous).

Scene 8 (finale, p. 233). "Ground-level vestibule above the castle prisons. Beatrice's maidens and servants emerge from the cells; all are in mourning. Sentinels everywhere." The orchestra introduces (F major, 4/4 time, moderato) the chorus of Beatrice's ladies and supporters; they pray that her fortitude under torture has convinced all of her innocence. Without interruption, this scene leads to the next.

Scene 9 (p. 237). *Andante mosso,* without modulation, but now in 3/8 time. "Beatrice emerges from the prison simply dressed and with her hair falling to her shoulders; she walks tentatively and with difficulty. Moved to pity, all surround her in silence." Proudly she says that she has not spoken under torture. As she converses with her friends, Agnese descends the staircase and interrupts (p. 239). Asking forgiveness in anguish and remorse, she confesses that her love for Orombello led her to steal the letters from Beatrice's room and thus bring about the tragedy. Idlebrando Pizzetti, whose admiration for Bellini was all but unbounded, hit upon one of the most debilitating flaws of *Beatrice di Tenda* when he wrote[15] of this recitative passage: ". . . when Agnese comes to confess her culpability in the false accusation that has caused her rival to be condemned to death, and precisely when to the more vivid and intense dramatic quality of the scene greater force and more varied richness of melodic accents should respond, precisely then the recitative appears exhausted, cold, and finally altogether inexpressive. Impeccable in prosody, perfect, but without the accents of emotion: the words here have the required rhythmic salience, but the musical intonation, reinforcing the sonority, does nothing but emphasize their logical value, adding nothing whatever to their value as emotion."

As the infuriated Beatrice tries to dismiss Agnese (p. 240), the key slides into A-flat major, 4/4 time. *Largo sostenuto*, the harp initiates the flowing accompaniment to which (p. 241), from inside, Orombello sings the exquisitely touching *"Angiol di pace"*—the melody of which Bellini adapted from the Sultan's *"Deh! se tu m'ami, o barbara,"* in Scene 2 of Act II of *Zaira* (see p. 370),[16] and which here is treated in part as a canonic trio. Orombello is urging Beatrice to inspire him to forgiveness by herself displaying it toward Agnese. As he repeats the melody, Beatrice forgives the girl, with whose voice hers is heard again in thirds (p. 242). Then the *a due* becomes an *a tre* as Orombello adds his voice (p. 242), beseeching Beatrice to continue setting the example of forgiveness.

Now (p. 244), *lugubre e maestoso*, Beatrice becomes aware of a funeral cortège as Rizzardo comes in followed by officers and halberdiers. All realize that hope must be abandoned. Proudly (p. 245), Beatrice says, *"Eccomi pronta"* (Here I am, ready). Agnese faints as Beatrice begins her farewell. Then, *assai sostenuto*, Beatrice sings (p. 245) the intensely moving aria *"Ah! se un'urna è a me concessa,"* in which she asks that her tomb not be left without flowers and that any prayers be offered for Filippo, not for her. As the chorus continues to lament, she embraces the unconscious Agnese and then (p. 248) sings the seemingly inappropriate but absolutely apt cabaletta, *"Ah! la morte a cui m'appresso"* (borrowed from Fernando's cabaletta *"Odo il tuo pianto,"* in *Bianca e Fernando*, p. 196 of piano-vocal score with plate numbers 9826–9842), asserting that in death she will find not pain, but victory. As the others sink to their knees, Beatrice is led away by the guards.

Here something should be said about the edition of *Beatrice di Tenda* prepared by maestro Vittorio Gui for staging at the Teatro Massimo, Palermo, in January 1959, and often repeated elsewhere since then. Gui himself wrote[17]: "Now, aside from some moments at which I, for my recent exhumation at Palermo, have thought it proper to so some retouching, but with the lightest hand, as in the accompaniment of the funeral march in the final scene, adding to the 'lugubrious' rhythm of the timpani such other percussion instruments as a single drum [*cassa*] and a bass drum [*tamburo grande*] (I still retained the memory of the Dead March in the recently performed *Saul* of Handel and remembered what in his time Handel had wanted to do, borrowing from the Tower of London the great funeral drums that had accompanied Charles I to the block), aside from that and the application of mutes to the strings in Beatrice's final aria, '*Ah! se un'urna è a me concessa*' . . . I hold that nothing more requires changing . . . in place of the mediocre 'cabaletta' that would have ended the opera and would have been like an icy shower upon the perturbation produced by both the situation and the music, I have had the chorus take up again, *sottovoce*, that divine theme of pardon [*"Angiol di pace"*], ending the opera in pianissimo as the condemned pair starts toward its death."

Maestro Gui's changes in *Beatrice*, except that of the closing moments, are not, though egregious, as damaging as Claudio Abbado's tampering with *I Capuleti e i Montecchi*. About that final change (which deprives Beatrice of the joyous transfiguration that was almost the only subtle development given her by Romani), William Weaver was facing theatrical realities rather than esthetic theory when he wrote[18]: "The theme [*"Angiol di pace"*] is, admittedly, a hauntingly beautiful one, but to deny Beatrice the last word is, in my opinion, a mistake. The cabaletta [*"Ah! la morte a cui m'appresso"*]—in this, as in so many other instances—is not just an occasion for vocal display, as some critics insist, but is also the dramatic assertion of the protagonist's character. Her death is not merely the concluding event of the opera, but the key to all her actions, given us when she says: 'The death I approach is a triumph, not suffering . . .' (Romani here uses the word *pena*, which can also mean punishment in the legal sense). If Bellini had lived longer and if he had rewritten *Beatrice*, he might well have created an ending still more appropriate. But these are *if's*. What he wrote is coherent with the rest of the opera . . ."

Bianca e Gernando
and Bianca e Fernando

I. Melo-dramma (*sic* in first libretto) in two acts. *Libretto*: by Domenico Gilardoni based upon the five-act prose play *Bianca e Fernando alla tomba di Carlo IV duca di Agrigento* (1820), by Carlo Roti.[1] *Composed*: 1825-1826. *Première*: Teatro San Carlo, Naples, May 30, 1826.[2] *Original cast*:

Bianca, *daughter of Carlo,* *Duke of Agrigento*	Henriette Méric-Lalande
Viscardo	Almerinda Manzocchi
Eloisa	Eloisa Manzocchi
Gernando, *son of Carlo, Duke of Agrigento*	Giovanni Battista Rubini
Clemente	Michele Benedetti
Carlo, *Duke of Agrigento*	Umberto Berettoni*
Filippo	Luigi Lablache
Uggero	Gaetano Chizzola

Published: 1826 by the Calcografia e Copisteria de' Reali Teatri (later by Girard and then by Cottrau), Naples, in incomplete piano-vocal score, as "*Bianca e Gernando*. Melodramma in two acts, Music by the Sig. M.º V. Bellini. Transcribed with pianoforte accompaniment by the Sig. F. Florimo," with some sections for piano, four hands; disjunct plate numbers (*Sinfonia*, 324). In 1828, the edition of Florimo's arrangement was changed by the addition of some numbers from the Genoa revision (*Bianca e Fernando*). Seldom performed elsewhere. Incomplete autograph score in the library of the Naples Conservatory, which also has an autograph of the "*Gran Scena ed Aria Finale*" in piano-vocal score, as well as an

---

* Spelled Berretoni in the first libretto.

incomplete manuscript copy ("*San Carlo 30 maggio 1826*") and two short scores. Some autograph sketches and a manuscript copy are in the Museo Belliniano, Catania, which also has two copies of the Florimo piano-vocal transcription which Bellini sent to his family; the manuscript copy includes most of the recitatives and shows instrumental indications, agogic instructions, and text-words in Bellini's script. It was donated to the museum by Carmelo Fazio, whom Pastura described (BSLS, p. 97) as "heir of the [Bellini] family"; its origin is unknown. Autograph incipits of several numbers in the Bibliothèque Nationale, Paris.

PERFORMANCE DATA. *Bianca e Gernando* was staged at the Teatro Carolino, Palermo, on May 30, 1829.[3] The cast was headed by Caterina Lipparini (Bianca), Ignazio Grifo (Viscardo, adjusted for a tenor), Maddalena Righetti (Eloisa), Giovanni Francesco Boccaccini (Gernando), Giambattista Placci (Clemente), Raffaele Scalese (Carlo), and Guglielmo Balfe[4] (Filippo). It seems to have had a few scattered performances elsewhere.

II. Revised version: *Bianca e Fernando* (*melodramma serio*), with libretto touched up and added to, probably by Felice Romani, and with the score supplied with a *sinfonia* and revised by Bellini (and possibly Francesco Florimo). *Prepared*: 1828. *Première*: Inauguration of the Teatro Carlo Felice, Genoa, April 7, 1828, preceded by an *Inno reale* especially composed for the occasion by Donizetti and coupled with the ballet *Gli Adoratori del fuoco*, choreographed by Giovanni Galzerani. *Original cast*:

BIANCA	Adelaide Tosi
VISCARDO	Elisabetta Coda
ELOISA	Marietta Riva
FERNANDO	Giovanni David
CLEMENTE	Agostino Rovere
CARLO, *Duke of Agrigento*	Giuseppe Rossi
FILIPPO	Antonio Tamburini
UGGERO	Antonio Crippa

Published: At least twice by Ricordi, Milan—(1) 1837, with plate numbers 9826-9842, in oblong piano-vocal score[5]; (2) in vertical format, with plate number 108911; also in piano transcription (108911-108912), with most of the recitative omitted. No complete autograph survives. The Museo Belliniano, Catania, has some autograph sketches. The *Album di autografi del Florimo* in the Naples Conservatory library includes the autograph of Bianca's final aria, "*Deh, non ferir*."[6]

PERFORMANCE DATA. *Bianca e Fernando* was staged at the Teatro alla Scala, Milan, on September 5, 1829, and ran for ten performances. The cast included Méric-Lalande (Bianca), Luigi Asti (Viscardo), Margherita Rubini (Eloisa), Giovanni Battista Rubini (Fernando, a revision of the role he had created as Gernando in 1826), Domenico Spiaggi (Clemente), Luigi Biondi (Carlo), Antonio Tamburini (Filippo), and Lorenzo Lombardi (Uggero); the stage settings were by Alessandro Sanquirico. An opera listed as *Bianca e Fernando,* but which may well have been *Bianca e Gernando,* was performed at Messina in 1828, with Amalia(?) Martelli (Bianca) and Giovanni Basadonna (Fernando). A *"Bianca e Fernando"* libretto printed at Messina specifies a performance at the Real Teatro Borbonico di Reggio [Calabria] "as the second score of the theatrical year 1829"; its cast is listed as Metilde [*sic*] Ruggiero (Bianca), Marietta Marconi (Viscardo), Giovanni Basadonna (Fernando), Andrea Tonti (Carlo), Giacomo Fortini (Filippo), and Giuseppe la Grua (Uggero), the composer as *"Maestro Sig. Vincenzo Bellini Siciliano."* This too may have been *Bianca e Gernando* or some mixture of the two scores. "Fernando" still could not be used on the San Carlo stage: on July 24 and October 30, 1829, and on June 7, 1830, the opera was performed there as *Bianca e Gernando,* and that disguise would have been necessary in Messina as well.

Bianca e Fernando was presented at the Teatro Valle, Rome, on July 1, 1837. Principe Agostino Chigi-Albani noted in his diary that the company was bad, the reception mediocre. In the *Rivista teatrale,* Rome, however, its publisher, Antonio Tosi, praised the leading singers and commented upon the altitudes to which Bellini's later operas had elevated him. He added: "In his *Bianca e Fernando,* he only followed the method of those numerous servile imitators of the Rossinian style who, lacking that master's genius and distinction, remained unaware that in the fine arts, not copies, but creations are wanted, not imitations, but originality."[7] Outside Italy, Bellini's second opera appears to have been staged only at the Teatro Principal, Barcelona, in 1830.

THE LIBRETTO. The adventurer Filippo has usurped the dominion of Carlo, Duke of Agrigento, and has proscribed the duke's son, Fernando, giving out false word that the duke is dead. Carlo's presumed heir is therefore his daughter Bianca, a widow with a baby son. She, believing Filippo's protestations of devotion to her and her family, has made him regent of the dukedom and is preparing to marry him so as to provide the people of Agrigento with a male ruler and defender.

As the opera opens, "Adolfo" (Fernando in disguise) arrives from

Britain, is presented to Filippo, and tells of having seen Fernando die in combat in Scotland. He places himself at Filippo's service. Deceived, Filippo orders him to murder the imprisoned duke—thus unintentionally informing Fernando that his father is alive. Fernando believes that Bianca is Filippo's accomplice, but she convinces him of her innocence and of her mistaken belief in Filippo's good intentions. Brother and sister agree that she will dress as a soldier to accompany him on a mission to rescue their father. She and Fernando find the dungeon cell in which Carlo has been all but buried alive. As brother and sister are reunited with their father, the people of Agrigento rebel successfully against Filippo. Carlo is acclaimed as the legitimate ruler.[8]

Bianca e Fernando differs from *Bianca e Gernando* by much more than the addition of the new *sinfonia* and several new numbers. Bellini deleted groups of measures from the original version, added instrumental passages, introduced new melodic-declamatory material into recitatives, had text-lines altered, probably by Felice Romani.[9] He described the changes to Florimo in a letter of February 27, 1829[10]: "P.S. You can tell Cottrau that of the entire *Bianca* [*e Gernando*], only the following pieces remain unchanged: the grand duet and the romanza; all the rest is changed, and almost half is new, and for that reason, the only pieces[11] that he can send to Genoa are those mentioned; do you understand? I shall change the cabaletta of David's cavatina, the same for Tamburini, and the same in the trio and perhaps also in Tosi's cavatina. The *stretta* of the finale has been changed, and [there is] a new *sinfonia*, the [original] introduction[12] serving as a largo. I may perhaps change the *stretta* of Tamburini's *scena*, where, if it satisfies him, I hope to put the cabaletta of David's cavatina, which he doesn't want because he wants to sing something sweet, and then I would put the cabaletta of Tamburini's *scena* into the first-act trio.[13] The romanza and duet will remain as they are. I shall compose David's *scena*, for which I have prepared an andante and cabaletta that seem to me very effective; in the second-act trio, I shall replace that little prayer with the one from the trio in *Adelson*, which, you will recall, produced lots of effect in the mouth of Marras,[14] and in that way I'll be able to interrupt the trio when Filippo enters, and won't have to do a cabaletta, which would tire Tosi and— because interest ends with the pardon by the father—would prove cold; and, finally, the *scena* for Tosi, which I have already finished along with the other pieces, and nothing remains for me to do but to write them out with the poetry that Romani will do."[15]

THE OPERA. The following analysis of *Bianca e Fernando* refers to the 1837 Ricordi piano-vocal publication, it being unlikely that *Bianca e*

Gernando will ever be performed or published complete.[16] Just as the surviving interest of *Adelson e Salvini* lies in its having been Bellini's first opera, so that of *Bianca e Fernando* lies chiefly in its having been his revision of his second opera, composed in its first form when he was twenty-five. Notably, it contains no *recitativo secco.* Its numbers are woven together more seamlessly than those of *Adelson*, the original *Bianca e Gernando*, and even, for the most part, *Il Pirata.* These proofs of increasing technical command could lead an otherwise uninformed analyst into dating *Bianca e Fernando* later than *Il Pirata*—which is certainly not to say that it is the better opera.

Sinfonia: After three and a half fortissimo measures of an *allegro risoluto* demand for attention, a pause, and three measures of piano hesitation, lento, the *sinfonia* proceeds through four measures of bare allegro A's to a delightful andante in which the cellos are employed melodically with charming results[17]—and then to another allegro, poor in ideas, blankly repetitious, and overlong—and unfortunately reminiscent of "Deck the hall with boughs of holly." Unfortunately, too, the rest of the *sinfonia* is inferior both in melodic and in other musical ideas, as well as in craftsmanship, to that of *Adelson e Salvini* and that of *Il Pirata*— which were composed earlier.

Act I: Bianca e Fernando opens upon a banal orchestral introduction (p. 16).[18] Interest freshens when Fernando enters: his expressive recitative *"Questa è mia reggia"* (p. 18)[19] expands into equally expressive cantilena (*"Io ti respiro,"* p. 18), with a reiterative accompaniment that outlasts its welcome. This is succeeded by a chorus for Fernando's followers, Uggero included, *"Sgombra quel duol"* (p. 19), for which vocal and instrumental lines are meshed in expert harmony. Next comes Fernando's "entrance" aria, *"A tanto duol"* (p. 27),[20] which begins larghetto and is succeeded by a short choral interjection, *"Ov'è il tuo cor intrepido?"* (p. 29) and a recitative-like passage for Fernando, *"Sì, a vendetta qui adulto ritorno"* (p. 30). That in turn leads (p. 31) to his cabaletta *"Ascolta, o padre,"* with choral comment supporting very Bellinian melody (at the words *"Sol di vendetta"*) of which more might have been made here—and would be made in Riccardo's *"Qui ti sfido a mortal guerra,"* in Scene 10 of Act I of *I Puritani* (see page 321).[21] A recitative scene involving Fernando, Clemente, Uggero, and Viscardo ensues: *"Uggero sol, non altri, meco resti"* (p. 37); at its conclusion, "Adolfo" misleads Viscardo by telling him that Fernando is dead.

In the recitative *"A noi viene Filippo,"* Viscardo foretells Filippo's arrival; later he carries out "Adolfo's" plan by reporting Fernando's supposed death to Filippo. In an *allegro maestoso* cavatina, *"Estinto! che ascoltai!*" (p. 42, leading into "*Ah no, sì lieta sorte,*" p. 43), Filippo voices joy at this news and sends Viscardo to fetch "Adolfo." Alone, he rejoices in events ("*Oh contento desiato!*" *allegro molto,* p. 50). Viscardo returns with "Adolfo" ("*E quegli il mio Signor,*" recitative, p. 54), who circumstantially recounts Fernando's death in Scotland. He displays a letter purportedly written by the dying man. Filippo, recognizing Fernando's script, reads it ("*Di Fernando . . . son le cifre,*" p. 57). In the succeeding allegro trio (Filippo, Fernando, Viscardo, p. 57), Bellini succeeds in externalizing the thoughts of each man, though all sing much the same words.[22]

The prevailingly impressive extended finale of Act I (pp. 71–136) is a single conception in three large sections: (1) a chorus for the people of Agrigento ("*Viva Bianca!*" p. 71); (2) a recitative and cavatina for Bianca ("*Miei fidi amici,*" p. 86, and "*La mia scelta a voi sia grata,*" p. 88); and (3) a "continuation of the finale" beginning with Filippo's "*Mira, o Bianca*" (p. 95). Section 1 is chiefly notable for muscular energy, a masculine vigor not always attributed to Bellini. In Section 2, after Bianca's similarly vigorous recitative, she sings to her subjects the announcement of her selection of Filippo as their ruler. This is interrupted by the people ("*Sì, nella sua virtude,*" p. 89), after which Bianca continues with "*Contenta appien quest'alma*" (p. 91), the chief melody of which would later pass into Norma's "*Ah! bello, a me ritorna.*" At the conclusion of Section 2, Bianca and the people rejoice together.

Filippo initiates Section 3—the "*seguito del finale*"—*alla marziale,* singing "*Mira, o Bianca*" (p. 95); the people again add their voices. What may be called the true finale begins (p. 99) as a recitative exchange among Bianca, Fernando, and Filippo. It flows into a concertato for them ("*Ah che l'alma invade un gel,*" largo, p. 102[23]), an attractive example of Bellini's melodic pathos, and extends into a choral-supported quintet (or sextet—Eloisa sings with the chorus) when the people, Viscardo, and Clemente join in (p. 104). Midway in this concertato, a dialogue between Bianca and Filippo starts in strength ("*Qual da folgore colpita,*" p. 109) but ends in cliché. The concertato is interrupted again (p. 115) when Bianca bursts out: "*Rode e lacera il mio petto quel suo detto quel furore,*" and Filippo and Fernando enter successively in fugato with slight variants of her words (respectively, "*Rode e lacera il mio petto il sospetto ed il timore*" and "*Rode e lacera il mio petto quell'aspetto il suo dolore*"), again allowing differentiation of personality and mood among characters singing together.[24]

Act II. Act II opens (p. 137) with recitative dialogue between Fernando ("*Che vuol tu dirmi?*") and Clemente. Filippo enters ("*Vis-*

cardo a te parlò," p. 138) and, in an aria of darkening power (*"Allor, che notte avanza,*" p. 142), informs Fernando that he intends to marry Bianca—and then orders him to murder the imprisoned duke. The people indicate their willingness to follow Filippo (chorus, *"Signor a compier l'alto incarco,*" p. 145, which is enfeebled by a monotonously iterative accompaniment). In an *allegro vivace* cabaletta, *"Bramato momento"* (p. 147), Filippo in turn expresses his pleasure in the new turn of events; the people again add approving comment.

Musical textures that Andrea Della Corte accurately judged "really pianistic, now in the bass, now in the vocal line,"[25] mark the orchestral introduction (p. 153) and the recitative-preceded romanza of Bianca and Eloisa (*"Sorgi, o padre," andante flebile,* p. 155), which is melodically and theatrically one of Bellini's finest achievements before *La Sonnambula*—it is superbly developed. It is followed by strong recitative dialogue (begun by Eloisa, *"Da te chiamato,*" p. 160), in which Bianca learns that "Adolfo" is her brother, Fernando.[26] This leads into a Fernando–Bianca duet begun when he denounces her: *"No! no! mia suora . . . più non sei"* (p. 165). When Fernando tells her that her father is still living, and then denounces Filippo, her demands for silence drive him to upbraid her again (*"Ahi donna misera,*" p. 171). She insists upon her innocence, whereupon Fernando tells her to put on a soldier's uniform and accompany him (*"Sorgi le spogli e indossati d'un mio guerrier,*" p. 174). Beatrice's animato solo section, *"Deh! fa ch'io possa intendere"* (p. 175), is of such persuasive brilliance that it aroused applause even at the Naples première. In a "recitative after the duet," *"Sai tu Clemente"* (p. 182), Fernando and Bianca joyfully discover that Clemente knows where their father lies incarcerated.

Mechanical employment of clichés from the circumambient over-supply of them enfeebles the *scena* for chorus and tenor which begins on p. 183 with an instrumental introduction.[27] The choral *"Tutti siam"* (p. 185) remained so strongly in Bellini's mind that he later reused it twice. In *Zaira*, it became the chorus *"Poni il fedel tuo martire"* (p. 109L of the autograph); in *Norma*, again transmogrified, it became the chorus *"Non partì"* (p. 189 of the piano-vocal score with plate number 41684). This continues monotonously until Fernando interrupts it by his entrance (*"Eccomi al fin, Guerrieri,*" p. 192)[28] and the people exculpate Bianca (*"Degna suora di Fernando,*" p. 194). The "cabaletta" of Fernando's cantabile (*"Odo il tuo pianto, o Padre,*"[29] p. 196) fails to lift the pervasive banality of this long *scena*. The prison scene, finally dispersing that pall, arrives as highly welcome contrast, beginning with its orchestral introduction (p. 203). Carlo's recitative (*"Sognai cader trafitto!"* p. 204) immediately calls the faltering drama back to vitality in a quickening intensified by his moving cantilena, *"Da gelido sudore"* (p. 206).

The closing scenes bring the best of *Bianca e Fernando*, starting with Fernando's recitative *"Ecco la tomba"* (p. 209), continuing with the simple, extraordinarily effective reunion of father with son and daughter (p. 211), achieving great emotional intensity when Bianca and Fernando foretell Filippo's downfall (*"Cadrà quell'empio cor,"* pp. 218–219), and ending with a recitative and aria finale beginning (p. 223) with recitative for Bianca, Fernando, and the people. The peak of excellence is reached last: Bianca's apostrophe to Filippo as he stands with dagger poised over her child (p. 225): *"Deh non ferir, deh sentimi,"*[30] inaugurating the *"scena* for Tosi" which had given Bellini so much trouble (he borrowed, for the passage beginning *"Crudele, alle tue piante"*—p. 229—a melodic idea from Nelly's *"Ah! Salvini, alle tue piante,"* in *Adelson e Salvini* [p. 286 of the piano-vocal score with plate number 108595]). This evolves into a trio for Bianco, Fernando, and Filippo. Its "cabaletta" (*"Alla gioja ed al piacer,"* for Bianca alone, p. 232) is much less imaginatively composed.[31] It announces the triumphant ending unhelpfully. But in it, as throughout this finale, individual passages and whole pages prefigure the dramatic abruptness and forward surge of the mature Verdi.

I Capuleti e i Montecchi[*]

TRAGEDIA LIRICA in two acts. *Libretto:* By Felice Romani, a reworking of his libretto for Nicola Vaccaj's *Giulietta e Romeo* (Teatro della Canobbiana, Milan, October 31, 1825), which had been derived very indirectly from Shakespeare's *Romeo and Juliet. Composed:* 1830. *Première:* Teatro La Fenice, Venice, March 11, 1830,[1] on a double bill with the ballet *Chiara di Rosemberg,* choreographed by Antonio Cortesi. *Original cast:*

GIULIETTA, *a Capulet,* *in love with Romeo*	Rosalbina Caradori-Allan
ROMEO, *head of the Montagues,* *in love with Giulietta*	Giuditta Grisi
TEBALDO, *a Capulet partisan,* *intended husband of Giulietta*	Lorenzo Bonfigli
CAPELLIO, *head of the Capulets,* *Giulietta's father*	Gaetano Antoldi
LORENZO, *physician,* *companion of Capellio*	Rainieri Pocchini Cavalieri

Published: in piano-vocal score by Ricordi, Milan, 1831, with plate numbers 5224–5234, separate numbers having been issued earlier (for a listing of them, see Friedrich Lippmann, *Vincenzo Bellini,* etc., p. 382); by Girard (later Cottrau), Naples, with disjunct plate numbers (*Sinfonia,* 4380); by Pacini, Paris, with plate numbers 1510–1520; again by Ricordi, undated (pl. no. 42043).† Autograph score in the Museo Belliniano,

---

* Often referred to by early writers as *Giulietta e Romeo.*

† In the 1960's, Ricordi also prepared an edition of the score by Claudio Abbado, available on rental. In it, the role of Romeo is assigned to a tenor. For criticism of it,

Catania; two manuscript copies in the Naples Conservatory library; another copy in the library of the Conservatorio Giuseppe Verdi, Milan; another in the Archivio Ricordi, Milan, with autograph interpolations (see Appendix M, p. 422); another in the archives of the Teatro La Fenice, Venice.

PERFORMANCE DATA. *I Capuleti e i Montecchi* was staged at the Teatro Comunale, Sinigaglia, during the 1830 *fiera*, with Giuditta Grisi and Bonfigli in the roles that they had created, but with Santina Ferlotti as Giulietta and a native *sinigagliese*, Natale Costantini, as either Capellio or Lorenzo. It was also staged at La Scala, Milan, on December 26, 1830, with Amalia Schütz-Oldosi, a mezzo-soprano, as Giulietta, Giuditta Grisi (Romeo), Lorenzo Bonfigli (Tebaldo), and Carlo Ottolini Porto (Capellio), and ran there for twenty-five performances that season. It spread rapidly to other Italian opera houses. In March 1831, it was staged at the Teatro Carolino, Palermo. On October 6 of that year, the Teatro Grande (later Comunale), Trieste, presented it, and on November 29, it was heard at the Teatro San Carlo, Naples, where the cast included Giuseppina Ronzi de Begnis (Giulietta), Luigia Boccabadati (Romeo), and Bonfigli (Tebaldo). It reappeared at the Carolino in 1832, when Bellini attended a performance there (April 11). The Giulietta of that evening was Annetta Fischer; the Romeo was Almerinda Manzocchi.

On October 27, 1832, at the Teatro Comunale, Bologna, Maria Malibran was the Romeo of the first performance of *I Capuleti* in which the tomb scene of Vaccaj's *Giulietta e Romeo* was substituted for Bellini's; with her were Sofia Dall'Oca Schoberlechner (Giulietta), Francesco Pedrazzi (Tebaldo), Carlo Ottolini Porto (Capellio), and Carlo Marcolini (Lorenzo). Writing of Malibran and her "caprices," Michele Scherillo said[2]: "Called in October 1832 to Bologna to sing the Bellinian opera there with Schoberlechner, after the first three acts[3] she put in [*azzeccò*] Vaccaj's third act. Some people say that this sacrilege had been advised personally by Rossini; however, whether the caprice was Malibran's or Rossini's, that heterogeneous fourth act did not sound any the less inharmonious. And the Bellinians screamed even under the powerful fascination of the diva; and what is more, when [Giuditta] Grisi herself, for whom the opera had been composed, later dared to adopt the Malibranian *pasticcio*, the one who screamed loudest was Felice Romani, in

see Fedele D'Amico, "*C'è modo e modo ('I Capuleti e i Montecchi' di Bellini nella revisione di Claudio Abbado)*," in the *Nuova Rivista musicale italiana*, I, 1, May–June 1967, pp. 136–142, and herein, p. 251.

the *Gazzetta piemontese;* and now Florimo has screamed, though he is a fanatic admirer and affectionate friend of that sorceress of song. The sacrilege is, in truth, ugly, gets on one's nerves: and in our view is improper and extremely unjustified." Scherillo then proceeds to analyze Bellini's final scene and Vaccaj's.

Scherillo also published[4] an interesting letter from Giuseppina Ronzi de Begnis to Florimo, introducing it thus:

"In the autumn of 1831, Ronzi, one of the most illustrious singers of the first half of the century, had sung Bellini's *Capuleti* at the San Carlo in Naples as prepared by Florimo, without alterations; and had won great applause. In 1834, invited to sing the opera again at the Pergola in Florence at a time when Malibran's dainty dish had had great success, she had the courage and the intelligence to perform the Bellinian opera integrally and to open the public's eyes. After the successful outcome, proud of having triumphed over her powerful rival's caprice, she wrote Florimo the following letter:

" 'Florence, June 18, 1834

" 'Friend Florimo,

" 'First performance of *I Capuleti* last evening. Everyone feared for the outcome because they had done it some time earlier and it had not pleased at all. Last evening, however, they saw that there is no failure where there is a Romeo like Ronzi (Modesty!)! In short, they no longer recognized it. Introduction—good; Romeo's Cavatina—two curtain calls; Duet—I was called out; and Finale—furor; what do you think of that? Second act: Giulietta's Aria—good; and Duet—also good, but no furor. The third [act] was supposed to fail but did not fail. Here they had been saying that Vaccaj's is better, and they wanted Ronzi to do the *pasticcio alla Malibran;* but I replied:—if I make a fiasco, at least it will be all Bellini—I assure you that I was trembling, as the Florentines have the vice of not listening; and you know that in this third act there are no things that flatter the ear, and that to enjoy the beauties, whether of music or of declamation, there must be religious silence. I obtained that, and once the audience had seen me, they remained as if unable to move. In short, to make the matter brief, it gave great pleasure, and after it we were all called out.

" 'Things seem to me to be going well; I really am content. To tell you the truth, I would have been very unhappy if this opera had failed; and I am the more content because it is all Bellini's work. There were people to say:—how does Malibran happen to change the third act? It seems to me that, as a singer who is said to be such an actress, she should be content. Does this seem to you a small triumph? . . .' "

On January 14, 1833, *I Capuleti* was staged at the Teatro Apollo, Rome; the cast consisted of Schoberlechner (Giulietta), Antonietta Galzerani (Romeo), Giovanni Basadonna (Tebaldo), Giovanni Campagnoli (Capellio), and Giuseppe De Gregorj (Lorenzo). It was revived at the Comunale, Bologna, on November 21, 1833, and again on May 10, 1834. Malibran sang it at the San Carlo, Naples, on March 6, 1834, as she did at La Scala, Milan—with Vaccaj's final scene—on October 9, 1834, when her colleagues were Schoberlechner (Giulietta), Domenico Reina (Tebaldo), Ignazio Marini (Capellio), and Pocchini Cavalieri (Lorenzo). During Bellini's lifetime, *I Capuleti* was also presented at the Teatro Valle, Rome (May 1834).

Extra-Italian performances of *I Capuleti* in Italian seem to have begun at Dresden on October 1, 1831; Madrid on June 1832; and at the Kärntnertortheater, Vienna, on December 1, 1832. Before Bellini's death, the opera was also staged (often with Vaccaj's tomb scene) at the Théâtre-Italien, Paris, on January 30, 1833; at London on July 20, 1833; at the Königsstädtischestheater, Berlin, on June 15, 1834; at Corfu on January 15, 1835; and at Lisbon on February 9, 1835. The first performance in the United States appears to have been that at the St. Charles Theatre, New Orleans, on April 4 (not April 1, as often stated), 1837, with Teresa Rossi (Giulietta), Clorinda Corradi Pantanelli (Romeo), Paolo Ceresina (Tebaldo), Pietro Candi (Capellio), and Federico Badiali (Lorenzo). Performances are also chronicled in Boston on May 13, 1847,[5] and in New York on January 28, 1848.

I Capuleti e i Montecchi soon was sung in more than one German translation: at the Königsstädtischestheater, Berlin, on June 18, 1832; at Graz on July 13, 1832; at the Theater in der Josefstadt, Vienna—as *Die Capulets und Montagues*, in a translation by Georg Ott—on November 23, 1832 and at the Kärntnertortheater in that city on December 1, 1832; at Brünn on April 10, 1833; Prague, June 8, 1833; Budapest, June 8, 1833; and Bucharest, March 1834. After Bellini's death, the opera was also sung in Czech, Danish, French, Hungarian, Polish and Russian.

During the centenary commemorations of Bellini's death the Teatro Massimo Bellini, Catania, presented *I Capuleti* on January 5, 1935. Gino Marinuzzi conducted, and the cast included Ines Alfani Tellini (Giulietta), Aurora Buades (Romeo), and Franco Lo Giudice (Tebaldo). On February 10, 1954, the Teatro Massimo, Palermo, revived this opera to open its season, with Rosanna Carteri (Giulietta) and Giulietta Simionato (Romeo). On October 14, 1958, the American Opera Society presented it in concert form at Carnegie Hall, New York. Laurel Hurley was the Giulietta, Simionato the Romeo, Richard Cassilly the Tebaldo, Ezio Flagello the Capellio, and David Smith the Lorenzo. When the Society offered *I Capuleti* again on April 28, 1964, Simionato was the Romeo; with her were Mary Costa (Giulietta), André Montal (Tebaldo), Raymond Michalski (Capellio), and Ron Bottcher (Lorenzo); the conductor (United States debut) was Lamberto Gardelli. Renata Scotto was heard as Giulietta at the Teatro São Carlos, Lisbon, on March 13, 1964 (commemmorating the quadricentennial of Shakespeare's birth). Anna Maria Rota was the Romeo, Michele Molese the Tebaldo.

On March 26, 1966, La Scala, Milan, inaugurated an unhappy train of events by presenting *I Capuleti e i Montecchi* with a tenor (Giacomo Aragall) as Romeo in a version of Bellini's score drastically revised by the conductor, Claudio Abbado; others in that cast were Scotto (Giulietta), Luciano Pavarotti (Tebaldo), and Mario Petri (Capellio). That distortion of Bellini's intentions was heard again on June 24, 1966, at the Stadsschouwburz, Amsterdam, as part of a Holland Festival, with Margherita Rinaldi as Giulietta, Walter Monachesi as Lorenzo, and the other singers from the La Scala cast. Those principals took the Abbado version to the Teatro dell'Opera, Rome, on April 8, 1967; it has also been heard at the Salle Pelletier, Montreal (October 7, 1967), and the Academy of Music, Philadelphia (October 22, 1968), both times with Scotto as Giulietta. Fedele D'Amico clinically dissected Abbado's revisions, demonstrating that they are at least as damaging to Bellini's opera as reorchestrations of Schumann's symphonies or Chopin's concertos and the "editions" of *Boris Godunov* have been to their originals.[6] But the Abbado version had become so entrenched that it was used at the Edinburgh Festival on August 30, 1967, with Anna Moffo (Giulietta), Giacomo Aragall (Romeo), Luciano Pavarotti (Tebaldo), Giovanni Foiani (Capellio), and Walter Monachesi (Lorenzo). English Bellinians noted gratefully that when the Opera Class of the Royal Manchester College of Music staged *I Capuleti* on March 7, 1967, Bellini's score, without benefit of either Vaccaj or Abbado, was used.

THE LIBRETTO. The story is set in Verona in the thirteenth century. As Franca Cella wrote[7] when discussing Romani's libretto: "One is dealing with Shakespearean thematic material, not with a true meeting with Shakespeare; F. Romani, in fact, modified for Bellini an earlier libretto of his (*Giulietta e Romeo*) which had already been used by Nicola Vaccaj (1825), for which he did not deny having drawn upon the earlier libretto by Giuseppe Foppa (*Giulietta e Romeo*), which had been set by Nicola Zingarelli (1796). Foppa's sources had not been translations of Shakespeare or the French interventions of [Jean-François] Ducis so much as Gerolamo Della Corte's *Storie di Verona*."

Notably, the Shakespearean characters of Mercutio, Benvolio, and the

Nurse to Juliet do not appear in Romani's libretto. Nor had Foppa been the first writer to base an operatic libretto upon the always attractive tragedy of Romeo and Juliet. Perhaps the earliest of the Romeo-Juliet operas was the *Romeo und Julie* of Georg Benda (Gotha, September 25, 1776), which set a libretto that Friedrich Wilhelm Gotter had based upon Shakespeare. In addition to the operas by Zingarelli, Vaccaj, and Bellini, other treatments of the subject have included Berlioz's *"symphonie dramatique," Roméo et Juliette* (1839), Gounod's *Roméo et Juliette* (libretto by Jules Barbier and Michel Carré, 1867), and Riccardo Zandonai's *Giulietta e Romeo* (libretto by Arturo Rossato, 1922)—not to mention Tchaikovsky's symphonic poem *Romeo and Juliet* (1870).[8]

Act I: Scenes 1–3. Gallery in the Capulet palace. Capellio, leader of the Capulets, who are Guelphs, announces to his followers that the Ghibellines (whose leader is a Montague, Romeo) are sending an envoy to negotiate a peace agreement; he adds that the Capulets will fight to avenge his son, killed in combat by Romeo. Tebaldo, who is enamored of Capellio's daughter, Giulietta, agrees to kill Romeo, whereupon Capellio promises him Giulietta's hand in marriage that day. Lorenzo, the Capulets' physician, attempts to delay the wedding by saying that Giulietta is ill. He knows that she loves Romeo, who has been visiting her clandestinely, and that they yearn for the peace that will permit them to marry. As Capellio is rejecting Lorenzo's arguments, Romeo, unidentified, appears as the Ghibelline envoy and suggests that the Capulet-Montague feud be terminated by the marriage of Giulietta to Romeo. In a rage, Capellio rejects the plan.

Scenes 4–7. Room in Giulietta's apartments. Giulietta bitterly laments that she must marry Tebaldo. Romeo, having come to her apartments in desperation, tells her that all hope for peace between their families is futile; he begs her to run away with him. But Giulietta, tortured by indecision, finally refuses to abandon her father. As Capellio and Tebaldo come in to lead her to the altar, Romeo escapes.

Scenes 5–12. An internal courtyard of Capellio's palace at night. A rear staircase leads to galleries affording entrance into rooms illuminated for a magnificent ceremonial. Romeo encounters Lorenzo, who has been befriending him and Giulietta, and tells the physician that he will lead his followers in an assault on the palace to rescue Giulietta. When the onset begins, Romeo again begs Giulietta to flee with him. Capellio and Tebaldo, preparing to defend the palace, find Romeo and Giulietta together. Romeo reveals to them his love for her; a scene of pandemonium precedes the battle.

Act II: Scenes 1–4. Night. An apartment in Capellio's palace illuminated by ancient torches. As the battle continues, Giulietta is terrified for both her father and her lover. Lorenzo suggests that she swallow a potion that will render her unconscious and apparently dead; after she has been entombed, she will be able to rise again and elope with Romeo. She takes the potion. Capellio orders her to await her husband at dawn, thinking thus to prevent Romeo from carrying her off. Lorenzo leads her out. Now suspicious of Lorenzo, Capellio has him arrested, thus making it impossible for Lorenzo to inform Romeo about the potion that Giulietta has swallowed.

Scenes 5–7. A deserted place near Capellio's palace; at the back, a great arch through which can be seen a gallery leading to the palace. The despairing Romeo is challenged to a duel by Tebaldo. As they prepare to fight, a funeral procession approaches and they learn that it is Giulietta's.

Scenes 8–11. The tombs of the Capulets; at the front, the tomb of Giulietta. All the mourners but Romeo depart. Maddened by grief, he swallows poison. Giulietta regains consciousness only to find Romeo dying. His death being beyond bearing to her, she too dies. Followed by Romeo's soldiers, Capellio and his men rush in to capture Romeo. When they find the bodies of the dead lovers, Capellio asks, "Killed—by whom?" and the others answer, "By you, ruthless man."

THE OPERA. *Sinfonia* (p. 1*): In D major, *allegro giusto*, the single-movement *sinfonia*, though of small interest for itself, serves to establish the somber and finally tragic urgency of the drama. Containing only one hundred and seventy-five measures, it presents two principal (and some subsidiary) melodic ideas, one of which is unmistakably Bellinian:

The *sinfonia* frequently depends upon the rhythmic figure that was almost Bellini's signature in his early operas: ♩ ♫ ♫ ♫ ♫ ♩ . As Andrea Della Corte noted,[9] "More than by inventiveness in melody and elaboration, the sober prelude is given substance by urgent dynamics and rhythm. . . . The motives themselves also have more rhythmic than lyric importance; the fourth [p. 4], which is more agitated than the

* Page references here are to the Ricordi piano-vocal score with plate number 42043, which contains as an appendix (pp. 137–153) the concluding "*Coro, Aria e Duetto Finale*" of Vaccaj's *Giulietta e Romeo.*

others . . . reappears in the accompaniment of the first chorus of the Capulets [where it leads into and underlines the words "*Già Cavalieri e militi*," p. 8]."

Act I: Scene 1 (p. 7). "*Coro d'introduzione*"; Gallery in the Capulet Palace; the followers of Capellio gather. The Introduction begins with a two-part chorus (t, bs) of the Capulets ("*Aggiorna appena*," C major, 4/4 time, *allegro moderato*, p. 7) that establishes the atmosphere of enmity between the Guelphs (Capulets) and the Ghibellines (Montagues).

Scene 2 (p. 14). The orchestra preludes, *marziale*, 4/4 time, for six measures, Tebaldo's recitative, "*O di Capellio, generosi amici*," which the chorus interrupts. Capellio and Lorenzo speak in recitative to convey the information that Romeo is the leader of the Montagues and has killed Capellio's son and that the wedding of Tebaldo to Capellio's daughter Giulietta is imminent. The musical texture changes to arioso (C major), 12/8 time, *andante* as Tebaldo sings (p. 16), "*E serbato, è serbato a questo acciaro*," revealing that revenge is reserved for his sword (the melody was borrowed from Corasmino's cavatina, "*Perchè mai, perchè pugnasti*," in Act I of *Zaira*). Capellio orders the wedding solemnized immediately, but Lorenzo reveals that Giulietta, who is feverish and unwell, can be taken to the altar only by force. In an ardent aria, "*L'amo tanto*" (p. 23), Tebaldo asserts that he would not cause Giulietta a single lament. The aria seems excessively praised by Della Corte, who found it[10] "marked by the taste and greater maturity of *Puritani*." Capellio and his followers reassure Tebaldo (p. 24) while Lorenzo sorrows for Giulietta. Capellio sends Lorenzo to prepare the girl for the ceremony. A trumpet announces (G major) the arrival of the Montague envoy (who is not known to be Romeo). Capellio asks (p. 29) whether anyone is inclined to accept the enemy's proposals. All present reply (p. 29), "*Odio eterno ai Montecchi, ai Ghibellini*" (Eternal hatred toward the Montagues, the Ghibellines). The next scene follows without interruption.

Scene 3 (p. 30). The unrecognized Montague envoy (Romeo) enters with soldiers and, in recitative, offers friendship and peace. Tebaldo and Capellio express utter distrust of the Montagues. The envoy suggests the marriage of Giulietta to Romeo as a way to peace; the Capulets abruptly reject the suggestion. Continuing in G major, now in 9/8 time, *larghetto cantabile*, the envoy sings (p. 32) the moving cavatina, "*Se Romeo t'uccise un figlio*," promising that as Giulietta's husband, Romeo—who constantly laments having killed Capellio's son in battle—would take that son's place. (The first melody of this cavatina was borrowed from Nerestano's "*O Zaira, in qual momento*," in Act II of *Zaira*.)[11] In 4/4 time, *allegro moderato*, (p. 33), Capellio tells the envoy to inform Romeo that another man will become his son. When the envoy asks who it will be, Tebaldo replies, "I." The Capulets shout for war (p. 34). *Allegro marziale sostenuto,* the orchestra introduces the melody of the envoy's challenging cabaletta (andante, p. 34), "*La tremenda ultrice spada.*" (Here the melody is an adaptation of Zaira's cabaletta, "*Ah crudeli, chiamarmi,*" in Act II of *Zaira.*) He warns the Capulets that Romeo will know how to extract revenge, that Heaven will accuse them of letting needless blood. Saying that only God can judge between them, the Capulets silence him.

Scene 4 (p. 41). Room in Giulietta's apartment. E-flat major, 4/4 time, *andante maestoso,* the orchestra brings forward a sad melodic fragment that Giulietta will pronounce in the unaccompanied recitative that begins (p. 41) "*Eccomi in lieta vesta,*" bitterly contrasting her happy ceremonial raiment and the multiple sorrows of her situation. Longing for Romeo, she sings, G minor, 4/4 time, *andante sostenuto* (p. 43) the beautifully effective romanza, "*Oh quante volte, oh! quante*"—a reshaping and major improvement of Nelly's "*Dopo l'oscuro nembo,*" in Act I of *Adelson e Salvini* (a comparison of the two numbers provides instruction in what Bellini had learned between 1825 and 1830). Giulietta's allure and vulnerability could scarcely have been created more appealingly or vividly.

Scene 5 (p. 45). Lorenzo and Giulietta, then Romeo. B-flat major, 4/4 time, in recitative, Lorenzo reveals to the distracted Giulietta that Romeo is in Verona—and then opens a secret entrance to let him in. After the lovers' first impassioned greeting, Lorenzo leaves.

*Scene 6** (p. 46). Giulietta and Romeo. Allegro, in recitative, Romeo urges that they conquer their future by fleeing together. "Flee—what are you saying?" is Giulietta's response. (Here a figure for the violins is borrowed from the accompaniment to Zaira's cavatina, "*Non è tormento,*" in Act I of *Zaira.*) *Allegro moderato* (p. 47), Romeo begins the nodal dramatic duet, "*Sì, fuggire*"; to his passionate urging that they run away, Giulietta opposes her duty to remain with her father, thus making the tragedy inevitable. (At Romeo's words, "*Miglior patria avrem di questa,*" in the cabaletta-like section, p. 48, Bellini quotes from the Zaira-Nerestano duet, "*Oh qual vibrasti,*" in Act I of *Zaira.*) Della Corte interestingly noted[12] the constant recurrence in these pages, especially in bridge passages, of the rhythm ♪♫♪♩ . (In the andante on p. 60, when, in A-flat major, Romeo sings, "*Ah! crudel, d'onor ragioni*" the melody is an adaptation from Nerestano's "*Segui, deh segui a piangere,*" in the second part of the Zaira–Nerestano duet in the first finale of *Zaira.*)

* Misnumbered "*Scena VII*" in the Ricordi piano-vocal score with plate number 42043.

Agonizingly torn between duty and impassioned love, Giulietta withstands
all of Romeo's pleading, even when he threatens to remain in her apartment and accept the consequences. Finally (p. 61), "defeated by Giulietta's
prayers, Romeo goes out through the secret entrance. Trembling, she
leaves." Their duet belongs among Bellini's most successful dramatic
achievements.

Scene 7 (p. 62). "An internal courtyard of Capellio's palace. Night.
At the back, a staircase to galleries affording entrance into palace rooms
illuminated for a magnificent ceremony. Knights and ladies come from
all sides to take part in the festivity." In "*Lieta notte*," G major, 3/4
time, *allegro moderato*, p. 62, the chorus (t, bs) salutes the occasion,
saying that it has ended the evil events of recent days. All ascend the
stairs and disperse.

Scene 8 (p. 67). "Romeo garbed as a Guelph; Lorenzo." Allegro,
Lorenzo begs Romeo to leave without trying to alter the already hopeless situation. When Romeo asserts that he has a thousand Ghibelline
soldiers with him, Lorenzo is horrified, torn between affection for
Giulietta and loyalty to Capellio. P. 69, *allegro vivace assai*: "A great
tumult is heard inside; the trumpets sound, shouts echo, and the guests
are seen dashing back and forth in confusion on the galleries." Romeo's
followers have launched an assault on the palace; the Capulets are being
summoned to its defense. Lorenzo persuades the exalted Romeo to avoid
the assembling people, and then follows him out. The orchestral postlude
dies to a whisper. The stage is left empty.

Scene 9 (p. 73). The place is deserted as the tumult ebbs, *più moderato assai*. Alone, Giulietta descends from a gallery. In fragmented, shifting G minor soliloquy ("*Tace il fragor*"), she bewails the bloodshed and
invokes "Heaven, Destiny, Love" for Romeo. The scene (lento, *lento col
canto, lento con espressione*,) does not really end, but leads on without
break.

Scene 10 (p. 74). *Primo tempo* [*più moderato assai*]. Romeo returns.
"*Con tutta la passione*," he all but orders Giulietta to follow him as he
creates a path to safety with his sword. Here the rhythmic variety, the
offbeat accents, and the rocking accompaniment of six beats in the 4/4
time* well intensify the distraction and terrible urgency. The chorus is
heard: "*Morte ai Montecchi!*" (p. 75). The scene flows into the next one
without interruption.

Scene 11 (p. 76). "Tebaldo and Capellio with armed men on one side,
Lorenzo on the other." This first finale is an ordered confusion that could
have served as a pattern for similar scenes in middle-period Verdi. Romeo's

---

* Not shown in the Ricordi score 42043, but see the Pacini piano-vocal score with
plate numbers 1510–1520, p. 85.

identity is revealed. Everyone either displays sanguinary fury or prays for peace. Romeo and Tebaldo confront one another; Romeo's followers irrupt into the palace, complicating the chaos. The fine quintet (p. 79) beginning *"Soccorso, sostegno accordale, oh cielo"*—for Giulietta, Romeo, Tebaldo, Capellio, and Lorenzo (A-flat major, 3/8 time, larghetto)—is succeeded by choral and recitative interjections and by (E-flat major, allegro, p. 84) a concluding *stretta* of the quintet, in which the chorus joins, ending the act. (In the *più vivo* section, to Romeo and Giulietta's words *"Se ogni speme,"* pp. 85–86, Bellini adapted the melody of the cabaletta *"Non si pianga"* in the Zaira–Nerestano–Lusignano trio in Act I of *Zaira*, shaping it into a continuous unison melody thirty-one measures in length.) This finale resolves nothing; a resolution would have ended the opera, and the intricacies of the sleeping-potion plot have not yet even been hinted.

Act II: Scene 1 (p. 97). "Apartment in Capellio's palace. It is still night; the place is lighted by ancient torches. (The music evokes a distant, gradually subsiding hubbub. Giulietta alone.)" After an introduction that is melancholy despite being D major, 4/4 time, *allegro moderato*, Giulietta expresses in recitative monologue her anguished uncertainty as to what has happened, who has been killed, for whom she must weep first. The next scene succeeds this one without interruption.

Scene 2 (p. 98). Lorenzo and Giulietta. In recitative, Lorenzo, after telling Giulietta that Romeo has survived, offers her a sleeping potion, assuring her that when she awakes, Romeo and he will be with her. She seems to hesitate, and then (A major, 4/4 time, lento, p. 100) begins a cavatina, the first part of her so-called "aria,"[13] *"Morte io non temo, il sai"* (its melody borrowed from Zaira's aria *"Che non tentai,"* in Act I of *Zaira*). She expresses horror at the possibility that she may never reawake. Lorenzo reassures her (p. 100), and she agrees to go with him (p. 101). No break follows.

Scene 3 (p. 102). Capellio, his followers, Giulietta, Lorenzo. Capellio orders Giulietta to her quarters to rest and to await the arrival of her husband (Tebaldo) at dawn. His followers attempt to intercede for her, but Capellio is unrelenting. *Più moderato*, Giulietta beseeches her father to forgive her, to embrace her, saying that she is near death (*"Ah! non poss'io partire,"* p. 105, its chief melody borrowed from the second part of Nerestano's aria, *"Sì, mi vedrà la barbara,"* in Act II of *Zaira*). Unable to soften her father's attitude, she leaves, supported by Lorenzo.

Scene 4 (p. 108). Capellio and his followers. In recitative, Capellio orders some of his men to find Tebaldo, others to spy upon the now-suspect Lorenzo. (Lorenzo's incarceration will, of course, prevent him from telling Romeo that Giulietta is not dead but merely sleeping.)

Scene 5 (p. 108). "A deserted place near Capellio's palace, with, at the back, a great arch through which can be seen a gallery leading to the palace itself. Romeo alone." Maestoso, E-flat major, 4/4 time, the orchestra introduces Romeo's bitter recitative beginning (lento), *"Deserto è il loco,"* in which he accuses Lorenzo of having forgotten him in his misfortune. He is about to go in search of Lorenzo when he hears someone approaching. The scene leads on without interruption into the next.

Scene 6 (p. 110). An enraged Romeo and Tebaldo insult and threaten one another. B-flat major, allegro, they sing the duet introduced by Tebaldo's *"Stolto!"* (p. 111) and including the *a due* begun by his *"Un nume avverso"* (p. 114). They are about to duel when they hear funeral music. Overwhelmed by foreboding, they abandon wrath and action. The scene ends without a break.

Scene 7 (p. 116). "A funeral cortege appears, filing along the gallery." The two-part chorus (s, t) sings a dirge, *"Pace alla tua bell'anima,"* which Bellini brought over from the funeral chorus, *"Poni il fedel tuo martire,"* in Act II of *Zaira.* Discovering that the funeral is Giulietta's, Romeo and Tebaldo both cry out—and stand in immobile silence for some moments. Then, in *"Ella è morta"* (p. 117, *allegro moderato assai*), Romeo attacks Tebaldo. Both men now want to die; they duel in blind grief and fury.

Scene 8 (p. 124). *"Coro, Aria e Duetto Finale."** "The tombs of the Capulets; at the front, the tomb of Giulietta. (The place is enclosed. After repeated knockings, a door opens and Romeo enters with his Montague followers.)" F major, *andante mosso*, the Montagues mourn; Romeo throws himself upon the stone at Giulietta's tomb. He asks that her casket be opened so that he may see her once more. "The silent Montagues pry open the cover of the casket and raise it; Giulietta is revealed laid out upon the sepulcher garbed in white. Romeo utters a shout and rushes to her." In extreme anguish (p. 127), he apostrophizes her, begging her to return from death. When his followers try to lead him out, he persuades them to leave him alone in the tomb.

Scene 9 (p. 129). After a brief recitative during which Romeo recognizes that Giulietta must remain deaf to his pleas, he nonetheless addresses her (C major, *andante sostenuto*, p. 130), saying that he will join her in death (*"Deh! tu bell'anima,"* its fine chief melody borrowed from Zaira's cavatina *"Non è tormento,"* in Act I of *Zaira*). Again in recitative (p. 131), he adds that now his sole hope is the poison that he

---

* Here the Ricordi piano-vocal score (plate number 32043) has a footnote: "If it is desired to replace this final number with that from the opera *Giulietta e Romeo* of M. Vaccaj, turn to page 137"—where Vaccaj's *"Coro, Aria e Duetto Finale,"* beginning *"Addio, addio per sempre, o vergine,"* is given with the note that "it is general practice to substitute it for the final number of Bellini's opera."

always carries. He swallows it, asking the tombs of his enemies to accept his final breath. There is no pause before the next scene.

Scene 10 (p. 132). Awakening, Giulietta makes a sound. The despair-crazed Romeo watches her emerge alive from the casket and piercingly realizes his own final folly. In recitative and arioso, fragmentarily, the lovers understand that Romeo has not received word from Lorenzo of Giulietta's feigned death and that he is dying of poison. Altogether free of tragic pseudograndeur, this whole scene is beautifully realized. It ends with Romeo's death, upon which Giulietta falls inert across his body. Again there is no interruption.

Final scene (p. 135). "Romeo's followers rush back precipitately, followed by Capellio and his men-at-arms, who come from several sides. The whole place is illuminated by torches. Lorenzo rushes in in dismay." *Allegro assai.* All are stricken by the sight of the lovers' bodies. "Both dead," Lorenzo says and, turning to Capellio, "Look!" When Capellio asks, "Killed—by whom?" (p. 136), Lorenzo's reply is: "By you, ruthless man." Capellio sinks down upon Giulietta's body, Lorenzo upon that of Romeo.

The entire scene in the Capulet tomb is miraculously held together by Bellini's mastery of varying, always just ways of responding immediately to his protagonists' situations and the words that convey them. With this emotion-packed, theatrically compelling scene, Bellini entered his brief period of mastery (which was to produce only one failure): he was entirely ready, with the genius that had always been latent in him and the experience that he had acquired, to compose *La Sonnambula*, *Norma*, and *I Puritani*.

Ernani

UNFINISHED OPERA. *Libretto* (incomplete?) by Felice Romani, derived from Victor Hugo's *Hernani* (Théâtre-Français, Paris, February 25, 1830). *Partially sketched:* 1830.

SINFONIA. In 1969, the Pierpont Morgan Library, New York, acquired an eighteen-page Bellini autograph of full orchestral score, bound, with this label on its front cover: *"Vincenzo Bellini/Sinfonia dell'opera Ernani/ Partitura/Autografi."* Its preceding owner had reported acquiring the autograph from the heirs of Giuditta Pasta, who in turn had reported Bellini's having presented it to Pasta and had said that it formerly had been enclosed in a wrapper on which was written, *"Sinfonia dell'opera Ernani donata a Giuditta Pasta da Vincenzo Bellini,"* but in handwriting that was neither Bellini's nor Pasta's.

The music is scored for flutes/piccolo, oboes, clarinets, horns, trumpets, trombones, strings, and timpani. It was written on an oblong twelve-staff paper measuring approximately 10″ × 9″ and watermarked CANSELL 1831.

The first notes are preceded by the customary instrumental indications and by a key signature of one flat (F major), but not by a time signature (the time is 4/4). This lack and the nature of the first four measures at least suggest the possibility that these eighteen pages represent only part of a longer manuscript, that its p. 1 is a sectional continuation rather than a beginning. And that possibility raises the question of whether this music could have been intended by Bellini as part of a purely orchestral composition about which no information survives.

The music opens (p. 1) with four melodic measures in F major, 4/4 time, which end on a fermata (⌒). The melody, assigned to the violins, is this:

B—First page of the eighteen-page autograph of the *"Sinfonia dell'-opera Ernani"* in The Mary Flagler Cary Music Collection of The Pierpont Morgan Library, New York.

That lento is followed, after a double bar-line, by the indication, allegro (p. 1); timpani in F then prelude alone for two measures. Thereafter, *sotto voce* and pianissimo (p. 1), comes what amounts to a thirty-two measure crescendo, the theme of which (see below) almost duplicates the accompaniment of Filippo's *"Ma . . . qual fragore! . . . Si taccia . . ."* near the beginning of Act II of *Bianca e Fernando**:

* Ricordi piano-vocal score, plate number 9835, page 144; plate number 108911, page 176.

After a two-measure clarinet link absent in *Bianca*, this conclusion ends on another fermata.

After the pause, at the indication "*attacca*," the tempo becomes *allegro vivace*. This twelve-page section (pp. 7–18) again thematically resembles the corresponding passage in *Bianca e Fernando* very closely, duplicating the melody and the accompaniment, in thirds, of Filippo's words "[*t'af*] *fretta, per te, già in me sento la pena calmar*" in the *allegro vivace* cabaletta, "*Bramato momento*,"* which follows his aria, "*Allor, che notte avanza*." The principal theme of this final *allegro vivace* section is:

Like the related passage in *Bianca*, this music ends (in F major) on what Richard Macnutt well called "an obviously conclusive orchestral tutti."

Did or did not Bellini compose this music (neither the word *sinfonia* nor the word *preludio* appears on it) as an overture for *Ernani*? We are unlikely ever to know. At least three other possibilities (they are no more than that) spring to mind: (1) it could have been a very early version of an orchestral introduction to the section of *Bianca e Gernando* containing Filippo's "*Allor, che notte avanza*" and the succeeding cabaletta, "*Bramato momento*"[1]; (2) it could have been a version of that introduction composed (or revised) for the 1828 Genoa revision of *Bianca* and then discarded; (3) it could have resulted from an intention on Bellini's part to compose an overture for *La Sonnambula*, which has none (in view of the nature of the music itself, this is the least likely of the possibilities suggested here). Before attaching more than passing interest to any surmise, we would have to know the exact significance of the 1831 watermark. If the paper was not made until 1831, the music can scarcely have been intended for either version of *Bianca* (1826, 1828) or for *Ernani*, which Bellini stopped composing before the beginning of that year. Conversely, proof that this music was not composed earlier than 1831 would slightly increase the possibility that it was intended for *La Sonnambula* (stylistic considerations completely rule out any consideration of its having been meant for *Norma*). We shall probably do best to accept, lacking any future proof to the contrary, the belief by the Pasta heirs that it was indeed intended as (part of?) a *sinfonia* for *Ernani*.

THE SKETCHES. As they now exist, the sketches clearly begin *in medias res*.[2]

The first group of pages contains a large part of a scene for Elvira

* Ricordi, plate number 9835, page 147; plate number 108911, page 181.

(soprano), Ernani (soprano), and the king, Don Carlo (tenor), as well as, on p. 1, Ines (whose only words are *"Qui . . . qui . . . son essi"*). Martial horns, trumpets, and timpani prelude the entrance of Elvira and Ernani, who converse in recitative dialogue before the indication *"attacca subito"* and two measures, ending on a fermata, of chords for horns and bassoons and two more measures of more general preluding which lead to a duet properly speaking, *"Muto e deserto speco."*[3] This duet begins:

This melody would reappear in *Norma:* in the *andante marcato* of the first finale (Ricordi 41684, p. 136), Norma's *"Oh! di qual sei tu vittima,"* still in the 9/8 time of this sketch. Also, the text-lines, but not the music, of the *a due* repetition—*"Sì, fino all'ore estreme . . ."*—would reappear, slightly modified, in Act II of *Norma* (Ricordi 41684, p. 182), in the cabaletta of the Norma–Adalgisa duet,*"Mira, o Norma."*

After this melody, Elvira and Ernani return to recitative, with interjections by Don Carlo as they plan to meet at midnight.[4] Don Carlo reveals his presence; the terrified Elvira throws herself into Ernani's arms; and Ernani demands that the intruder reveal his identity and purpose. The king replies, *allegro maestoso*—*"Io contemplar bramai/quel cavalier beato. . . ."*[5]—that he only wanted to see the knight for whom Elvira's heart sighed. Ernani threatens him; Elvira tries to intervene; and the fragment breaks off with Ernani's words *"Snuda l'acciar"* (Unsheathe your sword) and the beginning of a phrase from the king (*"t'ap—"*).

The second group of sketches is preceded by a one-page fragment for the strings in B-flat major, 4/4 time, without words, but with the indication that the singers are to be Don Carlo and Don Sancio; and by another discrete page, with the indication *"Cori,"* which contains a melody (six and a quarter measures in 4/4 time) that Bellini made use of in the chorus *"In Elvezia non v'ha rosa,"* in the *"Stretta dell'Introduzione"* in *La Sonnambula* (Ricordi piano-vocal score 41686, p. 14). That is followed by two discrete pages, in C major/A minor, 3/4 time, of recitative for Don Sancio and Don Carlo,[6] which break off incomplete.[7]

Next comes an Elvira–Don Carlo duet, *"Meco regna, io t'offro un trono."* When Antonino Amore first saw these sketches and had them examined as part of his determination to prove that *Ernani* had not been "disguised as *Sonnambula*," this duet was preceded by recitative[8] in which, after Elvira has given herself away by assuming that the man at her door is Ernani, the king asks her for "pity and love." Pastura asserted,[9] on what basis I cannot determine, that the duet itself begins with "an *Andante assai sostenuto*. Preceded by three measures of string tremolo (a group of sixteenth-notes arpeggiating a diminished-seventh chord), behold a C-major chord preceding the tenor's entrance by three measures." But the beginning of the duet in the sketch as I have seen it contains no tempo indication, though the measures of string tremolo and the C-major chord are there. As Pastura noted[10]: "The motif that sets these verses ["*Meco regna . . .*" and the rest of the duet] is the one that Bellini adapted to Oroveso's aria, *Ah, del Tebro al giorno* [*sic*, for *giogo*] *indegno*, in the second act of *Norma*. But two different versions of this motive appear in *Ernani*. The first shows it *alla breve;* but that was discarded when it became clear that the phrase was of eight measures rather than four. In the final version, in common time, the phrase appears contained within the regular four measures. There the melody—with respect to the definitive version of it which appears in *Norma*—is presented very differently in development, and above all is decked out with *fioriture* and cadenzas both when the tenor sings it and when the soprano takes it up a fifth higher:

DON CARLO

Me - co re - gna io t'of - fro un tro - no, o so-vra - na, o so - vra - na del mio cor . . . t'of - fri - re - i t'of - fri - rei la terra in do - no t'of - fri - rei la terra in do - no se ne fos - si se ne fos - si pos - ses - sor.

An *allegro agitato* section of recitative for Elvira and Don Carlo follows, leading into the central section of their scene, a lento beginning when Elvira sings, *"Ah, crudel, tu Re possente"*:

This melody is substantially the same as that of Bellini's romanza *"L'Abbandono,"* sometimes referred to as both *"Solitario zeffiretto"* and *"L'Ultima veglia,"*[11] which may have been composed either before or after the incomplete *Ernani*. On the penultimate page of this section, after a cadenza on the syllable *"-na"* (of the word *"piena"*), a melodic fragment strongly recalls the notes sung by Elvino soon after the introductory chorus of Act II of *La Sonnambula*, to the words *"il più triste de' mortali sono, o*

cruda" (Ricordi piano-vocal score 41686, p. 144). After that section, of which the autograph shows only the vocal lines, the sketches fray out and stop. Their last three pages, however, include a melodic line assigned to the doublebasses:

That melody also appears, in B major, in the sketches for *La Sonnambula* in the Museo Belliniano; and Bellini finally gave it permanence when composing, in D major, the opening of the orchestral introduction to *I Puritani*.

Norma

OPERA SERIA (*tragedia lirica*) in two acts. *Libretto:* By Felice Romani, based upon *Norma*, a five-act tragedy in verse by Alexandre Soumet (with some assistance from Jules Lefèvre) first presented at the Théâtre Royal de l'Odéon, Paris, April 16, 1831.[1] *Composed:* 1831. *Première:* Teatro alla Scala, Milan, December 26, 1831,[2] on a triple bill with the ballet *Merope*, choreographed by Antonio Cortesi to music by Luigi Viviani and Giacomo Panizza, and the demi-character ballet *I Pazzi per progetto*, also by Cortesi, composer unknown. *Original cast:*

NORMA, *Druidess, daughter of Oroveso*	Giuditta Pasta
ADALGISA, *young attendant in the*	
Temple of Irminsul	Giulia Grisi
CLOTILDE, *confidante of Norma*	Marietta Sacchi
POLLIONE, *Proconsul of Rome in Gaul*	Domenico Donzelli
FLAVIO, *a centurion, friend of Pollione*	Lorenzo Lombardi
OROVESO, *head of the Druids*	Vincenzo Negrini*

The stage settings were by Alessandro Sanquirico. *Published:* In full score by Ricordi, Milan, 189? (plate number 101966) and 1915 (pl. no. 115216); facsimile of the autograph score issued by the Reale Accademia d'Italia, Rome, in 1935. Piano-vocal scores published by Ricordi in 1832 (plate numbers 5900, 5775, 5911); possibly again in 1859 in large format (pl. nos. 30891–30995); and again in 1869–1870 (pl. no. 41684); by Girard (later Cottrau), Naples, with discrete pl. nos.; and by Pacini, Paris (pl. nos. 1600, 1617, *"ouvrage revu & corrigé par l'Auteur"*).[3] Autograph score in the library of the Accademia di Santa Cecilia, Rome, in which the

---

* Not, as often stated, Carlo Negrini, who was a tenor and was born only in 1826.

NORMA

TRAGEDIA LIRICA

DI FELICE ROMANI

DA RAPPRESENTARSI

NELL'I. R. TEATRO ALLA SCALA

IL CARNEVALE DELL'ANNO 1831-32.

MILANO

PER G* TRUFFI E COMP.

cont. del Cappuccio n. 5433

PERSONAGGI	ARTISTI
POLLIONE, Proconsole di Roma nelle Gallie	signor DONZELLI
OROVESO, Capo dei Druidi	signor NEGRINI
NORMA, Druidessa, figlia di Oroveso	signora PASTA
ADALGISA, giovine ministra del tempio d'Irminsul	signora GRISI GIULIETTA
CLOTILDE, confidente di Norma	signora SACCHI
FLAVIO, amico di Pollione	signor LOMBARDI
DUE FANCIULLI, figli di Norma e di Pollione	N. N.

CORI E COMPARSE

Druidi - Bardi - Eubagi - Sacerdotesse
Guerrieri e Soldati Galli

La scena è nelle Gallie, nella foresta sacra
e nel Tempio d'Irminsul

La Musica è del signor Maestro VINCENZO BELLINI

Le scene sono nuove d'invenzione ed esecuzione
del signor ALESSANDRO SANQUIRICO, Membro dell'I. R.
Accademia di Belle Arti in Milano, e di altre d'Italia.

C—Title page and cast list from the first printed *Norma* libretto.

"*Guerra, guerra*" chorus in Act II is not autograph; an autograph of four of the missing pages is in the Toscanini Collection, Milan (microfilm copy in the Library of the Performing Arts, Lincoln Center, New York).[4] Autograph copy of "*Casta diva*," with piano accompaniment, in the Bibliothèque Nationale, Paris. Manuscript copies of the score are in the Santa Cecilia library, Rome (1), the Naples Conservatory library (4), and the library of the Conservatorio Giuseppe Verdi, Milan (2).[5] Dedicated to "signor Nicolò Zingarelli . . . by his pupil V. Bellini."

PERFORMANCE DATA. From its second singing on, *Norma* was recognized as a successful and important opera. It was heard at La Scala thirty-four times during its first season.[6] By the end of the nineteenth century, the tally of *Norma* performances at La Scala had climbed to two hundred and eight. Malibran sang its title role for the first of seven times at La Scala on May 15, 1834. Pasta returned there for eleven performances as Norma in 1835, beginning on January 24. Barbara and Carlotta Marchisio were heard—respectively as Adalgisa and Norma—twice at La Scala, for the first time on January 29, 1839. Maria Meneghini Callas sang the first of her eighteen Scala Normas on January 16, 1952; the last of them was the opera's two hundred and forty-eighth singing in the house in which it had been heard for the first time almost exactly one hundred and twenty-four years before.

Norma was staged at the Teatro San Carlo, Naples, on January 20, 1832, when Giuseppina Ronzi de Begnis was the Norma, Domenico Reina the Pollione, Michele Benedetti the Oroveso. Malibran sang Norma at the San Carlo several times; on February 23, 1834, and again on December 4 of that year, her colleagues were Alexandrine Duperron-Duprez (Adalgisa), Teresa Zappucci (Clotilde), Gilbert-Louis Duprez (Pollione), Signor Rossi (Flavio), and Carlo Porto (Oroveso). *Norma* was staged under Bellini's direction at Bergamo during August 1832, with Pasta, Elisa Taccani (Adalgisa), and Reina (Pollione). It was presented at the Teatro La Fenice, Venice, on December 26, 1832, with Pasta, Anna Del Serre (Adalgisa), Alberico Curioni (Pollione), and Federico Crespi (Oroveso). Of that performance, the *Gazzetta privilegiata di Venezia* for December 27 said: "A learned and profound opera; the audience demonstrated great delight only at the chorus in the introduction, which was followed by a storm of applause . . ." During the 1834 *fiera*, *Norma* was sung at the Teatro Comunale, Sinigaglia, with Malibran (Norma), Giuseppina Ruiz-Garcia (Adalgisa), and Lorenzo Bonfigli (Pollione); during the next *fiera* there, the Norma was Eugenia Tadolini and Domenico Donzelli was the Pollione. On April 4, 1835, Malibran sang Norma in Venice (La Fenice), with Lina Balfe (Adalgisa), Donzelli (Pollione), and Giuseppe Paltrinieri (Oroveso). When the opera was played at the Fenice again on December 2, 1838, the title role was sung by Adelaide Kemble.[7]

Norma was staged at the Teatro Comunale, Bologna, for the first time on November 9, 1833, with Giuditta Grisi (Norma), Marianna Brighenti (Adalgisa), Curioni (Pollione), and Francesco Canetti (Oroveso). It was repeated at the Comunale on April 23, 1834, with Malibran (Norma), Giuseppina Ruiz-Garcia (Adalgisa), Lorenzo Bonfigli (Pollione), and Luciano Mariani (Oroveso); on September 30, 1834, with Pasta (Norma), Rosa Bottrigari Bonetti (Adalgisa), Donzelli (Pollione), and Celestino Salvatori (Oroveso); on July 26, 1836, with Giuditta Grisi (Norma), Ernestina Grisi (Adalgisa), Bonfigli (Pollione), and Carlo Ottolini Porto (Oroveso). After several intermediary productions, *Norma* returned to the Comunale on November 14, 1935, when Gina Cigna was the Norma, Ebe Stignani the Adalgisa, Francesco Merli the Pollione, and Tancredi Pasero the Oroveso; Gino Marinuzzi conducted. Trieste had heard *Norma* for the first time on November 5, 1834, when the cast at the Teatro Grande included Luigia Boccabadati (Norma), Fontana Talestri (Adalgisa), Lorenzo Bonfigli (Pollione), and Paolo Barroilhet (Oroveso); it was repeated there many times, nobably in 1859, when Carlotta Marchisio was the Norma, Barbara Marchisio the Adalgisa, Emanuele Carrion the Pollione, and Alessandro Lanzoni the Oroveso.

Norma was staged at the Teatro Regio, Turin, during the 1834 Carnival season. It reached the Teatro Apollo, Rome (first time there) as *La Foresta d'Irminsul*[8] on January 18, 1834, when Giuseppina Ronzi de Begnis was the "Delia" (Norma), Alexandrine Duperron-Duprez the Adalgisa, Giovanni Battista Millesi the "Galieno" (Pollione), and Porto the Oroveso. *La Foresta d'Irminsul* quickly became a favorite in the papal capital. It was repeated at the Apollo in 1835, when Caroline Unger at her benefit interpolated into the role of Delia an aria from Giovanni Pacini's 1826 opera *Niobe;* in 1837, with Amalia Schütz-Oldosi as Delia; again in 1843 and 1856; in February 1859, and again in May of that year, when Carlotta and Barbara Marchisio were, respectively, the Delia and the Adalgisa. The Apollo finally billed the opera as *Norma* in July 1871 and repeated it in 1879. Meanwhile, it also had been heard in Rome at the Teatro Valle in September and October 1834 and in the summer of 1835.

Norma has had several notable performances at Florence in the twentieth century: at the Teatro Comunale on May 26, 1929, when Gino Marinuzzi conducted a cast that included Claudia Muzio (Norma) and Stignani (Adalgisa); at the Comunale on April 19, 1932, with Vittorio Gui conducting and a cast headed by Bianca Scacciati, with Stignani again the Adalgisa; at the same theater on May 30, 1935, with Iva Pacetti (Norma), Gianna Pederzini (Adalgisa), Francesco Merli (Pollione), and Tancredi Pasero (Oroveso); again at the Comunale on November 30, 1948, with Tullio Serafin conducting and a cast including Callas (Norma), Fedora Barbieri (Adalgisa), Mirto Picchi (Pollione), and Cesare Siepi (Oroveso); and in the Giardino di Boboli on June 26, 1955, with Gabriele Santini conducting and a cast with Anita Cerquetti (Norma), Barbieri (Adalgisa), Franco Corelli (Pollione), and Giulio Neri (Oroveso). Catania, meanwhile, had signalized the exact centenary of the première of *Norma:* at the Teatro Massimo Bellini on December 26, 1931, Antonio Guarnieri conducted; and the cast included Fidelia Campigna (Norma), Irene Minghini Cattaneo (Adalgisa), Iesus De Gaviria (Pollione), and Antonio Righetti (Oroveso).

How swiftly and far *Norma* spread (leaving in its wake whole armies of baby girls named after its heroine) can be judged from a list of some performances heard outside Italy through 1850—

1833: Vienna, Kärntnertortheater, May 11 (in German translation by Joseph von Seyfried)[9]; London, His Majesty's Theatre, June 20 (with Pasta, Joséphine de Méric, Domenico Donzelli, and Vincenzo Galli).[10]

On July 12, "For the first and only time on this stage [Covent Garden], the Italian opera compressed into one act called *Norma*" was sung by Pasta (her only Norma at Covent Garden), Signora Castelli (Adalgisa), Domenico Donzelli (Pollione), and Galli (Ovoveso).

1834: Madrid, Teatro del Príncipe, January 16; Berlin, Königsstädtischestheater, March 26 (in German); Marseilles, summer; Teatro San Giacomo, Corfu, autumn; Brünn, October 24 (German); Budapest, November 3 (German).

1835: Prague, February 20 (German); Pressburg; spring (probably German); Vienna, Kärntnertortheater, April 29; Barcelona, June 4; Lisbon, summer; Agram, November (German); St. Petersburg November (German); Paris, Théâtre-Italien, December 8[11] (with Giulia Grisi as Norma, Laura Assandri as Adalgisa, Giovanni Battista Rubini as Pollione, Luigi Labache as Oroveso).[12]

1836: Lisbon, Teatro São Carlos, date unknown; Mexico City, February 12; New Orleans, St. Charles Theatre, April 1, with Signora Pedrotti (Norma), Signora Marozzi (Adalgisa), Signora Thilman (Clotilde), Signor Sapignoli (Flavio), Signor Montresor (Pollione), and Signor de Rosa, or Derosa (Oroveso)[13]; Clausenburg, May 23 (Hungarian translation by József Szerdahelyi); Havana, Teatro Tacón, August 12.

1837: Basel, March 6 (German); London, Drury Lane Theatre, June 24 (English translation by James Robinson Planché, librettist of Weber's *Oberon*); Vilna, summer; Mitau (Yelgava), summer; Algiers, autumn; St. Petersburg, October 15 (Russian); Budapest, October 28 (Hungarian); Lyon, November 14: Riga, December 23 (German).[14]

1838: Vera Cruz, Mexico, Teatro Italiano, Carnival; Berlin, Königliches Opernhaus, January 12; Liège, May 10 (German).

1839: Odessa, spring; Prague, April 7 (Czech translation by Vaclav Alois Swoboda); Amsterdam, May (German)[15]; Helsingfors, June 9; The Hague, October (French translation by Étienne Monnier).

1840: Palma de Mallorca, Carnival; Santiago, Cuba, spring; Copenhagen, March 20 (Danish translation by Adam Gottlob Oehlenschlager); Brussels, April; Moscow, April; Athens, spring; Valletta, Malta, spring.

1841: Nancy, January (French translation by Numa Lafont); Philadelphia, January 11, two theaters on the same day (English translation by William Henry Fry), New York, February 25 (the Fry translation); Stockholm, May 19 (Swedish translation by Niels Erik Willem af Wetterstedt); London, Covent Garden, with Adelaide Kemble as Norma, November 2 (English); Constantinople, the first Italian opera sung there, November; Lyon, December 18 (French, the Monnier translation).

1842: Bucharest, date unknown (German); Jassy, January 31 (German)[16]; Brussels, March 18 (French); London, Covent Garden (German); Smyrna, summer.

1843: Guayaquil, spring; Warsaw, summer; Gibraltar, spring-summer; Bucharest (the first opera sung there in Italian), September 15; Amsterdam, autumn; New York, September 20; Stockholm, October 10; Philadelphia, November 13.

1844: St. Petersburg, date unknown; Rio de Janeiro, January 17.

1845: Santiago, Chile, Carnival; Warsaw, May 8 (Polish translation by Jan Jásinski); Geneva, autumn.

1847: Budapest, October.

1849: Buenos Aires, June 26.

1850: Nizhni Novgorod, May 8 (Russian).

Additional translated performances of *Norma* have included: Portuguese (Rio de Janeiro, August 12, 1858); Finnish (Helsingfors, by Anders Törneroos, 1874); Norwegian (Christiania, 1875); Croat (Agram, by Dimitrije Demeter, 1876); Slovenian (Laibach, 1896); and probably Bulgarian (a translation by S. Christov was published at Sofia in 1901).

At His Majesty's Theatre, London, in 1833, *Norma* was presented as one integer of a benefit for the impresario Pierre-François Laporte. The rest of the monstrous program—at least, if a surviving poster[17] is to be credited—consisted of a performance by Paganini of "some of his celebrated variations"; Act III of Rossini's *Otello;* the ballet *La Sylphide,* with Marie Taglioni; and several *pas de deux* danced by Fanny Elssler and two different partners. Adelaide Kemble, daughter of Charles Kemble and sister of Fanny Kemble, made a sensational operatic debut in an English *Norma* at Covent Garden, London, on November 2, 1841, when Elizabeth Rainforth was the Adalgisa, William Harrison the Pollione, and Adam Leffler the Oroveso. Sir Julius Benedict conducted; the opera was repeated forty-one times before Easter.

Marie Stöckl-Heinefetter had the title role in *Norma* at Covent Garden on June 10, 1842; and Adelaide Kemble chose it for her premature retirement from opera on December 23 of that year. Giuseppina Ronzi de Begnis, by then forty-two, made her Covent Garden debut as Norma (in English) on April 26, 1843; the Oroveso was Joseph Staudigl, singing opera in English for the first time. Clara Novello's only Covent Garden Norma was sung on July 17, 1843. In 1847, Giulia Grisi, by then London's favorite *prima donna*, began her unprecedented reign as Covent Garden's Norma; from that year until 1861 (1856 and 1857 excepted because the theater presented no opera then), she sang the role there every year. During those fifteen seasons, she had as colleagues such outstanding singers as Enrico Tamberlik and Luigi Lablache, but her conductor was invariably Bellini's one-time schoolmate, Sir Michael Costa. In 1862, Covent Garden went *Norma*less, and when the opera returned there in 1863, the title role was sung by Antonietta Fricci.

Lacking Grisi, *Norma* continued to be heard at Covent Garden, often without stellar singers. During the 1868 autumn season, however, Therese Tietjens sang its title role there once, with Luigi Arditi as conductor; she also sang single performances of it in two different 1870 seasons. After Euphrosyne Parepa-Rosa (1872) and Maria Vilda[18] (1874, 1875), no Norma lifted her voice at Covent Garden for fifty-four years. Then, on May 28, 1929, Rosa Ponselle made her sensational London debut in the role; Vincenzo Bellezza conducted, and with Ponselle were Irene Minghini Cattaneo (Adalgisa), Nicolo Fusati (Pollione), and Luigi Manfrini (Oroveso). After Ponselle's three Covent Garden Normas that season and three the next, the opera lapsed there again, that time for only twenty-two years.

When Covent Garden next heard *Norma*—on November 8, 1952— the evening proved even more sensational than Ponselle's 1929 debut. Vittorio Gui conducted; the Norma was Maria Meneghini Callas,[19] and with her were Ebe Stignani (Adalgisa), Mirto Picchi (Pollione), and Giacomo Vaghi (Oroveso). The Clotilde of that performance was a young soprano who had made her debut as the First Lady in *Die Zauberflöte* eleven days before: Joan Sutherland. Returning to Covent Garden in June 1953, Callas elected to sing *"Casta diva"* in its original key (G) rather than in the traditional transposition—said to have been initiated by Pasta—to F.[20] But she returned to F in her Covent Garden performances of February 2 and 6, 1957,[21] when Stignani (Adalgisa), Giuseppe Vertecchi (Pollione), and Nicola Zaccaria (Oroveso) were her chief colleagues.

Norma was performed in New York for the first time (in the English translation by William Henry Fry) on February 25, 1841. Although it was also sung in New York in Italian on September 20, 1843, *Norma* did not establish itself among the city's favorite operas until October 2, 1854, when it was heard as the inaugural opera of the Academy of Music, with Giulia Grisi as Norma and Mario, her husband, as Pollione. Thereafter it was sung very often in New York before, on February 27, 1890, it was staged for the first time at the Metropolitan Opera House. The occasion was Lilli Lehmann's benefit performance.[22] Walter Damrosch conducted; the cast was completed by Betty Frank (Adalgisa), Louise Meisslinger (Clotilde), Albert Mittelhauser (Flavio), Paul Kalisch (Lehmann's husband; Pollione), and Emil Fischer (Oroveso). As the cast suggests, the opera was sung in German. Lehmann and Kalisch sang in two

*Norma*s during the 1891–1892 season, after which the opera disappeared from the Metropolitan for a quarter of a century.

On November 16, 1927, Rosa Ponselle sang the first of her nineteen Metropolitan Normas.[23] Other roles were taken by Marion Telva (Adalgisa), Minnie Egener (Clotilde), Giordano Paltrinieri (Flavio), Giacomo Lauri-Volpi (Pollione), and Ezio Pinza (Oroveso). Tullio Serafin conducted. Ponselle last sang Norma at the Metropolitan at a matinée on December 13, 1931. Gina Cigna became the house Norma on February 20, 1937, with Ettore Panizza the conductor, Bruna Castagna the Adalgisa, Thelma Votipka the Clotilde, Paltrinieri the Flavio, Giovanni Martinelli the Pollione, and Pinza the Oroveso. Two performances that season, three the next. Then, on December 29, 1943, the Norma was Zinka Milanov, with Cesare Sodero conducting, Castagna (Adalgisa), Votipka (Clotilde), Alessio de Paolis (Flavio), Frederick Jagel (Pollione), and Norman Cordon (Oroveso). Milanov undertook the role four times that season, four the next (when Nicola Moscona was the Oroveso). Then *Norma* went unheard at the Metropolitan for eight years. Milanov returned to the role there on March 9, 1954, when Fausto Cleva conducted and others in the cast were Fedora Barbieri (Adalgisa), Maria Leone (Clotilde), Paul Franke (Flavio), Gino Penno (Pollione), and Cesare Siepi (Oroveso). Four performances, the last on April 15, 1954, when Kurt Baum was Pollione and the Adalgisa was Blanche Thebom.

On October 29, 1956, opening night of the season, Maria Meneghini Callas made her New York debut as the Metropolitan's Norma; Cleva again conducted, and Callas's singing companions were Barbieri, Leone, James McCracken (Flavio), Mario Del Monaco (Pollione), and Siepi. After the five Callas Normas of that season, no Metropolitan performance of Bellini's opera was offered until the curtailed 1969–1970 season. *Norma* returned to the Metropolitan on March 3, 1970, with Joan Sutherland (Norma), Marilyn Horne (Metropolitan debut, Adalgisa), Carlo Bergonzi (Pollione), and Cesare Siepi (Oroveso), with Richard Bonynge conducting. Almost totally deprived of dramatic impact, the production nonetheless attracted capacity audiences for eleven performances during that season and eight more in the 1970–1971 season (with some substitutions in casting), largely because of the phenomenal singing, particularly in their two duets, of Sutherland and Horne. The opera's seventy-third performance by the Metropolitan company was heard on December 14, 1970.

Chicago had first heard *Norma* at the second of J. B. Rice's Chicago Theaters[24] in October 1853, when the title role was sung by Rose de Vries; Luigi Arditi conducted. In 1890, a German opera company headed by Walter Damrosch provided Chicago with an opportunity to hear Lilli Lehmann's Norma at the Auditorium. There too, at a matinee on

November 22, 1919, Rosa Raisa was heard as Norma, with Cyrena Van Gordon (Adalgisa), Alessandro Dolci (Pollione), and Virgilio Lazzari (Oroveso). When Raisa returned to the role of Norma at the Auditorium on December 31, 1928, Giorgio Polacco was the conductor and the singing cast included Coe Glade (Adalgisa), Charles Marshall (Pollione), and Lazzari. On November 22, 1937, at the Civic Opera House, the Chicago Norma was Gina Cigna; Glade was again the Adalgisa, but Giovanni Martinelli sang Pollione, and the Oroveso was Ezio Pinza. On November 1, 1954, at the Civic Opera House, Maria Meneghini Callas made her United States debut as Norma, opening the season. Nicola Rescigno conducted. The cast included Giulietta Simionato (Adalgisa), Mirto Picchi (Pollione), and Nicola Rossi-Lemeni (Oroveso). This proved to be Callas's only performance in Chicago of her most famous role.

The San Francisco Opera Company first staged *Norma* on November 13, 1937, when Gaetano Merola conducted; the leading singers were Gina Cigna (Norma), Bruna Castagna (Adalgisa), Giovanni Martinelli (Pollione), and Ezio Pinza (Oroveso).

In the Roman Arena at Verona on July 18, 1957, Anita Cerquetti was Norma; Francesco Molinari-Pradelli conducted, and the others in the cast were Simionato (Adalgisa), Laura Zanini (Clotilde), Mariano Caruso (Flavio), Franco Corelli (Pollione), and Giulio Neri (Oroveso). On the opening night of the 1958 season at the Teatro dell'Opera, Rome, Callas was the Norma. She declined to return to the stage after the first intermission—and Cerquetti sang the next performance (she had been singing the role at the Teatro San Carlo in Naples). On August 24, 1960, perhaps the most extravagant performance of *Norma* ever presented anywhere took place in the Greek Amphitheater at Epidauros. Twelve thousand people heard the octogenarian Tullio Serafin conduct; Callas was the Norma, and her stage colleagues included Kiki Morfonious (Adalgisa), Mirto Picchi (Pollione), and Ferruccio Mazzoli (Oroveso).

THE LIBRETTO. Felice Romani's *Norma* is dramatically one of the best librettos ever written. It is always described, with good reason, as having been derived from Alexandre Soumet's five-act *tragédie Norma*, which was staged for the first time at the Théâtre de l'Odéon, Paris, on April 16, 1831, when its principal roles were acted by Mlle George (Norma), Alexandrine Noblet (Adalgise), Lockroi (Pollion), and Eric Bernard (Orovèse). Certainly Romani used Italian versions of the names of Soumet's characters and reflected many scenes and actions in his *tragédie*. But other sources, one of them close, others more remote, also influenced him. Ten years before the appearance of Soumet's verse play, Romani himself had written, for setting by Giovanni Pacini, a libretto entitled

La Sacerdotessa d'Irminsul,[25] which contained a large foretaste of the atmosphere that pervades his *Norma*.[26] Its setting, however, is not the Gaul of *Norma*, but Saxony, A.D. 772, during the time of Charlemagne, and its principal characters are Romilda, Clodomiro, Ruggiero, and Sennone (the *"Gran Sacerdote"*).

The *Osservatore triestino* of May 22, 1820, writing of *La Sacerdotessa d'Irminsul*, began its critique by saying: "If the argument of this opera (resembling that of various dramatic presentations in which priestesses of Vesta, of the Sun, etc., and their fathers are taken together in the same tragedy)—if the argument of this opera lacks the virtue of novelty . . ." And in fact, the much-raided literature about erring priestesses and other vestals amorously involved with Roman legionaries harked back at least to Chateaubriand's epic romance of the early fourth century, *Les Martyrs* (1809). Chateaubriand's heroine, Velleda, was one of the more remote ancestresses of Romani's Romilda and Soumet's Norma.[27] *Norma* takes place in Gaul at an unspecified pre-Christian date.[28]

Act I: Scenes 1–6. "Sacred forest of the Druids . . ." Oroveso and the other Druids try to rouse the Gauls to a war of liberation against the Roman invaders. Pollione, the Roman proconsul, tells his friend Flavio that he no longer loves Norma, who broke her vow of virginity with him and has borne him two children: he now loves the priestess Adalgisa. After the two Romans leave, Norma ascends the altar and prophesies that Rome will fall of itself; she wants to prevent a struggle that would endanger her beloved Pollione. She prays to the chaste goddess of the moon to spread peace, but the assembly threatens death to the enemy proconsul. Adalgisa too prays nearby. Pollione then persuades Adalgisa to agree to return with him to Rome.

Scenes 7–9. "Norma's dwelling." Norma tells Clotilde of her suffering because of her children: she knows that Pollione is about to leave for Rome, and she would flee with him but for them. She knows, too, that she has a rival for his love. Adalgisa, deeply disturbed, comes to tell Norma of her love for a Roman. Herself guilty, Norma plans to free Adalgisa of her vows. But Pollione comes in, and Norma understands with rage that he is the man Adalgisa loves. Pollione tries to take Adalgisa away with him; but she will not go, finding herself unable to inflict such pain upon Norma.

Act II: Scenes 1–3. "Interior of Norma's dwelling. . . ." Tempted to kill her sleeping children, Norma is stopped by her love for them. Having decided despairingly to give Pollione up to Adalgisa if Adalgisa will promise to act as a mother to the children, Norma makes the offer. Still loyal, Adalgisa refuses; instead, she goes to Pollione in an attempt to recall him to his duty toward Norma.

Scenes 4–10. "Solitary place near the Druid woods . . ." The Gauls have assembled for battle. Norma, learning from Clotilde that Adalgisa has been unable to influence Pollione, thrice strikes Irminsul's shield—the signal for war. As the Gauls exult, Clotilde rushes in to announce that a Roman has been seized in the sacred cloister of the vestal virgins. Norma knows that it is Pollione, who has tried to abduct Adalgisa. The penalty for such a profanation, as Norma is aware, is death. But her love moves her to offer a substitute sacrifice, a faithless vestal: herself. Placing the children in Pollione's care, she confesses everything. The sacrificial pyre is prepared. But as Norma mounts it, Pollione—his love for her rekindled by her nobility and her love—joins her in fiery death.

THE OPERA. Although the best-known fact about Bellini's *Norma* is that it contains "*Casta diva*," the opera is much more notable for the strength and variety of its characterizations, achieved largely through an extraordinary and original employment of recitative, and for the unerring aptness of its orchestration. Domenico de Paoli well evoked the dramatic rightness of Bellini's writing[29]: "The first thing that strikes one when leafing through the score is to see the musician so taken by its argument, by the *interior* life of his personages, that there is not in the entire work a single measure dedicated to landscape, to ceremonies, in fact, not a single *decorative* touch, and that in a work in which the picturesque element nonetheless has a considerable place. But evidently Bellini thinks that the picturesque aspect of the milieu, of the ambiance, is the affair of the *régisseur*, of the scenographer, believing that he, the musician, must occupy himself only with the spirit and the life of his personages." And again[30]: "I want to say that, whereas with [Bellini's] contemporaries, the *aria* is always a 'dead point' in the development of the action, in *Norma* the *aria*, no less than the recitative, is always the drama *in action*. With the exception of Pollione's dream [*"Meco all'altar di Venere"*] (which is retold), the drama undergoes not a single moment of immobility; it is not interrupted because a character is singing; the melody in *Norma* is essentially dynamic, follows the action, envelops it, surrounds the characters, who here move, in Nietzsche's words, in the spirit of the music. The character sings and acts, and the melody follows the action and, moreover, displays it. It puts into relief the interior life of the character no less than the large Wagnerian orchestra does, but in a simpler and more evident way, and without the huge deployment of leitmotifs, symbols, etc."

Even more particularized and relevant was Henri de Saussine's comment[31]: "At the end of the admirable duet in *Norma*, one sees the exasperated blows of the betrayed priestess menace Pollione; how? By an E-flat major chord sounded by all the violins in the full tonality of G major. In

the final scene of *Norma:* a mounting progression of the basses—reproduced exactly, furthermore, in the death of Isolde—leading to the same
appoggiatura that expresses the climax of the emotion in the two works.
. . . Upon Chopin [as well as upon Wagner[32]] the Bellinian influence was
considerable. The entrance aria of the second act of *Norma* and the C-
sharp minor *Étude* (perhaps Chopin's *chef d'œuvre*) have a close relationship that perhaps can be found in other passages. . . ."

As for the instrumentation of *Norma*, Bellini himself was entirely
conscious of its exact nature. Writing to Florimo on August 13, 1835,
he said[33]: "Do you believe that, if I should take the risk of [re-]orches-
trating *Norma*, all the theaters in Italy would go to the expense of having
both the parts and the score recopied?—Therefore, if it is not to serve
for Paris, it will be useless work, and do you think, then, that I could
bring to it the manner of instrumentating *I Puritani*? you are mistaken: it
could be [done] in some places, but generally it will be impossible for me
because of the smooth and flowing nature of the cantilenas, which do not
permit another sort of instrumentation than what is there now; and I
have thought well about this." In short, the instrumentation of *Norma*,
which is a complete success, is what it is because Bellini planned it that
way, not out of any inadvertence.

Norma differs from Bellini's other operas in many ways, some of them
very difficult to name. As a setting of a libretto derived from a five-act
French tragedy in verse which in itself is very like "*grand opéra*," it responds to some of the intellectual and artistic surge that was culminating
in Paris when Soumet wrote his play (the première of Meyerbeer's *Robert
le Diable* occurred exactly five weeks before that of *Norma*). Bellini being
Bellini, his frequent use of librettos drawn from French sources did not
lead him to a true Italianate version of *grand opéra*. But into his less
"spectacular" opera he incorporated non-Italian elements that help to set
Norma and, somewhat less obviously, *I Puritani* apart from operas by his
Italian contemporaries using librettos based upon Italian writings. In its
theatrical integrity, the near-brutality of its *coups de théâtre*, its pervasive
vigor, *Norma* is closer to Scribe and Meyerbeer—and to Rossini in *Guillaume Tell* (which might be described as foretelling alternately the pastoral
atmosphere of *La Sonnambula* and the noble heroics of *Norma*)—than,
for example, to Rossini in such smaller-scaled operas as *Ricciardo e Zoraide*
and *Bianca e Falliero*, both of which set librettos derived from Italian
sources.[34] Those elements, added to the stylistic nobility of both libretto
and music, give *Norma* its unique position not only among Bellini's operas,
but also among all the operas of its era.

Sinfonia: Beginning in G minor, 4/4 time, *allegro maestoso e deciso*,
the overture to *Norma* announces martial atmosphere and tender personal

emotion outlined against a background of somber coloration.[35] A rapid pianissimo figuration of sixteenth-notes grouped in fours (many of them repeated notes, this being a Bellinian "sign" of emotional agitation [p. 2[36]]) leads to the principal melody in the thirds that intermittently lend their always very audible coloring to the entire opera (*"con voce nudrita"* —with sustained voice, p. 3*). After considerable development, this clearly outlined material gives way, by a shift to G major (p. 8), to a melodic, almost "impressionistic" pianissimo in which short violin trills rustle.[37]

Although Francesco D'Arcais stigmatized[38] this *sinfonia* as "exiguous in proportions for the grandeur of the subject," it establishes a *"Norma"* texture and voice that remain as unmistakable throughout the opera as those of *Die Zauberflöte* remain throughout Mozart's. The *Sinfonia* is architecturally the keystone of *Norma*, not music merely related to or presenting a foretaste of what is to follow. It is a far remove from the semi-Rossinian *sinfonia* for *Il Pirata*, and when played apart from the opera loses most of its significance. As Domenico de Paoli saw,[39] "This *sinfonia* has nothing of the character of a description or of a résumé of the drama; it is rather an *introduction* that does not evoke the atmosphere of the drama: it operates to create in the listener a 'state of spirit' or of spirit in unison with that of the milieu in which the action will take place. . . . In the drama to follow, a *warlike* world is opposed to a *religious-druidic* world: a *strong* expression is opposed to a *mystical* expression. Thus he constructed his *sinfonia*, and the listener is placed in harmony with the personages of the drama by the power of the music alone, without his being able to explain how. It is the *music* that operates upon him: even *before* the drama, but in the same sense."

Writing to Camille Bellaigue from Milan on May 2, 1898, Verdi discussed the judgment on Bellini that Bellaigue had made in a recently published book: "Bellini is poor, it is true, in harmony and instrumentation; but rich in feeling and in an individual melancholy of his own! Even in the least well-known of his operas, in *La Straniera*, in *Il Pirata*, there are long, long, long melodies such as no-one before him produced. And what truth and power of declamation, as for example in the duet between *Pollione* and *Norma*! And what elevation of thought in the first phrase of the *Introduction* [p. 10], followed after a few measures by another phrase [p. 12],† badly orchestrated, it is true; nevertheless, no one ever has created another more beautiful and heavenly."[40]

* Page references here are to the Ricordi piano-vocal score with plate number 41684.
† Verdi here refers to this melody:

Act I: Scenes 1–6. "Sacred forest of the Druids; in the center, an oak of Irminsul, at the foot of which is seen the Druidic stone serving as an altar. In the distance, wooded hills. It is night; lights gleam distantly in the woods. To the sound of a religious march, Gallic troops march in, followed by Druids in procession. Finally, Oroveso, with the chief priests":

Scene 1—Continuing in the G major of the conclusion of the *sinfonia,* the introductory *andante grave* (p. 10) employs a stage band.[41] It immediately evokes solemn mystery (and makes one of Bellini's infrequent uses of true four-voice counterpoint). The sacredness of the rite is majestically evoked by the chief melody (p. 11, entry of the stage band). The first voice heard is that of Oroveso intoning his renowned cavatina *"Ite sul colle, o Druidi,"* in which the vocal melody almost duplicates the instrumental melody, itself vocal in nature. The Druids ask if Norma will attend; Oroveso replies (p. 15) that she will—and the Druids echo his assurance in two-voice (tenor-bass) chorus. They then apostrophize Irminsul (p. 15) in the warlike, very impressive *"Dell'aura tua profetica,"* begging the god to inspire their priestess with such hatred for the Roman invaders that she will break the peace. Oroveso takes up their melody (p. 17), and is again joined by them (p. 18). The music intensifies in bellicosity (pp. 18–23). Then, *"Primo tempo"* (p. 24), with the instruction "All move toward the interior of the forest," the orchestra initiates a melody of which an arpeggiated eighth-note accompaniment foretells that of *"Casta diva."* And, in fact, Oroveso and the other Druids address the Moon (p. 25): *"Luna, t'affretta a sorgere!"* in which, singing only repeated D's, they are accompanied significantly by a condensed repetition of the principal melody (p. 11) of the instrumental introduction. The scene ends *morendo, piano-pianissimo.* "All leave, disappearing into the forest; from time to time, their voices can still be heard, sounding from a distance. Now Flavio and Pollione, wrapped in their togas, enter from one side."

Scene 2—Back in G minor, still in 4/4 time, after eight measures of instrumental prelude (p. 27), Pollione and Flavio converse in accompanied recitative, dialogue of remarkable suppleness which serves to inform us (pp. 27–31) that Pollione no longer loves Norma, the mother of his children, but is enamored of a temple priestess, Adalgisa, who returns his love. "And don't you fear Norma's wrath?" the centurion asks (p. 31); Pollione answers that her reaction will be *"atroce, orrenda,"* as he has learned from a dream. "Recalling it, I tremble," Pollione tells Flavio. Then (p. 31), C major, moderato, he retells the dream in the cavatina *"Meco all'altar di Venere,"* one of the least expressive passages in *Norma* largely because Romani here demands more intensity than Bellini supplies, partly because the drama has been arrested. With the instruction "a *sforzato* on the first beat of each measure," this cavatina climaxes as Pollione, "*con voce cupa e terribile*," tells of the end of his dream, in which "a horrible voice echoed through the temple: *Thus Norma destroys her treacherous lover.*" The key changes to E-flat major, the tempo to *allegro marziale*. The sacred gong (an onstage tamtam) is heard three times; its crashes are followed by fanfares from invisible onstage trumpets (pp. 37–38) in increasing numbers (2, 4, 6). Norma is approaching to preside over the rite. Flavio urges Pollione to flee with him, but Pollione remains behind. With a vulgarity that is one part of his nature, he sings (with Flavio and the offstage chorus) "*Traman congiure i barbari*" (p. 40). From near at hand, the approaching Druids order all outsiders from the sacred grove. *Poco più sostenuto*, still in E-flat major, Pollione sings (p. 42) the cabaletta "*Me protegge, me difende*," which makes clear why Bellini expressed dissatisfaction with the music that he had given the proconsul in this scene. After Pollione has boasted that he will destroy the altars of any god who dares to take Adalgisa from him, he and Flavio depart.

Scene 3 (pp. 49–55)—"Druids [enter] from the back; Priestesses, Warriors, Bards, Eubagi, Sacrificers, and, among them, Oroveso." Continuing the E-flat major in 4/4 time, but now *allegro assai*, the orchestra lays down in chords a menacing introduction (p. 49) that decreases from fortissimo to pianissimo. The stage band then joins in intermittently (pp. 50–55) in the characteristic military march, which increases in volume up to the three-voice (soprano-tenor-bass) chorus (pp. 51–55) "*Norma viene; le cinge la chioma*," which in turn rises to fortissimo, but whispers to its close.

Scene 4 (pp. 56–86)—"Norma amid her priestesses. Her hair is unbound, her head is encircled by a wreath of vervain, and she holds a golden sickle in her hand. She mounts the Druidic stone and gazes about her as if inspired. Everyone is silent." What now occurs is musical drama sufficiently powerful to justify the highest claims for the art of opera and to silence all ill-informed grumbling against both recitative and *fioriture*. Maintaining the E-flat major in 4/4 time, a forte chord followed by a rest (p. 56) preludes Norma's famous phrase in unaccompanied recitative, "*Sediziose voci,/voci di guerra avvi chi alzar si attenta/Presso all'ara del Dio?*" (Seditious voices, warlike voices—are there those who dare to raise them near the god's altar?). In accompanied recitative (pp. 57–58), Oroveso demands actions against the Romans: "*Omai di Brenno/Ozioso non può starsi la spada*" (The sword of Brenno [the Gallic chief] can no longer remain idle). The chorus interjects (p. 58) "Let it for once be brandished!" Commandingly, Norma replies (pp. 58–59) that the hour for rebellion is not yet: the Roman spears still are stronger than the Druid axes. The assemblage demands (p. 59) to know what the god has ordered her to do, what prophesied. Norma's reply (pp. 59–60) is that one day Rome will perish of its own vices, but that peace must be kept for the time being. Now she will cut the sacred mistletoe.

(P. 61). "The sickle cuts; the priestesses collect [the cut mistletoe] in wicker baskets. Norma moves forward and extends her arms toward the heavens. The moon shines forth with all its light. All prostrate themselves." After twenty-two pages of common time and the reign of E-flat major, a powerful change of both time and tonality occurs: to 12/8, F major (G major in the autograph score), *andante sostenuto assai.* After three measures of undulant, arpeggiated introduction, a solo flute is heard (p. 61) pianissimo in one of the longest-breathed and most enchanted melodies ever conceived: that of *"Casta diva"*—which, after a single measure continuing the arpeggiated accompaniment alone, Norma begins (p. 62): *"Casta diva, che inargenti/Queste sacre antiche piante,/A noi volgi il bel sembiante/Senza nube e senza vel"* (Chaste goddess, who silvers these holy, ancient trees, turn your beautiful face upon us free of cloud and free of veil).[42] After Oroveso and the others (three-part chorus) echo her prayer (pp. 63–66), while she sings it more slowly and with extremely apposite *fioriture,* she begins (p. 66) its second strophe: *"Tempra o diva, de' cori ardenti/Tempra ancora lo zelo audace,/Spargi in terra quella pace/Che regnar tu fai nel ciel"* (Restrain, o goddess, ardent hearts, still temper audacious zeal, spread on earth that peace which you cause to reign in the heavens). Again (pp. 67–69) Oroveso and the others add their voices while Norma decorates the melody, concluding with a cadenza and closing on the A of the tonic triad. The rite being concluded, Bellini returns from the "heavenly" F (or G) major to the more "earthly" E-flat major (p. 70), allegro, and the stage band reasserts the military march; *allegro assai maestoso* (p. 70), Norma orders all to leave the sacred grove, promising that when the God requires Roman blood, her voice will thunder forth. The assemblage demands (pp 71–73) that the first to fall be the proconsul, Pollione. Now the human, feminine aspect of Norma appears (p. 73) as, in recitative, she soliloquizes *"Cadrà . . . punirlo io posso . . ./Ma punirlo il cor non sa"* (He shall fall . . . I can punish him . . . but my heart does not know how to do it).

The key again shifts (p. 73) to F (or G) major, allegro ("pizzicato/vibrato"). To a rocking accompaniment (p. 73), the orchestra preludes the melody[43] of *"Ah! bello, a me ritorna,"* which Norma then sings (pp. 74–75), its compelling *fioriture* and descending chromatic runs revealing her agitated yearning: She is appealing to Pollione to return to her and restore the beauty of their first love. Oroveso and the others (pp. 76–77) insist that the irate god is hastening the downfall of Roman power, which they personify as Tebro— the Tiber. Norma, wholly rapt by her emotions and thoughts, again soliloquizes (pp. 77–80), singing a second strophe of the cabaletta to the same melody and accompaniment. Again Oroveso and the others pray for the destruction of Rome. Norma, still addressing Pollione in her mind, introduces another section of melody (pp. 81–84), asking him to be again what he was when she gave herself to him. And again Oroveso and the others, unaware of what she is thinking and feeling, assert their demand for revenge. As Norma leads them from the grove, the war march is repeated (pp. 84–85), *più mosso assai*, at first fortissimo, then diminishing in a varied extension to a final pianissimo. A single priestess remains near the altar: Adalgisa.

Scene 5—"Adalgisa alone." B-flat major, 4/4 time, andante (pp. 86–87), the orchestra foreshadows Adalgisa's inner torment in clusters of sixteenth-notes in groups of four, then brings in (p. 86) a melody that is the very voice of terrified anxiety. In unaccompanied recitative—"*Sgombra è la sacra selva*"—Adalgisa remarks on the loneliness of the grove after the rite; some of the immediately preceding orchestral matter appears in abridgment. Then, in *recitativo secco*, she soliloquizes on her love for Pollione, which has driven her to break her vows.[44] "Largo. She runs to prostrate herself on the stone of Irminsul" (p. 89), asking for the god's protection: "*Deh! proteggimi, o Dio!*" Of this first appearance of Adalgisa alone, Guido Pannain said illuminatingly[45]: "She begins her scene with a purely explanatory recitative: a musical stage-direction. It is the orchestra that takes the lyric initiative. An interior, collected movement, almost religious, like a prayer, then Adalgisa's invocation: '*Proteggimi o Dio!*' a phrase that jets forth, a powerful arc of song. Thus is revealed, modeled in her beauty, a living creature. The orchestra, all in shadows, finishes its brief passage; and the song of prayer which had begun the episode terminates and concludes it."

Scene 6—B-flat major, 4/4 time, andante. Pollione and Flavio enter. When Pollione sees Adalgisa, he tells the centurion to leave. He and Adalgisa converse in recitative (pp. 91–93): frightened by her lover's presence in the sacred grove, Adalgisa begs him to leave; he pleads his love, saying that he will follow her anywhere. Unmoved, she says that she will take refuge on the temple altar. "The altar!" he replies. "And our love?" Her halting answer is: "I shall forget it." The key changes to F minor, *allegro risoluto*, for an ominous prelude (p. 93) to Pollione's curiously unsuccessful "*Va, crudele*"[46]: above a rushing accompaniment in groups of four sixteenth-notes for the violins, he tells her to offer the god his blood, but not to believe that he ever can leave her (pp. 94–95). The melody of the second section of this aria-like introduction to the duet with Adalgisa ("*Sol promessa al Dio tu fosti*," p. 96) was borrowed by Bellini from his arietta "*Bella Nice, che d'amore*," published in 1829. When Adalgisa replies (pp. 98–101), expressing her helplessness (she sees Pollione's likeness even upon the altar) and begging Heaven to remove him or forgive her sin, the music repeats both sections of Pollione's introduction, robbing her reply of any dramatic contribution and weakening the intensity of the scene. Pollione, proffering purer sky and better gods in Rome (p. 101), continues to insist upon their fleeing together (pp. 101–102). Now, A-flat major, *più moderato assai* (p. 104), he expresses his desire tenderly in a fine melody, "*Vieni in Roma, ah! vieni.*" And when Adalgisa repeats the music that he has just sung (p. 105), this time the lack of change is effective because she is talking to herself in a way that reveals how his ardor persuades her. As they join in duet, *più mosso* (pp. 106–109), she agrees to renounce her vow and her god and go to Rome with Pollione. Several changes of tempo increase the pressure exerted by the increasing volume until (p. 109) the lovers sing in unison and then leave as the orchestra breaks out triumphantly in A-flat major.

Scene 7. A minor, 4/4 time, *allegro agitato* (p. 110). "Norma's dwelling; Norma holding her two small children by the hand; Clotilde." The splendidly evocative orchestral introduction (pp. 110–111) is marked by the Bellinian "sign" of agitation: groups of four rapid sixteenth-notes, many of them repeated notes. In its andante section (p. 111)—which, after a brief allegro, becomes the accompaniment of Norma's "*Oltre l'usato io tremo*," *assai più moderato* (p. 112)—the opera's only "leitmotiv" is heard, a melody related to the idea of the children which recurs near the end of the opera when Norma thinks of them (pp. 258–259). She now tells Clotilde to conceal the children. She is gripped by violently opposed emotions because Pollione has been recalled to Rome and has not said whether he will take her and their children with him. As Adalgisa approaches, Norma embraces the children, whom Clotilde then leads away.

Scene 8. B-flat major, 4/4 time, *andante sostenuto* (pp. 116–130). "Adalgisa and Norma." In extremely flexible and varied recitative dialogue (pp. 116–120), Adalgisa informs the warmly sympathetic Norma of her impassioned love, which has driven her to foreswear altar and fatherland. Then, F minor, *moderato assai*, the flute introduces (p. 120) the melody to which, in "*Sola, furtiva, al tempio*," Adalgisa will tell (p. 120) of her meetings with her as yet unnamed lover. Her melody (which unfortunately has an arpeggiated eighth-note accompaniment pointlessly recalling that of "*Casta diva*") is drenched in very Bellinian melancholy. Norma, recognizing a repetition of her own infatuation for Pollione, becomes increasingly agitated and often interrupts Adalgisa's narrative. Pitying the girl, still unaware that the lover is Pollione, in a shift to C major, *più animato*, on the words "*Ah! sì, fa core e abbracciami*" Norma frees Adalgisa from her vow so that she may live happily with her beloved. Enraptured by this promise ror

of liberated happiness, Adalgisa, to the same music, sings (pp. 127–128) *"Ripeti, o ciel, ripetimi/Sì lusinghieri accenti."* Then she and Norma sing in duet (pp. 128–130), often in the thirds that are one mark of their relationship—and indeed of the opera itself. A brilliant cadenza in thirds ends the scene (p. 130).[47]

Scene 9. C major, 4/4 time, *lo stesso tempo.* "Pollione, Norma, Adalgisa." After beginning in pianissimo orchestral sixteenth-notes in groups of four, the scene opens out (pp. 131–132) as Norma asks Adalgisa the name of her lover and Adalgisa replies that he is a Roman. As Norma is again asking for his name, Pollione comes in and Adalgisa indicates that he is the man. Enraged, Norma turns upon her (p. 133) and then upon Pollione. The score indicates (p. 134) "a few moments of silence" (which the conductor must provide for), after which (p. 134), with the stage direction "Pollione is confused, Adalgisa trembling, Norma raging," Norma launches *"con tutta forza"* a denunciation of Pollione which exculpates Adalgisa: *"Oh non tremare,"* the floridity of which incarnates Norma's emotional vehemence. Wholly at sea, Adalgisa seeks to learn the cause of Norma's sudden rage (*"Che ascolto!"* pp. 135–136). "She covers her face with her hands; Norma grasps her by an arm and forces her to look at Pollione; his eyes follow her." In 9/8 time, B-flat major (p. 136), Norma begins the great trio with *"Oh! di qual sei tu vittima/Crudo e funesto inganno"*[48] (Oh! of what a harsh and ruinous deception you are the victim). Adelmo Damerini described[49] this trio as ". . . resolving the drama of the three characters and surpassing it by the strength and the very expansion—which is a liberation—inherent in the single dominant line of song, where others would have introduced the contrast of varied themes. Bellini, eminently a lyric rather than a dramatic artist, finds the resolution of every struggle in the effusion, which he possesses in prodigal amount, of his faculty for song." Back in common time, *allegro risoluto* (pp. 144–145) and then *più mosso* (pp. 145–147), Pollione tries to pull Adalgisa away with him. As she too turns upon him for his faithlessness: *"Ah! no, giammai! pria spirar!"* (Ah! no, never! I would rather die)[50] (p. 147), Pollione at last loses all restraint. Now (pp. 147–148) the second section of the trio begins *allegro agitato assai* as Norma ("bursting out") sings: *"Vanne, sì, mi lascia, indegno"* (Go, yes, leave me, unworthy man).[51] Adalgisa and Pollione join in (p. 149). Norma is sending Pollione away with a warning that her hatred will pursue him[52]; Pollione continues to assert the greatness of his love for Adalgisa, and now curses the destiny that brought him from Rome; Adalgisa is saying that she will not be the cause of such sorrow for Norma, but will die in order to bring Pollione back to Norma and their children. "The sacred gongs of the temple sound, summoning Norma to the rites." The Druids are heard off-stage (p. 154)

calling to Norma as the trio continues to its close (p. 158). "[Norma]
repulses Pollione, grasping his arm and motioning to him to leave. He
departs in a fury" as the first act ends.[53]

Act II: Scenes 1–3. "Interior of Norma's dwelling. At one side, a
Roman bed covered with a bearskin. Norma's children asleep. Norma with
a lamp and with a dagger in her hand. She sits down and places the lamp
upon a table. She is pallid, distracted, etc.":

Scene 1—D minor, 4/4 time, *allegro assai moderato.* The orchestra
shouts fortissimo D octaves (p. 158). Silence.[54] The fortissimo D's are
repeated, as is the ensuing silence. Then, pianissimo, a deliberate orchestral
arpeggio in A climbs from the depths of the orchestra to a chordal ca-
dence—which is followed by another measure of silence, after which
both the arpeggio (a fifth higher) and the silence recur. Still pianissimo,
but animando, a syncopated quasi-melody depicts almost visibly, to quote
Pizzetti,[55] "a succession of anguished phrases and sobs." Above the simplest
of accompaniments, *"con dolore,"* the violins breathe (p. 160) the long
D-major cantilena that will shortly become Norma's *"Teneri, teneri figli."*
Silence. Then, forte, descending octaves—F, E, D—signal Norma's entrance into the room. Back to pianissimo for fifteen measures (p. 161) of
highly emotional atmospheric preparation. What follows (pp. 162–164,
andante, 165–166 allegro, recitative flanking the hushed, notably Chopin-
esque cavatina *"Teneri, teneri figli"*) is one of the greatest scenes ever to
exploit dramatic recitative. Between the disjunct phrases of Norma's soliloquy (*primo tempo, andante, lento a piacere, primo tempo* [the cavatina],
lento, allegro, allegro agitato) the chief elements of the orchestral introduction return dramatically. Norma is arguing with herself in a tone at
first inward, but increasingly urgent and outward: why must my children
die?—they are Pollione's—they are already dead for me—they must die
for him too—his anguish must exceed all others—stab them . . . "She
moves toward the bed; raises the dagger; gives a horrified scream; the
children awaken." She cannot strike them (she is not a witch like Medea,
but a very feminine woman). Weeping, she embraces them (p. 166) and
calls out *"Clotilde!"* thus concluding a scene that is as convincing proof
of Bellini's genius as *"Casta diva"* itself.

Scene 2—"Clotilde and Norma." In recitative (p. 166), Norma tells
Clotilde to bring Adalgisa to her. Clotilde replies that Adalgisa is wander-
ing about alone near by, weeping and praying. "Go," Norma orders.
"Let my sin be atoned . . . and then . . . to die."

Scene 3—"Adalgisa and Norma." B-flat major, lento, a comparatively
dull and inert double aria (pp. 170–174) begins, serving the purpose of
allowing Norma to tell Adalgisa that she has decided upon suicide and
wants to entrust her children to Adalgisa, who is to take them to Pollione

in the Roman camp; to say that she hopes that Pollione will be less cruel as Adalgisa's husband; to allow Adalgisa to say that she will renounce Pollione, whom she will persuade to return to Rome; and to let Norma insist that she will not permit any appeal to Pollione. And here it is as though Bellini's usually intense concentration had wandered—for, as Pizzetti pointed out,[56] the notes assigned to Norma and Adalgisa make it almost impossible for them to carry into action such a rubric as (for Adalgisa) "with fear . . . dismayed," and for the most part war with the clear implications of the text-words. Musically somewhat better, though not up to the level of Scene 1, is the double aria that Norma initiates (p. 170, C major, *allegro moderato*) with "*Deh! con te li prendi li sostieni*" and Adalgisa takes up (p. 172) with "*Norma! ah! Norma, ancore amata.*"

One of the peaks of *Norma* is the intensely expressive, very touching duet begun (p. 176, F major, andante) by Adalgisa with "*Mira, o Norma*" and continuing into a wonderfully plastic depiction of mutual sensibility expressed, mysteriously and effectively (beginning "*Un poco meno*," p. 177, with the subordinate second section of melody), largely by the two voices in parallel thirds. Norma, assuaged and convinced by Adalgisa's affection, gradually gives way to the girl's insistence: with some hope, she will live; they will confront outrageous fortune together. Their duet is interrupted midway (allegro, pp. 180–181) by a passage that hovers between recitative and arioso ("*Cedi . . . deh! cedi*") and is followed (pp. 182–187)—beginning in thirds with "*Sì, fino all'ore estreme*"[57] —by the cabaletta of the duet. Here this conventional quickening of tempo perfectly conveys the change from imminent tragedy to humanly shared hope, even to possible joy. A remarkable touch is Bellini's use (p. 182) of imitation when Adalgisa repeats Norma's words and melodic spurt on the phrase "*Teco del fato all'onte*" while Norma continues on with other words and notes (this is repeated, p. 185); Bellini brought over the melodic line for this phrase from a passage in the original version of *Adelson e Salvini*, where it occurs in the cabaletta of the Salvini-Bonifacio duet in Act I, "*Ah se a smorzar.*"[58] The voices end in unison on F, after which the orchestra concludes the scene with eleven mechanical measures of chordal repetition.[59]

Scenes 4–5. "Solitary place near the Druid woods, surrounded by gorges and caverns. In the background a lake crossed by a stone bridge":

Scene 4 (pp. 188–196)—"Gallic warriors." F major, 4/4 time, *allegro maestoso*. After ten alternately fortissimo and piano measures of introduction ending on a long pause, the orchestra begins the accompaniment of the two-part (tenor-bass) chorus "*Non partì? Finora è al campo.*"[60] The warriors know that Pollione has not left for Rome, and they promise to wait in silence until they can carry out their task and duty of rebellion.

Scene 5 (pp. 196–204)—"Oroveso and Gallic warriors." After a pause, and then continuing in F major, Oroveso speaks in recitative, telling the men that he is unable to spur them on to revolt. Is Pollione, then, not to return to Rome? Oroveso's sorrowful answer (p. 197) is that a "Latin condottiere" more dreaded and harsher than Pollione will succeed him. Does Norma know—and does she still want to restrain them? Oroveso admits that he has investigated Norma's state of mind in vain. They must submit, accept their failure, and disband. "And always dissemble?" the warriors ask. Above an altered version of the "Beethoven" accompaniment of "*Non partì*," Oroveso sings (pp. 199–200) "*con ferocia*" his renowned aria "*Ah! del Tebro al giogo indegno*" (Ah! against the base yoke of Rome).[61] He too longs to fight, but knows that the Gauls must feign docility. The warriors promise to obey (pp. 200–201), but will continue to nurse rancor in their hearts. After the second strophe of Oroveso's aria, he joins in the warriors' chorus. All depart.

Scenes 6–10 (pp. 205–270). "The Temple of Irminsul. At one side, an altar":

Scene 6—C major, 4/4 time, *andante maestoso*. "Norma, then Clotilde" (pp. 205–211). After a calm, brief orchestral prelude, piano and then pianissimo (p. 205), Norma expresses in recitative her belief that Adalgisa will have persuaded a penitent Pollione to come back to her. At the words "*come del primo amore ai dì, ai dì felici*" (p. 206), the recitative breaks into relevant *fioriture*. But after the indication "*primo tempo*," Clotilde runs in to say that Adalgisa has been unable to move the inflamed Pollione. Violently, Norma's mood shifts (p. 207) to conviction that Adalgisa has betrayed her. But what of Pollione? Clotilde says that he has sworn to take Adalgisa away with him even if that means dragging her from the god's altar. Norma's rage mounts (*primo tempo*, p. 208): saying that the faithless lover now has gone too far and that torrents of Roman blood shall flow, she rushes to the altar (presto, p. 209) and thrice strikes the shield (gong) of Irminsul (to agitated, rocking orchestral triplets in crescendo). Offstage fanfares of trumpets sound as Oroveso and the Gauls shout: "*Squilla il bronzo del Dio!*" (The sacred bronze sounds forth!).[62]

Scenes 7–8—After an orchestral introduction that increases in menace, *allegro e sempre crescendo, secche e marcate assai* (pp. 210–211), Oroveso, the other Druids, Bards, Priests, and Priestesses rush in as Norma mounts to her place upon the altar. In agitation, all ask her what has happened, why she has struck the shield of Irminsul. To vibrant tremolo accompaniment, she proclaims (p. 212) war, slaughter, extermination: "*Guerra, strage, sterminio.*" But she has only just imposed peace upon them! Her reply is that now she summons them to rage, slaughter, fury, and Roman deaths; they must raise their voices in the hymn of war.

Allegro feroce, fortissimo, marcatissimo, the assembled Gauls—with interjections by Norma ("*Guerra, guerra!* . . . *Sangue, sangue! vendetta!* . . . *Strage, strage!*")— sing the renowned "*Guerra, guerra!*" chorus (p. 214),[63] a thunderous summons to battle. Oroveso then (p. 221) asks Norma if she will announce the name of the intended sacrifical victim. She answers that he will soon appear—the awful altar never has lacked victims. Allegro. "But what is this tumult?" she asks as (Scene 8) Clotilde rushes in to say that a Roman has been seized in the sacred cloister of the virgins. *Allegro assai moderato* (p. 222), validating Norma's premonition that the prisoner is Pollione, he is led in.

Scene 9 (pp. 223–228)—Oroveso and the others call out: "It is Pollione!" and Norma tells herself: "Now I am avenged." In recitative, *assai maestoso* (pp. 223–224), Oroveso demands that Pollione explain his rash action. *Con fierezza*, Pollione replies: "Strike me but do not question me." Allegro (p. 224), Norma intervenes: "I should be the one to strike. Stand back." Oroveso and the assemblage agree (p. 225): she must use the sacred dagger and vindicate the god. "Yes," she concedes, "we shall strike" —and takes the dagger from Oroveso. *Allegro risoluto* (p. 225). But Norma, who could not kill her children, cannot strike Pollione. Can she be feeling pity? To gain time, she says that she must question Pollione; the others leave, not understanding. The scene closes (after one more irruption of repeated sixteenth-notes) on an orchestral modulation from C major to F major.

Scene 10 (pp. 229–240)—*Allegro moderato, piano e legato*. To the sort of rolling accompaniment so characteristic of this opera, Norma confronts Pollione, singing (p. 229) the superbly expressive aria *"In mia man alfin tu sei"* (At last you are in my hands), asserting that only she can save him. This becomes a melodic dialogue or near-duet as Pollione replies *"Tu nol dei."* Intensity increases gradually through repetitions of the melody and submelodies: Norma is demanding that Pollione never see Adalgisa again. He rejects her demand that he swear to obey. She tells him of her decision to murder their children and admits her inability to carry it out. But the moment will come, she warns, when she will kill them, when she will forget her motherhood. *Più mosso* (p. 233). Pollione asks for the dagger so that he may kill himself instead: he alone shall die. Modulation to A-flat major. Towering in majestic rage, Norma asserts (pp. 233–234) that, on the contrary, hundreds of Romans must die—and that Adalgisa, having violated her vows, must die by fire (here Norma's vocal line, *"con furore,"* becomes grisly with trills). Pollione continues to plead with her to kill him and spare Adalgisa. *Tutto a piacere* (freely throughout), she tells him in recitative that the time for pleading is past: she will strike at Adalgisa through him. After a pause, she launches (*più*

D—First two pages of the four-page autograph from the *"Guerra, guerra!"* chorus in *Norma* (Act II, Scene 7) in the Toscanini Collection.

animato, p. 236) into the violent aria *"Già mi pasco ne' tuoi sguardi/Del tuo duol, del suo morire!"* (Already in your glances I am feeding upon your anguish, upon her death!), the melody being that introduced midway through the *sinfonia* (*"con voce nudrita,"* p. 3). Repeating the melody (p. 237), Pollione again begs her to be satisfied with his suicide. Their voices finally unite (*più vivo*, p. 240), each repeating what he has sung earlier. Then (p. 241), in recitative, he brusquely insists that she give him the dagger. "You dare?" she asks. And when, beside himself, Pollione repeats "The dagger, the dagger!" Norma summons the others to return.

Finale: Allegro, fortissimo, the orchestral introduction modulates to A minor. In recitative, Norma announces that a priestess has violated her vows. When the people demand the betrayer's name, Norma, who remains deaf to Pollione's pleas, tells them to prepare the sacrificial pyre (p. 243). After tortured hesitation, to a trembling orchestral accompaniment, Norma tells them that the betrayer is herself: *"Son io"* (p. 245). Pollione is overwhelmed; Oroveso and the others are incredulous. Again a shift of tonality, this time to G major (largo p. 248), as Norma begins one of Bellini's most beautiful, apt, and emotion-saturated arias: *"Qual cor tradisti, qual cor perdesti"* (What a heart you betrayed, what a heart you lost).[64] This gradually develops into a dialogue with Pollione (who repeats the melody, p. 250) and then into a swelling ensemble in which they are joined (p. 252) by Oroveso and the assemblage (three-part chorus: soprano, tenor, bass), who beg for reassurance and insist that Norma vindicate herself. Half to herself, half to Pollione, Norma suddenly speaks of their children: *"Cielo! e i miei figli?"* (Heavens! and my children?), using the "Leitmotiv" heard in Scene 7 of Act I (p. 111).

A change in Norma's attitude toward Pollione is announced when she turns to him to ask (p. 257) *"I nostri figli?"* (Our [not your or my] children?). Oroveso and the people demand that she tell them whether or not she really is guilty (p. 258). "Yes, beyond any human idea!" They round upon her (*più moderato*, p. 258): *"Empia!"* Softly, to Oroveso—who is, after all, her father—Norma says: "I am a mother." In the accompaniment to this recitative, a very simple, very beautiful melodic phrase is repeated, with varying instrumentation, seven times, supplying variety and unity in a very Bellinian way. She asks Oroveso to take care of the children and Clotilde, preserving them from the "barbarians" (the Romans). He refuses, ordering her to leave him. She asks (p. 260), with a highly emotional rocket of *fioriture*, that he grant her final prayer. E minor, *più moderato, assai piano* (p. 261), Norma addresses Oroveso in the yearning, beseeching cavatina *"Deh! non volerli vittime"* (Oh! do not wish them victims). This is, like *"Casta diva,"* one of those numbers which Verdi must have had in mind when (May 2, 1898) he wrote to Camille Bellaigue of Bellini's operas that in them "there are long, long, long melodies such as no one before him produced."[65] Profoundly shaken, Oroveso says that love has won. But the people, *sotto voce*, murmur against Norma. Pollione adds his plea for the children, and Oroveso finally capitulates. A healing melody materializes (p. 262) as Norma sings *"Padre, tu piangi?"* (You weep, father?) She is joined by Pollione, Oroveso, and the people—who continue to insist that she be punished. The fortissimo (p. 264) will hold until the end. The Druids cover Norma's head with a black veil. Oroveso says to her: "Go, unhappy girl!" As she bids farewell to her father, Pollione's voice emerges from among the voices of the others: he will go to the pyre with Norma. There, eternal love will begin. As Oroveso bids his tears to flow at last—they are permitted, he says, to a father—the people go on cursing Norma. She and Pollione are led to the flaming sacrificial pyre as the opera ends on a thundered E-minor chord.

Il Pirata

OPERA SERIA in two acts. *Libretto:* By Felice Romani, based upon the three-act *mélodrame Bertram, ou Le Pirate,* by "Raimond" (Isidore J. S. Taylor), produced at the Théâtre du Panorama-Dramatique, Paris, on November 26, 1826, with music by Alexandre and choreography by Renausy[1]; *Bertram,* in turn, had been derived from Charles Robert Maturin's five-act verse tragedy *Bertram, or The Castle of Saint-Aldobrand* (Drury Lane Theatre, London, 1816). At its première, *Il Pirata* formed part of a triple bill with the ballets *Don Eutichio della Castagna* (choreographed by Salvatore Taglioni to unidentified music) and *Alceste* (choreographed by Antonio Cortesi to unidentified music). *Original cast:*

IMOGENE, *wife of Ernesto, Duke of Caldora,* *formerly in love with Gualtiero*	Henriette Méric-Lalande
ADELE, *Imogene's chief lady-in-waiting*	Marietta Sacchi
GUALTIERO, *ex-Count of Montalto, partisan* *of King Manfredi, now an exile and* *head of the Aragonese pirates*	Giovanni Battista Rubini
ITULBO, *companion of Gualtiero*	Lorenzo Lombardi
GOFFREDO, *former tutor of Gualtiero,* *now a hermit*	Pietro Ansilioni
ERNESTO, *Duke of Caldora, an* *Anjou partisan*	Antonio Tamburini

Published: Twice in piano-vocal score by Ricordi Milan; in 1827, with disjunct plate numbers (overture: 3364; Imogene's final aria: 3381), and in a later edition, with plate number 108189; by the Calcografia e Copisteria de' Reali Teatri (Girard, later Cottrau), with disjunct plate numbers (the *sinfonia:* 680), 1827–1828; also by Marquerie Frères, Paris, 1842. Auto-graph score in the Naples Conservatory library[2]; manuscript copy and separate sections there, including a short score of the *sinfonia;* manuscript copy, with autograph annotations, in the archives of the Teatro La Fenice, Venice; manuscript copy in the library of the Conservatorio Giuseppe Verdi, Milan. Dedicated to "*la Signora Duchessa Litta dei principi Bel-gioioso di Este*" (Camilla Lomellini, wife of conte Pompeo Litta Visconti Arese).

PERFORMANCE DATA. *Il Pirata* was staged at the Teatro San Carlo, Naples, on May 30, 1828, with Adelaide Comelli-Rubini (Imogene) and Giovanni Battista Rubini (Gualtiero).[3] Rome was introduced to Bellini on January 7, 1829, when *Il Pirata* was put on at the Teatro Argentina; Luigia Boc-cabadati was the Imogene, Giovanni David the Gualtiero, Luigi Mag-giorotti the Ernesto. During an 1829 summer season at the Teatro della Canobbiana, Milan, the original La Scala cast was heard in twenty-four performances of *Il Pirata*. Bellini adapted and rehearsed the opera for its first Venice hearing (Teatro La Fenice, January 16, 1830),[4] with Giuditta Grisi (Imogene), Clementina Pellegrini (Adele), Lorenzo Bonfigli (Gual-tiero), Rainieri Pocchini Cavalieri (Itulbo), Gaetano Antoldi (Goffredo), and Giulio Pellegrini (Ernesto). Trieste heard *Il Pirata* for the first time on December 28, 1830, at the Teatro Grande, with Caroline Unger (Imogene), Giambattista Genero (Gualtiero), and Celestino Salvatori (Ernesto). The Teatro Comunale, Bologna, presented *Il Pirata* on October 2, 1830, with Adelaide Comelli-Rubini (Imogene), Rubini (Gualtiero), and Maggiorotti (Ernesto). At Vicenza in the summer of 1830, the im-presario Perottin, who earlier that year had not accepted Bellini's terms for composing a new opera for the Teatro Eretenio, staged *Il Pirata* there with Emilia Bonini (Imogene), Rubini (Gualtiero), and Umberto Beret-toni (Ernesto); this production proved so popular that it was repeated, together with *La Straniera*, during the Carnival season of 1830-1831. *Il Pirata* was staged at the Teatro La Munizione, Messina, in 1831, and was played there on February 27, 1832, when Bellini was present. Soon there-after, the opera was staged all across Italy. Charles Jahant informed me that during the very early 1880's, a contralto named Eufemia Barlani-Dini sang the role of Ernesto in Rome, at the Teatro Carcano in Milan, and at the Teatro Nuovo, Naples.

   Il Pirata was staged outside Italy for the first time at the Kärntnertor-theater, Vienna, on February 25, 1828, with Comelli-Rubini (Imogene), Rubini (Gualtiero), and Tamburini (Ernesto). During the remainder of Bellini's lifetime, it was presented widely throughout Europe and America, in many places being the first Bellini opera to be heard. It was staged at

Dresden, October 31, 1829; London, His Majesty's Theatre, April 17, 1830, with Méric-Lalande as Imogene[5]; Madrid, May 9, 1830; Paris, Théâtre-Italien, February 1, 1832, with Wilhelmine Schröder-Devrient (Imogene) and Rubini,[6] the first of fifteen performances there that season; New York, Richmond Hill Theater, December 5, 1832; Lisbon, May 7, 1834; Havana, 1834; Mexico City, January 16, 1835. During the years from 1830 to 1835, *Il Pirata* was also sung in German translation, frequently in an "arrangement" by a local *Kapellmeister:* Graz, January 20, 1830; Budapest, August 23, 1830; Munich (as *Der Seeräuber*), October 31, 1830; Prague, summer 1831; Berlin, Königsstädtischestheater, August 31, 1831; Amsterdam, 1833.

To inaugurate the centenary commemoration of Bellini's death, *Il Pirata* was revived at Rome on New Year's Day 1935, when Tullio Serafin conducted. It was staged at the Teatro Massimo Bellini, Catania, on November 5, 1951, when Manno Wolf-Ferrari conducted, and the cast was headed by Lucy Kelston (Imogene), Renzo Pigni (Gualtiero), and Giangiacomo Guelfi (Ernesto). Kelston was again the Imogene when *Il Pirata* led off a season at the Teatro Massimo, Palermo, on January 21, 1958; with her in the cast were Mirto Picchi, Giuseppe Taddei, Enrico Campi and Mariano Caruso. The staging was by Franco Enriquez, with scenery and costumes by Piero Zuffi; that production was transferred to La Scala, Milan, where, on May 19, 1958, it became the most notable modern revival of *Il Pirata*. The cast was headed by Maria Meneghini Callas (Imogene), Franco Corelli (Gualtiero), Ettore Bastianini (Ernesto), and Plinio Clabassi (Goffredo); the conductor was Antonio Votto. Callas repeated her Imogene at Carnegie Hall, New York, on January 27, 1959, when the American Opera Society presented *Il Pirata* in concert form. On June 13, 1967, the Maggio Musicale Fiorentino offered *Il Pirata* at the Teatro Comunale, Florence, with Montserrat Caballé (Imogene), Flaviano Labò (Gualtiero), and Piero Cappuccilli (Ernesto). Caballé was again the Imogene (with her husband, Bernabé Martí, as Gualtiero, Vincente Sardinero as Ernesto) when *Il Pirata* was sung in concert form at Drury Lane Theatre, London, on June 22, 1969, and at Cincinnati on July 5, 1969, in a production by the Cincinnati Summer Opera.

THE LIBRETTO. The early printed librettos for *Il Pirata* include this *avvertimento* by Romani:

"Duca Ernesto di Caldora, a very powerful Sicilian leader, was hopelessly enamored of the beautiful Imogene, and desired to marry her; but her heart already belonged to Gualtiero, conte di Montalto. The duca di Caldora, in order to take revenge upon his favored rival—who, like Imogene's elderly father, is a partisan of Manfredi[7]—sets himself to favor the designs of Charles of Anjou, a project in which he succeeds so well that, upon Manfredi's death, the Angevin party triumphs in Sicily, and Gualtiero, defeated in battle, is persecuted and proscribed.

"Gualtiero fled to Aragon, the king of which, an enemy of the Angevins, was a claimant to dominion over Sicily; but he did not find in that kingdom the protection that he had hoped for. No alternative remained to him as a way of damaging his enemies but that of arming a squadron of Aragonese pirates, with whom, acting the pirate for a full ten years, he waged bitter war on the Angevins, always hoping to be able to vindicate himself and recover his beloved.

"But she was lost to him because the duca di Caldora had taken Imogene's old father prisoner and had forced the miserable girl to buy her father's life from him by giving him her hand.

"The pirates' boldness reached such intensity that Charles of Anjou was forced to send the full strength of Sicily against them, entrusting the command to the duca di Caldora. The two squadrons faced one another in the Straits of Messina, and Gualtiero was defeated after a long battle and forced to flee with a single vessel. Overtaken by a storm, he was cast up on the coast of Sicily not far from Caldora, where the unhappy Imogene languished, weak and afflicted.

"The action begins at this point. What happened thereafter will be seen in the *melodrama*. The author tried to be clearer than has proved possible; if he has not succeeded, the blame lies with the necessity of being brief."

In the libretto, Gualtiero encounters Imogene, tells her who he is, and castigates her for having betrayed him by marrying his rival and persecutor. He wants her to abandon Ernesto and flee with him: living together at sea, he says, they will find alleviation for their distress. But Imogene replies that she has sacrified herself to save her father's life and that now, a wife and mother, she belongs to her husband and infant son. Informed secretly of Gualtiero's presence in his home, Ernesto surprises his enemy and his wife together. The two men duel, and Gualtiero kills Ernesto. A council of knights condemns Gualtiero to death. Imogene goes mad.

Pastura wrote[8]: "This is the plot in its final version, as we can determine today from the autograph score of the opera surviving in the library of the Conservatorio San Pietro a Maiella at Naples. But it will be useful to add that the finale of *Il Pirata* underwent many variations in the libretto according to the epoch and theater in which it was being performed and because of the singer who was the protagonist, who certainly wanted the curtain to close upon a high note or some theatrical bravado).

"First of all, it must be noted that Felice Romani had the action conclude with an insurrection of the pirates, who rushed in to save their leader—who, rejecting any assistance, preferred to throw himself from a bridge into an abyss. This occurs in a scene of a few verses, of which Bellini did not set a single syllable, and which probably remains in the libretto at the poet's wish."

But the music for that alternative finale exists: it occupies the last pages of the very autograph in the Naples Conservatory which Pastura had just cited.[9] As Friedrich Lippmann wrote[10]: "The orchestra starts with the music from the early *Sinfonia* in E-flat major already used in the slow section of the overture; the chorus of knights (*'La tua sentenza'*) is in dialogue with Gualtiero; the chorus of pirates joins them; the last exclamation by the chorus—*'Che orror!'*—is followed by sixteen measures of orchestral epilogue. . . . Today we cannot tell whether the opera was given with this ending at the première or whether Bellini deleted it from subsequent performances (he did not do so in the autograph), or if this deletion was made only for the first edition of the piano reduction."

Pastura noted[11]: "As for the occasional variants referred to, we find that a libretto printed at the time of a performance of *Il Pirata* given at the Teatro Comunale in Catania in 1858* has, instead of the usual finale, the scene in which Gualtiero delivers himself over to his enemies to be judged. And thus the opera, rather than ending with Imogene's desperate invective: *'O sole! ti vela—di tenebre oscure,'* ends with Gualtiero's cabaletta (which in the original edition precedes the scene of Imogene's delirium): *'Ma non fia sempre odiata, la mia memoria, io spero,'* after which the Pirate, who has been disarmed, pulls a dagger from beneath his mantle and kills himself."[12]

The scene is Sicily in the thirteenth century.

Act I: Scenes 1–4. "Seashore near Caldora. In the background, an ancient monastery, the refuge of a hermit":

Scene 1—"When the curtain rises, a terrible storm has already begun. We see a ship in great danger, driven to and fro by the winds and the waves. The beach and the rocks are full of fishermen attempting to rescue the miserable men near shipwreck. The hermit urges them on. Little by little, the place becomes full of people. The storm is at its climax." The sailors are brought safely ashore.

Scene 2—"The people rush away; in the meantime, the shipwrecked men saved by the fishermen come from the beach. Gualtiero supported by Itulbo is among them. The Hermit runs up to them with the greatest interest." The Hermit (Goffredo) recognizes Gualtiero, who asks if Imogene has remained faithful to him, and Goffredo answers ambiguously.

Scene 3—"The returning fishermen and the others." The fishermen

* [Pastura's note]: It is preserved in the Museo Belliniano.

say that "the noble lady" is coming from Caldora to be of help. When Goffredo thereupon urges Gualtiero to hide, Gualtiero divines that the lady is Imogene—and repeats that without hope of having her he would want to die. Goffredo takes Gualtiero out of sight and then returns to Itulbo.

Scene 4—"Imogene, Adele, ladies-in-waiting, and the others. All go to meet her." Imogene questions Itulbo about the pirates and their leader; when he, hiding the truth, says that the leader may be in chains or dead, she reacts in horror. "At a signal from Adele, the pirates move some distance away; Imogene leads Adele aside." Imogene recounts a terrifying and mystifying dream that she has had about Gualtiero. Gualtiero, half-emerging, recognizes Imogene and starts toward her, but Goffredo forces him to go back inside. Imogene has heard his voice, which Itulbo assures her is that of a sorrowing, distraught shipwrecked man. Imogene herself is almost demented with grief. Goffredo, Adele, and the chorus urge her to return to the castle, assuring her that the strangers will be cared for.

Scenes 5–6. "In the Castle of Caldora, a loggia giving on the gardens. It is night":

Scene 5—"The pirates come in, drinking and giving themselves over to their disorderly joy. Then Itulbo enters to restrain them." He disperses them by telling them that the Duchess is approaching and that they must be prudent.

Scene 6—"Imogene and Adele, then Gualtiero." For a reason she cannot understand, Imogene has sent Adele to invite the stranger whose sorrowing voice she heard on the beach to come to her. "Gualtiero arrives upstage, walking slowly, and remains wrapped in his mantle without looking at Imogene." He refuses her offer of assistance. When she is about to leave, he reveals his identity to her and they embrace. Drawing away, she tells him to flee: "This is the court of Ernesto," with whom a fatal knot has joined her. She explains that she had to marry the Duke to save her father's life. "Imogene's ladies-in-waiting enter with her young son. She sees him and cries out in fear," calling him "my son." Gualtiero seizes the child and seems about to draw his dagger, but desists at Imogene's plea. Adele returns to say that the victorious Duke has arrived unexpectedly, that his people have gathered to honor him, and that Imogene is awaited. All leave.

Scenes 7–9. "Exterior of the Castle of Caldora, illuminated. Military march: applause by the knights; then Ernesto":

Scene 7—The knights and Ernesto celebrate his crushing defeat of the pirates.

Scent 8—"Imogene, Adele, ladies-in-waiting, and the others. Ernesto goes forward to receive Imogene." He tells her that the pirate leader escaped, and asks what succor she has given the shipwrecked men. When she replies that it was her thought to assist and interrogate them, he announces that he has ordered the Hermit, who saved their leader, to bring him to the Castle.

Scene 9—"The Hermit, Gualtiero, Itulbo, the pirates, and the others. They stop upstage." When Ernesto asks to speak with the leader of the shipwrecked men, Itulbo prevents Gualtiero from stepping forward, and himself pretends to be the leader. At first, Ernesto—suspicious of all who come from the sea—says that the men will remain respected prisoners. But at Imogene's request, he tells them that they may depart the next morning. Gualtiero is with difficulty restrained from attacking Ernesto. At last, Imogene leaves with her ladies; Gualtiero is led away by Itulbo and the Hermit, and Ernesto remains alone, lost in grave thought.

Act II: Scenes 1–4. "Salon leading to Imogene's rooms":

Scene 1—"Chorus of ladies, then Adele." The ladies and Adele discuss Imogene's agitation and depression; then the ladies leave.

Scene 2—"Adele and Imogene." Adele persuades Imogene to receive Gualtiero, who has sworn not to leave Caldora without seeing her. As the two women are about to go out, they hear Ernesto approaching.

Scene 3—"Ernesto and the others." Ernesto upbraids Imogene for her melancholy and accuses her of still loving Gualtiero. Replying "When I was taken from my father, this love was not hidden: you wanted my hand and did not care about my heart," she finally admits that she loves Gualtiero.

Scene 4—"A knight appears and hands a paper to Ernesto." Reading the message, Ernesto exclaims: "Gualtiero on these shores!" He is infuriated to learn that Imogene has already spoken to Gualtiero, and demands to know where he is. When she cannot tell him, he becomes enraged and rushes out, followed by the bewildered Imogene.

Scenes 5–7. "Loggia in the Castle of Caldora, as in Act I. Dawn is near":

Scene 5—"Gualtiero and Itulbo." Itulbo attempts to dissuade Gualtiero from his determination either to persuade Imogene to his "final proposal," or to sell his life dearly in avenging himself on Ernesto. But Gualtiero will not listen.

Scene 6—"Imogene and Gualtiero." Imogene warns Gualtiero that his presence at Caldora is known to Ernesto. He pleads with her to flee with him on one of the two ships he can provide. But Imogene remains firm and tries to bid him farewell.

Scene 7—"Ernesto at the back of the stage; the others, then Adele." Ernesto bursts in upon Imogene and Gualtiero as they are parting.

Gualtiero challenges him to combat, and they leave. Swooning, Imogene throws herself into her ladies' arms, but recovers to say that she must separate Ernesto and Gualtiero or die. Resisting Adele's attempt to stop her, she goes in search of the two men.

Scenes 8–10. "Ground-floor courtyard of the Castle. On both sides, passageways leading into the rooms; upstage, grand arcades beyond which can be seen the outdoors, with a cascade of water over which passes a bridge leading to the Castle":

Scene 8—"To the sound of a funeral march, Ernesto's soldiers enter with his weapons, of which they make a trophy. Then come the knights, afflicted and lost in thought; then Adele and the ladies. All group themselves around the trophy." They grieve over the death of Ernesto, killed by "a traitor, a vile pirate," and call for summary vengeance, which the knights swear upon the trophy.

Scene 9—"From one of the back galleries, Gualtiero, depressed and thoughtful, advances toward the others wrapped in his mantle. He throws down his sword, but asserts that his supporters still are capable of rescuing him. Against their will, the knights are awed by his spirit. After expressing the hope that the woman for whom he fought may one day forgive him and weep at his tomb, he leaves with the knights. Adele tells the others that the miserable, sorrowing Imogene is approaching.

Scene 10—"Imogene, leading her son by the hand. Her mind is wandering. She advances slowly, looking about her in confusion. She weeps. The ladies, staring at her and weeping, prepare to depart." Imogene does not know whether it is day or night, whether she is alive or has been buried. She imagines that she has seen Ernesto dying on the beach, that she saved her son from malefactors, and that Ernesto forgave her. She begs Adele to find her father and gain his forgiveness. "A lugubrious sound is heard from the Salon of the Council," and the knights are heard proclaiming that Gualtiero has been condemned to death. Raving, Imogene demands that Gualtiero be freed and allowed to leave. Adele and the ladies try to lead her away, but she runs from them. They follow her.

THE OPERA. *Sinfonia:* D major, 3/4 time, *allegro con fuoco,* a chordal introduction alternates between fortissimo and pianissimo, with intervening one- and two-measure pauses. *Andante maestoso* (p. 2*), Bellini now introduces an altered, greatly more interesting version of melodic material that he had adapted for the *Adelson e Salvini sinfonia* from his 1823 *Sinfonia* in E-flat major. The D-minor *allegro agitato* section that follows (p. 4) is in part newly composed, but again in part borrowed from the *Adelson sinfonia.*[13] Any *pastiche* effect is banished by the effective-

* Page references here are to the Ricordi piano-vocal score with plate number 108189.

ness with which the entire overture prefigures (despite its fortissimo formula close, p. 11) the alternately melancholy, amorously intense, and violent action of *Il Pirata* as Romani and Bellini created it.

Act I: Scenes 1–4. "Seashore near Caldora":

Scene 1 (p. 12)—"*Coro d'Introduzione,*" G minor 4/4 time, *allegro agitato assai.* This storm scene both owes something to Rossini's *Mosè in Egitto* and faintly prefigures the opening of Verdi's *Otello.* Andrea Della Corte evoked its character well[14]: "The tempest that is its motive, its inciting image, is represented by descriptive and psychological elements. Its motion is impetuous. Distant thunder, lightning, terror. The chorus intervenes quickly [*"Ciel! qual procella orribile,"* s, t, bs, p. 13], with anxious accents doubling the orchestral writing, in shouts of terror interspersed with fearful pauses. Elemental resources and means, but genuine and internal. Austerely, almost hieratically (the Rossinian *Mosè* had not been forgotten), the voice of the Hermit rises in the silence [*"Non disperate, o figli,"* p. 15]. The dynamics decrease, the agogics increase, p. 19; a long silence, then a collective shout: *'Ahi miseri!'* At this point the descriptive elements disappear and only feelings of horror and pity emerge." The prayer *"Nume che imperi"* (p. 24), impressively sung by the Hermit and the fishermen, is an improved borrowing from *Adelson e Salvini* (the orchestral part in Salvini's *"Nelly, che pena,"* p. 70). Up to a point, the rescue scene (begun on p. 30) is brilliantly conceived, but it tends to banality as it stretches on. It finally dies away (p. 41) in the orchestra, *"decrescendo poco a poco . . . mancando . . . morendo."*

Scene 2 (p. 42)—"*Scena e Cavatina,*" G minor, 4/4 time. Gualtiero and Goffredo (the Hermit) converse in recitative, in the accompaniment of which orchestral tremolos are used evocatively. *Allegro moderato* (p. 44), Gualtiero the fighter sings *"Di mia vendetta,"* but returns to recitative immediately, asking about Imogene. Then (p. 45), *allegro moderato,* his fine cavatina *"Nel furor delle tempeste"* tells how Imogene seemed to him an angel as he thought of her at sea; this in music of a purely Bellinian melodic texture which perfectly portrays Gualtiero the lover.

Scene 3 (p. 49)—G major, 4/4 time, allegro. The chorus of fishermen returning from the Castle (*"Del disastro di questi infelici"*) momentarily lowers the level of musicodramatic interest, which is raised only a little by Gualtiero's cabaletta-like *"Per te di vane lagrime"* (B-flat major, *allegro moderato,* p. 56), melodic material for which Bellini borrowed from *Adelson e Salvini* (Salvini's *"Oh! quante amare lagrime,"* p. 74), and it is somewhat enfeebled by an obvious lack of musical relevance to Gualtiero, especially when (after a choral interjection, p. 58) he repeats it (p. 61). The scene ends quietly (p. 65), after Gualtiero, Itulbo,

Goffredo, and the fishermen sum it all up somewhat repetitiously; Goffredo then leads Gualtiero inside and returns to Itulbo.

Scene 4 (p. 66)—"*Scena e Cavatina*," E-flat major, 4/4 time, maestoso. After an orchestral introduction of considerable variety in twenty-three measures, Imogene initiates (p. 67) the revelation of her strong character in recitative that becomes (p. 68) a dialogue with Itulbo. In B-flat major, *andante mosso assai*, Imogene recounts (p. 70) her horrible dream to Adele in another passage of pure Belliniana, the cavatina "*Lo sognai ferito.*" It is merely the beginning of an unusually extended series (pp. 70–91) of self-expressive melodic effusions (with contrasting coloration from the two-part—s, c—chorus and Itulbo), a series marred only by irrelevant *fioriture*. One of the choral interjections, "*Vane larve*" (p. 77, underlying solo lines of both Imogene and Itulbo), especially contributes to the strong dramatic effect. In the *allegro moderato* (G major, p. 81), Imogene's "*Sventurata*" beautifully continues the line of Bellinian melodies, as does its extension in her "*Ah! sarai, fin ch'io respiro*" (p. 87).

Scenes 5–6. "In the Castle of Caldora, a loggia giving on the gardens":

Scene 5 (p. 92)—"*Coro di Pirati*," F major, 6/8 time, *allegro brillante*. This vacuous scene for Itulbo and the chorus of pirates (t, b) contains the stage direction (p. 93) "they listen—an echo repeats the *evvivas.*" This is the echo effect of which Bellini boasted in a letter of October 29, 1827, to Vincenzo Ferlito when he spoke of "a chorus of pirates, with echo, which gave so much pleasure [at the opera's première] because of the novelty of my having imagined the echo so well," but the echo does not save the chorus from banality.

Scene 6 (p. 108)—"*Recitativo*," B-flat major, 4/4 time, *allegro moderato*. Imogene and Adele converse in recitative, preparing for the appearance of Gualtiero. "*Scena e Duetto*," 4/4 time, andante, p. 110. Imogene soliloquizes in recitative until Gualtiero's entrance, after which (G minor, moderato, p. 113) the recitative continues as dialogue up to (p. 114) Imogene's touching arietta "*Se un giorno*," *andante mosso*, which Gualtiero repeats to other words a tone higher (p. 115) as he begins to reveal his identity. The immediately succeeding recitative of mutual recognition (p. 115) is powerful in theatrical effect: it ends, on the word "*desso*" (G minor, allegro, p. 116), when Imogene sings a descending octave scale against an orchestral sixteenth-note downward plunge of almost two octaves, fortissimo, as they embrace. After a fermata, Imogene sings another quasi-aria "*Tu sciagurato*" (p. 116), telling Gualtiero that this is Ernesto's court and urging him to flee. The forceful dramatic tone is maintained as he answers "*Lo so . . .*" (p. 117) and they continue in melodic dialogue. Imogene's defense of her marriage ("*Il genitor cadente*," p. 120) ends in an *a piacere rallentando* descending chromatic run (p. 121).

With a change to E-flat major, 2/4 time, *andante sostenuto*, Gualtiero denounces her cruelty to him (*"Pietoso al padre!"* p. 122), wonderfully mixing hatred and love; he too breaks off, really unexpressed, after a descending (diatonic) run. For some measures, they join in duet (pp. 124–126), with a return to C major (p. 125). Then (allegro, p. 126) recitative is employed for the entrance of the ladies with Imogene's son and for Gualtiero's almost murderous reaction. The episode ends with Imogene pleading: *"Pietà! pietà!"* (p. 127). Now Gualtiero starts (*"Bagnato delle lagrime,"* allegro, p. 128) his duet with Imogene, the melodic beginning of which Bellini brought over from the *sinfonia* for *Adelson e Salvini* (page 7 of the Ricordi piano-vocal score with plate numbers 108595–108596)[15]; but even when Imogene joins him (p. 129), this duet provides only an ending that allows Gualtiero to leave rather than a solution or culmination for the intense theatrical drama that it follows. *"Recitativo,"* C major, *allegro moderato*, p. 134. Imogene is thanking Heaven for her son's safety when a band is heard from inside and Adele comes out to announce the unexpected arrival of Ernesto; the people are awaiting only Imogene to give him a victor's festal welcome.

Scenes 7–9. "Exterior of the Castle of Caldora, illuminated." Admirable passages do not conceal the fact that these scenes are the weakest in the opera:

Scene 7 (p. 137)—*"Marcia e Coro,"* F major, 4/4 time, moderato (then marziale). After an empty, overlong orchestral introduction, the warriors initiate the finale with the undistinguished chorus *"Più temuto"* (p. 139). Then, in an *"Aria . . . Seguito della Scena VII,"* F major, 2/4 time, *andante molto sostenuto*, in lieu of a traditional entrance aria, Ernesto breaks precipitately into his flowery, vacuous *"Sì, vincemmo"* (p. 149), which resembles one of the lesser baritone outbursts by Donizetti or the very early Verdi. Bellini borrowed it, altering only details, from Adelson's *"Obbliarti! abbandonarti!"* in *Adelson e Salvini* (p. 140 of the Ricordi piano-vocal score with plate number 108595). The tempo shifts to allegro (p. 151) as the chorus, needlessly, again celebrates Ernesto— and then to *allegro marziale* (p. 153) for what amounts to Ernesto's choral-supported cabaletta, though it reuses the text beginning *"Sì, vincemmo."*

The meaningless theatrical stasis introduced by that repetition of text is particularly difficult to understand because the libretto published for the première of *Il Pirata*, at La Scala in 1827, contains at this point Romani lines that Bellini apparently never set, though they both contain information about Ernesto's character and move the plot situation forward: Ernesto says that though he stained himself furiously with enemy blood, he could not satisfy his desires, as Gualtiero fled unpunished, without his blood having flowed. They would have been far more effective at this place than the device of having Ernesto twice repeat the "*Sì, vincemmo*" text in a new tempo and supported by the chorus until the end of the scene. Now only the emptiest, most offensive aspect of Ernesto's character has been displayed; the drama has not advanced a millimeter.[16]

Scene 8 (p. 161)—"*Recitativo*." After Imogene's strained greeting of Ernesto, she learns that he has summoned the Hermit and the leader of the shipwrecked men, who are now approaching.

Scene 9 (p. 165)—*allegro moderato*. The Hermit, Gualtiero, Itulbo, and the pirates enter at the back. When Ernesto asks that the pirate leader make himself known, Itulbo responds. "*Finale I . . . Seguito della Scena IX*," 2/4 time, allegro, p. 166. Ernesto, addressing Itulbo, denounces him as "a felon, the vile Gualtiero"; he orders the shipwrecked men held as respected prisoners. But Itulbo persuades Imogene to intervene, and Ernesto agrees to let the men leave for their home the next morning. In an aside (p. 170), Gualtiero denounces Imogene as a traitress. When Ernesto talks with his knights, Gualtiero furtively speaks to Imogene while the Hermit and Itulbo try to screen them from view.

"*Quintetto nel Finale I . . . Seguito della Scena IX*," A minor, 4/4 time, *largo agitato*, p. 172. Gualtiero initiates ("*Parlarti ancor*") a rich concerted number (pp. 172–191) strong enough as an entity and in detail to compensate largely for the feebleness of the immediately preceding scenes. Julian Budden wrote[17]: "[Bellini's] music never comments on the poet's lines: it dissolves them into a flow of song. The care which he brought to the exact scanning of words merely aids this process of fusion, giving to one of the most artificial of art-forms an illusion of complete naturalness. Shifts of mood are reflected less in the harmonies than in the physical contours of the cantilena. A particularly fine example in *Il Pirata* is the quintet in Act I, where the long-breathed melody, with its contrapuntal proliferations, derives entirely from the germinal motif embodying Gualtiero's desperate cry: '*Parlarti ancor per poco*.'" And Andrea Della Corte, after quoting Bellini's letter of October 29, 1827, to Vincenzo Ferlito—". . . the largo has been much praised as a work of great art, and also for making an effect by the domination of the principal song, and was much applauded"—criticized this ensemble incisively and with illumination[18]: "And the 'work of art' in this famous 'quintet' (which unites six voices and also the chorus) is certainly exquisite. In substance it is like a two-voice aria accompanied by soloists, chorus, and instruments. Adele's part moves almost parallel with Imogene's; Itulbo's often is united with Gualtiero's—logical associations, the one [Adele] being the lady's confidante, the other [Itulbo] the companion of the protagonist. Occasionally Ernesto emerges with a distinct phrase. The Hermit performs a simple bass's duty. The chorus, which has a triple function—harmonic, contrapuntal, rhythmic—fills out the harmony, replies to the solos, and fills spaces by means of marked beats. The orchestra doubles the voices, blends them, sustains them. The technical value of the composition is completed by sober means. The artistic value lies in the harmonious beauty of the constituents. The composition rouses and disturbs. The quivering of the rhythms sustains the disquiet. The sound-atmosphere sometimes trembles feverishly, sometimes envelops and soothes. The equilibrium is miraculous, as in the *concertato* of *I Puritani*. Life inheres in the secure motion, as constant as in a [Leonardo] Leo, Bach, or Handel largo. Each voice is integrated with the other voices and surrenders its own timbre. The first motive is Gualtiero's, alert and virile, peremptory, headstrong. The second is Imogene's, wearied by anguish and love, feminine and confused. A work of art and of theater. Not resolving the action, but expansive, a venting of sorrowful spirits and, as a venting, almost a catharsis."

After those masterly pages, the *"Stretta del Finale* I," allegro 4/4 time (pp. 192–229, with B-flat major established clearly at the *allegro molto agitato*, p. 196), is a near-disastrous fall into unchallenged conventionality. One can only agree with Della Corte[19]: "One would gladly make less of the *stretta* of the finale at its present length." For the ensemble beginning on page 200, Bellini took up, as accompaniment, a musical idea he had used first in his student *Sinfonia* in E-flat major and then had repeated several times in *Adelson e Salvini* (see pp. 25 and 218).

As the act ends, Ernesto remains alone, "wrapped in grave thoughts."

Act II: Scenes 1–4. "Salon leading to Imogene's rooms":

Scene 1 (p. 230)—*"Coro d'Introduzione,"* allegro moderato, 6/8 time, C major. After an undistinguished orchestral introduction, the Chorus of Ladies (p. 231) discusses Imogene's sad condition with Adele, who then asks them to leave. The charming harmonization of this chorus (of which Bellini was naïvely proud) is its only virtue.

Scene 2 (p. 240)—*"Recitativo."* Adele and Imogene are talking of Gualtiero, who has asserted that he will not leave Caldora before seeing Imogene alone; nearby noise suddenly informs them of Ernesto's approach.

Scene 3 (p. 242)—*"Scena e Duetto,"* 4/4 time, allegro. In recitative, Ernesto denounces Imogene for avoiding him only because she is sick at heart; she defends her state of mind by citing the oppression of her family and the death of her father, whereupon Ernesto accuses her of still loving Gualtiero. A major, 4/4 time, *allegro moderato*, Ernesto furiously attacks her, saying that she conceals her secret love badly: this arietta (*"Tu m'apristi,"* p. 244) does little to fill in Ernesto's facelessness; its essentially conventional baritonal character extends even to Imogene's reply (*"Quando al padre io fu rapita,"* p. 248), in which she asserts that Ernesto knew of her love for Gualtiero when he took her from her father: "You wanted my hand and did not care about having my heart." Imogene's admission (p. 253) that she still loves Gualtiero could have become a musicodramatic climax of great power; instead, it is entrusted to monotonous recitative *a piacere*, which places the singing actress in the position of having to create intense emotion almost unaided. The succeeding larghetto duet (F major, 6/8 time, p. 254) improves matters little. It succeeds, however, in expressing verbally Ernesto's sorrowing hunger for love, thus giving some chiaroscuro to his character (it is reminiscent, but only in its words, of the king's *"Ella giammai m'amò"* in Verdi's *Don Carlos*); it also underlines Imogene's longing for oblivion in death.

Scene 4 (p. 258)—C major, 4/4 time, *allegro moderato*. A knight brings Ernesto word that Gualtiero is in Caldora and has been seen with Imogene. To his demand that she tell him where Gualtiero is, she replies that she does not know, whereupon Ernesto asserts that he will find out. Della Corte spoke accurately of the "ugly tones" of Imogene's *"Ah! fuggi"* (p. 260), which soon becomes a duet emphasizing that ugliness by parallel motion of the two voices (pp. 261–262). She warns Ernesto that their son may die with him, but he is unheeding; referring to Gualtiero, his words are, "With his vile blood, yours will flow."

Mr. Stefan Zucker pointed out to me that this scene contains curious "reminiscences" of *Adelson e Salvini*. Beginning (p. 260) with Imogene's *"Ah! fuggi, spietato,"* it makes use of a brief melodic cell (see also line for Fernando, p. 261, and lines for Imogene, pp. 262 and 263) which similarly recurs several times in *"Amico, contento, contento pur sono!"* (*Adelson* score with plate number 108595, pp. 218, 219, 223, 224); there, however, it is given first to the deeper voice. Later (p. 266), for Imogene's words *"sta, sul capo ti sta,"* the last four repeated thrice, it adapts, from the Salvini–Bonifacio duet (p. 81) the four-tone descending phrase, followed by a wide upward leap and a small flourish of *fioriture*, sung there by Salvini to the words *"fier, sì, fier dolor, a così fiero dolor!"* (Bonifacio's simultaneous words are *"matti dovrò condurvi or, dovrò condurvi, sì, or, or!"*) Bellini clearly attached to this figuration some significance or value unrelated to the differing text-words that it sets.

Scenes 5–7. "Loggia in the Castle of Caldora, as in Act I":

Scene 5 (p. 267)—*"Scena,"* A minor, 4/4 time, *allegro molto*. Itulbo's pleas cannot deflect Gualtiero's determination to take revenge on Ernesto if Imogene refuses to set out to sea with him. As Imogene approaches, Itulbo leaves.

Scene 6 (p. 270)—"*Scena e Duetto*," 4/4 time, *allegro agitato*. In recitative, Gualtiero pleads with Imogene to run away with him. She refuses, saying "here I soon shall have revenge or death." This dramatic confrontation stirred Bellini to superb expressive dialogue (pp. 271–272). When Imogene breaks down in weeping (C major, *allegro moderato*, p. 272), though Gaultiero "is moved to pity," he in fact sings a conventional cavatina, "*Vieni, vieni*," which, though not ugly, is negative in effect. Imogene continues to refuse ("*Taci, taci*," A major, p. 275)— in this "*duetto*," the two never sing simultaneously, but repeat, rather, in increasingly florid measures, that the immense seas have no shore where they could hide. "*Scena e Terzetto . . . Seguito della Scena VI*," A major, 4/4 time, *allegro moderato*, p. 278. Telling Gualtiero that he must go on living and learn to forgive, Imogene starts to bid him farewell.[20]

Scene 7 (p. 279)—Ernesto enters and recognizes his enemy. In D major, 6/8 time, *andante sostenuto*, Gualtiero begins ("*Cedo al destin orribile*") the mediocre, *fioritura*-frilled trio, in which both tenor and baritone are required to perform difficult, extensive roulades (p. 286).[21] Ernesto accepts Gualtiero's challenge to a duel; the two men depart; and ("*Recitativo . . . Seguito della Scena VII*," pp. 298–300) Imogene resists Adele's attempts to stop her from following them.

Scenes 8–10. "Ground-floor courtyard of the Castle":

Scene 8 (p. 301)—"*Coro*," C major, 4/4 time, *allegro assai maestoso*. Gualtiero has killed Ernesto, whose supporters are preparing a funeral trophy. The ladies and knights (s, t, bs) and Adele sing the fine mourning chorus "*Lasso! perir così*," swearing upon their leader's weapons that they will have revenge.

Scene 9 (p. 310)—"*Scena*," 4/4 time, *allegro maestoso*. In this oddly matte and inexpressive connective tissue, Adele recognizes the approaching Gualtiero; the chorus of ladies and knights threatens him; he silences them and (p. 312) throws his sword on the ground. They agree to his being judged by the Council. "*Scena ed Aria . . . Seguito della Scena IX*," *allegro maestoso*. Gualtiero concurs in their decision. He turns toward Adele and (C major *larghetto maestoso*[22]) sings (p. 315) the waxingly dramatic if conventional cavatina "*Tu vedrai la sventurata*," asking her to tell Imogene of his hope that one day she will weep at his tomb. *Allegro moderato*, p. 318, trumpets are heard from the Council Chamber. Then (A-flat major, p. 318), Adele and the chorus further tighten the tension by telling Gualtiero to follow them to the Chamber to be judged: his answer is that he now thinks only of death. C major, *allegro cantabile*, p. 324, after almost nine measures of orchestral delay, Gualtiero sings a

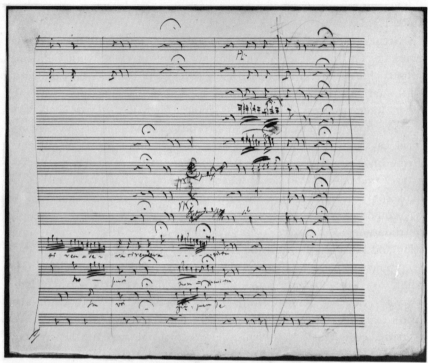

sort of coda to *"Tu vedrai"*: *"Ma non fia sempre odiata,"* pleading (with plenty of *fioriture* in sixteenth-notes grouped in fours) that he not be hated forever, that some future time have pity on his "traduced love." The knights and ladies assure him that his tomb will tell of his misfortunes. Gualtiero repeats (p. 328) his aria, which becomes most florid just before (p. 330) Adele and the chorus join in. With the knights, he starts toward the Council Chamber. *"Recitativo"* (p. 336, becoming lento, then allegro), Adele and the chorus comment on the approach of the distraught Imogene.

Scene 10 (p. 337)—*"Scena ed Aria Finale,"* F major, 4/4 time, *andante maestoso*. In effect, this is a "mad scene." Andrea Della Corte, again, analyzed it with accuracy and extraordinary insight[23]: "The final scene, Imogene's pitiful delirium, led Bellini to attempt pathetic effusions by means of the instruments, using them almost as musical expressions of the action [*mimica*]. If we examine carefully the stage directions prescribing the movements[24]—alternately more and less mournful—of Imogene and the development of the instrumental phrases, which also are varied in inflection, the relationship turns out to be very unsteady except during the final measures. The commentary on the action is unsuccessful. More important to notice is that these two pages [337–338] are the first of Bellini's to provide such fully instrumental songfulness. They do not consist of a melopoeia, but are made up of linked periods that are coherent in feeling, though the effort to prolong them is sometimes manifest. The Bellinian vocal drafting is incomplete if compared with later pages. In the accompaniment, and in some touches, it perhaps offers a point of departure for some pages in *L'Elisir d'amore*. However, the vocal episode that follows—initially [p. 340, *"Oh! s'io potessi"*] recitative, then arioso—is delicious. Now the delirium is described, sung, represented with evident, moving fondness. Also, the cantilena '*Col sorriso d'innocenza*' [F major, p. 344], preceded by a ritornello, moves in the direction of that expansion which will glow in *La Sonnambula*, and which here is agreeable without attaining profundity in the climaxes. The final aria belongs to another style—or, at least in features, recalls Spontini or Rossini. The outburst '*Oh, Sole*' [*allegro giusto, con forza*, p. 350] is powerful; the second phrase, '*Ma il sangue già gronda*' [p. 351] is pathetic. The final *fioriture* '*in modo lacerante*' [". . . *d'angoscia, d'affanno,*" p. 351] recall the practice of the period, make us see the end of the opera as more conditioned by its performance than determined by intrinsically

---

E—(Facing page) First two of eight autograph pages from *Il Pirata* in The Mary Flagler Cary Music Collection of the Pierpont Morgan Library, New York, beginning ". . . *ti renderà*" (Act II, Scene 7).

artistic elements." The last pages, that is, require Imogene to sing *"con gran forza . . . crescendo assai con gran forza"* above the voices of Adele and the soprano chorus in a terminal gesture that already had become banal.

As a musicodramatic whole, in an understanding performance, *Il Pirata* greatly exceeds the combined virtues of its separate scenes and diminishes its own flaws. The reason for its immediate popularity in 1827 is referred to obliquely by Della Corte when[25] he calls it "the work of a young Italian romantic composer of opera who—for ardor, sincerity in composition, and study of the passions—was unequaled in the Italy of the time, and who sings, not better than, but differently from any other contemporary." But that *Il Pirata* can still live upon the stage after nearly a century and a half proves that in general the ardor, artistic dedication, and passionate insights of the twenty-five-year-old Bellini were transmuted successfully in the music into which he absorbed Romani's libretto, the longest (*Zaira* possibly excepted) of his scores.

I Puritani[1]

Opera seria *(melodramma serio)* in three parts. *Libretto:* By conte Carlo Pepoli, based upon the three-act historical drama *Têtes Rondes et cavaliers*, by Jacques-Arsène Ancelot[2] and Joseph-Xavier-Boniface Saintine, first staged at the Théâtre National du Vaudeville, Paris, on September 25, 1833 (with Mme Albert [Marie-Charlotte-Thérèse Vermet] as Lucy Walton, the role that became Elvira in *I Puritani*). *Composed:* 1834–1835. *Première* (as *I Puritani e i cavalieri*): Théâtre-Italien, Paris, January 24, 1835. *Original cast:*

Elvira, *daughter of Lord Valton*	Giulia Grisi
Enrichetta di Francia, *widow of Charles I, King of England, known as the Dame de Villeforte*	Mlle Amigo[3]
Lord Arturo Talbo, *Cavalier, Stuart partisan*	Giovanni Battista Rubini
Sir Bruno Roberton, *Puritan official*	M. Magliano
Sir Ricardo [*sic* in first printed libretto] Forth, *Puritan colonel*	Antonio Tamburini
Sir Giorgio, *brother of Lord Valton, retired Puritan colonel*	Luigi Lablache
Lord Gualtiero Valton	M. Profeti

Published: in full score by Cottrau-Ricordi, Naples/Milan, 189?, with plate number 100716; twice in piano-vocal score by Ricordi, Milan/Florence, with plate numbers 8551–8557, 1836, and without date, plate number 41685; by Pacini, Paris ("*Publication Posthume*"), with disjunct plate numbers (Introduction: 3148) and later with plate numbers 4061–4077;

by Mills, London, without date, with plate number 2752; by Schott's Söhne, Mainz/Antwerp, without date, with plate number 4585; by Girard (later Cottrau), Naples, with disjunct plate numbers (Introduction: 3121); by Clausetti, Naples, without date, with plate numbers 4468–4483. Autograph score in the Biblioteca Comunale, Palermo; manuscript copy, with autograph annotations, in the Archivio Ricordi, Milan[4]; two manuscript copies in the Naples Conservatory library. The partially autograph score of the revision intended for Malibran is in the Museo Belliniano, Catania, as are some pages of a manuscript copy of the original version, with autograph annotations; these latter, include textless melodic sketches quoted by Pastura (BSLS, pp. 580–581 and 590).

PERFORMANCE DATA. *I Puritani* immediately became popular: it was sung seventeen times during its first season at the Italien (more than two hundred times there through 1909). It was staged at His Majesty's Theatre, London, on May 21, 1835; at the Teatro alla Scala, Milan, on December 26, 1835, possibly in a pirated edition orchestrated by Cesare Pugni, with Sofia Dall'Oca Schoberlechner (Elvira), Antonio Poggi (Arturo), Carlo Marcolini (Riccardo), and Ignazio Marini (Sir Giorgio)[5]; and at the Teatro Carolino, Palermo, during the 1835–1836 season, as *Elvira e Arturo,* with Giuseppina Démery (Josephine De Méric) as Elvira. Billed as *I Puritani e i cavalieri,* the opera was put on at the Teatro La Fenice, Venice, on April 23, 1836, with Giuseppina Strepponi (Elvira), Assunta Ballelli (Enrichetta), Bartolomeo De Gattis (Talbo), Antonio Banciolini (Sir Bruno), Giuseppe Paltrinieri (Riccardo), Giovanni Schober[lechner] (Sir Giorgio), and Saverio Giorgi (Walton).[6] The opera was heard at the Teatro San Carlo, Naples, for the first time on January 3, 1837, with Caterina Chiesa Barrilli-Patti, the future mother of Adelina Patti (who later sang Elvira), Margherita Spadaccini, Paolo Barroilhet, Giovanni Basadonna, and Luigi Lablache. It was staged at the Teatro La Munizione, Messina, on June 27, 1838, when the Elvira was Fanny Maray. Some of the hundreds of other stagings of *I Puritani*— not necessarily the first in the cities named—have been the following (performances listed here were probably sung in Italian unless otherwise specified)—

1836: February 5—Teatro Apollo, Rome, as *Elvira Walton*[7] (it appears not to have been billed in Rome as *I Puritani* [*e i cavalieri*] until January 28, 1880, when Zina Dalty was the Elvira, Roberto Stagno the Talbo); February 10—Königliches Opernhaus, Berlin, in German translation by Carl August Ludwig, Ritter von Lichtenstein; April 26—Kärntnertortheater, Vienna (as *Die Puritaner,* in Lichtenstein's

German translation); September 26 or 29—Teatro de la Cruz, Madrid; October 28—Brünn (language unknown); November 9—Teatro Comunale, Bologna, with Giulia Grisi (Elvira), Giuseppina Lega (Enrichetta), Napoleone Moriani (Talbo), Alessandro Giacchini (Sir Bruno), Giorgio Ronconi (Riccardo), Carlo Porto (Sir Giorgio), and Domenico Raffaelli (Walton).

1836–1837: December 26—Teatro Grande, Trieste, with Giuseppina Strepponi (Elvira), during a season that also offered *I Capuleti e i Montecchi, La Sonnambula,* and *Norma.*

1837: February 4—Dublin; March 18—Prague (German); April 17—Teatro São Carlos, Lisbon; May 5—Theater an der Wien, Vienna; spring—Teatro del Corso, Faenza, with Strepponi (Elvira), Moriani (Talbo), Domenico Cosselli (Riccardo), and Felice Varesi (Sir Giorgio).

1838: spring—Teatro Comunale, Sinigaglia, probably with Eugenia Tadolini (Elvira), Moriani (Talbo), Giorgio Ronconi (Riccardo), Pietro Scalese (Sir Giorgio); repeated there during the 1853 *fiera,* with Erminia Frezzolini (Elvira), Carlo Boucardé (Talbo) Alessandro Ottaviani (Sir Giorgio), and Bouché (Walton)[8]; November —Copenhagen (Danish translation by Christian Frederik Güntelberg); December—Laibach (German).

1839: February 27—Basel (German); April 20—The Hague (French translation by Étienne Monnier); November—Algiers.

1840: January—St. Petersburg; February—Brussels (French); May 3—Lille (French); November 12—Munich (German translation by Franziska Ellmenreich); date unknown—Teatro Grande, Trieste, with Eugenia Tadolini (Elvira), Napoleone Moriani (Talbo), Sebastiano Ronconi (Sir Riccardo), and Ignazio Marini (Sir Giorgio).

1841: Carnival—Havana; June 2—Königsstädtischestheater, Berlin.

1842: Carnival—Alexandria, Egypt; summer—Teatro Italiano, Zákinthos (Zante).

1843: January 14—Ragusa, Dalmatia; Carnival—Mexico City; March 16 —Princess's Theatre, London (English translation by Gilbert Arthur A'Beckett); July 22—Chestnut Street Theater, Philadelphia.

1844: Palmo's Opera House, New York; spring—Stadttheater, Hamburg (language unknown); September—Palma de Mallorca.

1845: date unknown Valletta, Malta; date unknown Rio de Janeiro.

1859: date undetermined—Chicago, by the Strakosch Company.[9]

1883: October 29—Metropolitan Opera, New York (fourth evening of the inaugural season), with Marcella Sembrich (Elvira), Ida Corani (Enrichetta), Roberto Stagno (Arturo Talbo), Amadeo Grazzi (Benno [*sic,* for Bruno]), Giuseppe Kaschmann (Riccardo),

Giovanni Mirabella (Sir Giorgio), and Achile Augier (Walton).[10]

1906: December 3—Manhattan Opera House, New York (inauguration), with Cleofonte Campanini conducting, Regina Pinkert (Elvira), Alessandro Bonci (Arturo), Emilio Venturini (Sir Bruno), Mario Ancona (Riccardo), Vittorio Arimondi (Sir Giorgio), and Luigi Mugnoz (Walton).[11]

1917: February 18—Metropolitan Opera House, New York, with María Barrientos (Elvira), Hipólito Lázaro (Arturo), Giuseppe DeLuca (Riccardo), José Mardones (Sir Giorgio), and Angelo Bada (Benno [*sic* for Bruno]). After the fourth performance of this season (matinee, April 6), *I Puritani* disappeared from the Metropolitan, having been heard there only five times.

1921: date undetermined—Teatro Colón, Buenos Aires, with Barrientos (Elvira), Dino Borgioli (Talbo), Carlo Galeffi (Riccardo), and Adamo Didur (Sir Giorgio).[12]

1933: May 25—Teatro Comunale, Florence (first Maggio Musicale Fiorentino), with Tullio Serafin conducting, Mercedes Capsir (Elvira), Nadia Kovaceva (Enrichetta), Giacomo Lauri-Volpi (Arturo), Adrasto Simonti (Bruno), Mario Basiola (Riccardo), Ezio Pinza (Sir Giorgio), and Carlo Scattola (Walton).[13]

1935: January 25—Teatro Massimo Bellini, Catania (centenary celebrations), with Attilia Archi (Elvira) and Aldo Sinnone (Talbo).[14]

1949: January 19—Teatro La Fenice, Venice, with Maria Meneghini Callas (Elvira),[15] Mafalda Masini (Enrichetta), Antonio Pirni (Arturo), Ugo Savarese (Riccardo), Guglielmo Torcoli (Bruno).

1955: October 31—Chicago Civic Opera House, Chicago (seasonal opening), with Callas (Elvira), Giuseppe di Stefano (Arturo), Ettore Bastianini (Riccardo), Nicola Rossi-Lemeni (Sir Giorgio), and William Wilderman (Walton).

1956: March—Teatro dell'Opera, Rome, with Virginia Zeani (Elvira), Giuseppe di Stefano (Arturo), Paolo Silveri (Riccardo), and Giulio Neri (Sir Giorgio).

1960: May 24—Twenty-sixth Glyndebourne Festival (seasonal opening), with Joan Sutherland (Elvira), Monica Sinclair (Enrichetta), Nicola Filaricudi (Arturo), John Kentish (Bruno), Ernest Blanc (Riccardo), Giuseppe Modesti (Sir Giorgio), and David Ward (Walton); Vittorio Gui conducted.[16]

1961: date not established—Teatro São Carlos, Lisbon, with Serafin conducting, Gianna D'Angelo (Elvira), Alfredo Kraus (Arturo), Dino Dondi (Riccardo), and Paolo Washington (Sir Giorgio).

1962: date not established—Wexford Festival, Eire, with Mirelli Freni

(Elvira), Luciano Saldari (Talbo), Lino Puglisi (Riccardo), and Franco Ventriglia (Sir Giorgio).

1963: April 16—American Opera Society, Carnegie Hall, New York (concert performance), with Joan Sutherland (Elvira), Nicolai Gedda (Arturo), Ernest Blanc (Riccardo), Justino Díaz (Sir Giorgio), and Raymond Michalski (Walton); Richard Bonynge conducted.

1964: February 12—Boston Opera Group, Boston, with Sutherland (Elvira), Charles Craig (Arturo), Richard Cross (Riccardo), and Spiro Malas (Sir Giorgio), Bonynge conducting.

1966: January 12—Bushnell Theater, Hartford, Connecticut, with Adriana Maliponte (Elvira), Gianni Jaia (Arturo), Enzo Sordello (Riccardo), and Ezio Flagello (Sir Giorgio).

1969: January 23—Teatro La Fenice, Venice, with Christine Deutekom (Elvira), Mirna Pecile (Enrichetta), Franco Castellana (Arturo), Ottorino Begali (Bruno), Giovanni Ciminelli (Riccardo), Agostino Ferrin (Sir Giorgio), and Carlo Micalucci (Walton)—a very far cry from earlier Fenice casts; March 18—Teatro Comunale, Bologna, with Mirella Freni (Elvira), Delia Lago (Enrichetta), Luciano Pavarotti (Arturo), Vittorio Pandano (Bruno), Walter Alberti (Riccardo), Silvano Pagliuca (Sir Giorgio), and Alfonso Marchica (Walton).

At Covent Garden, London, *I Puritani* has had a full history. It was first heard there, with Giulia Grisi in the role that she had created, in 1846. Grisi also sang it there in 1847 (with Mario as Arturo, Giorgio Ronconi alternating with Joseph-Dieudonné Tagliafico and Ignazio Marini as Sir Giorgio), in 1848, and in 1852. In 1853, Angiolina Bosio, as Elvira, appeared with Mario, Ronconi, and—in the role he had created eighteen years before—Luigi Lablache as Sir Giorgio. Rosina Penco was heard as Elvira in 1859 and 1860; Angiola Tiberini-Ortolani in 1861. Ronconi and Jean-Baptiste Faure were in the 1863 cast, when the Elvira was Mme Fioretti, who also sang that role in 1868, the year in which for the first time someone other than Sir Michael Costa (it was a Signor Li Calsi) conducted *I Puritani* at Covent Garden. In 1869, Ilma di Murska was the Elvira. Adelina Patti was heard as Elvira in 1870 and 1871, but in 1873 the role was sung by Elvira Trisolini. Emma Albani instituted her monopoly of Elvira in 1874, also singing the role in 1876, 1877, and 1878—always with Julián Gayarré as Arturo—and again in 1881 and 1882, seasons during which the Sir Giorgio was Édouard de Reszke, who also had that role on May 18, 1883, when Marcella Sembrich sang her only Covent Garden Elvira and Mattia Battistini made his London debut as Sir Riccardo. Albani took up the role of Elvira again for a single performance in 1887. Then *I*

Puritani vanished from the Garden for seventy-seven years, until March 20, 1964, when Joan Sutherland sang Elvira, with Margreta Elkins (Enrichetta), Charles Craig (Arturo), Gabriel Bacquier (Riccardo), Joseph Rouleau (Sir Giorgio), and David Kelly (Walton), with Richard Bonynge conducting. *I Puritani* has been sung about seventy times at Covent Garden since the Royal Italian Opera was established in 1847.

THE LIBRETTO. *Part 1: Scenes 1–3.* "Large open space in the Fortress [near Plymouth]. Some walls, towers, and other sorts of fortification, with drawbridges, etc. Mountains rise in the distance, making a beautiful view; the rising sun gradually illuminates them, then lights up the whole scene. The changing of the sentinels is seen on the ramparts."* The Puritan governor of the fortress, Lord Gualtiero Valton, has promised the hand of his daughter, Elvira, to the Puritan colonel, Sir Riccardo Forth, but the girl is enamored of a Stuart partisan, Lord Arturo Talbo. Such a marriage does not please Valton, but because he does not wish to coerce Elvira, preparations are being made to welcome Arturo. Riccardo, desolated by Elvira's rejection of him and enraged against his rival, tells his friend Sir Bruno Roberton of his bitterness over this sudden outrage.

Scene 4. "Elvira's apartment. The Gothic windows are open. The fortifications, etc., can be seen." Elvira thanks her uncle, Sir Giorgio, who has obtained her stern father's permission for her to marry Arturo. Her fiancé's arrival is heralded by trumpets.

Scenes 5–11. "Armor Hall. The back of the scene is open. Between the columns, one always sees some traces of the fortifications, etc. Lord Arturo enters from the right with equerries and pages bearing nuptial gifts, including a magnificent white veil. From the left, Elvira, Valton, and Sir Giorgio enter, with ladies-in-waiting and male and female courtiers carrying festoons of flowers, which they drape around the columns. Soldiers led by Bruno enter from the back to form a procession filling out the dignity of the celebration."

Arturo, bringing nuptial gifts, is solemnly received. Lord Valton gives his future son-in-law a safe conduct that permits him to leave the fortress with his bride; he places Elvira under the care of his brother, Sir Giorgio. He himself cannot attend the wedding, having been ordered to conduct to Parliament a female prisoner believed to be a Stuart spy. When Arturo sees this woman, she arouses his pity. When he manages to remain alone with her, she reveals that she is Enrichetta di Francia (Henrietta Maria, daughter of Henry IV of France and sister of Louis XIII), the widow of Charles Stuart. Parliament certainly will condemn her to death. Arturo will try to rescue his queen. Elvira enters in bridal dress and asks

* These descriptions of the settings are translated from the libretto.

Enrichetta to help her put on the veil. The girl is happy; laughing and joking, she amuses herself by covering Enrichetta's head with the veil. Arturo decides to take advantage of this action by using the safe conduct to leave the fortress with Enrichetta disguised as his bride. The two are preparing to leave when Riccardo rushes upon Arturo with drawn sword. Arturo defends himself, but when Enrichetta attempts to separate the two men, Riccardo recognizes her. But because he is happy to see Arturo depart, he swears not to reveal their flight until they have reached safety. When Elvira learns that Arturo has left with another woman, she believes herself betrayed and abandoned. The sudden grief troubles her reason. Sir Giorgio tries to console and sustain her; the others shout imprecations against the faithless Arturo.

Part II: Scenes 1–4. "Salon with lateral doors. Through one of them we see the English countryside and some fortifications." Puritans—male and female—and some officials, Bruno among them, await word of Elvira, who has shown clear signs of mental unbalance since the day of the unperformed wedding, going from excitement to depression. They cluster about Sir Giorgio, who comes from his niece's room and, in anguish, tells them of Elvira's sad state. They blame Arturo, declaring that he deserves the worst punishment. Riccardo announces, "And the punishment will not be long in coming": Parliament has ordered Arturo decapitated. As one of those most responsible for the civil war, he must be hunted down and killed. The Puritans depart to carry out the order. Elvira, her hair unbound and her clothes in disarray, comes in and speaks disconnected words that profoundly move Sir Giorgio and Riccardo. When she is persuaded to return to her rooms, Sir Giorgio tries to convince Riccardo to save Arturo; he believes that Elvira's reason might be restored by a sudden joy. But Riccardo is inflexible: even if, out of love for Elvira, he were disposed to save the man she loves, his political and religious convictions would stop him. And should he be fighting against the enemies of Parliament and England and come face to face with Arturo, he would kill him unhesitatingly.

Part III: Scenes 1–3. "Loggia in a shrubbery garden. Near Elvira's quarters; the doors and windows of the building are very transparent. We still see some fortifications, etc., in the distance. Day is beginning to wane. A storm is approaching, and as it increases, cries of alarm and an arquebus shot are heard from a distance, behind the stage. Soon Arturo appears wrapped in a great mantle. The moon begins to emerge. The interior of the house is illuminated by lamps."

Arturo is warily approaching the lighted windows when a drum roll and the voices of the guards force him to hide. But when Elvira comes out and vaguely calls him, he throws himself at her feet, asks her pardon for the harm that he unintentionally has done her, and explains that he was driven to flee in order to save the queen's life. Just as Elvira, convinced that Arturo did not leave her for the other woman, seems to be recovering her sanity, a drum roll disturbs her anew. Arturo realizes that her mind is wandering again. Armed men approach. Arturo attempts to get Elvira to flee with him, but she cannot understand the danger. Also, she fears that he means to abandon her again and seizes him by the knees and calls for help. Riccardo, Sir Giorgio, Sir Bruno, guards, and courtiers rush in. Arturo is recognized in the torchlight. The Puritans are ready to carry out Parliament's order by putting him to death. Their shouts startle and terrify Elvira, and violent emotion clears her mind. Sir Giorgio restrains the Puritans. While the two young people bid each other a moving farewell, a messenger brings word that the Stuarts have been routed and that a general amnesty has been proclaimed. All joyfully cluster around Arturo and Elvira, who embrace happily.

THE OPERA. *Part 1: Scenes 1–3*. "Large open space in the fortress [near Plymouth]":

Scene 1 (p. 1*)—*I Puritani* has no formal *sinfonia* or *preludio*,[17] but begins ("*Introduzione*," D major, 2/4 time, *allegro assai*) with an orchestral introduction (earlier versions of which appear in two groups of Bellini's sketches at Catania: those for *Ernani*, in which the chief melody is an inner instrumental voice in C major; and those for *La Sonnambula*, in which it is in B-flat major). After sixteen measures of on-the-beat quarternote chords marked *sforzato*, this moves, by way of a three-measure silence and a quiet orchestral section, to (p. 2) an *allegro sostenuto*, 6/8 time, of pastoral coloring, but marked by fortissimo agitations and closing on a five-measure crescendo (piano-fortissimo). Sir Bruno and the sentinels (3-part chorus, t1, t2, bs) announce (p. 4) the dawn (in part by the wonderfully onomatopoeic phrase, baffling to English translation, "*la tromba rimbomba*"), again with a crescendo ending (*pianissimo-forte*). *Allegro sostenuto e marziale*, 3/4 time, *marcato e staccato* (p. 6), the orchestra prepares for the offstage chorus (t1, t2, bs), "*Quando la tromba squilla*," of soldiers threatening to reduce the Stuart camp to ashes. On repeated D octaves, this too dies away pianissimo. The key shifts (p. 14) to F major, *larghetto maestoso*, as bell and organ, preluding religious music, are heard from inside. Sir Bruno urges "Cromwell's warriors" to turn their thoughts to the matins. When the soldiers kneel (p. 15), Elvira, Arturo, Riccardo, and Sir Giorgio join in prayer, "*La luna, il sole, le stelle*." Sir

---

* Page references here are to the Ricordi piano-vocal score the plate number 41685. For "Versions and Variants of *I Puritani*," see Appendix Q, p. 448.

Bruno and the soldiers comment (p. 18) that their prayer has been launched toward God upon the winds.

Scene 2 (p. 19)—B-flat major, 6/8 time, *allegro brillante*, the orchestra briefly announces festivity; from inside, the female courtiers sing "*A festa.*" As all emerge, the tenors and basses join to celebrate love, saluting the forthcoming wedding of Elvira and Arturo. A *stretto* occurs at the words (p. 23) "*Cantiam un santo amor.*" All leave; the orchestra prolongs the festive atmosphere.

Scene 3[18] (p. 25)—"*Recitativo ed Aria,*" E-flat major, 4/4 time, *allegro maestoso.* The grieving Riccardo, in recitative, bewails his loss of Elvira, expanding (*andante affettuoso*, p. 26) into touching arioso ("*O Elvira, o mio sospir soave*"), asking, "What is left for me in this life?" Sir Bruno's reply, "Your country and Heaven," naturally fails to satisfy Riccardo. A-flat major, 9/8 time, *larghetto sostenuto*, pianissimo (p. 28), the orchestra preludes Riccardo's archetypically baritonal aria, "*Ah! per sempre io ti perdei,*" which differs damagingly little in melodic outline from "*O Elvira, o mio sospir soave,*" but calls for considerable vocal agility. When soldiers file past (p. 30, G major, 2/4 time, *allegro moderato*), Sir Bruno tries to arouse Riccardo's martial, patriotic feelings; Riccardo answers that he flames only with love and rage. In the cabaletta, "*Bel sogno beato,*" however, he again dwells on the sorrow of thwarted love. He repeats the cabaletta (p. 34), but at last Sir Bruno is able to lead him toward the assembly hall (p. 37).

Scene 4 (p. 38). "Elvira's apartment." A minor, 4/4 time, *allegro molto.* Loudly, with punctuating *sforzati*, the orchestra (eventually ebbing to spaced-out pianissimo chords) prepares for the partly recitative, partly *a due* conversation between Elvira and Sir Giorgio, in which he tells her that she will marry, not Riccardo, but Arturo. The duetlike part begins (p. 40[19]) with Elvira's "*Sai com'arde in petto mio,*" in which the trills and rapid runs that are to help in characterizing her first appear. The happy girl is embraced by her uncle as he sings the aria-like "*Piangi, o figlia*" (p. 44). F major, 4/4 time, *meno allegro*, Elvira asks (p. 47) who persuaded her father to agree to her marrying Arturo. Answering, Sir Giorgio sings (p. 47) the equally aria-like "*Sorgea la notte,*" revealing his own part in convincing Lord Valton (and here the rapid, brief exclamation, "*Oh! mio consolator,*" with which [p. 48] Elvira interrupts to thank him—a mere thirteen notes—marvelously suggests her skittishness). As Sir Giorgio recounts his conversation with Valton (p. 48, "*Io cominciai: Germanno*") Elvira hovers between fear and joy. When hunting horns sound outside the fortress (D major, 2/4 time, *allegro moderato*, p. 51) "Elvira stands motionless, wholly attentive. Across her face should pass the increasing joy that reaches its climax at the words, 'Arturo Talbo.'" When the chorus announces Arturo's arrival, Elvira and Sir Giorgio sing (*più mosso*, p. 53) "*A quel* $\begin{cases} nome \\ suono, \end{cases}$" in which they give vent to their happiness. Again (*più allegro*, p. 56) the chorus greets Arturo. Elvira and Sir Giorgio repeat the joyful duet, extended to greater length. Then, as the orchestra noisily concludes the scene, they leave.

Scenes 5–11. "Armor Hall":

Scene 5 (p. 62)—"*Coro e Quartetto*," A major, 6/8 time, *maestoso assai* at first, then *allegro vivo*. After another festive orchestral introduction, the five-part chorus (s1, s2, t1, t2, bs) salutes (p. 63) Elvira and Arturo. Then the sopranos compare her (p. 64) to spring and the evening star, and all, at excessive length, call Arturo (p. 64) a forest cedar, a tempest in battle, a champion in jousting and love. An *allegro vivo* transition (p. 68) leads (p. 69, D major, 12/8 time, largo, *con grande espressione*) to the orchestral introduction of Arturo's entrance aria, "*A te, o cara*," which quickly becomes a chorus-supported quartet as Elvira, Sir Giorgio, Valton, and the five-part chorus join in (p. 70). When Arturo begins a second verse of his aria (p. 71), the ensemble continues in unclouded happiness.[20]

Scene 6 (p. 77)—"*Finale I*," C major, 4/4 time, maestoso. In recitative, Valton hands Arturo a safe conduct for Elvira and himself, says that he cannot attend the wedding, and tells Enrichetta that he will accompany her to Parliament. Arturo is disturbed by certainty that Enrichetta's fate is sealed. Page 79, 12/8 time, Valton salutes Elvira and Arturo. Then he leaves with his guards, Sir Giorgio and Elvira go out with her ladies, and Arturo manages to remain behind with Enrichetta.

Scene 7 (p. 79)—Arturo having offered (4/4 time, *allegro risoluto*) to help Enrichetta, she reveals her identity (p. 80, *allegro agitato assai*) in the aria, "*Figlia a Enrico*," while Arturo kneels before her as his queen. When he offers to save her by leading her from the fortress along a secret route, she attempts to dissuade him from that dangerous undertaking by telling him to think of Elvira. For a few measures, they sing *a due* (p. 83). Then Arturo replies (p. 83, A major, "*Non parlar di lei*"), saying that he will save Enrichetta or invoke Elvira while dying. The scene lengthens in repetitions.

Scene 8 (p. 87)—D major, 3/4 time, *allegro moderato*. Elvira enters in bridal dress; she carries a magnificent white veil given her by Arturo. She sings the flowery, lighthearted polonaise, "*Son vergin vezzosa*,"[21] which at once intensifies the candor of her nature and suggests a relationship to the Amina of *La Sonnambula*. The polonaise in effect becomes a quartet when (p. 88) Enrichetta, Arturo, and Sir Giorgio join Elvira, commenting upon her virtues. "Tell me if it is true that you love me," Elvira sings (p. 91), and the inoffensive naïveté of her self-esteem is excellently expressed (p. 92) in her *"Qual mattutina stella."* Thereafter, Enrichetta agrees to show her how to put on the veil. The scene evolves (p. 92) into a quartet (Elvira, Enrichetta, Arturo, Sir Giorgio), with Elvira repeating parts of the polonaise to changed words, which are harmonized with the others' vocal lines. Elvira places her veil on Enrichetta's head. Valton and the five-part chorus intervene (p. 96) to tell Elvira that the hour for her wedding is drawing near and that she should return to her quarters. After a flourish of descending and ascending scales (p. 98) and other happy *fioriture*, Elvira leaves with Sir Giorgio and her ladies.

Scene 9 (p. 101)—Moderato. Arturo takes the safe conduct from his belt. Enrichetta starts to remove Elvira's veil from her head, but Arturo prevents her from doing so, saying that it is a gift from Heaven (*andante risoluto*, p. 100): it will serve their escape by disguising her as his bride.

Scene 10 (p. 101)—E major, 4/4 time, *allegro agitato assai*. Riccardo enters with sword drawn (forte, risoluto, above deep tremolos, a chromatic ascending scale, crescendo in the orchestra). Mistaking the veiled Enrichetta for Elvira and desperate over his loss of her, in the ornate, violent *"Ferma, in van pretendi"* (p. 101), he challenges Arturo to a duel, *"Qui ti sfido a mortal guerra"* (p. 102), the melody of which Bellini borrowed from Fernando's cabaletta, *"Ascolta, o padre,"* in Act I of the Genoa version of *Bianca e Fernando* (see p. 243). Arturo accepts the challenge (*"Sprezzo, o audace,"* p. 103). As Enrichetta moves to separate them, her veil parts, revealing to Riccardo that she is the prisoner, not Elvira. Page 106, A minor, 4/4 time, in agitated, theatrically potent exchange, Riccardo tells Arturo that he and the prisoner may leave unharmed (he is, of course, delighted to be rid of Arturo). They do so as, in an aside *a piacere* (p. 107), Arturo bids farewell to the absent Elvira. No pause intervenes before the next scene.

Scene 11 (p. 110)—*Piano, pianissimo morendo*, Riccardo mentally follows Arturo and the prisoner through the fortress gates. The true finale begins, 3/4 time, *allegro veloce*, when (p. 111), Elvira having asked for Arturo, Sir Bruno says that he has left the fortress. F major, *piano-pianissimo, sotto voce*, p. 112, Sir Giorgio, Elvira, and the chorus (tenors alone at first, then sopranos alone, and finally in five parts), makes crescendo comment on the flight of Arturo and the prisoner. When Sir Bruno and the chorus point out the now-distant fleeing pair ("... *mirate colà!*" p. 113), Elvira screams. It is the onset of her delirium. Riccardo Sir Giorgio, Valton, and the chorus shout a call to arms, ordering the soldiers to "drag the traitors back by the hair." Elvira is reduced (p. 116) to a completely distracted state in which she can only repeat *"Ahimè!"* while the others call for revenge. Page 119, Elvira, "sorrowfully and with fixed stare," begins to give voice to her brain's stumbling fancies, speaking of "Arturo's lady" and the "white veil." Again calling Arturo (p. 121), she shouts a final *"Ahimè!"* Quite delirious (p. 123), Elvira now imagines Arturo with her; after a rapid descending diatonic scale on the word *"vieni!"* (p. 124), she sings (4/4 time, *larghetto sostenuto*) her plea to Arturo, *"Oh vieni al tempio"* ("declaimed with all the impetus of an innocent heart") to come to the church so that they can make their vows. Sir Bruno, Riccardo, Sir Giorgio, and the chorus intrude to express their intense pity for Elvira and their loathing of Arturo for having brought her to this demented state. (Here the constant use of three-against-four and the climaxing floridity, pp. 132-133, of Elvira's vocal line are employed creatively to establish the near-insane intensity of her emotional condition.) B-flat major, *allegro vivace*, p. 134 (*"Qual febbre vorace"*), Elvira, with Sir Bruno, Riccardo, and Sir Giorgio sing (*"Ahi! dura sciagura!"*) the concluding *stretta*, in which a certain musical squareness (perhaps brought on by too many on-the-beat notes) weakens rather than intensifies the extraordinarily varied and supple ensemble that just preceded it. But Bellini here was faced with an insoluble problem in Pepoli's libretto: nothing dramatic happens after the departure of Arturo and Enrichetta and Elvira's escape into dementia. The act necessarily has an ending, but it presents no resolution or final active climax.

Part II: Scenes 1–4. "Salon with lateral doors" (this Part is unusual among operatic acts in that the tenor hero makes no appearance in it):

Scene 1 (p. 150)—*"Introduzione e Romanza,"* G major, 4/4 time, *allegro moderato*. After a disturbed orchestral introduction bristling with agogic signals (fortissimo, piano, sforzato, crescendo, pianissimo, often changing after a single measure), the five-part chorus of courtiers mourns Elvira's delirium as she wanders about crying *"Pietà . . . pietà!"* They fear that she may die of love.

Scene 2 (p. 159)—G major, *allegro moderato assai, alla breve*. When Sir Giorgio comes from Elvira's quarters, the courtiers demand news of her. He tells them only that she is resting; they beseech him for an explanation of her state. Page 161, A-flat major, 4/4 time, *andante un poco mosso*, he replies in the romanza *"Cinta di fiori,"* which the chorus interrupts with shouts of grief and imprecation and finally (p. 165, *"Cada il folgor"*) with the hope that lightning may strike her betrayer. Page 166, Riccardo comes in with a paper and says that Parliament has condemned Arturo to death, but has proclaimed Valton's innocence of involvement in the prisoner's escape; Cromwell has ordered that Arturo be apprehended and killed. The people depart as the scene dies away in a *largo pianissimo* of tremolos.

Scene 3 (p. 171)—"*Scena ed Aria*," E-flat major, 4/4 time, andantino. In one of Bellini's greatest single scenes, the vacillations, blurrings, and refocussings of Elvira's mind are superbly evoked in passages not melodically inferior to "*Casta diva*." Elvira begins offstage, to pianissimo quivers in the orchestra, with the forthright prayer "*O rendetemi la speme, o lasciate, lasciatemi morir*" (Either give me hope or let me die). When seeking the reasons for the startling effectiveness of this lush melody, one scarcely knows whether to admire more the use of an opening appoggiatura for its first repetition or the uncannily apt ornamentation. After (p. 171) Sir Giorgio and Riccardo signal Elvira's approach, she comes in (p. 172) showing clear signs of madness[22] and sings one of the most purely sensuous melodies ever composed, the aria "*Qui la voce sua soave*," of which the second repetition of "*O [Ah!] rendetemi la speme*" proves to be the conclusion. After further comment by Riccardo and Sir Giorgio, Elvira addresses the latter (p. 175), asking him who he is and, with signs of happiness, mistaking him for her father. Instantly, "disconsolate," she asks, "And Arturo? And love? Speak . . . speak." In "*Ah! tu sorridi*" (p. 175), B-flat major (6/8 time, *allegro giusto*), she supposes that they will lead her to the altar, to dancing and singing, to the wedding feast. She grasps Riccardo's hand (p. 177), noticing that he is weeping; perhaps, she thinks, he too has loved someone. Sir Giorgio tells her to hope that Heaven will assuage her sorrow. "Never! never!" she replies and "with all the desperation of sorrow" (p. 179) again repeats the exquisite melody of "*Ah! rendetemi la speme*"—to the words "*Ah toglietemi la vita o rendete, rendetemi il mio amor*" (Ah, take my life from me or give me back my love). She stands exhausted and motionless. *Allegro moderato*, pianissimo, thinking herself with Arturo and singing "*sotto voce e con mistero*," she tells her lover not to fear her father, whom she will placate; everything will turn out well. A-flat major, 4/4 time, *allegro moderato*, p. 182, the orchestra introduces the melody of Elvira's bitersweet, insanely joyful cabaletta, "*Vien diletto*,"[23] which perfectly fulfills "*Qui la voce sua soave*," and in which she asks Arturo to come to her, to return to their first love. Riccardo and Sir Giorgio again comment upon her words; seeing that she is completely unhinged, they suggest that she leave, and the orchestral postlude fades to *piano-pianissimo* (p. 190). The desperately delicate, perilous balance of this entire scene requires of the soprano not only extremely agile, supple, and intelligently dramatic singing, but also acting of intensity among constantly shifting velleities. Without both, it can easily become "pinnacl'd dim in the intense inane," a meaningless festival of melody.

Scene 4 (p. 190)—"*Duetto—Finale II*," C minor, then F major, 4/4 time, *andante sostenuto*. Sir Giorgio, aware that Riccardo has allowed Arturo and the prisoner to escape, works upon Riccardo's love for Elvira in trying to persuade him to help save his rival; he prophesies (A-flat major, 3/4 time, *andante agitato*, p. 195)—beginning with "*Se tra il buio un fantasma vedrai*"—that the specters of Elvira and Arturo will follow Riccardo wherever he goes. But Riccardo is unable to yield. A-flat major, marcato, *crescendo e stringendo il tempo*, he hopes that the enemy troops will attack the fortress at dawn. Sir Giorgio agrees that should Arturo be one of the attackers, he must die. *Allegro, ma più maestoso*, to a rocking staccato accompaniment in eighth-notes, the orchestra introduces the melody of the renowned cabaletta (p. 202) for Riccardo and Sir Giorgio, "*Suoni la tromba*," which, sung partly in unison, brilliantly depicts the loyal patriotism and love of liberty that govern them (remote from those pastoral passages in *I Puritani* which recall *La Sonnambula*, "*Suoni la tromba*" would have served well for the Druidic warriors of *Norma*).[24]

Part III: Scenes 1–3. "Loggia in a shrubbery garden":

Scene 1 (p. 207)—"*Uragano, Romanza e Duetto*," D minor, 3/4 time. Amid the onset of a storm, pianissimo, armed men search for someone. After a temporary abatement of the storm, it rises to full fury (p. 208). Arturo enters (p. 209) as it gradually dies away. In recitative, he speaks his belief that he is safe at last, having thrown the pursuers off his trail. Page 210, *andante mosso*, he continues in recitative, apostrophizing his native soil and his love. Then (B-flat major, 6/8 time, *andante sostenuto*, p. 212) he hears Elvira's voice from inside singing "*A una fonte afflitto e solo*," a love song that he had sung to her—and which (C major, 6/8 time, *andante sostenuto*, p. 213), he now repeats. A major, 4/4 time, *allegro maestoso sostenuto*, p. 215, drumbeats alert Arturo; he hears the searching soldiers (t, bs) hastening to defensive positions and realizes that he must hide. After a few armed men pass by, he re-emerges and starts into Elvira's quarters, but stops, realizing that he might bring on tragedy. "*Primo tempo. Andante*," he sings (p. 219) the romanza "*Corre a valle, corre a morte*," the significance of which is left ambiguous by verses so pointless that Bellini's having accepted them from Pepoli even under duress is astonishing.

Scene 2 (p. 222)—C major, 4/4 time, lento. Sad because the sweet voice (Arturo's) has stopped, Elvira comes into the garden. "Ah! my Arturo, where are you?" she asks. Arturo, kneeling, asks her forgiveness. Sudden joy temporarily restores her reason, and she describes to him her long torment. Assuming that Elvira knows Enrichetta's identity, he describes (allegro, p. 227) her misery as a prisoner. Even after learning that her supposed "rival" is in fact the queen, Elvira asks for and receives asurances that Arturo still loves her (p. 229). His reply (4/4 time, *più moderato*, p. 229) begins the lively, restorative duet, "*Vieni vieni fra queste braccia*," in which she quickly joins him (on the word "*sì*," pp. 230 and 234, Arturo is required to sing high D's). The sound of a drum is heard. "*Finale III*," A major, 4/4 time, moderato. Elvira regresses into delirium, horrifying Arturo. Soldiers' voices are heard, and when Arturo tries to lead Elvira away (p. 238), she believes that he is planning to leave her again. Beside herself, she kneels and, weeping, embraces his knees and calls for help. People run in from all sides, and their presence appears to calm her.

Scene 3 (p. 240)—Riccardo, Sir Giorgio, and the chorus, recognizing Arturo, denounce him. After a funereal orchestral introduction, D minor, 2/4 time, *andante lugubre*, Riccardo asserts that God is punishing the betrayer. Elvira tries (p. 243) to convince Arturo that "the other woman" does not love him, that only she herself can bring him happiness. Riccardo and the people warn Arturo that God and England demand his death. As they pronounce (p. 244) the word "*morte*," a sudden change comes over Elvira, who cries out and repeats it. D-flat major, 4/4 time, *largo maestoso*, p. 246, Arturo explains ("*Credeasi misera!*") that Elvira had thought him faithless but that he is ready to defy fate if he can die with her. Elvira, Riccardo, Sir Giorgio, and the chorus join in, with Arturo repeating his thoughts, Elvira believing that she has sent Arturo to his death, Riccardo appalled by the lovers' fate, Sir Giorgio suffering, the women asking God's mercy for Elvira and Arturo, the men asserting that God is taking a harsh vengeance. *Sotto voce*, turning to Sir Giorgio and Riccardo, the men say "What are we waiting for? On to vengeance!" Ecstatic in love and renunciation, Arturo and Elvira sing to one another while Sir Giorgio and Riccardo accuse the increasingly vengeful men of cruelty and of deafness to pity. Not even Arturo's piteous "*Ella è tremante*" (p. 252), in which he tells them that the trembling Elvira will die, can weaken the Puritan demand for summary justice. The ensemble continues (pp. 253-255, with Arturo required to leap to a high F on the syllable "*po*" of the word "*poscia*," p. 254). The distant sound of a hunting horn is heard (A major, 3/4 time, *allegro marziale*, p. 255). Heralds enter with a message. When Riccardo and Sir Giorgio have read it, the latter bursts out (p. 256): "*Esultate*," which Riccardo repeats. The Stuarts have been defeated, and a general amnesty has been declared. "*Con gioia*," in a whirl of general rejoicing (pp. 257-263), Elvira and Arturo ("*Dagli affanni al gaudio estremo*"), with Riccardo, Sir Giorgio, and the chorus ("*A Cromvello eterna, eterna gloria!*") pour out (p. 258) their individual and collective happiness as the opera ends.

La Sonnambula

MELODRAMMA in two acts. *Libretto*: By Felice Romani, based upon the scenario for *La Sonnambule, ou L'Arrivée d'un nouveau seigneur*, a ballet-pantomine by Eugène Scribe and Jean-Pierre Aumer (choreographer), with music by Louis-Joseph-Ferdinand Hérold, first performed at the Opéra, Paris, on September 19, 1827, and in turn derived from *La Somnambule*, a two-act *comédie-vaudeville* by Scribe and Casimir Delavigne first performed at the Théâtre du Vaudeville, Paris, on December 6, 1819.[1] *Composed*: 1831. *Première*: Teatro Carcano, Milan, March 6, 1831, on a double bill with the ballet *Tutto al contrario*, choreographed by Louis Henry to music by Giacomo Panizza. *Original cast*:

AMINA, *orphan raised by Teresa*	Giuditta Pasta
LISA, *innkeeper, in love with Elvino*	Elisa Taccani
TERESA, *mill proprietress*	Felicità Baillou-Hilaret
ELVINO, *rich village landowner*	Giovanni Battista Rubini
A NOTARY	Antonio Crippa
CONTE RODOLFO, *lord of the village*	Luciano Mariani
ALESSIO, *in love with Lisa*	Lorenzo Biondi

Published: In full score by Cottrau-Ricordi, Naples/Milan, 189? (plate number 96343); in piano-vocal score by Ricordi, Milan, 1831 (pl. nos. 5271–5288)[2]; again, undated (pl. no. 41686), by Girard (later Cottrau), Naples (disjunct pl. nos). Autograph score in the Archivio Ricordi, Milan.[3] Manuscript copies in the Naples Conservatory library (2); in the library of the Accademia di Santa Cecilia, Rome (2); in the library of the Conservatorio Giuseppe Verdi, Milan. Autograph sketches in the Museo Belliniano, Catania. Autograph sketches of the libretto, with interpolations by Bellini, at the Accademia musicale chigiana, Siena. Dedicated to

Francesco Pollini. Only by consulting the autograph or the the facsimile of it can we know *La Sonnambula* as Bellini composed it. Andrew Porter rightly said (*Opera*, London, October 1960, p. 670): "As Bellini wrote it this Rubini role [Elvino] lies extremely high, as high as that of Arturo in *I Puritani*, but this has escaped comment owing to the practice, adopted already in the 19th century, of printing much of the tenor's music (and the duet 'Prendi, l'anel ti dono') in downward transpositions—a full major third lower in the case of 'Ah, perchè non posso odiarti'!"

PERFORMANCE DATA: Despite the favorable reception of *La Sonnambula* in Milan in 1831, the opera did not emigrate to other Italian cities as rapidly as might have been expected; it was staged in both London and Paris before being heard at Florence in the spring of 1832. A selection from its very extensive performance history follows (performances probably in Italian unless otherwise specified)—

1831: July 28— King's Theatre, London, with Pasta (Amina) and Rubini (Elvino); October 24—Théâtre-Italien, Paris (the first Bellini opera staged there), with Pasta and Rubini; during forty-four seasons, the Italien was to perform *La Sonnambula* 240 times down to 1909.

1832: Spring—Teatro della Pergola, Florence, with Rosalbina Caradori-Allan (Amina), Giuseppina Merola (Lisa), Faustina Piombanti (Teresa), Gilbert-Louis Duprez (Elvino), Celestino Salvatori (Rodolfo), Natale Costantini (Alessio), and Tersiccio Severini (Notaro); November 15—Teatro Carolino, Palermo, with Annetta Fink-Lohr (Amina), Pietro Gentile (Elvino), and Giovanni Schober(lechner) (Rodolfo); December 5—Budapest (German).

1833: May 1—Drury Lane Theatre, London (English translation by Samuel Beazley, with the score "adapted" by Henry Rowley Bishop); with Maria Malibran as Amina, the production was moved on June 17 to Covent Garden, where John Templeton was the Elvino and Arthur Seguin the Rodolfo (twenty-four performances at Covent Garden that season)[4]; October 26—Teatro Valle, Rome, with Adelina Speck (Amina), Antonio Poggi (Elvino), and Giorgio Ronconi (Rodolfo).

1834: April 9—Teatro Comunale, Bologna, with Malibran (Amina), Lorenzo Bonfigli (Elvino), Luciano Mariani (Rodolfo); April 24— Covent Garden, London, with Eugenia Garcia, the wife of Malibran's brother Manuel Patricio Garcia (Amina), William Harrison (Elvino), Adam Leffler (Rodolfo); summer—King's Theatre, London, with Giulia Grisi (Amina); July 21—Teatro del Príncipe, Madrid, where it was billed during thirty seasons down to 1878; September 27—

Dresden; October 1—Teatro alla Scala, Milan, with Malibran (Amina), Antonio Poggi (Elvino), Orazio Cartagenova (Rodolfo); November 11—Teatro San Carlo, Naples, with Malibran (Amina), Duprez (Elvino), and Carlo Porto (Rodolfo)[5]; November 12—Theater in der Josefstadt, Vienna (German, as *Die Nachtwanderlin*, translation by Georg Ott); December 9—Corfu; December 20—Pressburg (German).

1835: May—Prague (German); May 15—Kärntnertortheater, Vienna; November 13—Park Theater, New York (United States première); December 28—Boston.

1836: January—Teatro Italiano, Havana; February 1—Mexico City; February 11—Philadelphia; April 17—Teatro Comunale, Bologna, with Fanny Tacchinardi-Persiani (Amina), Giacomo Santi (Elvino), Carlo Porto (Rodolfo); May 25—Königliches Opernhaus, Berlin (German translation by Franziska Ellmenreich).

1837: January 17—Royal Theatre, Dublin; Carnival—Teatro La Fenice, Venice, with Tacchinardi-Persiani (Amina); March 10—Basel (German); May 29—St. Petersburg (Russian); autumn—Teatro dell'Opera Italiana, Algiers; October 6—Lisbon.

1838: January 4—St. Louis, Missouri.

1839: January 10—Antwerp (French translation by Étienne Monnier); March—Bordeaux (Monnier translation); June 26—Brussels (Monnier translation); July 7—Helsingfors (German); September 19—Odessa; no date—Amsterdam (German).

1840: Théâtre d'Orléans, New Orleans (French); Carnival—Palma de Mallorca; spring—Athens; June 2—Warsaw (Polish translation by Karol Kasimierc Kurpiński).

1841: Carnival—Ajaccio, Corsica; April 21—Teatro alla Scala, Milan, with Jenny Lutzer (Amina), Giuseppina Brambilla (Lisa), Lorenzo Salvi (Elvino), Ignazio Marini (Rodolfo); June 19—Budapest (Hungarian translation by Fülöp Sámuel Deáky); autumn—Teatro Italiano, Vera Cruz; November—Pera Theater, Constantinople.

1842: January 7—Königsstädtischestheater, Berlin; November 4—Copenhagen.

1843: January 9—Stockholm (Swedish translation by Niels Erik Wilhelm af Wetterstedt); spring—St. Petersburg.

1844: Carnival—Teatro Manoel, Valletta, Malta; May 13—New York; July—Agram (German); autumn—Port of Spain, Trinidad; no date—Valparaiso.

1845: February 17—Bucharest; December 9—Sydney, Australia (English).

1846: January—Théâtre de l'Opéra, Geneva; September 14—Rio de Janeiro.

1847: March 9—Edinburgh (English); late spring or early summer—Her Majesty's Theatre, London, with Jenny Lind (Amina).

1848: January 23—Christiania (Danish); May 9—Covent Garden, London, with Pauline Viardot-Garcia (London debut, Amina) and Signor Flavio, a last-minute replacement for Grisi's husband, Mario, as Elvino; October 18—Covent Garden, London, with Emma Romer (Amina) and, in his Garden debut, John Sims Reeves (Elvino).

1850: January 27—Buenos Aires; July 29—Chicago Theater, Chicago (the first opera performed in that city), with Elsa Brienti (Amina), Signor Manvera (Elvino).[6]

1851: February 12—Adelphi Theater, San Francisco (the first opera performed in that city).

1852: May 25—Marseilles (French); no date—Montevideo.

1853: Teatro Comunale, Bologna, with Virginia Boccabadati (Amina); *fiera*—Teatro Comunale Nuovo La Fenice, Sinigaglia, with Erminia Frezzolini (Amina), Carlo Boucardé (Elvino), Alessandro Ottaviani (Rodolfo).

1858: September 27—McVicker's Theater, Chicago, with Rosalie Durand (Amina) and Miss Georgia Hodson (Elvino).

1860: March 29—Teatro alla Scala, Milan, with Carlotta Marchisio (Amina).

1861: May 14—Covent Garden, London, the debut there of Adelina Patti (Amina), with Mario Tiberini (Elvino) and Joseph-Dieudonné Tagliafico (Rodolfo).[7]

1864: November 2—Copenhagen (Danish translation by Adolf Marius Rosenkilde).

1865: April 7—Prague (Czech translation by Bedřich Peška); May 20—Crosby's Opera House, Chicago, with Clara Louise Kellogg (Amina), who completed the evening by singing the "Mad Scene" from *Lucia di Lammermoor*, perhaps thus establishing an all-time record, having lost her reason at least three times during one performance.

1867: Théâtre-Lyrique, Paris (French).

1868: October 26—Covent Garden, London, with—her English debut—Minnie Hauk (Amina).

1871: January 4—New York (German); May 27—Teatro Apollo, Rome, with Carlotta Marchisio (Amina), Barbara Marchisio (Lisa), and Roberto Stagno (Elvino)[8]; autumn—Royal Theatre, Gibraltar.

1872: March 11—Teatro Apollo, Rome, with Giuseppina Vitali-Augusti (Amina), Italo Campanini (Elvino), and Giuseppe Del Puente (Rodolfo); April 2—Covent Garden, London, with Emma Albani in her Garden debut (Amina), Emilio Naudin (Elvino), and Jean-Baptiste Faure (Rodolfo).

1875: July 27—Teatro La Fenice, Venice, with Emma Albani (Amina).

1876: no date—Helsingfors (Swedish).

1877: February 8—Helsingfors (Finnish translation by Anders Törneroos); February 20—Teatro Apollo, Rome, with Adelina Patti (Amina), Ernesto Nicolini, one of Patti's future husbands (Elvino), and Alamiro Bettarini (Rodolfo); March 2—Teatro alla Scala, Milan, with Patti (Amina), and Nicolini (Elvino).

1879: no date—Her Majesty's Theatre, London, with, in her debut, the eighteen-year-old Marie Van Zandt (Amina).

1880: June 24—Covent Garden, London, with Marcella Sembrich (Amina).

1881: May 6—Teatro alla Scala, Milan, with Emma Nevada (Amina).

1883: November 14—Metropolitan Opera, New York, ninth (and second Bellini) opera of its first session, with Marcella Sembrich (Amina), Ida Corani (Lisa), Emily Lablache (Teresa), Italo Campanini (Elvino), Franco Novara (Rodolfo), Baldassare Corsini (Alessio), and Amadeo Grazzi (Un Notaro).

1889: February 3—Teatro La Fenice, Venice, with Emma Nevada (Amina); June 3—Covent Garden, London, with Marie Van Zandt in her Garden debut (Amina) and Édouard de Reszke (Rodolfo).

1890: May 29—Covent Garden, London, with Etelka Gerster in her Garden debut (Amina).

1897: Teatro alla Scala, Milan, with Regina Pinkert (Amina) and Alessandro Bonci (Elvino).

1905: December 15—Metropolitan Opera, New York, with Sembrich (Amina), Mathilde Bauermeister (Teresa), Enrico Caruso (Elvino), Pol Plançon (Rodolfo); no date—Teatro Massimo, Palermo, with María Barrientos (Amina).

1907: January 25—Manhattan Opera House, New York, with Regina Pinkert (Amina), Emma Trentini (Lisa), Bonci (Elvino), Luigi Mugnoz (Rodolfo), Vincenzo Reschiglian (Alessio).

1909: February 13—Manhattan Opera House, New York, with Luisa Tetrazzini (Amina), Trentini (Lisa), Angelo Parola (Elvino), Andrés de Segurola (Rodolfo), Reschiglian (Alessio); May 29—Covent Garden, London, with Tetrazzini (Amina), John McCormack (Elvino), and Angelo Scandiani (Rodolfo).

1910: January 12—Teatro alla Scala, Milan, with Rosina Storchio (Amina); April 2 (matinee)—Metropolitan Opera House, New York, with Elvira de Hidalgo (Amina), Bonci (Elvino), and Segurola (Rodolfo), on a double bill with the Glazunov ballet *Hungary*, in which Anna Pavlova and Mikhail Mordkin danced.

1916: March 3—Metropolitan Opera House, New York, with María Barrientos (Amina), Giacomo Damacco (Elvino), and Adamo Didur (Rodolfo).

1919: December 17—Auditorium, Chicago, with Amelita Galli-Curci (Amina), Maria Claessens (Teresa), Tito Schipa (Elvino), and Virgilio Lazzari (Rodolfo).

1922: no date—Teatro Massimo, Palermo, with Toti Dal Monte (Amina).

1923: January 20—Teatro La Fenice, Venice, with Graziella Pareto (Amina).

1924: January 13—Teatro alla Scala, Milan, with Toti Dal Monte (Amina), Dino Borgioli (Elvino), and Ezio Pinza (Rodolfo).

1931: December 28—Teatro Massimo Bellini, Catania, with Dal Monte (Amina), Anna Paguera (Lisa), Enzo De Muro Lomanto (Elvino), and Antonio Righetti (Rodolfo).

1932: March 16—Metropolitan Opera House, New York, with Lily Pons (Amina), Ina Bourskaya (Teresa), Beniamino Gigli (Elvino), Ezio Pinza (Rodolfo), Louis D'Angelo (Alessio), and Giordano Paltrinieri (Un Notaro); April 28—Teatro Comunale, Florence, with Maria Gentile (Amina), Enzo De Muro Lomanto (Elvino), and Luciano Donaggio (Rodolfo).

1934: no date—Teatro Massimo, Palermo, with Bidú Sayão (Amina).

1935 (centenary of Bellini's death): January 1—Teatro alla Scala, Milan, with Dal Monte (Amina), Ines Maria Ferraris (Lisa), Schipa (Elvino), and Tancredi Pasero (Rodolfo); July—Giardino Bellini, open air, Catania, with Maria Gentile, a *catanese* (Amina), Schipa (Elvino), and Santiago Font (Rodolfo); no date—Tunis.

1937: November 22—Civic Opera House, Chicago, with Gina Cigna (Amina), Giovanni Martinelli (Elvino), and Ezio Pinza (Rodolfo).

1942: May 9—Teatro Comunale, Florence (8th Maggio Musicale Fiorentino), with Margherita Carosio (Amina), Ferruccio Tagliavini (Elvino), and Tancredi Pasero (Rodolfo).

1951: November 22—Teatro Massimo Bellini, Catania, with Margherita Carosio (Amina), Cesare Valletti (Elvino), and Giuseppe Modesti (Rodolfo).

1955: January 25—American Opera Society, Town Hall, New York (concert performance), with Laurel Hurley (Amina), Nell Tangeman (Teresa), Charles Anthony (Elvino), and Cesare Siepi (Rodolfo).

1957: March 2—Teatro all Scala, Milan, with Maria Meneghini Callas (Amina), Eugenia Ratti (Lisa), Nicola Monti (Elvino), Niccola Zaccaria (Rodolfo); August 29—Edinburgh Festival, opening, with Callas (Amina), Fiorenza Cossotto (Teresa), Monti (Elvino), and

Zaccaria (Rodolfo), and with Renata Scotto replacing Callas on September 3.

1958: February 20—Drury Lane Theatre, London, with Renata Scotto (Amina), Luigi Pontiggia (Elvino), and Lorenzo Gaetani (Rodolfo).

1959: January—Teatro San Carlo, Naples, with Virginia Zeani (Amina), Nicola Monti (Elvino), and Nicola Rossi-Lemeni (Rodolfo).

1960: summer—Cincinnati Summer Opera, with Roberta Peters (Amina), Ugo Benelli (Elvino), and Ezio Flagello (Rodolfo); October 1— San Francisco Opera, with Anna Moffo (Amina), Nicola Monti (Elvino), and Giorgio Tozzi (Rodolfo); October 21—Covent Garden, London, opening night of the season, with Joan Sutherland (Amina), Agostino Lazzari (Elvino), and Joseph Rouleau (Rodolfo), Tullio Serafin conducting (the first Covent Garden *Sonnambula* since 1911).

1961: May 26—Teatro La Fenice, Venice, with Renata Scotto (Amina), Alfredo Kraus (Elvino), Ivo Vincò (Rodolfo)[9]; December 6—American Opera Society, Carnegie Hall, New York (concert performance), with Joan Sutherland (Amina), Betty Allen (Teresa), Eileen di Tullio (Lisa), Renato Cioni (Elvino), and Ezio Flagello (Rodolfo).

1962: February 10—Teatro alla Scala, Milan, with Sutherland (Amina).

1963: February 21—Metropolitan Opera, New York, with Sutherland (Amina), Nicolai Gedda (Elvino), and Giorgio Tozzi (Rodolfo).[10]

1964: October 22—New Orleans Opera House, New Orleans, with Gianna D'Angelo (Amina), Monti (Elvino), and Nicola Moscona (Rodolfo).

1965: August 3—Melbourne, Australia, with Sutherland (Amina), Luciano Pavarotti (Elvino), and Joseph Rouleau (Rodolfo).

1967: January 10—Philadelphia Lyric Opera, Philadelphia, with Renata Scotto (Amina), Pierre Duval (Elvino), and Ezio Flagello (Rodolfo).

THE LIBRETTO. Setting—a village in Switzerland.

Act I: Scene 1. "The village square. At one side, an inn, on the other a mill, in the background, gentle hills. . . ." Amina, an orphan who has been raised by Teresa, the miller's wife, is deeply in love with Elvino, and therefore has rejected the wooing of Alessio. She hopes that eventually Alessio will marry the young mistress of the inn, Lisa, who is in love with him (but who has hoped to marry Elvino). After Elvino has prayed at his mother's tomb, he gives Amina a ring that his mother had worn. As the local notary is preparing the marriage contract, a stranger arrives: Count Rodolfo, who had left his father's nearby castle when a young man and now becomes emotional over revisiting the scenes of his childhood. He is attracted by Amina's fresh beauty, and says that she reminds

him of another "*adorabile beltà*" of long before.* As the sunlight begins
to wane, the villagers tell the Count about the local specter, a woman
dressed all in white, her hair undone, who appears on dark, misty nights.
He is skeptical. Turning to Amina, he says: "Farewell, charming girl.
Until tomorrow, farewell. May your husband love you as I would know
how to." Instantly jealous, Elvino says: "Nobody outdoes me in declaring
his love . . ." The Count and Lisa enter her inn as the villagers disperse.
Alone, Amina and Elvino quarrel over the Count's attentions to her, but
finally part with happy hopes for their wedding the next day.

Scene 2. "Room in the inn. . . ." Lisa, while asking the Count—
whose identity she now knows—if his accommodations please him, shows
her flirtatious nature. Suddenly Amina appears in her nightdress. Lisa,
unaware that Amina is walking in her sleep, hides to spy on what she
believes to be Amina's amorous response to the Count's compliments,
and then goes to find Elvino. As Amina talks to Elvino in her dreams,
the Count understands her condition. Villagers wanting to pay their
respects to the Count are heard approaching. He leaves, and the intruders
find Amina alone and apparently asleep on his sofa. Awakened, Amina
naturally denies any wrongdoing and asserts her ignorance of how she
reached the Count's room. Elvino turns against her, breaking their
betrothal; only Teresa treats her with human kindness. As the villagers
leave in an ugly mood, Amina falls into Teresa's arms.

Act II: Scene 1. "A shadow-darkened dale between the village and
the castle." Discussing Amina's plight, the villagers agree to ask the
Count to defend her if he believes in her innocence or, at least, to help
her if he does not. Although Teresa is convinced of Amina's veracity,
the raging Elvino believes the worst of her. He tears his mother's ring
from her finger. Villagers enter to say that Count Rodolfo thinks Amina
truthful and innocent. Elvino, though not convinced, responds to Teresa's
anguished fear that Amina may die of grief: "Ah, why can't I hate you,
unfaithful girl, as I should like to? Ah! you still are not banished from
my heart at all." He rushes away in despair as Teresa leads Amina back
toward the village.

Scene 2. "The Village. Upstage, Teresa's mill; a stream turns the
wheel." Alessio now woos Lisa, who rejects him; Elvino decides that he
himself will marry her at once. The Count tries vainly to explain Amina's
somnambulism, which Elvino finds incredible. Teresa, hearing that Elvino

* Felice Romani much wanted the libretto to make clear that Count Rodolfo had
seduced a young village girl, who then had borne him a child—Amina—thus causing
him to leave the neighborhood. But Bellini vetoed the idea. Some rather puzzling
remnants of that notion remain to remind us how much better knit the imbroglio
would have been had Romani had his way.

proposes to marry Lisa, accuses Lisa of dishonesty and displays a hand-
kerchief that the girl had dropped in the Count's room. "We see Amina
emerge through one of the mill windows; asleep, she walks on the edge
of the roof: beneath her, the millwheel, which is revolving swiftly and
threatening to crush her if she should make a misstep. All turn toward
her in terror. Rodolfo restrains Elvino." Amina laments the loss of
Elvino, searches her hand for the ring he has taken from her, and weeps
over now-withered flowers that he had given her. Count Rodolfo orders
absolute silence and tells Elvino to approach her gently once she has
descended from the roof, and then to replace the ring upon her finger.
Convinced at last of Amina's innocence, Elvino does so, asking for her
forgiveness. She awakens amid general rejoicing.

THE OPERA. *Act I: Scenes 1–7.* "Upstage, Teresa's mill; a stream is turning
its wheel. Downstage, Lisa's inn":

Scene 1—The *"Coro d'Introduzione"* is prefaced by eighty-seven
measures of orchestral mood- and scene-evocation, which swiftly and
excellently establish the naïve, pastoral character that will suffuse the entire opera. G major, 6/8 time, allegro, the first forty-three measures end
on a fermata (p. 1*), after which a stage band is heard at a distance. As
the curtain rises without break in the music, offstage voices are heard:
"Viva! viva Amina!" (p. 3, three-part chorus: s, t, bs): the villagers are
assembling to celebrate Amina's betrothal to Elvino. "Lisa emerges from
her inn" and, A-flat major, 4/4 time, *allegro assai moderato*, p. 6, sings
her lamenting cavatina, *"Tutto è gioia, tutto è festa,"* complaining that
amid general joy only she must sorrow: Elvino is being taken from her.
Before she has finished, the villagers, still offstage, resume (p. 7) their
vivas; she then repeats the cavatina, resenting having to embrace Amina,
her successful rival. In the *"Stretta dell'Introduzione"* (p. 9), Alessio
comes down from the hills (G major, 6/8 time, allegro); as the villagers
persist in their gaiety, Lisa greets Alessio coldly. He, however, predicts
that her wedding day too will come.

Scene 2—The villagers arrive from the hills in festive garments and
carrying rustic instruments and flowers. Lisa becomes more and more
enraged. *Più moderato*, piano, the orchestra introduces, (p. 13) the cabaletta (p. 14) of the *Introduzione*—the dancelike chorus *"In Elvezia non
v'ha rosa"* (of which it becomes the principal melody). The villagers
praise Amina, and Alessio enthusiastically joins in. (Bellini brought this
melody over from the *Ernani* sketches, which contain a single page on
which six and a quarter measures of it appear in 4/4 time.) As Alessio
and Lisa continue at cross-purposes, the villagers turn (p. 18, *primo*

* Page references here are to the Ricordi piano-vocal score with plate number 41686.

La Sonnambula

7*La Sonnambula*   (335

tempo) to congratulating the still-absent Elvino, ending with a final
"Viva!"

Scene 3—Amina and Teresa enter. In recitative (p. 21), Amina thanks
her friends for their song; they wish her happiness; and she, continuing in
recitative, thanks Teresa for having saved her, an orphan, for this happy
day. E-flat major, 4/4 time, *cantabile sostenuto assai*, p. 22, she then
sings *"Come per me sereno"*—an aria remarkable for its melodic beauty,
its delineation of her simple, trusting nature, and its sure-handed estab-
lishment of light *fioriture* as natural exhalations of that nature. When the
villagers continue (p. 24) with their good wishes, Amina embraces Teresa,
taking her by the hand and drawing her close as she sings, moderato, p. 25
the cabalettalike *"Sovra il sen la man mi posa,"* which is supported by
Teresa and the chorus. After a brief *più vivo* section (pp. 27-28) and a
rapid twenty-note descending chromatic scale, Amina repeats (*primo
tempo*, p. 29) her cabaletta, again with choral support and highly relevant
colorature. Alessio, in recitative, p. 34, proudly tells Amina that it was he
who prepared this celebration, wrote the song, and assembled the musicians from neighboring villages. In thanking him, Amina artlessly refers
to his forthcoming marriage to Lisa, who interjects that it will not occur
soon.

Scene 4—As the conversation continues, the Notary enters (p. 35)
and Amina notices Elvino's continued absence. The Notary assures her
that Elvino is on his way—and very soon Elvino descends from the hills.

Scene 5—*"Recitativo e Duetto."* Elvino explains that he has been at
his mother's tomb to pray for her blessing upon Amina. The Notary lays
out the marriage contract and asks Elvino (p. 39) what he is giving his
wife; Elvino's response is "Everything I possess." Asked in turn what
she will bring her husband, Amina replies: "Only my heart." This leads
(p. 39, A-flat major, 12/8 time, *andante sostenuto*) to the signing of the
contract by Teresa and the witnesses as Elvino places a ring upon
Amina's finger and sings (p. 40) his exquisite *"Prendi: l'anel ti dono,"*
saying that it was his mother's wedding band. As all those present agree
(6/8 time, p. 44) that the vows are now sealed in Heaven, Elvino also
gives Amina a nosegay of field flowers (p. 42). Allegretto, *con brio*,
p. 49, Amina sings—again with almost dancelike skittishness—her wish
that she could express her love in words, *"Ah! vorrei trovar parole."*
Elvino's reply (pp. 45-46), *"Tutto, ah! tutto in quest'istante,"* has no
trouble finding ardent, amorous words. The sunburst of general happiness
proves almost more than the sulking Lisa can bear. As (B-flat major, 4/4
time, p. 54) Elvino speaks in recitative of the wedding at dawn the next
day, "Sounds of a whip and trampling horses are heard." Amina exclaims,
"A stranger!"

Scene 6—"*Recitativo e Cavatina*" (E-flat major, 3/8 time, allegretto, p. 55). Rodolfo and two postillions enter. When the Count asks whether or not he is still far from the castle, Lisa advises him to spend the night in her inn. Off guard, he says that he recognizes the place; all wonder who he may be. A-flat major, 4/4 time, *andante cantabile*, p. 57, he sings his extremely Verdian cavatina, "*Vi ravviso*," identifying these "beloved places" as the scenes of his youth; all join in, puzzled as to when he might have seen them before. Rodolfo too has his cadenza (p. 60): the role was composed for Luciano Mariani. When he learns that the festivities he has interrupted are a prelude to the marriage of Amina, he flatters her with compliments, to the scorn of Lisa and the dawning jealousy of Elvino,[11] but to the villagers' delight.

"*Coro*," E-flat major, p. 70. In recitative, Elvino asks the stranger if he formerly knew the village. Rodolfo replies that he was once with the lord of the castle, who is now dead—and that the lord's son still lives and will return one day to the castle. "The sound of bagpipes is heard, calling the flocks back to their fold." Teresa remarks (p. 71) that the sun is setting and that they should leave. When the others, Rodolfo excepted, ask why, she signals them to come closer to her and sings (4/4 time, *andante mosso*, "with great mystery," p. 72) "*Sapete che l'ora s'avvicina*," saying that it is the hour for the terrible apparition to manifest itself. As the people comment, "It is true, it is true," Rodolfo asks to be told about the fantasm. In the chorus "*A fosco cielo*" (E-flat major, *primo tempo*, "*con mistero*," p. 74), the villagers tell of the night-time appearance of a ghostly vision that walks wrapped in folds of white, with burning eyes and unbound hair. Henri de Saussine[12] wrote of this chorus: "In the first act of *La Sonnambula*: a syllabic chorus of peasants tells a ghost story in E-flat major. Suddenly: a D-major chord. One hears the phantom pass by." When Rodolfo asserts that the phantom is created for them by their own blind credulity, they repeat the music of their chorus (p. 76), this time insisting that when the phantom appears, even dogs lower their heads and howl. Amina, Lisa, Teresa, and Elvino assure him that the phantom is real (p. 78), and he expresses the hope of seeing it. In recitative (p. 81), Rodolfo prepares to retire for the night in Lisa's inn. He bids farewell to Amina with the wish (p. 82) that her husband will love her as he himself would know how to love her. Elvino stanchly insists that nobody can surpass the love he feels for Amina. "You are a happy man if you possess her heart," the Count tells him (p. 82) as, with Lisa, he goes into the inn. The others disperse. Amina and Elvino are left alone together.

Scene 7—"*Scena e Duetto*," C major, 3/8 time, moderato, p. 83. In recitative, Elvino reveals his jealousy to Amina. When she asks of whom he is jealous, he answers, "Of everyone," and begins, F major, *andante assai sostenuto, pianissimo, dolce,* p. 85, the naïvely winning duet *"Son geloso del zeffiro errante,"* during which Amina begs him to suppress his jealousy. Separately and together, they have high arcs of *fioriture* and a series of trills in thirds (pp. 86-87, 88-89) which emanate from youth, health, and impassioned love. Elvino promises not to doubt her, and they part regretfully.

Scenes 8–11. "A room in Lisa's inn; a window at the back; at one side, an entrance door; at the other, an inner room; a sofa and a small table":

Scene 8—*"Scena,"* Rodolfo alone (p. 91). After a brief orchestral prelude in F major, 4/4 time, moderato, the Count soliloquizes in recitative, realizing his pleasure in the village, its people, the attractive young bride-to-be, and the coy inn-hostess. Lisa enters (p. 92) and, in an exchange of persiflage, quickly makes her availability clear to the visitor, whom meanwhile she has identified as the Count. A noise at the window (p. 94) interrupts their amorous byplay. Not wanting to be found in her guest's room, Lisa runs out, dropping her kerchief in her haste; Rodolfo picks it up and tosses it onto the sofa.

Scene 9—Someone opens the window. Amina appears dressed in a simple white gown. She is asleep, a somnambulist. She advances slowly, uncertainly, to the center of the room. At once Rodolfo recognizes her as the pretty betrothed girl and realizes that she must be the villagers' "phantom." She is dreaming of Elvino and his jealousy. Debating whether or not to awaken her, Rodolfo goes to close the window. Watching from the inner room, Lisa says (p. 96), "Amina! o unfaithful girl!" and goes off without having been seen. *Allegro moderato,* p. 96, Rodolfo moves toward Amina, but then stops, saying to himself, "Oh God! What am I doing?" He swears to himself not to take advantage of her plight, but to help her. Maestoso, p. 98, the dreaming Amina imagines that the wedding ceremony is taking place and swears eternal fidelity to and love for Elvino. Rodolfo decides to leave her asleep. But as he goes toward the door, he hears voices approaching, and therefore leaves by the window, closing it behind him. Still sleeping, Amina lies down on the sofa.

Scene 10—*"Coro,"* F major, 4/4 time, *allegro moderato,* p. 100. Villagers, Alessio, and the mayor approach the door; Alessio and the mayor enter the room, having come to pay their respects to the Count. In three-part chorus (s, t, bs), they sing *sotto voce,* believing the Count to be asleep. When they see that the person on the sofa is a girl, they at first take the situation jocularly (*"È bizzarra l'avventura,"* p. 104): "How did she get in? What is she doing here?"

Scene 11—*"Quintetto,"* D minor, 4/4 time, *allegro assai agitato,* p. 105. Teresa, Elvino, and Lisa enter. Pianissimo, Lisa triumphantly indicates the recumbent Amina to Elvino, whereupon, fortissimo, the villagers break in: "Amina! It is she!" and thus awaken her. Seeing Elvino, she turns happily toward him, but he denounces her harshly for a reason she cannot understand. Dazed by grief, Amina turns toward Teresa while the others ask, "Are you convinced now?" They accept Lisa's story that Amina has yielded to the Count's flirtatious praise by going to him in his room. E-flat major, 12/8 time, *assai sostenuto*, p. 107, Amina begins the true act-finale, singing *"D'un pensiero e d'un accento,"* wholeheartedly swearing her fidelity to Elvino. No one but Teresa heeds her. All sing in swelling ensemble. Unnoticed by the others, Teresa picks Lisa's kerchief from the sofa and ties it around Amina's throat. *"Stretta del Finale Primo,"* A-flat major, 4/4 time, allegro, p. 115, Elvino sternly, righteously announces, *"Non più nozze"* (There will no longer be a wedding). The villagers turn against Amina with rustic cruelty. As Teresa sings her support of Amina—the maternal heart is not shut against her—the others leave threateningly. Amina collapses in Teresa's arms.

Act II: Scenes 1–4. "A shadow-darkened dale between the village and the castle":

Scene 1—*"Coro d'Introduzione," "Qui la selva è più folta,"* E major, 3/4 time allegretto, p. 128. On their way to the castle to ask the Count to tell them whether Amina—for whom they have begun to feel sorry—is or is not guilty, they sing respectfully of the Count (three-part chorus, s, t, bs), then continue on their way.

Scene 2—*"Scena ed Aria: Elvino,"* G major, *larghetto maestoso*, p. 139. Amina and Teresa come in. After a brief orchestral introduction in 9/8 time, Amina discusses with Teresa, in recitative, her terrible grief. Teresa tries to calm her by saying that Elvino too may be sorrowing. Then they see him approaching. Amina wants to hide from him, but cannot.

Scene 3—A minor, 4/4 time, *cantabile sostenuto assai*, p. 141, Elvino speaks to himself, saying that everything is over, sorrowing bitterly. Amina and he quarrel violently as the recitative shades into full song, first in duet, p. 142, then in Elvino's solo, *legato sempre, amaramente*, p. 143: *"Pasci il guardo e appaga l'alma."* (Toward the end of this solo, at the words *"il più triste de' mortali sono, o cruda,"* Bellini made use of a melodic fragment from an *allegro agitato* passage in the *Ernani* sketches; see page 265.) The villagers are heard approaching (p. 145) and singing *"Viva il Conte!"* Bitterly exclaiming, *"Il Conte!"* Elvino starts to leave. Amina delays him as the villagers return.

Scene 4—In chorus, the villagers happily announce that the Count has vouched for Amina's innocence. This further infuriates Elvino. Shouting (p. 147) that his rage knows no limits, he tears his mother's wedding ring from Amina's finger. When Teresa and the villagers warn him that the blow may kill Amina, he softens slightly, singing (p. 151) the intensely expressive and Bellinian *"Ah! perchè non posso odiarti,"* marveling that he cannot hate her—and wishing that she may find another man to love her as he has loved her. Allegro, p. 153, the villagers beg him to speak to the Count before abandoning Amina; fragments of his aria alternate with their choral interjections. In despair, he leaves as Teresa leads Amina away in the opposite direction.

Scenes 5–9. "The village, as in Act I, Scenes 1–7":

Scene 5—B-flat major, 4/4 time, allegro, p. 156. Lisa, Alessio, villagers. Alessio vainly tries to dissuade Lisa from her belief that Elvino will now marry her, saying that Elvino will come to recognize Amina's innocence and that he himself will invoke the Count's help. Offstage, the villagers sing that Lisa will now be Elvino's bride.[13]

Scene 6—Villagers, Lisa, Alessio, then Elvino. When the villagers congratulate Lisa, she replies (p. 159) in her aria *"De' lieti auguri,"* which does little more than allow her to display vocal agility. General happiness reigns. Elvino asserts his love for Lisa and is ready to lead the entire assemblage to the church for their wedding.

Scene 7 (p. 166)—Rodolfo with the others. The Count detains Elvino, assuring him that Amina still deserves his love. True, she was asleep in his room at the inn. But he explains (p. 169) that Amina is a somnambulist: when she went to his room, she was walking in her sleep. Unbelieving, Elvino (p. 170) tries to lead Lisa toward the church; the villagers share his disbelief.

Scene 8—Teresa and the others. B-flat major, 4/4 time, p. 172. Teresa enters and asks for silence: the exhausted Amina has fallen asleep at last. Teresa is appalled to learn that Elvino is about to marry Lisa. When Lisa says (p. 174) that she is worthy of Elvino because she was not found in another man's room, Teresa rounds upon her, accuses her of deceit, and displays the kerchief that she had picked up in the Count's room at Lisa's inn. Convinced of Lisa's perfidy, Elvino sings (A-flat major, 3/8 time, p. 176) *"Lisa mentrice anch'essa"* (Lisa too a liar), thus initiating a canonic quartet with, entering successively, Teresa, Lisa, and Rodolfo).[14] Lisa's obvious discomfiture convicts her in everyone's eyes. But when the crushed Elvino tries to persuade the Count to confirm Lisa's guilt, the Count will speak only of Amina's innocence. When Elvino asks (p. 184) who can supply proof of that, the Count replies, "Who? Look! She herself."

Scene 9 (p. 184)—*"Scena ed Aria Finale: Amina."* Amina emerges through the window of the mill; she is sleepwalking. Rodolfo warns everyone to remain silent: a single shout could awaken her—and cause her

death, for she is starting across the now-traditional shaky bridge (it is
not specified in libretto or score) leading from the mill above the whirl-
ing waterwheel. (This scene, until Amina's awakening, is a close parallel
to the "mad scenes" in many operas— *I Puritani* and *Lucia di Lammermoor* included—but could scarcely differ more from the guilty Lady's
sleepwalking scene in Verdi's *Macbeth;* as an entity it is the dramatic,
musical, and vocal climax toward which the entire opera has been leading.) The bridge shudders under Amina's light, slow step. At last she is
safe; she comes down among the others in complete silence, still asleep.
She dreams of seeing Elvino one more time before he marries another girl.
Forgiving him, she prays for his happiness. Then, *andante sostenuto*, p.
188, she laments the loss of her ring. Larghetto, p. 189, she takes Elvino's
now-withered flowers from her bosom and, after a brief recitative, sings,
A minor (-C major), *andante cantabile*, p. 190, one of the most exquisite
of Bellini's melodies, *"Ah! non credea mirarti sì presto estinto, o fiore"*
(Ah, I had not thought to see you dead so soon, o flower),[15] in which
the words *"al par d'amor"* (like love) burst into a rocket of melancholy
fioriture. Analyzing Bellini's melodic writing, Domenico de Paoli well
said[16]: "Sometimes he overtly breaks up a melody's geometric design and
writes absolutely asymmetric pages (*'Ah! non credea mirarti . . .'* in *La
Sonnambula*) which present, besides lyric beauty almost unique in the history of music, an astonishing cohesion despite their lack of traditional
architecture, despite the abolition of repetitions and recapitulations (the
melody begins, develops without ever returning upon itself: each note
appears to arise from the preceding one like a fruit from a flower, always
new, always unforeseen, always logical, and concludes without a single
recall of any one of its phrases)."

Elvino now can bear Amina's sorrow no longer. The Count tells him
(p. 192) to replace the ring on her finger. which he does. Gladdened
though still asleep, with Elvino kneeling at her feet, Amina addresses her
mother. Now, B-flat major, 6/8 time, *allegro brillante*, the villagers shout:
"Viva Amina!" and thus awaken her. In recitative, she dreads the thought
of being awakened from her recovered happiness. But Elvino (*"con gran
passione incalzante"*) assures her that she is already awake; he speaks of
himself as her husband and lover, and she throws herself into his arms.
Teresa and the chameleonlike villagers—who have now veered in Amina's
direction and have forgotten Lisa and Alessio—speak in chorus (p. 194)
of proceeding to the church for the wedding. B-flat major, 4/4 time,
allegro moderato, Amina sings (p. 196) the renowned cabaletta, *"Ah! non
giunge,"*[17] the vocal emanation of her ecstasy. Elvino and the villagers
join their voices to hers as *La Sonnambula* ends.

Because not one of the protagonists of Romani's *La Sonnambula* is of the slightest complexity or inherent interest, the opera depends, more than any other of Bellini's, wholly upon its music and the *bel canto* of its singers. But that is very far from meaning that its dramatic aspect can be neglected: the taste of the stage director and the singing actors must be unwavering and unflawed if the plot itself is not to strike most twentieth-century operagoers as absurd to the point of risibility. The scene in the room at the inn, in particular, requires a "suspension of disbelief" which can be won only by the most sensitive acting and stage direction to prove that the director himself believes in what is happening. It is difficult to do. But it can be done, and *La Sonnambula* repays faithful production by radiating a spell unlike that of any other opera. It is very unusual among operas still staged at all, not only because it is musically a Bellini masterpiece, but also because it is now the only surviving representative of a whole genre of pastoral tragicomedies which time has removed from the stage,[18] largely works by librettists and composers whose names are almost forgotten except by lexicographers and historians.

La Straniera

OPERA SERIA in two acts (eight scenes). *Libretto:* By Felice Romani, derived from *L'Étrangère*, a novel by Victor-Charles Prévôt, vicomte d'Arlincourt, and possibly in part from a free dramatization of that novel by barone Giovan Carlo Cosenza.[1] *Composed:* 1828–1829. *Première:* Teatro alla Scala, Milan, February 14, 1829, on a triple bill with two ballets—*Avviso ai maritati*, choreographed by Serafini to unidentified music, and *Buondelmonte*, choreographed by Giovanni Galzerani to music by Francesco Schira. *Original cast:*

ALAIDE (*"The Stranger"*)	Henriette Méric-Lalande[2]
ISOLETTA, *daughter of the Signore di Montolino, betrothed to Arturo*	Caroline Ungher*
ARTURO, *Count of Ravenstel*	Domenico Reina
THE BARON DI VALDEBURGO, *brother of Alaide*	Antonio Tamburini
THE PRIOR OF THE SPEDALIERI	Domenico Spiaggi
OSBURGO, *confidant of Arturo*	Luigi Asti
THE SIGNORE DI MONTOLINO, *father of Isoletta*	Stanislao Marcionni

The stage settings were by Alessandro Sanquirico. *Published:* In piano-vocal score by Ricordi, Milan, 1829, with plate numbers 4022–4041; again, undated, pl. nos. 35591–35607; again, undated, with pl. no. 108100; by the Calcografia e Copisteria de' Reali Teatri (Girard, later Cottrau), Naples, undated, with pl. nos. 17540–17557; and by both Launer and Maurice

---

* In Italy an *h* often was placed after the *g* in Unger's name to preserve the hard sound of the *g*.

Schlesinger, Paris. Autograph score in the Archivio Ricordi, Milan; manuscript copies in the Naples Conservatory library; in the library of the Conservatorio Giuseppe Verdi, Milan (two—one [Ms. 20] with autograph interpolations and passages); and in the Bibliothèque Nationale, Paris, which also has what appears to be an autograph fragment (four pages) of Alaide's final aria, "*Or sei pago, o ciel tremendo*." For further details concerning autographs and manuscripts, see Friedrich Lippmann, *Vincenzo Bellini*, etc., *op. cit.*, p. 379. Dedicated to Giuditta Turina.

PERFORMANCE DATA. *La Straniera* was presented at La Scala again in January 1830 (nineteen performances),[3] with Giovanni Battista Rubini as Arturo, and was revived there again on February 21, 1837 (nine performances) and January 22, 1841 (eight performances, with Giorgio Ronconi as Valdeburgo). As part of the centenary commemoration of Bellini's death, it was staged at La Scala for two performances in 1935, the first on April 22, when Gino Marinuzzi conducted and the cast was headed by Gina Cigna (Alaide), Gianna Pederzini (Isoletta), Francesco Merli (Arturo), Mario Basiola (Valdeburgo), and Duilio Baronte (Il Priore).

After the 1829 première of *La Straniera* at La Scala, the opera moved quickly to other Italian stages. Performances (not necessarily the first in the cities named) were put on at the Teatro Carolino, Palermo, on January 1, 1830; at the Teatro Riccardi, Bergamo, on August 17, 1830—when Reina repeated his Arturo and the Alaide was Stefania Favelli[4]; at the Teatro San Carlo, Naples, in December 1830, with Tamburini as Valdeburgo; during the 1830–1831 season at the Teatro Eretenio, Vicenza; at the Teatro La Munizione, Messina, during the Carnival of 1831; at the Teatro Comunale, Sinigaglia, during the 1831 *fiera*, with Unger as Alaide; at the Teatro Comunale, Trieste, in the autumn of 1831; on February 4, 1832, at the Teatro La Fenice, Venice, with Giuditta Grisi (Alaide), Anna Del Serre (Isoletta), Reina (Arturo), Domenico Cosselli (Valdeburgo), Natale Costantini (Il Signore di Montolino), and Alessandro Giacchini (Osburgo).[5] At the Teatro Apollo, Rome, on February 18, 1832, *La Straniera* became the second Bellini opera heard in that city; the cast included Clementina Fanti (Alaide), Teresa Zappucci (Isoletta), Andrea Peruzzi (Arturo), Luigi Battaglini (Valdeburgo), Federico Badiali (Osburgo), and Luigi Tabellini (Il Signor di Montolino).[6] Other Italian stagings of *La Straniera* included one at the Teatro Comunale, Bologna, on May 13, 1832, with Unger now in the title role, Artemisia Tarello (Isoletta), Antonio Poggi (Arturo), Giorgio Ronconi (Valdeburgo), Baldassarre Bazzani (Il Priore), Pietro Giacomini (Osburgo), and Francesco Grandi (Il Signore di Montolino).[7] The popularity of *La Straniera* in Italy endured for several decades.

Outside Italy, *La Straniera* was staged in Italian during Bellini's lifetime at least at Dresden (November 8, 1830); Madrid (Teatro del Príncipe, December 3, 1830); Vienna (Kärntnertortheater, November 24, 1831); London (King's Theatre, June 25, 1832); Paris (Théâtre-Italien, November 6, 1832), with Giuditta Grisi, Rubini (who interpolated a Pacini cavatina), and Tamburini; Maona, Minorca (Teatro Italiano, spring 1833); Corfu (Teatro San Giacomo, autumn 1833); Bastia, Corsica (Teatro dell'-Opera, autumn 1834); New York (Italian Opera House [Park Theater], November 10, 1834)[8]; Lisbon (Teatro São Carlos, June 25, 1835). During that period, *La Straniera* was sung in German: at Graz (February 19, 1831); Vienna (translation by Georg Ott, Kärntnertortheater, November 24, 1831); Prague (January 26, 1832); Berlin (Königsstädtischestheater, Februa̋ry 3, 1832); Budapest (July 30, 1832); Danzig (1833, with Sabine Heinefetter as Alaide); Klagenfurt (May 26, 1834); Amsterdam (1834); Agram (May 1835)—and in Danish (Copenhagen, December 4, 1834). Performances of which the language is not determined (it probably was German) were staged at Leipzig (Stadttheater, spring 1831) and Hannover (spring 1834).

La Straniera had been staged in Mexico City, Algiers, Constantinople, Odessa, Santiago (Chile), Rio de Janeiro, Warsaw, Buenos Aires, and Bucharest, but long since had become a musicological rarity when it was revived for a single performance at the Teatro Massimo Bellini, Catania, in 1954. It was used to open the 1968–1969 season at the Teatro Massimo, Palermo, on December 10, 1968, with Renata Scotto (Alaide), Elena Zilio (Isoletta), Renato Cioni (Arturo), Domenico Trimarchi (Valdeburgo), Maurizio Mazzieri (Il Priore), and Glauco Scarlini (Osburgo); Nino Sanzogno conducted. The American Opera Society presented *La Straniera* in concert form at Carnegie Hall, New York, on March 26, 1969, with Montserrat Caballé as Alaide. The opera has never been performed at Covent Garden, London, or the Metropolitan Opera House, New York.

THE LIBRETTO. The earliest printed librettos for *La Straniera* are preceded by one of Romani's informative but unfortunate *avvertimenti:*

"Although the romance from which I took the subject of the present *melodramma* may be well known to many readers, I may nonetheless be permitted to present them with a sort of summary clarifying what has occurred before the opera begins, which in a musical composition would have required introductory explanation that would have been, if not impossible, then very difficult to present.

"A courtier of the Duke of Pomerania promised the beautiful Agnès, young daughter of his lord [Berthold V, Count of Méran], that he would obtain for her the hand of Philippe-Auguste, King of France, for which reason she entrusted him with a ring, a lock of her hair, and her portrait. The rash Agnès lent herself to this ruse, and in fact became the wife of Philippe, who repudiated Isambour, Princess of Denmark, driven to do so, historians of that time say, by inexplicable aversion; however that may have been, on the very night of his wedding, he had fled the nuptial chamber terrified and filled with horror. Anathematized, the King of France was forced to take back his first wife. Agnès, banished from Paris, was imprisoned in the Château of Karency, in Brittany, where Philippe ordered that she be treated as Queen, even secretly sending to watch over her there her brother, Léopold, Prince of Méran, who settled down in the neighborhood as the Baron of Waldeburg. But the unhappy Agnès, bored in her splendid incarceration, took advantage of a prohibition against letting anyone see her, leaving behind in the château a friend who closely resembled her and retiring to a solitary cottage near the Lake of Montolino to weep in freedom over her guilt and her misfortunes. There, however, persecuted by her sad destiny, she could not find peace; also, the rough inhabitants of the surrounding countryside, seeing this 'Stranger' flee from all companionship and go about covered with a veil and weeping in the most deserted spots, began to fear and believe that she was a witch: for that reason, they persuaded Count Arthur de Ravenstel, descendant of the ancient princes of Brittany and a very importunate young man, to make her acquaintance. He became helplessly enamored of her and considered marrying her, though he was already betrothed to Isolette, daughter of the Lord of Montolino. The consequences of that love form the heart of the action, and I hope that in it they are made clear despite the obstacles erected by so fantastic a subject and, above all, despite the necessity placed upon me of not departing too far from the novelist's intention."

To understand what takes place in the two acts of *La Straniera* is impossible without some acquaintance either with D'Arlincourt's novel or with Romani's summary description of part of it in that *avvertimento*. In the libretto, everyone in the neighborhood of Alaide's retreat—including Isoletta, her father, and his vassals—becomes aware of Arturo's passion for "The Stranger" (Alaide—*i.e.*, Agnès). That awareness increases the peasants' dislike and fear of her, attitudes that only her brother, the barone di Valdeburgo, tries to calm and counteract.

Act I: Scenes 1–5. "Courtyard of the Castle of Montolino: at the back, the lake and, beyond it a view of the illuminated village":

Scene 1—"(Everything indicates that a celebration is taking place. In fact, what is being celebrated is the anniversary of the restoration of Brittany to Philippe-Auguste by the English and the forthcoming marriage of

Isoletta di Montolino and Ravenstel.) The lake is dotted with decorated
and illuminated boats. From a distance, happy singing and merry voices
of approval are heard. Little by little, the singing becomes more distinct,
and from this boat and that, men and women sing the following strophe
in chorus: ["*Voga, voga, il vento tace*"]."

Scene 2—"Valdeburgo and Isoletta." Isoletta explains her unhappiness
by telling Valdeburgo that Arturo has fallen in love with the Stranger—
whom she herself has seen and found divinely beautiful. Isoletta resists
Valdeburgo's horrified attempts to raise her spirits.

Scene 3—"Distant shouts are heard. A dark boat crosses the lake;
in it is seen the Stranger, veiled in black. Many boats follow her." The
agitated Isoletta still refuses to be calmed by Valdeburgo.

Scene 4—"From many sides, the Signore di Montolino, Osburgo,
Knights, and others rush in. Isoletta, leaning on Valdeburgo, is trembling."
Wildly, Isoletta talks of Arturo and the Stranger. Aside, she asks Valdeburgo to bring the ungrateful man to her. He tells her that he hopes to
help her, but that if she is to be a victim, she can find his breast a consoling place to weep. "Isoletta leaves with Valdeburgo, followed by the
chorus. Slowly the stage empties."

Scene 5—"Montolino and Osburgo." Montolino laments Arturo's
neglect of Isoletta and himself, offering to make Osburgo rich if he can
solve the problem caused by the Stranger. Osburgo's final words are:
"Rely upon me. Leave Arturo to me." They depart.

Scene 6. "Interior of the cottage in which the Stranger lives. Arturo
enters warily." The enamored Arturo longs to know the identity of the
Stranger. He sees a portrait of her in sumptuous attire. She once was,
then, happier and in richer circumstances. "The sound of a lute is heard
from a distance." Arturo recognizes Alaide's voice as she sings sorrowingly
of love's deception, all the while coming nearer.

Scene 7. "Arturo is about to leave; he meets Alaide, who is dressed
in black." In an impassioned scene, Alaide is finally driven to admit that
she returns Arturo's love—then tells him that they must part forever, but
will give him no explanation.

Scenes 8–10. "Forest in the neighborhood of Montolino. In the distance, Alaide's cottage. From far away are heard sounds of horns and confused shouting and noises indicating the hubbub of hunting. The shouts
approach nearer and become more distinct; some hunters cross the stage,
followed by Osburgo and the chorus":

Scene 8—All sing of the pleasures of the hunt. When Osburgo remarks upon the Stranger's cottage, the chorus joins in his wish that she
will soon be punished. They will spy upon her and learn her secrets and
ways, so as to take vengeance upon her for her "iniquitous deceptions."

Scene 9—"Valdeburgo and Arturo." Valdeburgo warns Arturo that everyone is agitated by his having fled from the festivities preceding his wedding. Arturo confesses that he no longer loves Isoletta. Arturo insists upon Valdeburgo's seeing Alaide—"and then, if you can advise me to run from her forever, I promise you this—I shall flee from her." Valdeburgo accepts the promise.

Scene 10—"As they approach Alaide's cottage, they see her come out of the forest." Alaide is astonished to see her brother, whom she embraces, thus arousing Arturo's suspicion. Valdeburgo, however, assures him that he and Alaide have been companions since childhood. Having realized that the Stranger is his sister, Valdeburgo vainly tries to drive Arturo away. Arturo becomes infuriated and puts his hand upon his sword. Alaide intervenes, however, and the two men finally depart in opposite directions.

Scene 11. "A remote place, with the Stranger's cottage shaded by forest growth. Facing it, some rocks rise; at their feet the lake. Arturo, then Osburgo and hunters. (The sky darkens gradually, threatening a storm, which in the final scene breaks out with extreme violence. Arturo remains motionless for some time, sunk in profound thought.)" The chorus tells Arturo that he has been betrayed, asserting that Valdeburgo and the Stranger, who are in love, are planning to run away. They bear him off to show him proof of their assertion.

Scene 12. "Alaide and Valdeburgo come out of the cottage; then, concealing himself, Arturo enters, etc." Brother and sister part affectionately; their promise to meet again the next day is misinterpreted by Arturo, especially when Valdeburgo tells her that she must avoid Arturo and flee with him. Calling her brother by his first name, "Leopoldo," Alaide promises to follow him.

Scene 13. "Valdeburgo takes Alaide back to the cottage; when she has gone in, Arturo emerges from hiding." He addresses Valdeburgo as "Leopoldo." When Valdeburgo asks what he wants, Arturo replies: "Vengeance!" The two men duel, and Arturo drives Valdeburgo to the lake shore, wounding him. "Die," Arturo exclaims—and the weakened Valdeburgo collapses into the lake, crying "Arturo!"

Scene 14. "Alaide emerges from the cottage with a torch in her hand." When Arturo tells Alaide that he has driven his rival into the lake, she reveals that Valdeburgo is her brother. Arturo is horrified, believing that Valdeburgo is probably dead; despite Alaide's pleas, he throws himself into the lake in an attempt to save Valdeburgo. Alaide calls for help and picks up Arturo's sword, staining her clothes with blood.

Scene 15. "Residents of the lake shore rush in from all sides, with torches. Osburgo, followed by armed men, appears on the rock on which the prostrate Alaide lies; he sees her, helps her to her feet." The chorus, seeing the blood on Alaide's garment, sings: "The Stranger! . . . blood is flowing." She accuses herself before them of having caused her lover's death. "A moment of silence; thunder, lightning, howling of wind in the forest. Alaide is delirious." Soliloquizing, Alaide increases her self-incrimination. At the height of the storm, Osburgo and the armed men surround her and take her away.

Act II: Scenes 1–5. "Grand salon of the Tribunal of the Spedalieri, which has jurisdiction over the province; at the back, a door":

Scene 1—"As the curtain rises, the Judges are all seated at their places; in their midst, on an elevated seat, the Priore, who presides over the Tribunal; at one side, before the Judges, is Osburgo, accompanied by villagers who, having been corrupted by him, will depose against Alaide. The salon is surrounded by guards." Osburgo, who knows that Arturo has been rescued and is under arrest, has no fear that his false story will be denied. The Priore orders the prisoner brought in.

Scene 2—"Alaide among the guards; she is covered with a large veil; her demeanor is noble and modest. The Priore stares at her breifly, as though reminded of something." When he questions her and she refuses to announce her true name, he is struck by her voice and accent, has her unveiled, and states the case against her: Valdeburgo was killed and thrown into the lake; she was found on the shore bloody and trembling. Is she guilty of the murder? "I am innocent," she answers. She denies having seen either the crime or the victim. "Why did you say that your love was fatal to the murdered man?" She will not answer, except to say: "That is my secret." Although death hangs over her head, she will advance no defense.

Scene 3—"Arturo rushes into the salon, oppressed and gasping." Arturo confesses to the murder of Valdeburgo, whom he had believed to be his rival in love. When the Stranger refuses to speak, the Priore warns her that she may be thought Arturo's accomplice.

Scene 4—"The door at the back opens, and Valdeburgo enters, pale and wrapped in a white cloak. (General astonishment.)" Valdeburgo scorns Arturo, but asserts his guiltlessness and Alaide's innocence. Planning to take Alaide away with him, he is stopped by the chorus's insistence that her identity be revealed. Valdeburgo has her unveil her face to the Priore, who (recognizing her true identity) allows her to leave with her brother.

Scene 5—"The Priore, Osburgo, Knights, and People." The Priore now accuses Osburgo of evil behavior, but allows him to depart with the people.

Scene 6. "Forest, as in Scene 8 of Act I. Arturo, then Valdeburgo." The sorrowing Arturo is about to enter Alaide's cottage when Valdeburgo

emerges. He forgives Arturo, but tells him that Alaide lies all but unconscious. When Arturo persists in his determination to face Alaide and
obtain her pardon, Valdeburgo urges him instead to return to Isoletta
and marry her. Arturo gives in, but extracts Valdeburgo's promise to
attend the wedding. They leave.

Scene 7. "Isoletta's room in the Castle of Montolino. Isoletta alone;
she is plainly dressed and profoundly sorrowful." Soliloquizing, Isoletta
bemoans her fate, her loneliness on what was to have been her wedding
day. She still loves Arturo, and sits awaiting him.

Scene 8. "Chorus of maidens and Isoletta." The maidens tell the enraptured Isoletta that Arturo has come to the Castle and that the wedding
ceremony will proceed.

Scene 9. "Porch of the Church of the Spedalieri. (The place is filled
by the nuptial procession.)" Knights and ladies sing in chorus of the happiness in store for Isoletta and Arturo.

Scene 10. "The Lord of Montolino, Isoletta, and Arturo, then Valdeburgo and Alaide. Isoletta wears a wreath of roses. Valdeburgo steps out
of the throng. A woman covered with a large veil appears and conceals
herself, unseen by the others, behind one of the monuments in the church-
yard. Arturo discovers Valdeburgo and runs up to him." The unsteady
Arturo finally pays attention to the worried Isoletta, but his thoughts
still clearly are with Alaide.

Scene 11. "The Priore comes to the great portal with some Knights."
The Priore and the Lord of Montolino try to persuade Arturo to enter
the Chapel, but he asks to be allowed to go in last. Montolino grants his
wish.

Scene 12. "Arturo, Isoletta, Valdeburgo, and the concealed Alaide."
As Arturo finally is preparing to take Isoletta's hand and enter the Chapel,
he sees Alaide. Isoletta bursts out that she is unloved, and she bravely tries
to free him from his torment, tearing the nuptial wreath from her head.
Alaide then steps forward, picks up the wreath, and in reply to Isoletta's
demand to know who is thus showing pity for her, uncovers her face and
says: "The Stranger!" Alaide takes Arturo and Isoletta by the hand and
leads them into the Chapel, with Valdeburgo following.

Scene 13. "After a few moments, Alaide emerges from the Chapel.
She is trembling, agitated, and almost beside herself." Kneeling and addressing Heaven, she asks acceptance for her sacrifice. The chorus intones a
wedding chant. Alaide thinks of running away, but when the interior
music stops and she realizes that Arturo and Isoletta are now husband and
wife, she sinks to the ground.

Scene 14. "A tumult and much shouting are heard from inside the
Chapel." In a moment, Arturo rushes out, beside himself. To the aroused

Alaide he says: "I mean to live or die with you"—and unsheathes his sword. She screams for help.

Final scene. "The Priore degli Spedalieri, Chorus, and People, all running from the Chapel; then Valdeburgo." The Priore's first words are: "Whom do I see? The Queen!" He tells Arturo that Alaide is really Agnès and—Isambour having died—now Queen of France. Understanding that his love for her is hopeless, Arturo addresses her: "Return to your homeland across my dead body!"—and stabs himself to death. While the others try to comfort the hysterical Agnès, she prays that she may die, swooning as the curtain falls.

THE OPERA. *Act I: Scenes 1–5.* "Courtyard of the Castle of Montolino; at the back, the lake and, beyond it, a view of the illuminated village":

Scene 1—Except for the first *Bianca e Gernando, La Straniera* was the earliest of Bellini's operas not prefaced with a formal *sinfonia;* instead, it begins (p. 1*) with a short orchestral *preludio* or *introduzione.*[9] In A major, 6/8 time, *allegro assai* then allegretto, this leads without pause to a chorus, "*Voga, voga, il vento tace*" (p. 5), a festive quasi-barcarolle (tenors in unison, then divided, sopranos, finally basses).

Scene 2 (p. 14)—"*Recitativo e Duetto,*" C major, 2/4 time, allegro. Valdeburgo and Isoletta, in recitative, discuss her unhappiness, the change in Arturo's attitude toward her, his passion for the Stranger. After a fermata, the signature becomes (p. 18) A-flat major, 4/4 time, *allegro moderato*, as Isoletta tells Valdeburgo of having seen the Stranger and heard her singing to herself, speaking Arturo's name; pianissimo, *movendo leggermente*, Isoletta repeats part of the Stranger's melancholy song ("*Ogni speme è a te rapita*, p. 19). Trying to console her, Valdeburgo sings, *più moderato*, "*Giovine rosa*" (p. 21); then, *più mosso;* "*Ma fa core,*" (p. 22), to which the sorrowing girl replies (p. 23) by again quoting the line from the Stranger's song. The profile of Valdeburgo's uninflected, stanch musical character, the tracing of which begins in this exchange, will become almost Verdian as the opera progresses, suggesting preliminary sketching for both the elder Germont (*La Traviata*) and Rodrigo (*Don Carlc*).

On this duet, Berlioz made an intensely interesting comment[10]: "In the first four measures of the song '*Giovine rosa*,' the cause of the particular hue of Bellini's melodies can be discovered. That cause, which it is easy to find, not only in all his operas, but even in most of his phrases, is the *predominance of the third note of the major mode.* By its proximity to the fourth, which is only a halftone above it, that note at times takes on the aspect of leading note, and gives the songs an expressiveness that

* Page references here are to the Ricordi piano-vocal score with plate number 108100.

is very tender, more often still sad and desolate. When it dominates in a melody that the composer has wanted to make brilliant or energetic, it almost always hides the phrase under a more or less vulgar physiognomy; we see an example in the famous unison duet in *I Puritani* ["*Suoni la tromba*"], the trivial redundancy of which made the success of the piece with part of the public while damaging the composer's reputation in the minds of musicians more than ten consecutive failures could have damaged it. In the duet in *La Straniera*, the expressiveness called for by the situation is, on the contrary, affectionate and melancholy, for which reason the melodic effect of the third [i.e., the note C, the key being A-flat major] is excellent, above all in the last lines:

> Ah! l'aurora della vita
> E l'aurora del dolor.

The same observation is applicable to the theme with which Isoletta begins the second part of the duet:

> O tu che sai gli spasimi
> Di questo cor piagato."

Scene 3 (p. 24)—C major, 4/4 time, *più allegro*. The distant chorus calls out: "*La Straniera! la Straniera!*" and, as she glides by alone in a boat, calls her "*l'iniqua fattucchiera*" (the evil witch), terrifying Isoletta. Here Romani's libretto catches the agitation and fright much more forcefully than they are caught in Bellini's music.

Scene 4 (p. 27)—The Lord of Montolino, Osburgo, knights, and others. Isoletta's father, the Lord of Montolino, tries to calm her. The effectiveness of the three-part chorus (p. 28, s, t, bs) is not served by the aridity of the somewhat square and unyielding accompaniment. Musical —but not dramatic—interest is increased when Isoletta sings her "aria" or cantilena, "*Oh tu che sai gli spasimi*," A-flat major, 4/4 time, *allegro animato* (p. 313). Valdeburgo joins in, their voices moving in parallel tenths. Banality of accompaniment again somewhat vitiates the chorus, "*Ritorna ai giochi*" (p. 34), urging Isoletta to emerge from melancholy. This leads (p. 36) to a repetition (with changed words) of the duet passage for Isoletta and Valdeburgo; the chorus too repeats its plea. The final ensemble (p. 38) is formed by Isoletta, Osburgo, Valdeburgo, the Lord of Montolino, and the chorus.[11]

Scene 5 (p. 46)—C major, 4/4 time, allegro. In recitative, Montolino, and Osburgo discuss how to solve the problem posed by Arturo's passion for the Stranger.

Scenes 6–7. "Interior of the cottage in which the Stranger lives": Scene 6 (p. 48)—"*Scena e Romanza*." F major, 4/4 time, *lento e mae-*

stoso, the orchestra preludes, shifting midway to a long-lined cantilena and leading to Arturo's recitative "*È sgombro il loco*" (p. 50). This is interrupted (p. 51, moderato) by a three-measure instrumental comment ending on a cadenza *a piacere;* it is followed by a strikingly expressive, forceful continuation of the recitative, which shifts to *allegro moderato* (p. 51) and then to *andante cantabile* (p. 52) for Arturo's romanza, "*Eri tu dunque un tempo,*" which Della Corte well called[12] "a sample of the smooth motives often written down in Bellini's notebook, and which he could place here and there without economizing." After a fermata, a cadenza for "lute" (onstage harp, p. 53) announces the distant presence of Alaide, who vocalizes floridly on the syllable "*Ah,*" her sighing being heard twice before she sings "*Sventurato il cor*" (G minor, andante, p. 53), another suave Bellinian melody that all but becomes a leitmotif identifying her, but fails either to individualize her or to transmit her tragic condition (it does, however, certainly foretell more pertinent passages in Bellini's later operas).

Scene 7 (p. 57)—"*Scena e Duetto.*" When, in recitative, Alaide tells Arturo that he cannot share her life or her sorrow, he sings ("*con passione,*" *allegro moderato,* p. 58) a plea that she believe in him, trusting the mysterious force that draws him to her. She prays (moderato, p. 59) that he may not be punished for his love—that she, the guilty one, may suffer alone—this in a highly emotional melodic fragment that passes almost in a single breath, to be succeeded (p. 60) by further recitative dialogue. B-flat major, 4/4 time, *allegro moderato* (p. 61), Arturo passionately restates his love: "*Serba, serba, i tuoi segreti.*" When Alaide confesses her love for him, he sings ecstatically "*M'ami adunque?*" (p. 65), asking how, then, she can hope to forget him. Bellini rises to his musicodramatic best in giving reality to the two lovers in the duet-recitative beginning with Arturo's "*Da regnanti io son disceso*" (p. 66). This (after relevant, extremely emotional vocal flourishes by Alaide, p. 67) glides, F minor, into a duet beginning with Arturo's vision of abandoning the world with her, "*Ah! se tuo vuoi fuggir*" (p. 67), the music of which is unquestionably that of Arturo as lover.[13] Alaide joins him (p. 69) as they exult (here the parallel thirds are an especially apt employment of Bellini's favorite device for projecting two people in shared passion). Giovanni Carli Ballola wrote[14]: "But the keystone of the opera undoubtedly is constituted by the admirable first-act duet between Arturo and Alaide: preceded by a no-less-inspired recitative that occasionally dissolves into pathetic arioso, this culminates in a central episode, '*Ah! se tu vuoi fuggir,*' the corrosive melodic élan of which somewhat resembles the principal theme of the Allegro of Mozart's Quintet in G minor, K.516." 6/8 time, allegro, the hunting horns are heard; Alaide urges Arturo to return to the Castle and marry Isoletta, but her grief breaks out in a cadenza *a piacere* (p. 73) before they sing (3/4 time, *allegro moderato*) the vividly revelatory duet *"Un ultimo addio,"* which increases in intensity and expressiveness to its end (p. 80).

Scenes 8–10. "Forest in the neighborhood of Montolino. In the distance, Alaide's cottage":

Scene 8 (p. 81)—*"Coro di Cacciatori,"* B-flat major, 6/8 time, *allegro brillante*. Repeating a motive heard earlier (p. 71), this is conventional hunt music, orchestral at first, then (p. 82) choral (Osburgo in chorus with the basses): *"Campo ai veltri,"* of which some writers have found it likely that it was stored in Verdi's memory when he composed *"Bella figlia dell'amore"* in *Rigoletto*. Osburgo advocates punishment of the Stranger (p. 86) and the hunters sing (pianissimo, *sotto voce*, p. 87) the ineffective *"Qui non visti,"* of which Andrea Della Corte accurately wrote[15]: "Expressions of cunning, of the vulgarly mysterious, were not really felt by Bellini."

Scene 9 (p. 92)—*"Recitativo e Terzetto,"* B-flat major, allegro. After a recitative exchange between Valdeburgo and Arturo, the former sings the rather featureless *"Ah! squarcia, amico"* (p. 95). When Valdeburgo and Alaide greet each other enthusiastically, rousing Arturo's suspicions, Valdeburgo tells him (p. 87) that he and Alaide have been companions since childhood. Some of this recitative is of Bellini's finest, particularly the very characteristic exchange between the two men begun by Valdeburgo's *"Ah! tu l'amavi"* (p. 93), which once more prefigures Verdi's noble baritones.

Scene 10 (p. 96)—Here Bellini's music fully responds to the intensity of Romani's text-words, particularly when Arturo asks Valdeburgo if Alaide perhaps has another lover (*"D'altri amante è forse?"* p. 99). Now Bellini entirely justifies the stage direction for Arturo (p. 101): "With all the impetus of jealousy." Della Corte was acute in calling[16] "Donizettian" Valdeburgo's reply (D-flat major, andante, p. 102), *"No, non ti son rivale,"* which begins the fine trio that starts in a peculiarly Bellinian atmosphere of melancholy (the French word *détresse* evokes the quality exactly) and thereafter soars and declines to the end of this scene (p. 119) by way of episodes of solo and duet capable of reflecting all of its varied moods and shifting thoughts.

Scenes 11–15. "A remote place, with the Stranger's cottage shaded by forest growth. Facing it, some rocks rise; at their feet, the lake":

Scene 11 (p. 120)—pianissimo, *alla breve, allegro assai*. The approaching thunderstorm is portrayed, with claps coming ominously nearer. Arturo enters (F major, 4/4 time, *allegro moderato*, p. 122) and music well exceeds nature in dramatic impact, particularly after a flash of lightning,

(p. 123, *allegro assai*), with the orchestra descending from fortissimo to pianissimo in six violent measures. Into Arturo's sorrowing soliloquy, the chorus breaks (p. 124) with curious irrelevance in the unison passage (A-flat major, *allegro assai moderato* p. 126) in which it sings "*La Straniera a cui fè . . . tu presti intera*," which would not sound out of place in a Rossini *opera buffa* or *Don Pasquale*, and which here long outlasts its dubious welcome.

Scene 12 (p. 138)—"*Terzettino*," E major (soon modulating to E flat), *andante sostenuto assai*. The orchestra introduces an expressive continuation of Arturo's bitter soliloquy and his overhearing of the parting of Alaide and Valdeburgo ("*Ah! non partir*," p. 138), whom she calls "Leopoldo." As Valdeburgo prepares to depart, the scene ends with an increasedly expressive passage in arioso texture ("*Addio per poco!*" p. 141), after which the orchestra leads through a crescendo to his confrontation with Arturo.

Scene 13 (p. 144)—"*Scena, Coro ed Aria—Finale I*," B-flat major, 4/4 time, allegro. The drama mounts swiftly, beginning with Arturo's suspicious exclamation "*Leopoldo!*" Against a relatively diaphanous orchestral background, the two men duel; wounded, Valdeburgo retreats to the shore before Arturo's onslaught. "Die," Arturo shouts (p. 146); Valdeburgo replies only "Arturo!" and falls into the water (his fall is represented, with almost Straussian realism, by a sixteen-note orchestral descending scale ending in trills).

Scene 14 (p. 136)—The storm approaches its climax as Alaide, torch in hand, emerges from the cottage. When Arturo tells her that he has killed Leopoldo, she replies that he has killed her brother. The theatrical force of this scene is propelled by Bellini's excellent employment of broken phrases, sudden pauses, and canny orchestral touches. Threatening suicide, Arturo runs to the lake, dropping his bloody sword, which Alaide picks up, thus staining her clothes.

Scene 15 (p. 149)—The two-part chorus (t, bs) is heard shouting that a man is in the water. All call for help. The men recognize the Stranger and see the blood on her. Osburgo and the others accuse her of murder (p. 151). In her splendidly evoked hysteria (pp. 151–152, E major, *di forza e crescendo sempre*), Alaide sings a sinuous, emotion-charged melody that is broken into by Osburgo and the now three-part chorus (s, t, bs): "*Tu omicida!*" (p. 152). The thunder is now directly overhead (p. 153); the key changes to a final G major, lightning flashes (p. 154), and the people's threat of punishment increases with the storm. Then, after a momentary silence that merely increases tension, the now-delirious Alaide, *moderato assai*, sings ("*Un grido io sento*," p. 155) of her love as evil and asks that more thunder accuse her (p. 156):

"*Non v'è perdona a tanto error*" (There is no forgiveness for such a sin). The act ends as the people chant against the climax of the tempest (p. 161): "*Paventa, indegna*" (Tremble, base woman).

Act II: Scenes 1–5. "Grand salon for sitting of the Tribunal of the Spedalieri, which has jurisdiction over the province; at the back, a door":

Scene 1 (p. 168)—"*Scena ed Aria,*" 4/4 time, allegro. In recitative, the Priore and the treacherous Osburgo discuss the accusation against Alaide, whom the Priore orders brought in. *Maestoso lugubre* (p. 169), in an orchestrally effective but vocally irrelevant fragment, Osburgo gloats because the imprisoned Arturo cannot be present to contradict him.

Scene 2 (p. 170)—the veiled Alaide is brought in by guards; she and the Priore dialogue in recitative with notably thin instrumental support, and her voice half-awakens the Priore's memory. Her intransigence arouses his anger; he orders her unveiled and recognizes that she is Agnès.

Scene 3 (p. 174)—*Allegro moderato.* The assemblage sings in two-part (t, bs) chorus ("*Morte è sospesa sul capo*"), excellently evoking a grave, threatening atmosphere. Arturo enters, asserts Alaide's innocence of the murder, and—demanding punishment for himself—faces Osburgo to say that he himself committed the crime. Pressed to confirm Arturo's statements, Alaide replies evasively.

Scene 4 (p. 177)—Valdeburgo enters. Alaide, Arturo, and the chorus express amazement at seeing him alive. In the A-flat major aria "*Sì, li scogliete*" (p. 178), he asserts that the prisoners must be freed as innocent: he fell in fair combat with Arturo, and God saved him from the water. But when Arturo joyfully turns toward him (p. 182), Valdeburgo asserts that for Arturo he is indeed dead. A-flat major, *meno mosso* (p. 183), the orchestra preludes Valdeburgo's exquisitely touching "*Meco tu vieni, o misera*" (p. 184), the aria in which he presses Alaide to leave Montolino with him, and which might be called Salvini's "*Ecco, signor, la sposa*" (in the finale of *Adelson e Salvini*, from which Bellini adopted it with ameliorations) half way to achieving the condition of "*Casta diva.*" Della Corte found it[17] "perhaps the most expressive of this opera's cantilenas." The chorus interrupts to say that the law forbids Alaide to depart still unidentified; the Priore, however, frees her. Valdeburgo repeats his aria (p. 187) with slight variation, and then leads Alaide out as the desolated Arturo departs alone and the chorus ponders the "inexplicable mystery." Of the cavatina, "*Meco tu vieni, o misera,*" Berlioz wrote[18]: "I come to a very short aria, scarcely fitted to its surroundings, lacking all development, without any orchestral plan, virgin of any ambitious vocalization—simple, in a word—but in my view offering the type of the young maestro's most touching elegies. It will be divined that I mean to speak of Valdeburgo's aria, one of Tamburini's triumphs.

> Meco tu vieni, o misera,
> Longe [*sic*, for *lunge*] da queste porte,
> Ove celar le lagrime
> Ti scorgerà la sorte,
> Tomba ove ignota scendere
> La terra a te darà.

All these ideas of sorrow, departure, separation, tears, death, the tomb, oblivion, are expressed with the most overwhelming truth. Certainly here is inspiration or it never existed; and that melody, which drives the indifferent to tears, should, by the memories it awakens and the images of mourning that it recalls, cruelly rend the hearts to which Bellini's memory has remained dear."

Scene 5 (p. 192)—"*Scena*," C major, 4/4 time, moderato. In recitative, the Priore turns upon Osburgo, accusing him and saying that he will be watched. Osburgo leaves with the others.

Scene 6 (p. 194). "Forest as in Scene 8 of Act I." "*Scena e Duetto*," E-flat major, 4/4 time, *andante sostenuto*. After a richly evocative, excellently orchestrated introduction (p. 194), Arturo's accompanied recitative expresses his willingness to suffer punishment if only he may see Alaide once more. Allegro (p. 196), just as he is about to enter her cottage, Valdeburgo emerges from it. Their recitative exchange (p. 196) is convincingly forceful. Then (B-flat major, 4/4 time, *allegro giusto*, p. 200), Valdeburgo opens his duet with Arturo ("*Sì . . . Sulla salma del fratello*"), in which Romani's words could serve a virtuous Verdian baritone, whereas Bellini's music for them sounds strained and unidiomatic. Arturo joins in ("*Ah pietà!*" p. 200). In protracted duet, Arturo extracts Valdeburgo's agreement to his seeing Alaide, but in return for a promise to Valdeburgo that he will marry Isoletta. One can sense Bellini's determination here to create contrast and variety: the tempo changes to *andante mosso* (Arturo's "*Tu togliesti al dolente*," p. 204); *allegro agitato* (Valdeburgo's "*Forsennato!*" p. 207); *allegro moderato* (Valdeburgo's "*Tergi il pianto*," p. 211); *più mosso* (p. 212); lento (p. 213); *allegro moderato* (Arturo's "*Ah! se me non vuoi*," p. 214); *più mosso* (p. 215); and *ancora più mosso* (p. 216)—all without achieving more than the forwarding of the plot.

Scenes 7–8. "Isoletta's room in the Castle of Montolino":

Scene 7 (p. 218)—"*Scena ed Aria*," A major, 3/8 time, *andante sostenuto*. A flute melody that Alfredo Parente rightly found[19] quasi-Mozartean invests the orchestral prelude with vague melancholy before

Isoletta's crushed recitative "*Nè alcun ritorna?*" After an *andante sostenuto assai* interlude (p. 220), the *primo tempo* returns (p. 221) with an altered fragment of the prelude, which in turn leads, pianissimo, to Isoletta's gazing at a portrait of Arturo and singing her romanza "*Ah! se non m'ami più*" (p. 222), in which the solo flute continues on its sad way (it could stand as proof that Bellini knew at least one of Donizetti's near-tragic soliloquies). Because Isoletta is an inert, acted-upon rather than active, character, this scene merely delays what is to follow.

Scene 8 (p. 224)—C major, 6/8 time, *allegro assai*. The soprano chorus exults to Isoletta that Arturo has finally arrived, will seek her forgiveness, still loves her, and will marry her this day. Isoletta's astonishment ("*Io . . . sua sposa!*" p. 226) and her change to radiant happiness ("*Ah! al mio sguardo*," *allegro moderato*, G major, 3/4 time, p. 228) are expertly set forth. General fortissimo exultation (p. 231) ends the scene.

Scenes 9–15. "Porch of the Chapel of the Spedalieri":

Scene 9 (p. 234)—"*Coro*," *allegro maestoso, alla breve*, B-flat major. The orchestra preludes impressively the prenuptial chorus (s, t, bs), "*È dolce la vergine*," in which Giovanni Carli Ballola[20] aptly found "Cherubinian grace," and in which Romani's verses floridly praise Isoletta and, with unwitting irony, Arturo.

Scene 10 (p. 245)—"*Scena e Quartetto*." After a recitative introduction (Arturo, Valdeburgo, Isoletta) this brief scene begins (*allegro moderato*, C major, 4/4 time) pianissimo. *Allegro moderato* (p. 246), the distraught Arturo offhandedly tries to reassure the rightly uncertain Isoletta.

Scene 11 (p. 246)—*Allegro moderato*, F major. The Priore and Montolino tell Arturo to take Isoletta inside to the altar, but he asks to be allowed to enter last. Montolino agrees, and all but Arturo pass into the Chapel.

Scene 12 (p. 248)—*Allegro moderato assai*, A-flat major, 4/4 time. As Alaide remains concealed behind a monument, Valdeburgo and Arturo address one another in recitative asides. Alaide sighs (P. 250), revealing her presence to Arturo, whose agitation mounts. Beginning with Valdeburgo's "*Si! si! tu il sei*" (p. 251), but known as "*Qual sarà dolor che uccide*" (p. 252), the impassioned quartet (Arturo, Isoletta, Valdeburgo, Alaide—not all of whom sing all the time) superbly presents the wildly disparate emotions, desires, and momentary beliefs of the protagonists.[21] Finally (pp. 258–259) Alaide leads Arturo and Isoletta, followed by Valdeburgo, into the Chapel.

Scene 13 (p. 260)—"*Scena, Coro ed Aria Finale*," allegro, D-flat major, 4/4 time: In culminating agitation, despairing and tottering,

Alaide emerges from the Chapel to bewail having erected a barrier between Arturo and herself. *Largo maestoso,* B-flat major, *"con grande espressione"* (p. 261), the orchestra begins a rocking eighth-note accompaniment that foretells that of *"Casta diva,"* as other details of the following aria confirm. Alaide kneels and intones her movingly intense and beautiful prayer, *"Ciel pietoso"* (p. 260), toward the end of which (p. 263) the meaning that her sacrifice has to her is revealed in *fioriture.* When the Chapel choir sings *"Pari all'amor degli angioli"* (*andante un poco mosso,* p. 264), she rises to her feet dismayed, realizing that the rite has begun. Hearing no further music from the Chapel, she sinks down at the foot of a monument, murmuring, pianissimo (p. 269), "The bond is sealed . . . I no longer live."

Scene 14 (p. 270)—F major. A tumult (chorus: *"Vaneggia . . . il passo sgombrisi"*) is heard inside the Chapel. Arturo rushes out to Alaide. Saying that he will live with her or die with her, he draws his sword. Alaide screams for help.

Final scene (p. 271)—The Priore, seeing Alaide unveiled, explains to the others that the Stranger is in truth Agnès, and now their Queen. At this revelation, Arturo shakes off restraint and dashes toward her, crying out: *"Sovra il mio corpo spento ritorna al soglio"* (Return to your homeland across my dead body), and stabs himself to death. The delirious Agnès cannot hear the calming phrases of Valdeburgo, the Priore, and the others. After three orchestral fermatas flanking bare chords, *"con tutta la forza"* (p. 275), she begins (B-flat major, *allegro moderato*) her shattering, death-desiring final aria, *"Or sei pago, o ciel tremendo,"* a strikingly close parallel in purpose and position (but not in musical ideas) to Imogene's mad scene at the end of *Il Pirata.* Her prayer for oblivion is answered as the chorus sings (p. 282) that her spirit is leaving her; after her last word (*"amor,"* against which the chorus sings *"terror"*), she swoons.

Turning to this last section of *La Straniera,* Berlioz wrote[22]: "I pass over several pieces clearly based upon the Rossinian formula so as to have praise for a prayer in the final scene: *Ciel pietoso,* beautiful and noble in color, though not very original, an inevitable recitative, full of movement, and Alaide's admirable aria at the moment of the catastrophe, in which she exhales her passion and her despair in frenetic accents. The chorus that then joins her offers nothing remarkable in itself, but does serve to sustain the cries of the half-mad Queen—sharp, violent, prolonged cries, nakedly presented—which could seem to be a disgraceful effect musically, but of which the strength, to a degree overlaid and at intervals veiled in the midst of the choral mass, suffuses this entire peroration with the most pathetic hue."

. . .

La Straniera cannot claim a position alongside Bellini's finest operas— *Il Pirata, La Sonnambula, Norma,* and *I Puritani.* Nor can it be listed with his secondary successes—*I Capuleti e i Montecchi* and the revised *Bianca e Fernando.* It is a strangely un-Bellinian, singular opera, partly because its libretto relies more on plot meshings and fractures than on the persuasiveness of its characters, and partly because its score, somewhat as in the case of the very different *Zaira,* represents Bellini's approaches and methods on the road from *Il Pirata* and the revised *Bianca* to the more purely melodic, tragically touching or sweetly sad *Capuleti* and *Sonnambula.* More than any of his other operas, perhaps excepting *Il Pirata,* it must rely for full effectiveness much more basically on the acting ability of its protagonists than on their *bel canto.* But even when superbly performed, it cannot be an opera by which the extremely individual Bellinian qualities best can be judged or appreciated. With *Il Pirata,* Bellini had succeeded more consistently two years earlier; two years later, with *La Sonnambula* and *Norma,* he would excel not only all of his own past creations, but those of his active contemporaries as well.

Zaira

TRAGEDIA LIRICA (*opera seria*) in two acts. *Libretto:* By Felice Romani, based upon Voltaire's *tragédie Zaïre* (1732), possibly with hints taken from Mattia Bo[u]tturini's libretto *Zaira, o sia Il Trionfo della religione*, as set by several composers, including Sebastiano Nasolini (*Zaira*, Teatro San Benedetto, Venice, 1797). *Composed:* 1829. *Première:* Inauguration of the Teatro Ducale (later Regio), Parma, May 16, 1829, on a double bill with *Oreste*, a five-act ballet choreographed and directed by Antonio Cortesi.[1] *Original cast:*

Mussulmans

Slaves of the Sultan {	ZAIRA	Henriette Méric-Lalande
	FATIMA	Marietta Sacchi
CORASMINO, *vizier*		Carlo Trezzini
MELEDOR, *an official of the Sultan*		Pietro Ansiglioni
OROSMANE, *Sultan of Jerusalem*		Luigi Lablache

Frenchmen

LUSIGNANO, *prince of the line* *of the onetime kings of Jerusalem*		Giovanni Inchindi
French knights {	NERESTANO	Teresa Cecconi
	CASTIGLIONE	Francesco Antonio Biscottini

Published: Two scenes (the *scena* and *duetto* "*Io troverò nell'Asia*" and the trio "*Cari oggetti in seno a voi*") were issued in piano-vocal score by both Ricordi, Milan (plate numbers, respectively, 4158 and 4157), and Girard (later Cottrau), Naples. Never published complete. Autograph score in the library of the Naples Conservatory. Seldom performed after the Parma singings of 1829.

PERFORMANCE DATA: *Zaira* was staged at the Teatro della Pergola, Florence, between May 14 and June 25, 1836,[2] with this cast: Sofia Dall'Oca Schoberlechner (Zaira), Giuseppina Lega (Fatima), Antonio Poggi (Corasmino), Stanislao Demt (Meledor), Carlo Marcolini (Orosmane), Luigi Battaglini (Lusingano [*sic*]), Teresa Cecconi (Nerestano, the male role she had created), and Tersiccio Soverini (*sic*—for Severini?—Castiglione). Below the cast-listing in the Florence libretto, this appears: "The music was composed by the Signor Maestro Vincenzo Bellini."

An anonymous writer in the *Gazzetta di Firenze* of July 14, 1836, after ticking off the ballets performed during the season at the Pergola, said: "Bellini's *Zaira* put in an appearance on the stage, but that audience, less sensitive than Orosmane, shouted at her, and she returned to the harem! Why so little delicacy? One sympathizes with the audience: *Zaira* was one of Bellini's first scores [*sic*], and because it was not happily received when first produced, the owner of this score kept it hidden, or in the harem. But Bellini took all of its happiest ideas to enrich other works of his, which were produced more happily and were thenceforward known by all. Thus, *Zaira* was like a mother who, having transferred her beauties to various daughters already admired by the best society, and having herself emerged again, but tardily, to seek adoration, is advised to go home." Bellini would particularly have disliked the next sentence of that chronicle: "[Donizetti's] *Belisario* followed, to demand not an offering but a triumph. And certainly the music merits a triumph, or at least an ovation."

THE LIBRETTO. Setting—The Sultan's palace and its garden, Jerusalem.[3]

Act I: Scenes 1–7. "A magnificent gallery leading to the Sultan's harem . . . The harem is *en fête* to celebrate the forthcoming marriage of the Sultan to Zaira. Male and female slaves enter from various sides; odalisques sing to the sound of Oriental instruments . . ."

The pre-nuptial music angers the vizier Corasmino and the other strict Mussulman officials, who oppose the enthronement of a Christian girl. But when rebellion is suggested, Corasmino remains faithful to the Sultan, promising to find another way of preventing the sacrilegious marriage. Zaira and Fatima discuss the knight, Nerestano, who left the year before, promising to return from France to free Zaira and ten of the other French knights. Fatima rails against Zaira's love for Orosmane. When a chorus of eunuchs announces Orosmane's arrival, Zaira's joy intensifies Fatima's fury. While Orosmane and Zaira express their mutual love, Fatima plans to separate them. Meledor, a palace official, tells the returned Nerestano that a hundred, rather than ten, French

knights may leave for home. Only one may not go: the elderly, ailing
Lusignano—who is descended from the hated onetime Lusignan kings
of Jerusalem. Nor, because of Orosmane's love for Zaira, will he now
keep his promise to release her: "No sum exists which could ransom
her." When the Sultan says that Zaira is happy to remain in Jerusalem
at his side, Nerestano is unbelieving; he upbraids Zaira, weakening her
resolution and darkening her joy.

Scenes 8–11. "Subterranean hall . . ."

Nerestano tells Castiglione that they are about to be freed, but
refuses to explain his distress. Finally he admits that Lusignano may not
accompany them. All of the imprisoned knights reject release without
Lusignano. Word is brought, however, that Orosmane has granted
Zaira's pleas and agreed to liberate Lusignano, too. Lusignano, struck
by the sight of the golden crucifix that Zaira wears, discovers that she
and Nerestano are his supposedly lost children, from whom his capture
by the Mussulmans had separated him. In the middle of this happy re-
encounter, Zaira tells her father that she will marry the Sultan. His new
happiness turns to intense sorrow: she will have to renounce Christianity
and become a Mussulman. Finally, she swears that she will do everything
possible to remain a Christian. Meledor tells Zaira that Orosmane has
sent for her.

Scenes 12–15. "Interior of the harem."

Orosmane orders the prisoners, Lusignano included, to be released
despite the objections of Corasmino, who predicts that all Europe will
denounce the Sultan for the sad condition to which imprisonment has
brought Lusignano. Zaira and Nerestano part in sorrow. Zaira then persuades Orosmane to delay their wedding. Corasmino supposes that Zaira
is in love with Nerestano and is planning to deceive the Sultan. Orosmane,
believing the accusation, swears revenge.

Act II: Scenes 1–2. "Zaira's quarters."

Fatima encourages Zaira to persevere in her refusal to marry Orosmane. When he enters, Zaira promises to tell him her secret if he will
again postpone their wedding.

Scenes 3–6. "Remote place near the quarters assigned to the French
knights."

Lusignano has died. Orosmane will permit his body to be taken
away for Christian burial. Zaira cannot attend the preliminary funeral
rites: she is to marry Orosmane the next day. This arouses Nerestano
and the other knights, who plan to rescue her.

Scenes 7–11. "Ground-floor hall in the harem . . ."

Corasmino reveals to Orosmane the supposed plan of betrayal, telling him that a slave bearing a secret message from Nerestano to Zaira has

trophizes her, calling her "light of our sky" and begging her to unveil her face for the Sultan's delight.

Scene 5 (60R–62R)—"Orosmane and the others." B-flat major, 4/4 time, *allegro maestoso e moderato*. Orosmane enters to an an impressive march rhythm (60R) and at once addresses Zaira in impassioned recitative (61L): *"Zaira, i bei concenti"* (Zaira, the beautiful harmonies), telling her that music, dancing, and perfumes speak his love for her. Zaira is enraptured (61R), but Fatima searches for a means to "rescue her from the seducer."[6] Orosmane continues his exulting praise of her (*"Dopo la gloria io t'amo"*—I love you next after glory, 62R); Zaira answers in his exalted tone.

Scene 6 (63R)—"Meledor and the others," B-flat major. Meledor tells Orosmane that the "slave" who left for France has returned and is seeking audience. Orosmane orders him admitted; and Zaira exclaims: "Oh Heaven, at what a moment he returns!"

Scene 7 (63R–83L)—"Nerestano, his attendants, and the others," *Allegro maestoso*, in continuing recitative, Nerestano and Orosmane outdo one another in courtly generosity. The Sultan announces that one hundred rather than the promised ten French knights will be freed; however, he excludes (64L) one knight from this amnesty: Lusignano, who is descended from a hated line, the ancient kings of Jerusalem. "And Zaira?" Nerestano asks (65L). F major, *allegro moderato*, the orchestra introduces the chorus-supported ensemble *"Prezzo non v'ha che basti"* (No ransom could suffice, 66L) of Orosmane, Nerestano, Zaira, and Fatima—a complex, uncommunicative piece. In it, the flute introduces a melody that Orosmane sings to explain why he now reneges on his promise to free Zaira: *con espressione* 67R, *"Or d'Orosmane al fianco"*# (Now beside Orosmane). This is interrupted by Nerestano's expressions of agitation and Zaira's of confusion. Undramatically, Nerestano sings to himself (70R) the melody just sung by Orosmane, saying that he cannot bear to hear of Zaira—who was "born to the faith"—as a Mussulman. *Più allegro* (71R), Orosmane orders the ceremony to continue, whereupon the three-voice chorus enters (*"Il temerario apprenda"*—May the rash man learn, 72), thus initiating the large, busy, somewhat vacant *stretta* that ends the scene. Nerestano turns upon Zaira (*"Misera!"* 73R); Zaira and Fatima lament. Orosmane asks Zaira the meaning of her sighs (74L) and then sings the chief melody of the *stretta*: *"Ritorni al tuo sembiante/ Il ben seren primiero"*# (Bring back to your face the first beautiful serenity,) *allegro maestoso*, 74R. Zaira and Nerestano take up the melody, singing in parallel thirds, while the three-voice chorus joins in (77L) and Orosmane repeats his earlier lines. And so the *stretta* stretches on, with

Nerestano swearing to save Zaira from God's enemies, Zaira in confused despair, Orosmane and the other Mussulmans rejoicing over his coming marriage.[7] At its end (83L), "Orosmane takes Zaira by the hand and leads her out; the others follow him. Nerestano departs with Meledor."

Scenes 8–11 (83R–138L). "Subterranean chamber leading to the cells in which the French slaves are incarcerated":

Scene 8 (83L–85L)—"Castiglione and Nerestano." After twelve measures of string introduction (83R), E-flat major, 4/4 time, *andante maestoso*, Castiglione and Nerestano discuss in recitative the forthcoming happy release of the prisoners. Nerestano refuses to disclose the cause of his depressed state. The tempo changes to *allegro moderato* as the tramping of the freed men is heard (84R). Nerestano exclaims: *"Beato istante!"*

Scene 9 (85R–98L)—"Chorus of French prisoners." *Allegro moderato*, the strings, soon backed by other instruments, introduce (85R) the two-voice chorus (87L) *"Chi ci toglie ai ceppi nostri"*# (He who frees us from our chain-blocks), which Pastura accurately described[8] as "mannered and weak despite the composer's obvious intention to confer dramatic interest upon the piece by introducing a series of unprepared modulations . . ." When (90L–91L) Nerestano tells the men that Orosmane refuses to free Lusignano, they and Castiglione reject their own liberation (91L–92R). The scene ends on too many repetitions of the chorus's high-flown lines *"Scritto in sangue è il giuramento./ Niun di noi tradir lo può"* (The oath is written in blood. None of us can break it, 95L–98L).

Scene 10 (98R–124L)—"Zaira and the others, then Lusignano supported by two slaves . . . Recitative and Trio" (98R). The protracted, largely ineffective recitative (98L–103L) is merely plot-forwarding.[9] From it we are meant to learn that Orosmane has agreed to free Lusignano; that Nerestano and Zaira were enslaved on the day of the taking of Caesarea; that on that same day Lusignano's two children were captured; that Lusignano recognizes the gold crucifix worn by Zaira; and that he knows that Nerestano bears a scar upon his breast. As Lusignano cries out *"Oh me felice!/Oh ineffabil dolcezza! . . . io li ritrovo,/Io riveggo i miei figli"* (What happiness I feel! oh ineffable sweetness! . . . I find them again, I see my children again, 103L–103R), Bellini writes above the top staff: *"Terzetto/ allegro vivo,"* though the actual start of the trio is delayed by two pages of recitative giving time for the family reunion and commentary by the chorus (104R).[10]

Lusignano begins the trio (104R) with the movingly set words *"Cari oggetti in seno a voi/Io rinasco a nuova vita"*#[11] (Dear ones, on your breasts I am reborn into new life). Nerestano and Zaira at once join in (105L);

all is joy until (106R) a sudden silence intervenes: Lusignano has noticed that Zaira is wearing Mussulman attire. She confesses that she has undergone conversion. A scene of desolated unhappiness follows (109R–112R), expressed equally well in Romani's words and Bellini's subtly modulating music. After another pause, the second section of the trio begins, *poco più moderato*, as Lusignano sings (113L) *"Qui, crudele, in questa terra,"* a melody that in profile and rhythm suggests the second part of the orchestral introduction to the chorus *"Norma viene,"* in Act I of *Norma*. After its first complete presentation (113L–115L), Nerestano repeats it a third higher (A-flat major), to words of different emotional temperature: *"Deh! ti calma,"* with agitated interjections by Zaira. Then she repeats the melody a second time—*"Ah perdona"* (117L); Nerestano and Lusignano join in. The unhappy girl now wishes to die. Again A-flat major, allegro, the third section of the trio begins. The knights comment (122R) that Zaira now is showing herself worthy of Lusignano. Considerable modulation prepares what follows. To her father's question (123R): "Are you a Christian?" Zaira replies: "I swear it to you." Everyone prays: *"Ciel! ricevi il giuramento!"*

Scene 11 (124L–135R)—"Meledor and soldiers." The Sultan has summoned Zaira (124L); she must accompany Meledor, who cannot explain why. All agree that she must obey, but that she will see happier days (124L–127R). Sadly, Lusignano says: *"Or basta, addio"* (Enough now, farewell, 127R). Then starts the most expressive, most musically alive, section of the scene, the concerted *"Non si pianga"*‡ (Do not weep, 129L),[12] the chief melody of which later became the ensemble *"Se ogni speme,"* in the Act I finale of *I Capuleti e i Montecchi*. This section fully deserves the praise that Pastura implied when he wrote[13]: "And, in fact, of the entire trio . . . it is the only section that does not merit oblivion, and which certainly must have been what most moved that Parma audience."

Scene 12 (136–138L). "Interior of the harem. Orosmane, Corasmino, and guards." After an eight-measure string introduction, *andante maestoso*, the first-act finale begins with this brief recitative scene as Orosmane defends (136–137L) his decision to free the French knight. His courtiers fear (137L) that Lusignano at liberty will spread reports of his treatment as a prisoner. The Sultan replies (137L) that Lusignano is near death. Besides, he has given his promise to Zaira (137R). Further, he has granted her wish to be allowed to say farewell to Nerestano (137R). By showing himself altogether human and open-spirited, he achieves the scene's only purpose.

Scene 13 (138L–138R). Continuing in recitative, this even shorter scene is begun by Meledor, who reports (138L) that he has, as ordered, brought Nerestano. Orosmane then sends for Zaira and commands (138L–138R) the outraged Corasmino to leave with Meledor, as no one is to listen to the farewell meeting of Nerestano and Zaira. Not obeying immediately, Corasmino momentarily lags behind, exclaiming (138R) that he is devoured by rage.

Scene 14 (138R–160L). "Meledor, Nerestano, and then Zaira." Meledor finally departs after telling Nerestano to await Zaira. Nerestano then (138R) soliloquizes, bewailing his coming separation from Zaira. *Allegro moderato.* She enters, and he tells her (139R) that their father is dying, dying unsure that she will cling to Christianity. She must, Nerestano tells her (140L), hate Orosmane and his nation. She protests (140L) that the Sultan is pitying, human, and generous—and reasserts her love for him. With the instruction *"Attacca subito"* (140L), the upper strings soar off, *allegro moderato*, on a flight of sixteenth-notes ending in a fortissimo orchestral chord (140R). A brief pause. Then *"(Tutto di forza) a piacere,"* Nerestano exclaims (140R–141L): *"Oh! qual vibrasti orribile/Colpo al mio cor, Zaira!"*[14] (Oh, what a fearful trembling strikes my heart, Zaira!). A pause. Then (142R), to pizzicato strings, the flutes and clarinets, pianissimo, give out a melody[#] that will recur, slightly modified, near the beginning of the Romeo–Giulietta duet *"Sì, fuggire,"* in Act I of *I Capuleti e i Montecchi.* To it, Nerestano sings (143L) the opening phrase of his duet with Zaira, *"Ah! con qual fronte riedere"* (Ah, with what a face I return), denouncing her afresh. In agitation flurried by groups of sixteenth-notes, Zaira replies (145L), *"Deh! non fuggirmi, svenami"* (Oh! do not run from me, kill me); later, the two argue until Zaira exclaims (150R): *"Speme per me non v'ha"* (There is no hope for me). A long pause. Andante, Nerestano begins (152R) the much more imposing second section of the duet: *"Segui deh! segui a piangere"*[#] (Go on, ah! go on weeping), the principal melody of which later became the second section of the Romeo-Giulietta duet in Act I of *I Capuleti e i Montecchi, "Ah! crudel d'onor ragioni."* Eventually (156L–159L), the two sing together, he urging her to return to Christianity, she begging for his support in her terrible internal struggle. They hear sounds (159R) of the Sultan's approach. Nerestano's last words to Zaira (159R–160L) are *"Sorella, ardire"* (Sister, take courage).

Scene 15 (160L–182L). "Orosmane, Corasmino, officials and slaves. The Sultan's entire retinue." The heading *"Quartetto finale"* having appeared on 159R, the new scene actually begins with fourteen pages (160L–167L) of plot-propelling recitative (*"Corsa è l'ora"*—The time has come, 160L) which serve to tell us that Nerestano may now leave for France; that Orosmane cannot understand Zaira's sadness; that Lusignano has died; that Zaira wants her wedding deferred; that Orosmane now suspects

Nerestano of being Zaira's lover. Orosmane, enraged, orders the marriage postponed and threatens Nerestano.

Allegro assai, 167R, the raging Orosmane, grasping Zaira by the hand, begins the quartet itself: *"Io saprò di qual deriva/Strana fonte il tuo dolore"*# (I shall discover from what strange source your sorrow arises). He continues denouncing and threatening Nerestano. Zaira, in *"Non cercar da qual deriva/Fatal fonte il mio dolore"* (Do not seek for the fatal source from which my sorrow arises), insists (p. 169R) that fate rather than any human being is depriving Orosmane of her. Parenthetically, Nerestano prays (*"Dio de' padri, in lei ravviva/Di tua Fede il puro ardore"*—God of our fathers, restore in her the pure ardor of Your Faith, 171L) that Zaira's love for Orosmane may die; what he fears is not revenge, but the power of love. Also parenthetically (and with brief exclamations from the others), as though to himself alone, Corasmino, more than sharing Orosmane's suspicions of Nerestano, promises revenge (*"Ben vegg'io da qual deriva/Rea cagione il suo dolore"*—I see clearly from what guilty cause her sorrow arises, 172R). The four voices ascend together (173L) *più mosso;* the chorus joins in (*"Tal ripulsa al suo signore"*—Such an affront to her lord, 174L), foreseeing Zaira's being punished with incarceration in the harem. The ensemble is skillfully worked out at some length (174L–181L), after which the orchestra closes Act I.

This terminal quartet, though lacking high melodic distinction, nonetheless is a very remarkable accomplishment. It not only displays the four protagonists and the courtiers expressing their separate, very divergent thoughts and emotions recognizably (to variations of the same text-words), but also moves the drama forward. Far from freezing the climax, it raises the dramatic pressure noticeably, leaving the listener theatrically eager to learn how, in Act II, the conflicting purposes and wills can evolve into action.

Act II: Scenes 1–2 (1R–31R). "Zaira's quarters":

Scene 1 (1R–3R)—"Fatima and Zaira." *Allegro maestoso*, a seventeen-measure string introduction leads to a recitative exchange in which Fatima tries to persuade Zaira that bitter sacrifice is required of her: she must give up Orosmane. But Zaira insists that no earthly help can save her now. She exclaims (3R) that she hears the Sultan approaching.[15]

Scene 2 (3R–30L)—"Orosmane, Zaira and Fatima; at a signal, Fatima* retires." In recitative, with horrified, lamenting interruptions by Zaira, Orosmane tells her (3R–4R) that she no longer deserves his love, but must languish neglected in the harem. A-flat major, *allegro moderato*, Orosmane begins (5L) the noted duet *"Io troverò nell'Asia/Donna a cui dare un trono"* (I shall find in Asia a woman to whom to give a throne), the other

* Not, as in the 1836 Florence libretto, Orosmane.

piece from *Zaira* to be published. A pause (6L). The clarinets announce (6R) a motive in thirds[16]; this leads into Orosmane's phrase "*Donna che più di te ne meriti*"# (A woman who deserves it more than you). Zaira gives voice to her misery (8R): she weeps not for a throne lost, but for Orosmane's formerly magnanimous heart. "And you love me?" Orosmane asks (11L); Zaira passionately reasserts her love. *Più moderato ancora*, Orosmane demands to know ("*Deh! se tu m'ami, o barbara*"#—Alas! if you love me, o barbarous girl, 12R) who, then, is taking her from him.[17] She begs him (13R) not to question her farther: she will die if he hates her, die if he loves her. Is a friend of hers conspiring against him? She will not explain, but again begs for his trust. Again in A-flat major, Zaira sings (19R) the curiously inappropriate melody "*Ah! questo dì concedimi*"# (Alas, grant me this day), beseeching him for one day of grace. With ill humor, Orosmane grants it, asking her to consider what a betrayal by her would mean to him. This scene is developed at excessive length (to 30L).

Scenes 3–6 (32R–76L). "Remote place near the quarters assigned to the French knights":

Scene 3 (32R–41R)—F major, 4/4 time, *andante mosso*. "Deeply afflicted, the freed knights emerge weeping over the death of Lusignano." After a longish orchestral introduction (32R–35R), during which the men totter from their cells, they murmur about Lusignano (34R–35R), "*tutti sotto voce*": "He is dead; he lies there forever, cold remains, a naked corpse," and then (35R–41R) sing the mourning chorus "*Ei mancò*" (He is gone).

Scene 4 (56R–62R)[18]—"Castiglione, Nerestano, and the others." This is the first of the two sections of Nerestano's so-called rondo—and the second of the only two numbers in *Zaira* which drew applause at its première. It begins (56R), F major, as Castiglione laments Lusignano. Nerestano tells (56R) how his father's final moments were shadowed by Zaira's absence. "*Attacca subito larghetto*" (57R): E-flat major, 3/4 time, the horns introduce (58R) the first melody, worked out at length, of Nerestano's rondo, which he sings (59L) to the words "*O Zaira! in qual momento*" (O Zaira, at what a moment).[19]

Scene 5 (62R–66R)—"Meledor, guards, and the others." E-flat major, 4/4 time, an orchestral introduction (62R–63L) leads to Meledor's announcement that the Sultan wishes the Frenchmen bearing Lusignano's body to be beyond the River Jordan by sunset. But Castiglione (64R) asks him to obtain permission for them to bury Lusignano in the Holy Land; Nerestano, in turn, asks (65R) if the marriage of the sorrowing Zaira cannot be delayed. Meledor accuses Nerestano (66L) of having caused Zaira's unhappiness—and adds that the wedding will be celebrated the next day. He then leaves.

Scene 6 (66R–76L)—"Nerestano, Castiglione, and the knights." D-flat major, allegro, Nerestano preludes (67L), in recitative exchange with the others, the second section of the rondo, swearing (68R) that he will not abandon Zaira to a "forever infamous" life: he would prefer to die with her. After a short orchestral interlude, Nerestano sings, allegro (70R) the second section of his rondo: *"Sì, mi vedrà la barbara"*# (Yes, the barbarous girl will see me.)[20] Castiglione and the knights swear (73L) that they will die with Nerestano rather than see him suffer such anguish.

Scenes 7–11 (76R–121R). "Ground-floor hall in the harem; at the back, great windowed arches, through which the mountain slopes can be seen":

Scene 7 (76R–77L)—"Orosmane, Meledor, and guards." This extremely brief recitative exchange serves to tell us that Orosmane has agreed to the burial of Lusignano on the holy mountain. Meledor departs.

Scene 8 (77L–99R)—"Orosmane, then Corasmino." Orosmane's forgiving mood is shattered when the courtiers assert (77R–78L): *"Fratelli, i franchi Essi ti sono fatali."* Corasmino says that a slave has been apprehended near the harem while bearing a letter to Zaira. He hands Orosmane the letter: it is from Nerestano (78L). To a violin tremolo, Orosmane reads (78R) rather than sings the contents of the letter: "Dear Zaira [three notes *"con tutta forza"* from the violas and cellos]: You will find a secret exit near the mosque [again three notes] through which you can reach the deserted garden unseen. Protected by the night, I shall await you [three notes] there; if you refuse to come, you will find me dead at dawn." *"Con forza,"* Orosmane exclaims: "Oh, treachery!" while Corasmino mutters to himself ("I triumph") and Orosmane, "as if struck by lightning, and with his eyes fixed on some point," repeats: "Oh, treachery!"

Now, B-flat major, 4/4 time, *andante mosso*, almost as though speaking to himself, Orosmane begins (79L) a duet with Corasmino: *"E pur ora al mio cospetto"*# (And yet, when she was with me). Corasmino works on the Sultan's offended sense of honor. Orosmane orders (81L) the letter taken to Zaira so that she may rejoice in it and then learn that he knows of it. The delighted Corasmino is about to leave when (84L) Orosmane detains him: what if Zaira were innocent? He has begun to doubt Corasmino, and he orders Zaira brought to him (86L). After protracted discussion, in which the characters' vacillating emotions—Orosmane's in particular—are evoked with a mastery worthy of *Norma*, a pause. Then this intensely expressive scene closes (92R–99R) as Corasmino and Orosmane sing what amounts to the cabaletta of their duet: *"Vieni meco; a me t'affida"* (Come with me; trust yourself to me)—and then leave. *"Fine del duetto/attacca subito recitativo di Zaira"* (99R).

Scene 9 (100R–101R)—"As Orosmane leaves, Zaira enters, moving toward him. He seems eager to remain. Corasmino takes him away. Zaira remains motionless, astonished." In soliloquy, Zaira regrets that Nerestano has not already passed the Jordan: with him gone, she could explain "this fatal mystery" to Orosmane, who does not see that she weeps out of love for him.

Scene 10 (101R–113R)—"Fatima, Zaira." Allegro, Zaira and Fatima talk. Fatima hands Nerestano's letter to Zaira; both girls read it. Fatima sees its contents as Zaira's salvation: now she can leave. But Zaira's love for Orosmane remains undiminished, as she demonstrates in a magnificent *scena: "Che non tentai per vincere/Questo fatale amore!"*#[21] (What have I not tried to overcome this fatal love! 103R–108R). Now she can only die. Fatima tries to calm her. Zaira is telling her to conceal the letter when (108R) "A sorrowful sound is heard. Struck, Zaira listens. In the distance, a chorus sings the following INNO FUNEBRE"—*andante lugubre*, the two-part (s, t) choral *"Poni il fedel tuo martire,"*#[22] until "In the background, the French knights are seen passing by, going to the grave of Lusignano." Zaira, learning thus of her father's death, becomes violently distracted. A second strophe of the funeral hymn is heard: *"Vegli beato spirito"* (110R). "Zaira swoons in Fatima's arms."

Scene 11 (113R 121R)—"Slaves and guards rush up from all sides." When the attendants see Zaira unconscious and want to hurry to the Sultan, Fatima explains that the sight of the Frenchman's funeral has afflicted Zaira. G minor, *allegro agitato*, *"con forza,"* the revived Zaira bursts (116L) into the cabaletta *"Ah, crudeli"*#[23]: having betrayed the faith of her fathers and disturbed a dying man, she now reiterates her desire to die. The attendants think her delirious. At last, "Fatima and the slaves bear Zaira away with them. The guards go off in another direction."

Scenes 12–14 (122R–153R). "Remote part of the harem gardens. In the distance, the minarets of a mosque rise above the trees":

Scene 12 (122R–133R)—"Orosmane, then Corasmino. *Finale/andante sostenuto assai.*" A lengthy orchestral introduction proclaims that the succeeding scene is to be an impressive one: *andante sostenuto assai*, it includes (123R) a solo for English horn# which lacks Bellinian melodic poignance. Awaiting his victim, Orosmane thinks of how particularly dark the night is and of how far from greatness he has fallen. Corasmino enters (127R). A slave has delivered Nerestano's letter to Zaira, who will accompany him to the rendezvous. Orosmane is beside himself with grief and lost faith. "Silence," Corasmino whispers (133R), "someone is coming." The two men hide.

Scene 13 (133R–143L)—"Zaira accompanied by Fatima, then Nerestano and the others." *In tempo*, after an orchestral prelude, Zaira appears, followed by Nerestano, who exclaims "*Zaira!*" as Orosmane and Corasmino eavesdrop. Zaira tells her brother: "I am worthy of your love" (137L–142L); he says that God has heard his prayers. Now, in F major, the voices of Zaira, Nerestano, Fatima, Orosmane, and Corasmino mix (137L–142L) in a peculiarly unmoving quintet: "*Lieto ci mira adesso*"#; borrowed from Bianca's "*Contenta appien quest'alma*," in *Bianca e Fernando* (p. 91 of piano-vocal score with plate numbers 9826–9842)—and to be heard again in Norma's "*Ah! bello, a me ritorna*" (p. 74 of piano-vocal score with plate number 41684)—it expresses almost nothing here, moves nothing forward, and, while lengthening the act and arresting the action, fails to satisfy as a musical set piece. Using loverlike words calculated to drive Orosmane to violence, Nerestano begs Zaira to flee with him (142R). She agrees to go. Orosmane irrupts from the shadows and stabs her (143L). "She is dead."

Scene 14 (143L–153R)—"At the shouts of Zaira, Nerestano, and Fatima, slaves and guards enter with torches from all sides." Very rapidly, Orosmane and the others learn that Nerestano was not Zaira's lover, but her brother. In an Othello-like self-accusation, Orosmane says (145L): "She loved me, and I have killed her." *Più allegro assai*, he sings (145R) his final cabaletta: "*Un grido d'orrore*"#24—and orders all to leave. But before they can obey, he stabs himself, saying (151R): "I follow you." As the curtain falls, the others say only: "He is dead."

Nonoperatic Compositions

1. Vocal Music
2. Instrumental Music

(In the following lists, these abbreviations are used: MB—Museo Belliniano, Catania; NC—library of the Naples Conservatory (San Pietro a Maiella); s—soprano; ms—mezzo soprano; c—contralto; t—tenor; bs—bass; chor.—chorus; orch.—orchestra. An asterisk preceding an item in the lists indicates one of the ten compositions that Bellini submitted to the authorities at San Sebastiano upon his arrival in Naples in 1819 [Florimo, CssSmdN I, pp. 771–772], autographs of which remain in NC.)

I am uncomfortably aware that—inescapably and unavoidably—these lists are both incomplete and, in details, almost certainly incorrect. Not only do autograph compositions by Bellini undoubtedly survive unlisted in private (and even public) collections, but also printed data, upon which a writer cannot avoid relying to some extent, are frequently incorrect and even contradictory. I should be indebted to anyone sending me, for possible later printings of the present book, any additional or corrective information concerning authentic compositions by Bellini.

H. W.

1. Vocal Music*

"*A palpitar d'affanno* [or *affanni*]": romanza, Milan, 1827–1833; see *Tre Ariette.*

"*Abbandono, L'* " ("*Solitario zeffiretto*"): romanza, ms. After saying that it was published by Ricordi (pl. no. 8361) and by Girard, Naples. *Omaggio* (p. 333) assigns its composition to Catania, 1824, almost certainly in error. Pastura (BSLS, p. 516) assigned it to May–July 1835 (Paris–Puteaux) and noted its resemblance to Elvira's "*Ah, crudel, tu Re possente*" in the *Ernani* sketches, from which he thought it adapted. But no proof exists that the dating is correct or that the *Ernani* melody was not in fact borrowed from the romanza. Included (#4) in the *Composizioni da camera,* q.v. It was also published by Ricordi (pl. no. 8821) in a bilingual (French-Italian) edition with the title "*L'Ultima Veglia*"; the French text begins "*Pourquoi ce chant.*" Autographs in NC and the Accademia di Santa Cecilia, Rome. The November 1965 catalogue of the Libreria Gaspare Casella, Naples, offered a Bellini autograph page dated Paris 1835 containing the *allegro agitato* beginning of an aria starting "*Solitario zeffiretto a che muovi i tuoi sospiri*" and described as coming from the Collezione Cherubini.

"*Ah! non pensai*": romanza, Milan, 1827–1833; lost.

"*Alla luna*" ("*Ode saffica*"): Said to have been setting of lines by Pepoli; lost.

"*Allegro a guisa di cabaletta,*" see "*E nello stringerti a questo core.*"

"*Allegro Marinaro, L'* " (also "*Allor che azzurro il mar*[*e*]"): ballata or arietta, G major, ms, Milan, 1827–1833; published by Ricordi (pl. no. 16715); included (#5) in *Composizioni da camera,* q.v.

"*Allor che azzurro il mar*(*e*)," see "*Allegro Marinaro, L'.*"

"*Almen se non poss'io*": arietta, ms, Milan, 1827–1833; published by Ricordi (pl. no. 4378) and by Girard, Naples; included (#5) in *Sei Ariette,* q.v., and (#13) *Composizioni da camera,* q.v.

"*Amore,*" see *Quattro Sonetti.*

arietta, unspecified, for Lady Christina Dudley-Stuart, Milan, 1828.

"*Bella Nice, che d'amore*": arietta, ms, Milan, 1827–1829; published by Ricordi, 1829 (pl. no. 4377) and by Girard, Naples; included (#3) in

* With piano accompaniment unless otherwise specified.

Sei Ariette, q.v., and (#12) *Composizioni da camera,* q.v. Melody used by Bellini in Pollione's *"Sol promessa al Dio tu fosti,"* in Act I of *Norma.*

canon (free): B-flat major, s, c (or t, bs); for Cherubini's album, Paris, 1835; published by Sonzogno, 1883, in *La Musica popolare,* II, No. 37. The text reads: *"Dalla guancia scolorita, dalla torbida pupilla, passa il duolo colla vita; sol con essa ha fine amor . . ."* In "Catalog Eleven" (1970 or 1971) of the autograph dealer Doris Harris of Los Angeles, a "beautiful manuscript" was offered for sale with this description: " 'Canone' for Soprano and Tenor [*sic*] with piano accompaniment in text which begins: 'Dalle [*sic*] guancia scolorita. . . .' At the lower right margin the composer identifies the work: 'Bellini compose per l'Album di Cherubini il Celebre—a Parigi 1835' and at the opposite corner: 'L'Autore al suo caro amico F. [Francesco] Pollini.' " What appears to be the same autograph was offered for sale by Paul C. Richards of Brookline, Massachusetts, in 1971 in his Catalogue No. 64, which contained a full-page reproduction of the Canon; the asking price was $1,500. This is, of course, a copy that Bellini sent for criticism to his seventy-two-year-old friend in Milan, as is proved by Pollini's letter of September 9, 1835 (transcribed in VB:V, pp. 395–396), replying in the gentle voice of a past age:

"You desired that I should express my opinion of your Canon; here it is, sincere and without the least reservation. If your piece be considered as an idealistic and free piece of music, it is embellished with many virtues, *rigorous imitation, ideal melody and charm.*

"If it be considered as a Canon in the true sense, it seems to me not to observe exactly, as you know perfectly well, some precepts established and prescribed by our oldtime Masters as essentials and characteristics of the nature of the true Canon.

"The great Cherubini, in his original and inimitable compositions, always rigorously observed those theories and laws; therefore, so that you should not incure some criticisms, and also so that you may be certain to reap just and well-earned praise, I would say: present your composition to this illustrious man exactly as it is, but omit the denomination *Canon, Duet, Duettino,* or any other, and say simply *And*[*ante*] *mosso.*

"In such a way, I believe, you will be sure of your achievement, and with no risk; but do not pay attention to me, govern yourself as seems to you most suitable and advantageous."

As Bellini died exactly two weeks after Pollini dated this letter, he may never have received it—or, receiving it, may not have been able to read it.

canon: F Major, 4 voices, Paris, Aug. 15, 1835, for Zimmerman; published in facsimile in Arthur Pougin: *Bellini, Sa Vie, ses œuvres*, preceding index; in part, the text reads: "*Chi per quest'ombre dell'umana vita talor non mira gli splendor celesti cade per via . . .*"

canzoni siciliane: Cicconetti (pp. 4–5) states that Bellini composed "some *romanze* and Sicilian *canzoni*" at the age of seven; they appear not to survive, but Pastura (BSLS, p. 35) reported examining "an autograph belonging to Professor Caldarella of the State Archive at Palermo which contains the sketch of a *canzone* that is a setting of dialect words of burlesque character."

cavatina, unspecified, for the album of a duchessa Litta.

Cerere, see *Scena ed aria di Cerere*.

Compieta: monsignore Giuseppe Coco Zanghy wrote (*Memorie e lagrime*) that in 1808–1813 Bellini composed "a Compline with *Salve . . .*"

Composizioni da camera per canto e pianoforte: published by Ricordi, 1935 and 1948. See (1) "*Farfalletta, La,*" (2) "*Quando incise su quel marmo,*" (3) "*Sogno d'infanzia, Il*" (4) "*Abbandono, L',*" (5) "*Allegro Marinaro, L',*" (6) "*Torna, vezzosa Fillide,*" (7) "*Fervido Desiderio, Il,*" (8) "*Dolente immagine di Fille mia,*" (9) "*Vaga luna, che in-argenti,*" (10) "*Malinconia, ninfa gentile,*" (11) "*Vanne, o rosa for-tunata,*" (12) "*Bella Nice, che d'amore,*" (13) "*Almen se non poss'io,*" (14) "*Per pietà, bell'idol mio,*" (15) "*Mi rendi pur contento.*"

Composizioni giovanili inedite: facsimile edition, with introduction by Francesco Cilea, Reale Accademia d'Italia, Rome, 1941. See (1) *Salve Regina*, (3) *Tecum principium* (*Dixit Dominus*), and, under Instrumental Compositions, (2) *Sinfonia*, D major, (4) Concerto for oboe, (5) *Sinfonia*, E-flat major (*largo assai, allegro vivace*).

Cor mundum crea (*motetto*) *a 2 voci, strofa del miserere con organo*: published in *Musica sacra*, 1879; according to Florimo (LSmdN III, p. 223), the autograph belonged to Filippo Cicconetti.

Coro (wordless): four voices, E-flat major, with orch.; autograph in NC.

Credo, C major: four-voice chorus, with orch., (1824?); unpublished.

Cum sanctis: autograph in NC.

"*De Torrente*": autograph in NC.

Dixit Dominus (psalm); soloists, four-voice chorus, with orch., Naples, 1819–1826; three sections; part of section 3 (*Tecum principium*) included in *Composizioni giovanili inedite*, q.v. Except for the *Tecum principium*, which is in full score, the autograph in NC consists only of parts for singers, violin, and doublebass, plus a few full-score fragments. Pastura wrote (BSLS, 64) that the complete choral parts of the *Dixit* appear with those of the *Magnificat*, q.v., "which assures us that they were performed together during some solemn Vesper."

"Dolente immagine di Fille mia": romanza or arietta, B-flat major, ms (c? or s?), Naples, 1821. Published by Ricordi (pl. no. 10208), 1824(?); by Girard (later Cottrau), Naples, 1825; and by Pacini, Paris; included in *Tre Ariette per camera*, q.v., in which it is described as "composed for and dedicated to signora Marianna Pollini," and in (#8) *Composizioni da camera*, q.v. Pastura wrote (BSLS, p. 57) that an old copy "certainly reproduced from an old edition by Cottrau" in MB contains the following inscription: "1st romanza for voice—with piano accompaniment—by Vincenzo Bellini—composed at the Real Collegio di San Sebastiano in 1821—dedicated by the composer to his friend Nicola Tauro"; autographs in the Naples Conservatory library and the Biblioteca Nazionale, Florence; autograph copy, with title *"La Tomba di Fille,"* inscribed *"al suo amico Pacini a Parigi, gennaio 1834,"* in the Bibliothèque Nationale, Paris.

Domine Deus: autograph in NC.

duet with unidentified Italian words: autograph in the Bibliothèque Nationale, Paris.

"E nello stringerti a questo core" ("Allegro a guisa di cabaletta"*) G major, s, with orch., Catania, 1817–1818; autograph in NC.

"Era felice un dì": arietta, ms, Milan, 1827–1833; unpublished.

"Farfalletta, La" (*"Farfalletta, aspetta, aspetta"*): ms, Catania, 1813(?); published in *L'Olivuzza*, Palermo, 1846; included (#1) in *Composizioni da camera*, q.v.

"Fervido Desiderio, Il" (*"Quando verrà quel dì"*): aria or arietta, A-flat major, Milan, 1827–1833; published by Ricordi (pl. no. 10207); included in *Tre Ariette per camera*, q.v., and (#7) in *Composizioni da camera*, q.v. In April 1965, the Libreria Gaspare Casella, Naples, offered an autograph described thus: "*'Quando verrà quel dì,'* composed expressly for and dedicated to the contessa Sofia Vojna ... Six autograph pages for voice and pianoforte, in the key of A-flat major, 6/8 time, *and/te sopr/to assai* ..."

"Fu che al pianger" (sometimes *"Tu che al pianger"*): arietta; published by Girard, Naples, n.d.

"Gallus cantavit": probably 1807; described by Cicconetti, Pastura, and Orrey as lost, but the Biblioteca Ursino, Catania, has a manuscript of it which may well be the autograph.

Genitori: the concluding line of the hymn beginning *"Pange lingua,"* just following the stanza *"Tantum ergo,"* this title is given to several conclusions of *Tantum ergos* composed by Bellini.

Gloria patris: a section of the *Dixit Dominus*, q.v.

*Gratias agimus: C major, s, with orch., Catania, 1817–1818.

"Guarda che bianca luna": romanza, Palermo, 1831, composed for and

dedicated to Almerinda Manzocchi (see Ottavio Tiby, *Il Real Teatro Carolino*, p. 156, ft. 12).

Ismene: wedding cantata, three solo voices, chorus, orch., Naples, 1824; said to have been composed for the wedding of Bellini's friend Antonio Naclerio to Gelsomina Ginestrelli. Considered lost, but see Pastura (BSLS, pp. 64–67, with four musical examples) for possible relation of it to a three-voice (s, t, bs) autograph epithalamium in MB. In a review of the première of *Il Pirata*, the Milan correspondent of the *Allgemeine musikalische Zeitung* (No. 5, December 1827, Leipzig, p. 872) mentioned the cantata *Imene* (*sic*).

Juravit: autograph in NC.

Kyrie: autograph in NC.

Laudamus te: autograph in NC.

Litanie pastorali in onore della Beata Vergine: 2s, with organ, Catania, 1817(?); Pastura (BSLS, p. 64) wrote that no trace of the *Litanie* survives; but he thereafter (idem, p. 710) listed the composition among those of which autographs have been traced.

"*Luna, La,*" see "*Alla luna.*"

Magnificat: four-voice mixed chor., with orch., Catania, 1818–1819 or Naples, 1819–1820. Autograph fragment in the Bibliothèque Nationale, Paris (from "*implevit bonis*" to "*et in secula secu-*"). See also under *Dixit Dominus*.

"*Malinconia,*" see *Quattro Sonetti*; see also "*Malinconia, La,*" below.

"*Malinconia, La*" ("*Ninfa gentile*"): arietta, ms. Milan, 1829; published by Ricordi (pl. no. 4375) and by Girard, Naples; included (#1) in *Sei Ariette*, q.v., and (#10) in *Composizioni da camera*, q.v. Verses probably by Ippolito Pindemonte.

"*Mammoletta, La*": romanza, Milan, 1830(?); unpublished, lost.

Mass, A minor: for four voices (s, c, t, bs) with orch. Naples, 1821(?), perhaps sung in Catania on Oct. 4, 1821; published in full score by Ricordi (pl. no. 15523) with alternative organ accompaniment (*Kyrie eleison, Gloria, Laudamus, Domine Deus, Qui tollis, Qui sedes, Cum Sancto Spiritu*). Incomplete autograph and complete copy in MB.

*Mass (*Kyrie, Gloria*), D major: 2s, t, bs, with orch., Catania, 1818; on the final page of the autograph (NC), Bellini wrote: "*Finis: Laus Deo et Beatae Mariae Semper Virgini, 1818.*"

*Mass (*Kyrie, Gloria*), G major: 2s, t, bs, with orch., Catania, 1818.

Mass, G minor: soloists, four-voice chorus, with orch., Naples, 1825(?); unpublished; autograph fragment of score and incomplete copy in MB, vocal and instrumental parts in NC (Mass reconstructed by Pastura; see BSLS, p. 63 and ft. 2). Probably sung in July 1825 at Gragnano.

"*Mi rendi pur contento*": arietta, ms, Milan, 1832(?); published by Ricordi (pl. no. 4380) and by Girard, Naples; included (#6) in *Sei Ariette*, q.v., and in (#15) *Composizioni da camera*, q.v.

"*Ninfa gentile*," see "*Malinconia, La.*"

"*No, traditor, non curo*": aria, s, Naples, 1819–1826(?); dedicated to donna Lauretta Caracciolo; autograph in MB.

"*Numi, se giusti siete*": romanza, Milan, 1827–1833(?); unpublished; lost.

"*Ô Souvenirs*": albumleaf; date of composition unknown; published by Ricordi, 1901.

"*Ombre pacifiche*": cantata, s, 2t, with orch., Catania, 1818(?); published by Ricordi, 1901, in a "*Rielaborazione di F. P. Frontini.*" Sixteen pages of autograph (incomplete) in the Pierpont Morgan Library, New York; manuscript copy (twenty-four pages) in MB.

Pange lingua: two voices, with organ, Catania, 1817–1818(?); unpublished; autograph in MB.

"*Per pietà, bell'idol mio*": arietta, ms, Milan, 1829(?); published by Ricordi (pl. no. 4379) and by Girard (later Cottrau), Naples; included (#4) in *Sei Ariette*, q.v., and (#14) in *Composizioni da camera*, q.v.

"*Pourquoi ce chant*," see "*Abbandono, L'.*"

"*Quando incise su quel marmo*": *scena* (recitative, andante, cabaletta), ms (c? or s?), with orch. (possibly intended to be preceded by "*Questa è la valle*," q.v.), Naples, 1821–182(?); published by Girard (later Cottrau), Naples, and by Ricordi (pl. no. 8985); included (with piano accompaniment) (#2) in *Composizioni da camera*, q.v.; autograph in NC.

"*Quando verrà quel dì*", see "*Fervido Desiderio, Il.*"

Quattro Sonetti: "*Amore*" (lost), "*Malinconia*" (lost), "*Ricordanza*" (autograph, dated April 15, 1834, in the Library of Congress, Washington, D.C.), "*Speranza*" (lost). To verses by conte Carlo Pepoli.

"*Questa è la valle*": romanza, Naples, 1821; later possibly intended as a prelude to "*Quando incise su quel marmo*," q.v.; said to have been included (as #2) in *Tre Ariette* (Mechetti), q.v.

Qui sedes: autograph in NC.

Qui tollis: autograph in NC.

Quoniam: autograph in NC. A fourteen-page autograph *Quoniam* for t., chor., and orch. in the Bibliothèque Nationale, Paris.

Quoniam with *Cum Sanctis*: autograph in NC.

"*Ricordanza*," see *Quattro Sonetti*.

romanze: Cicconetti (pp. 4–5) states that Bellini composed "some *romanze* and Sicilian *canzoni*" at the age of seven; the *romanze* appear not to survive.

Salve Regina, A major: four-voice chorus, with orch.; published in fac-

F—Autograph of the second B-flat clarinet part from the *Salve Regina* in F minor–major, composed at Catania in 1818(?). The reverse contains two autograph measures of apparently unrelated orchestral sketch.

simile in *Composizioni giovanili inedite*, q.v. Andrew Porter has speculated that this is in fact a copy by Bellini of a composition by his grandfather, Vicenzo Tobia Bellini—and that the title page, in Bellini's autograph, reads, not "V^{zo}B^{ni}F^{o}" (for Vincenzo Bellini Ferlito), but "V^{zo}B^{ni}I^{o}" (for Vincenzo Bellini primo). Notably, the related autograph on the title page of Bellini's D-major *Sinfonia* reads "Vincenzo Bellini 2do." Mr. Porter wrote me (April 17, 1970): "Stylistically I suggest that it [the A-major *Salve Regina*] could be the work of a pedestrian old man, rather than the talented but inexpert youth of the early masses," an opinion that I share, as I do Mr. Porter's reading of the abbreviated signature.

Salve Regina, F minor–major; bs, with organ, Catania, 1818(?); published by Ricordi (pl. no. 33244) with alternative organ accompaniment.

*Scena ed aria di Cerere: s, with orch., Catania, 1817–1818. Autograph in NC.

"*Se il mio nome*": canzonetta; included (#3) in *Tre Ariette*, q.v.

Sei Ariette per camera: ms; published October 1829 by Ricordi, dedicated to Marianna Pollini, and by Girard, Naples: (1) "*Malinconia, ninfa gentile,*" (2) "*Vanne, o rosa fortunata,*" (3) "*Bella Nice, che d'amore,*" (4)"*Per pietà, bell'idol mio,*" (5) "*Almen se non poss'io,*" (6) "*Mi rendi pur contento*"; all included in *Composizioni da camera,* q.v.

*"*Si, per te, Gran Nume eterno*": cavatina, s, B-flat major, with orch., Catania, 1817–1818; unpublished.

"*So che un sogno è la speranza*": aria, s(?), sketch of vocal line only, Naples, 1819–1826(?).

"*Soave sogno dei miei primi anni*": romanza, ms, Naples, 1824(?); published by Girard Naples. Because I have not been able to consult a copy of the published song, I am not certain that it is not identical with "*Sogno d'infanzia,*" q.v.

"*Sogno d'infanzia, [Il]*": romanza or arietta, Paris–Puteaux, May–July 1835; is included (#3) in *Composizioni da camera,* q.v.

"*Solitario Zeffiretto,*" see "*Abbandono, L'.*"

"*Speranza,*" see *Quattro Sonetti.*

*Tantum ergo (student), with *Genitori,* B-flat major: s, with orch., Catania, 1818(?).

Tantum ergo (student), with *Genitori,* E-flat major: s, with orch., Catania, 1815–1819(?); published by Ricordi, 1901, in a "*Revisione di F. P. Frontini.*"

*Tantum ergo (student), with *Genitori,* F major: 2s (*Genitori,* 4 voices), with orch., Catania, 1815–1819(?).

Tantum ergo (student), F major: s, with orch., Catania, 1815–1819(?); published by Ricordi, 1901, in a "*Revisione di F. P. Frontini.*"

*Tantum ergo (student), with *Genitori,* G major: four-voice chorus, with orch., Catania, 1815–1819(?).

Tantum ergo (four autographs, bound together, in NC, with autograph inscription "*Quattro Tantum Ergo—da Vincenzo Bellini—Ai 10 October 1823*"):

D major—bs, with orch. (string quartet, 2 clarinets, 2 bassoons, 2 horns)—published by Ricordi (pl. no. 3348);

E major—four-voice chorus (s, c, t, bs), with "normal orchestra"; published by Ricordi (pl. no. 33245);

F major—two voices, with "full orchestra"; published by Ricordi (pl. no. 3346);

G major—s, with orch. (string quartet, 2 horns, 2 bassoons); published by Ricordi (pl. no. 33246);

Tecum principium, see *Dixit Dominus.*

Te Deum, C major: four-voice chorus, with orch., Naples, 1824(?).

Te Deum, E-flat major: four voice chorus, with orch., Naples, 1819–1826(?).

"*Torna, vezzosa Fillide*": aria, s; published by Ricordi; included (#6) in *Composizioni da camera*, q.v. Autograph in the Noseda Collection at the Milan Conservatory.

Tre Ariette per camera: Ricordi published under this collective title "*Il Fervido Desiderio*" (pl. no. 10207), "*Dolente immagine di Fille mia*" (10208), and "*Vaga luna, che inargenti*" (10209). Mechetti, Vienna, is sometimes said to have issued a collection called *Tre Ariette* containing "*A palpitar d'affanno*," "*Questa è la valle*," and "*Se il mio nome*," but because no copy of it can be located, its existence is uncertain.

"*Tu che al pianger*," see "*Fu che al pianger*."

"*Ultima Veglia, L'*," see "*Abbandono, L'*."

"*Vaga luna, che inargenti*": romanza or arietta, ms, dedicated to Giulietta Pezzi; published by Ricordi (pl. no. 10209) and by Girard, Naples, Schott's Söhne, Mainz, and possibly Mechetti, Vienna; is included in *Tre Ariette per camera*, q.v., and (#9) *Composizioni de camera*, q.v.

"*Vanne, o rosa fortunata*": arietta, ms, Milan, 1829(?); published by Ricordi (pl. no. 4376) and by Girard, Naples; included (#2) in *Sei Ariette*, q.v., and (#11) *Composizioni da camera*, q.v.

Versetti da cantarsi il Venerdì Santo: 2t, with organ, Catania, 1815(?). Long thought lost, but see Pastura, "*Le Tre Ore di agonia*," in *Rivista del Comune di Catania*, 1953, on their rediscovery. Settings of eight verses in Italian and one Biblical verse in Latin. Autograph in the possession (1970) of signora Marusia Manzella, Rome.

Virgam virtutis: autograph in NC.

2. Instrumental Music

allegretto (piano): eleven-measure albumleaf dedicated to Angelica Paola [-Giuffrida]; autograph on final page of "*Dolente immagine di Fille mia*," q.v. (see Vocal Music, *above*), in the Biblioteca Nazionale, Florence.

Capriccio, ossia Sinfonia per studio, C minor, see *Sinfonia per studio*.

clarinet, piece(s) for: Florimo wrote (B:Mel, pp. 7–8) that Bellini composed a piece or pieces for clarinet at Naples (1819–1827).

Composizioni giovanili inedite: facsimile edition, with introduction by

Francesco Cilea, Reale Accademia d'Italia, Rome, 1941. See (2) *Sinfonia*, D major, (4) Concerto for oboe, (5) *Sinfonia*, E-flat major (*largo assai, allegro vivace*), and, under Vocal Music, (1) *Salve Regina*, (3) *Tecum principium* (*Dixit Dominus*).

Concerto for oboe and string orchestra, E-flat major: Naples, 1823(?); published by Ricordi (pl. no. 129978) in a *"Revisione e rielaborazione di Terenzio Gargiulo"* (*maestoso e deciso, larghetto cantabile, allegro "alla polonese"*); included in *Composizioni giovanili inedite*, q.v.; autographs in NC and the Library of Congress, Washington, D.C.

flute, piece(s) for: Florimo wrote (B:Mel, pp. 7–8) that Bellini composed a piece or pieces for flute at Naples (1819–1827).

oboe, piece(s) for: Florimo wrote (B:Mel, pp. 7–8) that Bellini composed a piece or pieces for oboe at Naples (1819–1827).

Polacca (piano, four hands, in *"tempo di polacca"*), n.d.

Sinfonia (student), B-flat major: *larghetto espressivo* (3/4), allegro (2/4); unpublished; autograph in MB.

Sinfonia per studio (*Capriccio, ossia*), C minor: lento, *in tempo ordinario, allegro tempo* (2/4); 1822(?).

Sinfonia for large orchestra, C minor; published by Ricordi, 1941, in a *"Revisione di Maffeo Zanon."*

*Sinfonia (student), D major: *andante maestoso* (12/8), allegro (6/8), Catania, 1817–1818; included in *Composizioni giovanili inedite*, q.v.*; published by Ricordi, 1941, in a *"Revisione di Maffeo Zanon"* and twice by Zanibon, Padua: 1953, as edited by Ettore Bonelli, and 1959, as edited by Santi di Stefano.

Sinfonia, D minor: orchestral parts of a *Sinfonia in re minore* were said by *Omaggio* (p. 334) to survive in the Noseda Collection, Milan; a *Sinfonia* in this key (*andante maestoso, allegro con spirito*) is also in MB. The Berlin autograph dealer Paul Gottschalk offered for sale in a 1930 catalogue a twenty-four-page Bellini item described as follows: "Autograph musical manuscript. Written with black ink, corrections in red ink by Bellini himself. Symphony. Title page and 23 pages. Folio oblong. Two movements: *Andante maestoso*. 12/8. D minor. Allegro 6/8. D major. Instruments: string-instruments, flutes, oboes, clarinets, bassoon, horns, trumpets, drums." A page of the autograph was reproduced in the catalogue.

Sinfonia, D minor (?): published in Milan (Ricordi?), 1961; see Guido

---

* Francesco Cilea, in his introduction to this facsimile edition, assigned the D-major *Sinfonia* to Bellini's Neapolitan years, though the autograph bears the date 1818. Pastura (BSLS, p. 34) assigned it, with convincing argument, to the final Catania years.

Pannain, in *La Musica: Enciclopedia storica UTET*, Turin, 1966, p. 466. Possibly an erroneous listing.

Sinfonia, E-flat major: *largo assai, allegro vivace;* included in *Composizioni giovanili inedite*, q.v.; autograph in MB.

Sinfonia, E-flat major: *larghetto maestoso, allegro moderato;* in part re-used in the *sinfonie* for *Adelson e Salvini* and *Il Pirata;* published by Ricordi, 1941, in a *"Revisione di Maffeo Zanon."*

sonata for piano, four hands: autograph in NC.

sonata for organ, G major: 4/4 time; autograph in the Pierpont Morgan Library, New York (*"Sonata per Organo Composta da Vicenzo Bellini allievo del Real Collegio di Musica Di Napoli"*); page 3 of the autograph contains a statement in Carmelo Bellini's handwriting that he sent it to the signora Peppina Appiani from Catania on May 21, 1846, and mentions the death of his mother (which occurred on December 2, 1842).

Theme for piano, with introduction and coda, F minor, two pages, with autograph inscription: *"Eccovi il tema, provatelo se vi viene regolare nello frammento"*; autograph in the Bibliothèque Nationale, Paris.

violin, piece(s) for: Florimo wrote (B:Mel, pp. 7–8) that Bellini composed a piece or pieces for violin at Naples (1819–1827).

APPENDIXES

APPENDIX A

Bellini's Baptismal Certificate

MAGNAE ARCHIEPISCOPALIS CURIAE GENERALE
NECNON ET CIVITATIS CATANENSIS
UNICUM PAROCHIALE ARCHIVIUM

Anno Domini Millesimo octingentesimoprimo.
Die quarta Novembris Sanctae Indictionis 1801, Catanae.
Reverendissimus D. Salvator Scammacca M. I. Doctor Decanus
hujus Sanctae Cathedralis Ecclesiae baptizavit in ipsamet Sancta
Cathedrali Ecclesia infantem hjeri natum ex D.a Agatha Ferlito,
et procreatum ex D. Rosario Bellini, jugalibus, cui imposita fuerunt
nomina Vincentius, Salvator, Carmelus, Franciscus: Patrinus vero
fuit D. Franciscus Ferlito: Unde ego quia ad haec omnia interfui
tamquam Cappellanus Coadiutor testor rem se ita haberi et propria
manu scripsi, et subscripsi. Benanti confirmo ut supra.

APPENDIX B

Florimo's References to the Romani-Bellini Ernani

Florimo published the following inexact account of his involvement with the Romani-Bellini *Ernani* in his CssSmdN II, pp. 780–781, unfortunately without citing any dates:

"*Ernani*, of which V. Hugo's fanciful drama was then recent, was a subject that aroused much sympathy in Bellini and in his poet, Romani. They both had decided upon writing it, intending it then for whatever theater would offer the best roster of performing artists.[1] I well remember that Bellini kept me informed about it all, and transcribed for me the poetry of a duet between Ernani and Elvira, and particularly the words of the andante were very beautiful: and he disclosed to me the satisfaction he felt at having set them to music well. That letter, which I have not since located among my papers so as to transcribe the poetry here, certainly was presented by me to one of the so-called collectors or lovers of autographs; one day, perhaps, the poetry of that duet can be brought to light. After that letter, Bellini never spoke about *Ernani* to me again, certain proof that he had laid the idea aside[2]; and it seems to me that Romani did not complete his libretto either."

When, in 1881–1882, Florimo published an expanded revision of his *Cenno storico* as *La Scuola musicale di Napoli*, the story had undergone interesting changes. Substantially unaltered through ". . . set them to music well," it now had a new concluding sentence: "But later, the motives prepared for this opera served for *La Sonnambula*, as is told in its place. Here we refer to a passage in a letter from Bellini to the publisher Giovanni Ricordi which confirms that fact: '. . . I cannot feel indifferent toward the grumblings of impresarios over the payments I ask. Couldn't I too, perhaps, write four operas in one year?[3] but I'd undergo the risk of ruining my fame and of feeling remorse over cheating whoever was paying me. Ah, perhaps I didn't compose *La Sonnambula*, beginning it on the 11th of January and going on stage on the 6th of March? But that was a special case, and then I had some ideas that I had composed for *Ernani*, which was prohibited.' "[4]

When, during the year in which publication of the four volumes of LSmdN was completed, Florimo also issued separately the Bellini materials from it as *Bellini: Memorie e lettere*, he omitted all of this story from "But later, the motives . . ." to the end, substituting: "I have been unable to locate that letter again among my papers, though I have looked hard for it. I certainly will have given it to one of the many collectors or lovers of autographs. After that letter, Bellini never spoke about *Ernani* to me again; sure proof that he had laid aside the idea; and it seems to me that Romani did not complete the libretto either."[5]

And when Michele Scherillo, a close friend of the aged Florimo whom Pastura described[6] as "in a certain sense Florimo's spokesman," asked the old man to recall the lines from the *Ernani* libretto, this is what Florimo gave him in reply:

> *Crudo e ferale speco*
> *È il mio brutal ricetto;*
> *Ivi compagni ho meco*
> *La rabbia e il dispetto.*[7]

When, however, sections of the *Ernani* score which Bellini had begun to compose were turned up, those lines were found to read:

> *Muto e deserto speco*
> *è il nuzial mio tetto;*
> *quivi compagni ho meco*
> *la veglia ed il sospetto.**

Florimo was not wholly frank with his readers or with Scherillo about other matters, but he surely can be forgiven for recalling incorrectly lines that he had not seen for more than forty years. Interestingly, it is precisely the music to which, in the *Ernani* sketches, Bellini set the lines beginning *"Muto e deserto speco"* which he later adapted for the middle section of the trio *"Oh! di qual sei tu vittima,"* for the Act I finale of *Norma*.

* Roughly "My nuptial home is a silent and deserted cavern; here I have as my companions wakefulness and suspicion"—whereas the lines as recalled by Florimo might be translated "My brutal refuge is a rough and gloomy cavern; here I have as my companions rage and vexation."

APPENDIX C

The Ernani–La Sonnambula
Polemic, 1882–1902

Beginning early in the 1880's, at a time when none of the music that Bellini composed for *Ernani* was known to survive, a prolonged, intemperate, and often foolish polemic broke out over the question of whether or not Bellini had made use of that music when composing *La Sonnambula*. The chief debaters were the former Emilia Branca Romani, Michele Scherillo, and Antonino Amore.

The debate involved both misunderstanding and misrepresentation of the reasons why *Ernani* had been dropped even before Romani had completed the libretto. Unaware that Bellini's letter of January 3, 1831, to Perucchini asserted that *Ernani* had been set aside incomplete because of threatened interference from censorship, Emilia Branca, by then the marchesa di Montezemolo—whose aim in writing her so-called biography of Romani was to magnify and glorify him at all costs—asserted that Bellini had approached Romani to insist upon the scrapping of *Ernani* because of the clamorous success that Donizetti's *Anna Bolena* (another Romani libretto) had won at the Teatro Carcano, Milan, on December 21, 1830 (the actual date was December 26, 1830). She also stated that Bellini had formed his frightened opinion of *Anna Bolena* at its first performance. But Bellini was not at the Teatro Carcano on that occasion: on the night of Donizetti's success, he was attending the opening performance of the season at La Scala: the first Milan hearing of his own *I Capuleti e i Montecchi*, a performance so wretched that it infuriated him.[1]

Recalling a longish conversation between Romani and Bellini, Emilia Branca represented the latter as explaining that for him to offer another *opera seria* after Donizetti's "beautiful, very beautiful, sublime music" would be to invite ruin. She seems to have been unaware that on December 23—three days before the Carcano première of *Anna Bolena*—"in the announcements of the Carcano [season] by the Milanese journals . . . the two operas already were announced by their definitive titles: on the one hand, *Anna Bolena,* 'expressly composed by Maestro Donizetti,' on the other, *La Sonnambula,* 'new music by Maestro Bellini.' "[2]

On January 1, 1882, Michele Scherillo, whom Emilia Branca had allowed to read some, if not all, of her book before its publication, himself published in *Il Preludio* (Ancona) an article entitled *"La Sonnambula (Note aned-dotiche),"* which gave a précis of her circumstantial anecdote about Bellini at the première of *Anna Bolena* and then added: "Half of the music of *Ernani* was completed, and Bellini could not, because of the pressure of time, re-place it with other music; he had to adapt the new words to that music. And *Ernani* was disguised [*camuffato*] as *Sonnambula*! ! !" He cited a single instance of the transfer: a "bolero that formed part of *Ernani*" had been transformed, he said, into the music of *"Ah! vorrei trovar parole"* in *La Sonnambula*.[3]

Scherillo's exaggerated assertion that *"Ernani* was disguised as *Son-nambula"* set off an explosive reaction by Antonino Amore, whose entirely erroneous rebuttal was based upon the idealistic conviction that no com-poser of quality could conceivably re-use for a new libretto music that he had composed in view of a very different one. Amore did not, of course, know that Bellini's *Ernani* sketches survived to prove that, at least symbolically, Scherillo had hit nearer to the truth than he had. Ironically, it was Amore who, three years later, made the discovery—among papers in the possession of the Bellini heirs in Catania—of Bellini autographs containing music to be sung not only by Ernani and Elvira, but also by Don Carlo and Don Sancio. Convinced by that discovery that he now had in hand the argument with which to give Scherillo the coup de grâce, Amore asked a local musician, Domenico Bonica, to examine the sketches and confirm that Bellini had not re-used anything from them in *La Sonnambula*. Bonica duly so reported. But he also reported—and this should have told Amore how faulty his basic esthetic-ethical argument was—that the andante of an Ernani–Elvira love duet (the one of which Florimo incorrectly recalled the verses) had become the middle section of the Norma–Adalgisa–Pollione trio in the finale of Act I of *Norma*.[4]

Other motives in the *Ernani* sketches went into other passages of *Norma* —and into *La Sonnambula*. Scherillo, who did not have the *Ernani* sketches at hand, went too far when asserting that *"Ernani* was disguised as *Sonnam-bula."* But he was correct, as Bellini himself made clear,[5] when asserting that some of *Ernani* became some of *Sonnambula*. The *Ernani* sketches include a first version of a duet for Don Carlo and Don Sancio, on the back of which appears a sketch for a chorus, the chief melodic phrase of which is that of *"In Elvezia non v'ha rosa,"* the first-act chorus in *La Sonnambula*.

Friedrich Lippmann has pointed out[6] that a bass instrumental part in the *Ernani* sketches:

reappears, in B-flat major, in the sketches for *La Sonnambula* which are now in the Museo Belliniano at Catania—and again in the *sinfonia* for *I Puritani*.

Amore's incandescent moral indignation was without foundation: it had resulted from lack of information. But all later Bellini scholars owe him a large debt for having uncovered the *Ernani* sketches in Catania and for first determining—with a patience equaled only by his inescapable limitations— what places they might have fallen into in that opera if Bellini had completed it.[7]

APPENDIX D

Bellini's Letter of July 30, 1831, to Luigi Remondini[1]

"To the Most Distinguished
"Signore Dottore Luigi Remondini
"Milan

"My dear Friend,

"I have been much gratified by your letter, as Signora Giuditta [Turina] has also, because it has brought us news of you and because we read there affirmation of the relief that poor Gaetano[2] has felt as a result of the quinine cure. Nevertheless, we have not written to you because Giuditta often gives news of herself to your family, whom you see daily, and from them you receive the news. Here is what you asked me for in the name of Signore conte Ritorni.

"1802.[3] I was born in Catania of Rosario Bellini: I shall complete my 28th year in the coming November. My grandfather, Vincenzo Bellini, who studied at the Naples conservatory under the great Piccinni,[4] gave me the first elements of composition. In 1819, I betook myself to the Naples college, and under Giacomo Tritto, then professor of counterpoint, I pursued my studies: after three years, he died, and thereafter I spent the other five years of college in the school of the celebrated Zingarelli.

"During the Carnival of 1825, I composed *Adelson e Salvini*, an *opera semiseria* in three acts, for the *teatrino* of our college, performed by all the collegians themselves, both as singers and in the orchestra: the success of that opera won me the Prize awarded by the King, which consisted of the honor of composing an opera for the Real Teatro di S. Carlo and of a sum of three hundred ducati: The opera was *Bianca e Fernando*, and it went on stage in May 1826: the singers in it were [Méric-]Lalande, Rubini, and Lablache. In 1827, I abandoned the college and betook myself to Milan, where I brought to light *Il Pirata*, which went on stage at La Scala in October of that year, and was sung by Lalande, Rubini, and Tamburini. In February 1829, I composed *La Straniera* for that same theater, and it was preformed by Lalande, Unger, Rubini, and Tamburini. In May of that same year, I put *Zaira* on the boards in Parma, for the Opening of the new theater; [it was] composed for Lalande *** Cec *** [Cecconi], Trezzini, and Lablache. In March 1830, I composed *I Capuleti e i Montecchi* for the stage of La Fenice at Venice,

an opera performed by Signora Giuditta Grisi, by Signora Carradori [Cara-
dori-Allan], and Bonfigli; finally, in March of this year, I gave *La Sonnambula*
on the stage of the Carcano in Milan: my sixth opera, sung by Pasta, Rubini,
Mariani, etc.

"There you have all the details of my theatrical career which your
friend wants.

"In the meantime, receive my embraces, and give your noble Gugino
[*cugino?*—i.e., cousin?] my respects. Signora Giuditta salutes you most
lovingly [*carissimente—sic*] and hopes [*s'agura—sic*] that you will always
give her good news of your Gaetanino.

"Your

Bellini"

APPENDIX E

Donizetti and Norma

Biographers and critics of Bellini and of Donizetti have given wide currency to two supposed communications from Donizetti purporting to contain his enthusiastic reactions to the first four performances of *Norma*. One of them is a letter addressed to a "Maestro Rebotti [or Rubetti]" of Pesaro, the other a fragment from a letter written by Donizetti to his Neapolitan friend Teodoro Ghezzi. The former is spurious, the second almost certainly misquoted.

The letter to "Rebotti" (of whom no other trace can be found) has been printed in several slightly differing versions. No autograph of it has ever been reported. When, as the centenary of *Norma* approached, the letter was published as a dispatch from Catania in the *Corriere del Tirreno*, Leghorn, on November 12, 1931, it carried the initials "v. r." This was Vincenzo Ricca, who at Catania in 1932 published an appalling book entitled *Vincenzo Bellini: Impressioni e ricordi, con documenti inediti*, a stew of nonsense interlarded with forged documents. Of Ricca's publication there of a letter from Bellini to Giuditta Turina, Frank Walker wrote[1]: "The love letter from Bellini to Giuditta published by Ricca is a forgery, as are all the 'unpublished documents' published in his book. They were rightly excluded from her *Epistolario* [BE] by Luisa Cambi."

Ricca asserted that he had found the "Rebotti" letter "in a book by a certain Carlo Nava, published at Genoa in 1854, which is a complete biography of the Bergamo composer [Donizetti]." No copy of that book has ever been brought to light. When the scrupulous, lifelong Donizettian scholar Guido Zavadini republished the letter,[2] he expressed his acute discomfort in this footnote: "Published in the *Voce di Bergamo* of November 13, 1931 [one day after its appearance in the *Corriere del Tirreno*], which in turn took it from the *Rassegna artistica*, which in turn, so I have been told, took it from a book by Carlo Nava issued at Genoa in 1854. I have searched as persistently as fruitlessly for that book, both at Genoa and elsewhere."

As published in the *Corriere del Tirreno*, the letter begins with a paragraph unrelated to Bellini and *Norma* which does not appear in Zavadini's transcription (the two versions also differ in several minor details). It reads:

"Milan, 31 December 1831

"Dear Maestro Rebotti,
"You ask me what important artistic events may have occurred in Milan

recently. The only musical event of extraordinary importance has been that of the performances of *Norma* by the young composer Vincenzo Bellini. I am exceedingly happy over the very happy success that the aforesaid opera has had in* the Teatro la Scala [*sic*] since the 26th of the current [month]†; a festal and joyful reception that has been repeated on the other succeeding evenings.

"A success the more significant because *Norma* had a reception that was a little chilly—even, to tell the truth, hostile—on the part of a large audience on the first evening when it was given at La Scala. For four evenings, on the other hand, an immense throng has taken by assault the loges, the galleries, the stalls, the pit; and has filled the enormous auditorium in an incredible way; applauding almost every piece in the opera with lively rapture and enthusiasm.

"Everyone exalts to the skies the music of my friend, my more than brother, Bellini; everyone is subjugated by his sovereign genius and finds there inestimable beauties and unknown treasures of sublime harmony. The entire score of *Norma* delights me; and for four evenings I have gone to the theater to hear Bellini's opera again to the final scene. The principal numbers in *Norma* which have captivated me most are: the introduction‡ of the first act, in which the musical ideas are distributed and managed with consummate skill and great knowledge of musical technique—the ending of this piece is highly original as well as of exquisite craftsmanship—and the introduction,¶ which closes with a martial chorus, [is] strong and vigorous, as well as being a very novel piece in form and development:

"The '*Casta diva*' is a very delicate, enchanting melody; just as the music of the cavatina is all grace and sweetness. The instrumental part* is carried out and performed with bravura.†

"Also, the recitative in *Norma* is most beautiful. The duet (Verdi says the same thing) '*In mia mano alfin tu sei*' is an admirable example of dramatic melody. Also Norma's final scene‡ '*Qual cor tradisti, qual cor perdesti*' moves me to tears. I shall never finish, and if I proceed farther, the letter will become too long¶; I should have to tick off all the beauties of *Norma*, which are abundantly profuse. I shall say only that I have been overcome and conquered by the genius of the composition, by the rich elegance of the orchestra; as also by the very lofty pathetic and dramatic feeling united to the grandeur of the inspiration.

"Your Gaetano Donizetti."*

* "*nel*," whereas the "v. r." version reads "*al*" (at the).

† "*del 26 corrente*"; "v. r.": "*del 26 dicembre corrente.*"

‡ Zavadini: "*l'introduzione*"; "v. r.": "*la introduzione.*"

¶ See the preceding note.

* "v. r." begins this sentence: "In the second, and final act" and comments: ". . . we should remember that *Norma*, which at first was in two acts, later was divided into three acts." He has "*dell'atto tutto*" (of the whole act) after "instrumental part," whereas Zavadini does not.

† "v. r." has "*grande bravura*" (great bravura).

‡ "v. r.": "*nella scena finale di Norma*" (in Norma's final scene).

¶ "v. r.": "*e*" (and).

* "v. r."'s version concludes: "*Addio. Sono con tutto l'animo Vostro Gaetano Donizetti*" (Farewell. With all my heart I am Your Gaetano Donizetti).

Of the elements constituting this letter, the most damaging to its credibility are its heading ("Milan, 31 December 1831") and its claim that Donizetti had been in Milan at least since December 26. The première of his opera *Fausta* (with a libretto by Bellini's onetime friend Domenico Gilardoni) was to take place at the Teatro San Carlo, Naples, on January 12, 1832, seventeen days after the première of *Norma* at La Scala, and Donizetti was in Naples preparing it for rehearsal, if not actually rehearsing it, when *Norma* received its first performances. For him to have made a special round-trip from Naples to Milan—approximately seven hundred miles by coach each way—to hear the first five performances of *Norma* would have taken him at least two weeks that he cannot have had free for so unlikely and costly an expedition.

Another very suspect detail is the letter's reference to "the '*Casta diva.*' " All the earliest references to this most famous of all Bellinian excerpts call it simply "the cavatina"; not until much later did it become known by the first two words of its text. Also, what could "the '*Casta diva*' " have been expected to signify to a musician in Pesaro a week or so after the first performance of an opera that he could not have heard?

The astonishing parenthesis "(Verdi says the same thing)" may, of course, be an editorial interpolation: it does not appear in the "v. r." version of the letter. But if it was intended to be taken as part of what Donizetti had written, it damns the letter out of hand: in 1831, Verdi was an unknown youth of eighteen whose opinion no one would have thought of seeking or, if it had been proffered, of considering seriously. Finally, as William Ashbrook wrote[3]: ". . . the style of these letters* lacks the characteristics of Donizetti's other letters." Except in the approximately impossible event that an authentic autograph of the "Rebotti" letter should be produced, it must be considered a deliberate forgery.

To cast doubt upon the reliability of either Francesco Florimo or Teodoro Ghezzi is not a pleasant action, but it is not possible to believe that the fragment of a letter from Donizetti to Ghezzi dated "Milan, 27 December 1831," published first by Florimo in 1869[4] with a note that it had been communicated to him personally by Ghezzi (again, no autograph has ever come to light) is authentic. It reads: "*Norma*, having gone on stage at La Scala yesterday evening, was not understood, and was judged inopportunely by the Milanese. As for me, I should be very content to have composed it, and should gladly place my name under this music. Just the introduction and the last finale of the 2nd act [would] suffice to establish the biggest of musical reputations; and the Milanese will quickly come to realize the rashness with which they rushed into a premature judgment of the merit of this opera."[5] The objections to this fragment are identical to those to the "Rebotti" letter: Donizetti was not in Milan on December 27, and these sentences are remote in manner from the intimate, relaxed, and often very jocular tone of the authentic letters from Donizetti to Ghezzi.

Pastura wrote of the "Rebotti" letter[6]: "I again repeat that I have transcribed Donizetti's letter as I found it,† and that the, in any case, slight variations between this version and the one reported by Zavadini show that the

---

* Mr. Ashbrook is also discussing the fragment of a supposed letter to Teodoro Ghezzi. See below.

† That is, in the *Corriere del Tirreno*.

original must have undergone manipulations every time it was transcribed." But then Pastura made an irrelevant point: "But I nevertheless do not think that doubts should be advanced as to its authenticity, given the frank and loyal heart of the Bergamo musician; though it would always be better to read the original text." As I wrote elsewhere[7]: "Donizetti might well have expressed these feelings—but it must be added that they are precisely the feelings that Florimo would have liked him to express about a work of his adored friend and idol, Bellini." Certainly, Donizetti liked Bellini and thought very highly of his best operas: he had none of Bellini's jealousy and was incapable of saying or writing the kind of things that Bellini more than once wrote about him. But to accept, for that or any other reason, the letter to "Rebotti" and the fragment of one to Ghezzi as accurate transcriptions of texts actually written by Donizetti is, for the reasons advanced, impossible.

APPENDIX F

Final Scenes of Il Pirata, *from the Libretto Issued for the Première*

SCENA XI

Gualtiero *e* Coro *di* Cavalieri, *indi* Coro *di* Pirati *ed* Itulbo.

Cavalieri   La tua sentenza udisti,
Il tuo destin t'è noto
Ma noi possiam d'un voto
Farti contento ancor.
Parla. Che vuoi?

Gualtiero   Null'altro fuorchè spedita morte.
Incontro alla sua sorte
Vola ansioso il cor.

Cav.   Pago sarai. Guidatelo
Tosto a morir . . . Quai grida! . . .
         (*s'odono delle grida nell'interno*)

Coro *di* Pirati (*di dentro*)
     Viva Gualtier!

Cav.   Ci assalgono i fidi suoi
         (*si precipitano da varie parti i Pirati*)
Si uccida.

Itulbo, Pirati Voi, soli, voi morrete.

Cav.   Ebben, il difendete.
         (*combattono fra di loro*)

SCENA ULTIMA

Imogene, Adele, Coro *di* Damigelle, *e detti.*

Imogene   Lasciatemi! lasciatemi!
Io vo' saper chi muor.
         (*Gualtiero attraversa il ponte seguito dai suoi*)

GUALTIERO   Scostatevi!
    (*ai Pirati*)
L'impone il vostro duce.
Un'abborrita luce
Fuggo così.
    (*s'uccide*)

TUTTI   Che orror!
    (Imogene *sviene nelle braccia delle Damigelle.*
    Quadro di terrore.)

FINE.

APPENDIX G

History of the Autograph Score of
I Capuleti e i Montecchi

An interesting glimpse into the sort of history acquired by operatic autograph scores was provided in 1956, when the late Franco Schlitzer wrote for the Florentine antiquarian book-dealer Leonardo Lapiccirella a brochure entitled *I Capuleti e i Montecchi di Vincenzo Bellini/L'Autografo della Partitura/Note Illustrative di Franco Schlitzer*. It includes this note on "The Provenance of the Bellinian Autograph":

"Related to the history of the provenance of the autograph of the score of *I Capuleti e i Montecchi*, there is preserved a letter from Antonio Lanari (Milan, July 30, 1882), son of the renowned Florentine impresario, Alessandro [Lanari], addressed to a signora 'Rosina,' not otherwise identified. In it, the writer declares that the Bellinian score, together with the scores of Donizetti's *Parisina* and of the second act of his *L'Elisir d'amore*, had belonged to his father, upon whose death he had inherited them. 'These autographs,' as Lanari writes, alluding to the three scores, 'the price of which must increase constantly with time, and which you want to purchase from me, will easily bring you, when it pleases you to resell them, a much bigger sum than you are now paying me.' Five years later, conte Bernardo Arnoboldi Gazzaniga, probably the fourth owner of the autographs, to whom the signora 'Rosina' must have sold them, turned to the music publisher Giulio Ricordi of Milan for a further authentification of them. Ricordi, in fact, on October 12, 1887, replied to the inquiry this way: 'Comparing the aforementioned scores with other autographs of the composers alluded to which exist in the Archive of the Stabilimento [Ricordi], and they having been carefully examined both by me and by Maestro Garignani, Director of the Copying Office, it becomes very obviously clear that the abovementioned scores are autograph manuscripts.' Perhaps through family inheritance, they became the property of baronessa Bice Airoldi di Robbiate, who in turn ceded the autograph of *I Capuleti e i Montecchi* to signora Paola Ojetti of Florence and those of *Parisina* and the second act of *L'Elisir d'amore* to the city of Bergamo.[1]

"Recently the Bellinian autograph became the property of the Libreria Antiquaria di Leonardo Lapiccirella in Florence."[2]

APPENDIX H

Sketch of a Letter (May 1834?) from Bellini to Romani [1]

"My dear Romani,

"Following on what sig. Bordese reported to me about the conversation that he had with you* in Milan, and after your letter addressed to Bordese sent to me by signor Bolselli [*sic*], I see that you still do nourish affection for me, as signor Bordese nourishes it for you. I did not insult you: I defended my innocence before the Venetian public, which accused me of a secret understanding with the impresario that my opera [*Beatrice di Tenda*] was to be given at the end of the season. What proofs could I adduce in the journals, if not that you were the chief cause? That declaration did you no damage, as the whole world knew about the large number of librettos ordered from you in a single year, knew that they placed upon you the hardship of not being able to satisfy composers and impresarios; but what an article you hurled against Bellini! If you say that you always have loved him and do love him, as you said in your letter to Bordese: 'Nonetheless, I have not ceased to love him, as I recognized that the blame was not his, that he was egged on by imprudent friends, that he was deceived by more than one person who wanted to divide us.' And if you were convinced of that, you should not have written with such bitterness as you wrote against me; and doesn't your conscience torment you for all the false assertions that you made? Wasn't I constantly at your door from August 10 on? I went to Bergamo for three weeks,† and then did not leave Milan until December 7. With regard to the selection of the story, didn't you assure me that you were awaiting dramas that you had ordered from Paris? And then didn't you needlessly add insults to what you called your defense? Oh! my dear Romani, you never loved me, never! ! ! I was always attached to you, and I showed that at every step. I—and Pappadopoli‡ is a witness—when I met you in Venice during that unhappy period, when my heart was lacerated from every side and my spirit wept—said to myself: then can I give up him who has won so much glory for me in my career? The man who up to now was the friend of my heart, of my most

* Bellini now addresses Romani again in the familiar second-person form.

† Actually about four weeks.

‡ Variously spelled: a Venetian friend of Bellini and of Giovanni Battista Perucchini.

delicate thoughts? But your final lines at the end of your preface to the libretto of *Beatrice* [*di Tenda*] drove me to defend myself before the most gossipy and smallest-minded public in the world, the Venetian. But let us draw a veil over so many unhappy things and, if it is possible, make up for them by mutual repentance, and let us go back to being what I think we always have been, friends, the one for the other. What I suggested to Bordese and now suggest to you (and this is a prime necessity) is that you write an article and have it inserted into the journals of Venice, Milan, Genoa, Turin, and that in it you state that signor Romani and signor Bellini, responding to their friends' desire that they return to their work, have agreed to regard as unsaid everything that was to be read in the journals, as in a momentary state of irritation, etc. etc. I tell you the tone of the thing; you in your expert way will express it in such a manner that it will leave our decorum intact for us both, and in that way we shall be worthy of one another and without shame [will] again take up our *attachment*, which was born with my career and will, I hope, die with my life."

APPENDIX I

Ferdinand Hiller's Impressions of
Bellini and His Music*

"Some time ago, I received from artist friends and the leading musical authorities at Naples a request that I collect contributions toward a Bellini monument. . . . I replied to those enthusiastic admirers of the composer of *Norma* that it might be very possible to obtain contributions for the planned monument, but that it would be wise to consider some of the likely consequences first. . . . My well-intended remarks seem to have met with a cool reception, for I have never received a reply. However, a few months later I received a letter from the learned librarian of the Naples Conservatory, cavaliere Florimo, asking me to contribute a composition to an international pianists' album, the proceeds from which were to go to the fund for the Bellini monument. As that appeal involved only myself, I was delighted to oblige my esteemed old friend. Hopefully, this album[1] will have substantial sales all the way from London to Yokohama, and thereby will pay for at least a few folds of drapery on the projected statue. . . .

"Everyone knows that Bellini, like others, went to the French capital during the first, good years of Louis-Philippe's reign in order to obtain Parisian confirmation of the laurels he already had won in Italy. We cannot deny it: an artist's fame may be more lucrative in London, more honorific in Berlin, noisier in Milan, but nowhere does it taste so sweet to the chosen one as in Paris. Bellini belonged to that group, and there was no one else upon whom one would rather have bestowed that acclaim. His personality was very like his melodies: it was beguiling, just as charming as it was likable. The slender figure of perfect proportions supported a head with a broad brow that could have been that of a great thinker. The rather sparse, light blond locks, the steady, cheerful glance, the finely chiseled nose, and the full, expressive mouth formed a countenance such as one might desire for a person dearest to one's heart. His external appearance in no way corresponded to the usual notion of a Sicilian. Rather, he looked more like one of those descendants of the sons of the North who had settled on his fertile native island, and who had longed to exchange pine trees for orange groves. Their children, in turn, now seem

* Translated by Esther Mendelsohn from "*Vincenzo Bellini*," in *Deutsche Rundschau*, Berlin, April–June 1878, pp. 308–317.

like the trunks of firs adorned with myrtle blossoms. Superior beings do not shine by their gifts alone: often their very imperfections evoke the greatest fascination. As a true Sicilian, Bellini spoke poor Italian, and, in addition to his bad pronunciation of French, was not really at home in it. But his intellect was keen and his perception lively; thus, the contrast between content and expression in his rather jumbled speech gave it a charm often missing from utterances by the greatest orators.

"I often had the pleasure of seeing the young Maestro during the all-too-few winters that he spent in Paris. There he came upon a new musical world, and many of its phenomena touched him profoundly. Earlier, in Milan, Josef Dessauer, one of the best of the Viennese Lieder composers,[2] had introduced him to the wondrous labyrinth of German instrumental music. Bellini was not satisfied merely to admire the trees of knowledge to which he was thus introduced: with courageous hand, he grasped many of their fruits. But those were nothing compared with the revelations he experienced upon hearing Beethoven's symphonies at the Concerts du Conservatoire! '*E bel comme la nature*,' he exclaimed to me when I encountered him in the lobby after the 'Pastorale.' His eyes were shining as though he himself had accomplished a great feat. He was equally interested in hearing piano music, even when it was not exactly a Chopin who was playing. I shall never forget the evening that he, Chopin, and I spent in the intimate circle of Frau Freppa's[3] house. Mme Freppa, a highly educated, extremely musical woman, was born in Naples, though she was of French descent: escaping from an embarrassing family situation, she had settled in Paris, where she gave singing lessons in the most elegant social circles. Her voice, though not large, was extremely pleasant and excellently trained. Even the devotees of Italian opera who had been spoiled most were charmed by her performances of Italian folksongs and the simple tunes of the older composers. We liked and admired her, and often went together to visit her at the extreme end of the faubourg St.-Germain, where she lived with her mother in a *troisième au-dessus de l'entresol*, high above the noise and hubbub of the city. And there we chatted, played, and sang music, and then chatted, played, and sang some more. Mme Freppa and Chopin alternated at the piano, and even I did my best, while Bellini made occasional remarks or accompanied himself in one of his cantilenas, more in order to explain what he had been saying than to perform them. He sang better than any German composer I have ever met: his voice was not so much beautiful as very expressive. His piano playing just sufficed to indicate the orchestral part, which, of course, is not saying very much. But he certainly knew what he wanted, and was very far from the sort of instinctive poet many imagine him to have been. Thus, I remember how on one occasion, when he heard a song without words in which the harmonic accompaniment infringed upon the melodic line, he explained, full of fire, how that had to be avoided upon the stage. He used such piquant ingredients only very rarely and sparingly 'for the improvement of a melodic standstill' [*Ausbesserung melodischen Stillstandes*]; as an example of that, he sang the yearning little F-minor passage from *La Sonnambula*, '*oh e vorrei trovar parola*,'[4] in which, for two half-measures, the progression is indicated chiefly by a few modulations. For the chief arias of an opera, he demanded charming expression and complete independence.

"Bellini's operas are, after all, chiefly 'Liederspiele.' That is true not only because each situation culminates in its own well-rounded, compact song, but also because the usual Lieder-repetitions are scarcely ever missing. What lies between those *da capos* is barely worth mentioning: it serves mainly to accompany applause, as a rest period for singers and audience, or as the cause for some commotion upon the stage. After the brief interruption, both listeners and singers are refreshed for more giving and receiving, for more applause and singing. A sort of passionate relationship develops between the two parties, and to decide which of the two is happier would be difficult.

"After the exceptional success (aside from some talented earlier attempts) that Bellini won with his *Il Pirata* at Milan's La Scala, the leading opera house of Italy, one really could say: 'Here inadequacy becomes an occasion.' How meager Bellini's musical powers were in comparison with Rossini's! Certainly no one ever was a more complete master of the Italian lyrical stage than Rossini was at that time. A friend once told him: 'You repeat yourself too often.' 'How can I help it?' the other replied. 'My own music is all that I hear anywhere!' On the other side of the Alps, everyone 'rossini-ized'—Mercadante, Carafa, Donizetti, and even the young German, Meyerbeer. Even though they could not attain to the verve of the great master, the breadth of his invention, the spectacular extravagance with which he thrust his melodies at people— nevertheless, they knew how to imitate the lively play of his orchestra, his brilliant treatment of vocal lines, the richness of his ensembles, and the routine but clear form of his compositions. And what ensued showed that they were clever people, those Rossinians: they all had much more to them than the twenty-five-year-old Bellini.

"What was it, then, that gave his awkward, almost clumsy muse such quick and almost universal recognition? In combination with his sensuous appeal, it was the sincerity of his emotion and the simplicity with which he expressed himself. One felt that the singing emanated from a soul—a loving, yearning soul. Even if the Maestro decorated it with all sorts of tinsel so as to make it presentable at the court of Prince Public, even if he always kept in mind who was destined to sing his melodies, he never lost his inmost self. When he sat at the piano and began to sing a poet's verses, turning and twisting the melismata a hundred times and testing their effect, probably also thinking of Rubini or Pasta, he never became torpid. Like a great actor, he was sensitive to the feelings of those whom he had to create as resounding human beings—he felt their joys and their sorrows. He lamented and rejoiced with them while his fingers indicated only a few supporting arpeggios. What were those cold players down there in the orchestra to him? Does a nightingale sing with accompaniment? Singing, always singing, everything had to be sung! That was his destiny, that is what he wanted, what he strove for; and a deity had endowed him with the ability to accomplish it.

"For quite some time, Bellini lived in a house on the boulevard des Italiens. Because it stood out from among the others there, many older visitors to Paris may remember it. A few smaller and larger houses, connected with one another and flanked by a four-cornered tower combined into a complex called 'bains chinois.' It glowed with the colors commonly seen on Chinese lacquer. There really was an ordinary public bath inside. It has since fallen to the axe of the architectural Reign of Terror, the Robespierre of which was called

Haussmann. Well, Bellini had a few rooms in the tower. They were elegant and snug, and for him had the great advantage of being very close to the Italian Opera and the people connected with it. The view, furthermore, was charming—and the bathers did not make music. At the time, Bellini was working on *I Puritani*, which went into production that season. When I called upon him one afternoon, he sat at his piano engrossed in the composition of its last finale. '*Écoutez,*' he called out to me, and began to sing with exuberant feeling the beautiful D-minor passage that precedes the last resolution. He had two, very slightly different versions of the tenor's final cantilena. He played both for me several times and wanted to know which I thought the more effective. I could not make up my mind: I liked them both. 'I'll have to have Rubini sing it for me,' he said in great agitation as he gathered up the score. So we went to the latter's house, where I modestly left him. . . .

"Bellini had the great good fortune to be able to compose for vocal artists who knew how to heighten the effect of every one of the composer's intentions. In the charming duet in *La Sonnambula* (just before the lovers retire ["*Son geloso del zeffiro errante*"]), Grisi and Rubini tossed trills at one another like blossoming roses; their sixths and thirds were sung kisses. No verses by Shakespeare could have been more overwhelming than the well-calculated and well-felt solfeggios by Pasta when, as Norma, she began: [final scene of Act I] '*Oh, non tremare, o perfido,*' and then flung her scale passages in Pollione's face.

"I called Bellini's operas '*Liederspiele,*' and I consider that term valid in view of their contents. But it would be unjust not to mention another aspect that the composer knew how to treat with great mastery: the recitative. Although but little disposed toward symphonic treatment of the orchestra and broad musical development of interdependent situations, Bellini reaches to the depths of his soul when he must endow spoken words with music. Not the slightest change in a character's mood escapes; for each he finds not only the appropriate accents, but also the proper changes in modulation and harmony. The occasional short orchestral interludes, the moments when declamation becomes melodic song—everything, everything testifies to his keen understanding, warm perception, and complete mastery of the medium. In Germany, due appreciation of that mastery is hindered by translation of the original Italian text. What is done and borne here in that respect is well known—what routine, inexact, crude translations have been the lot of many works, some by our greatest masters. The poorest text cannot harm music in those passages in which it emerges in full power; but in recitative, where tone is subservient to the word, a composer can be judged only when he is heard or read in the language that served him. Nothing is more ridiculous than North German admirers of Gluck enthusiastically praising their hero's recitative when they have never really heard it; or than Teutonic scorners of Italian opera citing their awful German text and maintaining that it does not fit the music. That compositions by tramontane composers still enjoy such great success here despite their being denied the melodic support of their sweet language, and despite their being performed by singers among whom the majority does not know how to sing them, proves that they contain something unkillable, though it may not be destined to survive much longer in one single momentary incarnation.

"Bellini had another good fortune, of a sort denied more or less to his predecessors since the age of Metastasio. Instead of the librettists whom Rossini could hardly escape in Paris, he found for his works a charming and sensitive poet. Felice Romani was no dramatist: he used the inexhaustible source of theatrical invention which existed in France. But he not only knew how to use the borrowed material operatically; he also gave the composer verses with the blood of true poetry in their veins. *Norma*, derived from a little-known tragedy by Soumet, contains both the loveliest songs (like that of the famous aria 'Casta diva') and dialogues aflame with the most intense passion. *La Sonnambula*, a really charming idyll, is based upon the plot of a Parisian ballet. At the same time, Romani never tries to show off his nice poetic gifts at the composer's expense. With the most self-sacrificing economy, he gives only what is relevant to the music, thus sparing the composer needless labor, the audience boredom. Instead of driving the singers breathless with protracted songs, he lets the composer create a long-breathed cantilena for four stanzas. I do not know the extent to which Bellini had to insist upon his rights as a musician. But when he wrote *I Puritani* in Paris with conte Pepoli, a talented dilettante, his activities certainly were not limited to composing: he more guided the librettist than was guided by him. To be sure, he already had succeeded in staging a half-dozen of his works. . . .

"Although nobody demanded of him more than that he should keep on singing, we must add, to his special glory, that he always aimed to give his cantilenas deeper significance and characteristic expression. *Norma* is far above *Il Pirata*. The whole composition is suffused by a significant, serious atmosphere. There is scarcely another tragic opera by an Italian which is its equal in coloring. Great care was bestowed upon the choral parts as well; many of them have been drawn with penetrating sharpness. A few instances appearing between recitatives and real sung passages (called 'scene' in operatic jargon) are truly pathetic. The great climax at the end not only has an overwhelming effect, but also has become the prototype, or at least the inspiration, for much that has been created since—in places, what is more, where one might least expect it. Many of the recitatives are exemplary in aptness of declamation and sincerity of perception. The only really routine work is in the interludes separating the repetitions of the cabalettas. The treatment of the orchestral parts is admittedly meager; nevertheless, at some places individual instruments are employed most effectively. Unisons are too prominent in the infrequent ensembles; the effect achieved by them barely hides the insufficiency of polyphonic treatment. Too many traditional cadenzas are used; finales often sound almost trivial. The more accustomed we become to the beauties and the more indifferent we are to the lyrical attractions, the more apparent these weaknesses become. But those imperfections must not prejudice us against much in the opera which is genuinely felt and inventive.

"*La Sonnambula*, no less than *Norma*, has its very own definite character. The fact that it is absolutely the opposite, having an idyll-like character perfectly suited to its little drama, testifies to Bellini's creative abilities. One can scarcely think of a 'Liederspiel' richer in charming, lovely, and endearing songs: it is like a bouquet of spring flowers with blossoms as modest as they are fragrant and appealing. Here too we find the weakness that we found in *Norma*; but the unpretentiousness of the work as a whole stresses them less.

If only it did not have so many, and so often unsuitable, concessions to the virtuosity of the singers for whom it was composed! Although I have already mentioned the effect that this work can make with those singers! Once I went to a performance of this opera with Chopin, with that same Chopin to whom the most original and extravagant harmonies were second nature. I have rarely seen him so deeply moved: during the finale of the second act, when Rubini seemed to be singing tears, he, too, had tears in his eyes. How very sad it is that even the beguiling creation of so virginal, almost childlike a fantasy sooner or later evokes the French saying: *'Tout passe, tout casse, tout lasse!'*

"The composition of *I Puritani* proves that the impressions to which Bellini was subjected in Paris were not without influence upon his composing. Whether that was to his advantage is doubtful. In this, his last opera, he obviously attempted to give the orchestra more freedom and fullness, to be more particular about transitions in the accompaniment, to give the melodic lines of the ensembles more independence, and to endow the entire structure, both as a whole and in detail, with more power and scope. In my opinion, the spontaneity of his invention suffered thereby. The most beautiful and effective passages are always those overflowing, sometimes slightly sentimental cantilenas which were characteristic of him. Toward their perfection he worked with his heart's blood. Next to them, one hardly knows whether or not to be pleased by the greater intricacies at which others were ever so much better than he was. What folly to believe that a lesser talent can achieve ultimate mastery through study. Further, it is very questionable that a unique nature like Bellini's would have created more significant works if he had received a stronger artistic training than was his lot. Had he lived longer, would he have composed something greater? Who can deny it? Who can estimate what the reaction of his inmost self might have been to the serious impressions of advanced age?

"Although Bellini was one-sided in the best he had to give—or perhaps because of that—he had many imitators. Not one of them did great things. Still, we must remember that Donizetti, though older and much his superior in the composing craft, had been greatly influenced by him. And it was only after he had assimilated what he had got from Bellini that he achieved his great popularity. *Lucia di Lammermoor* scarcely would have existed had there not been *Il Pirata*, and the often-heard and well-liked aria of the despairing Edgardo is a variation of the finale of that score.[5] Rossini cleared the path for his [Donizetti's] comic operas, which certainly can be regarded as his best and most durable; he also learned much from the French. Thus, with his extraordinary talent, he attained to creations that certainly cannot be denied a high degree of independence, their charm, wit, and vitality aside. Verdi, too, was not free of Bellini's influence; the Troubadour's last cantilena recalls Bellini's compositions.[6] And yet, it was Verdi who, more than any other, contributed to the displacement of Bellini's operas from the Italian stage. The energetic rhythms and pulsating dramatic vitality of his works could not help appealing especially to the agitated, revolutionary Italians. . . ."

APPENDIX J

Bellini's Death Certificate

"Deaths 1835 No. 46   Death   BELLINI VINCENZO September 23, 1835

"Mairie de Puteaux

"The year one thousand eight hundred thirty-five, the twenty-fourth day of the month of September, at ten o'clock in the morning, in our presence, Jullien Guillaume Jerôme, mayor and civil office of the Commune of Puteaux, canton of Courbevoie, arrondissement of Saint-Denis, department of the Seine, appeared the messieurs Jacques Louis Huché, aged fifty-three years, journeyman, woodworker, and Joseph Hubert, aged thirty-seven years, gardener, both domiciled in that commune and friends [*sic*] of the defunct hereinafter named. Who have declared that yesterday, at five o'clock in the afternoon, there died in the house of monsieur Legigan,[1] quai Royal, in that commune, *Vincenzo Bellini*, aged thirty-two years [*sic*], music-master, a bachelor, born at Catania in Sicily. Upon which, we, officer of the civil status named above, after having been transported with the declarants to the domicile where the corpse of the defunct was found, assured ourselves of the decease. In testimony whereof we have drawn up the act, which has been transcribed into the two registers and signed by the declarants and by us after reading it.

"JULLIEN

"Huché
"Hubert
  Joseph."

APPENDIX K

The Autopsy Performed on Bellini's Body, September 25, 1835

"It was on September 25, 1835, that I proceeded to the autopsy and the embalming of the body of Bellini, who had died thirty-six hours earlier at the house of M.ʳ Lewis [sic] in Puteaux, near Paris.

"The organs contained in the head and chest were intact and quite healthy; but I found those in the abdomen gravely altered and in the following state:

"The entire large intestine, from the anal extremity of the rectum to the ileocecal valve, was covered with innumerable ulcers of the average size of a lentil, quite gray, consisting of a layer of purulent detritus which could easily be squeezed out. The margins of these ulcers were very thin, slightly loose, and floating under water [sic]; no part of the mucous membrane was either thickened or hardened; quite the contrary, it was everywhere softened and detachable in the form of pulp wherever it was not ulcerated. Where it was, the ulceration covered the breadth of the mucous layer, some or all of the muscular layer, but no part of the serous layer, so that there were no perforations.

"The right lobe of the liver enclosed an abscess the size of a fist, which was full of thick, yellow, homogeneous, treacling pus. The abscess walls were formed of somewhat softened liver parenchyma, but without traces of cyst formation or of neoformed tissue of any description. No other abscess existed in the liver or elsewhere. The hepatic blood vessels were quite unaffected and normal in appearance. The gall bladder contained a small amount of blackish, viscous bile, but the orifices and passages constituting the biliary tract were not affected by any stenosis, so that the bile ran freely to the duodenum. There was no evidence of past or present jaundice.

"All the other viscera and organs were in the most satisfactory state, and it is evident that Bellini succumbed to acute inflammation of the colon, compounded by an abscess in the liver. The inflammation of the intestine had produced violent symptoms of dysentery during life. Because of its location, the abscess had not yet caused any accident, but, being so close to the convex surface of the liver, it could from one day to the next have opened into the abdominal cavity and thus have caused fatal peritonitis, as there were no adhesions between the parietal peritoneum and the liver, so that such a terminal episode was most probable.

"Paris, September 26, 1835

"A. Dalmas, Doctor and *professeur agrégé*
of the Faculty of Medicine, Paris,
Chevalier of the Légion d'honneur."

Commentary by Dr. Victor de Sabata, September 7, 1969

Responding generously to my request for his opinion of the cause of Bellini's death on the basis of that autopsy report and what I had been able to discover of Bellini's earlier medical history, my friend Dr. Victor de Sabata of Milan wrote me (September 7, 1969) as follows:

"From the description given by the worthy Dr. Dalmas some 135 years ago, it is quite obvious that Bellini died of a terminal flareup of chronic amebiasis.[1] It is, in fact, a wonder to me that the cause of Bellini's death can still be regarded by some as 'mysterious.' The preceding history of attacks of diarrhea, recurring for several years during the hot season, is itself sufficient, if not to diagnose the trouble with absolute certainty, at least to make any practicing doctor strongly suspect amebiasis. And then the findings at the autopsy are so typical of chronic amebiasis with amebic abscess of the liver that Dr. Dalmas's description could be lifted as it stands and printed in a treatise on pathological anatomy. The following excerpts are transcribed from the 1961 edition of *The Merck Manual,* doubtless the most reliable and updated source of medical information in abbreviated form:

" 'Gaining access to the mucous membrane chiefly in the regions of fecal stasis (the cecum, appendix, ascending colon, sigmoid colon, and rectum), the invaders penetrate the mucosa by direct histolysis and phagocytosis . . . later, ulcers form which tend to be ragged and undermined . . . they may be associated with . . . edema and sloughing of large areas of mucosa. The muscular coat limits penetration of the ameba, but occasionally it is destroyed with a resulting perforation. Amebas enter the radicles of the portal vein and are carried to the liver. Most of these probably are destroyed, but if the survivors are numerous, they may cause hepatitis, or one or more large abscesses. . . . Liver abscesses occur most frequently in adult males . . . only one-third of the patients with proved amebic liver abscess give a history of dysentery. . . . Abscesses usually are single and located in the right lobe of the liver. . . . Jaundice is unusual. . . . Perforation of the abscess into the subphrenic space, right pleural cavity, right lung, or other adjacent organs may occur. . . . Liver abscesses contain a thick, semifluid material composed of more or less cytolyzed remains of tissue.'

"I do not need to point out each of so many points of similarity between this modern, official version of the pathology of amebiasis and the Bellini autopsy report, as they are all so evident. Perhaps it is more rewarding to offer an interpretation of the mechanism of Bellini's terminal illness and death. Curiously, Dr. Dalmas ends his report by saying that 'if' the liver abscess had opened into the abdomen, that would in all likelihood have caused death; this is a very good piece of guessing—except that Bellini's abscess *did not* burst open, as Dr. Dalmas himself assures us; but poor Bellini died nevertheless. It is a thousand pities that Dr. Dalmas failed to give us a description of Bellini's *blood*—for I have good reason to suspect that the terminal episode was what our Latin forefathers called *inspissatio sanguinis*, i.e., thickening of the blood (caused by severe loss of water and electrolytes due to diarrhea) to the point at which it could not circulate through the smaller blood vessels, particularly in the brain and lungs. This is a common cause of death in any disease causing severe diarrhea of long duration (including cholera, to be sure; but also bacillary dysentery, amebiasis, several tropical infections, and even some malignancies), and would certainly include Bellini's case, particularly if we consider that he was in very poor shape to begin with. If Dr. Dalmas had had the astuteness to examine a specimen of Bellini's blood after his death, and had reported it as unusually thick (as he did in regard to the bile), we would have an entirely convincing explanation not only of the nature of Bellini's disease, but also of how he died even though his liver abscess had not exploded.

"At this point, the reader may find it difficult to understand how Dr. Dalmas could possibly miss so obvious a diagnosis of Bellini's disease—and, indeed, today this would amount to unforgivable ignorance. But the fact is that the first discovery of a pathogenic ameba (*Entamœba histolytica*) was made by Lösch in 1875—that is, forty years after Bellini's death—and no real progress was made in recognizing amebiasis as a disease distinct from what was broadly called 'dysentery' until 1911–1913, when Walker and Sellardz demonstrated that the ingestion of *Entamœba histolytica* produced full-fledged amebiasis in man. True, in the meantime (1903), Schaudinn had demonstrated the presence of the protozoan in the feces of patients with what would now be called acute intestinal amebiasis; but for some reason nobody paid much attention to him—and, at any rate, that would still be seventy years after Bellini's death. So if there is reason for wonder, it is not that Dr. Dalmas had no knowledge of amebiasis, but that more recent observers failed to recognize the true nature of Bellini's disease even though Dr. Dalmas had provided a description of truly marvelous clarity."

APPENDIX L

Sketches of Incomplete Scenes (Operas?)
in the Museo Belliniano at Catania
("Virginia"; An Oriental Scene; "Oreste")

Among the fragmentary autographs of music by Bellini in the Museo Belliniano at Catania, three may possibly represent operas that were projected and then abandoned; they are more likely, however, to have been student exercises and experiments. All were written out before Bellini left for Naples in 1819, and only one of them is of more than casual interest.

1. Sparse sketch using text-words taken from a libretto or drama dealing with Livy's story of Virginia, a plebeian girl of fifth-century Rome. The chief decemvir, Appius Claudius, becoming enamored of her, enslaved her, whereupon her father, Lucius Virginius, assassinated him.[1] The declamatory monologue begun by Bellini would fit in immediately after that assassination.

2. Almost illegible sketches dealing with an innocent girl imprisoned in an Oriental country. Pastura wrote[2]: "During the course of the scene, the acting personages have Oriental names that are given abbreviated and with changing orthography, among them only the name Delimano appearing clearly. . . . In these exercises, the declaimed style of the recitatives is interspersed with melodic phrases, certain of them presented in strophic forms, almost as if sketching an aria."

3. Orchestral sketches, very probably of an act finale, of a scene involving Achille, Agamennone, Clitennestra, Ifigenia, Patroclo, and a chorus. Pastura, who in the 1950's uncovered additional pages belonging to these sketches, noted[3]: "Looking at [this fragment] now, we note that it has all the characteristics of an exercise, in the ugliness of the verses as well, which Bellini never would have set to music for public performance. He probably was trying his hand at an ensemble scene, which (in view of the names of Ifigenia, Clitennestra, Achille, Agamennone, Patroclo, and the chorus, placed against their respective staves on the first sheet) certainly must have belonged to an *Ifigenia*, and would have given the musician a way of composing a large concerted piece, an act finale."

So far, so simple and so credible. But those autograph pages became enmeshed in one of the most confused, persistent, and incredible of the Bellini legends: that he considered composing—or even promised to compose— an opera by setting Alfieri's tragedy *Oreste* intact. On June 27, 1839, Benedetto

Castiglia said in an article in *L'Occhio* (Palermo): "Just before the calamitous illness that consumed him, [Bellini] wrote to Santocanale in Palermo that he intended to set the *Oreste* to music and to compose this entire opera in dramatic song, without any of the obligatory repeats, the interrupted sentences, etc., etc. which had been conventional until his time, but which he had tried to elimini- nate in some places in his earlier operas."

Writing about Bellini's 1832 visit to Sicily, Filippo Cicconetti said, twenty years after Castiglia's assertion[4]: "Then, almost a different man, he began to recite lines by Metastasio and by Alfieri, whose *Oreste* he had promised [whom?] to set as written if his occupations would permit him to. I think that if the world did not have infinite reasons for weeping over the untimely death of this divine [man], it would have reason for high sorrow on learning about this lost opera, which, in view of the quality of Bellini's genius, would have restored tragedy to the splendor with which it was surrounded in Greece, and at the same time would have altered the face of the dramatic theater." In fact, *Oreste* would have been impenetrable to Bellini's art—and probably to that of any composer earlier than, perhaps, the Carl Orff of *Antigonæ*, *Œdipus*, and *Prometheus*, which is to say that it could not be through-composed, but would have to be cast as some variety of play with incidental music.

Antonino Amore, taking up the *Oreste* argument, wrote[5]: "[Arthur] Pougin, who evidently took the information from the Roman biographer [Cicconetti], followed it with a very different observation: 'He conceived the project of setting to music Alfieri's *Oreste* just as the great poet had written it, a project that was never carried out. But was Bellini of the stature to attack such a subject, and ought one to regret that he was unable to do it? I am not certain; but it seems to me that his tender, elegiac, and melancholy genius would have communicated badly with *Oreste* and its furies.'[6]

"Florimo, on the other hand, denied the story flatly. He says[7]: 'This has always been a great wonder to me, as while Bellini lived, he never spoke or wrote to me about it.'

"Where do we stand? Was Cicconetti, then, fantasticating? And yet, he did not invent this item: as with all those items concerning Bellini's life for which some people want to call Cicconetti very credulous, he obtained it from [Bellini's] relatives and friends, such as Santocanale, Barbò, Rossini, and others. What, then, is the truth?

"The truth is that the information had been divulged in the press twenty years before the Roman biographer published (1859) his *Vita di Vincenzo Bellini*. . . ." Amore then quotes Castiglia's 1839 sentence cited above, and adds: "The letter addressed to avvocato Santocanale, which could have ended all doubt, has been lost like so many others; but it seems to me that it must have corrected Castiglia's statement in two details: 1st. The project to set *Oreste* must be placed not after *I Puritani* [*i.e.*, not just before Bellini's ter- minal illness], but after *Norma* [*i.e.*, on the 1832 trip to Sicily], nor in Paris, but in Catania, as Cicconetti understood clearly. 2nd. The opera [libretto] of which Bellini wrote or spoke to Santocanale must have been, not Alfieri's tragedy, but a text taken from that tragedy or something resembling it.

"Whoever has studied Bellini's disposition knows that he always avoided bloody scenes, so that it is true that nowhere in his operas is the death of a character presented upon the stage [*sic*], and that one of the causes to which he attributed the unfortunate reception of *Beatrice di Tenda* was precisely, as said, 'the libretto, which reeks of bloodshed at every point. . . .'

"In this conviction, I assert that I have found among the numerous autographs five sheets of very crumpled music, illegible here and there, which I believe to be fragments of the aforementioned opera.

"On the first of these, which is certainly the beginning of a scene, we read the following names: *Ifigenia, Clitennestra, Achille,*[8] and *Agamennone;* and then, on another, *Coro* and *Patroclo*. These names and the few verses that I transcribe below make me suppose that the argument is *Iphigenia in Aulis,* a story already treated by Gluck.

"I take from the pages themselves the words that I find it possible to read, and attempt to reconstruct the verses as well as possible:

> "—   *Signore,*
> *Da te chi mi difende?*
> *—Costui che vilipende*
> *La regal figlia* . . . (illegible)
> *—T'accheta.*

>   *A quai vicende*
> *Esposta io son!* . . .
> *—*   *Ma parla*
> *Ah tu che il sai!* . . .
> *—*   *Parlar! e lo potrei?*

"Some of the replies allow us to divine who is speaking, but they do not suffice to clarify the structure of the scene. Here, however, is another passage:

>   "CORO E PATROCLO.
> "*Tu la volesti vittima,*
> *Vittima è già al tuo piede,*
> *Anima senza fede,*
> *Mostro di crudeltà.*

> "*Ai tradimenti tuoi*
> *Chiedilo e ai pianti miei,*
> *E ti dirà che sei*
> *Mostro di crudeltà.*

"I do not find Oreste among the speakers, but the discovered pages are small fragments, and it is not difficult [to suppose], seeing that Agamennone and Clitennestra are here, that their young son Oreste also should have been. From this detail, certainly, the confusion arose.

"Some of our older people would have it that the poetry was written by Gioacchino Fernandez, a name forgotten but not obscure in the republic of letters. A fine orator in our criminal courts, a far from mediocre poet, and a student of the Greek and Latin classics, he acquired considerable fame by translating Ovid's *Heroides* and writing, in the Alfierian manner—he being, in independence of character, an Alfierianizer—four tragedies: *Atreo, Ermione,*

Antiope, and *Armino;* and two *melodrammi: Teresa al tempio* and *La Fanciulla repubblicana.*

"Fernandez may have induced [Bellini] to set a lyric tragedy borrowing its story from one of the bloody encounters of which the story of the Atridae is full; and the notion does not seem incredible when we remember that on the evening when Bellini went to theater as the guest of the principe di Manganelli in Palermo in 1832, precisely Fernandez's *Atreo* was being given.

"I note the tradition, but do not underwrite its truthfulness, and also confess my respectful doubts.

"The verses are too outlandish, and I should think myself offending Fernandez's memory if I were to attribute them to him. What is certain is that Bellini, leaving [Palermo], never spoke again of either *Oreste* or the Atridae."

No proof that Bellini ever considered composing Alfieri's *Oreste,* then, exists or is likely to be produced. No proof exists, what is more, that Oreste was to have been one of the characters in the scene (or opera) dealing with Ifigenia, the surviving pages of which were written out not later than 1819— thirteen years before Bellini's final visit to Sicily, when he could have discussed a possible libretto with Fernandez. And there, for the time being, and unless some such now unimaginable document as the dubious letter to Santocanale should be found, this entangled question must be left.

APPENDIX M

An Important Unpublished Addition by Bellini to I Capuleti e i Montecchi*

Friedrich Lippmann has written[1]:

"The autograph of the opera *I Capuleti e i Montecchi* is to be found in the Museo Belliniano at Catania. The most important copy, two manuscript volumes with the title 'I Montecchi e Capuleti/Melodramma in 2 Atti/Del Sig. r Maestro V. zo Bellini,' is preserved in the archives of the Ricordi publishing house at Milan. In reality, this is an entirely special copy, presenting large autograph sections, completely so on pages 111r. [recto]–118r., 122r.– 155v. [verso], 239r.–266v., and 339r.–343v., as well as limited isolated annotations *passim*. Several times Bellini has noted: 'Revised for mezzo soprano.' And in fact the variations from the autograph that was used for the first performance at Venice and for the published edition prepared by the Casa Ricordi† consist essentially of the adaptation of the role of Giulietta, originally for soprano, to the mezzo-soprano register.

"The most interesting thing is the autograph insertion of an 'Allegro agitato'—*Morir dovessi ancora*—into Giulietta's second-act 'aria.' Into this 'aria' are inserted, by means of reference marks, three pages (252r. and v., 253r.) containing an episode that has remained unremarked until now [see pp. 424–425 herein, where they are reproduced by special permission of the Archivio Ricordi].‡

"In all probability, Bellini composed this insertion, like this entire second version of *I Capuleti e i Montecchi,* for the performance of the opera in Milan during the Carnival of 1830–1831. The first Milanese performance occurred at the Teatro alla Scala on December 26, 1830. On January 3, 1831, Bellini informed [Giovanni Battista] Perucchini:

"'For me, then, the opera makes half the effect that one felt at Venice; whether because of the larger theater, because of the slower tempos used by [Alessandro] Rolla,[2] *because in all the ensemble pieces the voices of the two*

---

* All notes here printed as footnotes (bracketed additions excepted) are translated verbatim from Lippmann's text.

† First edition, Milan (1831), editorial number 5224–5234 (separate sections earlier). New edition *ibid.*, undated, editorial number 42043.

‡ See reproduction of them on pp. 142–144 [of Lippmann's article]. (Most grateful thanks to the Casa Editrice Ricordi for courteous permission to reproduce them.)

donnas cannot be effective because they are both mezzo-sopranos, because so large a theater is detrimental to [Giuditta] Grisi—in short, I no longer hear the 'Capuleti' of Venice, and even in a theater full of very abundant applause.'*

"The leading roles had been taken at Venice by the soprano Rosalbina Carradori [*sic*] Allan (Giulietta) and the mezzo-soprano Giuditta Grisi (Romeo). At Milan, instead, two mezzo-sopranos sang: Amalia Schütz [-Oldosi] (Giulietta) and again Giuditta Grisi (Romeo). One can understand how the blending of the two voices was more nearly complete in the ensemble pieces in the Venetian production.

"Whereas the libretto for the first Venice performance and that for a succeeding performance at Sinigaglia ('for the *fiera* of the year 1830') do not give the text of the fragment within Giulietta's aria referred to, it was printed in the libretto for the Milan staging (second scene of the third stage picture= second scene of the second act):

GIUL. Il Padre! ah! porgi, e salvami. *(spaventata)*
       (Lorenzo le consegna il sonnifero)

LOR. Salva sarai: costanza!

GIUL. Morir dovessi ancora,
       Per te, Romeo, si mora!
       Sol morte, mi può togliere
       Al fero genitor.
       (Beve rapidamente)

CAP. Arresta.

"These verses are also found in the libretto for the Neapolitan staging (Teatro San Carlo) in the autumn of 1831 and in the *Collezione delle opere teatrali poste in musica dal celebre Maestro Vincenzio Bellini,* issued at Naples in 1834 by the publisher Flautina.†

"With the 'Allegro agitato,' Bellini not only enriched the score of *I Capuleti* with another beautiful melody, but also by means of it increased the dramatic effectiveness of the first musical scene of the second act, which publishers very incorrectly have called 'Scena ed Aria' (for Giulietta). In reality, this is a conversation between Giulietta and Lorenzo and among Giulietta, Lorenzo, and Capellio (with intervention by the chorus), though it does reach its melodic climax in Giulietta's part. Bellini's scene must be numbered among the most modernly conceived and structured scenes in the repertoire of Italian *opera seria* around 1830. With respect to its musical drama- turgy, it is not far from one of the typical scenes of Verdi's middle period. Bellini has organized the scene (it corresponds to scenes I–IV of the second act in the libretto) this way: orchestral introduction, characterized by an in- dividual melody assigned to the cello and not repeated later—accompanied recitative (Giulietta's monologue and the dialogue of Giulietta and Lorenzo) —Giulietta's 'Lento' on the words *Morte io non temo,* and her '*a solo,*' into which, however, another dialogue for Giulietta and Lorenzo is inserted—dialogue a) between Giulietta and Lorenzo, in the course of which Giulietta receives and

* L[uisa] Cambi, *Vincenzo Bellini. Epistolario* [BE], Milan, 1943, p. 265. Italics mine.
† The copies H.2.4 and 24.3.1/2 in the library of the Naples Conservatory do not contain the musical addition.

G—Three autograph pages from the Ricordi manuscript copy of
I Capuleti e i Montecchi (pp. 252r. and v., p. 253r.): "*Morir dovessi
ancora,*" as discussed by Friedrich Lippmann.

drinks the sleeping potion (this is the point at which Giulietta's 'Allegro
agitato' is developed); b) among Giulietta, Lorenzo, and Capellio, with intervention by the chorus—Giulietta's 'Andante,' *Ah, non poss 'io partire,* repeated
later to the same text; before that repetition, the Giulietta-Lorenzo-Capellio
conversation (with chorus) continues; after it, a *stretta* again brings together
all the protagonists and the chorus—accompanied recitative (Capellio's monologue).

"For an 'aria,' that is truly an unusual form, even if we take into account
how often the Italian aria of the first three decades of the nineteenth century
attained great flexibility of structure in response to the dramatic situation.*

* On this point, see the chapter '*Stellung und Form der Arie*' in my dissertation
*Studien zu Libretto, Arienform und Melodik der italienischen opera seria im Beginn
des 19. Jahrhunderts (unter besondere Berücksichtigung Vincenzo Bellinis)*, Kiel 1962
(typescript), to be published shortly. [The resulting book was published in 1969
by Böhlau Verlag, Cologne/Vienna, as *Analecta Musicologica 6: Vincenzo Bellini
und die italienische opera seria seiner Zeit/Studien über Libretto, Arienform und
Melodik.* It is the most important musicological study of Bellini yet published, and
I am deeply grateful to Dr. Lippmann for blanket permission to quote from it, as
well as from his other published writings on Bellini.]

Certainly, the scheme is recognizable: Cantabile—Cabaletta *(Morte io non tempo— Ah, non poss 'io partire)*, the form standardized about 1810; but when one listens to the scene as a whole, one does not in fact hear it as a derivative of that scheme. With all the more reason, then, Giulietta's 'Allegro agitato' absolutely cannot be fitted back into that formal structure: rather, it is one of those solo-like episodes treated in aria style which Bellini inserted into his musical scenes more often than any other Italian composer of his time. Here, in *I Capuleti*, this episode has the function, from the dramatic point of view, of emphasizing the moment at which Giulietta takes the potion (which otherwise has little repercussion in the music), and, from a musical point of view, the function of an opportune interruption, by means of an ampler melodic arc, of dialogue carried forward in brief phrases.

"The second edition of *I Capuleti* for voice and piano issued by the Casa Ricordi (editorial number 42043), like the first (number of the scene: 5232), contains the Venetian version, in which Giulietta, immediately and in silence, drinks the poison that Lorenzo has brought her. (This action is marked musically by a fermata [⌒]. Immediately thereafter, Lorenzo exclaims: *'Salva già sei, costanza!'* words that Bellini left in the Milanese version, at the end, after the insertion of Giulietta's 'Allegro agitato')."

APPENDIX N

Friedrich Lippmann on Variants in Norma *Autographs, Manuscripts, and Editions*

Friedrich Lippmann has written[1]:

"A critical examination of the manuscript sources* and early editions of the opera *Norma* (December 26, 1831, at the Teatro alla Scala, Milan) is confronted by numerous problems. They chiefly concern the first finale and the chorus '*Guerra, guerra*' in Act II.

"In the fast section of the trio in the first finale (the text begins with Norma's '*Vanne, sì, mi lascia, indegno*'), the autograph† of the opera contains variants that are not given either in the copies I have seen‡ or in the printed editions.¶ In the autograph, page 142 recto and verso, Bellini subsequently

---

* All manuscripts to be mentioned originated during the first half of the nineteenth century. [All notes here printed as footnotes are translated verbatim (bracketed additions excepted) from Lippmann's article.]

† Conservatory, Rome, signature G.MS.1–2.

‡ I saw the following copies: Conservatory, Naples, 58.2.18/19, 24.3.3/4, 24.3.5/6, O^A.7.4. (with annotations probably by Donizetti); Rome, Conservatory, A. Ms. 47–/471; Milan, Conservatory, Ms. 2190 and Noseda C 23.

¶ The following are the most important editions (unless otherwise described, the piano arrangements mentioned always have text and separate vocal lines): first edition (piano arrangement), Milan (1832), Ricordi, plate nos. 5900–5775–5911. (This was preceded by an edition for piano only, plate numbers 5775, 5786; several numbers appeared earlier in arrangement for piano, four hands.) Almost contemporaneously with the Ricordi first edition, dependent upon it and upon manuscript material made available by Ricordi, piano arrangements appeared in other countries as well. Of them, I mention here those of Launer in Paris (plate number 3269, taken over later by Girod) and of T. Boosey & Co. in London (without plate number), noted on the title page and next to the plate number in each piece in the Ricordi first edition. But the two following piano arrangements also were certainly based upon contracts with Ricordi: B. Girard e C.i (later Cottrau) in Naples (disjunct, changing plate numbers—for example, *sinfonia* 2121, final aria 2103); A. Diabelli & Comp. In Vienna (plate nos. 5163–5177). Of the later editions (still in the first half of the nineteenth

entered a second version of the melody under Norma's part (Ricordi 1915 score, p. 247, middle; Ricordi piano arrangement, plate no. 41684, p. 148) without deleting the first*:

"This necessitates a few changes in the accompaniment, especially toward the end: Bellini wrote fermatas for the orchestra for the cadenza. In this second

century), the piano arrangement issued by Pacini, Paris (plate nos. 1600–1617) is especially valuable, as is indicated immediately by the subtitle: *Ouvrage revu & corrigé par l'Auteur*. Before 1850, other piano arrangements were published in Paris by Marquerie Frères (no plate nos.); in London by Cramer, Beale & Co. (plate no. 462, first about 1850); in Rome by Ratti, Cencetti e Co. (under the title *La Foresta d'Irminsul*), with very disjunct plate numbers (the first-finale trio 479, the 'Guerra' chorus 508). The most important piano editions to appear after 1850 are that issued by Ricordi, plate no. 41684, of 1869–1870 (it remains on sale today with a few plate corrections) and Ricordi's 1915 *Partiturdruck* (plate no. 115216). (According to the stock catalogues preserved in the Archivio Ricordi, an additional piano arrangement was issued in 1859 in large format, plate nos. 30981–30995, but I was unable to locate it in any library.) The best-known edition in Germany is the one issued by Peters, No. 391, plate nos. 4956 (new printing, plate no. 7995).

* Bellini's entry is without text. I have added the text of the familiar version, which stands above it.

version, the end of the substituted melody quoted is succeeded immediately (still Norma singing) by:

Te sul - l'on - de   e te sui ven - ti se - gui -

ran - no   mie fu - rie ar - den - ti

"The partly repetitive, partly modulating vocal measures before the section in major are omitted; only the rising scale in the orchestra remains.

"In the first autograph version (as in the Ricordi piano edition, plate no. 41684), the duet repetition of the melody by Pollione *('Fremi pure')* and Adalgisa *('Ah non fia')* follows. In the second version, Bellini struck out Adalgisa's part and reworked that of Pollione in a manner analogous to the reworking of Norma's cited above. Again the succeeding five measures are deleted. Just as in Ricordi 41684, the part in major is sung by the three voices in unison.

"It is difficult to tell when the composer made these changes, which, because they were made in pale-brown ink, are so obvious visually (as compared with the black-to-dark-brown of the first version).* If they were not made for the première and the performances immediately after it, the performances in Bergamo (first on August 22, 1832, with Pasta as Norma, Taccani as Adalgisa, and Reina as Pollione) and London (first on June 20, 1833, with Pasta as Norma, De Méric as Adalgisa, and Donzelli as Pollione) would have afforded Bellini an occasion to make the changes, both productions having been under his personal supervision. It could hardly have been the 1834 performances with Malibran at La Scala, Milan, or at the Teatro San Carlo in Naples, as Bellini was in Paris when they occurred. In a letter to Giuseppe Pasta of April 28, 1832, Bellini wrote: 'As regards *Norma*, I'll revise everything that the excellent Giuditta wants changed; but I'll not do a new note for the other singers.'†

"The composer did not consider his changes final. Above them, over the struck-out measures, he later wrote *'Si fa il Carattero nero'* (i.e., use what is written in black ink: the first version).

"Bellini must have made, or have given instructions for, a third version of the ending of the trio. The 1832 Ricordi piano arrangements shows a very different version from that in the 41684 printing (as does the 1915 score);

---

* Bellini made no other big changes in the score with this light-brown ink; the only other exception is the timpani accompaniment of *'Qual cor tradisti'* in the second finale.

† Cambi, *Epistolario* [BE], p. 312.

this would not have come about without Bellini's wish and knowledge.* [Here] Norma's melody, which (in the first version in the autograph) is divided into a section in minor and one in major *('Vanne, sì, mi lascia')*, is interrupted before the major section by Pollione, the first words of whose text *('Fremi pure')* anticipate this major motif by four measures. The second presentation of the ensemble melody is not entrusted to both Pollione and Adalgisa, but only to the former *('Fremi pure');* Adalgisa, in turn, again anticipates the major section by four measures with her first words *('Ah! non fia').* Then she goes on to sing the full stanza as a solo (Norma and Pollione merely interject occasional phrases during the section in minor); the usual interruption then is made by both Norma and Pollione. The chorus aside, only the *più mosso* section corresponds to the edition that Ricordi issued in 1869–1870† in accord with the first version in the autograph.‡ Furthermore, in the version in the Ricordi first edition

---

* In the trio, the following agree with the Ricordi first edition: a) manuscripts: Naples, Conservatory, 58.2.18/19, 24.3.4/5, 24.3.3/4, o 7.4; Milan, Conservatory, Noseda C 23. (That so many manuscripts—and surely many more that I did not see—should agree with Ricordi's first edition is not surprising. He was the only man with rights to publication of the manuscript). b) Reprints: Girard (Cottrau), plate numbers (see fourth footnote of this appendix for this and the following editions) (a much later edition by Cottrau for piano only, plate nos. 17941–17951, agrees with the autograph and with Ricordi 41684); Boosey; Launer (Girod); Pacini; Diabelli; Cramer, Beale & Co.; Ratti, Cencetti e C.; Marquerie Frères; Peters. (This list of reprints is as incomplete as the list of manuscripts.) Nonetheless, none of the manuscripts or printings cited, except the one by Boosey, shows the addition of the chorus at the end, as in the first version in the autograph. I ascribe that fact to neglect or to economizing (the shortening of ensembles by a few voices was very common at the time in piano arrangements) rather than to any intention expressed by Bellini. But we must not forget a passage in one of the composer's letters which refers to this trio, and most especially to the addition of the chorus. On August 24, 1832, he wrote to his librettist [Romani] from Bergamo: "The trio could not be performed better: they act it well and forcefully; it makes everyone shiver, and they find it a beautiful finale even without the help of supernumeraries, Druids, Druidesses, and other choristers to make noise. You were right to be obstinate about its being like this. They made you lose patience! but now I, too, am satisfied" (Cambi, *Epistolario* [BE], p. 320). Romani evidently had been more consistent in rejecting the audience's (anticipated) desire for a "big" finale with chorus; the verses for Bellini's chorus lines are not even in the libretto—where a simple instruction reads: "The sacred gongs of the temple sound, summoning Norma to the rites." Bellini's few lines of chorus appear to represent a compromise between dramatic conscience and the audience's demands. Is it possible that Bellini abandoned the chorus completely at Bergamo after all, and then suppressed it in the first edition as well?

† Curious as it seems, the Ricordi edition (and, what is worse, the 1915 score as well) neglects in turn to follow one detail of the autograph which had been faithfully observed in the first edition: in the accompaniment to the minor motif in the ensemble melody, Bellini wrote, not triplets, but syncopated eighth-notes.

‡ Of the manuscripts that I know, only the following correspond with the autograph in the trio: Rome, Conservatory, A. Ms. 470/471 (though the notation of the chorus is incomplete in it), and Milan, Conservatory, Ms. 2190.

(and in all the aforementioned printings dependent upon it), the beginning of the melody in major is not cited as above, but rather as:

Te - sul - l'on - de   e te   sui ven - ti se - gui - ran - no

"Only the *stretta* also goes 𝄽 𝅗𝅥| 𝅘𝅥

"In the first slow section of the trio (beginning with Norma's '*Oh! di qual sei tu vittima*') there is another big difference between the 1832 and 1869–1870 Ricordi editions (and all the editions that other publishers based on either of them from time to time). The first-edition version differs in the coda (starting twelve measures from the end in Ricordi 41684), in that Norma's cadenza is longer and the orchestra has no melodic postlude.

"That the version in Ricordi's first edition should not have accorded with Bellini's wishes is really out of the question. On the other hand, whether that version—the faster section of which has a strong dialogue character that intensifies the dramatic sweep—should be accepted as the 'final' version remains uncertain. Such a thing as a 'final version' scarcely existed then in dealing with opera in Italy. The basic musical substance was always retained, but the decisive factors always were the specific occasion and the vocal resources [available] for a particular performance. We can no longer determine what persuaded the Ricordi firm of the 1860's, when issuing its new edition, not to follow what we must assume was an autograph model for the first edition. Instead, it followed the autograph now in Rome. As already stated, the documents dealing with just such transactions were lost from the Archivio Ricordi during World War II. Possibly the model manuscript for the first edition had survived until then; perhaps there were entries concerning procedures in 1832 and 1869–1870. Perhaps!

"A note from Bellini to G[iovanni] Ricordi's secretary, [Giovanni] Cerri, has been preserved which deals with the '*Guerra, guerra*' chorus in Act II. According to [Luisa] Cambi [BE, pp. 289–290], this undated letter probably is of 1831, the time of the rehearsals for the première. But it could just as easily be from the period when the first edition was being prepared. Bellini writes: 'I believe that only the chorus "*Guerra, guerra*" needs correction; the rest should remain as you find it; so start with Grolli[2] so that by Friday he can have everything duplicated except the aforementioned chorus, which he can send on afterwards.' In the autograph score, this is the only piece not in Bellini's hand.[3] The version in Ricordi 41684 agrees with this copy.* The A-minor chorus ends on an A-major chord sustained on [the word] '*sol*' for five measures; in the ensuing four measures, the orchestra emphasizes the major

* This version also appears in Ricordi's editions of the score and in the editions by Girard (Cottrau), plate number 4461; Cramer Beale & Co.; and in the piano-solo edition by Ratti, Cencetti e C. (plate number 477). The abovementioned manuscripts in Naples, the Milan manuscript, Noseda C 23, and the manuscript 470/471 in the Rome Conservatory also agree with it.

coloration. But Ricordi's first edition and the several other editions based upon it* show—either in direct sequence (without other possibility) or as an alternative†—a longer A-major section for chorus, Norma/Oroveso, and orchestra; the vocal parts converge while repeating the last two lines of the chorus in chords sung *sotto voce e legatissimo,* and the orchestra accompanies them with this motif, first heard in the *sinfonia:*

"This furious piece thus ends solemnly and ceremoniously.

"A consultation, at the Museo Belliniano in Catania, of the sketches for the pieces discussed above in Acts I and II is extremely interesting.

"The melody of the slow section of the trio originates in the *Ernani* sketches. Pastura cites them with their original text on page 269 of his book [BSLS—see below, first quotation in the supplement to this appendix]. The melody of the fast section is to be found (in an earlier stage) among the sketches for the first, closed section of the Adalgisa–Pollione duet (Act I, beginning with Pollione's '*Va crudele*' [facing page].

"The chief motif of the section in major appears in the rhythmic form of the Ricordi first edition: ♪· ♪ |♪ ♪ ♪ . But the allegro melody of the finale can also be located in a longer sketch for this section. The ensemble melody (slightly different in detail) is still in A-flat minor–A-flat major at first (exactly as the composer had sketched it for the Adalgisa–Pollione duet); but on the following pages, Bellini proceeds to g/G. It is interesting to note, first, that the rhythm ♪· ♪ |♪ ♪ ♪ also appears here; second, that, as in the Ricordi first edition, the partners here also sing interjections that anticipate the melody in major. The chorus lines are not sketched.

"Several sketches for the '*Guerra, guerra*' chorus survive. The conventional first version is quoted in part by Pastura on pages 567–570 of his book [BSLS—see quotations below, in the supplement to this appendix]. There are also sketches for the familiar second version, including the postlude in major, together with the beginning of the following recitative. In the early stages of the composition,

---

* Girard, edition for piano only (plate no. 2122); Boosey; Marquerie Frères; Pacini; Diabelli; Ratti, Cencetti e C. (plate no. 508); Launer; Peters. Of the manuscripts known to me, only Ms. 2190 at the Milan Conservatory has the version of the Ricordi first edition.

† Ricordi's first piano-vocal edition has the addition in major as an alternative for the short chordal ending; in the preceding piano-solo edition it is given at once without comment.

(Allegro)

Va cru - de - le, al Dio spie - ta - to of - fri in

do - no il san - gue mi - o. Tut - to, ah tut - to ei sia ver -

sa - to, ma la - sciar - ti non pos - s'i - o, ma la -

sciar - ti non pos - s'i - o. Va cru - de - le al Dio spie -

ta - to, of - fri in do - no il san - gue mi - o, ma la -

sciar - ti, ah non pos - si'o, ah, non pos' - s'i - o.

Sol pro - mes - sa al Dio tu fo - sti, ma il tuo

co - re a me si die - de. Ah non sai quan - to mi

co - sti per - ch'io mai ri - nun - zi a te, per - ch'io

mai ri - nun - zi a te, per - ch'io ma - i,

per - ch'i - o mai ri - nun - zi a te.

then, Bellini already intended to follow the minor with a longer section making use of thematic material taken from the section in major in the *sinfonia*."

Quotations and Passages from
Pastura's Bellini secondo la storia
Referred to by Lippmann

1. Melody from the *Ernani* sketches at the Museo Belliniano, Catania, later adapted by Bellini in the slow section of the first-act trio finale in *Norma* (BSLS, p. 269):

2. Pastura on sections of the *"Guerra, guerra!"* chorus in the *Norma* sketches at the Museo Belliniano, Catania (BSLS, pp. 567–570):

"But one of the most noteworthy variants of the opera is that of the war hymn. In the autograph score, this famous piece appears written by another hand in the version commonly adopted—that is, with the finale ending on a loud chord held by the choruses. But two other completely different versions of the hymn exist. An autograph trace of the first is preserved in the score of the opera: it is that of the initial blasts of the hymn as it was first conceived. The rest of that first draft is preserved among the autographs at the Museo Belliniano. This is how the recovered fragments show the first draft of the hymn of war to have been [facing page].

"At this point, the variant is interrupted at the end of the page; it certainly was continued on the pages of the following sheet—which seems to have been torn from the fascicle—and very probably on other pages as well. Between this fragment and the one quoted below, the words and music are lacking for half of the first strophe and all of the second strophe of the war hymn. In the following fragment, in fact a '*ta*' at the beginning of a measure tells us—taking into consideration the words that follow—that it is the final syllable of the word '*s'affretta*,' the last in the verse '*già la vedo, si compie, s'affretta*.'

Guerra . . . Guerra! le gal - li - che sel - ve

quan - te han quer - ce pro - du - can guer rier . . .

In this small new fascicle, the variant continues complete to the end of the reappearance of the initial motif, which certainly was to end the hymn.

"From what it has been possible to quote, it is not difficult to understand that in its first draft the hymn of war possessed an academic form that certainly would have been ineffective. Perhaps at first Bellini was thinking of a song that would form part of a rite, and wanted to confer upon it a majestic and restrained character. To support this supposition, it would suffice to point out that polyphonic motion of the attacks by sections of the chorus in the second part. The musician evidently became aware that he had written something composite and academic. The Gallic warriors' hatred, their determination upon revenge, needed something that would be a cry of war and would, above all, immediately translate the violent explosion of their savage fury, repressed with difficulty until then. The hymn was altered. He changed the [trumpet] blasts, the introduction; he changed the rhythm; he changed the working-out; the conventional *allegro vivace assai* was replaced by an *allegro feroce*. Of the original hymn, in short, nothing remains but the faded record on the pages we have examined.

"The other hymn, the one that we have now, probably was composed after the opera was complete. A note from Bellini to the secretary of the publisher Ricordi tells us: 'I believe that only the chorus *"Guerra, guerra"* needs correction; the rest should remain as you find it; so start with Grolli so that by Friday he can have everything duplicated except the aforementioned chorus, which he can send on afterwards.'*

"In the autograph score of *Norma,* in fact, the only quinternion not written in Bellini's script is, as we know, that containing this hymn. But there are preserved at the Museo two pages that contain the final version of this piece, and to them we must add one other page that tells us what its finale was. Even for the final version, Bellini did not give up the idea that the hymn should form part of a sacred rite, and wanted to give it, so to speak, a religious ending; a sort of consecration—by the priests and the warriors—of spirits, arms, weapons to the god who lived in the trunk of an oak. After the final cadenza, which is resolved on A major (in which it customarily concluded), the continuing hymn suddenly changes character, as though, having reached the apex of fanaticism, the warriors' spirits suddenly had an instant revelation of a transcendental world. They have no new words to intone, but they take up—almost incomprehensibly—those final two verses of the hymn as if the evocation of the god, who appears upon a sunbeam to gaze upon the triumph of his faithful, immersed them in a state of beatitude. To create this stupendous contrast, the musician chose the 'Major' of the *sinfonia* of the opera, assigning to the chorus the lines performed in that passage by the clarinets and horns while the violin trills and the undulating chords of the harp create an atmosphere suffused in arcane luminosity.

"The finale as thus described is to be found in its complete form in the three first editions of the opera (in the third, it is for piano alone), whereas in the succeeding editions, the piece was printed as it was performed in the theaters—that is, without the finale in major. Evidently, that must have been deleted by Bellini himself, who would have sacrificed it to theatrical effect, but did not suppress it finally because that contrast between the ferocious

---

* [Pastura's note]: See Cambi, *op. cit.* [BE], pages 289–290.

shout and the ecstatic absorption remains artistically one of the most beautiful effects created by the musician. And many orchestral conductors have understood this and are restoring the *Norma* hymn of war to its original expressiveness."

APPENDIX O

Beatrice di Tenda: *Unpublished Passages and Variants*

Friedrich Lippmann has written[1]:

"Materials for Bellini's penultimate opera, *Beatrice di Tenda*, are to be found in some manuscript sources. Francesco Pastura revealed interesting details of the sketches for the opera preserved at the Museo Belliniano at Catania.* He deals with the sketch of a duet between Agnese and Beatrice belonging to the tenth scene of the second act of the libretto, which forecasts a regular duet between the two donnas,† thereafter amplified by the addition of the lines of Orombello (*Angiol di pace*), in the trio familiar in the published editions.‡ From the Catania sketches, from the autograph score, from manuscript copies preserved in Rome and Naples, we bring to light here other sections that deserve particular attention.

"One page of the Catania sketches contains a first version of the 'solo' with which Beatrice begins the last section of the first finale (*Nè fra voi si trova*):

* F. Pastura, *Bellini secondo la storia* [BSLS], Parma, 1959, pp. 573–580. [All notes here printed as footnotes are translated verbatim from Lippmann's article.]

† Cf. also E. Branca, *Felice Romani ed i più riputati maestri di musica del suo tempo*, Turin-Florence-Rome, 1882, pp. 179–180.

‡ In the autograph score (Rome Conservatory, Segn. G. Ms3/4), large parts of the Beatrice–Agnese dialogue and the trio significantly are in a copyist's hand.

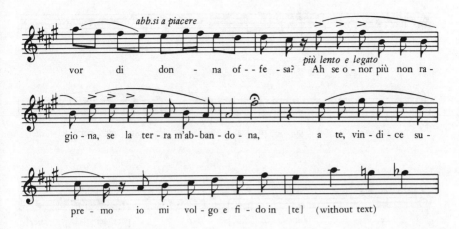

"The motive intoned to the words *Ah! se onor* is known from the first section of Beatrice's final aria.

"That first section of the final aria *(Ah! se un'urna)* is given in the Ricordi edition* in a form very different from that shown in the autograph. In the autograph, the sung melodic line reads as follows:

---

* First edition (1833), editorial numbers 6880–6950–6970 (the *Preludio* was issued earlier with the editorial number 6880). Two new editions, undated: editorial numbers 35566–35585 ("New edition, revised"); editorial number 45541.

It appears that way in the copies O^A.7.5 and 58.2.16/17* at the Naples Conservatory, and also in the full score issued by Pittarelli at Rome around the middle of the past century. The following coincide, except for insignificant variations, with the Ricordi edition: the copy 24.4.16/17 in the library of the Naples Conservatory; the copies A.Ms.430/431 and G.Ms.712/713 in the library of the Rome Conservatory†; the transcription for voice and piano issued by Girard (later Cottrau) of Naples (editorial number of the scene: 3377). Did Bellini perhaps—in answer to the request from Giovanni Ricordi (reported by Antonino Amore) that he make some changes in the score of *Beatrice di Tenda*‡—make ready the manuscript, probably lost, from which the Ricordi edition and other copies were made? And in that manuscript did there also appear the passages—the ones discussed here—in the form in which Ricordi printed them?

"A large difference between the autograph and the Ricordi edition is found in the dialogue between Beatrice and the chorus which precedes the first part of the final aria. In the autograph, in the manuscripts A.Ms.430/431 and G.Ms. 712/713 in the Rome Conservatory,¶ O^A.7.5, 58.2.16/17, and 24.4.16/17 at the

Naples Conservatory, and in the Pittarelli edition, fourteen measures that are not in the Ricordi edition appear. The text, which has been printed in librettos since that for the première goes like this**:

"SCENA ULTIMA

(Si presenta Rizzardo con Alabardieri e Ufficiali)
AGNESE, ANICHINO
  E CORO
            E più speme non v'è

BEATRICE   La mia costanza
            Non mi togliete. "Anche una stilla, e poi
            Fia vuotato del tutto e inaridito
            Questo calice amaro.

TUTTI   E iddio ritrarlo
            Dal tuo labbro non può!"

BEATRICE   Mi diè corragio
            Per consumarlo Iddio.
                (Rizzardo s'inoltra con gli Alabardieri)

BEATRICE   Eccomi pronta . . .

"Of Beatrice's solo-like section, only the initial and final measures appear in the Ricordi edition. Between '. . . *non mi togliete*' and '*Mi diè corragio*,' the following measures—which come to us instead from the sources cited—are missing. Thematically, they are inspired by what the orchestra has set forth:

* An insert in this latter manuscript contains in very abbreviated form the version accepted by the Casa Editrice Ricordi.

† As the frontispieces testify, these Roman manuscripts came from the Casa Cencetti, Rome.

‡ A letter from Giovanni Ricordi, published by A. Amore, *Vincenzo Bellini. Vita. studì e Ricerche,* Catania, 1894, Giannotta, pp. 402–405, says: "As to 'Beatrice,' I flattered myself that you would have sent me those changes which you had thought necessary to render this score not inferior to your others, and which you had promised me; but [. . .] I see that the distractions of London, and then those of Paris, have driven this promise from your mind [. . . .] Your forgetfulness, however, had the result that when this opera was given at the [Teatro] Carcano, though it won you the most flattering success, it nonetheless did not have the sort it would have attained had you taken the small trouble to change a few things here and there, chiefly the final aria, which would have procured you a full triumph despite the weakness of the company [. . .]"

¶ In the autograph and in the first-mentioned copy, posterior abbreviation symbols enclose the passage.

**For greater clarity, I have placed quotation marks around the verses omitted from the published edition of the opera.

(Lugubre maestoso)

An - che u - na stil - la, e po - i sia vuo - ta - to
e in - a - ri - di - to que - sto ca - li - ce a - ma - ro.

"Nor does the Ricordi edition follow the original version in the section that comes after the first part of the aria. Now Beatrice enters with the beginning of the cabaletta at the sixth measure of the 'Allegro.' The librettos give the missing verses*:

ANICHINO,
CORO
> Oh, infelice! "Oh! a qual serbate
> Fur le genti orrendo esempio!
> Tristo il suolo in cui lo scempio
> Di tal donna, oh Dio, si fè!

BEATRICE
> Per chi resta il Ciel pregate,
> Per chi resta, e non per me.
> Io vi seguo (ai Soldati)

CORO
> Deh! un amplesso . . .
> Un amplesso concedete . . ."

BEATRICE
> Io vi abbraccio . . . "non piangete.

CORO
> Chi non piange non ha cor."

BEATRICE
> Ah! la morte a cui m 'appresso . . .

Beatrice's 'a solo' reads as follows†:

(Allegro moderato)

Per chi re - sta il ciel pre - ga - - te, per chi
re - sta e non per me. Io vi se - guo.

* Part of the verses of the chorus follow in the Ricordi edition, within the cabaletta. In the autograph version, however, these are set also *before* the cabaletta.

† An earlier version is found among the sketches for *Beatrice* at Catania.

"The intermediate measures, which do not appear in Ricordi's edition, are found, other than in the autograph,* also in the manuscript copies O^A. 7.5 and 58.2.16/17 in the library of the Naples Conservatory and in the Pittarelli edition. The Ricordi edition, on the other hand, corresponds to the manuscripts G.Ms.712/713 and A.Ms.430/431 in the library of the Rome Conservatory and 24.4.16/17 in the Naples Conservatory library (later cuts were made in the latter two manuscripts).

"If the abbreviation of the final scene really was made by Bellini, one must assert that in truth he did not thus improve the opera. The two episodes cited (and the related choral episode) certainly do not belong among the composer's finest inspirations. But the two sections of Beatrice's aria, above all the cabaletta composed by adaptation of that for Fernando, *Odo il tuo pianto*, in the opera *Bianca e Fernando* (second version), are too feeble as compositions to carry the concentration of all interest solely upon them. A real amelioration would have required the remaking of the cabaletta as well as the melodic enrichment—rather than the reduction—of the dialogue between Beatrice and the chorus.

"A critical edition of Bellini's operas, or at least of the most important of them, appears to be one of the most urgent tasks awaiting students of the music of nineteenth-century Italy. I should like the present study to be understood as a small preparatory work in that direction."

* In the autograph, again, later indications for abbreviation occur which take us back to the version in the Ricordi edition.

APPENDIX P

Wagner and Bellini

Like Wagner's attitudes toward many other realities, his opinions of Italian opera, and in particular of Bellini's operas, fluctuated widely over the years. Robert W. Gutman noted[1] that Wagner's student Sonata in B-flat major for piano (1831–1832) showed "an enthusiasm for Bellini" in its "closing movement's second theme," and no one who has heard even just the overture to *Das Liebesverbot* (1835–1836) will doubt that Wagner had been listening very attentively to Italian opera. In 1834, he was deeply moved by Wilhelmine Schröder-Devrient's performance as Romeo in Bellini's *I Capuleti e i Montecchi* at Leipzig. In June of that year, he published anonymously an article on German opera[2] which contained clear indications of his dissatisfaction with the way singing melody tended to become lost in learned music-making in his compatriots' operas. In particular, he said: "I shall never forget the impression that a Bellini opera made on me recently after I had grown very weary of the eternally allegorizing hubbub, and at last a simple, noble song emerged again."

The lasting influence of that revelation of Bellini's melodic power was evidenced in another of Wagner's occasional essays; entitled "*Pasticcio*," it was signed Canto Spianato.[3] In it, he expressed longing for the very qualities in singing which were requisite for Bellini's operas: ". . . a really beautiful and technically correct trill . . . a perfect mordent . . . rounded coloratura . . . genuine, unaffected, soul-stirring portamento . . . complete equalization of the registers . . . steady intonation through all the varying shades of crescendo and diminuendo. . . ." At Magdeburg in 1835–1836, he conducted not only *I Capuleti e i Montecchi* and *Norma*, but also Paisiello's *La Molinara* and of Rossini both *Otello* and *Il Barbiere di Siviglia*.

At Königsberg on March 8, 1837, Wagner wrote (but apparently did not publish) a review of a local performance of *Norma* with Henriette Grosser in the title role.[4] Although his article is devoted largely to detailed, convincing criticism of Frau Grosser's singing, it constantly emphasizes Wagner's exalted opinion of *Norma*, which he places at the summit of Bellini's art while seeing in it that step toward the qualities of Greek tragedy through opera which Schiller had predicted in the preface to *Die Braut von Messina*. Wagner, though expressing reservations about the Italian construction of operas in separate numbers, nonetheless asserts that Bellini has employed it excellently in *Norma*. Also, he emphasizes the superior manner in which the passages of *fioriture*, if properly sung, can characterize Norma's "terrible anger." Toward the end of the review, he refers to *Norma* simply as "this beautiful opera."

At Riga in 1837, having decided to stage *Norma* for his own benefit night, Wagner wrote a propagandistic essay for insertion into the local *Zuschauer*, protectively signing it "O." In part, he said:

"What enchanted us in Bellini was the pure melody, the simple nobility and beauty of song. Surely it cannot be a sin to assert and believe that. Perhaps it is not even a sin if, before retiring to rest, one offers Heaven a prayer that some day it may occur to German composers to write such melodies, to acquire such a manner of treating song. Song, song, and again song. O Germans! Song is the language with which mankind should communicate, one with another, and you will not be understood if this language is not made and kept as arbitrary as any other cultivated language should be. Each of your village schoolmasters will do better what is bad in Bellini. Bellini probably would have learned more if he had served his apprenticeship with a German village schoolmaster, but he would have unlearned the art of song."

At Riga, also, Wagner composed a chorus-accompanied bass aria with full orchestra for the Oroveso to interpolate into that production of *Norma*. Later, in Paris, he either adapted that aria or composed another like it in the vain hope of persuading Luigi Lablache to interpolate it into a performance of *Norma* at the Théâtre-Italien. A Wagner aria with chorus was published in 1914 in Volume XV of his collected works: *"Einlage zu V. Bellinis Oper Norma von Richard Wagner/Arie (mit Männerchor) des Orovisto [sic],"* with text beginning *"Norma il predesse, o Druidi. . . ."* With a melodic line for the bass which is somewhat floridly decorated with trills, rapid descending scales, and other indications that Wagner was deliberately aping Bellini's manner, it runs to twenty-five pages of full score in the Breitkopf & Härtel edition.

The mature Wagner attacked bitterly almost all Italian opera, Bellini's included—this as part of his unflagging campaign in favor of German opera, by which he usually meant the operas of Beethoven, Weber, and Richard Wagner. As an old man, however, he found favorable things to say, not about Bellini only, but even about Rossini.[5] Francesco Florimo wrote[6]: "The very pontifex maximus of the music of the future, the anti-Rossinian par excellence, nourished a real admiration for Bellini in general and for *Norma* in particular. He made that certain in person during the visit he paid to Naples in the winter of 1880, when he said to me: 'They all think me an Orcus with regard to Italian music and place me in opposition to Bellini. But no, no, a thousand times no. Bellini is one of my predilections: his music is all heart, closely, intimately linked to the words. The music that I hate is that vague, indeterminate music which laughs at the libretto and at the situation!' "

Of that visit of Wagner to Florimo, Gutman wrote[7]: "Social intercourse was Wagner's salvation [in 1880]. He visited the conservatory of Naples to meet Francesco Florimo, who in 1876 had brought Bellini's remains back to his native soil from Paris, a service similar to that performed decades before by Wagner in respect to Weber. *The Destiny of Opera* [Wagner, 1871] had disdainfully called Bellini's music 'insipid and threadbare.' But now Wagner was returning to a love of his youth; crying, 'Bellini! Bellini!' he embraced the octogenarian musical scholar, both old men trembling with emoton."

APPENDIX Q

Versions and Variants of I Puritani

Friedrich Lippmann has written[1]:

"A genuine critical edition of *I Puritani* (Théâtre-Italien, Paris, January 24, 1835), would not only, like such editions of other operas, have an appendix giving all variants and alternatives; it would also require an entire second volume to show the second version of the opera. Only the first version, as performed in Paris in 1835, has been printed.* But for a staging scheduled that year in Naples, Bellini made a second version, altering it for the voices of the mezzo-soprano Malibran (Elvira), the tenors [Gilbert-Louis] Duprez (Arturo) and [Francesco] Pedrazzi (Riccardo), and the bass [Carlo Ottolini] Porto (Giorgio). In that version, the female lead is to be sung by a mezzo-soprano rather than a soprano (Giulietta Grisi in Paris), and the role of Riccardo is for a tenor rather than a baritone (Antonio Tamburini in Paris). Malibran would have had a splendid role. For example, the beautiful largo of the third finale ('*Credeasi misera*') is arranged to give her, and not the tenor, the predominant part (it starts with Elvira's words '*Qual mai funerea*'). The planned performance never materialized, and the Neapolitan version remained unused.†
It is now in the Museo Belliniano, Catania (the score was written out by a copyist, but contains annotations in the composer's script). Its great value would justify publication; confronted with current conditions in the supply of performers, modern opera house managers might prefer it to the Paris version.

"Because the second version was sent to Naples at the beginning of 1835,

---

* The most important editions (piano arrangements with texts and separate vocal parts): Milan (1836), Ricordi, plate numbers 8551–8577; Ricordi, undated, with plate number 41685 (still available); Paris, Pacini, as "*Publication posthume*," with disjunct plate numbers (*Introduzione* 3148; publication of individual numbers preceded the complete piano score); London, Mills, plate number 2752; Mainz and Antwerp, Schott's Söhne, plate number 4585; Naples, Girard (later Cottrau), disjunct plate numbers (*Introduzione* 3121); Naples, Clausetti, plate numbers 4468–4483. [Notes printed here as footnotes are translated verbatim (bracketed additions aside) from Lippmann's article.]

† See Pastura, *op. cit.* [BSLS], pp. 395–468 (Chapter: *I Puritani al Teatro Italiano de Parigi*), *passim*, and 581–585.

it lacks one section found in the Paris version: the closing second-act duet for Giorgio and Riccardo [preluding and including '*Suoni la tromba*']. Bellini worked on that until shortly before the performance.* He had, of course, already composed the fiery cabaletta ('*Suoni la tromba*') when he arranged the Neapolitan version, but it was set for different singers and had other slight variations. With a similar text, it was originally a *Coro di libertà*, a *Coro dell'alba*, or an *Inno di guerra* (Bellini used the terms interchangeably in his letters), and was part of the *Introduzione* to the opera. On May 26, 1834, the composer sent his friend Florimo verses for it, but unfortunately Florimo did not preserve them.† After having removed the warlike chorus from the *Intro-duzione* as early as May 1834 so as to insert it to greater effect later in the opera,‡ he decided in December to rework it into the cabaletta of a *Duetto per due bassi e cori* which was to precede the mad scene.¶ The final step was switching scenes and renouncing the chorus. In the known editions and manu-scripts, Giorgio and Riccardo sing the same text, which begins with the line '*Suoni la tromba, e intrepido*' and ends with '*E i pianti di pietà.*' Before the unison repetition, several words from the preceding dialogue are sung; the singing is interrupted several times by accented exclamations of '*All'alba!*'— and those repetitions allow us to recognize its having originated in the *Coro dell'alba*. That derivation becomes wholly clear in the version of the scene in the libretto of the paris première (Paris, 1835, Imprimerie de Pihan Delaforest). There, Riccardo and Giorgio *a due* sing text still to be found in the 'final ver-sion.' It is followed by these lines:

R.   All'alba!

G.   All'alba!

A 2   All'alba!

R.   Alba che surgi un popolo
      Che a libertà s'affidi

* The Giorgio–Riccardo conversation is in the form of a long recitative in the Naples version (it was originally planned that way for the Paris one). It precedes Elvira's mad scene. When Bellini altered the scenes and composed the Giorgio–Riccardo duet, he used part of its text there. In the first printed libretto, which is in only two acts (see below), the duet still precedes the mad scene.

† In reprinting the letter (Florimo, *Bellini. Memorie e lettere*, Florence, 1882, p. 413), Florimo shortened it precisely by omitting the statements of its contents and these verses. He mentions only the lines '*All'alba sorgerà—Il sol di libertà*,' adding Bellini's *N. B.*: 'This hymn was made only for Paris, where they love thoughts of liberty. Do you understand? For Italy, Pepoli himself will change the entire hymn and not even mention the word liberty, and in that way it will be changed if there are liberal phrases in the opera. . . . ' [BE, p. 401].

‡ Compare Bellini's letter to Pepoli of May 30, 1834 (Cambi, *Epistolario* [BE], pp. 402–403). In September (see his letter to Florimo of September 21, Cambi [BE], p. 439), he considered having Arturo's persecutor sing it at the beginning of the present Act III.

¶ Compare Bellini's letter to Florimo of December 21–22, 1834 (Cambi [BE], pp. 488–493). In it, however, Bellini wrote that the duet was not to be included in the Neapolitan version, 'first because it would not be within the capacity of Porto and Pedrazzi, and then because both love of country and Liberty enter into it.'

Giuliva a lui sorridi
Nunzia d'eterno Sol.

Alba che surgi ai perfidi
Tiranni della terra
Sii nunzia a lor di guerra,
Alba d'eterno duol.

>   (*Stanno per separarsi, nel fondo della scena* Giorgio *si rivolge a* Riccardo, *e lo prende per mano*.)

G.   Il patto è già fermato,
Se Artur è inerme o vinto? . . .

R.   Avrà pietà e conforto . . .

G.   Se vien ascoso e armato? . . .

R.   Ei sarà avvinto e morto!

"These verses, intended for Riccardo (but possibly sung by Tamburini at the première?), probably do not differ much from those in the *Introduzione* which Bellini sent to his Neapolitan friend. The final dialogue in recitative was musically a mistake, but it clearly tells the listener what the '*due Bassi*' really are deciding (in the 'final version,' he can hardly tell). Although crossed out, the beginning of the final recitative is preserved in the autography score (Biblioteca Comunale, Palermo). There, too, a remnant of the '*Alba che surgi*' text appears in a crossed-out measure.

"While at work on the rehearsals, and especially after the première, Bellini greatly shortened the opera. On January 26, 1835, he told Florimo about it.* Pastura, referring to the Neapolitan version,† describes two of the deleted sections: a trio for Enrichetta, Arturo, and Riccardo before the first finale [see below, p. 452] and a middle section in the duet for Elvira and Arturo in Act III [see below, p. 453]. Contrary to what Pastura asserts, the text for the deleted sections is not to be found only in a 'very early edition . . . preserved at the Museo Belliniano'‡; it even appears in present-day librettos. More than that: the music for the section of the duet beginning with Arturo's '*Da quel dì che ti mirai*' is not to be found only in the Neapolitan version; it is in the autograph of the Parisian version, at Palermo. There the part is marked only with small strokes. To the best of my knowledge, it did not get into any (surviving) hand-written copies, but it does appear in published editions. Although it is included in the first edition of the duet with Ricordi plate number N8576N, the second edition, with plate numbers N8576–N8573 no longer has it. It also appears in the following familiar piano arrangements: Girard-Cottrau, Naples, plate number of the scene 2754; Clausetti, Naples, plate numbers 4468–4483; Pacini, Paris, very disjunct plate numbers (*Introduzione* 3148); Mills, London, plate number 2752. A trace of the first-act trio—the two deleted initial measures—is still included in the Paris autograph score (Palermo). The piece does not appear in other copies or in printed editions.

"In Bellini's letter of January 26, mentioned above, the only deleted piece

---

* See Cambi, *Epistolario* [BE], p. 502.

† Pastura, *op. cit.* [BSLS], pp. 582–585.

‡ Pastura, *op. cit.*, p. 582, note [1].

to which he refers by name is the '*largo di mezzo*' of the duet for Elvira and Arturo; all other deletions are called only 'something still further' or 'an indifferent something that was there.' Pastura was convinced that he knew precisely what Bellini had deleted: in addition to the two passages mentioned, 'the repetition of the troubadour's romanza at the beginning of the third act.'* The question is on what he based that assumption. The autograph certainly does not agree with him; and, after all, in all editions the piece stands exactly as he had written it there: 1) musical stanza Elvira, 2) expanded musical stanza Arturo (beginning both times with '*A una fonte*'), after the pursuers' chorus, 3) musical stanza Arturo ('*Corre a valle*'), further expanded and varied. Pastura wrote of the third finale in the Neapolitan version: 'Nothing particularly important in the variant of the final chorus.'† But the Neapolitan version contains the third of the larger pieces by deletion of which Bellini shortened the opera after the première: a '*Più sostenuto*' of 54 measures (35, 19 of which are repeated) starting after the double line on p. 261 of Ricordi's piano arrangement with plate number 41685. The section beginning '*Più mosso assai*' (p. 262 in the abovementioned Ricordi edition) occurs only after that in Bellini's original plan. Its text, again, is to be seen in every edition of the libretto. The music is contained in the Neapolitan version, as well as in the individual parts for the Paris version, which are also preserved at Catania. (This fact is notable because those individual parts are the very ones that Bellini sent to Florimo to help him in inserting the Naples [changes] into the Paris version.‡ Bellini, that is, did not consider curtailing the third finale.) Another piece, in the appendix of the Neapolitan copy 3.8.21/22, very probably also is based upon the parts that Bellini sent to Florimo for the Palermo performance. I am led to assume its dependence on them because in both instances the first measures appear without text. The Archivio Ricordi includes a copy of the Paris version with autograph annotations which still shows two deleted measures.¶ The following quotation of the first eight measures of the '*Più sostenuto*' is taken from the Neapolitan version 3.8.21/22 because in it this section is in D major, the key in which the Paris version ends (in the score of the Naples version at Catania, it is, with slight variants, in B-flat major)* [p. 452].

"That is followed by brief contrasting B-minor measures, which revert to the major immediately. After a total of twelve measures of duet, the chorus enters ('*Sì, l'amor coronerà*').

"Because of the nonsensical genitive '*di voluttà*' in the text for Elvira and Arturo, the text of the *Più mosso*–close does not make sense. That genitive can be explained by what preceded it and was deleted. Bellini himself probably corrected '*di voluttà*' to '*oh (ah) voluttà*' in the abovementioned copy now in the Archivio Ricordi. The editors of the published Ricordi edition did not notice it.

* Pastura, *op. cit.*, p. 451.

† Pastura, *op. cit.*, p. 585.

‡ See Pastura, *op. cit.*, p. 462.

¶ That copy is all the more interesting because it has Rossini's verifying signatures as guardian of Bellini's estate; as well as signatures of the publisher Troupenas, of Robert, director of the Théâtre-Italien, and of Severini, that theater's administrator.

* But the text of the first three measures is that in the Catania score and the librettos.

"A new edition of *I Puritani* should offer all the deleted sections. First, the sources show that at least one of the curtailments was undertaken only halfheartedly by Bellini; second, present-day preference probably would choose other sections for omission."

Dr. Lippmann has also written[2]:

"Because Bellini sent it [the 'Malibran' version] to Naples before he had completed the Paris version, the Neapolitan one contains sections that Bellini deleted during rehearsals and after the première*:

"1. An Enrichetta–Arturo–Riccardo trio preceding the first finale. Pastura printed (*op. cit.* [BSLS], p. 583) the melody of the larghetto following Arturo's words '*Addio Elvira, addio mio ben.*' That solo is followed by an *a due* in which Arturo and Enrichetta continue to carry the melody while Riccardo mostly only makes interjections. For this melody, Bellini used a cabaletta that he had suppressed in *Norma*.

---

* For these, compare Bellini's letter to Florimo of January 26, 1835 (Cambi [BE], *op. cit.,* p. 502).

It is the one that Norma was to have sung after '*Casta diva*' ('*Ah, riedi ancor*') before the composer decided on the paraphrase of the *Bianca e Fernando* aria ["*Ah! bello, a me ritorna*"].

"2. The middle section (*andante sostenuto*) of the Elvira-Arturo duet in Act III.* The melody can be found in Pastura (*op. cit.*, pp. 584–585). The aforementioned solo for Arturo is followed by musical (solo) repetition by Elvira and by a section *a due* (in parallels).

"3. A kind of cabaletta in the ensemble of the third finale.† The following verses, which also appear in modern editions of the libretto:

ELVIRA/ARTURO	ENSEMBLE
Ah! sento, mio bell'angelo,	*Amor, pietoso e tenero*
Che poca è intiera l'anima	*Coronerà di giubilo*
Per esultar nel giubilo	*L'ansia, i sospiri, i palpiti*
Che amor ci donerà.	*Di tanta fedeltà.*
Benedirò le lagrime,	
L'ansia, i sospir', i gemiti,	
Vaneggerò nel palpito	
D'un'ebbra voluttà.	

had this melody,‡ which begins on p. 149r. of Act II in the Catania version [p. 454].

The Naples version includes these three sections complete. Some of them, and a few of them fragmentarily, can be found elsewhere. Because of the paging, the first two measures of the Act I trio remain

* In the Naples version, the second part of Act II corresponds to Act II [of the Paris version]. The opera was divided into three acts only just before the performance (the libretto of the première, Paris, 1835, Imprimerie de Pihan Delaforest, is still in two acts).

† Pastura, *op. cit.*, p. 585, is mistaken when he writes: 'Nothing particularly important in the variants of the final chorus.' Also, he incorrectly cites on p. 451, 'the repeat of the troubadour's romanza at the beginning of Act III' ["*A una fonte afflitto e solo*"] as one of the sections deleted after the première. [Florimo had advised Bellini to end *I Puritani* with a big *scena* for Elvira; on November 10, 1834, however, Bellini had replied (BE, p. 486): ". . . that was my intention; but because of the very reasonable changes in the second act, the donna's *scena* falls in the middle of the act . . . therefore another, final *scena*, and perhaps not well located, would do nothing but damage the opera as a whole. . . ." That he nonetheless provided a closing cabaletta for Elvira in the "Malibran" version may have weighed as heavily against performance of that version in Palermo[3] as the fact that there the Elvira was to be, not Malibran, but Josephine de Méric. And when *I Puritani* finally was heard at the Teatro San Carlo, Naples (January 3, 1837, with Caterina Chiesa Barrilli-Patti as Elvira, Lablache in the role that he had created), the Paris version was used.]

‡ I quote the first eight measures of the '*più sostenuto*' from the Naples version 3.8.21/22 because there the piece appears in D major, the key in which the Paris version ends (in the Catania score of the Naples version, it is, with slight variations, in B-flat major). The eight quoted measures are followed by brief contrasting measures in B major which revert immediately to D major. After a total of twelve measures of duet, the chorus adds: '*Sì, l'amor coronerà.*'

Allegro più sostenuto

ELVIRA

Ah, sen - to o mio bel - l'an-ge - lo che po-ca è in-te - ra l'a - ni - ma ad e - - sul - tar nel giu - bi - lo che a - mor ci do - - ne - rà.

ARTURO

in the autograph score of the Paris version, whereas those following have been deleted. Strangely, the duet section of Act III* remains in that score, being struck through only very lightly. In the copy of the Paris version now in the Archivio Ricordi, however, the duet section is missing completely. As the only section deleted later by Bellini, it appears in the piano[-vocal] scores issued by Pacini, Mills, Girard-Cottrau, Clausetti, as well as in the first Ricordi edition of the duet, with plate number N8576N (the edition with plate numbers N8576–N8573 no longer contains the andante). In the autograph score of the Paris version, only the first three measures of the Act III cabaletta have been struck out—and in the copy in the Archivio Ricordi, only two. In that copy, evidently, Bellini himself modified the text of the ending to make it accord with the shortened form. Unfortunately, the editors of the Ricordi edition ignored it. In the Ricordi edition,† non-

---

*Bellini wrote about exactly this section of the duet in his letter to Florimo of January 26, 1835: 'I had already taken out the middle largo at the final rehearsals because it is long, and particularly in being recognized . . .' (Cambi [BE], *op. cit.*, p. 502).

† The same is true of all other editions known to me (they all depend upon that edition or on material received from Ricordi).

sensically, the text of the deleted portion is continued in the voices of Elvira and Arturo: '*di voluttà.*' (When, in the copy, the '*di*' no longer made sense, it was altered to '*oh*' or '*ah*'). Interestingly, the 'cabaletta' is contained in the sections that Bellini sent for the Palermo performance,[4] though with some variations. Evidently, Bellini was very halfhearted about this cut. Probably depending upon the sections destined for the Palermo performance, this 'cabaletta' also appears in the appendix of the Neapolitan copy 3.8.21/22. (The following note appears on the title page of the second volume of that copy: '*N.B.* In this opera there is also Elvira's *scena* in the second act and the third finale as arranged by Bellini for Malibran.' The Paris version contained in this copy is then followed again by the mad scene and the third finale. However, the largo of the finale does not correspond to the Malibran version at Catania. The index, however, contains the 'cabaletta' of the last finale.)"

NOTES

*The following abbreviations are employed to denote
the sources most frequently cited:*

BdVB—Filippo Gerardi: *Biografia di Vincenzo Bellini*, Rome, 1835

BE—*Vincenzo Bellini: Epistolario*, edited by Luisa Cambi, Milan, 1943

B:LV—Luisa Cambi: *Bellini [La Vita]* Milan, 1934

B:Mel—*Bellini: Memorie e lettere*, edited by Francesco Florimo, Florence, 1882

BSLS—Francesco Pastura: *Bellini secondo la storia*, Parma, 1959

CssSmdN—Francesco Florimo: *Cenno storico sulla Scuola muiscale di Napoli*, 2 vols., Naples, 1869–1871

LSmdN—Francesco Florimo: *La Scuola musicale di Napoli*, 4 vols., Naples, 1881–1882

VB—Francesco Pastura: *Vincenzo Bellini*, Catania, 1959

VB:A—Antonino Amore: *Vincenzo Bellini: Arte, studî e ricerche*, Catania, 1892

VB:V—Antonino Amore: *Vincenzo Bellini: Vita, studî e ricerche*, Catania, 1894

VdVB—Filippo Cicconetti: *Vita di Vincenzo Bellini*, Prato, 1859

Chapter I

1. Vincenzo Bellini's seventeenth-century great-great-great-grandfather, Tobia Bellini, married Anna Pacifico. Their son Rosario also had a son named Rosario, born in 1711: the composer's great-grandfather, who is said to have played the violin. He married Francesca Mancini (born in 1717), by whom he had three children, of whom the son Vincenzo Tobia became a professional musician in Catania and the composer's grandfather.

2. They included Carlo Cotumacci (1689–1755), a pupil of Alessandro Scarlatti, and Giuseppe Dol (Dohl), who had studied under both Scarlatti and Francesco Durante.

3. After Michela Bellini's death, Vincenzo Tobia married (1796) Mattea Cognata, about twenty-six years his junior; that marriage proved childless. After his death, his widow was in part supported by the Benedictines.

4. The Ferlitos, in whose apartment in the present via Paternò the couple was married by a special dispensation granted by the vicar general, appear to have been Catanese of long standing. The composer's maternal grandfather, Carmelo Ferlito, a bookkeeper, had married Giuseppa Cristaldi, by whom he had three children: Agata, the composer's mother; Vincenzo, who would play a role of some importance in Vincenzo Bellini's life; and Francesco, later nicknamed "Don Ciccio."

5. See Appendix A, p. 392, for the text of Bellini's baptismal certificate. His birthday was given incorrectly by most writers down to 1882, when Francesco Florimo gave it correctly in *La Scuola musicale di Napoli* and in the separate publication—as *Bellini: Memorie e lettere*—of the Bellini section of that very long book. Filippo Gerardi (1835) had set the birthdate as November 28, 1804, Filippo Cicconetti (1859) as November 1, 1801—a date that even Florimo had repeated in 1869 in his *Cenno storico sulla Scuola musicale di Napoli*. In 1880, Michele Scherillo asserted that Bellini had been born in 1803 .

6. The massive Castello Ursino stood near the water's edge until the 1669 eruption of Etna, during which lava coursed around it and left it at almost its present considerable distance from the shore. Goethe, who visited Catania in May 1787, wrote: "We drove up the streets, where the lava which destroyed most of the city in 1669 has remained visible to this day. The solidified stream of fire had been used like any other stone; streets had been marked out on it and some even built" (*Italienische Reise*, translated by W. H. Auden and Elizabeth Mayer as *Italian Journey*, New York, 1962, p. 277).

7. In "*Urbanistica ed edilizia*," in *Catania nell'Ottocento*, Catania, 1934, p. 11.

8. In 1818, Catania was again severely damaged by an earthquake, which—occurring during a period of severe economic depression—reduced a large number of Catanese to real misery.

9. BSLS, Parma, 1959, p. 20.

10. In 1816, parents of seven children of whom the eldest was only fifteen, the Bellinis moved into larger quarters in a now-vanished house in the via di Sant'Agostino, near the church of Santa Maria dell'Aiuto.

11. The Teatro Comunale endured until 1890, but was used only intermittently. The first, inadequate Teatro Bellini, built in 1864, burned in 1869. The present Teatro Massimo Bellini, a handsome opera house, was planned as early as 1812; serious work on it started in 1880, and it was finished in 1890, when it was opened with a staging of *Norma*, with Virginia Damerini in the title role, Olympia Boronat as Adalgisa, Francesco Giannini as Pollione, and Giuseppe Rossi as Oroveso.

12. Catania, in which the centrally situated public park is called the Giardino Bellini, also has a much smaller Villetta Pacini.

13. The earliest attempt to publish the story of Bellini's life was the twenty-four-page *Biografia di Vincenzo Bellini* by Filippo Gerardi, issued in Rome in 1835, the year of the composer's death. Until the publication in 1959 of two books by Francesco Pastura—*Bellini secondo la storia* and the shorter *Vincenzo Bellini*, lacking the longer book's documentation—the chief sources of (frequently unreliable) information about Bellini's life were: the *Vita di Vincenzo Bellini* of Filippo Cicconetti, Prato, 1859; the extensive writings of Francesco Florimo, beginning with pp. 709–836 of his two-volume *Cenno storico sulla Scuola musicale di Napoli*, Naples, 1869–1871, later revised as the four-volume *La Scuola musicale di Napoli*, Naples, 1881–1882, in which the Bellini biography occupies pages 177–297 of Vol. III, and continuing through several other publications; the writings of Michele Scherillo, mostly issued in the 1880's; those of Antonino Amore,

which appeared from the 1870's to the early 1900's; and Luisa Cambi's
Bellini [*La Vita*], Milan, 1934, and *Vincenzo Bellini: Epistolario*, Milan,
1943. The best study of Bellini the composer in any language is Friedrich
Lippmann's *Vincenzo Bellini und die italienische opera seria seiner Zeit*,
Cologne/Vienna, 1969 (entire Vol. 6 of *Analecta Musicologica: Veröffent-
lichungen der Musikabteilung des Deutschen Historischen Instituts in
Rom*).

14. VB, Catania, 1959, p. 13.
15. L'Anonimo, p. 1.
16. L'Anonimo, p. 1.
17. The seven children of Rosario and Agata Bellini were: (1) Vincenzo
    (1801–1835); (2) Carmelo (1803–1884); (3) Francesco (1804–1884); (4)
    Michela (1806–1883), who married Ascanio Marziani; (5) Giuseppa (1807–
    1879), who married Ignazio Scammacca; (6) Mario (1810–1885); and (7)
    Maria (1813–1884), who married Paolo di Giacomo.
18. The best-remembered of the operas of Valentino Fioravanti (1764–1837)
    is *Le Cantatrici villane;* he also set (1816) the libretto by Andrea Leone
    Tottola entitled *Adelson e Salvini* which Bellini would reuse in 1825 for
    his first, student opera.
19. L'Anonimo, p. 1.
20. L'Anonimo, p. 1.
21. L'Anonimo, p. 2.
22. L'Anonimo, p. 3.
23. L'Anonimo, p. 2.
24. L'Anonimo, p. 2.
25. VdVB, p. 4.
26. Fulci's *Tri ottavi siciliani pri la morti di Vincenzo Bellini*, in Sicilian dialect,
    was issued at Catania in 1839; in these verses, Bellini is praised by a personi-
    fied Sicily.
27. *Op. cit.*, pp. 4–5.
28. L'Anonimo, p. 2.
29. *Memorie e lagrime de la patria sul sepolcro di Vincenzo Bellini*, Catania,
    1876, p. 9.
30. L'Anonimo, p. 2.
31. L'Anonimo, p. 3.
32. BSLS, p. 30.
33. BSLS, pp. 30–31.
34. *Op. cit.*, pp. 8–9.
35. Padre Don Giosuè Chisari (who in 1969 succeeded the late Francesco
    Pastura as director of the Museo Belliniano) wrote in *La Sicilia*, Catania,
    February 2, 1969: "The influence of this portentous instrument upon
    Bellini's spirit is undeniable, for from childhood he absorbed not only the
    extraordinary coloristic palette of the Benedictines' organ, but also the
    phonic scheme of its sound-masses (for example, the 'Echo' organ sys-
    tematized high near the vault of the apse gave him the point of departure
    toward achieving the echo in the fifth scene of Act I of *Il Pirata* '. . . *egli
    è il vento . . . il suon dell'onda che si frange sulla riva* . . .' and other similar
    effects in the *sinfonie* of *La Sonnambula* and *Norma*)."
36. L'Anonimo, p. 3.

37. Gallo was the supposed addressee of the most famous of Bellini's published letters, which is almost certainly apocryphal; see pp. 57–59.

38. It was published in *L'Olivuzza*, a *"numero unico,"* or commemorative brochure, issued at Palermo in 1846 in connection with the residence there in 1845–1846 of the Russian Imperial Family and Court (L'Olivuzza was the name of the villa that they occupied).

39. *"La Farfaletta* [sic], *Canzoncina, musica inedita, composta all'età di dodici anni dal Maestro Cav. Vincenzo Bellini di Catania,"* in *L'Olivuzza*, Palermo, 1846. Guglielmo Policastro reprinted the song in his *Vincenzo Bellini (1801–1819)*, Catania, 1935, making this comment: "The motive was adapted only to the first two strophes and then was repeated for the others, which do not exist. But Gallo completed the entire poetic part from memory . . ." *"La Farfalletta"* also was republished by Ricordi, Milan, (1948) in *Composizioni da camera per canto e pianoforte (ripristino)*.

40. In 1970, the autograph was in the possession of signora Marusia Manzella of Rome. Pastura told of his discovery of this manuscript and described the *Versetti* in *"Le Tre Ore di agonia,"* in the *Rivista del Comune di Catania*, Catania, 1953, pp. 59–66.

41. BSLS, p. 31.

42. L'Anonimo, p. 3.

43. Published in facsimile in 1941 in *Composizioni giovanili inedite*, by the Reale Accademia d'Italia.

44. Sixteen pages of the autograph (ending on a *fermata*) are in the Pierpont Morgan Library, New York. They are full of corrections and second thoughts. The first two strophes are in canon at the interval of eight beats; the three voices then join in the music of the other two strophes, alternate, and rejoin in the closing strophe. Antonino Amore (VB:A, p. 31) described this trio as being in 3/4 time, but the autograph begins in 9/8. A version of this piece, as "re-elaborated by F. P. Frontini," was published by Ricordi in 1901.

45. Autograph in the Naples Conservatory library. According to Florimo (CssSmdN I, pp. 771–772), this Allegro was one of the ten compositions that Bellini submitted to the authorities at San Sebastiano after his arrival in Naples in 1819 (see p. 15).

46. Autograph copy in the Naples Conservatory library.

47. VB, pp. 26–27.

48. L'Anonimo, pp. 3–4.

49. BE, p. 563.

50. Because Bellini was beyond the specified age limit for a beginning charity student, he would have to enter the Naples school as a paying student and bring bed linen with him.

51. The minutes of this meeting of the decurionate are now in the Museo Belliniano. One passage reads: "The decurionate, which knows the merits of the grandfather's and the father's labors in the science of music, discerning talent and vivacity in the applicant, persuaded that it would be to the honor of the comune to accede to Bellini's laudable wish . . ."

52. A *Pange lingua* for two voices and organ almost certainly was one of the last compositions that Bellini wrote out in Catania. Noting its unmistakable

resemblance to the second theme of the last movement of Beethoven's Sonata *"Appassionata,"* Pastura also described it (VB, p. 32) as a "sorrowing melody that begins with a sigh and culminates in an outburst of despairing affliction."

53. The generally unreliable Policastro (*op. cit.*, p. 100) set the date at June 3.

Chapter II

1. See asterisked items in list, pp. 377–387.
2. BSLS, p. 46.
3. BE, p. 20. Only three of Bellini's letters from the period of his nearly eight years in Naples seem to have survived.
4. Letter of October 13, 1819, in Don Giosuè Chisari's *"Vincenzo scrive allo zio Guerrera,"* in *L'Opera*, V, 16–17, Milan, 1970, pp. 28–30.
5. The best-known of the Riccis' collaborative operas, *Crispino e la comare*, to a libretto by Francesco Maria Piave, had its première at the Teatro San Benedetto, Venice, on February 28, 1850, and became a longtime favorite. It was staged at the Metropolitan Opera House, New York, on January 18, 1919, with a cast that included Frieda Hempel, Sophie Braslau, Thomas Chalmers, Andrés de Segurola, Paolo Ananian, Giordano Paltrinieri, and Antonio Scotti.
6. Della Corte–Pannain: *Vincenzo Bellini: Il Carattere morale, i caratteri artistici*, Turin, etc., 1935, p. 50.
7. *Ibid.*, pp. 50–51.
8. Conti's student opera, *Le Truppe in Franconia*, was staged in the San Sebastiano *teatrino* in 1819.
9. Bellini's Masses are *messe di gloria*: as was the Italian custom of the period, that is, they do not include all six sections of the Ordinary, but end with the Gloria; the Credo often was set as a separate composition.
10. For soprano, contralto, tenor, and bass, the published score calls for violins, violas, flutes, oboe, clarinets in C, horns in D, trumpets in C, bassoons, trombones, cello, and doublebass; it has an alternative accompaniment for organ. It consists of the *Kyrie elesion, Gloria, Laudamus, Domine Deus, Qui tollis, Qui sedes*, and *Cum sancto spiritu*. It was also published in Paris in about 1860 in piano score and separate parts.
11. Michele Scherillo: *Vincenzo Bellini: Note aneddotiche e critiche*, Ancona, 1882, p. 38.
12. If, like Donizetti, Bellini was at the Teatro San Carlo on March 14, 1822, when Rossini conducted there a performance of Giovanni Simone Mayr's oratorio *Atalia*, the three foremost Italian operatic composers of the first half of the nineteenth century were then under one roof.
13. B:Mel, pp. 129–130. It is not possible to accept uncritically Florimo's detailed reproduction of conversations that had occurred more than sixty years earlier, but that fact does not diminish the general reliability of their contents.
14. VB:V, frontispiece.
15. B:LV, p. 18 and ft. 1.
16. LSmdN III, p. 233.

17. Autographs of both pieces survive in the Naples Conservatory library. Both were republished in 1948 by Ricordi, Milan, in *Composizioni da camera per canto e pianoforte (ripristino)*. Pastura ascertained that the *scena* was composed after "*Dolente immagine di Fille mia*." As originally published, neither was dedicated to Maddalena Fumaroli: the dedicatee of the romanza was Nicola Tauro, a friend of Bellini; of the *scena*, "Her Excellency Donna Lauretta Caracciolo."

18. *Op. cit.*, p. 235.

19. *Vincenzo Bellini: La Vita, l'uomo, l'artista*, Brescia, 1935, p. 19.

20. *Op. cit.*, p. 236.

21. *Op. cit.*, p. 237.

22. BE, p. 39.

23. *Op. cit.*, p. 55.

24. *Op. cit.*, p. 95.

25. *Op. cit.*, p. 104.

26. *Op. cit.*, p. 561.

27. B:Mel, p. 5.

28. CssSmdN I, p. 486.

29. LSmdN II, p. 412.

30. The autograph of the E-flat *Sinfonia* is at the Museo Belliniano, that of the Oboe Concerto at the Naples Conservatory library. The *Sinfonia* was published in facsimile by the Reale Accademia d'Italia in *Composizioni giovanili inedite*, edited by Francesco Cilea (1941), and by Ricordi. The Oboe Concerto appears in the same facsimile volume, and also was published by Ricordi in 1961 in an edition prepared by Terenzio Gargiulo.

31. Among those whom Bellini tutored were Giuseppe Bornaccini, Michele (later Sir Michael) Costa, Giuseppe Curci, Paolo Fabrizzi, and Lauro Rossi.

32. *Semiramide* was introduced to Naples at the Teatro San Carlo on December 20, 1823, not quite eleven months after its première at Venice on February 2.

33. CssSmdN II, p. 716.

34. *Op. cit.*, p. 679.

35. About $403 in 1971 purchasing power.

36. The staging of student operas was a longtime custom in Naples. Zingarelli had begun his opera-composing career in 1768 with *I Quattro Pazzi*, an *intermezzo* staged at the Conservatorio di Santa Maria di Loreto. In 1819, he reinstituted the custom by authorizing the production at San Sebastiano of Conti's *Le Truppe in Franconia*, which was followed there by Nicola Fornasini's *Il Marmo* (1822); Luigi Ricci's *L'Impresario in angustie* (1823), using the libretto by Giuseppe Maria Diodati which Cimarosa had set in 1786; Bellini's *Adelson e Salvini* (1825); and—the last such opera before the royal music school was moved to San Pietro a Maiella —Francesco Stabile's *La Sposa al lotto* (1826).

37. Fioravanti's *Adelson e Salvini*, sung at Lisbon in 1815, was first heard in Italy at the Teatro dei Fiorentini, Naples, during the Carnival season of 1816, with a cast that included Margherita Chabrand, Giovanni Battista Rubini, Felice Pellegrini, and—in the dialect role of Bonifacio, which

had been arranged especially for him—the *buffo* Carlo Casaccia. It was not a success.

38. A comparison of the text of the Ricordi edition of *Adelson e Salvini* and the printed edition of Tottola's libretto as used by Fioravanti shows that considerable changes were introduced into it as Bellini set it. They could have been made by Tottola, who lived until 1831.

39. The scores issued by Ricordi do indeed give the date of the première as January 12, 1825, but that day fell during the period of official mourning for the king. That period ended on January 15 (the Teatro San Carlo, for instance, reopened on that day), and the first singing of *Adelson e Salvini* could have occurred on that day or any day shortly thereafter. Florimo, who naturally attended the première, said that it took place during Carnival, between February 10 and 15. Unless new evidence to the contrary should materialize, his statement must be accepted as correct.

40. LSmdN III, p. 249.

41. Guido Zavadini: *Donizetti: Vita—Musiche—Epistolario*, Bergamo, 1948, p. 245.

42. BE, p. 94.

43. The nature and verbal quality of some of the new text-lines (and especially those for Salvini's *"Ecco, signor, la sposa,"* p. 301 of the Ricordi piano-vocal score) suggest that Bellini obtained help in altering the libretto from Felice Romani, whose *Il Pirata* he was setting during the period likeliest for his work on the revision of *Adelson e Salvini*.

44. BE, p. 187. Bellini does not mention *Adelson e Salvini* in any letter surviving from after 1829.

45. The Museo Belliniano has an incomplete autograph of the first version of *Adelson e Salvini;* it also has a complete manuscript copy, in full score, of the important separate numbers as issued by Ricordi in 1903. See p. 215 and—for full, detailed information on autographs, manuscript copies, and published versions of *Adelson e Salvini*—Friedrich Lippmann: *Vincenzo Bellini und die italienische opera seria seiner Zeit*, Cologne/Vienna, 1969, pp. 367-374.

46. LSmdN III, p. 181.

47. BSLS, p. 78.

Chapter III

1. An incised stone set into a wall of the Gragnano church read: "In this sacred temple in July 1825, VINCENZO BELLINI, student at the Musical College of Naples—the Solemn Festival of S.a Ma. del Carmine being celebrated—directed a *messa di gloria* especially composed by him. In everlasting memory, the Municipality of Gragnano [placed] this stone 1881." For the meaning of *messa di gloria*, see footnote 9 for Chapter II.

2. BSLS, p. 80. The Museo Belliniano has an incomplete manuscript copy of this G-minor Mass, with interpolations in Bellini's writing, and a fragment of it in his autograph.

3. VdVB, p. 14.

4. Seven years of absence would place this trip in 1826. Cicconetti was probably correct when giving its year as 1825, but lack of documentation of Bellini's activities during parts of 1824 and 1826 leaves those years too as possibilities for it.

5. L'Anonimo, p. 5. Had Bellini visited Palermo as well as Catania in August 1825, he would have found there, at the Teatro Carolino as *"maestro di cappella*, director of the music, and composer of the new operas," a very disgruntled Donizetti. See William Ashbrook: *Donizetti*, London, 1963, pp. 75–82, and Herbert Weinstock: *Donizetti*, etc., New York and London, 1963, pp. 41–47, for accounts of Donizetti's Sicilian misadventures; both accounts rely heavily upon Ottavio Tiby: *Gaetano Donizetti a Palermo*, Rome, 1951.

6. BE, p. 167.

7. In *Omaggio, op. cit.*, p. 66:

8. BSLS, p. 81.

9. *"Una Bocciatura di Vincenzo Bellini,"* in *La Scala: Rivista dell'opera*, Milan, December 1953, p. 68.

10. Roti (1781?–after 1854), a Venetian, was a professional actor when, in 1820, he won his first success as a theatrical writer with *Bianca e Fernando*. Among his later dramas, *I Due Sergenti* became popular and was played well into the twentieth century. Roti's plays were published in two volumes at Naples in 1835.

11. LSmdN II, p. 413.

12. The king never managed to hear Bellini's opera, a fact that destroys the amusing story that, wanting Bellini to appear on stage to accept the applause, he called out in Neapolitan dialect: *"Fora 'o guaglione"*— roughly, "Let the young fella come out!"

13. B:Mel, p. 14.

14. BE, p. 143.

15. The Calcografia e Copisteria de' Reali Teatri (i.e., Girard and, later, Cottrau) issued an incomplete piano-vocal score of *Bianca e Gernando* (the piano arrangement is Florimo's); this lacks nearly all of the recitatives and gives the choral passages in piano transcription. The existence of this score caused Bellini some embarrassment when Ricordi decided to issue the revised version of the opera—*Bianca e Fernando*—in 1828; see pp. 49–50.

16. Zavadini, *op. cit.*, p. 245.

17. *Le Mie Memorie artistiche*, Florence, 1875 edition, p. 53.

18. Antedating Bulwer-Lytton's novel by nine years, this setting of a Tottola libretto was heard first, on November 19, 1825, at the Teatro San Carlo, Naples. When staged at the Teatro alla Scala, Milan, on August 22, 1827, it won sufficient popularity to be sung there forty-three times by the end of that season.

19. Bellini never was required to fulfill the clause in the original grant which specified repayment of the total amount should he not return to live and work in Catania. Further, the decurionate confirmed a pension of 36 onze annually to Bellini's father (December 3, 1832), and after Rosario Bellini's death, extended an annual pension of 108 ducati to his widow, the composer's mother (January 1842). Much later, the king of

united Italy accorded pensions of 500 lire and 300 lire, respectively, to Bellini's surviving siblings, Carmelo and Mario, and early in 1885, Carmelo having died in 1884, extended the combined amount of 800 lire annually to Mario Bellini, who died shortly thereafter at the age of eighty-one.

20. BSLS, p. 97.

21. The only Bellini letters from this period of which we have information are the lost one to the Catania decurionate (June 18, 1826) and the cited one to Cristina Guerrera (July 19, 1826). The possibility exists, of course, that it was during August 1826 that Bellini visited Catania.

22. Pastura (BSLS, p. 100) recorded an oral tradition, collected from surviving friends of Florimo, that Bellini's room at San Pietro a Maiella was "the second on the right of the corridor on the first floor [above the street floor], where the rooms for male students are."

23. BSLS, p. 96.

24. This refers to autograph pages in the Museo Belliniano which some writers mistakenly have supposed to be indications of an intention on Bellini's part to set Alfieri's *Oreste*, unchanged, as an opera. Actually, the pages contain the full score of an ensemble scene for Ifigenia, Clitennestra, Achille, Agamennone, Patroclo, and a chorus. The text is not from Alfieri's tragedy, but does suggest that at some time Bellini may have toyed with the notion of composing an opera on the Iphigenia story. See Appendix L, p. 418.

25. LSmdN III p. 358, ft. 1.

26. Cammarano (1766–1850), a member of a longtime dynasty of theatrical and musical men and women, was a son of the actor Vincenzo Cammarano, called Giancola, and the father of the librettist Salvatore Cammarano.

27. The original of the Cammarano portrait seems not so survive, but the Museo di San Martino, Naples, has a purported copy of it; see Plate 3a. Everything about this likeness is more credible than the slick, idealized painting of Bellini in late adolescence attributed to Federico(?) Maldarelli. This latter (which can be seen on the wall in Plate 1, and which was reproduced in the *Vincenzo Bellini* edited by Pizzetti, Milan, 1936, between p. 40 and p. 41) certainly was painted from other portraits and from imagination, without Bellini's actual presence.

28. After Bellini's death, Florimo sent a list of these belongings to the lawyer for the heirs in Catania. It includes eighteen bound volumes of music, two published selections, three separate vocal pieces by Mayr, three poplar-wood tables, two high-backed iron chairs, and a quilted coverlet. Among the music, Florimo listed: incomplete copies of Rossini's *Elisabetta, regina d'Inghilterra* and Spontini's *La Vestale;* complete copies of Rossini's *La Donna del lago, Ricciardo e Zoraide,* and *Mosè in Egitto;* chamber music by several composers; Mozart symphonies; and a copy of Boniface Asioli's *Trattato d'armonia e d'accompagnamento* (Milan, 1813). Florimo believed that Bellini had promised these possessions to him in the event of his not returning to Naples to live, but had no wish to keep them against the expressed desires of the Bellini heirs. He had sold Bellini's piano for him early in February 1828.

29. The *Gazzetta privilegiata di Milano* for April 12, 1827, publishing a list of travelers who had arrived by diligence that day, mentioned *"Bellini, maestro di cappella da Napoli,"* but not the Rubinis.

30. Leslie Orrey wrote (*Bellini*, London and New York, 1969, p. 21): "Among the letters of recommendation he brought to Milan was one from the Catanian poet [Felice] Bisazza to Andrea Maffei. When they met, Maffei, experienced in the theatrical world, warned Bellini of the difficulties of La Scala and its singers . . ." Bisazza appears only once in Bellini's available correspondence: in a stiff formal letter of March 8, 1832, from Catania, Bellini thanked him both for an envelope that had failed to reach him in Naples and for laudatory words about him which Bisazza had included in a poem (*"Settentrionale,"* in his *Saggi poetici*) mentioning *Il Pirata* and *I Capuleti e i Montecchi*.

31. Donizetti set ten Romani librettos, including *Anna Bolena*, *L'Elisir d'amore*, and *Lucrezia Borgia*.

32. *Il Turco in Italia*, *Bianca e Falliero*, and *Adina*, the last as rewritten by Gherardo Bevilacqua-Aldobrandini.

33. *Felice Romani ed i più riputati maestri di musica del suo tempo*, Turin, etc., n.d. (but 1882).

34. Quoted in Livia Miragoli, *Il Melodramma italiano nell'Ottocento*, Rome, 1924, p. 146, from Guido Mazzoni's *L'Ottocento*, 1-vol. edn., Milan, 1964 (first published in 2 vols., 1913).

35. Besides many pieces for solo piano and two pianos, Pollini composed a miscellany of other instrumental music; a *Stabat Mater;* at least two operas—*La Casetta nei boschi* (Teatro della Canobbiana, Milan, 1798) and *L'Orfana svizzera* (posthumous, Milan Conservatory, 1856); and a cantata celebrating the peace of Lunéville: *Il Trionfo della Pace* (Teatro alla Scala, Milan, April 30, 1801).

36. In 1820, Pollini had published his *Trentadue Esercizi in forma di toccata*, in which he advocated writing piano music on three staves so as to propound the principal melody in the middle of the keyboard and provide passagework above and below it. This procedure had been adumbrated by Muzio Clementi and Johann Nepomuk Hummel, and was to be developed farther by Sigismond Thalberg and Liszt. Pollini's publication was dedicated to his friend Giacomo Meyerbeer; a second, enlarged edition of it was issued later.

37. *Op. cit.*, pp. 128–129.

38. Between the date of Bellini's arrival in Milan and that of the première of *Il Pirata*, he could have heard at La Scala: Mercadante's *Il Montanaro;* Rossini's *La Donna del lago* and *L'Inganno felice;* Felice Frasi's *La Selva d'Hermanstadt;* Rossini's *Il Barbiere di Siviglia;* a *pasticcio by* several composers entitled *Il Trionfo della Musica;* Pacini's *L'Ultimo Giorno di Pompei*, and Rossini's *Mosè in Egitto*—which together accounted for 155 performances in 198 days.

39. A friend of Bellini and author of *Cenni illustrativi alla nuova opera La Straniera*, Milan, 1829.

40. VdVB, p. 24.

41. Either that in Act I—*"Se un giorno fia che ti tragga degli altari"*—or that in Act II—*"Vieni, vieni."*

42. *Don Eutichio della Castagna* had choreography by Salvatore Taglioni; the composer(s) of the music remain unknown. *Alceste* had been choreographed by Antonio Cortesi; "The Music is by various Maestros."

43. BE, p. 25.

44. A condensed misquotation of the line *"Macte nova virtute, puer; sic itur ad astra,"* from the *Aeneid*, 9, 641. Addressing Iulus, Apollo says (translation by C. Day Lewis, from *The Aeneid of Vergil*, London and New York, 1952): "More power to your young valour, my son! You're going the right way to starry fame . . ." The same version of Vergil's line (by Publius Papinius Statius) had been addressed to Donizetti nearly six years earlier, in a critique of his *Zoraide di Granata*.

45. This portrait, which no one who knew Bellini liked well or regarded as even an approximate likeness, is in the Museo Teatrale alla Scala, Milan.

46. BE, p. 134.

47. The king's advisers had their reasons. According to Ottavio Tiby (*"Una Bocciatura di Vincenzo Bellini,"* in *La Scala: Rivista dell'opera*, Milan, December 1953, p. 69), Giuseppe Mosca sent in for approval a Mass of which the *Kyrie* had been taken from a chorus in the opera *Nina* (Paisiello or Coppola); the *Domine Deus* from a trio in *Gli Orazi ed i Curiazi* (Cimarosa or Zingarelli); and the *Qui tollis* from an aria in Mayr's *La Rosa bianca e la rosa rossa*. The *Quoniam*, finally, had been composed in the manner of an *opera buffa* chorus.

48. One of the members of this commission was Andrea Monteleone, later a friend of both Donizetti and Bellini, who mentioned him in letters.

49. The six pieces by Bellini passed by the commission—and now difficult to identify—were a *Credo*, two Masses, a *Messa da Requiem*, a *Sinfonia*, and a *Dixit*—all of which, the *Requiem* excepted, Florimo assigned to Bellini's Neapolitan years.

50. French by birth, Adèle Chaumel had married Rubini in 1819, after which she generally was billed as Adelaide Comelli-Rubini. She had sung in Naples during Bellini's years there and had created the role of Calbo in Rossini's *Maometto II* at the Teatro San Carlo on December 3, 1820.

51. BE, p. 43.

52. BSLS, p. 121.

53. BE, pp. 42–45.

54. The immediate propagator of this false first report seems to have been Luigi Pacini, a *basso comico* then on the roster of the Kärntnertortheater; he was the father of Bellini's bête noire, Giovanni Pacini.

55. *Gazzetta privilegiata di Milano*, March 11, 1828; *I Teatri*, March 11 and 20, 1828; *L'Eco*, March 10, 1828.

56. BE, p. 62.

Chapter IV

1. BE, p. 41. Like several of Bellini's other letters to Florimo, this one was addressed to Gabriele Nigri, first flutist of the Teatro San Carlo; its salutation, however, is *"Mio caro Florimo."* The reason for this subterfuge is not clear. Luisa Cambi (BE, p. 35, ft. 1) surmised that it was "probably

to avoid the indiscretions of the Andreanna family," a large, tightly knit group that Pastura (BSLS, p. 49) called "one of those peaceful and prosperous tribes spoken of in the Bible." Bellini many times asked to be remembered to eight or nine different Andreannas (Andreani and other variant spellings occur) in letters to Florimo, who for a time may have lived in their capacious home.

2. Bartolomeo Merelli (1793–1879), a childhood friend and fellow student of Donizetti at Bergamo, had become a Milanese agent for opera houses elsewhere. He also wrote librettos for Donizetti, Mayr, Morlacchi, and Vaccaj. At various later times, he was an impressario at Vienna (Kärntnertortheater, 1836–1848; 1853–1855), Paris (Opéra and Théâtre-Italien), London, Berlin, and St. Petersburg in addition to several Italian cities, including Milan (La Scala, 1836–1850; 1861–1863) and Turin (Teatro Regio, 1859). Almost all of the foremost singers of his era—as well as the dancers Fanny Cer(r)ito, Fanny Elssler, and Marie Taglioni—were under contract to Merelli at one time. Among the operas that as impresario he had a hand in commissioning were Rossini's *Guillaume Tell*, Donizetti's *Lucia di Lammermoor*, Pacini's *Saffo*, and Verdi's *Oberto, conte di San Bonifacio, Un Giorno di regno, Nabucco, I Lombardi alla prima crociata*, and *Giovanna d'Arco*.

3. This decision had to be concurred in by Giovanni David, who had the contractual right to select the opera in which he would open the Carlo Felice.

4. He was to be paid 2,500 francs and to have free lodgings in Genoa. From there, on April 16, he told Florimo (BE, p. 84): "This morning I received two thousand five hundred francs from the management, and though signor Peluso had promised me to have my lodgings paid for, now he has told me that the impresario has not been able to take care of that, and I myself therefore have had to pay it. I figure that, deducting all the expenses that I must incur in supporting myself in Genoa and returning to Milan, and paying for the house and giving the hundred and twenty-five francs to the theatrical correspondent [Merelli] at five percent, I'll have two thousand francs net, and perhaps more. See what economies I make without forcing myself to do without anything!" Two thousand francs (i.e., lire) of the Kingdom of Sardinia and Piedmont of the period would have had a value about equivalent to $1,035 in 1971 purchasing power.

5. Morlacchi's *I Saraceni in Sicilia*, to a Romani libretto, was staged at the Teatro La Fenice, Venice, during the Carnival season of 1828.

6. Bellini naturally was embarrassed vis-à-vis Cottrau, whose plates of separate numbers from *Bianca e Gernando* would require revision in view of *Bianca e Fernando*.

7. BE, pp. 57–58.

8. BE, p. 65.

9. Ruggi, a clarinetist, had played the solo in *Bianca e Gernando* at the San Carlo in 1826.

10. BE, pp. 74–75.

11. Literally "pieces in a trunk," a *pezzo di baule* being a discrete number, by no matter what composer, which a star singer carried about, interpolat-

ing it into any opera at all as a way of displaying his or her voice with special effectiveness.

12. In fact, Donizetti's *Alina, regina di Golconda* was not heard until five weeks after *Bianca e Fernando*, being preceded at the Carlo Felice by two Rossini operas: *Il Barbiere di Siviglia* and *Otello*. The most curious result of Bellini's struggle with Tosi was that he later borrowed the melody of the fought-over cabaletta ("*Contenta appien quest'alma*") for use in *Norma*, where it became famous as the cabaletta following "*Casta diva*": "*Ah! bello, a me ritorna.*"

13. BE, p. 73.

14. The first two performances thus were on consecutive nights, the première having been scheduled for April 7, a Monday.

15. The solos in Donizetti's hymn with chorus were sung by Letizia Cortesi, Giovanni Battista Verger, and Antonio Tamburini.

16. On March 24, Bellini wrote to Florimo (BE, p. 69): "The [scene of the] demolition cannot be used, as there is one in the ballet, and more impressive, with a conflagration; and mine, coming after that, would be a mere hubbub, as they do the ballet between the two acts." On April 12, he told Florimo (BE, p. 80): "The King has ordered that from Saturday forward —that is, from this evening—it [the opera] is to be done in sequence, and the ballet last, as this latter is long and boring, and nothing in it pleases [the audience] except a trio . . ." Bellini objected on principle to the performance of ballet between the acts of his operas, finding it "damaging to the staging of the spectacle" (*Verdi: Bollettino*, I, 1, Parma, April 1960, p. 93).

17. BE, pp. 75–76.

18. That is, in a royal theater in the capital of his kingdom.

19. BE, p. 80.

20. BE, pp. 76–77.

21. BE, p. 77, ft. 1, quoting a writer in *I Teatri*, Milan, of April 16, 1828.

22. BE, p. 83.

23. The "terrible donna" was Letizia Cortesi, the "very mediocre tenor" Giovanni Battista Verger. Also in the cast was the *basso buffo* Giuseppe Frezzolini.

24. BE, p. 88.

25. After Bellini left Genoa at the end of April, the season at the Carlo Felice continued with Donizetti's *Alina, regina di Golconda* (première, May 12, with Bellini's bugbear, Adelaide Comelli-Rubini, singing the title role), Morlacchi's *Colombo* (première, June 21), and Rossini's *L'Assedio di Corinto*, for insertion into which Donizetti composed his immediately and enduringly popular cabaletta "*Pietosa all'amor mio*," sung at Genoa by Tosi and Tamburini, and thereafter frequently interpolated into Rossini's opera everywhere. Donizetti was very much easier to deal with than Bellini.

26. BSLS, p. 137.

27. Bellini agreed to bear one third of the costs of this publication and to share any ensuing profits with Ricordi, but that understanding appears to have been changed to read that he would not bear any of the costs, but would take printed copies in lieu of profits that might accrue to him.

28. BE, p. 78.
29. Letter of April 12, 1828, BE, p. 82.
30. BE, pp. 85–86.
31. As Camporesi was born in 1785, Bellini was exaggerating her age by two or three years.
32. BE, p. 95.
33. Christina Alexandrina Egypta Bonaparte (1798–1847), a daughter of the Prince de Canino, had married in 1824 Lord Dudley Coutts Stuart, a son of the first Marquess of Bute. Bellini had met her in Genoa in March or April 1828.
34. BE, p. 98.
35. BE, p. 93.
36. Issue of June 14, 1828, p. 170. The article also said: "The impresario Barbaja persuaded the illustrious Zingarelli [then seventy-six years old] to accept one of the largest loges for himself, his family, and his friends, there to witness the glories of his favorite disciple. Throughout the performance, tears of contentment overflowed from the eyes of that most illustrious veteran of song."
37. BE, p. 106.
38. BE, p. 103.
39. BE, pp. 103–104.
40. BE, pp. 106–108.
41. The illegible word here was probably *"avrò"* (I shall have).
42. BE, p. 109.
43. As Florimo would have understood, Bellini meant that he had a very low opinion of the tenor signed up for La Scala: Berardo Calvari, called Winter. See p. 63.
44. BE, pp. 109–112.
45. René-Charles-Guilbert de Pixerécourt's play *La Femme à deux maris* had run for 1,346 performances in Paris after being introduced at the Ambigu-Comique on December 27, 1802. It could scarcely have been overlooked as a source by more than one Italian librettist.
46. BE, p. 111, ft. 5, gives this humorous aside: " 'A very apposite battle,' *L'Eco* says ironically (Milan, 1828, June 13, p. 284). This battle gave rise to burlesque comments. The stage direction in the libretto said that [after] Ramiro flung himself into an assault upon the walls, followed by some of his companions: 'some bastions fell. The others, remaining ashore, sing in chorus.' And the chronicler in *L'Eco* recounted that the audience eagerly awaited this *chorus of bastions*, which naturally did not exist."
47. Not Pacini's popular opera by this title, but Valentino Fioravanti's 1812 opera *Adelaide maritata*, which was sometimes billed as *Adelaide e Comingio*.
48. Bellini's wishful prediction proved unreliable: Pacini's *Il Talismano* received its première at the Teatro San Carlo, Naples, on June 10, 1829, his *Giovanna d'Arco* its première at La Scala, Milan, on March 14, 1830— and he went on composing operas until just before his death in 1867.
49. BE, p. 115.
50. BE, p. 113.
51. BE, p. 134.

52. Cosenza's free Italian rendition of D'Arlincourt's French novel had been staged for the first time in the private theater in Cosenza's Naples palazzo on March 21, 1825. Earlier (1822), an opera with a French libretto derived from the novel, the score by Michele Enrico Carafa, had been staged at the Opéra-Comique, Paris. Bellini was aware, also, that Stefano Pavesi's opera *Il Solitario ed Elodia* (Teatro San Carlo, Naples, 1826) had used a Tottola libretto based upon either the novel or Cosenza's play. The Sienese composer Rinaldo Ticci (1805–1883) later wrote an opera to a Gaetano Rossi libretto entitled *Il Solitario* (Teatro dei Rinnovati, Siena, 1838).

53. BE, p. 146.

54. *L'Étrangère*, a two-volume novel, Paris, 1825. The fact that in this letter Bellini gives some of the characters their French names suggests that, despite his faulty knowledge of French, he had read the original novel. No translation of it into Italian was published before 1830, but *La Straniera*, the five-act play that the barone di Cosenza had derived from it, was staged at the Teatro dei Fiorentini, Naples, in 1827. For further details, see p. 342 and Franca Cella's *Indagini sulle fonti francesi dei libretti di Vincenzo Bellini*, Milan, 1968, pp. 478–479.

55. This forecast closely resembles what Romani actually put into the libretto, which, however, was parceled out into eight scenes in two acts.

56. From 1824 on, while Ricci remained a student at San Pietro a Maiella, operas by him had been heard at the Teatro Nuovo, Naples; on January 28, 1828, his *Ulisse in Itaca* was produced at the San Carlo.

57. BE, p. 136.

58. BE, pp. 136–137. Coccia (1782–1873), a Neapolitan, had since 1807 been a prolific composer of operas, some of which had won wide success. His *Caterina di Guisa* (Teatro alla Scala, Milan, February 14, 1833) was generally called his best work; its libretto was by Romani.

59. Rieschi (sometimes Riesck, 1779–1880) finally reached La Scala on December 26, 1829, with his *Bianca di Belmonte*, to a Romani libretto; but even with a cast including Méric-Lalande, Unger, Rubini, and Tamburini, it lasted for only nine performances. His *La Fidanzata di Lammermoor* (Trieste, autumn 1831) preceded Donizetti's *Lucia di Lammermoor* by four years.

60. BSLS, p. 509.

61. Mercadante was then about to try his luck in Paris. His opera *I Briganti* (Théâtre-Italien, March 22, 1836) was staged there with Rossini's help, but proved unsuccessful. His finest opera, *Il Giuramento*, followed the next year, but at La Scala (March 10, 1837).

62. At the time of the Ricci imbroglio in 1828, Bellini also had failed to satisfy Florimo that he had been properly helpful to Conti, who had been their *maestrino* and friend at the conservatory. Nevertheless, the only one of Conti's operas to receive its première in Milan was staged at La Scala on October 31, 1829, with a libretto by Romani and the leading roles sung by two of Bellini's favorite singers, Méric-Lalande and Rubini; this was *Giovanna Shore*.

63. Possibly Luciano Andreatini, a student at San Pietro a Maiella at the time.

64. BE, p. 155.

65. BE, p. 157.
66. BE, p. 160.
67. Perhaps Gilardoni and Andreatini had suspended work on their opera because news of the Romani-Bellini project had reached Naples.
68. BE, pp. 181–182.
69. BSLS, p. 547.
70. VB:A, Catania, 1892, pp. 102–103.
71. BE, p. 181, ft. 2.
72. This is no longer true.
73. Perhaps—but as it was published by a Sicilian, Miss Cambi's rather feeble point is not invalidated even if the "Letter to Gallo" was first published outside Sicily.
74. See Appendix L, pp. 418–421.
75. BSLS, pp. 546–550.
76. B:Mel, p. 81.
77. BE, p. 157, where it is undated, though it was taken from Florimo's B:Mel, p. 371, where it is dated September 20, 1828. The autograph was thought lost until the late Frank Walker located it in the Raccolta Piancastelli at Forlì: it bears the date assigned to it by Florimo. See Walker: *"Lettere disperse e inedite di Vincenzo Bellini,"* in the *Rivista del Comune di Catania*, October–December 1960, for his corrections in the text as published by Luisa Cambi in BE.
78. Rossi (1780–1855?) was an official librettist to La Scala. He provided Donizetti, Mayr, Meyerbeer, Rossini, and other composers with workmanlike texts, usually devoid of creative imagination, including (Rossini) *La Cambiale di matrimonio, Tancredi*, and *Semiramide*; (Donizetti) *Maria Padilla, Linda di Chamounix;* and (Meyerbeer) *Il Crociato in Egitto*.
79. A phrase in Gualtiero's Act I cavatina *"Nel furor delle tempeste,"* these words occur at the moment when the ambiguousness of his character— Guido Pannain called it his duplicity (*Bellini*, ed. Pizzetti, Milan, 1940, p. 50)—is made clear.
80. BE, p. 158.
81. BE, p. 162.
82. The grandeur of two of the Turina homes, the present *municipio* at Casal-buttano (about ten miles north of Cremona) and the former Villa Salterio at Moltrasio on Lake Como, silently testify to their wealth. Ferdinando Turina and his brother Bortolo owned large tracts of land and silk factories. Giuditta's father, in turn, was also a wealthy silk merchant; her mother had been a baronessa Sopransi.
83. Born on February 13, 1803, Giuditta was actually only twenty-five when Bellini met her in Genoa and when he wrote this letter to Florimo.
84. BE, p. 163.
85. BE, pp. 163–164.
86. BE, pp. 164–165.
87. Giuditta's fear eventually proved justified, but the damaging correspondence was from Bellini to her, not to Florimo.
88. BE, p. 165.
89. BE, p. 165.

90. BE, p. 154.
91. Donizetti's opera, sung first at the Teatro San Carlo, Naples, on January 1, 1828, was in fact a mild success even at La Scala (ten consecutive performances). But Bellini was disturbed by what he took to be its failure "because I see that there is good music in it, but that Milan is too enthusiastic about the greatly blessed *Pirata* and Rubini, and I see that all other scores fail. Serenades, academies, the mob, the ones who frequent the taverns, all, all breathe only *Il Pirata*, and that, my dear Florimo, disturbs me greatly, for what shall I do without Rubini even if I produce divine music?" (letter to Florimo, July 14, 1828, BE, p. 139).
92. Reina (1797–1843), born at Lugano, had first studied painting. Turning to singing, he showed special promise, soon fulfilled. Making his La Scala debut on January 12, 1829, as Ilo in Rossini's *Zelmira*, he rapidly became a leading tenor. He was to create the roles of Arturo in Bellini's *La Straniera* and Tamas in Donizetti's *Gemma di Vergy*, both at La Scala, and to sing Pollione opposite Pasta's Norma there.
93. BE, pp. 161–162.
94. VdVB, p. 35. Antonino Amore said incorrectly that *La Straniera* was composed at Moltrasio, which Bellini almost certainly did not visit before September 1829. Cicconetti and others also have said that the subject of the opera was suggested to Bellini by Giuditta Turina, though Bellini stated clearly that Florimo had brought it to his attention.
95. Data related to Bellini's activities immediately after December 27, 1828, are few because only one letter from him is available between that date and February 15, 1829, the day after the première of *La Straniera*. That single exception—which is quoted from on p. 65—is dated January 7, 1829. It is in the Raccolta Piancastelli at Forlì and is cited complete in Walker, "*Lettere disperse e inedite di Vincenzo Bellini*," in the *Rivista del Comune di Catania*, Catania, October–December 1960, p. 6.
96. BE, pp. 170–175.
97. BE, pp. 170–171.
98. Giuseppe Persiani (1805–1869) was only twenty-two when his *Gastone di Foix*, a setting of one of Romani's poorest librettos, was a failure at the Teatro La Fenice, Venice, on December 26, 1827. He was later to win considerable fame as an operatic composer, particularly with two operas to better Romani texts—*Eufemio di Messina, ossia La Distruzione di Catania*, Teatro del Giglio, Lucca, September 20, 1829, and *Il Fantasma*, Théâtre-Italien, Paris, December 14, 1843—and one to a libretto by Salvatore Cammarano—*Ines di Castro*, Teatro San Carlo, Naples, January 27, 1835. In 1830, he married the great soprano later known as Fanny Tacchinardi-Persiani, for whom Donizetti composed the title role of *Lucia di Lammermoor*.
99. BE, p. 172.
100. Walker, *op. cit.*, p. 4.
101. BE, p. 172.
102. Walker, *op. cit.*, p. 5.
103. Walker, *op. cit.*, p. 6. Walker also quoted (p. 4) from the *Catalogue de la belle Collection de Lettres Autographes de fu M. le Baron de Trémont,*

Paris, 1852, an entry reading: *"Bellini. Quatre vers et 3 lig. aut. sig. Milan, 27 octobre 1828,"* which may have referred to still another set of Romani verses for *La Straniera* transcribed by Bellini and possibly sent to Florimo.

104. Giuditta appears to have been suffering from particularly intense gynecological disorders.

105. Romani went to Venice to work on the libretto of *Rosmunda d'Inghilterra,* Carlo Coccia's opera first sung at the Teatro La Fenice on February 27, 1829.

106. VdVB, pp. 39–40.

107. *L'Assedio di Corinto,* first heard at Parma on January 26, 1828, was an Italian adaptation-translation of Rossini's *Le Siège de Corinthe* (Opéra, Paris, October 9, 1826), which in turn had been a French translation-adaptation of his *Maometto II* (Teatro San Carlo, Naples, December 3, 1820). In the 1828–1829 La Scala season, *L'Assedio di Corinto* was sung more often than any other opera (29 performances); it was followed on January 2, 1829, by Rossini's *Zelmira,* which reached 17 performances there that season.

108. *La Straniera* was performed 26 times during the rest of the regular La Scala season, which it closed on March 18. On March 19, a special performance of it was presented for the benefit of the orchestra. Then, from March 22 to April 7, La Scala offered ten "extraordinary performances," at least seven of which were of *La Straniera.* By April 7, 1829, then, Bellini's new opera had been sung at least 34 times in Milan in little more than seven weeks.

109. Quoted by G. Cenzato in *"Le 'Prime' celebri: Il Centenario della 'Straniera,'"* in *Corriere della sera,* Milan, February 14, 1929.

110. From about $14 to about $63 in 1971 purchasing power.

111. Cenzato, *op. cit.* For extensive quotations from articles about *La Straniera* in *L'Eco,* Milan (February 16, 20, 23, 1829), *I Teatri,* Milan (February 25, March 6 and 19, 1829), and other periodicals see BE, pp. 195–209.

112. *I Teatri,* Milan, 1829, Vol. I, Part 1, p. 72; quoted in Livia Miragoli: *Il Melodramma italiana nell'Ottocento,* Rome, 1924, p. 133.

113. Reproduced both in facsimile and textually in Franco Abbiati's *"L'Incorregibile Vincenzillo,"* in *La Scala,* Milan, March 1950, pp. 20–21.

114. BE, pp. 182–183.

115. BSLS, pp. 157–158.

116. Letter of February 14, 1829, from Francesco Pollini to Zingarelli, quoted in BSLS, pp. 155–156.

117. BSLS, p. 159.

118. Writing to Giovanni Ricordi almost six years later to announce the success of *I Puritani* (BE, pp. 518–519), Bellini remarked that the audience's approval had transported him back to La Scala on the first night of *La Straniera,* and added ". . . at that first performance of *La Straniera,* at the end of the second act, I was so content that my knees would not hold me up . . ."

119. Donizetti in his finest *opere serie* and Verdi in many places owed more than a little to this "melodramatic" opera by Bellini.

120. *Le Tre Arti considerate in alcuni illustri italiani contemporanei,* Milan, 1874, p. 37.

Chapter V

1. BE, pp. 173–174.
2. Giuditta Pasta, the great soprano who was to be Bellini's first Amina (*La Sonnambula*), Norma, and Beatrice di Tenda, recently had sung in London, where she was very popular. Bellini seems to have met her in midsummer 1828, when she was thirty.
3. BE, pp. 113–114.
4. For Merelli's part in arranging for Bellini's revision of *Bianca e Gernando* for Genoa, see pp. 45 and 72.
5. The Grand Duchess's lover, Count Adam Adalbert von Neipperg, whom she married morganatically in 1821, seems to have had some executive control over this commission.
6. Quoted in Cesare Alcari: "*La 'Zaira' fu veramente fishchiata?*" in *Musica d'oggi*, July 1935, p. 262. Alcari, attached to the Biblioteca Maria Luisa at Parma, quoted many letters and other fugitive documents dealing wtih the fortunes of Bellini's *Zaira*.
7. BE, p. 149.
8. BE, p. 159.
9. BE, pp. 175–176.
10. BE, pp. 177–178.
11. Antonio Sartorio, to a text by Giacomo Francesco Bussani, had composed a *Cesare in Egitto* that was staged at the Teatro Vendramin di San Salvatore, Venice, during the Carnival season of 1667. At the Teatro Regio Ducal, Milan, in January 1735, a setting of Bussani's text by Geminiano Giacomelli had been staged. Other operas dealing with Caesar in Egypt had been composed by such men as Jommelli (1751), Piccinni (1770), Bellini's onetime teacher Tritto (1805), and Pacini (1821).
12. Torrigiani first sent his libretto to Bellini in Milan, interleaving it with blank pages on which the composer was invited to pose any questions and make suggestions for changes.
13. Alcari, *op. cit.*, p. 263.
14. Unavailingly, Torrigiani also offered a substitute libretto dealing with the Chevalier Bayard.
15. Giovanni da Procida (1210–1298) was to be a principal character in the libretto by Scribe and Charles Duveyrier which Verdi set in French as *Les Vêpres siciliennes* (Opéra, Paris, January 13, 1855).
16. Alcari, *op. cit.*, p. 265.
17. BE, p. 185.
18. BE, p. 186.
19. *Zaïre*, 1732. Bellini did not know or did not care that on September 3, 1802, the Teatro Carcano, Milan, had staged another opera derived from Voltaire's tragedy: *Zaira, o sia Il Trionfo della religione*, with a libretto by Mattia Botturini and music by Francesco Federici; and that on January 29, 1805, another *Zaira*—librettist undetermined, but probably either Lorenzo da Ponte or Filippo Pantani—with a score by Peter von Winter, had been staged at His Majesty's Theatre, London. As late as May 28, 1890,

still another was presented at the Opéra, Paris: *Zaïre*, libretto by Édouard Blau and Louis Besson, score by Paul Véronge de La Nux.

20. Now the via Cavour. Some days later, Bellini and Romani moved into the house of a signor Gibertini at No. 58, strada Santa Lucia.

21. Alcari, *op. cit.*, p. 266.

22. Alcari, *op. cit.*, p. 266.

23. VdVB, p. 45.

24. BSLS, p. 170. The "documents," to be found in Cesare Alcari's article already cited, were the two letters from conte Sanvitale calling Bellini to account.

25. The final postponement, from May 12 to May 16, was necessitated by Lablache's inability to reach Parma from Naples on time.

26. BE, pp. 213–214.

27. If Bellini was being precise, neither he nor Romani had sat down to real work on *Zaira* until mid-April, a full month after they had reached Parma.

28. For the full text of Romani's *"Proemio,"* see BSLS, pp. 183–184.

29. It may also have been an apprehensive audience. Rumors had persisted that postponement of the première had really been dictated by discovery of a serious defect in the structure of the theater itself. Both *I Teatri*, Milan, and the *Gazzetta privilegiata di Venezia* (respectively, May 10 and May 12) had felt called upon to deny the rumor, which in fact appears to have been baseless.

30. As listed by Alcari, *op. cit.*, that first audience included Giovanni Ricordi, the principessa Amalia di Belgiojoso, and several other titled Milanese. Marie-Louise also attended the second performance of *Zaira* and at least part of the third—the latter because it was a grand gala honoring her palace guests, Francesco IV, duca di Modena, and his family.

31. VdVB, pp. 46–47.

32. Quoted in BSLS, p. 186.

33. Alcari, *op. cit.*, p. 267.

34. In his obituary tribute to Bellini published in the *Gazzetta piemontese*, October 1835. See pp. 210–211 for a complete translation of it.

35. For the only known revival of *Zaira* to date, see p. 361.

36. BE, pp. 185–187.

37. BE, pp. 386–387.

38. From this 1829–1834 period, I have read in autograph or transcription: (1) a letter dated at Venice on January 20, 1830 (BE, p. 232); (2) one dated at Como on September 19, 1831 (BE, pp. 282–284); (3) a probably tampered-with letter dated at Milan on December 26, 1831 (BE, p. 290); (4) a letter dated September 24, without year (but very probably 1831), in the Pierpont Morgan Library, New York, mentioned in BE, p. 287, as having been sold by N. Charavay on November 29, 1924; and (5) fragments of letters from London covering the period from May to August 1833, which Luisa Cambi (BE, p. 363) well described as "of dubious authenticity."

39. BSLS, pp. 215–216.

40. BSLS, pp. 216–217. The manuscript notebook, now in the Museo Belliniano, also mentions a letter from Bellini dated August 5, 1829, which appears to

have vanished. The date suggests that news of his grandfather's death was slow in reaching him.

41. The libretto of *Il Talismano* had been derived by Gaetano Barbieri from the 1825 installment of Sir Walter Scott's *Tales of the Crusaders: The Talisman*.

42. *Guillaume Tell* had been sung for the first time on August 3. The Rossinis had left Paris ten days later.

43. BSLS, pp. 220–221, where the autograph is described as lacking its first page and as belonging to professore Antonio Caldarella of the Archivio di Stato, Palermo. A photographic copy of it is in the Museo Belliniano.

44. At the time of Rossini's call, Bellini seems still to have had quarters in the contrada Santa Margherita, but may already have moved to the via San Vittore e Quaranta Martiri (now the via Pietro Verri), where he certainly was living shortly afterwards.

45. Rossini's *La Gazza ladra* was sung 23 times, Pacini's *Il Talismano* 18, Vaccaj's *Saul* 11, *Bianca e Fernando* only 10.

46. BSLS, p. 223. Letter and medal in the Museo Belliniano.

47. "*Un Amico torinese di Vincenzo Bellini*," in *Atti della Reale Accademia delle Scienze di Torino*, XLVII, 1–5, 1932, pp. 101–136.

48. In 1829, Lamperi was Under-Secretary of State in the Ministry of Foreign Affairs of the Kingdom of Sardinia and Piedmont. Before Luzio's publication, only two letters from Bellini to Lamperi had been known. Sixteen autograph letters from Bellini to Lamperi are now in the Houghton Library of Harvard University.

49. The letter is dated at Milan but postmarked at Cremona and was certainly written at Casalbuttano, which is near the latter: in it, Bellini remarks: "The day after my arrival [in Milan], I left for the country place where I'll remain some days longer."

50. Grosson was a very active member of the Turinese Accademia filarmonica. He achieved some notoriety for his violent opposition to the cacophony that orchestras create when tuning up before playing.

51. Quoted complete by Luzio, *op. cit.*, p. 104.

52. Eventually, by a roundabout route, this contract led to Bellini's composing *La Sonnambula* for Crivelli as co-impresario with Lanari of the Teatro Carcano, Milan. On January 28, 1832, writing to Perucchini from Naples, Bellini explained: "The contract that I made with Crivelli to write an opera for Venice was signed before I wrote *I Capuleti*, and signor Crivelli, in association with signor Lanari, ceded that contract to Marietti [one of the lessees of the Carcano in 1830–1831] for a price of 1500 francs" (BE, pp. 299–300).

53. This publication was listed in Ricordi's catalogue dated October 29, 1829. The title page reads: *Sei ariette per camera—composte e dedicate—alla esimia dilettante—la Sig.ra Marianna Pollini—dal maestro V. Bellini*. The six songs, which appear originally to have been love-offerings to Giuditta Turina despite the perhaps collusive dedication to Marianna Pollini, are: (1) "*Malinconia, ninfa gentile*," (2) "*Vanne, o rosa fortunata*," (3) "*Bella Nice che d'amore*," (4) "*Per pietà, bell'idol mio*," (5) "*Almen se non poss'io*," and (6) "*Mi rendi pur contento*."

54. Perucchini had been born at Bergamo in 1784. An accomplished pianist, he composed *"romanze di camera"* and *"canzonette popolari veneziane,"* some of them with guitar accompaniment, which became popular.

55. For one thing, the role of Imogene had been composed for Méric-Lalande, a soprano, whereas Giuditta Grisi was a mezzo-soprano. Also, Bonfigli was far from being a Rubini or even a Domenico Reina, Pellegrini equally far from being a Tamburini.

56. Letter in the library of the Conservatorio Luigi Cherubini, Florence, quoted in BSLS, p. 229. The fact that Bellini's arrangement was with Lanari rather than Crivelli meant that the earlier contract with Crivelli remained in force, later allowing its transfer to the lessees of the Teatro Carcano, Milan.

57. In Romani's libretto, Juliet's father is called Capellio.

58. The libretto used by Zingarelli had been set as early as 1784 by Luigi Monescalchi; it was the work of Giuseppe Maria Foppa; but another setting of the libretto that Romani had prepared for Vaccaj was staged at the Teatro Eretenio, Vicenza, in the summer of 1828: the *Giulietta e Romeo* of a composer identified only as E. Torriani.

59. LSmdN III, pp. 227–228.

60. Neither Bellini's letter nor Zingarelli's reply appears to survive.

61. BSLS, p. 231.

62. BE, pp. 231–232.

63. BE, pp. 232–233.

64. Although Vaccaj's *Giulietta e Romeo*, to Romani's libretto, had gone on to long-lasting popularity after its première at the Teatro della Canobbiana, Milan, on October 31, 1825 (eighteen performances there that season), Romani may well have felt that he was entirely free merely to touch up the libretto for Bellini: he had never been paid for it.

65. BE, p. 233.

66. That first libretto, in turn, had been based to some extent upon Foppa's treatment of the Romeo and Juliet story as set by Zingarelli; its source had not been Shakespeare so much as Gerolamo Della Corte's *Storie di Verona*. None of these librettos is in any real sense Shakespearean.

67. Bellini's score contains other self-borrowings as well, most notably in Giulietta's first-act romanza, *"Oh! quante volte, oh! quante,"* which is a happy adaptation of Nelly's romanza in Act I of *Adelson e Salvini, "Dopo l'oscuro nembo."*

68. BE, p. 239.

69. Bellini believed that the première would occur on March 10; it actually took place on Thursday, March 11.

70. Giuditta, whose health always was uncertain, had been seriously ill.

71. To the modern question: why did Bellini assign the role of Romeo to a mezzo-soprano rather than to a tenor, several partial answers can be suggested. Many composers both earlier than and contemporary with Bellini felt that characterization of a boy, youth, or very young man could be achieved more convincingly by a contralto, mezzo-soprano, or even soprano than by a post-adolescent male singer. The Romeos of Zingarelli's and Vaccaj's operas both are mezzo-sopranos. Related feelings undoubtedly help to explain—beyond the force of mere tradition—the assigning to a female voice of such roles as Cherubino in *Le Nozze di Figaro*, several

Rossinian male characters (Tancredi, Arsace in *Semiramide*, Malcolm Graeme in *La Donna del lago*, Isolier in *Le Comte Ory*), several in Donizetti operas (Pierotto in *Linda di Chamounix*, Maffio Orsini in *Lucrezia Borgia*, Smeton in *Anna Bolena*), Urbain in Meyerbeer's *Les Huguenots*, Vanya in Glinka's *A Life for the Tsar*, Oscar in Verdi's *Un Ballo in maschera*, Siebel in Gounod's *Faust*, Stéfano in his *Roméo et Juliette*, Frederick in Thomas's *Mignon*, Hänsel in Humperdinck's *Hänsel und Gretel*, Prince Orlovsky in Johann Strauss's *Die Fledermaus*, and Octavian in Richard Strauss's *Der Rosenkavalier*. It was said, also, that Bellini assigned the role of Romeo to a mezzo-soprano to please Giuditta Grisi, then at the brief climax of her vocal prowess, who intensely wanted to sing the role.

72. Only one opera not by Bellini was sung at the Fenice during this season. The work of a young French composer named Albert(o) Guill(i)on, it had been newly composed to a libretto by Gaetano Rossi. That *Maria di Brabante* was sung at the Fenice between *Il Pirata* and *I Capuleti e i Montecchi*.

73. This is one of the astonishingly few comments upon the quality of stage settings in contemporary accounts of early-nineteenth-century Italian operatic performances.

74. Quoted in BE, p. 240, ft. a. For quotations from other press commentaries on *I Capuleti*, see BSLS, pp. 237–239.

75. LSmdN III, p. 191.

76. BE, p. 250.

Chapter VI

1. The obverse of this medal shows a head of Bellini facing left and encircled by this inscription: VINC. BELLINI CATANENSIS MUSICAE ARTIS DECUS. The reverse bears the date 1829 and shows a standing Minerva bearing a wreath in her right hand, a spear and shield in her left, and the inscription: MERITIS QUAESITAM PATRIA. An engraving of the obverse was used as the frontispiece of Cicconetti's VdVB and is reproduced on the title page of the present book.

2. The score, bound in red morocco with gold stamping and gilt edges, is now in the Museo Belliniano. For Bellini's dedicatory inscription in it, see p. 115.

3. The original of this portrait later belonged to Verdi; it is now in the collection at the Verdi house at Sant'Agata. See Plate 3b.

4. The society also included Lanari and Barbaja.

5. BE, p. 252.

6. In terms of 1971 buying power, Bellini had been promised about $4,155 by Crivelli. From the new society, he was to receive about $6,040 outright, and could hope for an additional $1,760 or so from half of the rights in the score, a total of about $7,800.

7. BE, pp. 252–253.

8. Emilia Branca said (*op. cit.*, p. 129) of this doctor, whose name was either Prini or Prina, that he was one of Bellini's "intimate friends" and an "eminent cultivator of music (and later Bellini's personal physician)."

9. Bellini expressed some of his feeling of obligation to Francesco Pollini by dedicating *La Sonnambula* to him.

10. BSLS, p. 249.

11. *Indagini sulle fonti francesi dei libretti di Vincenzo Bellini*, Milan, 1968, p. 450.

12. The Teatro Carcano as it existed in 1830 had opened on September 3, 1803, with Francesco Federici's opera *Zaira*, followed by Zingarelli's *Ines de Castro*.

13. Considerable confusion exists about who lived exactly where, and at what periods, in Moltrasio. With the much-appreciated help of signor Rodolfo Caramazza of Moltrasio, I have been able to determine a few facts. In the center of the village, Ferdinando Turina owned the Villa Salterio, in which Bellini probably spent some time. Bellini also stayed at Moltrasio for considerable periods as the guest of a conte Passalacqua in the Villa Passalacqua, on a hill rising above the lakeshore at the south end of the village. On September 8, 1908, Alessandro Gallone, a later owner of the Villa Salterio, placed on the former Turina house—by then known as the Villa Gallone—a stone incised with words arranged by Antonino Amore: "To the quiet asylum of this pleasant resort, Vincenzo Bellini came for inspiration, and here wrote *La Straniera* and here found the ravishing melodies of *La Sonnambula*. So that posterity may remember the fact, Alessandro Gallone placed [this stone] 1908/Prof. Antonino Amore dictated [this text]." Actually, though Bellini may have sketched or composed parts of *La Sonnambula* while a guest of the Turinas or conte Passalacqua, no indication survives that he had ever stayed in Moltrasio until some time after the first performance of *La Straniera*. When I visited Moltrasio in 1969, the Villa Gallone was inhabited, but the Villa Passalacqua stood empty, though its gardens were flourishing and its fountains playing.

14. In 1825, when Manuel del Popolo Vicente García took to New York the first Italian opera troupe ever to visit there, he invited the Pastas to join it. Giuditta flatly refused, but Giuseppe made the trip, only to fall ill and have to return to Italy six months later. He seems, however to have sung secondary roles in some of the García performances at the Park Theater late in 1825 or early in 1826.

15. BE, pp. 254–255. Letters written at Moltrasio had to be posted at Como.

16. Vincenzo's oldest sister, Michela, had married Ascanio Marziani in 1827; presumably, she no longer required support by her father. In 1829, the third of the brothers, Francesco, had married Rosa Rossi; he no longer lived with his parents and probably had become self-supporting.

17. The tarì of the Kingdom of the Two Sicilies was equivalent to about eighty-five one-hundredths of the then existing Sicilian lira. In 1971 purchasing power, six tarì would be about $1.50.

18. The onza was equivalent to 12.75 of the then existing Sicilian lira. In 1971 purchasing power, thirty onze would equal approximately $227.

19. Two months before writing this letter to his brother, Bellini had worked out two very favorable contracts for the coming year, and they in addition to other arrangements signed earlier.

20. BSLS, p. 258; see also p. 87 above. Pastura was able to read canceled passages of this letter through the ink that had been used to cross them out.

He believed that the deletions had been made by Vincenzo Ferlito in response to a request from Bellini that the financial matters under discussion be kept secret between them.

21. Another canceled passage in the letter *(op. cit.)* reads: ". . . therefore, if some misfortune should come to me, or if I should not have further success [with] operas, or if another physical ailment should leave me unable to compose more, I should be left in misery; whereas if I succeed in putting aside a hundred thousand francs [about $60,000 in 1971 buying power], I assure the . . ."

22. Pasta had sung at the Carcano for the first time on April 21, 1829, in Rossini's *Semiramide* (with Marietta Brambilla as Arsace). She had also been heard there as Rossini's Tancredi (a travesty role, with Stefania Favelli as Amenaide) on May 8, 1829; in Rossini's *Otello* (May 24), in her renowned impersonation of Medea in Mayr's *Medea in Corinto* (June 21), and in Vaccaj's *Giulietta e Romeo* (July 31).

23. Quoted in LSmdN III, p. 195, ft. 1.

24. Mercadante evidently failed to extract the long-awaited libretto from Romani: the next Romani text that he set was the *Zaira* that Bellini had set earlier. Mercadante's *Zaira* was first heard at the Teatro San Carlo, Naples, on August 31, 1831, and was a considerable success.

25. Few of the qualities that brought *Hernani* its central position in the annals of contemporary politics and of literary romanticism survive in the libretto that Francesco Maria Piave wrote for Verdi's *Ernani*, which was first sung in Austrian-controlled Venice on March 9, 1844. The provenance of that libretto nonetheless had to be disguised on several occasions: Verdi's opera was staged at Palermo in 1845 as *Elvira d'Aragona* and at Naples in 1847 as *Il Corsaro di Venezia*, both times with consequent alterations in the text as sung.

26. BE, p. 256.

27. BE, pp. 259–260.

28. B:Mel, p. 392.

29. VB:V, p. 136, ft. 1.

30. Bellini's letter to Romani is in BE, pp. 319–320; that to Barbò in BE, pp. 318–319.

31. "La Straniera *a Bergamo, ovvero Pietosa Storia di Una Balena a Milano,*" in the *Rivista del Comune di Catania*, September–October 1934, p. 288. The quoted sentence from Bellini's letter of August 3, 1830, is in BE, p. 260.

32. In that letter, furthermore, Bellini mentions that *La Straniera* had been scheduled for "Saturday, the 14th of the current month," i.e., August. In 1830, August 14 was a Saturday; in 1832 it was not.

33. In the cited article. Luisa Cambi again reprinted the article from *L'Eco* in BE, p. 259, ft. 1.

34. Luisa Cambi noted (BE, pp. 259–260, ft. 1) that in *Le Comte de Monte-Cristo*, Dumas wrote of "the famous Henri, who as a choreographer, had made a colossal reputation in Italy, which the unhappy man came to lose in a nautical theater." The ballet given with the première of *La Sonnambula* on March 6, 1831, *Tutto al contrario*, was choreographed by Henry.

35. Quoted in BE, p. 259, ft. 1.

36. BE, p. 259.

37. The cast included Favelli (Alaide), Filotea Reina (Isoletta), Domenico Reina (Arturo), and Giovanni Giordani (Valdeburgo); two of Donizetti's particular friends, Pietro Rovelli and Antonio Dolci, acted, respectively, as director (first violinist) of the orchestra and chorusmaster. In a letter dated at Como on August 30, 1830, to conte Ottaviano Tasca, Bellini said: "Advise Giordani to take *un poco più mosso* the tempo of his aria at the words '~~Vieni tu meco!~~ Meco tu vieni,' etc., as that is the only fault that can be charged against him, and to sing the rest as he conceives it." The letter was first published in Niny Ganguzza's "*Inediti Belliniani: Agosto 1830—'La Straniera' a Bergamo,*" in *L'Opera*, V, 16–17, Milan, 1970.

38. BE, pp. 262–263.

39. No letters from Bellini are available between that of August 24, 1830, to conte Ottaviano Tasca, from Como (transcribed and reproduced in fac-simile in *L'Opera*, Milan, V, 1969, Nos. 16/17, pp. 24–26), and one of November 10, 1830, to Giovanni Battista Perucchini, from Milan (quoted in BSLS pp. 254–255). Pastura wrote (BSLS, p. 255, ft. 1) that Bellini was in Milan from September on, a statement that I have been unable to document. The possibility certainly exists that he went from Bergamo to Milan and then to either Moltrasio or Casalbuttano before returning to Milan again on November 8.

40. BE, p. 254.

41. Quoted in full by Franco Schlitzer in "*Nell'intimità di Vincenzo Bellini: Lettere inedite sparse o disperse,*" in *Il Mattino d'Italia*, Naples, June 8, 1951; reprinted in Schlitzer's *Tommaso Traetta, Leonardo Leo, Vincenzo Bellini*, Siena, 1952, pp. 63-64. In his *Mondo teatrale dell'Ottocento* (Naples, 1954, p. 14), Schlitzer asserted that the libretto not yet begun was that of the opera with which Bellini and Romani had decided to replace *Ernani*. But the decision to drop *Ernani* was not arrived at until December.

42. The Pierpont Morgan Library, New York, has an eighteen-page full orches-tral score in Bellini's autograph which its preceding owners had described as having been in a paper wrapper on which had been written "*Sinfonia dall'opera Ernani donata a Giuditta Pasta da Vincenzo Bellini,*" the hand-writing not having been that of Pasta, her husband, or Bellini. For a dis-cussion of this autograph, see p. 260. Although the possibility must be recognized that this music, which uses melodic ideas that also appear in *Bianca e Fernando*, was in fact intended to prelude *Ernani*, proof probably always will be lacking. Also, its likelihood is undermined somewhat by the fact that the paper on which the score was written is watermarked CANSELL 1831, whereas the decision to abandon *Ernani* was made in Decem-ber 1830. If, however, this music in fact was intended for *Ernani*, another bare possibility must be considered: that, despite evidence to the contrary, and while still lacking any of Romani's text, Bellini in the late summer, autumn, or early winter of 1830, composed it then for that purpose.

43. BE, pp. 265–266.

44. Writing from France to Giovanni Ricordi on June 14, 1834, Bellini would refer (BE, p. 407) to "*Hernani,* which was prohibited." For Florimo's references to Bellini's *Ernani*—he published three differing versions of an anecdote related to it—see Appendix C, p. 394.

45. BSLS, pp. 256–276.
46. Hugo's *Hernani* became the source of several later opera librettos, including those of Vincenzo Gabussi's *Ernani* (libretto by Gaetano Rossi, 1834); Alberto Mazzucatto's *Hernani* (libretto by Domenico Bancalari, 1843, not quite eleven weeks before the première of Verdi's greatly more successful opera); Verdi's *Ernani* (libretto by Francesco Maria Piave, 1844); and Henri Hirschman's *Hernani* (libretto by G. Ribet, 1908).
47. The frequently repeated assertion that Bellini's chief reason for wanting to drop *Ernani* was his wish not to challenge the popular success of Donizetti's *Anna Bolena* with another *opera seria* is unfounded.
48. For information and speculation about Giuseppina Appiani's age and the identity of her husband, see Frank Walker: *The Man Verdi*, London and New York, 1962, pp. 100–103.
49. *Il Salotto della contessa Maffei*, 4th edn., Milan, 1895, pp. 101–102.
50. BSLS, p. 278.
51. Bellini apparently moved in 1832 to quarters shared only with his manservant, Giovanni. These were in the contrada dei Tre Monasteri and were furnished during that summer. This was the apartment that he closed up when he departed for London in April 1833; its furnishings are detailed in a list now at the Museo Belliniano. These included a carpet embroidered with large bouquets of flowers; in each of its corners, surrounded by laurels, appeared the name of one of his operas first staged in Milan: *Il Pirata, La Straniera, La Sonnambula*, and *Norma*. It had been a gift from several of his female Milanese friends. Also in those quarters was a bedside carpet said to have been cross-stitched by Giuditta Turina: it showed a popular depiction of the final scene of *La Straniera*.
52. BE, p. 267.
53. Letter at the Villa Sant'Agata in an album that belonged to Verdi. Quoted in full in BSLS, p. 280.
54. The Charavay catalogue listed a letter of February 26, 1831, from Bellini to Giuseppe Ruggeri and stated that the remark about the production of *La Sonnambula* occurred in it. The present whereabouts of the letter is not known.
55. See Bellini's letter of June 1834 to Giovanni Ricordi (Pougin: *Bellini*, etc., p. 147, in French translation, and BE, p. 407, Amore's translation of that translation) for Bellini's statement that he had composed *La Sonnambula* between January 11 and March 6, 1831, a total of fifty-four days. Three years after the event, he had forgotten his own statement that he began the introduction on January 2. Also, in giving the day of the opera's première as the terminal date of its composition, he was surely mistaken.
56. *Op. cit.*, pp. 163–164, and *Vincenzo Bellini: Note aneddotiche e critiche*, Ancona, 1882, p. 71.
57. See p. 537 for two of the alternate texts as quoted by Emilia Branca.
58. In assaying the credibility of Emilia Branca's report, it is essential to remember that she did not marry Romani until 1844 and wrote her book in 1881–1882, fifty years after the dress rehearsal so circumstantially described. But Bellini well may have been recalling doubts about the text of *"Ah! non giunge"* when, on September 27, 1834, writing to Giovanni Ricordi from

Paris, he said (BSLS, p. 430): "The first act of *La Sonnambula* was greatly preferred to the second at the rehearsals; then, at the Carcano, the latter, instead, succeeded in producing almost more effect than the first."

59. BE, p. 268.

60. Friendly with Bellini and Lamperi, De Angelis is mentioned in several of Bellini's letters, for the last time in April 1835.

61. *Mikhail Ivanovich Glinka/Memoirs.* Translated from the Russian by Richard B. Mudge, Norman, 1963, p. 61. Glinka also wrote (*op. cit.,* p. 72): "In the spring [1832] I . . . started work on a serenade based on a theme from *La Sonnambula,* for piano, two violins, viola, cello, and bass. I dedicated this piece to one of Pollini's pupils, who performed it very nicely in July of 1832, accompanied by the best musicians in Milan."

62. Evgeni Petrovich Shterich (1808–1833), a friend of Glinka, was an amateur composer.

63. Quoted in BE, pp. 268–269.

64. BE, pp. 269–270.

65. BE, p. 272.

66. BSLS, pp. 281–282, where its source is not specified; it is dated March 4.

67. BSLS, pp. 282–283.

68. "1831" was added to this dating by someone else (see photograph of the letter following p. 272 of BE), but that it is correct is made sure by the contents, for which see BE, pp. 275–276.

69. BE, pp. 273–274.

70. Federico Girard (who was succeeded by Guglielmo Cottrau) was then the most important publisher of music in the Kingdom of the Two Sicilies. He operated from Naples, where he died in 1877.

71. See pp. 103–104.

72. The Carcano season had closed with *La Sonnambula* on March 23 and *Anna Bolena* on March 25.

73. BE, p. 274.

74. *Norma,* Alexandre Soumet's five-act *tragédie,* had had its very successful première at the Théâtre de l'Odéon, Paris, on April 16, 1831, when the principal roles had been acted by Mlle George (Norma), Alexandrine Noblet (Adalgise), Lockroi (Pollion), and Éric-Bernard (Orovèse). See pp. 276 and 526–527 for other sources of Romani's *Norma.*

75. Rubini had been born in 1795 near Bergamo (at Romano), Donzelli in 1790 in Bergamo itself.

76. Quoted in BSLS, p. 287.

77. Quoted in BSLS, pp. 287–288.

78. A letter dated at Como on July 30 is to Luigi Remondini (for it, see Frank Walker: "*Lettere disperse e inedite di Vincenzo Bellini,*" in the *Rivista del Comune di Catania,* October–December 1960, pp. 6–8). Remondini, a Milanese acquaintance, had written Bellini to ask him, in the name of a conte Ritorni, to send him autobiographical data (see Appendix D, p. 397, for complete translation of this letter). The other, dated at Como on August 19 (Walker, *op. cit.,* p. 8), is to Giuseppe Bornaccini, a friend of Bellini and Florimo in their Neapolitan student days, who had written for assistance in securing a contract to compose an opera.

79. BE, p. 278.

80. BE, p. 278. Evidently these figurines were costumed as the characters in Soumet's *Norma*.

81. BE, p. 280. Now in the library of the Naples Conservatory, this is a draft rather than a posted letter. See Pastura: *Lettere di Bellini (1819–1835)*, Catania, 1935, p. 118, ft. 2, for his argument that it cannot have been intended, as Antonino Amore stated, for Filippo Santocanale, whom Bellini first met during his 1832 visit to Palermo.

82. Here Bellini crossed out the phrase "I have taken on the new fatigue of . . ."

83. BE, p. 281.

84. The letter to Giuditta Turina cited above is dated at Milan; in a letter to Florimo dated September 19 at Como, Bellini wrote: "I find myself in these regions; but next Wednesday or Thursday at the latest I'll be in Milan, where I'll continue to compose as I am composing here." Another letter to Florimo, now in the Pierpont Morgan Library, New York, is dated from Milan on September 24.

85. BE, pp. 282–284.

86. At one time, Marianna Lewis, who was English, had studied with Pasta in Paris. As early as 1827, *I Teatri*, Milan (September 13, p. 357), had described her voice as "tired, weak, and cold."

87. When *I Capuleti e i Montecchi* was staged at the San Carlo on November 29, 1831, Romeo was sung, not by Marianna Lewis, but, as Bellini wished, by Giuseppina Ronzi de Begnis.

88. BE, pp. 283–284.

89. BE, pp. 284–286.

90. Equivalent to about $6,000 in 1971 purchasing power.

91. Equivalent to about $7,500 in 1971 purchasing power.

92. That is, the page announcing the singers, librettists, composers, and sometimes other participants in the operas of a forthcoming season.

93. Bellini's annual summer intestinal difficulties were probably on his mind.

94. A few short interims excepted, Barbaja continued as impresario for the Neapolitan royal theaters until 1840.

95. Because Amore believed that Bellini composed *Norma* at Casalbuttano, in 1901 he devised the inscription that was cut into a stone placed on the façade of the Casalbuttano *palazzo municipale*, the building in which the Turinas had lived. That inscription proclaimed his belief as a fact. But Bellini is very unlikely to have spent time at Casalbuttano while composing *Norma*. None of his surviving letters of the period mentions the place. As those letters are few, however, a bare possibility exists that he spent some days at Casalbuttano late in October or early in November.

96. Letter in the library of the Naples Conservatory.

97. Mercadante was in Turin to prepare the performance of his new opera, *I Normanni a Parigi*—which, however, did not reach its première at the Teatro Regio until February 7, 1832.

98. Pp. 579–580, quoted in BE, p. 287.

99. Quoted in Amore: VB:V, pp. 311–312.

100. *L'Eco*, Milan, October 21, 1831, p. 504, quoted in BE, p. 288, ft. 1.

101. Stefano Pavesi's *La Donna bianca d'Avenello*, to a libretto by Gaetano Rossi, had been heard for the first time at the Teatro della Canobbiana, Milan, on November 13, 1830.

102. *Op cit.*, p. 84. Earlier, Bellini had struggled to persuade Romani to recast many of the verses in his libretto. The first version of *"Casta diva,"* for example, had been delivered to Bellini in this form:

> Casta diva, che inargenti
> questo suol con vergin volto,
> nel tenace umor raccolto
> spandi influssi di virtù.
> Sia quel balsamo alle genti
> che le piaghe disacerbi
> che costanti ancor le serbi
> in si lunga servitù.

Only after Bellini rejected those lines as unsatisfactory did Romani produce the lines finally set. Seven different autograph versions have survived of the Pollione–Adalgisa duet lines.

103. Bellini originally composed *"Casta diva"* in G, but from the beginning it was customarily lowered a whole tone, to F.

104. BSLS, p. 295, where a footnote reports that the objects survived as properties of a Martinez family in Catania; they are now in the Museo Belliniano.

105. *Il Corsaro*, with a libretto by Jacopo Ferretti, has been staged for the first time at the Teatro Apollo, Rome, on January 15, 1831; its La Scala première occurred on January 10, 1832.

106. *La Vendetta*, with a libretto by Calisto Bassi, had its first performance at La Scala on February 11, 1832. Pugni is now remembered only for some excerpts from his more than three hundred ballet scores.

107. *Ugo, conte di Parigi*, the first singing of which took place at La Scala on March 13, 1832.

108. Giulia (often Giulietta) Grisi (1811–1869), a younger sister of Giuditta Grisi, became the leading Italian operatic prima donna of the era after Pasta and Maria Malibran.

109. In fact, Grisi sang in both *Norma* and *Il Corsaro*. The La Scala season also included thirteen performances of Rossini's *Otello*, with Donzelli in the title role and Pasta as Desdemona, and one performance of his *L'Inganno felice*. Between December 26, 1831, and the close of the season early in April 1832, both Grisi and Donzelli sang in sixty-two performances, Vincenzo Negrini in fifty-nine, and Pasta in fifty-one.

110. The role of Adalgisa, who is younger, not older, than Norma, is now unfortunately almost always sung by a mezzo-soprano or even a contralto, though it was composed by Bellini for a soprano.

111. Bellini jettisoned some of his original conception of the role of Oroveso —which, for example, was to have included, in the finale, a cabaletta denouncing Norma—because Negrini suffered from a weak heart and had to conserve his strength.

112. BE, pp. 290–291. No autograph of this letter is known to exist. It was published in French translation in 1868 by Arthur Pougin (*Bellini: Sa Vie, ses œuvres*, Paris, 1868, pp. 112–114), with a note that it had been communicated to him "with charming good grace by cavaliere Francesco

Florimo. . . ." Florimo in turn published it in Italian in 1882 (B:Mel, pp. 31–32 and pages 397–398—two versions differing in orthography), with this footnote (p. 32): "To the cavaliere Temple, brother of Lord Palmerston, who was then Minister of Her Britannic Majesty at Naples, I gave this autograph letter from Bellini, contenting myself, so as to do something pleasing to that lofty personage, with keeping a simple copy for myself." Luisa Cambi wrote (BE, p. 290, ft. 1): "This letter probably was retouched and prettified by Florimo; but not invented; to demonstrate that, it would be enough to cite . . . the note reported here above; Florimo would not have named such important people. What is more, as I have said, Pougin showed that he knew the letter as early as 1868." The authenticity of the letter is unquestionable; but its phraseology as we now know it is almost certainly apocryphal.

113. *L'Olimpiade,* setting a libretto by Metastasio, was notoriously unsuccessful at its Roman première (Teatro Tordinona, January 8, 1735), but then became popular; it is regarded as the finest of Pergolesi's *opere serie.*

114. Bellini was about to leave Milan for Naples and Sicily.

115. Pougin's translation is remarkably close to the Italian version published fourteen years later by Florimo. Some details differ: where Florimo has ". . . e spero arrivare prima della presente," Pougin's translation reads: ". . . et j'espère arriver à Naples avant la présente"; where Florimo has ". . . ricevi un abbraccio dal tuo affezionatissimo Bellini," Pougin reads: ". . . reçois un baiser de Ton affectionné Bellini."

116. BE, p. 292.

117. Cicconetti (1859) reported (VdVB, pp. 61–62) that when he asked Pacini about Bellini's reaction to the first reception of *Norma,* Pacini answered: "I saw Bellini in Milan again under the circumstances in which he put on his masterpiece, *Norma,* and I well remember that at the first, second, and third performances, that sublime work had an almost hapless reception, which afflicted the young composer, and I saw him shed some tears." Charity might suggest that perhaps, some twenty-seven years after the event being discussed, Pacini's memory had dimmed about the audience reactions at the second and third performances of *Norma.*

118. BE, p. 292.

119. Both ballets had been choreographed by Antonio Cortesi. Despite Bellini's stricture about them, *I Pazzi per progetto* was danced fifty-one times that season, *Merope* forty-one.

120. BE, p. 292.

121. In letters of December 31 to Perucchini and Giuseppe Ruggeri (BE, pp. 296–298), Bellini substantially repeated the points about the *Norma* performances made in his letter of December 28 to Vincenzo Ferlito.

122. At the Teatro degli Accademici Filodrammatici in an opera by her teacher, Giuseppe Scappa.

123. Born a Countess Pahlen in Russia in 1803, the contessa Samoyloff died in Paris in 1875 after an extraordinarily variegated life.

124. BE, p. 296.

125. For supposed comments by Donizetti on the first four performances of *Norma,* see Appendix E, p. 399.

126. Glinka, *op. cit.,* p. 204.

Chapter VII

1. Bellini left Milan unaccompanied on January 5, and Cicconetti reported (VdVB, p. 64) that one Fabio Cavalletti had told him of finding Bellini the only passenger in a carriage bound for Rome from Foligno. Giuditta Turina and Gaetano Cantù traveled to Naples in their private carriage.
2. BdVB, p. 16.
3. LSmdN III, p. 204.
4. BSLS, p. 312.
5. BSLS, p. 312. Now in the Museo Belliniano, Catania.
6. The ailing sixty-year-old Scott, ordered to recuperate in Italy, had reached Naples in December 1831. Donizetti almost certainly was there too in January 1832, and the fact that either he or Bellini could have met Scott leads to fascinating idle speculation because each of them was to produce a "Scottish" opera in 1835: respectively, *Lucia di Lammermoor* and *I Puritani*, the former based on a Scott novel, the latter influenced indirectly by Scott's popularity.
7. In a letter of October 29, 1827, to Vincenzo Ferlito, Bellini had asked his uncle to pass some news on to "D. Tatà Zappalà," evidently another Catanese. In 1876, a Carlo Zappalà Scammacca published a semifictional *Vincenzo Bellini* at Catania. I have not been able to identify Fortunato Giardina.
8. See p. 87 for information about the medal ordered by the decurionate of Catania from Sebastiano Puglisi after the success of *La Straniera*.
9. This clearly had to do with Bellini's forthcoming visit to Sicily.
10. VdVB, p. 68.
11. One of the king's brothers.
12. Possibly Bellini had Giuditta Turina with him and did not want to flaunt her presence in the theater.
13. BE, p. 300.
14. In his letter of February 3, Bellini told his uncle that he had decided not to embark for Palermo on February 10 because doing so might necessitate his spending seventeen or eighteen days en route to Catania; he would take the steamer for Messina on February 25—if, indeed, it would sail then: the steamer that had been scheduled to sail from Naples on January 25 was still being held there by stormy weather as he wrote.
15. BE, p. 304.
16. BE, pp. 301–302.
17. Letter not in BE. For it, see Marcello Conati: *"Lettere di musicisti dell' 1800: Vincenzo Bellini,"* in *L'Opera*, II, 5, Milan, October–December 1966, p. 99.
18. BE, p. 483.
19. CssSmdN III, p. 744.
20. The fullest (not entirely reliable) sources of information on Bellini's stay in Messina are: Giuseppe Arenaprimo, barone di Montechiaro: *"Bellini a Messina,"* in *Omaggio a Bellini nel primo centenario dalla sua nascita*, Catania, 1901, pp. 237–246, and Nitto Scaglione: *Vincenzo Bellini a Messina*, Messina, 1934.

21. Arenaprimo mentions as among them: Giuseppe La Farina, Vincenzo Amore, Felice Bisazza (see p. 468), Giuseppe and Carlo Falconieri, Letterio Stagno, Giacomo Rol, Gaetano Grano, Carlo Gemelli, barone Placido Arenaprimo, Domenico Ventimiglia, Giuseppe Morelli, Antonio Catara, Anastasio Cocco, Giuseppe Monasta, Domenico Pavone, abate Giovanni Saccano, and Riccardo Mitchell.

22. The cast included Angelina Borroni (Imogene), Elena Alessandri (Adele), Giovanni Francesco Boccaccini (Gualtiero), Giovanni [Johann] Schober [lechner] (Ernesto), and Matteo Buonconsiglio (Itulbo).

23. La Farina: *Elogio del Cavaliere Vincenzo Bellini letto nell'Accademia Peloritana il giorno 26 novembre 1835*, Messina, 1835.

24. *Op. cit.*, p. 245.

25. In *"Musica e musicisti,"* in the *Archivio storico messinese*, 1918–1919, pp. 158–159 (reprinted by Nitto Scaglione in *Vincenzo Bellini a Messina*, pp. 6–7), Leopoldo Nicotra wrote: "In speaking of Bellini in relationship to Messina, it is proper to refer to a musical composition attributed to the great master and performed in this city for so many years in the church of the Padri Crociferi. I still have an arrangement of it consisting of the complete part for 'two sopranos' and a few hints at the organ accompaniment. This is the 'Seven Words' of Jesus, and in it one truly senses the composer of 'Giulietta e Romeo.' When playing it, I always have showed my admiration for this truly felt work, saying that if the music is not by Bellini, it is by someone who certainly had something in common with the Swan of Catania. It was said that when very young, Vincenzo Bellini was assisted financially by a pious Catanese lady, who thereafter induced him to compose the music, giving it to the Padri Crociferi in that city. I am certain that the Catanese Crocifero, Padre Corsaro . . . brought it from Catania to our city." This is, of course, the *Versetti da cantarsi il Venerdì Santo*, for two tenors (not sopranos) and organ. See pp. 10 and 385.

26. The trip occupied three days because no coastal road was then available: the Messina–Catania route was very indirect and in part clambered across the lower slopes of Mount Etna.

27. Bellini also made short trips to places on the Etna slopes, very probably to show them to Florimo. On one such trip, he stopped in Maugeri at the home of his cousin Pasquale Bellini (a son of his father's brother Carlo). There he played through *Norma* on a piano now in the Museo Belliniano.

28. Because Pietro Antonio Coppola had left Catania a few months earlier, the city had no operatic conductor. Had Coppola remained available, a frustrated plan to present *La Sonnambula* in Bellini's honor might have been carried out.

29. The spring 1831 season had consisted of Donizetti's *L'Esule di Roma*, Coppola's *Artale d'Aragona*, and Bellini's *La Straniera*, all with Coppola conducting.

30. *Omaggio, op. cit.*, pp. 249–250. In a footnote, Menza thanked "my cultured friend avv. Antonio Ursino-Recupero" for the historical data in his article, not all of which are accurate.

31. Bellini introduced his father to the audience, whereupon the applause increased greatly.

32. *Elogio biografico del Cav. Vincenzo Bellini, scritto in occasione del trasporto delle sue ceneri da Parigi a Catania,* Catania, 1876, p. 137, ft. 141.
33. BSLS, p. 326.
34. These "poems," together with Mario Musumeci's flatulent introductory speech, are reprinted in *Omaggio, op. cit.,* pp. 251–263.
35. On April 10, 1872, one Franco Abate wrote from Catania to ask Florimo for a copy of the recently issued Vol. I of CssSmdN, containing a biography of Bellini. In the letter (now in the Naples Conservatory library), Abate said: "In April 1832, we made the trip from here to Palermo together; there was the never sufficiently lamented Bellini; there were Angelo Urzì [probably either a relative of Bellini's paternal grandmother, whose name was variously spelled Urzì, Burzì, Wirzì, Virzì, and Borzì, and/or of his aunt Agata Urzì Ferlito, the wife of his uncle Francesco], Carmelo Ferlito, his uncle and aunt, a Dominican, and I. I have never been able to forget thàt period, very beautiful for a hundred reasons. . . ." Carmelo [sometimes Carmine] Ferlito was Bellini's first cousin, a son of Francesco Ferlito; the "uncle and aunt" were Vincenzo Ferlito and his wife, Sara.
36. BE, pp. 307–309. Pastura surmised that this lady was the daughter of Ignazio Giuffrida-Moschetti (see p. 109 for the letter probably addressed to him by his nephew, an otherwise unidentified "Giovanni"). The Giuffrida family evidently had been on intimate terms with Bellini and Florimo in Catania. Except for the address and two brief postscripts, the letter of April 16 was written by Florimo. It is signed *"Florimo e Bellini."*
37. Letter in the Biblioteca Nazionale Vittorio Emanuele, Rome.
38. Santocanale, who lived to an advanced age, was also a close friend of Rossini.
39. On the façade of the building at number 272 in the present via Marqueda (formerly the strada Nuova), a commemorative incised stone, its wording almost certainly Santocanale's, reads: "Vincenzo Bellini, the Angel of Music, was received and welcomed as a guest in this house, the year 1832."
40. *La Cerere,* Palermo, April 12, 1832.
41. In *Omagio, op. cit.,* p. 266.
42. The program performed that evening by the dilettantes of the Accademia filarmonica was in two sections: I. 1. Introduction and duet from *La Straniera*; 2. Duet from *Il Pirata*; 3. Theme and Variations for pianoforte by Czerny; 4. Duet *"Serba, serba, i tuoi segreti,"* from *La Straniera*; 5. Finale from *I Capuleti e i Montecchi* (as this last was sung by five singers, it must have been the finale of Act I). II. 1. Concerto for pianoforte by Moscheles; 2. Duet from *I Capuleti e i Montecchi*; 3. Duet from *Bianca e Gernando*; 4. Concerto for pianoforte by Hummel; 5. Finale of *Il Pirata* (again, as five singers took part, certainly the finale of Act I).
43. *Omaggio, op. cit.,* p. 267.
44. During the 1901 centenary celebrations of Bellini's birth, an incised stone was set into a wall in the entrance corridor of the Palermo Conservatory. The inscription, written by Guardione, reads: "On the 14th day of April 1832—Vincenzo Bellini—fêted guest of Palermo—visiting this institute—inspired in the young lovers of melody—the sublime ideals of the art—a sure omen of the new greatness of Italy."
45. BE, p. 308.

46. See Plate 4a. Patania later made a lithographic version of this portrait.
47. In *"Prime Scintille del genio di Vincenzo Bellini di Catania,"* in *L'Olivuzza*, *op. cit.*, p. 52.
48. Bellini retained happy memories of this group, to which he referred later as "the old guard," as well as by the slang or dialect word *conciaroti*, to which widely varying meanings have been attributed, one of them being "bordello patrons."
49. BE, p. 311.
50. BE, p. 311.
51. The letter mentioned appears to have disappeared. However, in a letter to Vincenzo Ferlito of April 28, 1832, now in the Pierpont Morgan Library, New York, Bellini specified that whereas Lanari originally had offered him only 8,000 francs, he now had fattened the offer to 12,000.
52. Lanari was then administering the Teatro della Pergola at Florence.
53. Mamma Rachele was Giuditta Pasta's mother, Rachele Negri; Clelia was the Pastas' fourteen-year-old daughter.
54. Giuseppe Pasta evidently had written Bellini that the tally of *Norma* performances at La Scala had risen to thirty-four.
55. Another Bellini letter dated at Naples on April 28, 1832, is to Giovanni Ricordi. It is not in BE. The autograph is in the British Museum. Dealing largely with the agitated problem of pirated versions of *La Sonnambula*, the letter is quoted complete in BSLS, p. 336.
56. In the letter of April 28, 1832, written from Naples to Vincenzo Ferlito, cited in note 51 above, Bellini wrote that he intended to leave Naples "within ten days," an intention that he clearly carried out.
57. Alberto Cametti, a tireless researcher into Roman operatic lore, could produce no reports of it beyond the passing references by Cicconetti and Florimo.
58. Antonino Amore wrote (*Belliniana*, Catania, 1902, p. 107): "I recall having seen it gleam on his [Santocanale's] chest when, a venerable old man, he came to Catania [1876] to render more solemn by his presence the sad ceremony of the homecoming of the mortal remains of his beloved friend."
59. *Bellini a Roma*, Rome, 1900, pp. 18–19.
60. Probably Filippo Co[l]lini, 1811–1863, the future great Verdi baritone. A Roman, he had made his first public appearance in a concert of the Accademia filarmonica romana in 1831.
61. Teresa Terzetti, the wife of Jacopo Ferretti.
62. Giuliani wrote librettos that were set by—among others—the Verdi imitator Antonio Buzzi.
63. Unless Cametti was referring to a return of *La Straniera* to the stage of the Apollo after Easter, these dates appear to be one of his rare mistakes. He himself, earlier in the same essay (p. 8), refers to the intention of the Apollo's impresario to put *La Straniera* on as "the third opera of the 1832 Carnival"; he also (p. 9) gives the date of its first Roman performance as February 18. The Easter of 1832 fell on April 22; Carnival therefore ended on March 6—for which reason the "third opera of the 1832 Carnival" cannot have been given first as late as April 30. In any case, the first Roman *La Straniera* occurred on February 18, 1832.
64. BE, p. 314.

65. *Enciclopedia della Musica UTET*, Turin, 1966, note on p. 464.
66. This letter was incomplete as published by Florimo (B:Mel, pp. 398–399) and in BE, p. 312. The entire text is reprinted in BSLS, pp. 337–338.
67. At the Teatro della Pergola, of which Lanari was acting impresario. This production of *La Sonnambula* had first been heard there on May 13, when the chief roles had been sung by Rosalbina Caradori-Allan (Amina), Giuseppina Merola (Lisa), Gilbert-Louis Duprez (Elvino), and Celestino Salvatori (Rodolfo). For a review of that performance from the *Giornale di commercio*, Florence, of May 16, 1832, see BSLS, p. 339.
68. Crivelli, with whom Bellini had signed a contract for a Venice opera, had died in 1831. Lanari had thereafter acquired the contract from Crivelli's heirs, and at Florence was merely substituting a new arrangement for the old one.
69. Giacomo Zamboni was director of the copying office at the Teatro La Fenice, Venice.
70. BE, pp. 315–316.
71. BE, p. 316.
72. *La Stagione d'opera alla Fiera di Agosto (1784–1936)*, Teatro Donizetti (*già Riccardi*), Bergamo, 1937.
73. Other members of that summer troupe at the Riccardi included Brigida Lorenzani, Erminia Gebauer, Elena Fanny, Carolina Franchini, Vincenzo Negrini (who sang Oroveso in *Norma*), and Edoardo Spech. Pietro Rovelli served as first violin and director of the orchestra, Vincenzo Schira as *maestro dei cori*.
74. BE, pp. 318–319.
75. A review of the Bergamo performance in *L'Eco*, Milan, of September 3, 1832, p. 424, fully bears out Bellini's description of it. Passages from that review are quoted in BE, pp. 318–319, in several footnotes.
76. BE, pp. 319–321.
77. Giovanni Simone Mayr (1763–1845), born Johann Simon Mayr in Bavaria, was a very talented and successful composer of operas (*La Rosa bianca e la rosa rossa*, *Medea in Corinto*, etc.); he served as *maestro di cappella* at Bergamo and was the first musical instructor and lifelong friend of Donizetti. He had been the first composer to set a Romani libretto: *La Rosa bianca e la rosa rossa* (1813).
78. BE, p. 323.

Chapter VIII

1. Letter not in BE; quoted in full in BSLS, pp. 348–349.
2. This probably refers to Almerinda Manzocchi, who created roles in three of Donizetti's operas, rather than to her less prominent sister, Eloisa. Both Manzocchis had sung in the 1826 première of *Bianca e Gernando*.
3. Letter not in BE; quoted in full in BSLS, pp. 353–356.
4. BE, p. 324.
5. When Dumas's play was restaged in 1841, it was retitled *Christine, ou Stockholm et Fontainebleau*.
6. Pasta had gone to Paris late in October to sing at the Théâtre-Italien.

7. *Beatrice di Tenda*, a ballet choreographed by the Milanese ex-*ballerino* Antonio Monticini, had been danced between the acts of Mercadante's opera *Donna Caritea* at the opening of La Scala on September 15, 1832. It was to be performed thirty-nine times that season, always coupled with an opera.

8. Even before the final decision to drop the Dumas subject was made, Romani may have dashed off a few verses for *Beatrice di Tenda* so that Bellini could show them to Pasta. As for Dumas's *Christine*, Romani would take up the subject again in 1853, writing as his last libretto a *Cristina di Svezia* for the pianist-composer Sigismond Thalberg. The Romani-Thalberg opera was staged at the Kärntnertortheater, Vienna, on June 3, 1855, with Giuseppina Medori in the title role. The libretto is discussed in Mario Rinaldi's *Felice Romani*, Rome, 1965, p. 481.

9. The occasion was reported in *L'Eco*, November 26, 1832, with mention of "the mastery of a Bellini, who accompanied her [Pasta]."

10. The *Gazzetta privilegiata di Venezia*, December 11, 1832.

11. See page 154 for Giuditta Turina's comment about this gossip in a letter that she wrote to Florimo on February 19, 1834.

12. BE, p. 329.

13. BE, p. 330.

14. Not in BE; quoted complete in BSLS, pp. 358–359.

15. VB, p. 301.

16. Zavadini, *op. cit.*, p. 304.

17. The contessa Giulia Samoyloff, with reference to Pacini? Or Giuditta Turina—who seems to have played no active role in the strained relations between Bellini and Romani? Or even Giuseppina Appiani?

18. Articles of December 27, 1832, and January 11, 1833.

19. BE, p. 331.

20. BE, p. 333.

21. This was the unfortunate Alberico Curioni, whose noted good looks greatly exceeded his talents as a singer.

22. Not in BE; published in facsimile in Franco Abbiati: "*L'Incorreggibile Vincenzillo*," in *La Scala: Rivista de l'opera*, 5, Milan, March 15, 1950; complete transcription in BSLS, p. 364.

23. BE, pp. 334–335.

24. A (tentative) postponement to March 2 had been announced for the première; it was soon moved ahead to March 6.

25. BE, p. 355.

26. *Vincenzo Bellini: Note aneddotiche e critiche*, Ancona, 1882, p. 107.

27. BE, pp. 345–346.

28. That is, the other two performances during which Bellini sat at the cembalo.

29. Bellini was overstating Rossini's productivity by at least two dozen operas (the actual number varies according to the way they are counted).

30. Possibly authentic is a purported letter from Bellini to Giuseppe Bornaccini, who had been a student with him in Naples, and who was in Venice in 1833 to stage his *opera buffa Aver moglie è poco, guidarla è molto* (Teatro San Grisostomo, February 13). The story was spread about that Bornaccini was so disgusted when his own trifling opera succeeded while *Beatrice di Tenda* failed that he stopped composing operas. In the sup-

posed letter to him (BE, pp. 344–345), Bellini is represented as writing: "All my efforts for Venice have been thrown to the winds; you will have heard of the solemn fiasco of *Beatrice*. I could adduce in explanation the public's irritation over the great delay, certain anticipatory articles in the journal, an *avvertimento* by Romani in his libretto which smells of the executioner at every point; but now such excuses would be untimely. All that now consoles me is that the second performance of *Beatrice* brought the management one third more entrance tickets than the first performance; and twice as many at the third. Lanari, who believed that he would do better with *Tancredi*, was screwed yesterday evening. Saturday or Sunday, *Beatrice* will be given, and we'll await the outcome. Then time will answer everything. *Zaira* was revenged by *I Capuleti; Norma* by itself; what will happen to *Beatrice*? I love her the same as my other daughters [and] I hope to find a husband for her too." This letter was published first by Florimo (CssSmdN II, p. 746, ft. 1), who said that he had found it "in a biography of Bellini written by Professor F. J. Polidoro" and who misdated it (May 21, 1833, for March 23, 1833). Republishing it, Luisa Cambi wrote (BE, p. 345): "According to Pastura, the autograph would be found at the Naples Conservatory, where it has been impossible to find it despite the most careful search." In the absence of the autograph or a facsimile of it, the letter remains suspect.

31. This village in the province of Belluno was selected for its very obscurity. The letter is reprinted complete in BE, pp. 336–337.
32. Reprinted complete in BE, pp. 338–339.
33. Pietro Generali's opera *Beniowski* had had its première at the Fenice on March 17, 1831.
34. Pacini's *Ivanhoe* had been sung for the first time at the Fenice on March 19, 1832.
35. This second letter to "A. B." is reprinted complete in BE, pp. 339–341.
36. See, as examples, the reviews from two Milanese journals (*L'Eco*, March 20, 1833, and *Il Barbiere di Siviglia*, March 21, 1833) as reprinted complete in BE, respectively, pp. 341–342 and p. 343.
37. Quoted complete in BE, pp. 347–348. Pastura wrote (BSLS, p. 372): "We do not know to whom to attribute the paternity of this explanation, but it must surely have been someone friendly with Bellini and rather close to the management of the Theater [La Fenice], as in the course of the defense, he is able to cite the protocol number of the letter informing the Governing Director of the Fenice of the declaration that Romani had made to the Milan police."
38. "*Nulla è un regno a core amante*" and "*Ma la sola, ohimè! ohimè! son io,*" both in Act I.
39. The pieces indicated were Beatrice's entrance aria. "*Come, ah come ogni cosa il suo sorriso allegra,*" which was thought to resemble "*Casta diva,*" and the concerted number that follows the introductory chorus of Act II—it begins with Anichino singing "*O troppo a mie preghiere*"—in which resemblances were detected to sections of the closing scene of *Norma* and to the *stretta* "*Se ogni speme è a noi rapita,*" in the Act I finale of *I Capuleti e i Montecchi*.
40. The complete original text of this letter is reprinted in BE, pp. 350–351.

41. These references to Minerva have been interpreted as allusions to Giuditta Turina, but this passage indicates that Romani—who must have known the facts—was alluding to Pasta.

42. The unhappy signore di Ventimiglia in *Beatrice di Tenda*.

43. Supplemento No. 11 to No. 40. This version of Romani's letter is reprinted complete in BE, pp. 352-353.

44. Reprinted complete in BE, pp. 354-358.

45. Romani's *Caterina di Guisa* was set by five composers: Carlo Coccia (1833), Giuseppe Mazza (1836), Fabio Campana (1838), Beniamino Rossi (1861), and Riccardo Gandolfi (1872). His *Conte d'Essex* was set by Mercadante (1833). Donizetti's *Roberto Devereux, ossia Il Conte di Essex* (1837), however, used a libretto by Salvatore Cammarano.

46. Donizetti's *Parisina*, to Romani's libretto, was staged at the Teatro della Pergola, Florence, the day after the Venice première of *Beatrice di Tenda*, and was a considerable success. Its libretto was set again in 1878 by Tommaso E. Giribaldi.

47. Lodovico Grossi, called Viadana (1564?-1645), to whom has been attributed —many musicologists believe incorrectly—the "invention" of unfigured *basso continuo*.

48. Reprinted in BE, p. 358.

49. Quoted complete in BE, pp. 358-361.

50. The garrulous, amiable quack in the Romani-Donizetti opera *L'Elisir d'amore*.

51. Coviello is a bragging Neapolitan poltroon mask in old Italian *commedia*.

52. Here, in a small flourish of erudition, Romani uses the obsolescent word *calepino*, originally a Latin-Italian dictionary named after its compiler, Ambrogio da Calepio, a monk (1440?-1510).

53. Here an untranslatable pun probably was intended: "*caratteri di speziale*" are large letters or block capitals, but "*speziale*" is also the word for druggist, as well as being a former spelling of the adjective *speciale*, meaning "special."

54. Quoted in BE, p. 361. In 1827, in the journal *La Vespa*, Romani had published what became a notorious classicizing attack upon the so-called romanticism of Alessandro Manzoni's historical novel *I Promessi Sposi*. A year before that, using the pseudonyms "Don Libero" and "Don Sincero," Romani had attacked in the same vein Tommaso Grossi's *I Lombardi alla prima crociata*.

55. See pp. 165-70.

56. Long incorrectly attributed to Pelagio Palagi, this portrait is now in the Naples Conservatory museum, to which Florimo presented it. See Plate 2.

57. Discussing Giuditta with Florimo by letter from Puteaux on August 13, 1835 (BE, p. 582), Bellini was to say: "She has my money, about six thousand francs [roughly $3,750 in 1971 purchasing power], in addition to all of my furniture, which she will sell at the first public auction." But on May 2, 1835, Giuseppe Pasta had written Bellini to say that Giuditta Turina had sold his piano for "37 zecchini d'oro" [about $300]; he enclosed a list of pieces of Bellini's furniture which Giuditta Turina had selected as better sold directly, and for which she had obtained a total amount (including the money received for the piano) of 1,527.20 Austrian

lire (about $950); he added that because of her "ill-omened affairs with the Turina family," she could not, for the time being, return the funds that Bellini had left with her in 1833. Bellini seems never to have obtained either that sum or any money realized by the sale of his effects. Either Bellini did not receive Giuseppe Pasta's letter of May 2 or Antonino Amore mistranscribed its date when publishing it (VB:V, pp. 145–147)— for if Bellini had read it in May, why should he have written to Florimo as he did on August 13?

58. The leading singers of that season were to be—in addition to Pasta— Joséphine de Méric (not, as often asserted, Henriette Méric-Lalande), Laure Cinti-Damoreau, Domenico Donzelli, Filippo Galli, Giovanni Battista Rubini, and Carlo Zucchelli. The operas originally announced were: (Bellini) *Il Pirata, Beatrice di Tenda* (for which *I Capuleti e i Montecchi* was substituted), *La Sonnambula,* and *Norma;* (Donizetti) *Anna Bolena;* (Mayr) *Medea in Corinto;* and (Rossini) *Tancredi.* Unlike Rossini's contract with Giovanni Battista Benelli, impresario of the King's Theatre, ten years earlier, Bellini's arrangement with Laporte did not foresee his composing a new opera especially for London.

59. BE, p. 362. Cicconetti, who published this fragment for the first time (VdVB, p. 77), supposed that it had been addressed to Filippo Santocanale; he also supplied the dating "*Parigi, 23 aprile 1833,*" which is entirely credible.

60. Bellini repeated this assertion on April 1, 1835, in a letter to Vincenzo Ferlito from Paris (BE, p. 536). Unlike Rossini, Donizetti, and Verdi, Bellini never composed an opera to a libretto in French.

61. Whom the paper incorrectly (prudishly?) identified as Malibran's husband, though she would not obtain her divorce from the Americanized Frenchman Eugene Malibran until 1835, or marry De Bériot until March 26, 1836. Her illegitimate son, Charles-Wilfred de Bériot, had been born on February 12, 1833.

62. The first "two scenes" of *Bianca e Gernando,* or just possibly of *Bianca e Fernando,* had been sung at the King's Theatre on May 10, 1828, being interpolated into a performance of Rossini's *La Donna del lago,* the cast of which included Henriette Sontag, Amalia Schütz-Oldosi, Alberico Curioni, Matteo Porto, and Carlo Zucchelli. Where the score of Bellini's early opera had been obtained and what sort of score it was (it may have been a pirated one orchestrated by someone else) cannot be determined.

63. Leslie Orrey wrote (*Bellini,* London and New York, 1969, p. 50) that at a meeting of the Philharmonic Society directors on April 27, 1833, it was "resolved that Sigr. Paganini, Mr. Bellini and Mr. Herz be presented with a free admission for the season."

64. *Leaves from the Diary of Henry Greville,* ed. by the Viscountess Enfield, London, 1883, cited by Orrey, *op. cit.,* p. 52.

65. CssSmdN II, pp. 824–826. Florimo reprinted the letter in LSmdN III, pp. 256–257, and again in B:Mel, pp. 137–139. See BE, p. 364.

66. This deletion is indicated in all three of Florimo's publications of this passage; in itself, it seems a strong argument in favor of the authenticity of the letter, though not necessarily of the phrasing exactly as Florimo gives it.

67. After conte Rodolfo has reunited Amina and Elvino, she turns toward her mother and (in published librettos and scores) says: "*Mi abbraccia* [or *M'abbraccia*], *tenera madre*"—roughly, "Embrace me, loving mother."

68. In CssSmdN II, p. 826, Florimo adds: "What hopes! . . . what dreams! . . . Only a year and some months would elapse before these two geniuses of melody and song, who had embraced one another in this world, would be suddenly summoned back to the ethereal regions and, as if by agreement, on the same day a year apart! Bellini died at Puteaux on September 24, 1835, Malibran died at Manchester in 1836, and on that same doleful September 24. A mysterious coincidence! ! ! . . ." Unfortunately for Florimo's "coincidence," Malibran died on September 23, not 24, 1836.

69. BSLS, pp. 382–383.

70. BE, p. 368.

71. The word is *gusto,* which may have been intended to mean gusto in the English sense.

72. Dated June 25, 1833; BE, pp. 371–372.

73. BSLS, p. 393. This miniature of Bellini is now in the Museo Belliniano at Catania. See Plate 5a.

74. After Bellini's death, Rossini sent this brooch to the Bellinis in Catania. Now in the Museo Belliniano there.

75. In Ferranti-Giulini: *Giuditta Pasta e i suoi tempi,* Milan, 1935, p. 159.

76. Whether the parenthetic explanations were in Pasta's letter, or—what appears more likely—were inserted by Maria Ferranti Nob. Giulini when preparing the book in which it appears is not clear.

77. As quoted in *Lady Morgan's Memoirs: Autobiography, Diaries and Correspondence,* 2nd edn., rev., 2 vols., London, 1863, Vol II, p. 359.

78. Vincenzo Gabussi (1800–1846), a Bolognese composer and friend of Rossini, long resident in London.

79. *Album-Bellini/a cura di F. Florimo e M. Scherillo/Publicato il Giorno dell'Inaugurazione del Monumento/a Vincenzo Bellini/in Napoli,* Naples, 1886.

80. Translated from the Italian version in the *Album-Bellini,* the original being unrecoverable. Mrs. Geale appears to have been quoting from her aunt's manuscript diary rather than from the published version of it.

81. Pastura wrote (BSLS, p. 383) that it opened on May 1. But in a letter that Pasta wrote to her mother on May 2 (Ferranti-Giulini, *op. cit.,* p. 158), which Pastura himself cites, she said: "The second performance of *Medea* took place last night."

82. BE, pp. 367–370.

83. Alessandro Luzio, who first published this letter (*Atti della Reale Accademia delle Scienze di Torino,* Vol. LXVII, Turin, 1932, pp. 122–124), footnoted this reference: "Does this refer to a woman he had loved? I do not know, but she may be the Lucchina mentioned at the end of the same letter." See note 87.

84. Lady Morgan, then, either had misunderstood Pasta or was misquoting her as having said on July 1 that the "second rehearsal" of *Norma* had taken place that day.

85. Ambassador in London of the Kingdom of Piedmont and Sardinia, of which Lamperi was a subject.

86. The Bilottis and Grossons were active in Turinese musical life.
87. Luisa Cambi (BE, p. 370, ft. 1) thought that this might refer to a musical child prodigy know as La Lucchi, of whom enthusiastic notice had appeared in *I Teatri*, Milan, on December 24, 1832.
88. BSLS, pp. 390–391.
89. See p. 50.
90. Ferranti Nob. Giulini, *op. cit.*, pp. 159–160.
91. That Pasta's benefit on June 21 was the first London performance of *Norma* is established by other references to it. What, then, did Giuseppe Pasta mean by *"la terza reappresentazione al* 'King's Theatre' "? It was not the third opera of the season there—and he himself just had referred to the *Norma* of the preceding night as *"questa prima rappresentazione di* Norma."
92. The trio for Norma, Adalgisa, and Pollione, "*Oh non tremare, o perfido,*" ends, not the prayer, but the act.
93. *Enciclopedia dello spettacolo*, Florence/Rome, 1960, Vol. VII, p. 1759.
94. BE, pp. 371–372.
95. *Beatrice di Tenda* had received its first Milan performance, at the Teatro Carcano, on July 19. There the cast had been headed by Fanny Tacchinardi-Persiani (Beatrice), Teresa Brambilla, then a student at the Milan Conservatory (Agnese), Claudio Bonoldi (Filippo, the role evidently having been adapted to his tenor range), and Magnani (Orombello). The generally enthusiastic press reviews of the performance expressed some doubts about the quality of the opera itself.
96. BE, p. 334, ft. 2.
97. VdVB, p. 78.
98. If Bellini received French francs, 12,000 of them would have been roughly equivalent to $7,400 in 1971 buying power; if Lombardo-Veneto francs (*i.e.*, lire), about $6,450.
99. Writing to Santocanale on June 26, 1833 (BE, p. 372), Bellini had said: "Don't write to London in reply to this letter; your answer will not find me in this city, as before the end of next month I must go to Paris, where I believe that I'll stay until August 20; therefore, if you'd like to tell me your news, send it to Paris or to Milan, where I'll arrive about August 26 or 28." None of these plans was carried out exactly.

Chapter IX

1. BE, pp. 370–371.
2. The probability exists that Ferdinando Turina had been aware for some time that his wife had become Bellini's mistress, that he merely used the incriminating letters as a pretext for action when action suited him. That he had remained unaware of Romani's reference to Bellini as "a new Rinaldo . . . idling on Armida's island" or had been alone among Bellini's acquaintances in not knowing what it meant is altogether unlikely.
3. B:LV, p. 226.
4. BE, p. 392.

5. The contessa Virginia Martini (1778–1836), a daughter of conte Lodovico della Torre Rezzonico, was Giuditta Turina's most intimate female friend. She was of great assistance to Giuditta during the period of Ferdinando Turina's action against her, and also corresponded with Florimo.

6. See p. 158.

7. BE, pp. 424–425.

8. First published by Frank Walker (*Music and Letters*, London, January 1959, pp. 23–25) in English translation, in an article entitled "Giuditta Turina and Bellini"; then in an Italian version of that article (*"Amore e amori nelle lettere di Giuditta, Bellini e Florimo,"* in *La Scala*, Milan, March 1959, pp. 17–18). Walker had located it in one of the thirty-seven volumes of correspondence which Florimo left to the library of San Pietro a Maiella, where the cataloguing of them was begun many years later by the librarian, professoressa Anna Mondolfi.

9. Of a portrait or portraits of Bellini.

10. In "Giuditta Turina and Bellini," *op. cit.*, p. 25.

11. This refers to Luisa Cambi's assertion quoted on p. 153.

12. For the final raveling-out of even their cool friendship by letter, see p. 165.

13. BE, p. 536.

14. Letter in the library of the Naples Conservatory, cited in BSLS, p. 397.

15. BE, p. 379.

16. The Opéra, the Théâtre-Italien, and perhaps the Opéra-Comique as well.

17. Giuseppe Consul, impresario at Turin.

18. BE, p. 531.

19. BE, p. 536.

20. Alejandro María Aguado, Marqués de las Marismas, was an international banker and Gallicized Spaniard. Some possibility exists that Bellini accompanied Giuditta Pasta on a visit to Rossini at Aguado's villa at Petit-Bourg before Rossini's return to Paris.

21. BE, p. 431.

22. BSLS, pp. 399–400.

23. In a letter to Florimo from Puteaux on August 13, 1835 (BE, p. 583), Bellini wrote: ". . . you will receive, with the fan and the waistcoat, a canon that I composed for Cherubini's album; tell me how you like it." An autograph copy of the canon, with Rossini's seal in its margin, is now in the Museo Belliniano, Catania. It was published in 1833 by Sonzogno in *La Musica popolare*. Amore and others confused it with another canon, which Bellini wrote for Zimmerman's album on August 15, 1835, almost certainly the last music that he composed. That less strict canon, for four voices, carries this inscription: "Bellini composed [this] for his friend and famous composer [*sic*] M.ro Zimmerman Paris August 15, 1835." It is a setting of these lines: *"Chi per quest'ombre dell'umana vita/talor non mira gli splendor celesti/cade per via"* (He who because of these shadows of human life does not sometimes look up at the celestial splendors, falls by the wayside). It is reproducd in facsimile in Pougin's *Bellini*, preceding the index.

24. BE, pp. 381–382; reproduced in facsimile in *Omaggio*, p. 270.

25. *Gianni di Calais*, to a libretto by Domenico Gilardoni, had been very

popular in Naples after its première there, at the Teatro del Fondo, on August 2, 1828, and again at the Teatro Carcano, Milan, after its first performance there on January 2, 1831. Rubini had been the frantically acclaimed Ernesto in both stagings, but his presence in the cast at the Italien did not save Donizetti's opera when it was sung there in 1833 and again in 1834.

26. BE, p. 391.
27. BE, p. 385.
28. BE, p. 386.
29. BE, pp. 389–391.
30. BE, p. 394.
31. BE, p. 382.
32. BE, p. 387.
33. BSLS, pp. 412–413, where the autograph is said to belong to the Auteri family of Catania.
34. The play is interspersed with *"airs,"* one of which (Act I, Scene 11) is headed: *"AIR: Le bon vieillard sentant sa fin (Violette de Caraffa [sic])"*; another (Act II, Scene 8) is listed as *"AIR du BRAVO (Romance de Troupenaz [sic])."* Already existing songs, then, were used.
35. Leslie Orrey, *op. cit.*, p. 119, ft. 1, pointed out that Scott's *Old Mortality* was published in French translation as *Les Puritains d'Écosse*, but rightly added that the plot and characters of Pepoli's libretto have only the most tenuous connection with *Old Mortality*. Scott and Scotland simply were drifting through the intellectual atmosphere.
36. The orthography of this man's name is an unconquerable confusion: it appears as Levy, Levys, Lewis, and Lewys. Pastura wrote (BSLS, p. 414, ft. 4): "Among the orthographic variants of this name, I chose that used by Levys himself in an autograph letter addressed to Bellini's father, preserved in the Museo Belliniano." I follow Pastura's decision.
37. BE, p. 422.
38. On April 1, 1835, to Vincenzo Ferlito, Bellini was to write (BE, p. 541): "Did you know that of the ten thousand francs that I lost in the Spanish funds last year, I have got back almost five thousand? And I hope to recover the other five thousand, but without risking one soldo more."
39. BE, p. 401. In Levys's house, Bellini had a large second-floor room with a window on a garden and another facing the Seine.
40. BE, p. 392.
41. BE, pp. 536–537.
42. The actual date of the première of *Anna Bolena* was December 26, 1830.
43. Première: March 13, 1832. It received only four repetitions.
44. BE, p. 397.
45. BE, p. 403.
46. BE, pp. 404–405.
47. BE, p. 405.
48. The present location of this letter is not known. See note in BE, p. 406: "The Charavay catalogue mentions a three-page letter to conte Rinaldo Belgiojoso, from Paris, June 18, 1834. Bellini announces that Pepoli has finished the libretto of *I Puritani;* regrets *la Malibran* [probably the fact that she would not be his Elvira]; wishes to write for the French theaters."

49. BE, p. 398.
50. BE, pp. 418–419.
51. BE, pp. 444–445.
52. BE, pp. 411–413. Now in the Museo Belliniano.
53. Words scored through in the autograph.
54. VB:V, pp. 334–335.
55. BE, p. 411.
56. Amore: VB:A, pp. 248–250, reprinted in BE, pp. 412–413; see Appendix J, p. 414, for a complete translation of it.
57. BE, pp. 401–402.
58. *Grandi e piccole memorie*, Florence, 1910, p. 484. Barbiera's version is quoted complete in BSLS, pp. 375–377, with this footnote: "The letter published in the volume cited [Barbiera's] must have undergone restoration, we do not know whether by Barbiera or by the first transcriber." In addressing Romani, Bellini here returns to the intimate *tu*.
59. Spelled variously; a Venetian friend of Bellini and of Rossini's close friend Giovanni Battista Perucchini.
60. Pepoli's name, clearly intended, is omitted from the letter as published by Barbiera.
61. BE, p. 444.
62. King Carlo Alberto had appointed Romani editor of the *Gazzetta ufficiale piemontese*.
63. Letter first published by Florimo in B:Mel, p. 99. Reprinting it, Luisa Cambi added this footnote (BE, p. 447, ft. 1): "Published by Florimo with the date summer '35 in the 1882 collection, no. 99, pages 504 ff; but it was enclosed in the letter to Lamperi on October 7, 1834. According to Pastura, the autograph was to be found in the Naples Conservatory— where, however, it could not be located."
64. BE, pp. 399–400, where—as transcribed from the *Corrispondenze del Conte Carlo Pepoli*, Bologna, 1881—it is both incorrect and incomplete. In October 1968, the letter was in the possession of Mr. Paul C. Richards of Brookline, Massachusetts, who kindly allowed me to examine a Xerox reproduction of it.
65. This clause ("... *e sai tu perchè io ti dissi che il buon dramma per musica è quello che non ha buon senso?*") has been carelessly or tendentiously interpreted as proof that Bellini believed that an opera should make no sense. What he really meant is clear: in writing a libretto, Pepoli should ignore the formal rules, proclaimed as "good sense," to which Italian writers of the period paid constant lip-service.
66. BSLS, p. 422.
67. Letter in the Museo Belliniano, Catania. A purported letter from Bellini to Lanari, with a postmark of arrival at Florence on July 27, 1834, is in the Museo Teatrale alla Scala, Milan, where it is bound with manuscript notes by the tenor Napoleone Moriani. It may be a copy of an actual letter (BE, pp. 409–411), but as an autograph it is of dubious authenticity.
68. BE, pp. 414–420.
69. Bellini probably was referring to the fact that the society controlled not only the Teatro San Carlo, but also the Teatro del Fondo, the Teatro Nuovo, and probably one or more other Neapolitan theaters.

70. BE, pp. 416–417.
71. Letter in the Naples Conservatory library; quoted complete in BSLS, p. 425.
72. BE, p. 422.
73. Mercadante's opera *Elisa e Claudio, ossia L'Amore protetto dall'Amicizia*, to a libretto by Luigi Romanelli, received its première at La Scala, Milan, on October 30, 1821, and won long-lasting popularity.
74. On September 21, 1834, Bellini reported to Florimo (BE, p. 436): "I hope that you won't have forgotten that the director of the *Grand'opéra* [*sic*] came to invite me to write an opera for him and that, because I demanded a fee like that paid Rossini, in addition to the author's rights, the matter died; so I was asked, as perhaps Donizetti will be; he will accept; I have refused." No new opera by Donizetti was staged at the Opéra until 1840 (*Les Martyrs*). Something of Bellini's ethical ambiguity had been evidenced early in these negotiations with the Opéra: writing to Florimo on September 4, 1834, he had foreseen writing for the French theaters, and then had added (BE, p. 430): "With this contract and with this career, if I succeed, I'll not suffer any more from Romani's indolence, nor with the laziness or weakness *** [the mutilated words are almost certainly "of the other"] poets. Scribe, Dumas, and other good poets full of merit will give me their poems and I'll be at peace." This was a very different song from the one he sang to Romani (see p. 166).
75. BE, p. 434.
76. BE, p. 437.
77. Quoted by Orrey, *op. cit.*, p. 57.
78. As Bellini wrote to Florimo the next day (BE, p. 462): "*La Sonnambula* was given in Paris four years ago, but for two evenings only, and with Pasta extremely tired because just back from London, so that almost nobody remembers it." *La Sonnambula* also was welcomed enthusiastically at La Scala on October 1, 1834, with a cast including Malibran, Domenico Reina, and Ignazio Marini.
79. François-Henri-Joseph Blaze, called Castil-Blaze (1784–1857), the first man to be designated music critic of a Paris paper (*Journal des débats*), was translator, impresario, librettist, and composer as well as critic. His distortion of Weber's *Der Freischütz* as *Robin des bois* (Odéon, Paris, 1824), became both extremely popular and notorious. He was the father of Henri-Ange Blaze de Bury (1813–1888), a well-known litterateur and music critic.
80. Letter from Castil-Blaze quoted in full in French in Florimo: LSmdN III, p. 210.
81. BE, pp. 453–460.
82. Mr. Andrew Porter wrote ("Bellini's Last Opera," in *Opera*, London, May 1960, p. 318): "And there can be little doubt that Malibran, not Grisi, was the real inspiration of Elvira in *I Puritani*."
83. Instead, Bellini adapted Tamburini's role (Riccardo) for tenor—in addition, of course, to adapting the originally soprano (Giulia Grisi) role of Elvira for Malibran's lower range.
84. Dalayrac's one-act *Nina, ou La Folle par amour* (Paris, 1786), with a libretto by Benoît-Joseph Marsollier, had been a continuingly popular

entertainment in France. Its libretto had been translated and adapted more than once in Italy, most successfully by Giuseppe Carpani for Paisiello's use in *Nina, o sia La Pazza per l'amore* (Caserta, 1789). In 1835, to a libretto by Donizetti's friend Jacopo Ferretti, Pietro Antonio Coppola's *Nina pazza per amore* was to be produced successfully at the Teatro Valle, Rome.

85. BE, p. 460.

86. BE, p. 483.

87. On August 13, 1835, Bellini said in a letter to Florimo (BE, p. 582): "I know that there is gossip in Milan about [Clelia] Pasta's marrying her cousin, who is a stupid beast, for which reason I don't believe that Pasta will commit such an absurdity in spite of the affection that she has for the young man's father, who is her uncle." In December 1836, Clelia married an engineer named Eugenio Ferranti, who, faced with irretrievable financial losses, committed suicide in a Turin cemetery in 1862.

88. It takes up seven pages (480–487) in Luisa Cambi's *Epistolario* (BE).

89. Horace Vernet—who for a time had been the lover of Rossini's second wife, Olympe Pélissier—was then director of the Académie française at Rome. His daughter Louise was also to be discussed in connection with a possible marriage to Donizetti.

90. A reference to Giuditta Turina?

91. BE, pp. 522–524. Undated—but internal evidence places it not long after February 18, 1835.

92. Points of suspension occur in the letter as first published by Florimo in B:Mel, pp. 482–484. No autograph is known to survive.

93. Points of suspension occur in the letter as published.

94. BE, pp. 476–479.

95. Bellini was once again engaged in futile negotiations with the Opéra about composing a full-length work to a French text.

96. Principe Ottajano was an official of the royal theaters of Naples.

97. Vincenzo Gabussi's *Ernani*, to a libretto by Gaetano Rossi, was sung at the Théâtre-Italien, Paris, on November 25, 1834.

98. Here Bellini is citing, as a possible source for the libretto of one of the operas that he planned to write for Naples, Scribe's libretto for Auber's very popular opera *Gustave III, ou Le Bal masqué*. Like Bellini's project to set an *Ernani* libretto, this one would be carried out later by both Gabussi (Venice, 1841, libretto by Gaetano Rossi, as *Clemenza di Valois*) and Verdi (*Un Ballo in maschera*, Rome 1859, libretto by Antonio Somma), as well as by Saverio Mercadante (*Il Reggente*, Turin 1843, libretto by Salvatore Cammarano).

99. *Un Duel sous le Cardinal de Richelieu,* a three-act drama by Lockroy (and Edmond Badon), had been produced at the Théâtre National du Vaude-ville, Paris, on April 9, 1832. It became the basis of several operas, including Federico Ricci's *Un Duello sotto Richelieu* (La Scala, Milan, August 17, 1839, to a libretto by Antonio Gazzoletti and Antonio Somma), Giuseppe Lillo's *Il Conte di Chalais* (San Carlo, Naples, October 1839, to a libretto by Salvatore Cammarano), and Donizetti's *Maria di Roh* ̄ ̄ ̄e Cammarano libretto, Kärntnertortheater, Vienna, Ju

100. BE, pp. 429–430.
101. Rossini had returned to Paris from the country.
102. BE, p. 435.
103. BE, pp. 437–438.
104. BE, p. 443.
105. *Vincenzo Bellini,* by Andrea Della Corte and Guido Pannain, Turin, 1935, p. 25.
106. *"Gioacchino Rossini: Appunti di viaggio,"* in *Rivista romana di scienze e lettere* I, 3, 4, Rome 1878; reprinted as a pamphlet, Rome, 1878, and again in De Sanctis's *Memorie: Studie dal vero,* Rome, n. d.
107. For a complete translation of this passage, see Weinstock: *Rossini,* New York and London, 1968, p. 320.
108. BE, p. 463.
109. Earlier in this letter, Bellini had burst out: "Oh, if I could come to be director of the Théâtre-Italien, how I'd have all my operas mounted, for Rossini's now have been reduced to boredoms, almost as in Italy." Luisa Cambi quoted (BE, p. 573, ft. 4) this item from *L'Eco,* Milan, of March 2, 1835: "The French journals, since Bellini presented *I Puritani ed i Cavalieri* on the Paris stages, do not hesitate to proclaim him, amid admiration and ecstasy, the only, the true reformer of music, the one who, more than any other, has known how to adapt it to the circumstances and taste of the time, and, coming to a parallel between Bellini and Rossini, do not hide the hope that Rossini, setting aside his unique and prodigious system, will want, in view of the demands and inclinations of our age, to give his support to the party of the restoration. From that it can be inferred that Rossini no longer pleases and that there is need for a reform."
110. BE, p. 474.
111. B:Mel, p. 54.
112. BE, p. 479.
113. BSLS, pp. 447–448. Letter in the Naples Conservatory library.
114. BE, pp. 501–502.
115. Bellini forgot to close the parenthetical expression begun here.
116. LSmdN III, p. 208.
117. Composed to a libretto by Emmanuele Bidera (with additions by Agostino Ruffini), *Marin(o) Faliero* had as its leading singers the *"Puritani* Quartet": Grisi, Rubini, Tamburini, and Lablache. The opera was to have a long career, being received more enthusistically in Italy and elsewhere than in Paris.
118. Zavadini, *op. cit.,* pp. 158–159.
119. BE, pp. 536–542.
120. Counting three juvenilia, Donizetti had composed fifty operas in nineteen years. Bellini, who had had ten premières (if that of the Genoa *Bianca e Fernando* be included), found Donizetti's facility especially reprehensible.
121. In view of Donizetti's statement to Antonio Dolci, quoted above, that the second and third evenings of *Marin Faliero* had been brilliant, it is impossible to accept Bellini's opinion as unbiased: Donizetti was a cool-minded witness, and never attempted to conceal his own failures or half-successes.

Chapter X

1. Donizetti too was named a *chevalier* of the Légion d'honneur at this time, though the official decree was not issued until February 2, 1836. He dedicated the published score of *Les Martyrs* to Queen Marie-Amélie.
2. See Cicconetti, p. 86, and B:Mel, p. 46.
3. BSLS, p. 456; the version given in BE, p. 314, is incomplete.
4. BE, p. 515.
5. *Norma* did not receive its first Paris stage performance until after Bellini's death (Théâtre-Italien, December 8, 1835).
6. BE, p. 528.
7. BE, p. 520.
8. BE, p. 515.
9. Halévy's opera, to a Scribe libretto, had had its extremely successful première at the Opéra on February 23, 1835. Donizetti and Bellini both disliked it violently.
10. BE, p. 545.
11. BE, p. 566.
12. BE, p. 572.
13. BSLS, p. 488.
14. BE, p. 575.
15. BE, p. 535.
16. BE, p. 555.
17. The San Carlo management agreed to pay Bellini 1,800 ducati for *I Puritani*, 3,600 ducati for each of two later new operas.
18. BE, p. 486.
19. In a letter of December 21–22, 1834, to Florimo, Bellini said (BE, p. 489): "Now listen to the change that I have made for Malibran. There is no place for a cavatina in the book; therefore she will make her entrance in a duet with [Carlo] Porto [who was meant to play Sir Giorgio opposite her], and then, in place of an insignificant little quartet, I have made her a piece so curious and so brilliant that she will be utterly content, it being of the kind that she likes most: this piece is worth more than ten cavatinas because it occurs at a good place, so much so that I'll also give it in Paris, for it makes a big effect." The piece referred to was the familiar "*Son vergin vezzosa.*"
20. The plan was for the role of Riccardo to be transposed for Francesco Pedrazzi, a tenor, the San Carlo having no baritone who could sing the role satisfactorily as composed for Tamburini.
21. Having obtained annulment of her marriage to Eugene Malibran on March 6, 1834, Malibran had left London for Naples, where she was to sing at the San Carlo.
22. The "Naples version" of *I Puritani*, now in the Museo Belliniano at Catania, is in the script of a copyist (Pugni), but has extensive annotations in Bellini's script.
23. BE, p. 493.

24. BE, p. 494.
25. BE, p. 519.
26. See pp. 448–455 for a discussion of the differences between the "Paris" and "Naples" (or "Malibran") versions of *I Puritani*.
27. BE, pp. 536–542.
28. Donizetti, by no measure "convinced of his fiasco," actually left Paris on March 20 or 21.
29. *Sic*. Possibly comte Joseph de Flahaut, natural son of Talleyrand and father, by Queen Hortense, of Napoleon III's illegitimate half-brother, the duc de Morny.
30. Possibly baron Sellières, husband of the baronne Sellières mentioned on pp. 175 and 176 as trying to arrange a marriage for Bellini.
31. Basically as meaningful as any of Bellini's confused statements on the subject of marriage are some sentences in a letter that he wrote on April 7, 1835, to the contessa Virginia Martini (BSLS, pp. 470–471): ". . . I greatly want to apply myself more constantly [to composing operas], especially now that I have no love relationship, from which may God free me for my whole life! You cannot imagine how happy and peaceful I am now. Not to speak badly of women, but I think it impossible to be happy loving a woman who is not one's own, and who cannot dispose of herself as she wishes. Perhaps I should be enamored of my wife, but I don't think that I shall ever find her as she is pictured in my thoughts; for the rest, I find diversion here and love only in friendship . . ."
32. Lamperi's copy of the Dantan bust eventually became the property of senatore Carlo Rizzetti, who presented it to the Museo Belliniano in Catania, where it remains.
33. BSLS, p. 485.
34. BE, pp. 560–562.
35. Giuseppe Morelli, whom Bellini had met in Messina.
36. Luisa Cambi wrote (BE, p. 561, ft. 4): "The poetry of Morelli's *Due speranze* begins: 'My first hope! o rosy dreams of first youth.' Bellini's arietta '*Il sogno dell'infanzia*,' published in 1835, begins: 'Soft dreams of my earliest years, my heart has become drunk on memories of you,' etc., I think it is the promised answer . . ." Justly, she then adds: ". . . for the rest, the poetry and the music are of little value." The arietta is most often called "*Sogno d'infanzia*."
37. BE, p. 556.
38. Bellini had mentioned favorable reviews of *I Puritani* in *The Times* and the *Courier*.
39. Letter in the Museo Belliniano, Catania.
40. BE, p. 558.
41. BSLS, pp. 500–501.
42. BE, pp. 573–574. Bellini also wrote Pasta about Grisi's failure (letter dated July 24, 1835, now in the Library of the Performing Arts, Lincoln Center, New York).
43. Grisi became the first Paris Norma, at the Théâtre-Italien on December 8, 1835, with Laura Assandri (Adalgisa), Rubini (Pollione), and Lablache (Oroveso).
44. According to Amore (VB:A, p. 370), in 1880, conte Carlo Pepoli wrote

Florimo a letter including this passage: "I long to know if you ever have been able to turn up certain choruses written by me and already set to music by Bellini for the *dramma Cola di Rienzi.* For all the investigations I have made in Paris and elsewhere, no one ever has been able to give me information about them." Nothing is known of Bellini's having considered an opera dealing with Rienzi, about whom Wagner would write his own libretto, basing it upon Bulwer-Lytton's novel.

45. VB, p. 411.
46. BSLS, p. 489.
47. BE, p. 589.
48. BE, pp. 571–575.
49. Rossini did not leave Paris for his years in Bologna and Florence until 1836. He composed no opera after 1829, though he lived until 1868.
50. BE, pp. 575–577.
51. Fieschi was badly wounded when the device blew up as he triggered it. He and two accomplices were guillotined on February 19, 1836.
52. The canon for Zimmerman, which is reproduced in facsimile just before the table of contents of Pougin's *Bellini,* is not known to survive in autograph. The autograph copy of the canon for Cherubini which Bellini sent to Florimo is now in the library of San Pietro a Majella. The library of the Accademia di Santa Cecilia, Rome, has an autograph of *"L'Abbandono"*; another autograph of its first page was reproduced in facsimile in the November 1965 catalogue of the Libreria Gaspare Casella, Naples, which offered the page (twenty-one measures) for 120,000 lire (then approximately $195).
53. BE, pp. 585–589.
54. BE, pp. 589–592.
55. BE, pp. 592–593.
56. BE, p. 592, ft. 6.
57. *Lo Spigolatore* added as a note this public letter: "Théâtre-Royal Italien. We, the undersigned, declare that the only true original score of the opera *I Puritani* which has been sent to Italy is that which we have ceded to monsieur Ricordi, music publisher at Milan, initialed by us on the first and last page of each piece. Consequently we declare false and apocryphal any other copy that may have been circulating in Italy before the present declaration. In testimony whereof we have issued the present certificate so that it may be given all the publicity that the said Ricordi may judge suitable. Paris, the eleventh December, one thousand eight hundred thirty-five. E[ugène] Troupenas, *publisher of the score,*/[Édouard] Robert, director of the Théâtre-Italien,/[Carlo] Severini, administrator of the abovementioned theater/G[ioachino] Rossini, authorized agent of the powers of the Bellini heirs." The authorized score appears to have been used when La Scala presented *I Puritani* for the first time, on December 26, 1835, with Sofia Dall'Oca Schoberlechner (Elvira), Antonio Poggi (Arturo), Ignazio Marini (Giorgio), and Carlo Marcolini (Riccardo), thus initiating a seasonal run of twenty-three performances.
58. Heine: *Sämtliche Werke,* Insel Verlag, Leipzig, n.d., Vol. II *(Prosadichtungen, Florentinische Nächte: "Erste Nacht"),* pp. 807–808.
59. Heine, *op. cit.,* p. 807.

60. *Souvenirs*, Paris, 1881. Mme Jaubert was intimate with many people whom Bellini knew. The Pasta Collection at the Library of the Performing Arts, Lincoln Center, New York, includes a letter from Lady Hunloke to Giuditta Pasta discussing Bellini's final illness. Heine's remarks about Bellini appeared in several publications, including his *Reisebilder*, and were translated often into Italian.

61. Mme Jaubert dates this dinner four days before Bellini's death—that is, on September 19. But it must have taken place not later than September 8 or 9, as Bellini had been confined to his bed for more than a week by the 19th, and had been attended by Dr. Montallegri from the 11th on.

62. Francesco Giugni, in his *L'Immatura Fine di Vincenzo Bellini alla luce di nuove circostanze*, Lugo, 1938, and his *La Malattia e la morte di Vincenzo Bellini*, Faenza, 1939, wrote that Montallegri was from Faenza, had been a physician with the Napoleonic army in Italy, was a liberal patriot, was friendly with conte Carlo Pepoli—with whom he had been associated in the Romagna insurrections of 1825–1831—and underwent imprisonment in Venice and exile in France. Lady Hunloke, in a letter in French to Giuditta Pasta (September 25, 1835), said simply that Bellini had been taken care of by Doctor Montallegri, sent by Princess Belgiojoso.

63. Amore published them in VB:V, pp. 213–215; they have been reprinted several times—for example, in BE, pp. 594–595. They are now in the Museo Belliniano.

64. This appears to have been Montallegri's Paris address.

65. In "*Nuovi Importanti Documenti assicurati al Museo Belliniano,*" in the *Rivista del Comune di Catania*, October–December 1958; reissued as an undated pamphlet.

66. The quotations from Aymé d'Aquino's diaries were published first by Florimo (B:Mel, pp. 61–63), as part of a letter that Aymé d'Aquino had written him in reply to a request that he put on paper what, during a visit to Naples, he had told about Bellini's death. They have been reprinted often—for example, in BE, pp. 593–596.

67. Under date of September 26, 1835, Henry Greville wrote in his diary an account of Bellini's last days which closely parallels Aymé d'Aquino's: "A sad event has happened. Poor Bellini is dead after an illness of three weeks! The last time I saw him was at the Barrière de l'Étoile, where Lady Hunloke, with whom I had been dining, brought us. He came into town from Puteaux to make an arrangement about our opera box, but I missed him, and we were to have dined together, on a day which he was to fix, at Madame Graham's, and I had written to him by her desire, and receiving no answer wrote again, and was answered by a note from a Mr. Levy, at whose house he was staying, to say he was ill and unable to write. I wrote again, and Levy answered he was still ill. I went [to Puteaux] to inquire, but they assured me there was no danger, but would not permit me to go up, as he was forbidden to see any one. I then wrote again to Levy to inquire about him, and he answered that, having been better the preceding day, his night had not been good, and he was less well, but hoped to be able to send me better news shortly. At the moment that I received that letter *he had ceased to live*, and it was from the newspaper of Thursday [September 24] that I learnt that at four o'clock [*sic*] of the preceding day

he had expired. Poor fellow! Those Levys have much to answer for, as they not only kept away and in ignorance all his best friends, but neglected to call in fresh advice." But why, with Dr. Montallegri in attendance— and especially if cholera was strongly suspected—should Mr. and Mrs. Levys have called in "fresh advice"?

68. Alari (or Alary) was a twenty-one-year-old Mantuan composer.
69. The two lines of verse are in Italian in the published version of the diary entries.
70. For a translation of Bellini's death certificate, see Appendix J, p. 414.
71. Dr. Dalmas's report of the autopsy is now in the Museo Belliniano. For a translation of it, see Appendix K, p. 415.
72. Dr. de Sabata's commentary, written in answer to a request from the present writer, was dated at Milan on September 7, 1969. The complete text of it follows the report of Dr. Dalmas on the autopsy in Appendix K, p. 415.
73. In 1938, Francesco Giugni wrote (*L'Immatura Fine di Vincenzo Bellini*, p. 8): "It turned out that Bellini was suffering from ulcerous colitis caused by the dysenteric amoeba . . ." Curiously, Leslie Orrey (*op. cit.*, p. 60) wrote as late as 1967 (date of preface to his book): "There was no evidence of any infective or amoebic dysentery . . ."
74. Quoted in BSLS, p. 527.
75. Three masks of Bellini exist. The first, taken by Dantan on September 24, 1835, produces a staring effect because no one had taken the trouble to close Bellini's eyes (see Plate 6). Another was taken in 1876, when the body was transported from Paris to Catania; it very clearly reveals time's erosions (see reproduction of it in *Omaggio*, p. 294). The third, not a true mask, was modeled by a sculptor named Tripisciano, who used the 1876 mask as the basis of a reconstructed and idealized face. At least one photograph was taken of Bellini's re-embalmed body in 1876; the faded photograph now in the Museo Belliniano appears as an illustration on p. 293 of *Omaggio*. The body was exhumed again in 1959 so that the decaying casket might be replaced. Again, at least one photograph was taken; it is now in the Museo Belliniano. I have talked to people in Catania who saw Bellini's body in 1959—a century and a quarter after his death. They agreed that though decay was advanced, an unmistakable resemblance to the best of the Bellini portraits remained.
76. BE, p. 600, where a footnote incorrectly states that it was published by Giorgio Barini in his "*Noterelle belliniane*," in the *Rivista musicale italiana* (Bocca), Turin, I, 1902.
77. Fromental Halévy was the noted pedagogue and the composer of *La Juive*; François-Antoine Habeneck the famous conductor; Auguste-Mathieu Panseron a prominent teacher of singing and minor composer; Adolphe Nourrit the great tenor; Jean-Baptiste-Marie Chaullet (Chollet) a popular baritone turned tenor; and Eugène Troupenas a leading publisher of music. Rossini made the first contribution to the fund. Subscriptions came in from King Louis-Philippe, Queen Marie-Amélie, other members of the Royal Family, and many private citizens. In a short time, a sum of about 20,000 francs was raised.
78. The autograph of this letter was described in a catalogue published at

Bologna in 1888 in connection with an exhibition of the Raccolta Succi. Its full text appears in Giorgio Barini's *"Noterelle belliniane,"* in the *Rivista musicale italiana* (Bocca), Turin, I, p. 70. Identical or similar letters undoubtedly were sent to other professional musicians.

79. Published in mutilated text by Amore (VB:V, pp. 233 *et seq.*); reprinted complete in BE, pp. 601–603. The autograph is in the Museo Belliniano.

80. Mazzatinti-Manis: *Lettere di G. Rossini,* Florence, 1902, pp. 62–63. Autograph in the Biblioteca Comunale, Palermo; a copy sent by Santocanale to the Bellinis in Catania is in the Museo Belliniano. Despite Pastura's statement (BSLS, p. 535) that this letter was "published without date and lacking the following final section . . ." both the date and the "final section" that he quotes appear complete in Mazzatinti-Manis.

81. A son of Bellini's "enemy," Giovanni Pacini, Émilien was a poet and opera librettist.

82. Barini, *op. cit.*, p. 71, published a list of the expenses which was found in an autograph notation by Carlo Severini: they totaled 4,765.12 francs. Barini also asserted that the subscription had raised 13,796 francs, but other evidence suggests that the amount of it finally rose to about 20,000.

83. This refers to Santocanale's having intervened, partly at Bellini's behest, in some financial matters connected with land held in Sicily by Rossini's wife, Isabella Colbran.

84. The published text here reads *servitori:* servants. But Bellini had no servants in Sicily, and this was unquestionably a mistranscription of *genitori:* parents.

85. Rather than the more formal *Lei.*

86. Zavadini, *op. cit.*, p. 388.

87. Donizetti gave three "proofs" of his friendship for Bellini: a *Messa da Requiem* (1835), a very considerable musical work (for descriptions of it, see Guglielmo Barblan: *L'Opera di Donizetti nell'età romantica,* Bergamo, 1948, pp. 223–226, and William Ashbrook: *Donizetti,* London, 1965, pp. 173 and 371); the *"Lamento in morte di V. Bellini,"* setting verses by Andrea Maffei for solo voice and piano (1836); and an ingenious potpourri of Bellini melodies, the *Sinfonia per orchestra sopra motivi di V. Bellini* (1836).

88. The casket had been installed in the Duomo temporarily on the forty-first anniversary of Bellini's death—that is, on September 23, 1876.

89. For a description of all the events and ceremonies connected with the transfer of Bellini's remains from Père-Lachaise to the Catania Duomo, see Giuseppe Giuliano: *"Traslazione in Catania delle ceneri di Vincenzo Bellini: Diario,"* in *Omaggio,* pp. 271–294. Florimo, aged almost seventy-six, was present throughout the ceremonies, from Paris to Catania. Also present in Catania were all six of Bellini's siblings: Carmelo (73), Francesco (72), Michela Marziani (70), Giuseppa Scammacca (69), Mario (66), and Maria Castorina di Giacomo (63), as well as the septuagenarian Santocanale.

90. Published in the *Gazzetta piemontese,* Turin, October 1, 1835.

91. The transcription of this *Necrologia* published by Romani's widow, Emilia Branca (*op. cit.*, pp. 188–190), omits the passage beginning "It was then . . ." and ending ". . . few composers in Italy." She thus deleted any

reference by title to the Romani-Bellini operas, almost certainly out of a desire not to mention *Zaira* and *Beatrice di Tenda* and the notorious Romani-Bellini polemic.

92. Although Romani lived until 1865, he never published any of the materials foreshadowed.

Adelson e Salvini

1. Friedrich Lippmann wrote (*Vincenzo Bellini und die italienische opera seria seine Zeit, Analecta Musicologica*, 6, Cologne/Vienna, 1969, p. 29, ft. 57) that Tottola's libretto probably was based upon a comedy of the same name performed at Esterháza in 1778, but of which no copy has survived at either Esterháza or Eisenstadt. The 1816 libretto for Fioravanti's opera lists the cast this way: Margherita Chabrand (Nelly), Francesca [Gimignani] Checcherini (Madama Rivers), Francesca Cardini (Fanny), Giovanni Battista Rubini (Lord Adelson), Felice Pellegrini (Salvini), Carlo Casaccia (Bonifacio), Francesco Spanora (Struley), and Giovanni Pace (Geronio). After Bellini's death, another *Adelson e Salvini*, with a score by Luigi Savj, was staged at the Teatro della Pergola, Florence (January 24, 1839).

2. The archives of the Accademia filarmonica at Bologna contain seventeen pages of autograph: 219 measures of the Nelly–Salvini "*Felice istante!*"

3. The "*fogli sparsi*" (separate pages) include: (1) a single page (rubber-stamped as No. 1) roughly corresponding to p. 99 of the Ricordi piano-vocal score of Version II; (2) pp. 11–18 and 27–34, roughly corresponding to pp. 208–213 of that published score; (3) pp. 3–6, related to pp. 286–287 of that score; (4) pp. 7–10, related to pp. 296–297; and (5) pp. 19–24, the first of which is headed "*Scena e Finale del Atto 3⁰*," which are not continuous, and which it seems impossible to identify accurately (one contains the words "*Barbaro cielo! ancora mi persegue il tuo sdegno?*"; another the words "*grida Nelly vendetta*"). Unless something happened to these pages after Friedrich Lippmann examined them, his statement (*op. cit.,* p. 367) that they contain the "*Finale des II. Akts vom Solo* 'Salvini, alle tue piante' *bis einschliesslich Chor* 'Lieto facciamo ritorno' " is slightly inexact: rubber-stamped pages 3–6 (see above) begin with "*-manta, se a quella mano aspiri, Salvini, a' suoi sospiri chiude le vie del cor . . .*" and end (p. 288 of piano-vocal score) in mid-word just before Struley sings "*Stanco de' suoi lamenti . . .*"; p. 7 begins with the chorus singing (p. 296 of piano-vocal score) "*Lieti facciam ritorno.*"

4. The Ricordi editions contain a few passages that do not appear in available autographs, separate pages, or manuscript copies.

5. Comic characters using dialect were not uncommon in operas whose chief protagonists sang in standard Italian. An interesting example is conte Asdrubale in Donizetti's 1824 opera *Emilia di Liverpool*, a role also designed for Carlo Casaccia. As *Emilia* received its première while Bellini was still in Naples (Teatro Nuovo, July 28, 1824), he very probably was familiar with it.

6. In "*Adelson e Salvini*," in *Vincenzo Bellini: L'Uomo, le sue opere, la sua fama*, ed. by Ildebrando Pizzetti, Milan, 1936, p. 42.

7. Bellini re-employed ideas from this passage as the point of departure for Gualtiero's "*Per te di vane lagrime*," in Act I, Scene 3, of *Il Pirata* (p. 56 of the piano-vocal score of that opera). "*Oh! quante amare lagrime*" was the replacement (Version II) of the cabaletta (Version I) "*Ah se a smorzar l'ardire*"—one phrase of which (to the words "*con questa mano il core saprò dal sen strappare*") would reappear, adapted, in *Norma* (in the allegro cabaletta of the second-act Norma–Adalgisa duet "*Mira, o Norma,*" at the words "*Teco del fato all'onte ferma opporrò la fronte,*" p. 182 of the Ricordi piano-vocal score of that opera with plate number 41684).

   Mr. Stefan Zucker pointed out to me that the cadenza sung by Salvini on the words "*così fiero dolor!*" (p. 81 of the piano-vocal score with plate number 108595) is substantially repeated by Imogene at the end of Act I, Scene 4, of *Il Pirata* (to the words "*capo ti sta,*" p. 266 of the Ricordi piano-vocal score with plate number 108189), and is more than hinted at by Bianca in her last three measures in *Bianca e Fernando* (to the words "*fa a me, a me si fa,*" p. 238 of the piano-vocal score with plate numbers 9826–9842).

   In this connection, its is worth noting that a few passages in the first version of *Adelson e Salvini* were not reused by Bellini either in the second version of that opera or elsewhere (see Friedrich Lippmann, *Vincenzo Bellini*, etc., *op. cit.*, p. 373).

8. Della Corte (*op. cit.*, p. 46) noted that the melody of Adelson's "*Di piacer la voce echeggi,*" p. 154, closely echoes "*Lo conosco a quegli occhietti,*" in Pergolesi's *La Serva padrona*, with which Bellini was familiar—and which was to be echoed again by Donizetti in *Lucrezia Borgia* ("*Maffio Orsini, signore, son io,*" in the *stretta* of the prologue).

9. The melody sung here by Nelly was used later by Bellini for "*Crudele, alle tue piante,*" an *allegro agitato* that he inserted into the finale of the Genoa version of *Bianca e Fernando* for Adelaide Tosi (1837 Ricordi piano-vocal score with plate numbers 9826–9842, pp. 229–230).

10. *Op. cit.*, p. 47.

Beatrice di Tenda

1. Romani's chief source was the *dramma* (mentioned by Goethe and praised by Sismondi) *Beatrice di Tenda*, by Carlo Tedaldi Fores (Milan, 1825). Other more remote possible sources are: Andrea Biglia (or de Billis): *Rerum Mediolanensium historiae*, published after 1431; Giuseppe Ripamonti: *Historiarium patriae in continuationem Tristani Calchi*, seventeenth century; Diodata Saluzzo-Roero: *Il Castello di Binasco*, a novel, 1819; and the scenario for the ballet *Beatrice di Tenda*, choreographed by Antonio Monticini (La Scala, Milan, 1832). The historical Beatrice di Tenda (1370–1418), widow of the *condottiere* Felice Cane, married Filippo Mario Visconti, duca di Milano, who later had her convicted of adultery and decapitated. Romani's libretto, exactly as Bellini had set it, was used again for a *Beatrice di Tenda* by Rinaldo Ticci which was presented at the

Teatro Bianchi in the composer's native Siena in 1837. It was set at least once more, in Portuguese translation, as *Beatriz*, by Federico Guimarães (Teatro São Carlos, Lisbon, March 29, 1882).

2. See p. 237.
3. BE, p. 394.
4. BE, p. 406.
5. Revived at La Scala on March 2, 1841, with Erminia Frezzolini in the title role, and again on September 16, 1843, *Beatrice di Tenda* had been sung there twenty-six times when its first twentieth-century revival in that house occurred on May 10, 1961. Joan Sutherland was then the Beatrice, Raina Kabaivanska the Agnese, Giuseppe Campora the Orombello, and Dino Dondi the Filippo (five performances that season).
6. *Beatrice di Tenda* won perhaps its greatest suffrage in Rome. The Teatro Apollo revived it on January 17, 1839, July 1, 1840, December 26, 1844 (to wild applause for Erminia Frezzolini as Beatrice and for her husband, Antonio Poggi, as Orombello), and on April 11, 1872. It also was sung elsewhere in Rome.
7. The Clément-Larousse *Dictionnaire lyrique, ou Histoire des opéras* (Paris, 1869, p. 94) said: "In Paris, *Beatrice di Tenda* given in 1840 for the benefit of Mme Persiani, with the participation of that singer and of Mario, a fugitive from the Opéra, obtained no better than mediocre success. It was no happier the next year despite the efforts of Ronconi and the curiosity aroused by the debut, in the role of Orombello, of a Spanish tenor, Don Manuel Ojeda. *Beatrice di Tenda* was revived on April 22, 1854, with the participation of Graziani and Mme Frezzolini; but that retrospective attempt served only to prove that the work would never succeed in France."
8. This description is adapted from that used in the 1964 Fenice libretto.
9. In the 1964 Venice production, *Beatrice di Tenda* having been divided into three acts, Act I ended here; the rest of the original Act I thus became Act II; the original Act II now was called Act III.
10. At this place, the 1964 Fenice program continues: "Exactly at this point, the restoration of the finale arranged by maestro Vittorio Gui is fitted in." See p. 237.
11. I want to thank Mr. Fabrizio Melano for calling to my attention the resemblance of this section of Romani's libretto to a scene for Eboli and Don Carlos in Schiller's *Don Carlos*.
12. In this scene, Beatrice sings the words that Pasta was said to have addressed effectively at the restive first-night Venetian audience: ". . . *se amar non puoi, rispettami . . .*"
13. In March 1968, Richard Macnutt of Tunbridge Wells, England, offered for sale an autograph described as follows: "Autograph musical MS. 2 pages in full score from Beatrice di Tenda, oblong folio. The leaf is numbered 5/1 and is folded. The music is from the Coro d'Armigeri in Act I. The MS starts with the più lento passage for orchestra, 42 bars before the final '[an]diam'. The first 4 bars of MS are as published. After 'Arte egual si ponga in . . .' there is an indication that 28 bars, presumably as at present, follow. The next MS bar starts with '[secur]tà' on a crotchet, after which Bellini has set the words 'Vel non fia, per quanto il copra che da noi non

sia squarciato, s'ei si stima inosservato, s'ei si crede in securtà. Vel non' . . .
This 9-bar setting is completely different from the published score.
Whether it is a rejected version or a final version lost in the transfer of
Bellini's MSS from Paris to Catania we are unable to say." The autograph
is now in the collection of Mr. O. W. Neighbour, London.

14. In *Ottocento musicale italiano; Saggi e note*, Milan, 1952, p. 43.
15. In *Intermezzi critici*, Florence, n.d., p. 74.
16. For the survival, in the Museo Belliniano at Catania, of Bellini's sketches for
    a Beatrice–Agnese duet intended to precede *"Angiol di pace,"* see Pastura,
    "Un Duetto inedito della Beatrice di Tenda," in *La Scala: Rivista dell'opera*,
    Milan, March 1951, p. 44 (reprinted, with musical examples, in BSLS, p.
    573).
17. *"Beatrice di Tenda,"* in *Musica d'oggi*, Milan, May 1959, p. 194.
18. In the booklet accompanying the Decca-London recording of *Beatrice di
    Tenda* with Joan Sutherland as Beatrice.

Bianca e Gernando *and* Bianca e Fernando

1. The extremely prolific Francesco Antonio Avelloni, called *"Il Poetino,"*
   also wrote a *dramma* entitled *Bianca e Fernando*. Roti's play was published
   in *L'Ape teatrale, ossia Nuova Raccolta di drammi, commedie e tragedie*,
   II, Naples, 1825.
2. Another operatic *Bianca e Fernando* was staged in the spring of 1826: to a
   libretto by Martino Cuccetti, it had been composed by Pietro Capiuti
   (dates unknown) and presented at the Teatro San Benedetto, Venice; it
   was restaged successfully at the Teatro dei Compadroni, Pavia, on November 11, 1830. Still another was performed for the first time by the Accademia filarmonica at Treviso on March 31, 1827; it had been composed
   by Giovanni Belio (1806–18??).
3. That this was the original, not the Genoa, version is indicated by the libretto
   published at Palermo in 1829 for these performances.
4. Michael William Balfe (Dublin, May 15, 1808—October 20, 1870, Rowney
   Abbey) did not begin his career as a composer of English operas until
   1835. Before then, he had been a violinist and a popular operatic baritone
   at the Théâtre-Italien, Paris, and several opera houses in Italy. His best-
   remembered opera, *The Bohemian Girl*, was first heard at Drury Lane
   Theatre, London, on November 27, 1843.
5. Plate numbers in this score indicate that the *sinfonia* (3553), the soprano-
   tenor recitative and duet *"Mia suora più non sei"* (3567), and the choral
   scena and tenor aria *"All'udir del padre afflitto"* (3577) had been issued
   separately earlier, probably late in 1828. I am particularly indebted to Mr.
   Philip Gossett for assistance in interpreting Ricordi plate numbers.
6. For a detailed listing of autographs, manuscript copies, and published editions of both versions of *Bianca*, see Friedrich Lippmann, *"Vincenzo
   Bellini und die italienische opera seria seiner Zeit,"* in *Analecta Musicologica*, 6, Cologne/Vienna, 1969, pp. 374–377, and his *"Quellenkundliche
   Ammerkungen zu einigen Opern Vincenzo Bellinis,"* in *Analecta Musicologica*, 4, Cologne/Graz, 1967, pp. 134–136.
7. See Alberto Cametti, *Bellini a Roma*, Rome, 1900, p. 17.

8. Pastura, who believed incorrectly that the play upon which Gilardoni had based the *Bianca e Gernando* libretto was called simply *Carlo, duca d'Agrigento* (BSLS, p. 85), surmised that the title had been changed to *Bianca e Gernando* because the librettist gave less weight to the character of Carlo than the dramatist had given it. But in fact Gilardoni and Bellini had merely shortened Roti's title. The change from Fernando to Gernando was not their choice: it was insisted upon by the Bourbon authorities because the hereditary prince's name could not be used on royal stages in the Kingdom of the Two Sicilies.

9. For a detailed discussion of these alterations, see BSLS, pp. 129–135.

10. BE, pp. 58–59.

11. That is, in the Girard-Cottrau incomplete publication of the opera in piano-vocal score.

12. *Bianca e Gernando* opens with a very brief instrumental introduction.

13. Bellini's comments here demonstrate that he did not always feel strongly the connection between text-words and their meanings and the music used to express or accompany them.

14. Giacinto Marras had sung the role of Nelly in *Adelson e Salvini.*

15. In some instances, then, Romani was required to adapt words to music already composed, a far cry from the belief that Bellini always responded solely, directly, and immediately to text words when composing.

16. The incomplete 1826 edition of *Bianca e Gernando* consists of:

    Act I

    1. Introduction and chorus of warriors, pf. 4 hands
    2. Gernando's cavatina *"A tanto duol quest'anima,"* tenor
    3. Filippo's aria *"Estinto! che ascoltai!"* bass
    4. Trio, *"Di Gernando sono le cifre,"* tenor, contralto, bass
    5. Dance-march and chorus, pf. 2 hands
    6. Bianca's cavatina *"Per lui che in sen racchiude,"* soprano
    7. Finale: march, pf. 2 hands
    8. Finale: *quintettino "Ah! che l'alma invade un gel!"* soprano, contralto, tenor, bass-baritone, bass
    9. Finale: *stretta,* pf. 4 hands

    Act II

    1. Filippo's recitative and aria, with chorus, *"Allor, che notte avanza,"* bass
    2. Romanza for Bianca and Eloisa, soprano and contralto
    3. Recitative and duet for Bianca and Gernando, soprano and tenor
    4. Carlo's *scena* and cavatina, bass
    5. Finale: trio *"Oh Dio! qual voce!"* soprano, tenor, and bass

17. Writing to Florimo on March 2(?), 1828, Bellini said (BE, p. 62): "How can I convince you that the introduction remains as it was? I am using it as the largo [lento] of the *sinfonia . . .*"

18. Page references are to the 1837 Ricordi piano-vocal score. *Bianca e Gernando,* after its short orchestral introduction, begins with a recitative for Clemente, an elderly henchman of the duke. In the letter to Florimo cited in the preceding note, Bellini said: ". . . the opera then begins with Fernando's entrance, without Clemente's recitative, which is useless because it neither says anything nor prepares the way for anything, and the fact

that he is an old, loyal friend *** of Carlo will be learned in the recitative after David's cavatina" (BE, p. 62).

19. That Fernando is also Giovanni David, a star tenor, is made clear in his second sentence: *"Oh gioja, felice io son!"* The vocal writing for the word *"felice"* is this:

20. This is the first of the six numbers about which Bellini told Florimo (letter of April 5, 1828, BE, p. 73): "The pieces upon which I base my hopes are the three cavatinas and the finale of the first act and the duet and the two *scene* of the second . . ." The other two first-act cavatinas referred to are Filippo's *"Estinto! che ascoltai!"* (p. 42) and Bianca's *"La mia scelta a voi sia grata"* (p. 88). As Guido Pannain wrote (*Ottocento musicale italiano*, Milan, 1952, p. 24): "But in fact these three cavatinas seem not to offer much." The first-act finale, however, is a genuinely impressive climax. The second-act duet, *"No! no! mia suora . . . più non sei"* (p. 165) and the two scenes just mentioned, beginning respectively on pp. 183 and 205, come closer to justifying the hopes that Bellini had rested upon them.

21. A variorum edition of *Bianca e Fernando* would include three existing cabalettas for Fernando's entrance *scena*: *"Ascolta, o padre,"* from the Genoa revision; *"Il brando immergere,"* from the first version; and a third —which may be an early, discarded sketch for either version. See note 30, below.

22. Andrea Della Corte pointed out that the otherwise meaningless break between Fernando's words *"Di mia sorte già l'iniquo"* and his *"gode, esulta!"* resulted from Bellini's wish to bring Viscardo's voice into the musical fabric at this juncture. He well described Fernando's *"Col braccio di morte"* (p. 66) as "Bellinian but meager" (Pizzetti, ed., Milan 1936, p. 59).

23. The melody of the repetitive accompaniment beginning in measure 6, p. 102, is (difference of key excepted) all but identical with that of Nelly's *"Oh qual raggio di speranza"* in Act I of *Adelson e Salvini* (p. 116 of the Ricordi piano-vocal score).

24. The last melody introduced into this *stretta* was borrowed from the first theme of the allegro of Bellini's student *Sinfonia per studio (Capriccio)* in C minor, almost certainly composed for Tritto's class in 1822.

25. Pizzetti, ed., *op. cit.*, p. 61.

26. Although the character is called Fernando in the 1837 Ricordi piano-vocal score, he is referred to as Gernando on some pages evidently incorporated into it from partial earlier publication.

27. This orchestral introduction makes use of what many commentators have called a quotation from Beethoven's *Sonata quasi una fantasia*, op. 27, no. 2 (the "Moonlight"):

Bellini repeated his use of this simple figuration in both *Zaira* and *Norma*.

28. The autograph sketches in the Museo Belliniano, Catania, include a preliminary version of "*All'udir del padre afflitto,*" with most of the instrumentation lacking.

29. Bellini later reused music from this cabaletta in the finale of Beatrice's last aria in *Beatrice di Tenda*, "*Ah! la morte a cui m'appresso*" (p. 248 of modern Ricordi piano-vocal score, plate no. 45541).

30. Friedrich Lippmann pointed out ("*Quellenkundliche Anmerkungen,*" *op. cit.,* p. 135, ft. 14) that when revising Gilardoni's libretto, Romani and Bellini brought back from Roti's drama Filippo's attempt to save himself by threatening to stab Bianca's son, which Gilardoni had not included. "The composer," Lippmann wrote, "certainly did not induce him [Romani] to do so for pure theatrical effect, but rather so as to give Bianca occasion to sing the touching '*Deh, non ferir.*'" He added that the finale of the original version is found only in a manuscript copy of the score in the Museo Belliniano, Catania, and in another copy in the library of the Naples Conservatory which (like still another copy at Naples, dated "Firenze 18 ottobre 1869") contains a conflation of the two versions. Dr. Lippmann writes: "It [the copy at Naples, signature 64–88] contains, in addition to Fernando's well-known *aria di sortita*, first version, another one (*Coro e Cavatina Gernando*) not to be found in other sources*:

1st Section.

Se qui cad - de e-stin - to il pa - dre per vi - gor d'av - ver - so fa - to

2nd Section.

Cie - co al - le lagri - me, sor - do ai la - men - ti

* [Lippmann's note]: Thus no less than three cabalettas for Fernando's entrance scene exist: "*Il brando immergere*" in the first version, "*Ascolta, o padre*" in the second, and the one cited here.

"The chorus begins with the words '*Calma signor l'affanno*.' Both solo melodies are characteristic of the usual average of contemporary Italian opera. When they were composed is uncertain. Is this the first, later discarded, form of the *aria di sortita* of the Neapolitan version, or is it the first attempt for the Genoese one?"

31. Cicconetti (p. 34) asserted of this cabaletta that Bellini "improvised [it] in a few moments immediately after lunch, when they [Bellini and Tosi] were together." Because Cicconetti was contemporary with the events that he recounted and knew many of the singers, composers, and other musicians of his period, credence must be given to his undocumented anecdotes—and certainly this cabaletta sounds hastily improvised.

I Capuleti e i Montecchi

1. *Capuleti* was repeated at the Fenice in 1832, with Caradori-Allan, Grisi, and Pocchini Cavalieri in their original roles, but with Domenico Reina as Tebaldo and Natale Costantini as Capellio; it was heard there again in 1835 and 1840, but has not been revived there since.

2. *Belliniana: Nuove note*, Milan, 1885, p. 27.

3. Like Vaccaj's opera, *I Capuleti* is described in its first printed libretto as being in two acts; but both operas often were divided into three, and even four, acts at the whim of impresarios, managers, and star singers. Referring to Malibran's substitution of Vaccaj's act for Bellini's, Julian Budden wrote (*The Listener*, London, Aug. 11, 1966, p. 216): "It may seem strange that this outrage should have been committed by an artist who owed a large part of her reputation to Bellini. But a glance at Vaccai's final scene will show why she did it: the earlier setting throws the mezzo-soprano part far more strongly into relief than do Bellini's simple melodies. Vaccai gives effective prominence to the lower notes; Bellini does not." The unconventionality of Bellini's final scene—like that of the finale of *Norma*—undoubtedly left many early listeners dissatisfied. Vaccaj's handling was charming in an entirely expected way. It was as simple as that.

4. *Op. cit.*, p. 35.

5. The present writer owns a libretto in English. "Romeo and Juliet: A Lyrical Tragedy in Three Acts by Signor Vicenti [*sic*] Bellini, as performed by the Italian Opera Company at the Howard Athenæum, May 13, 1847. Boston, 1847. Eastburn's Press." It lists this cast: Signora Caranti de Vita (Juliet), Signora Fortunata Tedesco (Romeo), Signor L[uigi] Perozzi (Tybalt), Signor Pietro Candi (Capulet), and Signor Frederico [*sic*] Badiali (Lorenzo).

6. D'Amico reported that Ricordi had been distributing the Abbado version in orchestral parts that lacked mention of their not being copies of the originals—and that, at the same time, the publisher was also distributing the score in anastatic reproduction without the Abbado alterations but still containing, as an appendix, Vaccaj's final scene, with this note: "To be substituted, as is generally done, for the final scene of Bellini's opera."

7. *Indagini sulle fonti francesi dei libretti di Vincenzo Bellini,* Milan, 1968, p. 451.
8. Other operatic or quasi-operatic treatments of Romeo and Juliet include Luigi Monescalchi's *Giulietta e Romeo* (the Foppa libretto, 1784); Daniel Steibelt's *Roméo et Juliette* (libretto by Joseph-Alexandre-Pierre de Ségur, 1793); Pietro Carlo Guglielmi's *Romeo e Giulietta* (1810); Manuel del Popolo Vicente García's *Giulietta e Romeo* (Park Theater, New York, 1826); E. Torriani's *Giulietta e Romeo* (Romani's libretto, 1828); Melesio Morales's *Romeo y Julieta* (1863); Richard d'Ivry's *Les Amants de Vérone* (libretto by the composer, 1864); Filippo Marchetti's *Romeo e Giulietta* (libretto by Marco Marcelliano Marcello, 1865); John Edmund Barkworth's *Romeo and Juliet* (libretto by the composer, 1916); Heinrich Sutermeister's *Romeo und Julia* (1939); and Boris Blacher's *Romeo und Julia* (radio première, 1947; staged, 1950).
9. "*Le Prime Opere,*" in *Vincenzo Bellini,* ed. Pizzetti, *op. cit.,* p. 70.
10. Della Corte, *op. cit.,* pp. 70–71.
11. This melody also recurred in the arietta, "*Mi rendi pur contento,*" No. 6 of the *Sei Ariette* published by Ricordi in 1829.
12. Della Corte, *op. cit.,* p. 74.
13. See Appendix M, p. 422.

Ernani

1. Perhaps indicatively, the manuscript copy of *Bianca* in the Museo Belliniano at Catania with autograph indications by Bellini contains this opening scene of Act II much as it was published by Ricordi in the piano-vocal score with plate numbers 9826–9842, whereas the autograph score at Naples is incomplete at this point. The first page of music in the autograph after the ending of Act I begins with the single dangling word "*mora,*" and then proceeds directly into the beginning of "*Allor, che notte avanza*"; "*mora*" is the last word of Filippo's preceding that aria (see Ricordi 9826–9842, p. 142), the rest of which is lacking from the autograph, as is everything found on pp. 137–141 and in the first two measures of p. 142 of the Ricordi score (in which p. 142 is the first with the plate number 9838).
2. As supplied to me by the Museo Belliniano in microfilm, the *Ernani* sketches run to 69 pages. Many signs point to the earlier existence of other pages— which almost certainly were given away by one or another of the Bellini heirs. A possibility must be mentioned that a few of the 69 pages were not original sketches for *Ernani,* but became mixed with them inadvertently.
3. See p. 393 for Florimo's faulty memory of these text lines as they had been reported to him by Bellini in a letter that he later lost or gave away.
4. The text of this recitative is given in BSLS, pp. 267–268. In a footnote there, Pastura points out that Amore (VB:A, pp. 165–166), quoting from the libretto, gave four concluding lines that do not appear in the autograph sketch as we have it (had Amore seen a copy of the unfinished libretto?):

ERNANI—Pensa, mio bene, a te, mi lascia, Elvira . . .
ELVIRA — M'ami così?
>   Speme del triste Ernani,
>   S'io t'ami, non lo dicon sensi umani.

5. This passage is transcribed in BSLS, p. 270.
6. The melody sung by Don Carlo is transcribed in BSLS, p. 271. The notes of its first measure, allowing for the difference in key, are identical to those of the first measure of Norma's "*Ah! bello, a me ritorna.*"
7. The second of these pages is illustrated after p. 129 in Benedetto Condorelli's catalogue *Il Museo Belliniano*. It contains this inscription: "I the undersigned certify that this page of autograph music is in the handwriting of the celebrated Maestro Vincenzo Bellini. Catania. October 8, 1922. Avv[ocato] Riccardo Chiarenza." Chiarenza was descended from Bellini's younger brother Mario.
8. Quoted from Amore in BSLS, pp. 272–273.
9. BSLS, p. 273.
10. BSLS, p. 273.
11. See p. 377 for discussion of "*L'Abbandono.*"

Norma

1. For possible more remote sources of the libretto story, see p. 276.
2. Another *Norma*, with music by the Dutch composer Jan Hendrik Laurens Rijken (1857–1921), was staged at Rotterdam in 1890.
3. For an extended list of editions of *Norma* published during the nineteenth century, see Lippmann, "*Quellenkundliche Anmerkungen*, etc.," p. 141, ft. 27.
4. The Toscanini autograph is contained in a leather binder stamped "A Arturo Toscanini/La 'Scala'/Riconoscente al suo Maestro." The collection also contains: (1) a page of sketches including three vocal lines only of Norma's "*Qual cor tradisti*," which show slight variations from both the Santa Cecilia autograph (page 88 right) and the modern Ricordi piano-vocal score (plate no. 41684); this fragment ends with "*con te*"; (2) three pages of single-line and other sketches without words; (3) two pages of sketches for the introductory second-act chorus "*Qui la selva è più folta e ombrosa*," from *La Sonnambula* (see p. 338); (4) autograph of Bellini's letter of August 23, 1832, from Bergamo to Barbò (BE, p. 318; in facsimile in Cicconetti, after p. 111); and autograph of his letter of March 11, 1835, from Paris to Ricordi (see BE, p. 532, with quotation from the Charavay catalogue).

In the Santa Cecilia autograph of *Norma* (Vol. II, p. 561 left), Norma's "*Il cantico di guerra alzate, o forti*" occupies the first half of the page; it is followed by a half-page heavily struck through in pen and then by the copyist's version of "*Guerra, guerra!*" This leaves open the question of whether the four pages in the Toscanini Collection (the last of which also is lined through for deletion) were originally part of the complete autograph or are a sketch or discarded version. Both the Toscanini autograph and the copyist's version at Santa Cecilia give the third line of the *Inno Guerriero* as "*Qual sui greggi fameliche belve*," as does the original published libretto; but the modern Ricordi piano-vocal score has "*Qual sul gregge fameliche belve*." Where modern scores have "*Sangue, sangue!*" after "*Sui Romani van essi a cader*," the Toscanini shows that Bellini wrote out those words but then crossed them through and substituted for them part of a text line that occurs later in the published versions: "*Strage, strage!*" which here is followed by "*Ster-[minio]*."

The fourth page of the Toscanini autograph is not a continuation of the third: between the text words on the two pages, at least "*-minio*" and "*vendetta!*" are lacking. (Two pages—clearly 4 and 5—of this version were reproduced in facsimile on p. 38 of *Omaggio a Bellini*, where they are described as being "From the collection of the cavaliere [Giuseppe] Giuliano," who was director of the Circolo Bellini of Catania at the turn of the century.) The fourth page of the Toscanini autograph, marked for deletion, begins "*galliche scuri/Fino al tronco . . .*"

The first page of the Toscanini autograph, numbered "1" in the upper righthand corner, carries two inscriptions: "*Autografo di Vincenzo Bellini/ I suoi fratelli/Mario Bellini/Carmelo Bellini*" and "*Regolato al carissimo/ R. E. Pagliara da/Peppino Auteri*": Rocco Pagliara, a poet and librettist, succeeded Florimo as librarian of the Naples Conservatory. The second page is unnumbered. The third page has "3" in the upper righthand corner and also carries the attestation by Mario and Carmelo Bellini. The fourth page has number "6" in the upper righthand corner; its (deleted) words end "*Sovra i flutti del Ligeri impuri/ne gorgoglia con funebre suon*," text that also appears in the copyist's version—whereas the Ricordi score and most recent librettos read: "*Sovra i flutti del Ligeri impuri/ei gorgoglia con funebre suon*." Many small variations occur in the music as among the Toscanini autograph, the copyist's version, and published scores.

5. For an extended list of autograph sketches for *Norma* in the Museo Belliniano, Catania, see Lippmann, *Vincenzo Bellini*, etc., pp. 386–387.

6. Glinka wrote (*op. cit.*, p. 75): "I heard Norma in the spring of 1832 at the Teatro della [*sic*] Scala with Pasta, Donzelli, and Giulietta Grisi. The latter, just beginning her career, was not as fat as she was later in Paris and consequently she looked remarkably good, but she sang in a sort of caterwauling manner, that is, wishing to soften or modify a given musical phrase, she more or less miaowed in her nose."

7. Later performances of *Norma* at the Fenice occurred in 1844, 1856, 1859, 1866, 1912, 1922, 1926, 1931, 1935, 1950, 1954, and 1966–1967 (Elinor Ross as Norma, Fiorenza Cossotto as Adalgisa, Mario Del Monaco as Pollione, Ivo Vincò as Oroveso). The name role had been sung there in 1912 by Ester Mazzoleni; in 1922 by Iva Pacetti; in 1926 by Vera Amerighi Rutili; in 1931 by Cigna; in 1935 by Rosa Raisa; in 1950 by Maria Meneghini Callas (with Elena Nicolai as Adalgisa, Gino Penno as Pollione, Tancredi Pasero as Oroveso); and in 1964 by Lucille Udovick.

8. The pontifical censor insisted upon the change of title and several alterations in the text.

9. *Norma* was sung at the Kärntnertortheater for the three-hundredth time in 1867.

10. Performances in this dated list were probably sung in Italian unless otherwise described.

11. This was after Bellini's death. But on February 6, 1835, the finale of *Norma* had been sung at a Court Concert, with Bellini present to savor the reactions of Louis-Philippe, Queen Marie-Amélie, and the courtiers. See p. 188. Chopin heard *Norma* at the Italien. Frederick Niecks, discussing Chopin's "liking for Bellini and his music," wrote (*Frederick Chopin*, London and New York, 1888, Vol. I, p. 285): "[Ferdinand] Hiller relates that he rarely saw him so deeply moved as at a performance of *Norma*, which they attended together, and that in the finale of the second act, in which Rubini seemed to sing tears, Chopin had tears in his eyes." The familiar legend that Chopin asked to be buried near Bellini is completely without basis in fact.

12. By 1909, *Norma* had been sung more than two hundred times at the Italien. It was presented at the Opéra for the first time on June 6, 1935, when Gina Cigna was the Norma, Gianna Pederzini the Adalgisa, Francesco Merli the Pollione, and Tancredi Pasero the Oroveso.

13. *The Bee* (New Orleans) for April 8, 1836, said: "The third representation of La Norma, by Bellini, was witnessed by about 2000 persons—most of whom were of the most fashionable and respectable class of our citizens. . . . The opera will be repeated this evening. It is probably the best of Bellini, and has delighted all amateurs of music."

14. In December 1837, Wagner conducted *Norma* as his benefit performance at the Riga Opera. The following notice appeared in the *Neue freie Presse* of that city on December 11: "The undersigned believed that he could not better prove his esteem for the public of this city than by selecting this opera. Among all the operas of Bellini, *Norma* is the one that has the most abundant melodic vein joined to the most profound reality, personal passion. All the adversaries of Italian music render justice to this great score, saying that it speaks to the heart, that this is the opera of a genius. And it is for that reason that I invite the public to attend in large numbers. Richard Wagner."

15. An undated anonymous translation of Romani's *Norma* into Dutch was published, but no performance in that language has been documented.

16. The *Norma* libretto had been published at Jassy in a Romanian translation by Gheorghe Asachi; this was said to be the first libretto ever issued in Romanian.

17. See Ian Woodward, "Rare Romantic Ballet Prints," in *The Christian Science Monitor*, Boston, April 15, 1968.

18. This Austrian soprano's real name was Marie Wilt. At Leipzig in 1878, she would be the Brünnhilde of the first complete *Ring* cycle sung in Germany outside Bayreuth—thus preceding Lilli Lehmann in singing both Norma and Brünnhilde.

19. Callas had first sung Norma at the Teatro Colón, Buenos Aires, on June 17, 1949, when Tullio Serafin conducted and others in the cast were Fedora Barbieri (Adalgisa), Antonio Vela (Pollione), and Nicola Rossi-Lemeni (Oroveso).

20. See Andrew Porter, "Opera on the Gramophone. 3—'Norma,' " in *Opera*, London, January 1958, p. 12, ft. 1. Mr. Porter pointed out that the auto-

graph score has *"Casta diva"* in G, as does the Boosey "Royal Edition"
edited by Sir Arthur Sullivan; the autograph also shows the "cabaletta"—
"Ah! bello, a me ritorna"—in G. Whatever Bellini's reasons for permitting
Pasta to transpose them down a whole tone to F, the transposed version
makes infinitely more effective the sudden shift from the preceding prolonged E-flat major.

21. Harold Rosenthal wrote (*Two Centuries of Opera at Covent Garden*,
London, 1958, p. 665): "At the second performance on 6 February, the
applause after the first Norma-Adalgisa duet was so great that [John]
Pritchard was unable to continue, and eventually granted an encore of
the *cabaletta*. This was the first encore at Covent Garden since the es-
tablishment of the post-war company, the first of Callas' career, and the
first Stignani had ever been accorded in *Norma*."

22. Lehmann also sang Norma at Oscar Hammerstein's Harlem Opera House
on March 25 and 27, and on March 22 had been the Brünnhilde in a
matinee *Siegfried* at the Metropolitan.

23. One of the nineteen—that of December 26, 1931—occurred exactly on the
centenary of the première of *Norma* at La Scala. On that occasion, Serafin conducted; Ponselle's singing companions were Gladys Swarthout
(Adalgisa), Minnie Egener (Clotilde), Angelo Bada (Flavio), Giacomo
Lauri-Volpi (Pollione), and Ezio Pinza (Oroveso).

24. See p. 536.

25. Norma too is a *"sacerdotessa d'Irminsul."* Irminsul is thus defined by
Webster's New International Dictionary, 2nd edn.: *"Teut. Relig.* Great
tree trunks or carved columns worshiped in Germanic territory, esp. among
the continental Saxons, orig. as the seat of ancestral souls, later as the seat
of the gods."

26. Different years (1817, 1818, 1820) have been given for the première of
Pacini's *La Sacerdotessa* (sometimes *Foresta*) *d'Irminsul*. Pacini himself, in
his *Le Mie Memorie artistiche* (posthumous, Florence, 1875, p. 13), said: "In
the spring of 1816 I was signed up by the shrewd but honest impresario
Maestro Adolfo Bassi for the Trieste theater, where I put on *La Sacerdotessa d'Irminsul*, poetry by the celebrated *cavaliere* Felice Romani, an opera
that was performed by the highly praised [Emilia] Bonini, by the celebrated
[*castrato*, Giovanni Battista] Velluti, by the tenor Bolognesi, and by the
baritone [Carlo] Zucchelli." In the list of operas in that book, this one is
assigned to "1817/spring/Trieste." However, "Luigi Lianovasani" (*i.e.*,
Giovanni Salvioli), in his *Saggio bibliografico relativo ai melodrammi di
Felice Romani* (Milan, 1878), assigned its première to 1818 and specifically
ruled out 1817 as its possible date. Mario Rinaldi (*Felice Romani*, Rome,
1965, pp. 120–121) gives conclusive evidence that the first performance of
La Sacerdotessa d'Irminsul took place at Trieste on May 11, 1820, a date
underwritten by Ireneo Bremini in *Il Comunale di Trieste* (n.d., but 1962),
p. 117 (where he lists Carolina Pellegrini, but not Emilia Bonini, among
the singers at the première). Had Soumet ever seen that opera—or read
Romani's libretto for it?

27. Disregarding the fact that *Les Martyrs* was not published until 1809, writers
sometimes described Velleda as also ancestral to Giulia, the erring priestess-
heroine of Gaspare Spontini's opera *La Vestale* (Opéra, Paris, December

16, 1807, libretto by Victor-Joseph Étienne de Jouy). Vincenzo Pucitta's *La Vestale*, composed for Angelica Catalani to sing in London in 1810, used an Italian translation of Étienne de Jouy's French libretto. But the libretto that Salvatore Cammarano wrote for Saverio Mercadante's *La Vestale* (Teatro San Carlo, Naples, March 10, 1840) came enough later to show acquaintance not only with Chateaubriand and Étienne de Jouy, but also with Romani's texts for *La Sacerdotessa d'Irminsul* and *Norma*. Friedrich Lippmann has pointed out (*Vincenzo Bellini*, etc., *op. cit.*, p. 23) the resemblance between the subject matter of Romani's *Norma* and that of Giuseppe Bernardoni's libretto for Giovanni Simone Mayr's opera *Alonso e Cora* (La Scala, Milan, December 26, 1803).

28. Andrew Porter, in "Footnotes on Norma," in *About the House*, Vol. 2, No. 8, Christmas 1967, London, p. 14, wrote: "Before leaving Soumet, we might just note that his Clothilde is a Christian nanny, and that her charges, Agénor and Clodomir [the children of Norma by Pollion], are speaking roles, Agénor indeed being quite voluble. Act III begins with a conversation in which Agénor says that he doesn't care much for mummy's god, Irminsul, and is rather uncertain about his father's, Jupiter. Clothilde produces a picture of *her* God—only a baby in his mother's lap, but more powerful than either of the others. It is not an important motif in the play and was not taken up in the opera."

29. In "*En relisant Norma: Bellini, musicien dramatique*," in the special Bellini issue of *La Revue musicale*, Paris, 1935, pp. 54–55.

30. *Op. cit.*, pp. 60–61.

31. In "*Sur Bellini harmoniste*," in the special Bellini issue of *La Revue musicale*, Paris, 1935, p. 64.

32. See Appendix P, p. 446, for a discussion of Wagner's attitudes toward Bellini, and toward *Norma* in particular.

33. BE, p. 581.

34. The marchese Francesco Berio di Salsa had taken the libretto material for *Ricciardo e Zoraide* from the *Ricciardetto* of Niccolò Forteguerri (1674–1735), Felice Romani that for *Bianca e Falliero* from an episode retold in histories of seventeenth-century Venice.

35. In measures 29–30 of the *sinfonia*, Domenico de Paoli found "the cell from which will emerge the Bacchanale in *Tannhäuser*" (*loc. cit.*, p. 52).

36. Page references are to the Ricordi piano-vocal score, plate number 41684, from which the Schirmer piano-vocal score with plate number 44001 was reproduced with small editorial changes.

37. This G-major section is nearly always destroyed in performance by excessive loudness and a closing fortissimo rather than the tranquil hush leading to a forte, as clearly indicated in the autograph twelve measures from the end. Also, Bellini's instruction at the end, "*Attacca l'Introduzione*," is always countermanded by applause, which further weakens the effect. Bellini's care as an orchestrator is illustrated by the fact that he wrote a harp part into this *sinfonia* from its opening measure, but then scratched it out, having decided to employ the harp timbre only where it can truly be heard, in the concluding section in G major.

38. In "*La 'Norma' di Bellini*," in *Nuova Antologia*, December 15, 1882, p. 807.

39. *Op. cit.*, p. 55.

40. Gaetano Cesari and Alessandro Luzio, eds.: *I Copialettere di Giuseppe Verdi*, Milan, 1913, p. 416.
41. The stage band should never be seen, modern trombones, bassoons, etc., being too visibly anachronistic.
42. The definitive text of "*Casta diva*" was not reached at first attempt. Benedetto Condorelli (in "*Genesi e vicende della 'Norma,'*" in *Norma: Numero unico*, Catania, 1931) quoted this preliminary version of its two strophes:

> *Casta diva che inargenti*
> *questo suol con vergin volto,*
> *nel tenace amore raccolto*
> *spansi influsso di virtù.*
>
> *Sia quel balsamo alle genti*
> *che le piaghe disacerbi,*
> *che costanti ancor le serbi*
> *in si lunga servitù.*

43. This melody, in simpler form, was originally that of the cabaletta "*Contenta appien quest'alma*" in the revised *Bianca e Fernando* (p. 91 of the Ricordi piano-vocal score); it recurs again in *Zaira*, in the heroine's "*Lieto ci mira adesso*" (p. 138L of the autograph).
44. That Adalgisa has taken only preliminary vows is indicated when (pp. 124–125) Norma says to her: "*Ah! tergi il pianto: te non lega eterno nodo all'ara*" (Cease weeping: no eternal knot ties you to the altar). She is, then, less of a sinner than Norma.
45. In "*La Norma*," in the special Bellini issue of *La Revue musicale*, Paris, 1935, p. 48.
46. This is sometimes referred to as the first section of a Pollione–Adalgisa duet.
47. The illusion-destroying custom of assigning the role of Adalgisa to a mezzo-soprano or contralto deprives us of Bellini's conception of their relationship. The original Adalgisa, for whom he composed the role, was a soprano: Giulia Grisi. One result of the change to a deeper color and throatier timbre is to make Adalgisa sound somewhat older than Norma— an effect that Bellini certainly would have disliked: Grisi was fourteen years younger than Pasta, and Adalgisa is supposed to be a young girl.
48. The melody of this *andante marcato* is a revision of that of the opening of the Elvira–Don Carlo duet "*Muto e deserto speco è il muzial mio tetto*," in Bellini's autograph sketches for the unfinished *Ernani*. See p. 263.
49. *Norma*, Milan, 1923, pp. 116–117.
50. Here the score is starred with directions to the singers: ". . . with great fire . . . bursting out . . . desperately . . . to Norma, supplicatingly . . ." etc.
51. Much of the dramatic effect here is produced by the rhythms of the accompaniment, in which the cellos and doublebasses play groups of four sixteenth-notes while the violins are playing equivalent triplets, of which the first integer is always a rest. See Appendix N, p. 427, for a translation of Friedrich Lippmann's description of the variants in *Norma* autographs, editions, and manuscript copies.
52. Here the emotional force is increased by a modulation from G minor to G major with the words "*Te sull'onde*" (p. 149).

53. In the four-act version, this is the end of Act II.
54. Norma's exceedingly right words for this scene appear in the original (1831) libretto as:

> Dormono entrambi . . . non vedran la mano
> Che li percuote.—Non pentirti, o core;
> Viver non ponno . . . Qui supplizio, e in Roma
> Opprobrio avrian, peggior supplizio assai . . .
> Schiavi d'una matrigna.—Ah! no: giammai.
>
> Sorge
>
> Muoiano, sì. Non posso (fa un passo e si ferma)
> Avvicinarmi: un gel mi prende, e in fronte
> Mi si solleva il crin.—I figli uccido! . . .
> Teneri figli . . . in questo sen concetti (intenerendosi)
> Da questo sen nutriti . . . essi, pur dianzi
> Delizia mia . . . ne' miei rimorsi istessi
> Raggio di speme . . . essi nel cui sorriso
> Il perdono del ciel mirar credei! . . .
> Io, io li svenerò! . . . di che son rei?
>
> Silenzio
>
> Di Pollïon son figli:
> Ecco il delitto: Essi per me son morti:
> Mojan per lui: n'abbia rimorso il crudo,
> N'abbia rimorso, anche all'amante in braccio,
> E non sia pena che la sua somigli.
> Feriam . . . (s'incammina verso il letto: alza il
>   pugnale; essa da un grido inorridita: i
>   figli si svegliano)
>   Ah! no . . . son figli miei! . . . miei figli!
>   (li abbraccia e piange)
> Clotilde!

55. *Intermezzi critici*, Florence, n.d. (but 1921), p. 76.
56. *Op. cit.*, pp. 80–81.
57. The text words were borrowed, very little altered, from a passage in the Ernani–Elvira duet in the autograph sketches for *Ernani*. There they were also sung in thirds, but to the melodic line of the opening of the duet ("*Muto e deserto . . .*"), which in Norma has become that of "*Oh! di qual sei tu vittima*"; see p. 263.
58. For these melodic phrases, see Friedrich Lippmann, *Vincenzo Bellini*, etc., p. 373.
59. In the four-act version, this is the end of Act III.
60. Bellini borrowed this, with small but effective changes, from *Zaira* (the Act II chorus of French knights mourning the death of Lusignano: "*Poni il fedel tuo martire*"— found on p. 109L of the autograph of *Zaira* at Naples). The *Zaira* chorus, in turn, he had borrowed from the revised *Bianca e Fernando* (Act II chorus "*Tutti siam, sì, tutti uniti,*" Ricordi 1837 piano-vocal score, p. 184). See pp. 367 and 245 for those earlier passages; for the supposed "quotation" from Beethoven's "Moonlight" *Sonata quasi*

una fantasia, op. 27, no. 2, see also note 27 for *Bianca e Fernando,* p. 518.

61. The principal melodic idea of "*Ah! del Tebro*" first appeared, in only slightly different form, as that of the *andante assai sostenuto* Don Carlo-Elvira duet in the *Ernani* autograph sketches, where (in two differing versions) it set the text beginning "*Meco regna io ti offro un trono/O sovrana del mio core.*"

62. At this point, the original 1831 libretto and many librettos issued later indicate a line for Clotilde: "*Cielo! che tenti?*" But that line does not appear in the autograph score or in the Ricordi piano-vocal score with plate number 41684.

63. The assertion, apparently made first by Luigi Ricci, that this chorus was borrowed from a chorus of Turks in *Zaira* is incorrect. See Appendix N and footnote 3 above for discussion of the partial autograph and published variants of the "*Guerra, guerra!*" chorus.

64. Of "*Qual cor tradisti,*" Domenico de Paoli wrote (*loc. cit.,* pp. 58–59): "Aria? no: the true *melody* does not begin until '*Deh! non volerli vittime.*' Before that, this is a little melodic-rhythmic lead-in born from the inflection of the poetic phrase, which the musician transposes onto the different steps of the scale and varies, but never to the point of rendering the original *cell* unrecognizable. Recitative in the usual sense of the word? not at all. Melody or *bel canto*? again, no; something shaped out of the elements of both, but belonging solely to Bellini, something of which the formative elements are easily analyzable, but of which the result always remains a mystery, especially if one thinks of the simplicity of the means employed."

65. *I Copialettere di Giuseppe Verdi,* ed. by Gaetano Cesari and Alessandro Luzio, Milan, 1913, p. 416.

Il Pirata

1. Raimond's *mélodrame* was an immediate popular success. In *Un Grand Homme de province à Paris* (1839), Balzac's Lucien de Rubempré and Lousteau go to the Panorama-Dramatique to see "a very good *mélodrame* entitled *Bertram,* a play derived from a tragedy by Maturin which was very highly esteemed by Lord Byron and Walter Scott." Raimond's play was closely based upon Charles Robert Maturin's five-act verse tragedy, *Bertram, or The Castle of Saint-Aldobrand* (Drury Lane Theatre, London, 1816, having been secured for the theater by Byron on the recommendation of Scott [see Leslie A. Marchand, *Byron: A Biography,* New York, 1951, II, p. 542]). A French translation of Maturin's tragedy, by Charles Nodier and Isidore Taylor ("Raimond"), was published in Paris in 1821, but may not have been staged. Raimond's play followed the next year. M. A. Ruff, in his edition of the Nodier-Taylor translation of Maturin's play (Paris, 1956), pointed out the possible derivation of elements in it from Scott's *Rokeby,* a French translation of which had been issued in 1820. Coleridge violently attacked Maturin's *Bertram* at the end of his *Biographia Literaria.*

2. Many pages of this score—the *sinfonia* included—are not autograph; some of them appear to have been inserted by mistake.

3. Of this performance, *I Teatri* (Milan, June 14, 1828) reported: "The impresario Barbaja persuaded the illustrious Zingarelli [then seventy-four] to accept one of the most spacious loges for himself, his family, and his friends, as from there he could look out upon the triumphs of his favorite disciple. Throughout the performance, tears of contentment ran from the eyes of that very renowned veteran of the singing art." When *Il Pirata* was staged at the San Carlo again on November 14, 1834, the cast was: Caroline Unger (Imogene), Marietta Sacchi (Adele), Gilbert-Louis Duprez (Gualtiero), Alessandro Giacchini (Itulbo), Carlo Novelli (Goffredo), and Domenico Cosselli (Ernesto).

4. *Il Pirata* has not been restaged at the Fenice since 1830.

5. The first Bellini opera heard in England, *Il Pirata*, was followed by the ballet *La Sonnambule* (libretto by Scribe; choreography by Aumer, music by Hérold), upon the scenario of which Romani and Bellini were to base *La Sonnambula* the following year.

6. If Bellini was given a detailed description of this performance, he must have been infuriated: not only did Schröder-Devrient interpolate into it an aria from Pacini's 1825 opera *Amazilia*, but also a duet by Pacini brought the opera to a "happy ending." When the Italien repeated *Il Pirata* on October 8, 1833, however (with Caroline Unger, Rubini, and Santini in the leading roles), Bellini's tragic ending was restored.

7. Manfredi (1232–1266), natural son of Frederick II of Swabia, became king of Sicily in 1258, but was defeated and killed by Charles of Anjou, who succeeded him.

8. BSLS, p. 114.

9. See Appendix F, p. 403, for the text of the concluding scenes of *Il Pirata* as printed in the first libretto.

10. "*Quellenkundliche Anmerkungen zu einigen Opern Vincenzo Bellinis*," in *Analecta Musicologica*, 4, Cologne/Graz, 1967, p. 139.

11. *Op. cit.*

12. Lippmann, *op. cit.*, describes other performance variants.

13. The borrowings from the *sinfonia* for *Adelson e Salvini* are: p. 5, measures 9–18 (*Adelson e Salvini*, Ricordi piano-vocal score with plate numbers 108595–6, p. 6, measure 11, to p. 7, measure 6); the second theme of the *allegro agitato*, measure 11, p. 6 (*Adelson*, p. 9, measure 2)—and, in fact, forty-three measures, from measure 11, p. 6, through the three-measure bridge passage that ends p. 7 (*Adelson*, p. 9, from measure 2 through measure 11, p. 10); the repetition, D major, measure 5, p. 9, of the second *allegro agitato* theme (*Adelson*, p. 13, measure 9). Lippmann pointed out (*Vincenzo Bellini*, etc., *op. cit.*, p. 371, ft. 23) that this second theme of the *allegro agitato* is used in the form in which it is sung in *Adelson e Salvini* (p. 74), not as Gualtiero sings it in *Il Pirata* ("*Per te di vane lagrime*," p. 56). He believes that this seeming anomaly was caused by Bellini's borrowing for the *Pirata sinfonia*, not from the published overture to *Adelson* (almost certainly as used for the 1825 première), but from a revision of it intended for later use, of which an incomplete non-autograph

copy exists in the library of the Naples Conservatory, where it is cata-
logued as Rari 4.3.2.[48]

14. Della Corte, Pizzetti, ed., *op. cit.*, p. 50.
15. Della Corte (*op. cit.*, p. 54) found echoes of Rossini's *L'Italiana in Algeri* in "*Bagnato delle lagrime.*"
16. Friedrich Lippmann (*Vincenzo Bellini*, etc., pp. 101–102) speculated that Bellini's reason for not using these excellent Romani lines was difficulty in fitting them comfortably to an already existing melody that he had de-cided to place at this point.
17. In *The Listener*, London, May 26, 1966, p. 772.
18. Della Corte, *op. cit.*, pp. 54–55.
19. Della Corte, *op. cit.*, p. 55.
20. Have Imogene and Gualtiero been lovers? As Andrew Porter wrote (In-troduction to booklet supplied with the recording of *Il Pirata* in which Montserrat Caballé sings Imogene): "An adulterous heroine! Not only Coleridge was morally indignant. And yet, unless we assume that something of the kind happened, Imogene's wish to "corregere l'error di cui siam rei' [atone for the sin of which we are guilty] (in her duet with Gualtiero [p. 278]) does not really make sense. There is a loose end in Romani's otherwise tidy work."
21. In the autograph score of *Il Pirata* in the library of the Naples Conserva-tory, the pages beginning with "*ti renderà*" (p. 281 of the Ricordi piano-vocal score, with plate number 108189) and ending with "*virtù, virtù*" (p. 286) are not autograph. Those pages are in the Pierpont Morgan Library, New York. With the generous permission of that library, I had the pleasure in 1969 of taking a reproduction of the autograph pages to the Naples library.
22. Rubini is said to have sung "*Tu vedrai*" transposed up a tone to D major; Domenico Donzelli to have had it transposed down to B-flat major.
23. Della Corte, *op. cit.*, p. 56.
24. The stage directions are: "Here Imogene enters holding her son by the hand. She is delirious. She moves forward slowly, looking about her in confusion. She weeps. The Maidens stand to one side, observing her and weeping . . . She seems to search for something in the empty air . . . Sighs of contentment . . . She falls back into sorrow . . . She moves farther forward on the stage with irregular steps and lets go of her son; crying, he tries to console her, but she does not hear him . . . The boy runs to Adele's arms and, tugging her toward his mother, begs her to help her . . . Adele presses him to her heart, weeping, and approaches Imogene; but, realizing that she is out of her mind, moves a little distance away."
25. Della Corte, *op. cit.*, p. 58.

I Puritani

1. Sometimes billed as *I Puritani e(d) i cavalieri*, sometimes as *I Puritani di Scozia*, though, except for references to the Stuarts, the opera has nothing to do with Scotland.

2. As Andrew Porter wrote ("Bellini's Last Opera," in *Opera*, London, May 1960, p. 318), plays by Ancelot were also used for the librettos of two operas by Donizetti (*Roberto Devereux* and *Maria Padilla*) and one by Emanuel Chabrier (*Le Roi malgré lui*). Mr. Porter also wrote: "At least two drafts for the scenario [of *I Puritani*] have survived. Pastura in his recent volume [BSLS, pp. 418–419] transcribes one [from Tommasino D'Amico's *Come si ascolta l'opera*, Milan, n.d., but shortly after World War II], and I have recently acquired another, earlier one, in Bellini's hand, dictated by Pepoli when (as he notes in the margin) 'the infirmity of my poor eyes entirely prevented me from writing.' In this quite detailed draft, the heroine is called Eloisa, and one number is described as 'Duetto di Lablache e Eloisa.'" This latter was probably what became "*Sai com'arde in petto mio*," early in Part I.

3. Probably the less accomplished of the two Amigo sisters—a soprano—but possibly the more prominent elder sister, usually listed as a mezzo-soprano.

4. The Ricordi copy consists of two bound volumes in which each piece is attested to by signatures of Rossini, who acted as the Paris executor of Bellini's estate; the publisher Eugène Troupenas; and the director and administrator of the Théâtre-Italien, respectively Édouard Robert and Carlo Severini. The Conservatorio Giuseppe Verdi, Milan, also has a manuscript copy of "*I Puritani/Dal Sig^{re} Maestro V^{zo} Bellini*," of which Friedrich Lippmann wrote (*Vincenzo Bellini*, etc., op. cit., p. 390, ft. 39a): "It must be viewed as fraudulent. It is evidently one of those unauthorized [read: pirated] copies which distort the text, and which caused Bellini so much concern. It begins with a 'newly composed' overture. All the recitatives, similarly, are pure inventions. The arialike passages inserted by Bellini into the recitatives are missing. The instrumentation is not Bellini's. The creator of this score most probably 'fashioned' it after the model of the first published separate numbers and the libretto (the melodies included are on the whole correct)."

5. At the end of the 1960–1961 season, *I Puritani* had been performed 114 times at La Scala. It was also sung at the Teatro della Canobbiana, Milan, seventeen performances beginning on September 29, 1855, with Enrico Delle Sedie as Riccardo.

6. *I Puritani* was repeated at the Fenice in 1837, 1838, 1866, 1875, 1900, 1949, and 1966. On December 31, 1900, the cast included Regina Pinkert (Elvira) and Alessandro Bonci (Arturo).

7. It was still *Elvira Walton* when, on December 26, 1842, it was restaged at the Apollo with Clara Novello (Elvira), Adelaide Gualdi (Enrichetta), Baldassare Mirri (Walton), Pietro Balzar (Sir Giorgio), Napoleone Moriani (Talbo), and Felice Varesi (Riccardo).

8. Of that occasion, Giuseppe Radiciotti wrote (*Teatro e musicisti in Sinigaglia*, Milan, etc., 1893, p. 102): "Frezzolini no longer had her onetime voice, but always was the excellent singer whom we all knew; Boucardé was good; very good, Ottaviani, who each evening had to repeat, with Bouché, the second bass, the magnificent duet ["*Suoni la tromba*"] in Act II." Radiciotti also noted that various censors demanded the replacement (in "*Suoni la tromba*") of "*Gridando: Libertà*" by "*Gridando: Lealtà*."

9. *I Puritani* was also played in Chicago in 1865, at Crosby's Opera house, with

Clara Louise Kellogg as Elvira; and, to open the season, at the Civic
Opera House on November 31, 1955, with Maria Meneghini Callas (El-
vira), Giuseppe di Stefano (Arturo), Ettore Bastianini (Riccardo), and
Nicola Rossi-Lemeni (Sir Giorgio).

10. *I Puritani* had been sung only five times at the Metropolitan through the
1970–1971 season: once in 1883 and four times in 1918, beginning on Febru-
ary 18, when the cast consisted of María Barrientos (Elvira), Flora Perini
(Enrichetta), Hipólito Lázaro (Arturo), Angelo Bada (Benno [*sic*]),
Giuseppe DeLuca (Riccardo), José Mardones (Sir Giorgio), and Giulio
Rossi (Walton); Roberto Moranzoni conducted.

11. *I Puritani* was also presented at the Manhattan on February 26, 1909, when
Luisa Tetrazzini was the Elvira, with Gina Severina (Enrichetta), Floren-
cio Constantino (Arturo), Emilio Venturini (Bruno), Giovanni Polese
(Riccardo), Andrés de Segurola (Sir Giorgio), and Giuseppe de Grazia
(Walton).

12. *I Puritani* was offered again at the Colón in 1961, with Leyla Gencer
(Elvira), Gianni Raimondi (Talbo), Manuel Ausensi (Riccardo), and
Ferruccio Mazzoli (Sir Giorgio).

13. *I Puritani* was sung in Florence again on January 9, 1952 (Teatro Comu-
nale); Serafin conducted, and the cast was made up of Maria Meneghini
Callas (Elvira), Grace Hoffman (Enrichetta), Eugene Conley (Arturo),
Alberto Lotti Camici (Bruno), Carlo Tagliabue (Riccardo), Nicola
Rossi-Lemeni (Sir Giorgio), and Silvio Maionica (Walton); and again at
the Comunale on December 20, 1963, when Alberto Erede conducted and
the cast was made up of Virginia Gordoni (replacing an indisposed Renata
Scotto as Elvira), Flora Rafanelli (Enrichetta), Alfredo Kraus (Arturo),
Gino Sarri (Bruno), Sesto Bruscantini (Riccardo), Paolo Washington
(Sir Giorgio), and Giovanni Antonini (Walton).

14. *I Puritani* was repeated at the Massimo Bellini on November 8, 1951, with
Callas (Elvira), Wenko Wonkoff (Arturo), Carlo Tabliabue (Riccardo),
and Boris Christoff (Sir Giorgio); again on November 3, 1955, with Virginia Zeani (Elvira), Mario Filippeschi (Arturo), Aldo Protti (Riccardo),
and Giulio Neri (Sir Giorgio); and again in 1960, with Anna Moffo
(Elvira) and Filippeschi (Arturo).

15. Having opened that Fenice season as Brünnhilde in *Die Walküre* (in
Italian), Callas replaced an indisposed Margherita Carosio in the role of
Elvira, which she learned in six days. She sang Brünnhilde on the opening
night (January 13) and January 15 while learning *I Puritani*—and was
ready for the dress rehearsal of the latter on January 17. That night, she repeated Brünnhilde; she sang her first Elvira on January 19. Her Italian debut
as La Gioconda at Verona on August 3, 1947, had made her famous; after
this conjunction of Wagner and Bellini, she became an international phenomenon.

16. Defending his "editing" of Bellini's score, Maestro Gui wrote (in a note,
"Vincenzo Bellini and 'I Puritani,'" in the Glyndebourne Festival program): "It was the custom of the period for composers to adapt the vocal
parts of their operas to circumstances, that is to say, to singers' requirements, for they still ruled supreme on the lyric stage. Bellini, intimate
friend and warm admirer of Malibran, thought of adapting the part of

534) *Notes to* I Puritani

Elvira to the famous *diva*'s voice and at Catania, the composer's birthplace, there is a manuscript in the Bellini museum which, besides this arrangement and some important variants in the tenor part, contains three ensembles which do not appear in the current edition. What would Bellini have done to Arturo's part with its impossible *tessitura*, the part he wrote expressly for the exceptional talents of the famous Rubini, if he had had the time and the means to adapt the part for a less . . . exceptional tenor? That is what we wonder today and although a concrete answer must for ever elude us, we can find consolation in the thought that a few slight, inevitable revisional touches to the vocal 'eccentricities' in Arturo's part can never betray the composer's intention and in any case we cannot ask him for his direct authorization. If as we know the entire soprano part (Elvira) was transposed and adapted by Bellini for Malibran (mezzo-soprano), why could not the same treatment have been given to the tenor part (Arturo)—and with greater justification—written as it was for Rubini's individual vocal technique and perhaps also to satisfy the demands of the *divo* of the moment?"

The answer to Maestro Gui's special pleading is, of course, that for a composer to alter his score or let someone else alter it under his supervision is one matter, but that for anyone else, even a distinguished conductor, to alter it—particularly more than a century after its composition —is to tamper dangerously with an established document.

17. Bellini originally intended *I Puritani* to begin with a *sinfonia*. But at the eleventh hour, the time taken up by the final shaping of the Riccardo–Sir Giorgio cabaletta (*"Suoni la tromba"*) and by the adaptation of the Paris score for Naples made composition of the *sinfonia* impossible. Pastura commented (BSLS, p. 447): "But it is also to be believed that, hearing the rehearsals of the first act with the choruses and soloists, he [Bellini] became aware that the introduction of the opera is in itself a vocal and instrumental *sinfonia* that immediately reveals to the listener the spirit and character of *I Puritani*."

18. The partially autograph "Malibran" score in Catania begins with this scene, transposed down to A major.

19. The melodic figuration in thirds which begins in the orchestra at measure 10 of p. 40 is borrowed from flute-clarinet writing in the Lusignano–Nerestano–Zaira trio in Scene 10 of Act I of *Zaira* (see p. 366).

20. At the word *"rammento"* (p. 72), Arturo sings a high C sharp as the first note of a downward sixteenth-note run. Desmond Shawe-Taylor noted (" A 'Puritani' Discography," in *Opera*, London, June 1960, p. 394) that in the recording of *I Puritani* in which Maria Meneghini Callas is the Elvira, Giuseppe Di Stefano as Arturo "rises four times to a rather anxious C sharp; once in '*A te, o cara*', twice in '*Vieni fra queste braccia*' (transposed down by a semitone), and once during the final ensemble, '*Credeasi misera!*', in which he sings a D flat at the point where the score has a famous and virtually inaccessible high F." Rubini, of course sang those C sharps and equivalent D flat—and the high F—without strain or anxiety.

21. Bellini almost certainly composed *"Son vergin vezzosa"* with Malibran in mind after learning that she was scheduled to sing Elvira at Naples, and then included it for Grisi in the first Paris performances. One of his

reasons for cutting from thirty to forty minutes of playing time from the score after its première was that *"Son vergin vezzosa"* (like *"Suoni la tromba"*) was so much applauded that it had to be repeated, thus tending to lengthen the performance unduly. He also cut the trio leading up to the flight of Arturo and Enrichetta in Scene 10 of Part I and the andante of the Elvira–Arturo duet near the end of Part III.

22. Sopranos singing Elvira ought to know that in the Palermo autograph of *I Puritani*, Bellini wrote in just before the beginning of *"Vien, diletto"*: *"molto silenzio primo d'attacare"* (a long silence before attacking). That silence can greatly increase the effect of the cabaletta.

23. Friedrich Lippmann acutely observed that it would have been difficult for any other composer of Bellini's time to remove the chorus from the stage before Elvira's mad scene (*Atti del I Congresso internazionale di studi verdiani*, Parma, 1969, p. 188).

24. Bellini originally intended *"Suoni la tromba"* to be sung by the chorus of Puritans after *"La luna, il sole, le stelle"* in Part I, Scene 1, which it would have concluded. Feeling it excessive there, he considered having it follow the storm in what is now Scene 1 of Part III. Some time later, however, he foresaw it as a duet with chorus for Riccardo and Sir Giorgio, to be placed before the scene of Elvira's first delirium, "perhaps," as Pastura suggested (BSLS, p. 441) "as a sequel to the invocation of divine punishment upon the traitor and betrayer, Arturo." Rossini appears to have seen the score with it so placed, and a credible tradition says that he then suggested to Bellini the division of *I Puritani* into three acts by cutting the second act in two and the use of *"Suoni la tromba"* as the cabaletta of the duet of the two basses, as which it would end what thus became the second of three acts. In a sense, this new division returned to an earlier three-act plan, which at one point Bellini himself had asked Pepoli to change to two acts.

La Sonnambula

1. Earlier operas dealing with somnambulism had included Luigi Piccinni's *opera buffa Il Sonnambulo* (libretto anonymous, Stockholm, 1797) and Ferdinando Paër's *La Sonnambula* (libretto by Giuseppe Maria Foppa, Venice, 1800). The Palermitan composer Antonio D'Antoni reset Romani's *Sonnambula* libretto as *Amina, ossia L'Orfanella di Ginevra*; the opera was successfully staged at the Teatro Comunale, Trieste, during the Carnival season of 1824–1825 (according to *Memorie del Teatro Communale di Trieste*, by "Un Vecchio Teatrofilo," *Amina* was that season's only success, despite the fact that the other three operas, all Rossini's, were *L'Equivoco stravagante, Il Barbiere di Siviglia*, and *La Cenerentola*).

2. A new edition of *La Sonnambula* in piano-vocal score announced as among the complete operas published by Ricordi through December 1859 may or may not have been issued; no copy of it is known.

3. The full score of *La Sonnambula* was issued in facsimile of the autograph by Ricordi, Milan, in 1934.

4. *La Sonnambula* being considered too brief to occupy an entire evening, it was played (as examples) with *Der Freischütz* and with *Fidelio,* in which latter Malibran also sang, in English.

5. The first performance of *La Sonnambula* at the San Carlo appears to have occurred on June 20, 1834, when Giulia Toldi was the Amina, Nicholas Ivanoff the Elvino.

6. *La Sonnambula* was repeated on July 30. Just as Manvera began to sing *"Tutto è sciolto,"* the frame theater was found to be ablaze. No one was injured, but the theater and some twenty nearby buildings were destroyed. J. B. Rice, owner of the theater, built a second Chicago Theater, and in October 1853 continued introducing opera to the city. With Luigi Arditi conducting and Rose De Vries as *prima donna* very *assoluta,* the operas presented during 1853 were *Lucia di Lammermoor, Norma,* and again *La Sonnambula.*

7. Patti sang Amina at Covent Garden every year for twelve years—and again in 1878.

8. Carlotta added (interpolated or post-performance) the final rondo and cavatina from Rossini's *La Cenerentola;* Barbara joined her and Cornelia Castelli in the trio from Cimarosa's *Il Matrimonio segreto.*

9. A note in the Fenice's typed list of performances reads: "The part of Amina was to have been interpreted by the soprano Joan Sutherland: because of artistic differences with the director of the orchestra [Nello Santi], the artist canceled the performances."

10. From the 1883–1884 season through that of 1970–1971, the Metropolitan gave forty-eight performances of *La Sonnambula* in eleven seasons.

11. When conte Rodolfo says (p. 62), *"Tu non sai con quei begli occhi/ Come dolce il cor mi tocchi,/Qual richiami ai pensier miei/Adorabile beltà"* (You can't know how those dear eyes/Gently touch my heart,/ What adorable beauty/Is recalled to my thoughts), we are half in the presence of Romani's idea that Amina should be the count's illegitimate daughter by a village girl he had seduced and left. Friedrich Lippmann said of this passage: "Rodolfo's allegro *'Tu non sai con quei begl'occhi'* in *La Sonnambula,* Act I . . . evidently made a great impression [upon Verdi]; in fact, many Verdian melodies recall it . . ." and then cites as examples Zaccaria's cabaletta *"Come notte a sol fulgente,"* from Part I of *Nabucco,* and Silva's cavatina *"Infelice!"* from Act I of *Ernani.*

12. *"Sur Bellini harmoniste,"* Bellini number of *La Revue musicale,* Paris, 1935, p. 384.

13. This brief scene and Scene 6 until Lisa addresses Elvino (*"E fia pur vero,"* p. 165) were omitted from the recording of the opera in which Maria Meneghini Callas sang Amina.

14. That Bellini should have availed himself of this "learned" device of imitation surprises only those commentators who have forgotten that he also used it both in his 1821(?) Mass in A minor and in *Beatrice di Tenda.*

15. This phrase is incised upon the stone of Bellini's tomb in the Cathedral at Catania.

16. *"Bellini, musicien dramatique,"* in Bellini issue of *La Revue musicale,* Paris, 1935, pp. 52–62.

17. According to Emilia Branca (*Felice Romani,* etc., pp. 16–17), the verses

for this "hymn of joy" were rewritten ten times. She quotes two of the versions not used:

1. *Oh! si unisca in un amplesso*
   Alma ad alma, core a core,
   Ah! non possa il fato istesso
   Separarci, o mio tesor.

   Sempre uniti, uniti insieme
   In un voto, in una speme,
   Della terra in cui viviamo
   Ci formiamo un ciel d'amor.

2. *Al pensar che a tanto bene*
   Mi ha serbato amor pietoso
   Di sua sorte il cor dubbioso
   Giunge, o madre, a diffidar.

   Questa gioia, questo Imene
   Si presenta al mio pensiero
   Come un sogno lusinghiero
   Da cui m'abbia a risvegliar.

18. *La Sonnambula* differs from (for example) Donizetti's *L'Elisir d'amore* in entirely doing without elements of farce.

La Straniera

1. Cosenza's five-act *La Straniera* was played for the first time at the Teatro dei Fiorentini, Naples, on December 8, 1827, by an acting company headed by Alberto Tessari and his wife, Carolina Cavalletti-Tessari. It was published in Naples in 1827; Mr. William Weaver generously lent me a copy of the play as republished in Venice in 1830.

2. Florimo wrote (LSmdN II, p. 187): "*La Straniera* proved tragic to the artist who enacted its principal role. Méric-Lalande, obliged to sing throughout the opera in an extremely high range, drove herself to surmount triumphantly all the great vocal difficulties. And she succeeded; but her voice succumbed to the unprecedented exertions." What Florimo may have had in mind (notably, the passage had not appeared in CssSmdN) it is impossible to determine. Bellini would not knowingly have written a role consistently too high for his leading soprano; Méric-Lalande went on singing until at least 1838: later than the first performance of *La Straniera*, she appeared at Her Majesty's Theatre, London, in *Il Pirata* (1830), at the Teatro Regio, Turin, in *Norma* (1835–1836)—and created the title role in Donizetti's *Lucrezia Borgia* (Teatro alla Scala, Milan, December 26, 1833).

3. Bellini almost certainly adjusted Arturo's vocal lines for Rubini.

4. See page 93 for these performances.

5. The only other Fenice staging of *La Straniera* occurred in 1834.

6. See the handbill reproduced in Alberto Cametti, *Il Teatro di Tordinona poi di Apollo*, Tivoli, 1938, Vol. II, p. 439. Conte Chigi-Saraceni noted in

his diary that *La Straniera* "pleased despite the awful singers." In fact, it was a notable success. It was repeated at the Apollo in May 1832 with better singers, and at another Roman theater, the Valle, in November 1832 and in 1836.

7. Bologna had had *La Straniera* earlier: at the Teatro del Corso in the spring of 1831.

8. *La Straniera* was staged at the St. Charles Theatre, New Orleans, on May 11, 1836, the year after Bellini's death.

9. *Adelson e Salvini, Bianca e Fernando* (Genoa), *Il Pirata, I Capuleti e i Montecchi, Norma,* and *I Puritani* each had a *sinfonia. Bianca e Gernando* (Naples), *La Straniera, La Sonnambula,* and *Beatrice di Tenda* each had an orchestral *preludio* or *introduzione. Zaira* may be said to have had no orchestral prelude at all.

10. In *"Notes nécrologiques," Journal des débats,* Paris, July 16, 1836.

11. The melody of Isoletta's "aria" in this scene is the same as that of Bellini's arietta *"Quando verrà quel dì,"* which probably was composed at Milan in 1827–1828 and has also been known as *"Il Fervido Desiderio,"* as which it was published by Ricordi (plate number 10207), who reprinted it in 1948 as No. 7 of the *Composizioni da camera per canto e pianoforte.*

12. In Pizzetti, ed., *op. cit.,* pp. 64–65.

13. Pointing out the resemblance between Alaide's *"Ah! no, ah! non ti lusingar!"* (p. 68) and the elder Germont's *"Di Provenza il mar,"* in Act II of *La Traviata,* Friedrich Lippmann added: "The two melodies proceed to the same rhythm throughout and, given that insufficient other compositional resources are in contrast to the rigidity of the rhythmic motion, both of them end up becoming a little monotonous" (*Atti del I Congresso internazionale di studi verdiani,* Parma, 1969, p. 190).

14. In the house program (pages unnumbered) of the 1968–1969 performances of *La Straniera* at the Teatro Massimo, Palermo.

15. In Pizzetti, ed., *op. cit.,* p. 66.

16. In Pizzetti, ed., *op. cit.,* p. 66.

17. In Pizzetti, ed., *op. cit.,* p. 67.

18. *Loc. cit.*

19. In the house program of the 1970 performances of *La Straniera* at the Teatro La Fenice, Venice, p. 115.

20. In the house program of the 1968–1969 performances of *La Straniera* at the Teatro Massimo, Palermo, pages not numbered.

21. At Valdeburgo's words *"Che far vuoi tu? Rammenta i giuramenti tuoi"* one can only think that Verdi remembered this music, unconsciously or half-consciously, when composing the Alvaro–Carlo duet *"Solenne in quest'ora,"* in Act III of *La Forza del destino.*

22. In *"Notes nécrologiques [1836],"* in *Les Musiciens et la musique,* Paris, 1903, p. 178.

Zaira

1. Romani's *Zaira* was set by at least three other composers: Alessandro Gandini (whose *Zaira* was heard first at the Teatro di Corte, Modena, on

November 7, 1829, not quite six months after the Parma première of Bellini's); Saverio Mercadante (*Zaira*, 1831); and Antonio Manni (*Zaira*, 1845). Operas with other librettos derived from Voltaire's tragedy have included: *Zaira*s by Sebastiano Nasolini (libretto by Mattia Bo[u]tturini, 1797); Marcos Antonio Portogallo (Bo[u]tturini, 1802); Francesco Federici (Bo[u]tturini, 1803); Peter von Winter (libretto by either Filippo Pananti or Lorenzo Da Ponte, 1805); Ernst II, Duke of Saxe-Coburg-Gotha (libretto by M. Tonelli, 1846); and Paul Véronge de la Nux (libretto by Édouard Blau and Louis Besson, 1890). Antonio Caldara's three-act "*operetta*" *Zaira* (anonymous libretto, 1722) preceded Voltaire's *tragédie*.

2. The libretto printed at Florence "*nella Stamperia di F. Giacchetti presso il Teatro Nuovo*" for this 1836 production includes Romani's "*Proemio dell'autore*" and lists Andrea Nencini as "*maestro e direttore dell'opera*," Nicola Petrini Zamboni as "*Capo e Direttore d'Orchestra*." The costumes are listed as the property of the impresario Alessandro Lanari.

3. Stage directions translated from the autograph score and the 1836 Florence libretto. The description of the action is taken from the autograph, the libretto, and BSLS, pp. 193–195.

4. A manuscript copy of the score (nine pp. R and L—*i.e.*, 18 pp.) up to this point survives in the library of the Naples Conservatory; it is headed "*Introduzione Ballabile/Atto I/Foglietto Ripetitore*," and was intended for rehearsal use. The library also has a similar, but incomplete, manuscript copy headed: "*Primo Cambiamento in tutte le parti d'Orchestra/dell'Introduzione e Duetto Atto 2°/Fogli 17* [18?]," which now consists of only eleven pages.

5. Somewhat altered, Corasmino's melody became the opening of Tebaldo's cavatina "*È serbato questo acciaro*," in Act I of *I Capuleti e i Montecchi*.

6. In the autograph, following Fatima's word "*seddutor*," Orosmane continues to address Zaira in recitative beginning "*Te sua Sultana già saluta*"; this continues for nine measures (61R–62L), at the end of which Bellini wrote a *dal segno* symbol and scratched out the rest of 62L, placing the related symbol at the beginning of 62R.

7. Pp. 81R–82L are in a copyist's writing.

8. BSLS, p. 200.

9. The opening word, spoken by Zaira, begins on 98L and ends on 98R. In the 1836 Florence libretto, it is given as "*Fermatevi*," which it certainly is not in the autograph, in which it seems to be "*Arrestate*."

10. This remarkable three-section trio (104R–124L) was one of the only two numbers that drew applause from the unfriendly audience at the Parma première of *Zaira*. About it, just before that performance, Bellini wrote to Vincenzo Ferlito (BE, pp. 213–214): "I am very content, and especially with the trio, a piece that [in rehearsal] has amazed everyone so much that I myself don't believe that I have composed so effectively in that manner . . ." He thought well enough of the accompaniment to Lusignano's opening words (104R–105L) to use it again in *I Puritani*, with a different melody above it, at the opening of the Act I Elvira–Sir Giorgio duet "*Sai com'arde in petto mio*."

11. This trio was published in piano-vocal score by Ricordi, Milan, and Girard (later Cottrau), Naples.

12. Bellini originally scored this section for soloists and chorus throughout, but deleted the choral lines until the middle of 133L. He evidently wanted the massed voices to increase the effect at that point. Parts of this scene, from 129L on, do not appear to be in Bellini's script; this is notably true of the orchestral lines on 129R, 130R, and 132R, and of 135L and 135R. Confusion in these final pages suggests that some of them were bound erroneously with the autograph.

13. BSLS, p. 203.

14. A quotation from the beginning of this introduction to the Nerestano–Zaira duet occurs in *I Capuleti e i Montecchi*, in Act I, the Giulietta–Romeo duet, at Romeo's words "*miglior patria avrem di questa.*"

15. This rather aimless scene is considerably longer in both text and music in the autograph than is indicated by the mere eight lines of text allotted to it in the 1836 Florence libretto; that performance may well have been shortened.

16. This motive would be reused in *Beatrice di Tenda*, as accompaniment to the first-act Beatrice–Filippo duet "*Duolo d'un cor piagato*" in Act I.

17. Reshaped and subtilized, this melody became that of Orombello in the trio of the finale in *Beatrice di Tenda* ("*Angiol di pace*"). A clarinet motive from this duet also reappears in *Beatrice di Tenda*, as an oboe motive in the Beatrice–Filippo duet in Act I, "*Duolo d'un cor piagato.*"

18. Pp. 45R–55L of this second bound volume of the autograph score, not in Bellini's script, merely repeat Scenes 4–6, often with a difference in key, suggesting that they were prepared for a tenor Nerestano and were included in the autograph in error.

19. In *I Capuleti e i Montecchi*, Romeo sings a variant of this melody, in 9/8 time, G major, in his first-act cavatina "*Se Romeo t'uccise un figlio.*"

20. Bellini made use of this melody in *I Capuleti e i Montecchi*: in Giulietta's cabaletta "*Ah! non poss'io partire,*" in Act II.

21. The opening of this *scena*, marked by a melodic rise over a ninth, was to be adapted by Bellini for Giulietta's "aria" in Act II of *I Capuleti e i Montecchi*, "*Morte non temo, il sai.*"

22. Borrowed in part from the chorus "*Tutti siam,*" in *Bianca e Fernando* (p. 185 of piano-vocal score with plate numbers 9826–9842), this would later figure in the choral "*Non partì,*" in *Norma* (p. 189 of piano-vocal score with plate number 41684).

23. Bellini used the first two and a half measures of this melody as the opening of Romeo's first-act cavatina "*La tremenda ultrice spada,*" in Act I of *I Capuleti e i Montecchi*, where their effectiveness is multiplied many, many times.

24. Pastura wrote (BSLS, p. 213): "Despite his despair, Orosmane intones a motive that much resembles the cabaletta of the Alaide–Arturo duet in *La Straniera*: '*Un ultimo addio,*' and though there the time is ternary, whereas in *Zaira* it is binary, the derivation is evident, not only in the phrase, but also in the accompaniment written with pizzicato chords. Evidently the composer felt drawn to imitate himself not so much by the vehemence of the situation as by the very rhythm of his verse."

Appendix B

1. *Ernani,* of course, was intended for the Teatro Carcano, Milan.
2. To believe that Bellini did not inform Florimo of a matter so important as a change of subject for his next opera is all but impossible.
3. This is probably one more expression of Bellini's feeling of bitter disdain toward Donizetti, though Rossini and several other composers of the era also were capable of turning out four operas in a single year.
4. LSmdN III, p. 229; the letter to Ricordi is in BE, p. 407. No autograph of the letter is known; it was first published, in a French translation, by Arthur Pougin, in his *Bellini: Sa vie, ses œuvres,* Paris, 1868, pp. 147–151, where the quoted passage reads: *"Je ne peux donc voir avec indifférence les plaintes des directeurs sur les prix que je demande. Est-ce que je ne pourrais écrire quatre opéras en un an? Mais je ruinerais ma réputation, et j'aurais les remords de tromper qui me paie. N'ai-je pas écrit* la Sonnambula *du 11 Janvier au 6 Mars? Mais ce fut un accident, et puis j'avais déjà quelques réminiscences de mon* Ernani *qui avait été défendu."*
5. B:Mel, pp. 91–92.
6. BSLS, p. 257.
7. BSLS, p. 257.

Appendix C

1. In the letter to Perucchini (January 3, 1831), Bellini said: "By now you will know about the success of *I Capuleti;* I want to give you a report. I didn't write you after the first night because my poor opera could not have been performed worse, so that, though it made some effect and the audience wanted me on the stage, I was so infuriated that I didn't want to go out. . . ." Then he reported: "On the succeeding nights, the effect increased in direct ratio to the better performance, and now the impresarios console themselves because they see the big theater crowded every night." This well may have indicated that Bellini did not attend any of the early performances of *Anna Bolena* at the Carcano. Nor is he likely to have been present at one of its pre-première rehearsals, especially as rehearsals for *I Capuleti e i Montecchi* at La Scala were held simultaneously with them.
2. Eugenio Gara, in *"La seconda moglie di Re Barbablu,"* in the house program of La Scala for the 1958–1959 performances there of *Anna Bolena.*
3. How Scherillo reached this conclusion it is now impossible to know: either he had read the statement in a now-unknown source or, what seems very unlikely, he had seen at least some of the *Ernani* sketches. The likeliest explanation is that Florimo had showed him a now-lost letter from Bellini in which the borrowing was stated explicitly or had reported it to him on the basis of such a letter.
4. As late as 1902, astonishingly, Amore published his side of the argument as *Belliniana (Errori e smentite),* neither quoting Scherillo's rebuttals nor retreating a millimeter from his own untenable position.

5. See Bellini's undated letter to Giovanni Ricordi, BE, pp. 407–408, quoted in part herein.
6. "*Quellenkundliche Anmerkungen,* etc.," in *Analecta Musicologica*, 4, Cologne/Graz, 1967, p. 140.
7. See Amore, *Vincenzo Bellini: Arte, studî e ricerche*, Catania, 1902. For further discussion of the *Ernani–La Sonnambula* question, see herein, pp. 94–95 and 260–266.

Appendix D

1. Letter in the Archivio di Stato di Reggio Emilia, quoted in full in Frank Walker, "*Lettere disperse e inedite di Vincenzo Bellini,*" in *Rivista del Comune di Catania*, 4, October–December 1960, pp. 6–8.
2. Unidentified, but apparently Remondini's son.
3. An error (conscious or unconscious?) for 1801.
4. A mistake on Bellini's part? Or had he been given this incorrect detail by Vincenzo Tobia Bellini himself?

Appendix E

1. In "*Amore e amori nelle lettere di Giuditta, Bellini e Florimo,*" in *La Scala*, Milan, March 1959, p. 20, ft. 10.
2. *Donizetti: Vita—Musiche—Epistolario*, Bergamo, 1948, pp. 287–288.
3. *Donizetti*, London, 1965, p. 125.
4. CssSmdN II, p. 819.
5. Quoted also in Zavadini, *op. cit.*, p. 287, and BSLS, pp. 300–301.
6. BSLS, p. 302.
7. *Donizetti*, New York and London, 1963, p. 81.

Appendix G

1. The Donizetti autographs mentioned are now in the Museo Donizettiano at Bergamo.
2. The autograph of *I Capuleti e i Montecchi* is now in the Museo Belliniano at Catania.

Appendix H

1. Amore: VB:A, pp. 248–250; reprinted in BE, pp. 412–413.

Appendix I

1. No such album appears to have been published before the unveiling of the Bellini monument in Naples in 1886: the *Album-Bellini* edited by Florimo

and Michele Scherillo in connection with the unveiling contains no music by Hiller.

2. Dessauer (1798–1876) was actually a Bohemian. In addition to numerous songs, he composed operas, most notably *Ein Besuch in Saint-Cyr* (Dresden, 1838), to a libretto by Eduard von Bauernfeld.

3. Lina Freppa, to whom Chopin dedicated the four mazurkas of his opus 17, was a singer; her salon was a focal point of interest for the best-known musicians in Paris, particularly those of foreign birth.

4. In Act I, Scene 5, of *La Sonnambula*, Amina sings: *"Ah! vorrei trovar parola."*

5. Hiller seems to mean that *"Tu che a Dio spiegasti l'ali"* is related to Imogene's *"Col sorriso d'innocenza"*—and though the dramatic situations are very different, a certain resemblance in melancholy mood can be detected.

6. To know exactly what Hiller had in mind here is impossible. Manrico has no aria after *"Di quella pira l'orrendo foco"*—which assuredly does not sound Bellinian. Probably he was thinking of Manrico's part in the Miserere, the lines beginning *"Sconto sul sangue mio,"* or of his part in the duet *"Ai nostri monti,"* the lines beginning *"Riposa, o madre."* The most Bellinian number in *Il Trovatore*, however, is Leonora's *"D'amor sull'ali rosee."*

Appendix J

1. Legigan appears to have been the man from whom Levys had rented the villa.

Appendix K

1. My friend Dr. Richard J. Fauliso of Wethersfield, Connecticut, to whom I showed the autopsy report and the commentary by Dr. de Sabata, kindly sent me quotations from two standard medical texts: *Manson's Tropical Diseases: A Manual of the Diseases of Warm Climates*, by Sir Philip H. Manson-Bahr, 16th edition, London, 1966, and *Pathology of Tropical Diseases*, by J. E. Ash, M.C., U.S.A., and Sophie Spitz, M.D., Philadelphia and London, 1945. I quote from the former: "**Definition.**—Amœbiasis denotes infection with the protozoan, *Entamœba histolytica*. When confined to the intestinal canal it produces *amœbic dysentery*, or primary intestinal amœbiasis. This is insidious in its onset, chronic in its course, and with a marked tendency to relapse. Metastatic lesions may be produced in the liver and elsewhere."

Appendix L

1. The ensuing insurrection ended the rule of the decemvirs in 449. Several Italian writers, including Vittorio Alfieri, wrote tragedies on the story of Virginia.

544)   *Notes to Appendixes L, M, & N*

2. BSLS, p. 69.
3. BSLS, p. 69.
4. VdVB, p. 73.
5. VB:A (1892), pp. 222–227.
6. The quotation is from Pougin's *Bellini: Sa Vie, ses œuvres,* p. 127.
7. B:Mel, pp. 90–91. Florimo's paragraph on the *Oreste* problem reads: "In more than one biography of Bellini, I have read that he manifested the desire to put Alfieri's *Oreste* to music; this has always been a great wonder to me, as while Bellini lived, he never spoke or wrote to me about it. When I traveled with Bellini on the voyage to Sicily and the return to Naples, he never said a word about this tragedy; nor did he make the smallest reference to it in the many hundreds of letters that he wrote me. I find even less credible that he wanted to set the tragedy exactly as it had been written by the great poet, of whom he was an enthusiastic admirer; and, sharing M. Pougin's feeling, I say that his elegiac, tender, and melancholy genius would have found itself unsuited to, even in positive battle with, the impetuosity and violence of the great Italian tragedian. The lamb (permit me the comparison) would have been wrestling with the lion; but Bellini had too much good sense to gird up his loins for such an undertaking. Add to that, then, his exacting standards with respect to poetic form, verbal harmony, and the rhythm of verses! He who was scarcely satisfied with Romani! For those reasons, what has been written about the *Oreste* must be put among the false legends unless someone appears with valid proof to the contrary."
8. Achille is not a character in Alfieri's *Oreste.* Benedetto Condorelli convincingly suggested (*Il Museo Belliniano: Catalogo Storico-iconografico,* Catania, 1935, pp. 126–127) that the text Bellini had before him while composing the surviving sketches was based upon Euripides' *Iphigenia in Aulis.*

Appendix M

1. In *"Pagine sconosciute de 'I Capuleti e i Montecchi' e 'Beatrice di Tenda' di Vincenzo Bellini,"* in *Rivista Italiana di Musicologia* II, 1, Florence, 1967, pp. 140–146. Here, as everywhere, I am deeply in Dr. Lippmann's debt for his blanket permission to quote him at length in translation.
2. Alessandro Rolla was the noted leader of the orchestra at La Scala.

Appendix N

1. In *"Quellenkundliche Anmerkungen,* etc.," in *Analecta Musicologica,* 4, Cologne/Graz, 1967, pp. 131–153.
2. Evidently a Ricordi employee, very probably a copyist.
3. An autograph of part of this chorus exists. It was presented to Arturo Toscanini in 1946 by La Scala, and later was in the Toscanini Collection in Riverdale (New York). It can be seen in microfilm at the Library of the Performing Arts at Lincoln Center, New York City. See illustration, p. 290.

Appendix O

1. In "*Pagine sconosciute de 'I Capuleti e i Montecchi' e 'Beatrice di Tenda' di Vincenzo Bellini*," in *Rivista Italiana di Musicologia*, II, 1, Florence, 1967, pp. 146–151.

Appendix P

1. In *Richard Wagner: The Man, His Mind, and His Music*, New York, 1968, p. 32.
2. In Heinrich Laube's *Zeitung für die elegante Welt*.
3. In the *Neue Zeitschrift für Musik*, Leipzig, November 6 and 10, 1834.
4. Autograph in the collection of the Juilliard School of Music, New York; quoted by permission.
5. See Edmond Michotte, *Richard Wagner's Visit to Rossini*, etc., translated from the French by Herbert Weinstock, Chicago, 1968.
6. LSmdN III, pp. 198–199.
7. *Op. cit.*, p. 401.

Appendix Q

1. In "*Quellenkundliche Anmerkungen, etc.*," in *Analecta Musicologica*, 4, Cologne/Graz, 1967, pp. 148–153.
2. In *Vincenzo Bellini und die italienische opera seria seiner Zeit*, *Analecta Musicologica*, 6, Cologne/Vienna, 1969, p. 392.
3. In March 1835, the Palermo opera asked for the "Malibran" version of *I Puritani*, then in Naples. But Bellini decided against its use, asking Florimo to have copied out only those sections of it which were identical in the two versions: he himself sent Florimo amended and annotated copies of the sections that were different in the Paris version or absent from the Naples one. Some time after Bellini's death, Florimo turned over to the Bellini family in Catania both the manuscript of the Naples version and manuscripts of some separate sections; they are now in the Museo Belliniano at Catania.
4. In a Decca-London recording of *I Puritani*, Joan Sutherland sings the "cabaletta" ("*Ah! sento, mio bell'angelo*") with some alterations in the text-words. Discussing that recording, Andrew Porter wrote (*The Financial Times*, London, March 24, 1964): "Between the first and second nights of *I Puritani*, Bellini cut, by his own account, 30–40 minutes of music. In the published score the ending is weak. The magnificent largo ensemble growing out of the tenor's 'Credeasi misera' has no *allegro* section to balance it, only a conventional little close. Both on the records and at Covent Garden [Richard] Bonynge [the conductor] has restored from Bellini's manuscript the necessary brilliant ending, which is effective. On the other hand he has cut the corresponding section of the Act I finale to

an extent where it no longer complements 'Oh vieni al tempio.' Another commendable restoration is the few bars of introduction to the baritone's 'Bel sogno beato'—reserving the surprise effect of the 'foreshortened' entry for the second verse. . . ."

BIBLIOGRAPHY

Rather than include here all the periodical and other minor, though highly particularized, sources quoted from and cited in the notes, I have made the following a list of major, generalized sources in which readers may be interested in pursuing additional information, analysis, and criticism.

A Vincenzo Bellini (Bollettino dei Musicisti: Mensile del Sindicato Nazionale Fascista [dei] Musicisti, II, 3, Rome, 1934).

Album-Bellini, see Florimo–Scherillo.

Album Bellini—Premio Bellini, see Florimo.

Amore, Antonino: *Belliniana (Errori e smentite)*. Catania, 1902.

———: *Vincenzo Bellini: Arte—Studî e ricerche*. Catania, 1892.

———: *Vincenzo Bellini: Vita—Studî e ricerche*. Catania, 1894.

Ashbrook, William: *Donizetti*. London, 1965.

Bauer, Anton: *Opern und Operetten in Wien*. Graz–Cologne, 1955.

Bauwr, Mme de: *Mes Souvenirs*. Paris, 1853.

Blaze de Bury, Henri, Baron: *Musiciens contemporains*. Paris, 1856.

Branca, Emilia (Romani): *Felice Romani ed i più riputati maestri di musica del suo tempo*. Turin/Florence/Rome, n.d. (but 1882).

Brockway, Wallace, and Weinstock, Herbert: *The World of Opera: The Story of Its Development and The Lore of Its Performance*. New York, 1962; London, 1963.

Cambi, Luisa: *Bellini [La Vita]*. Milan, 1934.

———, ed.: *Vincenzo Bellini: Epistolario*. Milan, 1943.

Cambiasi, Isidoro: *La Scala: 1778–1906*. Milan, n.d. (but 1906?).

Cametti, Alberto: *L'Accademia filarmonica romana dal 1821–1860*. Rome, n.d. (but 1924).

———: *Bellini a Roma*. Rome, 1900.

———: *Il Teatro di Tordinona poi di Apollo*. 2 vols. Tivoli, 1938.

Caselli, Aldo: *Catalogo delle opere liriche pubblicate in Italia*. Florence, 1969.

Castil-Blaze (François-Henri-Joseph Blaze): *L'Opéra-Italien de 1548 à 1856*. Paris, 1856.

Catania nell'Ottocento. Catania, 1934.

Cavazzuti, Pietro: *Bellini a Londra*. Florence, 1945.

Cella, Franca: *Indagini sulle fonti francesi dei libretti di Vincenzo Bellini*. Milan, 1968.

———: *Prospettive della librettistica italiana nell'età romantica*. Milan, 1968.

Cento Anni di vita del Teatro di San Carlo 1848–1948. Naples, 1948.

Cicconetti, Filippo: *Lettere inedite di uomini illustri*. Rome, 1886.

———: *Vita di Vincenzo Bellini*. Prato, 1859.

Clayton, Ellen Creathorne: *Queens of Song.* London–New York, 1865.

Clément, Félix: *Les Musiciens célèbres depuis le seizième siècle jusqu'à nos jours.* Paris, 1878.

———— and Larousse, Pierre: *Dictionnaire des opéras (Dictionnaire lyrique).* Updated by Arthur Pougin. Paris, n.d.

Collezione delle opere teatrali poste in musica dal celebre maestro Vincenzio [sic] *Bellini.* Naples, 1834.

Colombani, Alfredo: *L'Opera italiana nel secolo XIX.* Milan, 1900.

Condorelli, Benedetto: *Il Museo Belliniano: catalogo storico-iconografico.* Catania, 1935.

Cottrau, Guglielmo: *Lettres d'un Mélomane pour servir de document à l'histoire musicale de Naples de 1829 à 1847.* Naples, 1885.

Curzon, Henri de: *Meyerbeer.* Paris, n.d.

Damerini, Adelmo, ed.: Norma: *Guida attraverso il dramma e la musica.* Milan, 1923.

D'Arienzo, N.: *La Musica in Napoli.* Naples, 1900.

De Angelis, Giuseppe Tito: *Vincenzo Bellini: La Vita, l'uomo, l'artista.* Brescia, 1935.

De Biez, Jacques: *Tamburini et la musique italienne.* Paris, 1877.

De Filippis, F., and Arnese, R.: *Cronache del Teatro di S. Carlo (1737–1960).* 2 vols. Naples, 1959.

Della Corte, Andrea, and Pannain, Guido: *Vincenzo Bellini: Il Carattere morale, I Caratteri artistici.* Turin, etc., 1935.

Di Ferrer, Cav.: *Rossini e Bellini.* Cesena, 1843.

Di Giacomo, Salvatore: *I Quattro Antichi Conservatori di Napoli.* 2 vols. Palermo, 1923–1924.

Duprez, Gilbert-Louis: *Souvenirs d'un chanteur.* Paris, 1880.

Edwards, Henry Sutherland: *The Prima Donna: Her History and Surroundings from the Seventeenth to the Nineteenth Century.* 2 vols. London, 1888.

Elwart, Antonio Elia: *Duprez: Sa Vie artistique.* Paris, 1838.

Enciclopedia dello spettacolo, 9 vols., Rome, 1952–1962; *Aggiornamento,* 1955–1965, Rome, 1966; *Indice-Repertorio,* Rome, 1968.

Escudier, Léon: *Mes Souvenirs.* Paris, 1863.

———— with Escudier, Marie: *Études biographiques sur les chanteurs contemporains.* Paris, 1840.

———— with Escudier, Marie: *Vie et aventures des cantatrices célèbres.* Paris, 1856.

Fantoni, Gabriele: *Storia universale del canto.* 2 vols. Milan, 1873.

Ferranti (Nob. Giulini), Maria: *Giuditta Pasta e i suoi tempi.* Milan, 1935 (probably written in 1869).

Ferrari, Paolo-Emillio: *Spettacoli drammatico-musicali e coreografici in Parma dall'anno 1628 all'anno 1884.* Parma, 1884.

Ferrarini, Mario: *Parma teatrale ottocentesca.* Parma, 1946.

Fétis, François-Joseph: *Biographie universelle des musiciens et Bibliographie générale de la musique.* 2nd edn. 8 vols. 1873. And 2 vols. of *Supplément et complément,* ed. Arthur Pougin, Paris, 1878.

Florimo, Francesco, ed.: *Album Bellini—Premio Bellini.* Naples, 1887.

————: *Bellini: Memorie e lettere.* Florence, 1882.

————: *Cenno storico sulla Scuola musicale di Napoli.* 2 vols. Naples 1869–1871.

————: *La Scuola musicale di Napoli.* 4 vols. Naples, 1881–1882.

————: *Translazione delle ceneri di Vincenzo Bellini.* Naples, 1877.

————, ed., with Scherillo, Michele: *Album-Bellini.* Naples, 1886.

Gatti, Carlo: *Il Teatro alla Scala nella storia e nell'arte (1778–1963).* 2 vols. Milan, 1964 (with "*Cronologia completa degli spettacoli e dei concerti a cura di Giampiero Tintori*").

Gerardi, Filippo: *Biografia di Vincenzo Bellini.* Rome, 1835.

Giugni, Francesco: *L'Immatura Fine di Vincenzo Bellini alla luce di nuove circostanze: Chi fu il suo medico curante?* Lugo, 1930.

————: *La Malattia e la morte di Vincenzo Bellini.* Faenza, 1939.

Gray, Cecil: *Contingencies.* London, 1947.

Greville, Henry: *Leaves from the Diary of Henry Greville,* ed. by the Viscountess Enfield. London, 1883.

Gutierrez, Beniamino: *La Scala nel 1830 e 1930.* Milan, 1930.

————: *Il Teatro Carcano (1803–1914).* Milan, 1914.

Heine, Heinrich: *Florentinische Nächte: "Erste Nacht,"* in Vol. VI of *Sämtliche Werke,* Leipzig, 1912.

Hogarth, George: *Memoirs of the Musical Drama.* London, 1838.

Incagliati, Matteo: *Figure meridionali d'altri tempi.* Lanciano, 1913.

Jaubert, Mme C.: *Souvenirs.* Paris, 1881.

Kolodin, Irving: *The Metropolitan Opera 1883–1966.* New York, 1966.

Levi L'Italico, Primo: *Paesaggi e figure musicali.* Milan, 1913.

————: *Vincenzo Bellini a Santa Cecilia.* Rome, 1900.

Lianovosani, Luigi (Giovanni Salvioli): *La Fenice, Gran Teatro di Venezia: Serie degli spettacoli dalla primavera 1792 a tutto il carnovale 1876.* Milan, n.d. (but 1876?).

————: *Saggio bibliografico relativo ai melodrammi di Felice Romani.* Milan, n.d. (but 1878).

Lippmann, Friedrich: "*Quellenkundliche Anmerkungen zu einigen Opern Vincenzo Bellinis,*" in *Analecta Musicologica* 4, Cologne/Graz, 1967, p. 131.

————: *Vincenzo Bellini und die italienische opera seria seiner Zeit, Analecta Musicologica,* 6, Cologne/Vienna, 1969 (entire issue, 402 pp.).

Lloyd, William A. C.: *Vincenzo Bellini: A Memoir.* London, n.d. (but 1908).

Locatelli, Agostino: *Cenni biografici sulla straordinaria carriera teatrale percorsa da Giovanni Battista Rubini.* Milan, 1884.

Loewenberg, Alfred: *Annals of Opera 1597–1940.* 2nd edn. 2 vols. Geneva, 1955.

Luzio, Alessandro, ed.: *Carteggi verdiani.* 4 vols. Rome, 1935, 1947.

Maccolini, Giuseppe: *Della Vita e dell'arte di Antonio Tamburini* . . . Faenza, 1842.

Malvezzi, Aldobrandino: *Cristina di Belgiojoso.* 3 vols. Milan, 1936 1937.

Manferrari, Umberto: *Dizionario universale delle opere melodrammatiche.* 3 vols. Florence, 1954.

Marangoni, Guido, and Vanvianchi, Carlo: *La Scala.* Bergamo, 1922.

Mastrigli, Leopoldo: *La Sicilia musicale.* Bologna, 1891.

Mattfeld, Julius: *A Handbook of American Operatic Premieres 1731–1962.* Detroit, 1963.

Megali del Giudice, G.: *Francesco Florimo, l'amico di Vincenzo Bellini.* Naples, 1901.

Mezzatesta, Girolamo Guido: *Vincenzo Bellini nella vita e nelle opere.* Palermo, 1935.

Mila, Massimo: *Cent'anni di musica moderna.* Milan, 1944.

Miragoli, Livia: *Il Melodramma italiano nell'Ottocento.* Rome, 1924.

Mitjana y Gordon, Rafael: *Discantes y contrapuntos.* Valencia, 1905.

Mocenigo (M. Nani-Mocenigo): *Il Teatro La Fenice.* Venice, 1926.

Monaldi, Gino: *Cantanti celebri del secolo XIX.* Rome, n.d. (but 1906).

———: *Impresari celebri del secolo XIX.* Rocca San Casciano, 1918.

———: *Le Prime Rappresentazioni celebri.* Milan, 1910.

———: *I Teatri di Roma negli ultimi tre secoli.* Naples, 1929.

Monteverdi, Mario, ed.: *Scene di Alessandro Sanquirico nelle Collezioni del Museo Teatrale alla Scala* (catalogue). Alessandria, 1968.

Monti, Antonio: *Milano romantica 1814–1848.* Milan, 1946.

Morgan, Lady (Sidney Owenson): *Lady Morgan's Memoirs* . . . rev. edn. 2 vols. London, 1863.

Moschino, Ettore: *Vincenzo Bellini e la sua origine abruzzese.* L'Aquila, 1940.

Musumeci, conte Libero (Liborio): *Parallelo de' due maestri Bellini e Rossini.* Palermo, 1832.

Naumann, Emil: *Italienische Tondichter von Palestrina bis auf die Gegenwart.* Berlin, 1883.

Norma, Numero unico. Catania, 1931.

Omaggio a Bellini nel Primo Centenario dalla sua nascita. Catania, 1901.

Opera, L': "*Teatro Massimo Bellini, Catania*" (Anno V, N. 16/17, Milan, 1970), with articles on Bellini and his operas by Niny Genguzza, Don Giosuè Chisari, Domenico Tempio, Benedetto Condorelli, "Gani," and Vittorio Consoli.

Orrey, Leslie: *Bellini.* London–New York, 1969.

Pacini, Giovanni: *Le Mie Memorie artistiche.* Florence, 1875.

Pagliara, Rocco; *Intermezzi musicali.* Naples, 1889.

Pannain, Guido: *L'Opera e le opere.* Milan, 1958.

———: *Ottocento musicale italiano.* Milan, 1952.

———: *Il R[eal] Conservatorio di Musica "San Pietro a Maiella" di Napoli.* Florence, 1942.

———: see also Della Corte, Andrea.

Pasolini-Zanelli, G.: *Il Teatro di Faenza dal 1788 al 1888.* Faenza, 1888.

Pastura, Francesco: *Bellini secondo la storia.* Parma, 1959.

———, ed.: *Le Lettere di Bellini (1819–1835).* Catania, 1935.

———: *Vincenzo Bellini.* Catania, etc., 1959.

Pepoli, conte Carlo: *Ricordanze biografiche* . . . Bologna, 1881.

Persiano, Filippo: *La Sonnambula di Felice Romani.* Florence, 1903.

Pinzauti, Leonardo: *Il Maggio musicale fiorentino dalla prima alla trentesima edizione.* Florence, 1967.

Pizzetti, Ildebrando: *Intermezzi critici.* Florence, n.d. (but 1921)

———: *La Musica italiana dell'Ottocento.* Turin, 1947.

———: *La Musica di Vincenzo Bellini.* Milan, 1916.

———, ed.: *Vincenzo Bellini: L'Uomo, le sue opere, la sua fama.* (Essays by

Luisa Cambi, Andrea Della Corte, Gianandrea Gavazzeni, Carl Holl, Edward J. Dent, Jean Chantavoine, Adelmo Damerini.) Milan, 1936.

Poggi, Cencio: *Vincenzo Bellini a Moltrasio*. Como, 1891.

Policastro, Guglielmo: *Catania nel Settecento*. Turin, 1950.

——: *Vincenzo Bellini (1801–1819)*. Catania, 1935.

Pougin, Arthur: *Bellini: Sa Vie, ses œuvres*. Paris, 1868.

Pugliatti, Salvatore: *Chopin e Bellini*. Messina, 1952.

Quicherat, Louis-Marie: *Adolphe Nourrit, sa vie, son talent, son caractère, sa correspondance*. 3 vols. Paris, 1867.

Radiciotti, Giuseppe: *Gioacchino Rossini, Vita documentata*. 3 vols. Tivoli, 1927–1929.

——: *Teatro, musica e musicisti in Sinigaglia*. Milan, etc., 1893.

Raffaelli, Pietro: *Il Melodramma in Italia dal 1600 fino ai nostri giorni*. Florence, 1881.

Raggi, Alessandro and Luigi: *Il Teatro Comunale di Cesena . . . (1500–1905)*. Cesena, 1906.

Regaldi, G.: *Cenni biografici su V. Bellini*. Naples, 1942.

Reina, Calcedonio: *Vincenzo Bellini (1801–1835)*. Catania, 1902 (later edn., as *Il Cigno catanese: Bellini—La Vita e le opere*, Catania, 1935).

Ricca, Vincenzo: *Vincenzo Bellini: Impressioni e ricordi, con documenti inediti*. Catania, 1932.

Ricobi, Nicodemo: *Norma: Opera nuova del Maestro Bellini*. Milan, 1832.

Ricucci, Giuseppe: *Vincenzo Bellini: Le Sue Opere e i suoi tempi*. Naples, 1899.

Riehl, Wilhelm Heinrich: *Musikalische Charakterköpfe*, I. Stuttgart, 1853.

Rinaldi, Mario: *Felice Romani: Dal melodramma classico al melodramma romantico*. Rome, 1965.

Rognoni, Luigi: *Gioacchino Rossini*. Turin, 1968.

——: *Rossini*. Parma, 1956.

Rolandi, Ulderico: *Il Libretto per musica attraverso i tempi*. Rome, 1951.

——: *Malefatte contro opere belliniane*. Rome, 1931.

Roncaglia, Gino: *Invito all'opera*. 2nd edn. Milan, 1954.

Rosenthal, Harold: *Two Centuries of Opera at Covent Garden*. London, 1958.

Rossini, Gioachino: *Lettere di G. Rossini, raccolte ed annotate per cura di G. Mazzatinti, F. e G. Manis*. Florence, 1902.

Rovani, Giuseppe: *Le Tre Arti considerate in alcuni illustri italiani contemporanei*. 2 vols. Milan, 1874.

Salvioli, Giovanni: *Lettere inedite di Bellini*. Milan, 1884.

Santagata, Ettore: *Il R[egio] Museo storico di S. Pietro a Majella*. Naples, 1930.

Scaglione, N.: *Vincenzo Bellini a Messina*. Messina, 1934.

Scala Theatre Museum, The (in English). Milan, 1966.

Scherillo, Michele: *Belliniana: Nuove Note*. Milan, 1885.

——: *Vincenzo Bellini: Note aneddotiche e critiche*. Ancona, 1882.

Schlitzer, Franco: *I Capuleti e i Montecchi di Vincenzo Bellini: L'Autografo della partitura*. Florence, 1956.

——: *Cimelli belliniani*. Siena, 1952.

——: *Tommaso Traetta, Leonardo Leo, Vincenzo Bellini*. Siena, 1952.

Schmidl, Carlo: *Dizionario universale dei musicisti*. 2 vols. Milan, n.d.

Sciuto, Agatino: *Vincenzo Bellini: Profilo biografico*. Catania, 1876.

Scuderi, Luigi: *Biografia di V. Bellini.* Catania, 1840.

Scudo, Paul (Paolo): *Critique et littérature musicales,* I. Paris, 1852.

———: *Donizetti et l'école italienne depuis Rossini.* Paris, 1852.

Seltsam, William H.: *Metropolitan Opera Annals.* New York, 1947. *First Supplement, 1947–1957,* New York, 1957; *Second Supplement, 1957–1966,* New York, 1968.

Soubies, Albert: *Histoire du Théâtre-Lyrique.* Paris, 1899.

———: *Le Théâtre-Italien de 1801 à 1913.* Paris, 1913.

Succi, Egidio: *Catalogo* (of his autograph collection). Bologna, 1888.

Tari, Antonio: *Vincenzo Bellini: Reminiscenze.* Naples, 1876.

Tiby, Ottavio: *Il Real Teatro Carolino e l'Ottocento musicale palermitano.* Florence, 1957.

———: *Vincenzo Bellini.* Rome, 1935.

———: *Vincenzo Bellini.* Turin, 1938.

Trezzini, Lamberto, ed.: *Due Secoli di vita musicale: Storia del Teatro Comunale di Bologna.* 2 vols. Bologna, 1966.

Vaccai, Giulio: *Vita di Nicola Vaccai.* Bologna, 1882.

Verga, E.: *Storia della vita milanese.* Milan, 1931.

Vincenzo Bellini: Numero commemorativo. Catania, 1935.

Viola, Orazio: *Bibliografia belliniana.* Catania, 1902. 2nd, rev. and enl., edn., Catania, 1923.

———: *I Maggiori e più antichi Interpreti delle opere belliniane.* Catania, n.d.

Vittadini. Stefano, comp.: *Catalogo del Museo Teatrale alla Scala.* Milan, 1940.

———: *Museo teatrale alla Scala, Il: Catalogo.* Milan, 1962.

Voss, Paul: *Vincenzo Bellini.* Leipzig, n.d. (but 1901).

Walker, Frank: *The Man Verdi.* London–New York, 1962.

Weinstock, Herbert: *Donizetti and the World of Opera in Italy, Paris, and Vienna in the First Half of the Nineteenth Century.* New York, 1963; London, 1964.

———: *Rossini: A Biography.* New York–London, 1968.

Zavadini, Guido: *Donizetti: Vita–Musiche–Epistolario.* Bergamo, 1948.

INDEXES

General Index

Index of Bellini Compositions
Mentioned in Text

Page numbers in italics indicate an in-depth description of the composition.

A Note About the Author

Herbert Weinstock is a well-known historian and critic of music and the author of six biographical studies of composers: *Tchaikovsky* (1943), *Handel* (1946, revised 1959), *Chopin: The Man and His Music* (1949), *Donizetti* (1963), *Rossini* (1968), and *Vincenzo Bellini: His Life and His Operas* (1971). He has also written *What Music Is* (1966) and has collaborated with Wallace Brockway on *Men of Music* (1939, 1950) and *The World of Opera* (1941, 1962). His annotated translation of Edmond Michotte's *Richard Wagner's Visit to Rossini (Paris, 1860)/An Evening with Rossini at Beau Séjour (Passy) 1858* was published in 1968. Mr. Weinstock's reviews of recordings frequently appear in *Saturday Review,* and he is the New York correspondent of *Opera* (London).

A Note on the Type

This book was set on the Linotype in Janson, a recutting made direct from type cast from matrices long thought to have been made by the Dutchman Anton Janson, who was a practicing type founder in Leipzig during the years 1668–87. However, it has been conclusively demonstrated that these types are actually the work of Nicholas Kis (1650–1702), a Hungarian, who most probably learned his trade from the Master Dutch type founder Dirk Voskens. The type is an excellent example of the influential and sturdy Dutch types that prevailed in England up to the time William Caslon developed his own incomparable designs from them.

The book was composed, printed, and bound by The Haddon Craftsmen, Inc., Scranton, Pa. Typography and binding design by Anthea Lingeman.